The Civil War and the Press

The Civil War and the Press

David B. Sachsman

S. Kittrell Rushing

Debra Reddin van Tuyll

EDITORS

with Ryan P. Burkholder

Transaction Publishers
New Brunswick (U.S.A.) and London (U.K.)

Copyright © 2000 by Transaction Publishers, New Brunswick, New Jersey.

All rights reserved under International and Pan-American Copyright Conventions. No part of this book may be reproduced or transmitted in any form or by any means, electronic or mechanical, including photocopy, recording, or any information storage and retrieval system, without prior permission in writing from the publisher. All inquiries should be addressed to Transaction Publishers, Rutgers—The State University, 35 Berrue Circle, Piscataway, New Jersey 08854-8042.

This book is printed on acid-free paper that meets the American National Standard for Permanence of Paper for Printed Library Materials.

Library of Congress Catalog Number: 99-16865
ISBN: 0-7658-0008-X
Printed in the United States of America

Library of Congress Cataloging-in-Publication Data

The Civil War and the press / edited by David B. Sachsman, S. Kittrell Rushing, Debra Reddin van Tuyll.
   p. cm.
Includes bibliographical references and index.
ISBN 0-7658-0008-X (alk. paper)
   1. United States—History—Civil War, 1861–1865—Press coverage.
2. United States—History—Civil War, 1861–1865—Journalists.
3. Press and politics—United States—History—19th century.
I. Sachsman, David B. II. Rushing, S. Kittrell. III. Van Tuyll, Debra Reddin.
E609.C58   1999   99-16865
                                                                           CIP

Contents

List of Tables   ix

Introduction
    David B. Sachsman   xi

Part I. Setting the Agenda for Secession and War

1. Western Maryland Newspapers, 1820-1860:   3
   American Culture in Transition
   Yvonne Carignan

2. Consensus and Public Debate: The Washington Press
   During the Nullification Crisis, 1832-1833   21
   Steven G. Saltzgiver

3. Mississippi Newspapers and the Secession Convention:
   The Influence on Anti-Secessionist Porter Jacob Myers   37
   Nancy McKenzie Dupont

4. "John Brown Still Lives!": The Case of John Brown   49
   Bernell E. Tripp

5. Censorship, Racism and the Antebellum Press:
   Harper's Weekly Reports Harper's Ferry   63
   Robert C. Kennedy

6. Abolitionism at the Crossroads: Lydia Maria Child and the
   National Anti-Slavery Standard, 1841-1843   75
   Leonard Ray Teel

7. "I hear nothing about me now but politics --
   slavery, and antislavery *ad nauseam*.": Paul Hamilton Hayne
   and the Editorial Policy of *Russell's Magazine*, 1857-1860   93
   J. Michael Robertson and *Alton Loftis*

8. The Lion's Roar: Cassius Clay's *The True American*   107
   Gene Murray

9. Preserving a Denomination: The Promotion of Women
   by North Carolina's Antebellum Baptist Press   123
   David A. Copeland

10. Mississippi's Fire-Eating Editor Ethelbert Barksdale
    and the Election of 1860   137
    Nancy McKenzie Dupont

11. Agenda-Setting in Antebellum East Tennessee 147
    S. Kittrell Rushing

12. Between Tradition and Innovation: The Nature of
    Antebellum News in the *Courant* 161
    Robert Dardenne

Part II. In Time of War

13. Edwin M. Stanton, the Inverted Pyramid, and Information Control 179
    David Mindich

14. For Women and the War: A Cultural Analysis
    of the *Mayflower, 1861-1864* 209
    Janet M. Cramer

15. Isaac Leeser and *The Occident*: A Jewish Leader's Response
    to the Civil War 227
    Barbara Straus Reed

16. *The Albany Patriot,* 1861-1865: Struggling to Publish
    and Struggling to Remain Optimistic 245
    Ford Risley

17. Images of Women in Civil War Newspapers:
    Leave the "Proper Sphere" 257
    Hazel Dicken-Garcia and *Janet M. Cramer*

18. Two Men, Two Minds: An Examination of the
    Editorial Commentary of Two Georgia Editors
    During Sherman's March to the Sea 275
    Debra Reddin van Tuyll

19. The Paradox of Samuel Medary, Copperhead Newspaper Publisher 291
    Reed W. Smith

20. Picturing the News: Frank Leslie and the
    Origins of American Pictorial Journalism 309
    William E. Huntzicker

21. Jewish Press Coverage of an Anti-Semitic Act:
    Grant's Order No. 11 325
    Barbara Straus Reed

22. Visibility of Women in Newspaper Advertisements
    During the Civil War 349
    Hazel Dicken-Garcia

23. Samuel Chester Reid, Jr.: Confederate Correspondent, 1861-1864 373
    Lisa M. Daigle

	Table of Contents	vii

24. Devil to Clown: News Coverage of the Capture of Jefferson Davis 389
    Robert Dardenne

25. Journalistic Impedimenta:
    William Tecumseh Sherman and Free Expression 407
    John Glen

26. The Role of the First Lady and the Media:
    A Preliminary Case Study of *New York Times* Coverage
    of Mary Todd Lincoln, 1861-1865 419
    Katherine E. Roberts

27. Journalists First, Rebels Second: An Examination of
    Editorial Reaction to the President's
    Proposed Conscription of Newspapermen 437
    Debra Reddin van Tuyll

28. Isaac Mayer Wise, *The Israelite*, and the Civil War 451
    Barbara Straus Reed

Part III. Reconstructing a Nation

29. Republican Newspapers and Freedom of the Press
    in the Reconstruction South, 1865-1877 473
    Richard H. Abbott

30. Suffrage for Freedmen: The Specter of *Dred Scott* 485
    Kenneth Rystrom

31. The Michigan Democratic Press and the Fifteenth Amendment:
    A Divided Party United 503
    Janice L. Bukovac

32. Partisan News in the Early Reconstruction Era:
    Representations of African-Americans in Detroit's Daily Press 519
    Richard Kaplan

33. Wanted Dead or Alive: How Nineteenth Century
    Missouri Journalists Framed Jesse James 547
    Cathy M. Jackson

Index 571

Tables

Chapter 11

Table 1. Newspapers and Editorial Slant 1860-1861 and 1860-1861 Vote	151
Table 2. Democratic Newspapers 1860-1861 and 1860 Vote	152
Table 3. Democratic Newspapers 1860-1861 and 1861 Vote for Secession	153
Table 4. Democratic Newspapers 1850-1861 and 1861 Vote for Union	154
Table 5. Whig Newspapers 1850-1861 and 1861 Whig Vote	155
Table 6. Whig Newspapers 1850-1861 and Secession Vote	156
Table 7. Whig Newspapers 1850-1861 and Vote for Union	157

Chapter 22

Table 1. Adveriesments in the *New York Times*	358
Table 2. Advertisements in the *Richmond Dispatch*	359
Table 3. Classification of Advertisements in the *Richmond Dispatch*	362
Table 4. Advertisements in the *Richmond Enquirer* (by category)	362
Table 5. Advertisements in the *Richmond Enquirer* (by date)	362
Table 6. Advertisements in the *New York Times*	363
Table 7. Advertisements in the *New York Tribune* (by category)	363
Table 8. Advertisements in the *New York Tribune* (by date)	364
Table 9. Advertisements in the *Cincinnati Commercial* (by category)	364
Table 10. Advertisements in the *Cincinnati Commercial* (by date)	365
Table 11. Advertisements in the *Charleston Mercury* (by category)	365
Table 12. Advertisements in the *Charleston Mercury* (by date)	365
Table 13. Advertisements in the *Charleston Courier* (by category)	366
Table 14. Advertisements in the *Charleston Courier* (by date)	366
Table 15. Summary of Advertisements Reflecting Images of Women in Seven Newspapers on Two Dates in 1861 and 1864	367

Introduction

What was American journalism like in the 19th century? Did newspapers look the way they do today? Were there reporters and columnists? Did many people read 19th century newspapers? Or only the elite? Or city dwellers?

Were 19th century newspapers influential? Were some of them powerful? Many people believe that by the end of the century, some big city newspapers were so powerful that publishers like William Randolph Hearst and Joseph Pulitzer could and did set the agenda for the United States to go to war. But while newspaper publishers took the credit for the Spanish-American War, historians generally do not blame publishers for starting the Civil War. Weren't the newspapers of the 1830s, 1840s, and the 1850s influential enough to set the regional public agendas of the North, South, and West, regional agendas that became so fractional that Abraham Lincoln couldn't even get one electoral vote in the South in 1860?

These are a few of the questions that led to the creation of the Symposium on the 19th Century Press, the Civil War, and Free Expression at the University of Tennessee at Chattanooga. What follows are some of the answers provided by historians, political scientists, and scholars of journalism, among others. While they tend to be highly specific, as is most good scholarship nowadays, taken together they point to broader answers: That the antebellum press was more influential than is commonly thought, though maybe not powerful enough to support the concept of agenda-setting. And that the 19th century media were more diverse than is usually acknowledged. Most of all, they tell fascinating, little-known stories about larger than life but very real characters, the editors and publishers of the day.

The 19th Century Press, the Civil War, and Free Expression Project

This project on the 19th Century Press, the Civil War, and Free Expression started in 1993 when the George R. West Jr. Chair of Excellence in Communication and Public Affairs and the Department of Communication at the University of Tennessee at Chattanooga invited leading 19th century journalism historians and Civil War journalism historians to join Kit Rushing and me in Chattanooga to discuss the possibility of creating an annual symposium.

The "Antebellum and Civil War Press and Freedom of Expression" conference took place on November 5, 1993 at UTC. It was attended by 11 leading experts in 19th century and Civil War press history, representatives from the Chattanooga community and the university, and more than 50 students. The journalism historians gave presentations about their work in Civil War press history and then voted to form a steering committee to support future conferences in November 1994, 1995, and 1996 on the Antebellum and Civil War Press and Freedom of Expression. The journalism and Civil War historians who voted with Kit Rushing and me to form the steering committee and serve as judges for what would become a refereed symposium were: Edd Applegate (Middle Tennessee State University), Charles Caudill (University of Tennessee, Knoxville), Lloyd Chiasson (Nicholls State University, Thibodaux, LA), Robert Dardenne (University of South Florida at St. Petersburg), David Mindich (New York University), Barbara Reed (Rutgers University, New Brunswick, NJ), Don Reynolds (East Texas State University, Commerce), Leonard Ray Teel (Georgia State University, Atlanta), Dwight Teeter (University of Tennessee, Knoxville), Gary Whitby (East Texas Sate University), and Gene Wiggins (University of Southern Mississippi, Hattiesburg). Many of these scholars have continued to serve on the steering committee and as referees throughout the life of the conference, and several of them have submitted papers for judging. A number of these papers are included in this volume.

Two of the papers in this book were presented at the November 5, 1993 organizational meeting. (David Mindich presented his just-published monograph on the inverted pyramid and Kit Rushing delivered his paper on agenda-setting.) The rest of these papers were presented at annual conferences in November 1994, 1995, 1996, and 1997. In 1997 the name of the conference was changed from the Symposium on the Antebellum Press, the Civil War, and Free Expression to the

Symposium on the 19th Century Press, the Civil War, and Free Expression in order to broaden the scope of discussion.

The overall goal of the annual conferences has been to lay a foundation for the development and sharing of scholarship on the 19th century press, the Civil War and the press, and 19th century concepts of free expression. My personal goal for the conference has been to encourage research on the role of the 19th century press in setting the agenda for the Civil War. (The conference regularly includes an opening night discussion on "Did the Antebellum Press Set the Agenda for Civil War?")

The first section of this volume, "Setting the Agenda for Secession and War," discusses the antebellum press. The second section concerns the press "In Time of War," while the third section, "Reconstructing a Nation," concerns the role of the press in the Reconstruction era.

Setting the Agenda for Secession and War

The book begins with Yvonne Carignan's examination of "Western Maryland Newspapers 1820-1860: American Culture in Transition," which sets the scene for our examination of 19th century American life. The newspapers of their time reflect the changing nature of American culture from community-centered family economics "toward the consumer society of modern America," says Carignan.

Steven G. Saltzgiver reminds us that the states' rights position of nullification and even secession were very real issues in the antebellum period as he discusses "Consensus and Public Debate: The Washington Press During the Nullification Crisis 1832-1833." The threat of armed resistance in South Carolina was real enough to President Andrew Jackson to cause him to make preparations, explains Saltzgiver.

Nancy Dupont then takes us (in "Mississippi Newspapers and the Secession Convention: The Influence on Anti-Secessionist Porter Jacob Myers") to the Mississippi of 1860 and 1861, when most Mississippi newspapers favored secession while a few cooperationist papers either called for resistance within the Union (Unionists) or for the secession of all slave-holding states *en masse* (Southern Cooperationists).

Southern fears had been fueled in October 1859 by John Brown's attack on Harper's Ferry, explains Bernell E. Tripp in "'John Brown Still Lives!': The Case of John Brown." "Are the thinking men of the

North ready for civil war -- a war of vengeance, embittered by the hottest fanaticism? Will they recognize the desperado, Osawatomie Brown, as a martyr in a good cause...?" asked the *New Orleans Daily Picayune* on October 27.

"The news coverage of John Brown's Raid of 1859, the subsequent trial, and execution, represent 'a milestone in the development of American journalism,'" says Robert C. Kennedy in "Censorship, Racism and the Antebellum Press: *Harper's Weekly* Reports Harper's Ferry." Kennedy argues that it was the coming of age for modern field reporting: "Never before in American history had so many reporters and illustrators been sent by distant urban newspapers to cover a breaking story." Kennedy concentrates on the coverage provided by *Harper's Weekly* and its writer and illustrator David Hunter Strother, known by the pen name "Porte Crayon."

Leonard Ray Teel takes us back to an earlier period in the development of the abolitionist movement in "Abolitionism at the Crossroads: Lydia Maria Child and the *National Anti-Slavery Standard*, 1841-1843." His paper is of particular interest because it concerns one of the first women to serve as an abolitionist leader "at a time when women in the movement were excluded from meetings and relegated to supporting roles as fundraisers." As a journalist, Lydia Maria Child also was an early feminist who refused to publish stories "which tell of countries where they raise 'fine wine and fine women,' or where they have 'the handsomest horses and the handsomest wives.'" She had "thrown aside all poetry about 'tempting lips and voluptuous forms,' all jokes about matrimony and women."

J. Michael Robertson and Alton Loftis believe that scholars tend to oversimplify the antebellum South and Southern periodicals as being preoccupied with slavery and politics. They note that journalism historian Frank Luther Mott considered Charleston, South Carolina's *Russell's Magazine* one of a number of Southern publications that were made "ardently sectional" by proslavery arguments. In "I hear nothing about me now but politics--slavery and antislavery *ad nauseam*: Paul Hamilton Hayne and the editorial policy of *Russell's Magazine* 1857-1860," Robertson and Loftis argue that while *Russell's Magazine* was "passionately pro-Southern," its editor Paul Hayne attempted to find a middle way between hating and tolerating "the North and all things Northern." Literature, not slavery or politics, was the principal interest of the periodical, they say.

Kentucky was a slave state, but it was also the home of an antislavery newspaper. In "The Lion's Roar: Cassius Clay's *The True*

American," Gene Murray tells the story of the birth of the newspaper in June 1845, its temporary suppression in August, and its revival in September ("bearing a Lexington dateline but printed in Cincinnati"). *The True American* lasted until October 1846 and was succeeded by another emancipation newspaper, the *Louisville Examiner*, which died from lack of funds in December 1849.

Slavery and politics were not the only two issues in the antebellum South, or the rest of America for that matter. Religion was a central issue of the day, and in 1850 there were 191 religious newspapers and other periodicals publishing in the United States. David A. Copeland tells the interesting and little known story of "Preserving a Denomination: The Promotion of Women by North Carolina's Antebellum Baptist Press," the story of the female readership of religious newspapers.

What role did the newspapers of the South play in support of secession? In South Carolina, the *Charleston Mercury* led the call for secession, and in Mississippi "when the [*Jackson Mississippian*] roared... all the little papers yelped." Nancy Dupont describes the overpowering influence of the politician/editor of the *Mississippian* in "Mississippi's Fire-Eating Editor Ethelbert Barksdale and the Election of 1860."

Examining East Tennessee, Kit Rushing compares the results of the presidential election of 1860 and the secession election of 1861 with the political positions of the 16 newspapers then published in the region. In "Agenda-Setting in Antebellum East Tennessee," Rushing argues that "rather than fomenting the secession shift that occurred in the South between the elections of 1860 and 1861, antebellum newspapers at most reflected existing opinion."

The newspaper industry changed dramatically from the advent of the penny press in the 1830s to the beginning of the Civil War. This was especially true in the urban Northeast. Robert Dardenne discusses these revolutionary changes in journalism by focusing on the *Hartford* (Conn.) *Courant* in "Between Tradition and Innovation: The Nature of Antebellum News in the *Courant*."

One of the most significant innovations of this period was the development of the inverted pyramid form of presentation, the format in which the most important information is given first (and the least important comes last). Dardenne's analysis of the development of the inverted pyramid style makes reference to David Mindich's research on this topic, which is presented in the next chapter.

In Time of War

All of the articles in this book were presented at one or another of the annual conferences on the 19th Century Press, the Civil War, and Free Expression held at the University of Tennessee at Chattanooga in the middle 1990s.

One of these papers was actually published first, David Mindich's "Edwin Stanton, the Inverted Pyramid, and Information Control," which was published in *Journalism Monographs* in August 1993. When the conference organizers read this monograph, they invited Mindich, then a graduate student at New York University, to present his paper at the meeting which established the annual Chattanooga conference.

Mindich argues in his groundbreaking paper that the earliest examples of the use of inverted pyramids were not written by journalists but rather by Edwin M. Stanton, Abraham Lincoln's Secretary of War. Stanton's "terse impersonal dispatches," which were published "unedited on the front pages of newspapers across the Union," were written in inverted pyramids, explains Mindich.

The women's rights movement in the United States began in the antebellum era and by the 1850s supported a number of periodicals. In the Civil War period of 1861-1864 only one women's rights periodical was published, the *Mayflower*, an eight-page semimonthly edited in Peru, Indiana by Lizzie Bunnell. In "For women and the War: A Cultural Analysis of the *Mayflower*, 1861-1864," Janet Cramer discusses the images and ideas of womanhood presented in the pages of the *Mayflower* and the fate of the women's rights movement in the Civil War era.

The Jewish press in America essentially began with the publication in 1843 of Isaac Leeser's monthly magazine *The Occident and American Jewish Advocate*. Published in Philadelphia, it circulated throughout the country, making Leeser a leader of the Jewish community. During the Civil War, Leeser was loyal to the Union, but refused to condemn the South, explains Barbara Reed in "Isaac Leeser and the *The Occident*: A Jewish Leader's Response to the Civil War." In this chapter, and in two more in this book, Reed discusses the role of the Jewish press concerning the major issues facing Jews during the Civil War.

What was the Southern press like during the Civil War? Some newspapers, like the small, weekly *Albany* (Ga.) *Patriot* were so fiercely optimistic about the Confederacy's chances of winning that they tell us much more about the public opinion of the time than about the events. "True to its nature," says Ford Risley in "The *Albany Patriot* 1861-1865: Struggling to Publish and Struggling to Remain Optimistic," "the *Patriot* concluded the account of Appomattox with this proclamation: 'We are yet unconquered, and until the sword of the enemy is at our throats, we upbraid our fellow citizens for their nefarious conduct. God help our country.'"

What images of women were presented by newspapers during the Civil War? To answer this question, Hazel Dicken-Garcia and Janet Cramer examined 100 news items about women carried in five different newspapers plus items quoted in secondary sources from ten other papers. Most of the stories they read came from Northern newspapers from 1861 to 1863. They concluded (in "Images of Women in Civil War Newspapers: Leave the 'Proper Sphere'") that "the war created a way for women to enter the public sphere" and that this was reflected in the newspaper coverage of women during the period.

After reading about the *Albany Patriot*, one would expect that a Georgia newspaper's news coverage would reflect the state's politics. "Interestingly enough, this was not always so for most newspapers in Georgia," says Debra Reddin van Tuyll in "Two Men, Two Minds: The Editorial Commentary of Two Georgia Editors During Sherman's March to the Sea." No matter how divergent their editorials were, most Georgia newspapers carried similar news stories, says van Tuyll, in her comparison of the *Augusta Chronicle* and the *Macon Telegraph*.

Was Samuel A. Medary a great journalist and defender of freedom of the press or was he a traitor and "one of the devil's own children"? That is "The Paradox of Samuel Medary, Copperhead Newspaper Publisher," writes Reed Smith. Medary was an Ohio Peace Democrat politician and newspaper editor whose newspaper office was attacked twice, once by soldiers and once by civilians, in response to his "flagrant opposition journalism."

Nowadays when we think of national news media we think of the television networks and the weekly news magazines. During the Civil War, three illustrated newspapers -- *Harper's Weekly, Frank Leslie's Illustrated Newspaper,* and the *New York Illustrated News* competed in the national market, at least in the North. In "Picturing the News: Frank Leslie and the Origins of the American Pictorial Journalism," William Huntzicker tells the story of the creation of illustrated periodicals in America and of the Civil War correspondents and "special artists, the illustrator/reporters who sent back both written and artistic sketches from the field."

On December 17, 1862, General Ulysses S. Grant issued order number 11 to expel all Jews from the Department of Tennessee. In "Jewish Press Coverage of an Anti-Semitic Act: Grant's Order No.

11," Barbara Reed tells the story of this shocking incident and of the Jewish periodicals that responded to it.

"Given attitudes about women's sphere at the time of the Civil War, plus the need for everyone to assist during the war and women's unprecedented activities, did notions about women's 'proper sphere' change, and, if so, what propelled the change?" asks Hazel Dicken-Garcia in "Visibility of Women in Newspaper Advertisements During the Civil War." Specifically, in this article, Dicken-Garcia is interested in "whether newspaper advertisements revealed changing notions of gender roles" and "the degree to which women seemed to be recognized as part of the newspaper audience and as exercising purchasing power."

Samuel C. Reid, Jr. was a special correspondent who wrote for a number of Southern newspapers during the Civil War. In telling his story (in "Samuel Chester Reid, Jr.: Confederate Correspondent, 1861-1864") Lisa Daigle gives us a sense of what life was like for Southern reporters during this time. She peppers her article with quotes from Reid's dispatches that are often as interesting as they are informative. Of particular delight to a reader from Chattanooga, Tennessee is Reid's description of the region: "East Tennessee is the Switzerland of America, and presents views of river, mountain and valley scenery not excelled by any in the world."

What does the coverage of the arrest of Jefferson Davis tell us about the news and newspapers of 1865? asks Robert Dardenne in "Devil to Clown: News Coverage of the Capture of Jefferson Davis." In this article, Dardenne shows that some Northern newspapers blamed Davis for the assassination of Abraham Lincoln, thus setting a mood that resulted in the dissemination of wild rumors about Davis' whereabouts and finally even the circumstances of his capture.

William Tecumseh Sherman did not see the virtues of a free press in times of war, says John Glen in "Journalistic Impedimenta: William Tecumseh Sherman and Free Expression." This short article provides an overview of Sherman's problems with the press in the early years of the Civil War.

Kate Roberts' "The Role of the First Lady and the Media: A Preliminary Case Study of *New York Times* Coverage of Mary Todd Lincoln, 1861-1865," is the fourth article in this volume concerning women and the media during the Civil War. They come from the University of Minnesota, the home of journalism professor Hazel Dicken-Garcia. In this article, Roberts discusses Mary Todd Lincoln's entrance into the public sphere, and how the *New York*

Times refused to criticize Mrs. Lincoln while Lincoln was alive, depicting her "in a manner that would lead a reader to believe her behavior never deviated from the proper sphere and women's traditional role."

In November 1864, President Jefferson Davis asked the Confederate Congress to begin drafting newspaper employees, among others. His speech "provoked howls of protest by Southern newspaper editors," reports Debra Reddin van Tuyll in "Journalists First, Rebels Second: An Examination of Editorial Reaction to the Proposed Conscription of Newspapermen." Van Tuyll says this "was but one of Davis' several mistakes at the end of the war... which were to weaken Confederate morale and fighting spirit." Clearly, the press reacted to the speech by publishing "divisive commentaries."

This volume has three papers on the Jewish press and the Civil War, all by Barbara Reed. While there necessarily is some duplication among these papers, we are including all three because together they give a fairly complete picture of the Jewish periodicals of the period. The reaction of the Jewish press to General Ulysses S. Grant's notorious General Order No. 11 is a unifying feature of the three papers, but each stands on its own. This chapter is about the most distinguished organizer and leader of the Reform Jewish movement, "Isaac Mayer Wise, *The Israelite* and the Civil War."

Reconstructing a Nation

After the Civil War, nearly 400 Republican party newspapers were started in the former Confederate states, reports Richard Abbott in "Republican Newspapers and Freedom of the Press in the Reconstruction South, 1865-1877." They were supported not by subscriptions and advertising but by "printing contracts provided by federal, state, and local governments."

"When federal subsidies ended, and as Republicans in the South lost control of the state and local governments, their party newspapers, deprived of patronage, all but disappeared. From the perspective of the Southern Republicans," says Abbott, "government, rather than threatening freedom of the press, was the only means of sustaining it."

In "Suffrage for Freedmen: The Specter of Dred Scott," Kenneth Rystrom charts the reactions of both conservative Southern editors and Radical Republicans to the developing issue of voting rights for freedmen. He concludes that after 1876, with the return of Southern conservatives to political power, it would become clear that the end of slavery did not necessarily guarantee "the full enjoyment of the blessings of freedom."

In the period following the Civil War, the Democratic newspapers of the North, like their Southern counterparts, continued to argue against black civil rights legislation, reports Janice Bukovac in "The Michigan Democratic Press and the Fifteenth Amendment: A Divided Party United." The editorials of Michigan Democratic newspapers against black suffrage "were frightening in their predictions," says Bukovac.

Detroit's Democratic newspapers editorialized "against civil rights for blacks, by selecting news that depicted the negative consequences of Republican Southern policies, and by elaborating stereotyped images of the emancipated blacks," says Richard Kaplan in "Partisan News in the Early Reconstruction Era: Representations of African-Americans in Detroit's Daily Press." And by 1876, continues Kaplan, the Republican party was abandoning its support for civil rights for blacks, acceding "to the racist depiction promulgated by the Democratic media."

Jesse James became a folk hero, according to historian Kent L. Steckmesser, "because he operated outside the law during the post-Civil War days, a time when Reconstruction laws and conquering unionists were considered unjust by many Southerners, including western Missourians," reports Cathy Jackson in "Wanted Dead or Alive: How Nineteenth Century Missouri Journalists Framed Jesse James." Jackson tracks down the role of contemporary newspapers in creating the myth of Jesse James and finds John Newman Edwards, the editor of the *Kansas City Times* and a friend of the James family. This is a fascinating story and the fitting end to this volume on the Civil War and the Press.

In conclusion, we would like to thank the *Chattanooga Times Chattanooga Free Press*, Publisher Walter E. Hussman, Jr., Associate Publisher Paul Neely, Managing Editor Bob Lutgen and President Frank McDonald for institutional support for the publication of this book; and we would like to thank Augusta State University senior communications major Michelle Violette for her editorial assistance in preparing this volume.

David B. Sachsman
Chattanooga, Tennessee
March 1999

I

Setting the Agenda for Secession and War

1

Western Maryland Newspapers, 1820 -1860: American Culture in Transition

Yvonne Carignan
University of Maryland

The culture of Western Maryland and the role of its newspapers as a mirror of that culture deserve attention. In Western Maryland lay the busy crossroads through which passed much of the activity that drove the growing young country before the Civil War. From the northeast to the southwest, the great valley migration route passed through Hagerstown and Williamsport. Germans and Scots-Irish, so important in pushing back the American frontier in the eighteenth century, stayed in Western Maryland and permanently shaped its character. From southeast to northwest, the development of a route out to the Ohio River focused on the turnpikes, canals, and, finally, the railroads.[1] Farming, milling, and mining produced the commodities for trade back down the new transportation routes to the commercial center of Baltimore.

The inland portion of a "middle state,"[2] by the mid-nineteenth century Western Maryland no longer formed the frontier, yet remained remote in character from bustling eastern cities. The newspapers of

Hagerstown, Frederick, Williamsport, and Cumberland traded information with newer western centers such as Cincinnati, as well as with older urban areas such as Philadelphia and New York. The many credits to sources of articles in these newspapers testified to that exchange.[3] At the same time, Western Maryland's local papers contained meetings, obituaries, advertisements, opinion, and news of interest only to the locality. These newspapers served their communities, in between an old and a new civilization, with the ideas and values of both cultures. The old community-centered culture, characterized by scarcity and an appreciation of character over fashion and appearance, was inhabited by the pious, the patriotic, and a surprising lot of hard-drinkers. The new culture was composed of individualists, interested in making something of themselves and partaking in the growing American industrial society with its increasingly available and affordable consumer goods.

Western Maryland stood not only in between two geographic areas, but two chronological periods as well. America's family farm economy moved toward industrialization and even toward the consumer culture that dominates America today. Improvements in transportation not only facilitated the vast westward movement of Americans and settlement of the country, but made possible the coming national market economy. A new relationship had to be negotiated between localities and what historian Daniel Boorstin has called "the national experience."[4] Factory goods became more affordable to the mass of Americans even while the gap between the rich and the poor grew larger. The economic changes were accompanied by social changes as the cohesive fabric of integrated communities gave way to the individualism and self-promotion that Michael Schudson terms "society."[5]

As part of my objective in this paper, I hope to describe the culture of Western Maryland in the early 19th century as reflected in its newspapers. For this paper, I am defining culture narrowly as "intellectual and artistic activity" (American Heritage Dictionary, 1970 ed.) and as the leisure activities that people pursued when they were not working, praying, or politicking.[6] I also hope to investigate whether those newspapers communicated a culture grounded in the values of the old producer ethic, or whether that culture had already assumed the tastes of the coming age of consumerism. I will examine the newspapers to decipher the variety of cultural messages they sent, and draw some conclusions about the significance of that message in American history.

In drawing such conclusions, the works of several scholars will guide my efforts. Jürgen Habermas, while focusing more on politics than culture, provides useful theory for understanding the changes underway. In *The Structural Transformation of the Public Sphere*, Habermas writes of the change in the function of the press from an "exchange of communications among the members of a public" to "circulation of a commodity." He explains how big advertising agencies bought up space in newspapers of the mid-nineteenth century and soon translated their large payments into control over the newspapers. To Habermas, that control bode ill for the public sphere because "privileged private interests" ultimately used mass media to falsify and commodify public opinion.[7]

While the phenomenon of advertising agencies occurred in eastern cities rather than in western Maryland, Habermas's concerns relate to the centralization and commercialization of culture, precisely the transition that this paper will document. Michael Schudson, in *Discovering the News*, deals with similar themes when he writes of the change from community to society during the Jacksonian period. Most likely, Western Maryland of the Jacksonian era had communities with some semblance of "the old world of face-to-face human ties — of family, kinship, neighborhood, and social circle." Meanwhile, the rise of a democratic market society — in contrast to self-sufficient family economies — led to the admiration of a new virtue: "self-interest."[8] While Schudson seems to associate the early growth of individualism with big cities, another historian, Lawrence Frederick Kohl, maintains that new transportation networks transformed the whole country during the Jacksonian era. Not just urbanites and town people, but "even simple farmers were caught up in the restless pursuit of wealth. Enticed by new opportunities, they increasingly turned from a household economy of self-sufficiency and barter to production for the market and the cash nexus. . . . The idea of the self-made man emerged as individuals scrambled to improve their station in life."[9]

The Frenchman, Alexis de Tocqueville, writing of his travels in 1831 and 1832, testified to his firsthand experience of the shift from community to society through American individualism. Tocqueville saw individualism as "a mature and calm feeling" which disposed "each member of the community to sever himself from the mass of his fellows. . . ."[10] While he found the origins of individualism in democracy, Tocqueville argued that individualism would sap "the virtues of public life" and lead to selfishness. From his perspective in the 1830s, Tocqueville, unlike Habermas, thought newspapers the solution to the destruction of a public sphere:

> When men are no longer united amongst themselves by firm and lasting ties, it is impossible to obtain the co-operation of any great number of them, unless you can persuade every man whose help you require that his private interest obliges him voluntarily to unite his exertions to the exertions of all the others. This can be habitually and conveniently effected only by means of a newspaper: nothing but a newspaper can drop the same thought into a thousand minds at the same moment.11

The dichotomy between a world of family and community versus individualism and self-fulfillment receives analysis by Warren I. Susman in *Culture as History*. Susman identifies traditional America as "Puritan-republican, producer-capitalist culture that envisioned a world of scarcity, . . . hard work, self-denial, . . . sacrifice, and character." By 1852, Susman finds Rev. Henry W. Bellows preaching about advertisement as "a scheme for creating wants."12 Here we find roots for the culture of buying, selling, and consuming — a "leisure ethic" — that has dominated the United States throughout the Twentieth Century.13 While the age of abundance did not fully arrive during the period under study here, this examination of selected Western Maryland newspapers finds ample evidence of the transitions from traditional to consumer culture.

The Newspapers of Western Maryland

A number of newspapers survive to document this area from the foot of the Catoctin Mountains at Frederick, through Maryland's Hagerstown Valley at Hagerstown, over to the Potomac River and C & O Canal towns of Williamsport and Cumberland.14 Those four towns each supported one or more papers between 1820 and 1860.15 To cover both the time span and the geographic area, I chose to examine six titles: two from Hagerstown and Frederick, and one from Williamsport and Cumberland. From each run of newspapers, I then selected one issue per year. To provide for seasonal variety and a sense of newspaper content at all times of the year, I followed a pattern of selection demonstrated by the following example: January 1821, April 1822, July 1823, October 1824, February 1825, and so on. Altogether, sixty-two issues comprise the sample read for this paper.16

Advertisements might appear on any page in these newspapers which seemed to have few rules about where different types of material appeared. Front pages typically ran a poem or two, short stories, and excerpts of books and periodicals. The same newspaper that published such a combination one time, however, might also run a front page full of advertisements and notices the next time, placing poetry on page four.

If the layout of Western Maryland newspapers varied, so did the content. Richard T. Stillson, in his thesis "Virginia Newspapers in the 1830s," found that those newspapers included a "diverse range of topics, features, and advertising. . . ." Western Maryland newspapers also featured a diverse range, and also bore out Stillson's findings that while politics appeared in some of these papers, others ran "little or no political party coverage."[17] One can, however, identify certain patterns of coverage that remained consistent throughout the period. For instance, books and medicines consistently dominated advertisements.[18] A large quantity of notices also invited the public to taverns or advised them of the availability of such taverns for rent or sale. In volume, perhaps the most space in these newspapers went to stories and anecdotes. Sometimes books appeared chapter by chapter over a space of several weeks, and covered most of the front page. Taking up less space or appearing less frequently, a variety of other items — such as notices of organizations, exhibitions, or parades — expressed values, made judgements, or in some other way provided clues to illuminate the transition underway.

Cultural Life in Western Maryland

Western Maryland newspapers reveal that the culture of the area in the early nineteenth century equated Schudson's "community." Towns revolved around a self-sufficient family farm and shop economy. People focused their lives around their church, celebrated patriotic events, and participated in local, community related activities. The town provided the places where neighbors and friends met to conduct their community activities and share their common interests. Although these patterns dominated cultural life at the time, signs of commercialization, individualism, and changes in the national culture began to appear in the newspapers.

Ample press coverage of patriotic events during the first decades of the nineteenth century, for example, reflected community oriented celebrations: by the late 1850s, signs of a commercialized patriotism appeared. Among the myriad occasions for local patriotism in the early nineteenth century, speeches, parades, and even public art in the form of memorial sculpture and monuments resulted in community gatherings. When in 1824 the popular Revolutionary War hero, LaFayette, visited America, citizens of Frederick Maryland organized a welcoming celebration. The *Frederick-Town Herald* of 11 September 1824 announced completion of preparations for the "Grand Fete," the effort to assemble a procession of 20,000 by adding 5,000 children to the number of marchers, and a meeting at the court house to organize a committee to "wait on" General LaFayette. Nowhere in reports of Frederick's local feting of the hero appeared any hints of buying and selling: the event appeared to be a purely patriotic community celebration.

Community-centered patriotic celebration came to the forefront, naturally enough during the early nineteenth century, in newspaper coverage of holidays commemorating the birthday of the young nation, or of its "Father," George Washington. The newspapers not only announced these holidays, but editorialized on the proper ways to celebrate them. The *Frederick Herald* of 7 July 1827 complemented the local Fourth of July festivities which were done "in a becoming manner" — with the roar of cannon, peels of merry bells, music of fife and drum, and parades, orations, reading of the Declaration of Independence, and soldiers in neat uniforms. The 4 July 1835 *Republican Banner* of Williamsport, however, found in all of Washington County only one "manifestation of patriotism . . . worthy of its inhabitants." That model event occurred in Smithson where "the waving of banners, the sound of guns, the stirring notes of music, and the voice of eloquence and song" provided appropriate entertainment. The author of the report condemned the "orgies of Bacchus" that the rest of the county apparently used to celebrate the Fourth. Whether held "in a becoming manner" or not, these patriotic celebrations provided indigenous entertainment, organized locally and immune to outside conceptions of propriety.

A hint of the commercialization of patriotism to come appeared in the fund drives to erect statuary and monuments. The *Hagerstown Torch Light and Public Advertiser* reported a new monument at Bunker Hill on 5 October 1824, and a drive in New York to fund a statue in memory of George Washington. During 1822 and 1823, both the *Frederick-Town Herald* and the *Torch Light* advertised lotteries to benefit the District of Columbia's Washington Monument. But these advertisements did not solely appeal to patriotism. To that theme they added the easy money from the lottery's "splendid scheme."[19]

Commodification — the reduction of patriotism to a sales strategy — occurred a few decades later. By 1859, an appeal to patriotism for support of a public monument in the 1820s had given way to the use of that sentiment for the sale of a print of Mount Vernon. In the 9 July 1859 *Cumberland Democratic Alleganian*, the celebrated orator Edward Everett recommended the print whose subject — the home of George Washington — "endears itself to the heart of the country" and cost only fifty cents. Here, instead of rousing people to support their country, patriotism simply sold a product. The transition from patriotic values to commercialism had begun.

By the 1850s, Western Maryland newspapers reported on an organization which promoted both commercialization and a nationally — versus a locally —oriented project. The Colonization Society represented the infiltration of a national movement into a local interest. A long report in the *Cumberland Alleganian* of 15 February 1851 praised the Society for "attracting the attention of philanthropists and statesmen in every section of our country." The Colonization Society, its goals described glowingly as "this great work . . . with motives of humanity," appealed to "the duty of our people to aid in ridding themselves of a population that cannot improve our condition while here. . . ." In other words, this Society planned to deal with free Blacks by exiling them from the United States and shipping them to Liberia, Africa. Apparently, horrible health conditions in Liberia resulted in a loss of enthusiasm for the Colonization project, but the *Examiner* of 17 September 1851 reported a new plan to send Blacks to Trinidad instead. That report clearly outlined the reasoning:

> popular opinion in this country, . . . especially in the non-slave holding States, is eventually to expel the free people of color. Already, they are excluded from some, — tolerated only under oppressive restrictions in others, — and regarded as a growing evil in all the states.

Racism, hopes for trade benefits — former U. S. Blacks were to produce cotton — and missionary zeal — to bring Christianity to Africa — all joined together to justify this project.[20]

Besides the foremost motivation, the expulsion of unwanted African-Americans, the Colonization Society preached commercial advantages to potential supporters. One Society report quoted Thomas Jefferson on that very issue: "Exclusive of motives of humanity, the commercial advantages to be derived from it might defray all its expenses."[21] Another report elaborated by pointing out that the population of Africa numbered 10,000,000 people who would trade "gold dust, ivory, gums, and hides" for "tobacco, a yard of muslin, a string of beads, shoes, hats, hatchets, &c." In addition, "laboring men may be employed to any extent, at the lowest rates." The Colonization used these tempting profit opportunities to appeal to specific groups as it concluded its request for funding:

> To the cotton manufacturer we can say, here are many millions of naked people, all of whom would be clothed if they could barter the productions of the soil for cotton cloth. The cheapest yard of cotton manufactured in this country will sell in the interior for fifty cents and the natives will return you rich dye stuffs in exchange. To the blacksmiths we will say, here is a demand for millions of axes, hoes, hatchets, &c. if you will give them in exchange for the productions of the soil. The shoe maker, tanner, potter, and almost every other mechanic in our country, can find a sale of their productions on equally favorable terms. . . . Will not a discerning public always awake to its own interests; come forward and set this vast machine in motion.22

Commercialization thus drove the Colonization Society which commodified both the settlement of Liberia and the population of potential customers in Africa.

The work of the Colonization Society provided a chilling view of profit-driven society, but Western Maryland newspapers continued to reflect the values of an older culture before the Civil War. Stories, poems, and anecdotes published in those newspapers throughout the first half of the nineteenth century preached against the superficiality of material gain. The poems, for instance, usually related to one of the following themes: death, the superficiality of beauty, and the importance of charity. The emphasis on death ranged from grief over the loss of a young wife or small child, to a yearning for heaven, to the morbid refrain, "Ye are hastening to dust!"23 The modern reader begins to glimpse the fragility of life during that time. Garry Wills has observed that not just the high mortality rate, but the nineteenth century romantics' fascination with dreams, spiritualism, and the rituals of mourning led to this pre-occupation with death.24 In *Western Attitudes toward Death: From the Middle Ages to the Present*, Philippe Aries elaborated further about the rituals of mourning. By the nineteenth century, Aries sees a new ostentation in grieving which passed fixed social conventions of mourning.25

Western Maryland newspapers, however, documented not excess of mourning, but stoic acceptance and faith in heaven. Even heart wrenching descriptions of a child's death focused on the hereafter. For instance, The *Cumberland Alleganian* (31 January 1857) printed a poem by Daniel Webster about the death of his three year old. While his "house is sad and dreary," Webster believed his darling "safe in Heaven" and asks the child to "guide me there." Other poems praised the same outlook. One lost beloved, "although she was happy in life, she trusted alone to heaven."26 Another approach, found in a poem entitled "To Miss Sally Rudd," called for a life of love together:

> "And when we've had a pleasant swing,
> We'll drop together in the valley.
> While still the tree of life shall wave,
> And bend the fraitage o'er our grave."27

The attitude expressed in these newspapers connoted comfort with the prospect of death, not over-reaction. Furthermore, apart from a handful of tombstone carvers' notices, the newspapers sampled offered no advertisements of funeral accoutrements, or of mourning clothes or jewelry. If the industry that profited from death already existed in Western Maryland before the Civil War, these newspapers provided no evidence of it. Seekers of commercial opportunity apparently had not yet discovered the industry of mourning.

The theme of submission to death received amplification in the obituaries found in those newspapers. The *Frederick-Town Herald* of 11 September 1824 reported that a local merchant faced his death with "patience and resignation." Mrs. Harriet Kemp exhibited "modest and retiring excellence of character," as well as "Christian fortitude," and Mrs. Rebecca Scrogin met death with "calmness of resignation."28 One short story in the *Herald of Freedom* of 3 July 1844 pessimistically pointed out that life could turn out so badly that "you may live to wish you died in the morning of your life." Perhaps the constant nearness of death contributed to a culture of self-denial and impatience with vanity. Certainly, the values expressed about death in the press upheld the traditional culture in contrast to newer trends of excessive display, self-indulgence, and consumerism.

In *The Refinement of America: Persons, Houses, Cities,* Richard Bushman argued that the eighteenth century saw the rise of gentility, refinement, and the consequential emphasis on material comfort and display. Such a leisure and consumer ethic contradicted the resident values of republicanism, work ethic, and religion. Bushman admitted the uncomfortable co-existence of the two value systems but maintained that gentility co-opted work ethic. In the resulting culture, one worked hard to produce and equally hard to get and spend. Before 1860 in Western Maryland, this compromise between materialism and self-denial held no share of the morals offered by the newspapers.29

Throughout the years between 1820 and 1860, the poems, stories, and anecdotes that dominated the newspapers taught the superiority of plain good sense over beauty and fashion. A "Parable for Ladies," in the *Cumberland Alleganian* of 25 December 1847, scolded women about envying the gaudy peacock. Instead, the parable taught the virtue of the dove, and advocated a character of meek constancy. The *Republican Banner* defined "loveliness" not as the "tinsel ornaments of the body, but in the reflection of the rectitude and serenity of a well spent life, that soars above the transient vanities of this world."30 On the top center of the front page, the *Cumberland Alleganian* of 31 January 1857 began a short piece: "Fashion kills more women than toil or sorrow." The hearty strength of the kitchen maid, the washer woman, and the slave women appeared as paragons compared to the "fashion-pampered" lady who had "to be nurtured like a sick baby." The piece concluded with a glance at the country's great men and women, who "nearly all sprang from plain, strong-minded women who had about as little to do with fashions as with the changing clouds." The 12 October 1850 *Cumberland Alleganian* ran a similar piece about men. In that story, young men made fools of themselves and ruined their credit by buying fancy clothes. Although newspapers accepted paid advertisements for the splendid new goods from the democratic market economy, they continued to deliver the moral message of the old producer ethic. Thus older values survived in the press of Western Maryland even as signs of the new consumer culture began to appear.

The Roots of a Commercial Culture

Through the evidence of newspapers of Western Maryland, one finds a culture that valued simplicity, as well as community activities, patriotism, and faith in heaven. At the same time, the newspapers reflected the region's exposure to America's increasingly individualistic society that brought changes, subtle but ultimately important. The evolution of attitudes about pianos illustrates. An article in the *Herald of Freedom*, 6 May 1846, played on the earlier attitude with a humorous tale of foolishness of vanity in fancy, new objects. In the story, "A Piano in Arkansas," the whole town became excited when a piano arrived. It was the first piano in town, and no one had ever seen one before, except for Mo Mercer, the proud owner, who "had seen more Pianos in the 'Capital' than he had ever seen wood-chucks." Mo continued in popularity until someone —

who could read — noticed the words "washing machine" on the side of the new wonder. "The fashionable vices of envy and maliciousness were that moment sown in the village of Hardscrabble," Mo slunk away, having dealt the blow of consumerism to a community previously forged by scarcity.

The earliest advertisement for pianos in this sample appeared in the *Frederick-Town Herald* of 24 April 1830 and reflected the old values of frugality and utility. The town's manufacturer of carpeting and coverlets had come by one piano which it offered not only as "the cheapest instrument ever offered in this place," but one "warranted to stand up in all climates." Nineteen years later, the *Herald of Freedom*, 28 March 1849, advertised grand and square pianos from the Piano Forte Manufactory in Baltimore. The pianos received the endorsement of Mr. Knoop, the "Great Master," and with an "elaborate finish," made a "splendid piece of furniture for the Drawing Room."

The advertisement of a luxurious piano marked a significant change from advertisements previously run by the newspapers in this sample. Formerly, advertisements announced local goods and services, mostly necessities with a few new "fancy" articles included. The new style of advertising transcended necessities, and, indeed, created a new class of necessity — the need to acquire luxury. When the piano became transformed from an instrument for home-made music to a drawing room ornament, industry and improved transportation routes had begun to succeed in creating the consumer culture. The conflicting tensions between the old and new cultures appeared in the newspapers of Western Maryland. At that time, in that culture, people struggled to pick between basic values, and the pursuit of possessions.

Newspapers showed simultaneously the power of the old ways and the allure of the coming changes. By 1850, the *Examiner* notified farmers of a two-year old periodical, *The Plough, the Loom and the Anvil*, designed for their "instruction and benefit."[31] While "this was acknowledged to be one the most instructive Agricultural works ever published in the country," no farmer in the region subscribed to it. The article asked farmers if they felt "so secure in their rich soil as not to feel the necessity of instruction or the want of information in the Agricultural pursuits?" For the small expense of this periodical, farmers might increase their crop yield by fifty percent! Clearly, this periodical appealed to farmers' interest in increasing their wealth, and disparaged those content with their current earnings. The fact that no farmers had so far taken the bait, provides another clue to the status of the consumer culture in Western Maryland. Lawrence Frederick Kohl argues that "Even simple farmers were caught up in the restless pursuit of wealth."[32] But it seems from these newspapers that Frederick area farmers still opted for their old ways, without the help of periodicals.

Still, transformations brought about by new technologies could not be denied. "The environment in which people lived and worked was altered. . . . Chemically produced colors made possible a world of color never before seen. Photography and new methods of printing flooded the world with images. . . ."[33] The *Examiner* (7 February 1855) announced that the American Artists Union had the "purpose of cultivating a taste of enabling every family to become possessed of a gallery of engravings." The Artists Union thereby attempted to create a need for goods where no need existed before, and equated democracy to the ability to own prints.

The rise of a democratic market economy brought enough prosperity to Frederick by the 1850s to result in a number of specialized, new buildings. Throughout the 1820s to the 1850s, newspapers noted that meetings and events occurred in taverns, church buildings, warerooms, or over stores. A different trend appeared in the *Frederick Examiner* of the 1850s — a trend found neither in earlier newspapers of any of the Western Maryland towns in this survey, nor in the *Cumberland Alleganian* of the 1850s.[34] In the pages of the *Examiner,* new buildings specifically designed for cultural activities begin to appear. For instance, by 1852, Frederick apparently afforded its own Lyceum, a popular institution of the time intended for public educational and social programs. The Frederick Lyceum's opening lecture offered the topic, "The Relation of the Action of the Mind to the Physical Structure of the Brain."[35]

While support for a Lyceum suggests the achievement of a certain level of public spirit in Frederick, another new public building, called Junior Hall, appeared as well. Besides offering meeting quarters for organizations — the Mechanics,' Mercantile and Literary Institute, according to the Examiner of 3 November 1858, held its organizational meeting there — between 1854 and 1858, "Junior Hall" hosted the Baltimore Museum Drama Corps, the "Grand National Panorama," the "Grand Tournament Ball," and the "Grand Vocal & Instrumental Concert."[36] These events embodied cultural change. As lavish entertainment packages, the grand events contrasted with, say, the ladies church fair over Swartzweder's store (*Herald of Freedom*, 28 November 1848). Besides the performances offered at Junior Hall, P.T. Barnum's "Grand Colossal Museum and Menagerie!" advertised its arrival with elephants, lions, tigers, freaks, and wax statuary among other exotic oddities.36 Such extravaganzas held no hint of a culture of scarcity and self-denial. These big shows also represented other trends, including the selling of cultural events by outsiders and the commodification of culture for a profit. The modest, self-contained, community activities of earlier times pale beside them.

Buildings in Frederick provide other evidence of transition away from the culture of scarcity and self denial. During the period of 1820 to 1860, real estate advertisements described local buildings as brick or frame, with such accessories as out buildings, convenient wells, and acreage. In the *Examiner* (Frederick) of 7 February 1855, however, appeared a description of an "elegant mansion" designed by a professional architect. The details of refinement inside and out occupied a column with, in part, the following description:

> The superb brown stone edifice . . . just completed for Charles E. Trall, Esq., of this City, is a chef d' oeuvre of architectural beauty and taste. . . . This elegant mansion of brown stone, with its basement, portals, windows and capitals of sculptured Parisian marble, rises to the height of three stories, and is surmounted by a cupola. . . . The style of architecture is distinguished as the Anglo-Italian bracketed, and was designed by Samuel Sloan, Esq., of Philadelphia.37

Effusions continued on about the layout of the interior, with its stuccoed ceilings, "elaborately chiselled fireplaces," and sliding doors. The article identified the proud painters and grainers, as well as the plasterers, bricklayers, roofers, and plumbers. Frederick had come a long way by 1855 from the "new two story log house, a good barn, and other suitable out-houses, with a well of good water within about fifteen yards of the door . . ." advertised in the *Frederick-Town Herald* of 9 March 1822.

The description of the log house seems an age away from the library, veranda, bath rooms, and gas and water pipes of the brownstone mansion. None of the earlier newspapers sampled even hinted at the existence of such niceties. Yet here the *Examiner* broadcast lodging not just equipped with necessities for people and their livestock, but with extravagance and luxury. While such a fine mansion surely fell out of reach of all but a few elite, the inclusion of the crafts people's names in the *Examiner* article implies that others might be interested in hiring them for similar projects. Before long, perhaps plumbers and plasterers would join the American Art Union in marketing their product to "all families." Whether they presented art prints or fine houses as desirable commodities, these items in the newspapers begin to show "how consumption became a cultural ideal," a goal in itself.38

From the 1820s through the 1850s, holidays rarely appeared in newspapers as occasions for buying and selling, but rather for attention to traditional values of communal worship and sharing. Newspapers in the three towns of Williamsport, Hagerstown, and Frederick all marked Thanksgiving Day, for example, with notices of the governor's proclamation for a day of thanksgiving to God, church attendance, and refraining "secular employment."[39] The *Hagerstown Herald of Freedom* (29 December 1841) urged its readers to celebrate Christmas with thankfulness to God as well as with "those time-honored festivities" of gifts and feasting. Most of all, the editorial continued, "We hope the wealthy and benevolent have celebrated the day by relieving the poor and needy; and thus rendered it one of hilarity and happiness, to the whole community." A Charles Dickens story published in the *Frederick Examiner* (22 December 1852) concluded with the same theme; "the sweet and secret satisfaction of doing good" with charity to the sick, aged, poor, and needy.

Here and there, however, the spirit of Christmas provided a marketing strategy. The proprietors of Henderson's Cheap Book Store "hope the festive season will not be suffered to pass without remembering the sick. They require a double share of our attention and to those suffering with Coughs, Colds, etc., nothing could be more suitable than a bottle of Ross's Expectorant. . . ."[40] While other advertisements in the same issue more simply and directly announced "Christmas goods . . . suitable for Christmas presents," no one else followed Henderson in twisting Christmas charity to sell a product. Yet a story as early as 1841 hints at Christmas as a time focused on acquisitions and spending money. In the 15 May 1841 *Republican Banner* (Williamsport), a short story called "A Married Man's Reverie" featured a narrator who whined that "my wife has made out a list of the presents she means to put in [the children's] stockings. More expense — and their school bill coming too. . . ." Throughout the rest of the story, the protagonist came across either as a misogynist grouch, or as a man embittered by his inability to adequately support his family. His brief depiction of Christmas as a financial burden may point to the commercialization of the holiday as well as a common experience of scarcity and indebtedness.

Still another holiday, Valentines Day, provided a commercial opportunity. Several Valentine advertisements in the *Examiner* (7 February 1855) made pitches similar to the following: "YOUNG MEN, who too long already, have delayed to dare to win the heart you'd

American Culture in Transition

hope to call your own, come and arm yourselves for LOVE'S GENTLE STRUGGLE. . . . Come, ye bright-eyed MAIDENS, LAUGHING GIRLS and SPINSTERS." Smith's Variety Store freely harnesses — and commodifies — love, sex, and Valentine's Day to sell cards.

By the 1850s the growing democratic market economy offered increasing quantities of affordable products. Luxury goods, once an oddity in small communities, became readily available. Prospering towns built new public halls and lyceums. Communities opened up to lavish new entertainments from afar. Extravagant architecture set new standards for a wealthy life style and opened up the possibilities for using new technologies in home building. Western Maryland had begun to develop a commercial culture where shop keepers saw holidays as commercial opportunities.

Conclusion

In *The Culture of Consumption*, Fox and Lears try "to discover how consumption became a cultural ideal, a hegemonic 'way of seeing' in twentieth century America..."[41] Richard T. Stillson has concluded that advertisements in Virginia newspapers of this period set standards of living, fashion, and education, and, in addition, enhanced a sense of community and provided connections with a larger culture.[42] The newspapers of Western Maryland, during the decades of the 1820s to the 1850s, embodied much continuity of traditional American values while carrying ever increasing examples of a commercialized culture.

The culture of Western Maryland was still traditional. Community-centered activities dominated leisure and recreation. Self-restraint, economy, simplicity, patriotism, and religious faith made up the value system. People were enjoined to bear sickness and loss stoically, and to live economically, eschewing expensive frivolities.

During this period, however, commercialism began to accompany traditionalism. Patriotic celebrations gave way to patriotic products. National organizations, such as the Colonization Society, applied centrally controlled, profit motivated solutions to local problems.

By the end of the period, consumerism and commodification become apparent. Technological developments created affordable new wonders — and new consumer markets where none existed before. A new elite built and furnished mansions with the products of big eastern factories. Even farmers were urged to participate by new periodicals teaching them how to extend profits dramatically.

The newspapers of Western Maryland documented a culture going through the changes that Schudson described: people living in communities of "self-sufficient family economies" becoming "unstuck from the cake of custom."[43] In a region with emerging ties with the East and the West, within a nation developing transportation and communication linkages to form a national culture, the transformation was probably inevitable. The culture moved slowly but surely toward the consumer society of modern America.

Notes

Newspapers

Cumberland Alleganian, 1845 - 1859.
Frederick Examiner, 1849 - 1859.
Frederick Town Herald, 1822 - 1834.
Herald of Freedom (Hagerstown), 1839 - 1849.
The Torch Light & Public Advertiser (Hagerstown), 1821 - 1830.
Republican Banner (Williamsport), 1830 - 1841.

1. See maps of Maryland and its early routes in Appendix A.
2. For historians's views of Maryland as a state in-between, see Barbara Jeanne Fields, *Slavery and Freedom on the Middle Ground* (New Haven: Yale, 1985) and Robert J. Brugger, *Maryland: A Middle Temperament 1634 - 1980* (Baltimore: Johns Hopkins University, 1988).
3. For a description of similar connections in American newspapers, see John C. Nerone, "A Local History of the Early U.S. Press: Cincinnati, 1793-1848 in William S. Solomon and Robert W. McChesney, eds., *Ruthless Criticism: New Perspectives in U.S. Communication History* (Minneapolis: University of Minnesota Press, 1993), 38-65; and John W. Miller, "Frontier Newspapers and National News: Indiana in the Early Nineteenth Century," *The Maryland Historian* XIV (Fall/Winter 1983): 1-14.
4. Daniel J. Boorstin, *The Americans: The National Experience* (New York: Vintage Books, 1965).
5. Michael Schudson, *Discovering the News: A Social History of American Newspapers* (New York: Basic Books, 1978), 58-59.
6. Social Scientists have devoted much research to the definition of culture. In *Religion and the Solid South*, Samuel Hill Jr. comments on the many possible definitions of culture, but selects "a system of conventional understandings general enough to influence everyone included within it." (Nashville: Abingdon Press, 1972), 80. Michael Agar, in his recent book, *Language Shock*, spends a whole chapter examining scholarly definitions of culture, and finally settles on culture as "frames."
7. Jürgen Habermas, trans. Thomas Burger, *The Structural Transformation of the Public Sphere: An Inquiry into a Category of Bourgeois Society* (Cambridge, Mass.: The MIT Press, 1989), 181 - 194.
8. Schudson, 58-59.
9. Lawrence Frederick Kohl, *The Politics of Individualism: Parties and the American Character in the Jacksonian Era* (New York: Oxford University Press, 1989), 4.
10. Alexis de Tocqueville, *Democracy in America*, ed. Richard D. Heffner (New York: New American Library, 1956), 192-193.

11. Ibid., 202.
12. Warren I. Susman, *Culture as History: The Transformation of American Society in The Twentieth Century* (New York: Pantheon Book, 1984), XXIV - XXV.
13. Richard Wightman Fox and T. J. Jackson Lears, eds., *The Culture of Consumption: Critical Essays in American History, 1880 - 1980* (New York: Pantheon Books, 1983), xii.

14.

	Laid out	Population in in 1860	Population in 1820
Cumberland	1784	1,162	7,300
Frederick	1745	3,640	8,143
Hagerstown	1762	2,690	4,132
Williamsport	1787	827	1,016

In contrast, Baltimore City grew from 13,503 in 1790 to 62,738 in 1820, and to 212,418 in 1860. William Paul Walker, *Certain Financial Aspects of Local Government in Maryland* (NP: Maryland State Planning Commission, 1934).

15. For the titles sampled for this paper, see list at beginning of the notes.
16. Throughout the forty year period surveyed, the style and appearance of these newspapers varied little over time or from each other. All consisted of a single sheet folded in half to make four printed pages. The number of columns varied from five to seven, but within each title, the number of columns never changed from page to page. I found only a few instances of two-column width items for the whole period. For instance, an advertisement for an auction, complete with an engraving of an auction scene, occupied a square two columns wide on page four of the *Cumberland Alleganian* of 12 October 1850. The Frederick *Examiner* of 22 December 1852 had a two-column wide headline for balsamic cough syrup. All of these papers appeared weekly (three came out on Saturday, two on Wednesday, and one on Tuesday); sold subscriptions for $2.00 to $2.25 per year; requested at least six months payment in advance; and sold squares of advertisements at one dollar for three or four appearances. Politically, these newspapers differed strikingly from each other. Williamsport's *Republican Banner* spoke for itself. Other newspapers in this group ranged from the Democratic *Cumberland Alleganian* to the Know Nothing *Examiner* (Frederick). The last three newspapers; the *Frederick-Town Herald*, the *Herald of Freedom* (Hagerstown), and the *Torch Light and Public Advertiser* (Hagerstown), all supported the Whigs.
17. Richard T. Stillson, "Virginia Newspapers in the 1830s: A Diverse Communications Network" (Thesis, George Mason University, 1994), abstract.
18. Charles E. Clark points out that book and medicine advertisements dominated English language newspapers from the very beginning. Charles E. Clark, *The Public Prints: The Newspaper in Anglo-American Culture 1665-1740* (New York: Oxford University Press, 1993), 38.
19. *Frederick-Town Herald*, 9 March 1822; *Torch Light and Public Advertiser* (Hagerstown), 9 April 1822; 22 July 1823.
20. See, for example, *Frederick-Town Herald*, 31 January 1829.
21. *Cumberland Alleganian*, 15 February 1851.
22. *Frederick-Town Herald*, 11 September 1824.
23. *Torch Light and Public Advertiser* (Hagerstown), 6 November 1828; see also *Frederick-Town Herald*, 4 May 1833; *Republican Banner* (Williamsport), 30 September 1837.
24. See the chapter "Gettysburg and the Culture of Death" in Garry Wills, *Lincoln at Gettysburg: The Words that Remade America* (New York: Simon & Schuster, 1992), 63-89.

25. Philippe Aries, *Western Attitudes toward Death: From the Middle Ages to the Present* (Baltimore: The Johns Hopkins University Press, 1974), 67.
26. *Frederick-Town Herald*, 31 January 1829.
27. *Hagerstown Herald of Freedom*, 29 November 1848.
28. *Frederick-Town Herald*, 24 April 1830; *Cumberland Alleganian*, 28 July 1849.
29. Bushman, Richard, *The Refinement of America: Persons, Houses, Cities* (New York: Knopf, 1992).
30. *Republican Banner* (Williamsport), 15 February 1834.
31. *The Examiner* (Frederick) 12 June 1850.
32. Kohl, 4.
33. Susman, XXV.
34. For the decade of the 1850s, the sample of newspapers for this paper included the Frederick *Examiner* and the Cumberland *Alleganian*. The cultural content of the *Alleganian* bore more resemblance to that of newspapers of earlier decades than to the "grand" new events in the *Examiner*.
35. *Examiner* (Frederick), 12 August 1857.
36. *Examiner* (Frederick), 19 July 1854; 7 February 1855; 12 August 1857; 3 November 1858.
37 *Examiner* (Frederick) 19 July 1854.
38. Fox and Lears, x.
39. *Examiner* (Frederick) 3 November 1858; a Thanksgiving proclamation also appeared in the *Republican Banner* (Williamsport) 10 November 1832; and the *Herald of Freedom* (Hagerstown), 29 November 1848, noted celebration of Thanksgiving according to the Governor's prescription.
40. *Examiner* (Frederick), 22 December 1852.
41. Fox and Lears, x.
42. Stillson, 94.
43. Schudson, 59.

2

Consensus and Public Debate: The Washington Press During the Nullification Crisis, 1832-1833

Steven G. Saltzgiver
Federal Judicial History Office

"Treason!" "Disunion!" "Civil War!"[1] The newspapers of Washington, D. C. showed no decorum during the winter of nullification. The capital city anxiously awaited news traveling north from the state of South Carolina, but an individual's understanding of the crisis depended upon his or her source of information. Party newspapers chose their articles very carefully and printed precious little that did not square with party beliefs.

What did the public know about the crisis that gripped the United States during the winter of 1832-33? Because South Carolina nullified the tariffs of 1828 and 1832 instead of succumbing to what they considered oppressive national policies, the state's behavior posed a threat to the existence of the Union. As political leaders from around the country searched for resolutions to the situation, the newspapers in the nation's capital waged a consistent and open debate on the various constitutional, sectional, and partisan issues. Traditionally, historians of this era portrayed the press as obsequious to their respective parties responding with frequently vitriolic rhetoric to any politician, organization, or publication in disagreement with party tenets. The major newspapers in Washington were the Jacksonian *Globe*, the opposition *United States Telegraph*, and the unaffiliated *National Intelligencer*. The differing perspectives and agendas of the papers led, not surprisingly, to a wide variety in reporting on particularly divisive issues. South Carolina's Ordinance of Nullification, Andrew Jackson's Annual Message, and his Nullification Proclamation represent significantly contentious issues and present an opportunity to study the positions of these prominent newspapers. By exploring the available evidence this paper seeks to ascertain what information the newspapers presented to the public and what they withheld. Furthermore, in a city where all sides of the nullification issue found support, this study will show that the cumulative rhetoric of papers sought to bring about consensus and resolution rather than division and war.

As part of a network of papers that reprinted and thus spread the national news around the country, the Washington press held an important role in the nation's communication system. In an effort to dominate public opinion, the Jacksonians tried to control the content of information put out and then disperse it as widely as possible. Using newspapers to reach voters, these Jackson partisans endeavored to lower the campaign "down to the level of the average citizen."[2] Charged with the duty of spreading Andrew Jackson's message around the country, Duff Green, a Missouri-born friend of Vice President John C. Calhoun, made the *United States Telegraph* the mouthpiece of the administration.[3] The *Telegraph* displaced the *National Intelligencer*, which had held the honored position as the presidential press throughout the Jefferson, Madison, and Monroe administrations. Joseph Gales and William W. Seaton, the *National Intelligencer*'s editors, did not regain the patronage of the presidency until the William Henry Harrison administration in 1841.[4] Duff Green also acquired both the House and Senate printing contracts and left the *Intelligencer* free of party affiliation, allowing it to remain relatively neutral during the Nullification Crisis.

Government patronage served as a method to both reward past loyalty and ensure future support. In the 1830s, the three Washington papers vied for lucrative government printing jobs, and in such a small city the absence of public funding could doom a paper to bankruptcy. Therefore, the revocation of patronage constituted an effective means of punishing dissenters "who refused to support the party's principles or nominees."[5] Duff Green received the presidential patronage in 1828 as a reward for his unending and influential efforts to unseat President John Quincy Adams. During the first Jackson administration, Green lost favor with the president partly due to his close personal ties to Jackson's Vice President, Calhoun, with whom the president had become increasingly disenchanted. Also, a series of soured business ventures forced Green to borrow large sums of money from the Second Bank of the United States. Green's indebtedness to the Bank, Jackson's *bête noire*, suggested a conflict of interest and cinched his removal as Jackson party editor.6 By revoking the patronage from the *Telegraph,* Jackson not only had the opportunity to punish Green but to reward another supporter at the same time. The administration awarded the newly available patronage to Francis P. Blair of Kentucky. Blair's efforts to swing Kentucky in favor of Jackson during the 1828 election attracted the Old Hero's attention and ultimately led to an invitation to move to Washington and set up the Washington *Globe*.7 Blair quickly endeared himself to the administration by championing the president's favorite issues.

A long standing opposition to debt, credit, and speculation fueled Jackson's desire to retire the national debt, but this endeavor required the government to raise large sums of money.8 For many years, Congress used tariff measures as a means to acquire the necessary funds to meet the federal government's obligations. The passage of tariffs dating back as early as 1816 revealed an increasing tendency to favor one region of the country over another. Not only did these tariffs highlight the economic difference of the North and South, but also exposed slavery as a potential area of sectional conflict. Some historians have suggested that the Southerners' vehement response to the tariffs of 1828 and 1832 masked their greater anxiety over the additional financial strain which might expose slavery, the cornerstone to the Southern economy, to the actions of abolitionists.9 The protective tariffs propped up falling consumer prices resulting from the currency contraction and overproduction of cotton.10 Since the tariffs did not rescue the dropping prices of raw cotton, Southerners, particularly South Carolinians, seized the opportunity to assign blame and labeled the new protective measures of 1828 the "Tariff of Abominations." Active opposition to the tariff could have resulted in defeat for the Jackson-Calhoun ticket, so anti-tariff advocates abandoned their protest until 1832 when Jackson supported another tariff also more beneficial to Northern interests. Under the leadership of John C. Calhoun, the South Carolinians developed a scheme to nullify the tariff legislation.

A group of delegates elected by the residents of South Carolina arrived in Charleston, on November 19 to discuss the nullification of the tariffs of 1828 and 1832. The *Telegraph* carried the announcement of the Convention, which did not merit mention in the other Washington papers for over a week.[11] The *Telegraph's* interest in the convention surprised no one in light of Duff Green's long standing personal ties to Calhoun and the editor's estrangement from the Jackson administration. As the nullification movement drew Calhoun into its ranks as the chief spokesman for the constitutional justification of nullification, Green's newspaper moved toward a position of unrestrained support for South Carolina's struggle. Around the time of Jackson's reelection in 1832, nullification had become an explosive political issue that locked the President and his former Vice President in an intense battle of political survival with undeniable constitutional overtones.

The delay in time before the other Washington papers recognized the convention showed their reluctance to acknowledge an event that could threaten the existence of the Union. A correspondent for the *National Intelligencer* on November 28 reported a brief and innocuous summary of the first day's proceedings. The absence of an immediate response by the *Globe* appeared conspicuous, because the paper had run a long article the preceding week alleging that the South Carolinian Convention had intended to subvert the actions of a proposed convention in Hartford, Connecticut also aimed at a tariff reduction. Timing became crucial, reasoned the *Globe*'s editors, since it would be a blow to Calhoun's reputation and stature, "to see the war debt paid, and the tariff reduced to the lowest point, consistent with the wants of economical government, before he can get his...followers fairly into rebellion."[12] The editors of the *Globe* viewed the tariff issue as the means by which the nullifiers hoped to elevate their national stature. Without prompt action, Calhoun and his fellow nullifiers would discover "their whole pretext of quarrel will be taken from them, and they will find nothing nullified but their own self-importance."[13] When the nullifiers did meet in convention, the Jacksonian paper perceived their actions as a threat, and decided against acknowledging the meeting.

Once the nullifiers began their convention and the debate shifted from a desire to simply nullify the tariff to a call for South Carolina to secede from the Union, Duff Green began to express some concern in the *Telegraph* that the overly enthusiastic proceedings might result in something other than tariff reduction, such as civil war. Agreeing with Calhoun's belief in tariff reduction through legal and constitutional means, Green expressed apprehension that threats of secession might draw the wrath of the federal government. Green appealed to the convention to avoid being "so blinded by passion or prejudice, as to precipitate their State into a position hostile to the laws of the country."[14] The *Globe* assured its readers that the federal government did not anticipate "forcible opposition to the laws of the people of South Carolina," but rumors around Washington of a military build-up caused the *Telegraph* to question the sincerity of the disavowal of federal violence. Through its admonition, the *Telegraph* hoped to avert an armed conflict. The *Telegraph*'s words of caution, after months of attempting to incite just such an action, drew a quick response from its rival.

Crediting the *Telegraph*'s repeated calls for "immediate and active resistance" with responsibility for the now militant actions of previously reluctant politicians, the *Globe* derided the "assumed moderation" articulated by the *Telegraph*. Although Green now hoped to slow down the escalating crisis, Francis P. Blair seized the opportunity to hold the *Telegraph* responsible for being "the instrument that [first] sounded the blast of nullification."[15] The *Globe*'s editors reasoned, "[w]e must either understand this [call for restraint by Green] as a *secession* from nullification, on the part of one of its special organs, from principle—or we must construe it into a submission on the part of the public printer to Congress for the sake of interest."[16] Duff Green continued to be an advocate of nullification despite his congressional patronage, but he could not countenance anything more extreme that might imperil the Union. Just days later the *Telegraph* responded to the attack on its motives by claiming it was Blair's jealousy and desire to be the congressional printer that lay behind the accusations. Green maintained that his support for South Carolina in its time of crisis remained foremost in his mind, and he would continue even if it cost him reelection.[17] It would not have been the first time the politically astute Duff Green had maneuvered to maintain political favor. In the early months of 1831 after already losing the patronage of the Jackson administration, Green delayed his publication of the controversial *Correspondence Between General Andrew Jackson and John C. Calhoun* until after he had secured his reelection as printer to both the House of Representatives and the Senate.[18] However, this time Green attempted to prevent any precipitous action that might forestall a political resolution.

Like Green, Francis P. Blair also recognized the importance of preserving the Union, which he viewed as endangered if nullification succeeded, but as support for nullification grew in South Carolina in the fall of 1832, interest emerged in an opposition party to undermine the efforts of the nullifiers. In support of those who believed in a perpetual Union, and felt at odds with their government in South Carolina, the *Globe* proposed the formation of a Union party, which would take its motto directly from the words of Andrew Jackson, "the federal Union must be preserved."[19] A strong party in opposition to the nullifiers would ensure continued debate and provide an opportunity to restrain South Carolina's activities before they led irretrievably to violence.

The *Telegraph* responded by downplaying the need for a Union party as opposition saying "[w]e trust that there is no necessity for the regular organization of such a party, as we hope that the doctrine of nullification is too generally abhorrent to the principles and the feelings of the people of this country, to need an organization to resist it."[20] Green later went so far as to deny the existence of an active opposition in South Carolina. The *Telegraph* criticized the administration organ for "seem[ing] to talk as if the spirit of resistance existed with the people of South Carolina alone, when they know it is almost universal in the south. The only difference is, that one says, let us resist now; another, let us bear it a little longer."[21] As much as the *Globe* sought to arouse dissent in South Carolina, the *Telegraph* attempted to give support to the nullifiers by painting them as a united and patriotic movement. Even Duff Green knew that nullification lacked the "universal" support he attempted to describe, as illustrated in a letter he sent to John C. Calhoun prior to the Convention. Green wrote Calhoun that Mitchell King, "The agent of the Union Party has made a formal communication to the Legislature of Tennessee appealing from the majority of your state, and arraigning you for dangerous and treasonable doctrines."[22] Publicly, Green portrayed the South Carolinians as united in support of nullification, while in private he reluctantly admitted that the secessionists continued to give the federal government an issue around which to build opposition.

The *National Intelligencer*, which had attempted to avoid the nullification issue, also noted the presence of the Union party at the convention in Columbia. Even then the *Intelligencer* refrained from an outright condemnation or endorsement of nullification, saying only that the Unionists at the convention "made no opposition to the whole proceedings, except a silent vote in the negative."23 As with the reporting of the convention's first day, the *Intelligencer* report attempted to use the most unbiased language possible.

By the time South Carolina's convention issued the Ordinance of Nullification, the Washington newspapers agreed with the necessity of reducing the irritating tariff, but the parties endorsing the particular papers remained far from an actual resolution. The Jackson administration's *Globe* appeared to suggest the possibility of a bargain when it reported that the tariff would no longer be set or "established," but would be "modified" in accordance with all the "reasonable expectations of the south."24 Their rival's assertion that "Jackson and Van Buren were elected under an implied understanding that the tariff was to be reduced to the 'economical wants of government'" confounded the *Telegraph*, the nullifiers' press in Washington. In Duff Green's opinion, "repeal [of] the obnoxious portions of the tariff" would end the crisis in South Carolina. With the possibility of consensus at hand, Green remarked that the once "roaring lion" of nullification had become a "gentle lamb."25 Still, Jackson and the nullifiers remained at loggerheads forcing their respective presses back to the attack.

Knowing that a threat of secession still existed in South Carolina, the editor of the *Telegraph* fired off an attack at the *Globe* for its reluctance to effect a reform in the tariff at an earlier date. The passage of a "certain fixed gradual reduction of the tariff" in the previous session of Congress would have averted all these difficulties.26 In response to the charge of laggardness, the editors of the *Globe* countered by charging "that the ordinance of nullification [was] passed to anticipate and prevent the healing of the divisions in our country—to keep up a contest among the states, and to gratify the selfish purposes of ambitious leaders." Duff Green dismissed this as simply "nonsense." Responding to the *Globe*'s report that duties would be reduced to the lowest level to sustain government or what they called a "mere revenue standard," Green intimated that South Carolina might accept this as a new proposal. In reference to the President, Green wrote, "it is but for him to speak and it is done."27 This enthusiasm for the "mere revenue standard" apparently caught the editors of the *Globe* off guard and they were forced to argue that the President had advocated this in many speeches, and "in frank and unreserved conversations with members of Congress opposed to a reduction of the Tariff, he urged the necessity of mutual concession as indispensable to . . . *the preservation of the Union.*"28

In essence, the Washington papers engaged in a public dialog that seemed aimed at defining the terms for compromise amid the tumult of nullification.

For a short time, it appeared as though at least the party organs were in agreement on a reduction in the tariff, until Francis P. Blair's *Globe* renewed its accusation that "the selfish purposes of ambitious leaders" had subverted a possible consensus.29 The *Globe* had singled out John C. Calhoun as the personification of the evil created by nullification. When challenged on this charge by the *Telegraph,* the *Globe* responded simply that as a potential presidential candidate, Calhoun needed to be answerable for his involvement as the constitutional theorist and nominal leader of the nullifiers. The *Telegraph* remarked that an individual's actions should in no way have been "sufficient cause to refuse a repeal of oppressive and unnecessary taxes." Green speculated, "these facts show that the *Globe* is enlisted in the cause of a Presidential candidate, who makes the public interest subservient to his own personal advancement."30

In an effort to make the impact of nullification understandable to the general public and to provide spirited reading, Blair's comments personalized the political issues. The idea of distilling complex or abstract ideas down into understandable images had long been a device of the *Globe*'s editor. For example, the sweeping economic plan proposed by Senator Henry Clay of Kentucky, known as the "American System," became too elaborate to explain in the pages of a newspaper; so the editor used Henry Clay to personify all the perceived evils of the American System. Likewise, Nicholas Biddle would soon represent all the financial troubles the Second Bank of the United States had inflicted as well as all the other economic woes of the country.31 Identifying individuals with political crises creates a problem if the person does not embody all the aspects of the issue. Indeed, even the Jackson administration knew that, though Calhoun believed in nullification as a constitutional tool, he did not wholly subscribe to secession as a solution.32

Since the Washington papers all agreed with the need for tariff reduction, their major disagreement lay with whom to blame for the controversial tariffs in the first place. The *National Intelligencer* did not engage in the finger-pointing, since it did not suit their aim of acquiring government patronage. However, just as Calhoun provided a target for the *Globe*, Martin Van Buren served the purpose for the *Telegraph*. Speaking in New York on the tariff, Van Buren called for an end to the sectional strife. Duff Green claimed, "more than any other individual, [Van Buren] is responsible for the Tariff of 1828" and the resulting sectional controversy. Green accused Van Buren of adopting the tariff measures of Henry Clay's "American System" as a means of elevating his own political standing. The *Telegraph*'s editor speculated that the only way Van Buren could abandon the opprobrious tariff would be "by such means, as will act on the popularity of Mr. Calhoun."33 If Van Buren brought about a tariff reduction, the demands of the nullifiers would have been met and Calhoun and the South Carolinians emerge victorious. This debate possessed additional significance considering the rivalry between Calhoun and Van Buren to succeed Jackson to the presidency. By blaming Van Buren for the tariff, the *Telegraph* gave support to a Calhoun candidacy for the high office.

A week later, the Democratic party paper attempted to call attention to some facts in an effort to clear the reputations of the administration and Vice President-elect Van Buren. The *Globe* pointed to the Jefferson Birthday Dinner of 1830 as evidence of Jackson's position on the tariff. The President toasted that "the confidence with which the extinguishment of the Public Debt may be anticipated, presents an opportunity for . . . a modification of the Tariff, which shall produce a reduction of our revenue to the wants of the Government."34 After being placed on the ticket with Andrew Jackson, Van Buren claimed to hold the same position on the tariff as his running mate. Despite their campaign rhetoric against the tariff in 1832, both Jackson and Van Buren held positions influential to the legislation's initial passage. A strong case has been made that, as a senator from New York in 1828, Martin Van Buren conceived of the tariff as a way to attract the middle and western states to support Jackson. If Jackson convinced those regions of his belief in protectionism, he could win their votes. Van Buren's resulting bill became necessarily weighted against the South, but the Democrats were confident Jackson's popularity would sustain his advantage in that region. Interestingly, when Senator Van Buren's constant presence at the congressional hearings and his strong influence over the issue found its way into the Washington newspapers, Duff Green came to his defense. Green at that time still retained the position of editor of the Jackson party organ, and would have been in a fine position to know about Van Buren's maneuvering on Jackson's behalf.35 His assertions in 1832 that Van Buren was sole author of the Tariff of Abominations could reflect either his inside knowledge gained in 1828 or simply the accusations of an opposition editor.

Yet by accusing Van Buren of engineering the tariff for political reasons, Duff Green hoped to divert attention from one of the more vexing eventualities of nullification: secession.

The *Globe* responded with great indignation to the *Telegraph*'s efforts at provoking Jackson and Van Buren to justify their conduct on the tariff issue. The editors of the *Globe* thought that "turn[ing] the war directly on the administration—to represent it as heretofore deaf to the complaints of the South" suggested a "new aspect" in the dispute.36 This "new aspect" referred to an attempt to make the president responsible for the Nullification Crisis. Francis P. Blair suspected the idea of drawing Jackson into the tariff debate had originated from the nullification party's headquarters in South Carolina. The *Globe* quickly returned to its attack on Calhoun by asserting that the South Carolinian had planned to use the tariff question as a tool to "drive the Federal Government."37 Despite the *Globe*'s consistent attacks upon Calhoun and the Nullifiers, Green denied embarking upon a systematic attack of presidency in the hope that Jackson would indeed reduce the tariff as friends and members of his administration claimed he would.38

Beyond the rhetoric of assigning blame, the press appeared to be laying the groundwork for a consensus until the publication in the District of Columbia of South Carolina's Ordinance of Nullification drove a wedge between the parties and sent their respective papers back into their partisan corners. The Ordinance declared the federal tariffs of 1828 and 1832 "null and void" and authorized the state legislature to pass the necessary legislation to ensure compliance with its pronouncements. The administration's press, the *Globe*, responded swiftly and dramatically. After exalting the benefits of Union, such as a strong navy, economic strength, and peace, the *Globe* painted an imaginary picture of "Bloody Wars," "invading armies," "and oppressive taxes" to illustrate life after nullification. In the view of the editors, the only possible result of nullification could be "eventual separation from the Union."39

Previously reluctant to take a side in the nullification controversy, the *National Intelligencer* finally entered the public debate with its December 1 publication and critical analysis of the Ordinance. The editors, who went to great lengths not to offend anyone with political influence in the hope of one day regaining their government patronage, sided with the administration in its belief that South Carolina had gone too far. The *Intelligencer* raised primarily constitutional concerns, such as the Ordinance's lack of judicial authority. Rhetorically, the *National Intelligencer* queried about the "precedent for so strange a use of the term [ordain]," which preceded the clauses of the Ordinance. The editors considered the religious implications of "ordain" and mused about the holy authority of the document.[40] The editors also questioned the Convention's legal authority to "legislate" on matters such as the oath of allegiance. The oath required all of South Carolina's military and civil officers to swear an oath of allegiance to uphold the pronouncements of the Ordinance. Regardless of their feelings about the oath, the *National Intelligencer* took the South Carolinians to task for trying to legislate at a convention. Most people familiar with nineteenth-century law viewed conventions "legally deficient bodies existing outside of the regularly constituted authority."[41] Passage of any legislation should have been left to the South Carolina legislature following the convention.

Despite the technicality of not being able to legislate in a Convention, the nullifiers believed it totally within a states' rights to establish its own Constitution and set its own qualifications for public office holders. But this did not convince the editors of the *Globe*, who found the oath a particularly vile construction. Upon entering any State office, elected officials were required to take an oath to support and defend the Constitution of the United States of America. In the judgment of the editors of the *Globe*, the South Carolinian Ordinance of Nullification required men to "take an [additional] oath to subvert [the] Constitution, become traitors to their country, and plunge it into anarchy and civil war."[42] The proscription of Union loyalists from their military and civic offices for refusal to take the oath appeared to be the most disturbing result for the Jacksonians. If carried into effect, the oath could have undercut the federal government's support by removing all of their supporters from positions of power and influence. This provision was amended slightly later to allow for an exception for members of the legislature. The party newspaper implored its loyal party members to resist submission to oppressive state laws. The *Globe* editors stopped just short of calling for the Unionists to rise up against the insurrectionists. The *Globe* suggested provocatively that "[i]t is impossible that the Union men in South Carolina should submit to this tyranny, nor is it to be expected that they will abandon the land of their fathers without a struggle. We do not advise them."[43] Yet the implications of their suggestion could not have been more clear.

In the face of the overwhelming denunciation of the Ordinance, the *United States Telegraph* faced the difficult task of presenting the document in the best light possible and attempting to salvage the integrity of South Carolina. The actions of the convention in South Carolina denied Green the consensus that had seemed so close at hand and forced him to defend a document that threatened the Union. Yet Green publicly denied being against conciliation, as the *Globe* had charged. In fact, the *Telegraph* professed its efforts in "laboring to do all that is in our power to awaken a spirit of inquiry and conciliation." As the states surrounding South Carolina moved to criticize and condemn the Ordinance, Green beseeched the other southern states to "consult together" before passing judgment. The *Telegraph* wrote, "we entreat you to preserve the Union; but we warn you that this is not to be done by assailing South Carolina." The Ordinance forced the nullifiers' torch-carrier to soften its rhetoric against the administration and appeal for consensus at least among the South. Green even resorted to quoting from his former nemesis, John Quincy Adams, who declared, "the United States of America, and the people of every state of which they are composed, are each of them sovereign powers. . . . *Each is sovereign within its own province.*"[44]

Amid this rabid public discourse, President Andrew Jackson submitted his Annual Message to Congress. Having just defeated Henry Clay and the National Republicans in the presidential election of 1832, Jackson's Message laid out his plan for the next term, which included tariff reform as well as curtailing many internal improvements, closing the Second Bank of the United States, and effecting Indian removal. The *Telegraph* printed the document reluctantly while explaining that it did so in the name of "truth."[45] The *Globe* hailed the Message as "probably the most important document of the kind which has been submitted to Congress since the organization of the General Government."[46] As expected, the *National Intelligencer* came down in the middle. The *Intelligencer* noted the import of the Message and applauded its foreign policy efforts, but skimmed over reporting on nullification to focus on the banking issue.[47] Overall, the Message reflected the agrarian nature of Jackson's old republican beliefs, but this document was soon overshadowed by the president's own Proclamation.

On December 10, 1832, Jackson released his Proclamation on Nullification. The Proclamation denounced the idea of nullification and threatened the use of force to collect the tariff. As with the President's Annual Message, the press reaction reflected the party to whom they pledged their loyalty. The *National Intelligencer* reacted with expected ambivalence, but assumed that it "originated in the best of intentions."48 The *Telegraph* offered the president no such latitude. With a "single cursory reading," the editor of the opposition press protested that Jackson had endeavored to "appoint himself *dictator*, to place himself above the laws as *sole* expounder of the Constitution." Green attributed Jackson's aggressive posturing to his "strong personal animosity" toward Calhoun. Some papers strongly in support of nullification, such as the *Charleston Mercury*, welcomed the Proclamation in the hope that Jackson's militant stand would arouse sympathy from other states. The President's abandonment of the states' rights position he had asserted less than a week earlier dismayed Green. With the release of the Proclamation, Green had forsaken his earlier conciliatory manner and resumed his attacks on the administration.49 South Carolina Governor James A. Hamilton's did not lash out at Jackson's stern Proclamation, but rather he noted in a complimentary letter to the President the "masterly manner" of the Proclamation. The Governor intimated that South Carolina might soon disavow nullification in favor of the tariff reforms included in the President's Annual Message.50 Reconciliation appeared close at hand. Hamilton's letter resembled the tone of Duff Green's public calls for reconciliation of the previous weeks.

Throughout the Nullification Crisis, a great deal of apprehension and uncertainty existed over the possibility of an armed conflict. Military action would have signalled a breakdown in the political process and an end to any hope of consensus on the tariff issue. Aware that any fighting would end negotiations, the press of both parties disclaimed any knowledge of their own party's troop movements or stockpiling of arms. The press did accuse their rivals of military buildup in an effort to berate them into a less militaristic stand. In late November, the *National Intelligencer* reported the movement of some artillery and the fortification of a garrison in Charleston, but insisted that this did not reflect the "difficulties" in that city. The *Intelligencer* concluded that the revenue cutters and customs officers possessed sufficient means to enforce the laws, and in the case of a rebellion too great for those officers to handle, President Jackson possessed enough authority to bring about peace. In this instance, the first blow would originate when a state refused to pay customs.51 The *Telegraph* set aside the rumor of a blockade of Charleston's harbor as plainly unconstitutional. Blockades constituted a belligerent right that would amount to an act of war, a power residing in Congress, not the presidency.52

The editors of the *Globe* reported Governor Hamilton's Message asking the legislature for "the services of two thousand men" for the defense of Charleston with an additional request for 10,000 troops in reserve. The *Globe* interpreted this as an effort to organize an offensive, since the federal government had not even threatened to attack Charleston.53 President Andrew Jackson's correspondence indicates that the administration considered the threat of armed resistance in South Carolina serious enough to begin preparations. The Jackson administration directed the Secretary of the Navy to replace the forts in Charleston with men loyal to the Union.54 Jackson sent at least two men down to South Carolina to assess the situation: George Breathitt and Joel R. Poinsett. Breathitt traveled "ostensibly as a post office inspector; but his real business was to observe the situation with respect to nullification and report to Jackson," and Joel R. Poinsett reported to Jackson on tactical positioning and Unionist support in that state.55 In the week following his Proclamation, Jackson began inquiring of his Secretary of War, Lewis Cass, about the availability of muskets, swords, and pistols. "We must be prepared to act with promptness," wrote the president, "and crush the monster in its cradle before it matures to manhood."56 On 16 January 1833, the president took the next step of asking Congress to authorize him to take the necessary action in the Charleston harbor to ensure collection of the tariff. This request soon became known as the Force Bill Message.

Once again the Union appeared endangered by the threat of violence, and the consensus the press had so long sought to encourage seemed lost until Henry Clay entered the debate. Still reeling from his defeat in the 1832 presidential election, Clay hoped to restore his personal credibility through a resolution of the Nullification Crisis by reducing the tariff and averting an armed conflict. For months, the Washington press had promoted these very resolutions, and now it seemed their public discourse had moved into the halls of Congress. On 1 March 1833, Congress voted in approval of the Compromise Bill assembled by Clay, which included both the tariff reduction measures and the now unnecessary enforcing legislation for tariff collection proposed by the president.57

The newspapers of the 1830s clearly evidenced their strict adherence to party dictates. Some papers even suppressed matters that did not suit their purposes. Even Andrew Jackson's party paper, the *Globe*, neglected to comment on the President's Proclamation for more than a week and then endeavored to "explain" the president's justification for such a strong threat of force. But eventually the *Globe* did respond by seeking to justify and elucidate the president's position and necessarily so, since Jackson could easily have withdrawn his patronage, committing the paper to a slow death. In the midst of the Nullification Crisis, Duff Green wrote, "[i]t is our duty to lay before our readers the truth—to keep them informed of public opinion. Nothing has contributed more to the present crisis of our public affairs than the subserviency of the press—its blind devotion to party mandates, which has forbidden the publication of anything in the party press that may be unpalatable to the party taste."[58] Written at a low point for the nullifiers, Green surged back with a vengeance in response to the President's confrontational Proclamation.

The political parties of the Jacksonian era did not overlook the importance of the press's influence on the public opinion. With this in mind, the parties attempted to control the newspapers. During the 1830s, the party organs never lacked for divisive issues around which they could attempt to manipulate the public debate in their favor by selective publication of only the most supportive opinions available. Most importantly, this study revealed the press's reluctance to validate through publication any radical policy of a party that appeared to lead to war or secession. Though rarely in agreement on the major issues, these newspapers continually sought to move toward a political consensus when a possible conflict threatened the public safety. The press served less as a mouthpiece for party propaganda as previously asserted than a public forum for political debate aimed at resolving a crisis and reuniting the country.

Notes

1. *United States Telegraph*, Nov. 23, 1832.
2. Harry L. Watson, *Liberty and Power: The Politics of Jacksonian America* (New York: Noonday Press, 1990), 90.
3. *Ibid.*, 89; William W. Freehling, *Prelude to Civil War: the Nullification Controversy in South Carolina, 1816-1836* (New York: Harper and Row, 1965), 142.
4. Culver Smith, *The Press, Politics and Patronage: The American Government's Use of Newspapers, 1789-1875* (Athens, Ga.: University of Georgia Press, 1977), 249.
5. Watson, 174; Culver Smith, passim.
6. Kenneth Laurence Smith, "Duff Green and the 'United States' Telegraph,' 1826-1837" (Ph. D. diss., The College of William and Mary, 1981), 134-137.
7. Culver Smith, 128.
8. Robert V. Remini, *Andrew Jackson and the Bank War* (New York: W.W. Norton, 1967), 19, 120-121.
9. Freehling; Frederic Bancroft, *Calhoun and the South Carolina Nullification Movement* (Baltimore: Johns Hopkins Press, 1928).

10. Freehling, 36.
11. *U. S. Telegraph*, Nov. 20, 1832.
12. *Washington Globe*, Nov. 15, 1832.
13. *National Intelligencer*, Nov. 28, 1832.
14. *U. S. Telegraph*, Nov. 23, 1832.
15. *Globe*, Dec. 1, 1832.
16. *Ibid.*
17. *U. S. Telegraph*, Dec. 4, 1832.
18. Culver Smith, 120.
19. *Globe*, Nov. 26, 1832.
20. *U. S. Telegraph*, Nov. 29.
21. *Ibid.*, Dec. 1, 1832.
22. Duff Green to John C. Calhoun, 23 October 1832, *The Papers of John C. Calhoun*, XI, 667.
23. *National Intelligencer*, Dec. 4, 1832.
24. *U. S. Telegraph*, Nov. 27, 1832.
25. *Ibid.*, Nov. 29, 1832.
26. *Ibid.*
27. *Ibid.*, Dec. 1, 4, 1832.
28. *Globe*, Dec. 6, 1832.
29. *Ibid.*
30. *U. S. Telegraph*, Dec. 1, 1832.
31. Culver H. Smith, 131.
32. Joel R. Poinsett to Andrew Jackson, 16 November 1832, *Correspondence of Andrew Jackson*, IV, 486-487.
33. *U. S. Telegraph*, Nov. 29, 1832.
34. *Ibid.*, Dec. 4, 1832.
35. Robert V. Remini, "Martin Van Buren and the Tariff of Abominations," *American Historical Review* 63 (July 1958): 903-917.
36. *Globe*, Dec. 6, 1832.
37. *Ibid.*
38. *U. S. Telegraph*, Dec. 4, 1832.
39. *U. S. Telegraph*, Nov. 29, 1832; *Globe*, Nov. 29, 1832.
40. *National Intelligencer*, Dec. 1, 4, 1832.
41. Gordon Wood, *The Creation of the American Republic, 1776-1787* (New York: W.W. Norton, 1969), 306-312.
42. *Globe*, Nov. 29, Dec. 6, 1832.
43. *U. S. Telegraph*, Dec. 11, 1832.
44. *Ibid.*, Dec. 4, 1832.
45. *Ibid.*
46. *Globe*, Dec. 8, 1832.
47. *National Intelligencer*, Dec. 6, 8, 1832.
48. *Ibid.*, Dec. 11, 18, 1832.
49. *U. S. Telegraph*, Dec. 11, 13, 1832.
50. James A. Hamilton to Andrew Jackson, 13 December 1832, *Correspondence*, IV, 498-499.
51. *National Intelligencer*, Dec. 11, 13, 1832.
52. *U. S. Telegraph*, Dec. 13, 1832.
53. *Globe*, Dec. 6, 1832.
54. Andrew Jackson to Levi Woodbury, 11 September 1832, *Correspondence*, IV, 474.
55. Jackson to George Breathitt, 7 November 1832, ibid., IV, 484-485; Joel R. Poinsett to Jackson, 24 November 1832, ibid., IV, 491-492.
56. Jackson to Lewis Cass, 17 December 1832, ibid., IV, 502-503.
57. Merrill D. Peterson, *Olive Branch and Sword,* (Baton Rouge: Louisiana State University Press, 1982); Richard E. Ellis *The Union at Risk,* (New York: Oxford University Press, 1987).
58. U. S. Telegraph, Dec. 4, 1832.

3

Mississippi Newspapers and the Secession Convention: The Influence on Anti-Secessionist Porter Jacob Myers

Nancy McKenzie Dupont
Loyola University - New Orleans

On December 20, 1860, registered voters in Mississippi were called to the polls by act of the state legislature to elect delegates to a Constitutional Convention. The legislature, meeting in special session in November, called the convention after learning that Abraham Lincoln had won the 1860 presidential election, a development that was viewed as a crisis point for the state (Rainwater 1938). The purpose was to develop a plan of resistance to the election of the abolitionist Lincoln who believed that the United States must be "all slave or all free." While several types of resistance were considered, it became obvious that the convention would favor secession from the Union. Most of the state's newspapers, including the *Jackson Mississippian*, the *Vicksburg Sun*, and the *Natchez Free Trader*, made it clear from the start that secession was their choice of resistance plans.

Despite widespread statewide support for the secessionist cause, anti-secessionists ran for election to the constitutional convention in 34 of Mississippi's 60 counties (Rainwater 1938). The vote was close in some counties (Wooster 1962), including Perry County, located in the Piney Woods of southeastern Mississippi where, because two pro-secessionists split the vote, the anti-secessionist was able to win election by a slim margin (1860 election returns). His name was Porter Jacob Myers, and he would go down in history as one of the 15 men at the Constitutional Convention who stood in a packed chamber and announced they were voting against the secession of the state of Mississippi.

Myers was well-known to the voters of Perry county. By the age of 45, he had served as tax collector, sheriff, and as a representative in the state legislature. He owned 13,000 acres of Perry County land; in fact, he was the largest land owner to be elected to the Constitutional Convention of 1861 (Wooster, 1954). By the end of the convention, Myers was the only delegate from his section of the state still voting against secession, yet the newspapers of his day and the historians who came after him never mention him by name in their descriptions and analyses of Mississippi's secession crisis. Clearly, Myers was not a leader of any particular party or movement, nor was he prone to speeches and public appearances. Still, he is deserving of study because he cast a dissenting vote during a turning point in Mississippi's history.

The Newspaper Influences

Perry county did not have its own newspaper in 1860, but its information needs were supplied by the *Eastern Clarion* published in Paulding about 35 miles away. Even before Lincoln's election, the *Clarion* supported secession and was frequently quoted in the pro-secessionist *Mississippian*. The *Clarion*, like so many other Mississippi newspapers in the 1860s, had fallen under the spell of the *Mississippian* and its dynamic editor, Ethelbert Barksdale. His influence in regional journalism was such that "when the paper roared in Mississippi all the little country papers yelped." (Sloan, Stovall and Startt 1993, 158). The *Mississippian* must be considered the leading fire-eater newspaper of Mississippi. The South's fire-eating newspapers were solidly pro-slavery and, as their nickname implies, were not opposed to inflammatory language to promote the cause.

Barksdale's personal position on secession was militant, and he was willing to go to unusual lengths to show support for his position. He represented Mississippi at the Democratic National Convention in Charleston, South Carolina, in 1860; most Southern editors avoided this kind of direct political participation because the demands of their newspapers kept them too busy. Barksdale's appearance in Charleston was noticed by a fellow journalist who wrote: "He is full of fire and prone to fly off the handle...there is a dangerous glitter in his eye (Reynolds)." But when the time came for Mississippi to make its decision on secession, Barksdale preferred the role of fire-eating editor to convention delegate. No Mississippi newspaper editor sought election to the Constitutional Convention (Wooster 1954).

Still, the power of these newspaper editors must be considered. In 1860s Mississippi, personal journalism was the rule, and what the editor wrote in his column was more important than coverage of local news. Antebellum newspapers in Jackson did not write about the arrival of the first train in the city nor about the completion of the railroad between Jackson and Vicksburg (Andrews 1970). Advertisements were frequently on the front page and, despite the success of the Penny Press newspapers sold on the streets in the North, Southern newspapers in the 1860s depended on mail subscriptions to stay in business (Andrews).

It is possible, then, that Myers read many different Mississippi newspapers, although he would have received the publications some time after their release. In the 1860s, the rural Piney Woods got twice monthly mail service, although receivers had to travel to a local center to pick up the post (Knight 1951). Newspapers might have been shared by businessmen at trading centers such as Augusta in Perry County, Ellisville in Jones County, and Paulding in Jasper County.

The Cooperationists

A few Mississippi newspapers took a more conservative view of secession following Lincoln's election. Among these were the *Vicksburg Whig* and the *Natchez Courier* whose editors frequently wrote in support of Southern cooperation. This position soon became a political party of its own and was often capitalized and referred to as the "Cooperation Party." Historians have had difficulty defining the ideological boundaries of this party, but in general the name referred to a belief that the cotton-growing states should not secede individually but rather take one of two actions: 1. Stay in the Union as long as possible while making trouble for Lincoln and seeking protection for slavery through the protection of the Constitution, or 2. Secede from the Union en masse with all slave-holding states, not just the cotton-growing states (Rainwater 1938). Cooperationists were further defined as "Unionists" who held the former position and "Southern Cooperationists" who held the latter position. At the Constitutional Convention, the parameters of these positions would become clearer.

Fire-Eaters versus Cooperationists

The contrast between the Fire-Eaters and the more conservative newspapers was never more apparent than when the editors discussed the possiblity of war. The Fire-Eaters tried to convince readers that immediate secession would not cause civil war and, if it did, the South would win. This example is from the Mississippian, November 13, 1860:

> Why, Lincoln could not control this little establishment of an army against us if he would. Probably one half the number are composed of Southern men; and when the fighting comes on they will be found on the side of the South.

Cooperationist newspapers, on the other hand, took the position that immediate and individual secession would almost certainly mean war. These examples are from November and December issues of *Natchez Courier* and the *Vicksburg Whig* :

> (Secession is) a hypocritical, cowardly word used to deceive patriots into treason. (The resulting war will be) the most prolonged, extensive and horrible ever recorded in Time's bloody volume. (Rainwater 1934, 181 and 184).

Days of Decision

As Myers made his decison about whether to run for election to the Constitutional Convention and, if so, what position to take, Missippi newspaper editors wrote volumes about the crisis. The Cooperationists continued their arguments, hoping to sway public opinion and convince those seeking election to the convention. On November, the *Vickburg Whig* wrote:

> We shall submit to the evils, confessedly great though they may be. (The Union's) pillars ought not to be overthrown through passions of disappointed demagogues. . .Our heart sickens at the rashness of a misguided and demagogue-ridden commonwealth. (Reynolds 1966, 155 & 149).

Despite the strong language, there is some evidence that Southern Cooperationist newspapers began to lose their conviction (Reynolds). Note the qualification in this statement from the January 2, 1861 *Vicksburg Whig* : "It is therefore the part of wisdom to maintain our rights and settle this question in the Union, if it can be done." This hesitance could have been caused by a growing support for immediate secession among the populace or by the constant battering of the anti-secessionist position by the more numerous Fire-Eaters. The *Mississippian* wrote on November 30, 1860:

> It is now a significant, gratifying, and cheering fact that there is no party, nor scarcely a semblance of a faction in Mississippi, which opposes disunion and the formation of a Southern Confederacy. . . .this great end is gained -- the idea of "saving the Union" has been abandoned by almost everybody in Mississippi, and the idea of saving the South is enthusiastically embraced! . . .All hail this glorious era.

The *Natchez Free-Trader* declared on December 1 that two-thirds of the people of Mississippi supported "immediate secession and no compromise." The *Mississippian*, on December 11 and 18, admonished its readers to work hard to elect secessionist candidates to the Constitutional Convention: "Don't grow weary of well doing on Thursday the 20th. Recollect that you are then to choose between the alternative of living under a Northern free Negro despotism, or in a confederacy of free and equal Southern States."

As Myers prepared for the December 20th election, his newspaper hammered away the secession line. On December 12, the *Eastern Clarion* printed a letter from ardent secessionist W.A. Ward:

> Here is the matter in a nutshell: let Mississippi disconnect herself from all those who would oppress her; she has wealth and intelligence; she had a capacious harbor to export and receive in return a just and equivalent remuneration for her vast production. We can trade direct with Europe, ship our cotton there. . .

On December 18, the *Mississippian* printed this prediction from the *Eastern Clarion*

> The greatest enthusiasm prevails in this and the adjoining counties. The Cooperation

> Southern Convention Submission party will be so weak in East Mississippi that it will be with difficulty that they can procure candidates to lead their forlorn hope.

The "Submission" party was a term of insult used frequently by the Fire-Eaters to describe the Cooperationists. But in Perry and Jones counties, the insult did not have its intended effect, and the forlorn hope not only found candidates but managed to elect anti-secessionists to the upcoming convention.

Destination: Jackson

Myers had exactly 18 days to prepare for the Constitutional Convention. He spent his last Christmas and New Year's holidays as a healthy man. Though he was only to be in Jackson for a few days, Myers would see the peace of his home state shattered by the time he returned to Perry county. During these days, he and his fellow Mississippians learned of the secession of South Carolina. On December 24, the *Natchez Free Trader* wrote: "Brave South Carolina: Long enduring South Carolina!. . .It leads the van of the great army of the Southern Confederacy" (Reynolds 1966, 162).

The *Mississippian* spent two issues, December 25 and 28, reporting the election results of December 20. Though the elections of some anti-secessionists were reported, Myers's election in Perry county and J.H. Powell's in Jones county were not mentioned. But the *Mississippian* rejoiced in the overall outcome: "The convention will meet on the 7th of January and will proceed at once to give form and effect to the purpose which has been so unmistakably pronounced at the polls." The secessionists had won, a fact that would be confirmed as soon as the delegates were called into session.

Myers went to Jackson, the Mississippi capital. Though he was in a minority politically, Myers found himself to be more like than dislike the 100 delegates in a number of categories. For example, Myers was a native of South Carolina which contributed more delegates to the convention than Mississippi or any other state. He was a farmer, as were 41 of his fellow delegates. Thirty-three of the delegates were lawyers, and while they were not in the majority, the lawyers dominated the convention according to secession delegate Thomas Woods (1902) who wrote his memoirs late in life. Other delegate occupations were doctor, saddler, clerk, marshal, and professor of law. As a landowner and a slave owner, Myers was clearly in the majority: Ninety-nine of the delegates owned land and 85 owned slaves.

Because their positions changed during the convention, it is impossible to determine just how many delegates belonged to which parties when the convention convened on January 7, 1861 (Rainwater 1936 and Wooster 1954). However, it is accurate to say that, in general, the Cooperationists came from two sections of the state: the Delta, especially Adams and Warren counties, and the extreme northeastern section of the state, especially Tishomingo county. Myers and Powell, both Cooperationists, were from adjoining counties, but together they do not represent a "region of dissent" because, at the end, Powell changed his position.

Secessionist William S. Barry, a 53-year-old farmer from Tippah county, was elected convention president; his opposition was James L. Alcorn, a 43-year-old lawyer and farmer from Coahoma county, who would also change his position and vote with the majority. A committee of 15 delegates, led by law professor and future United States Senator L.Q.C. Lamar, was appointed to write an ordinance of secession. On January 9, the convention met to consider the ordinance ("Journal" 1861). Since South Carolina's vote had been unanimous, it may have seemed that the decision had been made, but Myers and his fellow Cooperationists were determined to have their say.

Three measures were introduced to the convention, all of them designed to defeat or at least postpone the immediate secession of Mississippi. The record of these votes is important because it has allowed historians to define the exact political positions of the delegates. In his exhaustive work on secession begun in the 1950s, Wooster (1954) has placed Myers in the most conservative of all of the groups at the convention. Myers's voting record reveals him to have been a "conditional Unionist," meaning he believed Mississippi should secede only as a last resort; Myers and only eleven other delegates were in this group (Wooster).

First, J. Shall Yerger of Washington County, introduced a substitute ordinance that would have called for the slavery controversy to be solved by seeking Constitutional protection in the Union. Myers voted for this ordinance; it failed 78 to 21. Alcorn then introduced an amendment that Mississippi's secession not go into effect until other lower South states had seceded. Myers voted for this amendment; it failed 74 to 25. Finally, Walter Brooke of Warren county proposed putting the ordinance to a vote of the people of the state on February 1, 1861. Again, Myers voted yes, but the amendment failed by a vote of 70 to 29 ("Journal" 1861).

Just one decision was left for the Cooperationists: would they now change their positions and vote for secession in order to present a united front? Myers's neighbor and colleague Powell decided, at his later peril, to drop his anti-secessionist stance and vote with the majority (Leveritt 1984). Alcorn had a particularly tough decision because he was relatively young and had political ambitions. He was unnerved by the pro-secession faction at the convention and throughout Mississippi. He wrote: "Should we fail to commit ourselves, it will be charged that we intend to desert the South. The people will be urged to deny us a hearing. The epithet of coward and submissionist will be everywhere applied to us. We shall be scouted by the masses!" (Pereyra 1966). Given his fright, it is not surprising that Alcorn voted yes, but he admitted his reluctance as he announced his vote: "...the die is cast- -the Rubicon is crossed- -and I enlist myself with the army that marches on Rome" (Rainwater 1936).

Without making a speech or any comment for the record, Myers voted no to the ordinance of secession. The final vote was 84 to 15. What can be said about those 15 dissenters? Historians agree on the futility of their vote, but many scholars admire the anti-secessionists' determination to record their opposition. Myers and his fellow anti-secessionists had "uncommon courage" (Barney, 309). They were "uncompromising...diehards" (Rainwater 1936, 211). They had nothing left to accomplish except to make it clear forever that they were opposed to Mississippi's leaving the Union at that time. This they had to do in full view of a packed House of Representatives, announcing their votes after their names were called, knowing that the next day the Fire-Eaters would malign them. Accounts of the moment leave no doubt as to the tension they must have felt. Historians Lowery and McCardle wrote in 1891: "The hall of the House of Representatives was wrapped in silence as deep and still as death." Lamar wrote:

> "A strained and eager audience received the instrument amid a silence so intense as to be oppressive. As slowly and with suppressed emotion, the passages, one by one, were read, a number of hearts in the solemn assembly seemed well nigh bursting as their deep significance dawned upon the mind...The hour was big with destiny; not only the destiny of one people, but that of much of the human race hung in the balance. The Muse of History held her pen aloft..."(Rowland 1925)

The solemnity of the vote was in stark contrast to the tumult that erupted as soon as the results were known. There was applause in the chamber, and cheering crowds screamed in the capitol halls and continued shouting until they reached the street. Cannons fired in celebration. A blue silk flag, made by the women of Jackson, was delivered to the capitol building (Rowland, 1925). One can imagine that it must have been unnerving for Myers and his fellow anti-secessionists to walk out of the capitol building and into such a celebration that day.

On January 15, all but two of the delegates to the Constitutional Convention signed the Ordinance of Secession. Of the two who stayed away, one refused and the other was already in military service to the state of Mississippi (Rainwater 1936). Myers affixed his name in the third row of delegate signatures. It was his last act as a politician and public servant.

Back home in the Piney Woods

Less than 30 days after demonstrating that he did not want to live under a Southern government, Myers was in its service. Myers returned to his home in Perry County and stayed just long enough to join the 24th Mississippi regiment which was dispatched soon after Florida's secession to service in the Army of Pensacola (Myers 1970; McFarland 1906). Powell of Jones county could not return home immediately (Leverett 1984). He had been elected as an anti-secession candidate, and when word of his vote for secession reached his constituents, an angry, drunken mob gathered in Ellisville. They built bonfires and hung a dummy with a sign that read: "Powell, the Anti-Secessionist Candidate" (Knight 1951).

Myers resigned his officer's commission in December 1861; he was given an honorable discharge for medical reasons by the Confederate States of America. Though there is no known reason for his medical problems, Myers was paralyzed for the rest of his life (Myers 1970).

On May 3, 1862, the Seventh Battalion of the Mississippi Infantry was mustered into service (Rowland 1978). Myers's oldest son, David Crockett Myers, joined the Battalion's Company B, which became known as the Beauregard Defenders. Throughout the war, the battalion was active, fighting in Vicksburg, Alabama, Georgia, and Tennessee. David almost survived the war, but on January 1, 1865, just four months before the Confederate surrender at Appomattox, he died during an amputation of his left leg while a Union prisoner of war. Union soldiers buried David's remains in an unmarked grave in the Nashville City Cemetery (Confederate Records 1865). The elder Myers never entered David's death in the family Bible even though later significant events are recorded in the same handwriting found on the Mississippi Ordinance of Secession (Myers Bible). At the end of the war, Myers gave 40 acres of his land to each of his former slaves who wanted to remain on the homestead (McKenzie 1994). He died in 1889, having been paralyzed for 28 of his 74 years.

Conclusion

Writing in 1966, Reynolds made a direct link between the actions of Southern newspapers and the Civil War, the most catastrophic event in United States history. Reynolds holds Southern newspapers responsible for operating a monopoly on Southern news. Southerners were not reading what Northerners thought; they were reading what Southern editors supposed Northerners thought. In Reynolds's view, the anti-Northern bias came through even in Unionist journals. He engages in a "what-if" and condemns Southern editors:

> Had a majority of the South's newspapers maintained even a modicum of integrity in reporting Northern views in general, and the Republican party's slavery intentions in particular, the South's 'Republicanphobia' almost certainly would have been less virulent than it was... (Reynolds, 215)

Could a different type of journalism in Mississipi have prevented the secession vote? One can only speculate, but it does seem that the lesson of Mississippi secession is that the media must pay attention and give coverage to alternative views, no matter where or from whom they spring. There were far fewer outlets for the Cooperationist viewpoint than for the Fire-Eating secessionists, and there were no outlets for any viewpoints from the North. It seems clear that Myers and his few colleagues who made up the anti-secession contingent should have been given their due -- an open discussion in the press. As difficult as it must be for journalists to accomplish, the goal of the media must always be to tell all sides as thoroughly as possible so that the marketplace of ideas will produce a well-informed citizenry capable of self-government. In 1861, the result of not having such a journalistic goal was as Alcorn described it: (Mississippi) was hurled from its seat of prosperous repose and unquestioned power into the embrace of causeless, cruel, and bloody war" (Rainwater 1936, 214).

Notes

Andrews, J. Cutler. *The South Reports the Civil War* (Princeton: Princeton University Press, 1970).

Barney, W.L. *The Secessionist Impulse: Alabama and Mississippi in 1860* (Princeton: Princeton University Press, 1974).

Confederate Service Records (Jackson, MS: Mississippi State Department of Archives and History).

Election Returns by Counties for the Election of Delegates to the Convention of 1861, Secretary of State Office, Jackson, Mississippi.

Journal of the State Convention and Ordinances and Resolutions Adopted in January 1861 with an Appendix, The (Jackson, MS, 1861).

Knight, Ethyl. *The Echo of the Black Horn* (Published by the author, 1951).

Leverettt, Rudy H. *Legend of the Free State of Jones* (Jackson, MS: University Press of Mississippi, 1984).

Lowery R. and W. H. McClure. *A History of Mississippi* (Jackson: R. H. Henry & Co., 1891).

McFarland, B. "A Forgotten Expedition to Pensacola in January, 1861," *Publications of the Mississippi Historical Society* 9, (1906), 15-23.

McKenzie, Tate Myers. Taped Oral History in the Possession of the Author.

Myers Family Bible in the Possession of Dorothy Mae Craft, Petal, MS.

Myers, Katheryn. Signed Personal Statement in the Possession of Robert T. Myers, Jr., Hattiesburg, MS. (1970).

Pereyra, L.A. *James Lusk Alcorn: Persistent Whig* (Baton Rouge: Louisiana State University Press, 1966).

Rainwater, Percy L. *Mississippi, Storm Center of the Secession, 1865-1861* (Baton Rouge: Otto Claitor, 1938).

Reynolds, Donald E. *Editors Make War* (Nashville, TN: Vanderbilt University Press, 1966).

Rowland, D. *History of Mississippi: Heart of the South* (Chicago and Jackson, MS: The S.J. Clarke Publishing Company, 1925).

Sloan, W. D., J. G. Stovall and J. D. Startt. *The Media in America: A History*(2nd ed.). (Scottsdale, Az: Publishing Horizons, Inc., 1993)

Woods, Thomas H. "A Sketch of the Mississippi Secession Convention of 1860-Its Membership and Work," *Mississippi Historical Society Publications*, 6, (1902):91-104.

Wooster, R. A. "The Membership of the Mississippi Secession Convention of 1861," *Journal of Mississippi History,* 16, 1954: 242-257.

Wooster, Ralph A. "The Secession Conventions of the Lower South: A Study of Their Membership" (Ph.D. diss., University of Texas at Austin, 1954)

Wooster, Ralph A. *The Secession Conventions of the South (*Princeton: Princeton University Press, 1962).

Newspapers

The Eastern Clarion (Paulding, MS)
The Natchez Courier
The Natchez Free-Trader
The Semi-weekly Mississippian
The Vicksburg Whig

4

"John Brown Still Lives!": The Case of John Brown

Bernell E. Tripp
University of Florida

A gaping mob watched in silence as the prisoners straggled from the jail and proceeded diagonally across the street to the courthouse, filing between rows of troops holding bayoneted rifles. Rumors circulated that 80 soldiers had been dispatched to guard the five men, three whites and two Negroes, who had been in custody since October 17. Hordes of spectators filled every space in the courtroom —pressing around the bar area surrounding the prisoners and along the walls, before spilling out into the hallways and onto the porch. Charlestown, West Virginia teemed with newspapermen, milita and citizens anxious to catch a glimpse of the man and his followers who had staged the vicious attack against peaceful citizens in Virginia. Despite the short trip, one prisoner, Aaron Stephens, had to be supported by two bailiffs—his body smeared with blood and grime

---

Originally pubished in *The Press on Trial: Crimes and Trials as Media Events*, Lloyd Chiasson, Jr., ed. (Greenwood Press, an imprint of Greenwood Publishing Group Inc., Westport, CT.). Copyright 1998 by Lloyd Chiasson, Jr. Reprinted with permission. All rights reserved.

as he suffered from three balls in his head, two in his breast, one in his arm. His forehead also bore the mark of a rifle bullet that had failed to penetrate his skull.

However, it was the leader who strode at the head of the bedraggled band at whom most of the spectators gawked. Old John Brown marched into the midst of his foes, head erect and eyes glaring defiantly around him at the crowd and the eight magistrates presiding over the court of examination. Reporters would later point out that capture and confinement by his enemies appeared not to have softened and certainly not broken Brown's spirit. Like Stevens, the 6-foot-tall Brown also bore signs of the pitched battle at Harper's Ferry a week earlier. His peculiarly shaped head was covered with long gray hair matted with grime and caked blood from a sabre cut. In sharp contrast to the dirt, blood, and gunpowder residue, pale blue eyes, almost a clear gray, challenged the hostile faces that surrounded him. His only allies seemed to be the four men standing next to him: Stevens, Edwin Coppic, John Copeland, and Shields Green.

As the prisoners stood before the eight Justices of the Peace, the sheriff read the commitment charges, each carrying the death penalty — treason, murder, and inciting slaves to insurrection. Two lawyers, C. J. Faulkner and Lawson Botts, both Virginians and slavery advocates, were called forward from their places in the crowd, and the prosecution, Charles B. Harding, attorney for Jefferson County, and Andrew Hunter, counsel for the State, asked the prisoners if they would accept the two men as counsel. Twice Brown refused, while the other four assented to the arrangement. After the first request, Brown remarked:

> Virginians: I did not ask for any quarter at the time I was taken. I did not ask to have my life spared. The Governor of the State of Virginia tendered me his assurance that I should have a fair trial; but under no circumstances whatever, will I be able to attend to my trial. If you seek my blood, you can have it at any moment without this mockery of a trial.[1]

And so began the most partisan, political trial of the 19th century. So began the end for Old Osawatomie Brown. So began one of the final Fransteps of the long path leading the country toward civil war.

Previously thought killed in the fight against the Virginia militia, but later discovered to be wounded only slightly despite several sabre cuts, Old Osawatomie Brown was very much alive, and eager to plead his own case before the press and the world. Consequently, the press, as well as the people, would be forced to decide for themselves if Brown was indeed a madman or a martyr. The question still lives.

Thus began the preliminary hearing of a man whose life and actions were at one moment atrocious to many Americans, yet understandable to others, applauded by the North, yet feared by the South. John Brown was at the heart of the matter, and the matter was human bondage. His crimes and trial perhaps marked the cusp of public opinion in a struggle older than the country.

Let there be no drama. Brown was guilty under the law. He was found guilty; he was condemned; he was hanged. But there is much more to the trial and death of John Brown than benign statements of fact. Newspapers for and against Brown attempted to use the raid, the trial, the sentencing, and the execution to propagate their beliefs across a country rapidly heading for the unthinkable: war within.

John Brown's trial, then, would become a crucible in deciding the question of slavery. It was important to newspapers simply because it was the news, and at the same time, it was propaganda. It was *the* event and readers throughout the country would look to journalists to provide them with information and guidance.

This is not to suggest that the country wasn't already charged with the excitement and controversy surrounding slavery. Newspapers, as well as citizens, were choosing sides, and each new event was judged for its media impact and persuasive value in garnering support for either pro-slavery advocates or abolitionists. The Nat Turner and Denmark Vesey uprisings were "proof" in the South that slaves needed to be controlled. The 1837 murder of St. Louis editor Elijah Lovejoy had already provided the abolitionists with a martyr and concrete evidence of the brutality of those who promoted the continuance of slavery. As time passed, there was no reconciliation between the regions and the only significant change was the strength of feelings. The last thing slavery sympathizers needed was another martyr, something feared when rumors abounded that Brown had been lynched by the soldiers who had captured him.

Journalists first viewed Brown's capture as a victory for slavery supporters. One of the more violent and radical abolitionists — a madman who served as an example of just how unstable anti-slavery advocates were — would no longer plague southern slaveholders.[2] However, this sense of triumph gradually disintegrated into fear. By his very nature, and by his treatment of the blacks around him, Brown easily inspired blacks to rally in support of his efforts. Since the Nat

Turner rebellion of 1831, southerners had begun to fear their own creation: the enemy within; the one working in the kitchen, or in the barn, or in the fields.

To free blacks and slaves, the leader at Harper's Ferry was more than a man — he was a symbol who conferred dignity and worth upon his black followers. This devotion to Brown, with his condemnation of slavery as the sin of all sins, motivated many blacks to follow him without question.[3] Fear that Brown's failed raid at Harper's Ferry might ignite a great slave uprising was real. Andrew Hunter, appointed as special prosecutor by the governor, seemed to agree that the "raid was not the insignificant thing which it appeared to be before the public, but that it . . . was the incipient movement of the great conflict between North and South . . . ."[4]

This was perhaps the greatest fear of southerners: not the threat of war so much as the potential for slave insurrections and the crumbling of a way of life. Activities of all blacks in the South, even seemingly innocent actions, were viewed with suspicion. Initial reports of the raid stated that as many as 600 to 900 Negroes were expected to revolt.[5] Even during Brown's incarceration, rumors circulated that an army of slaves and abolitionists were plotting to march across Virginia's borders and free Brown. This scenario had the anti-slavery army massacring all white men, women, and children, while burning everything in their path.[6]

Newspapers capitalized on this hypothetical, citing numerous incidents of southern paranoia. According to a Richmond *Enquirer* article reprinted in the New York *Times,* the raid was proof that abolitionists were madmen determined to undermine the rights of slaveholders in the South.[7] During the siege at Harper's Ferry, Baltimore newspapers printed detailed stories of a dangerous ringleader who commanded 300 "strapping negroes" (later 500 to 700) who were slaughtering whites and causing a great deal of trouble.[8] And on October 27 the New Orleans *Daily Picayune* asked the question no one in either region wanted answered: "Are the thinking men of the North ready for civil war — a war of vengeance, embittered by the hottest fanaticism? Will they recognize the desperado, Osawatomie Brown, as a martyr in a good cause . . . ?"

By comparison, some northerners viewed southern fear of Brown's actions as advantageous to the anti-slavery cause. Abolitionist Thomas Wentworth Higginson, one of six well-known men thought to have been part of the conspiracy, wanted Brown to disprove the theory that all slaves were as submissive as Harriet Beecher Stowe's ultimate propaganda figure, Uncle Tom. By doing so, the slaves would prove that they possessed the core of American political, social, and economic ideals — the willingness to fight for their freedom — and force whites to understand the reasoning behind their need for enfranchisement.[9]

At the heart of this slave uprising was a New Yorker raised to abhor slavery and discrimination in all forms. John Brown was born May 9, 1800, in Torrington, Litchfield County, Connecticut, the second son of Owen and Ruth Mills Brown. His father, a tanner and shoemaker, had also been an abolitionist, a legacy that son John would pass on to his own children.[10]

By 1856, Brown was a contributor to the *Ram's Horn,* a black weekly owned and operated by Willis A. Hodges in New York City, and he often sent money and supplies to be used in aiding the runaways' assimilation into a new life in Canada.[11]

However, after Brown and his sons waged war on the pro-slavery settlers in the Kansas territory, and after he butchered five pro-slavery settlers near Osawatomie, Kansas, in 1856, many people in both regions saw Brown's "executions" as either the work of a madman or a religious zealot. The following year, President James Buchanan labeled the man now widely known as Old Osawatomie an outlaw and offered a reward for his capture.[12]

Brown escaped to Canada, however, and remained free until October 1859. Then on Sunday, October 16, Brown and 21 men took control of the town of Harper's Ferry. By the next day, Brown's forces were embroiled in an unrelenting battle with the state militia, having killed or taken several residents hostage and controlling the United States armory and both bridges leading into town. At dawn on October 18, Brown and his followers were overrun by a company of United States Marines, under the direction of then-Colonel Robert E. Lee, who had moved into the town during the night.[13]

Only 12 of the 22 men survived, and Brown's two sons, Watson and Oliver, were casualties of the raid. Oliver died at the armory, and his body was wrapped in the arms of free black Dangerfield Newby as a joke, before both were tossed into an unmarked hole on the bank of the Shenandoah River.[14] Watson, bleeding internally, died 20 hours later in the guardhouse after the group was captured. After his death, Watson's body was supposedly shoved into a box and taken away to Winchester Medical College for medical dissection.[15]

The conditions and the treatment of the prisoners provided ample opportunity for both sides to analyze Brown and the U.S. slavery policy. Separated from his son after their capture, Old Brown lay more than 30 hours on the floor of the superintendent's office of the armory, listening to the drunken carousing and the gunfire from his own Sharps rifles and revolvers taken by looters who were threatening to lynch him. For Brown, a lynching might have been preferable to a public trial and execution. It could have provided the abolitionists with yet another martyr — this time, one who had a stronger connection to blacks, who were becoming an increasingly integral part of the movement.[16] A lynching, however, could never have had the impact of a capture, an indictment, a trial and, finally, an execution. So began partisan and regional media campaigns that shoved the slavery issue to the top of the news agenda.

Despite Brown's hopes, the prisoners were transported to Charlestown, the Jefferson County seat, before a lynching could occur. After the five men were safely ensconced in the jail, Hunter was determined to indict, try, and execute Old Brown and his men within 10 days. According to Virginia law, anyone involved in a slave insurrection could be tried under this accelerated process.[17]

The men remained in jail five days before they were brought into the court for their arraignment.[18] During the incarceration, newspapers were limited to providing analysis of Brown's life and philosophies, as well as background material on the prisoners. Many editors used this opportunity to contemplate the outcome of the trial and its effect on the slavery issue.[19] However, because of rumors that Hunter was attempting to limit access to the prisoners, Brown soon became fearful that the people would never hear the truth about his actions and beliefs. In a hastily arranged press conference in his cell, the old renegade bluntly, guiltlessly, righteously, preached his innocence of wrong-doing. Said Brown: No acts of violence except those necessary to implement his plans were ever committed. Yet Brown's beliefs were of little interest to the reporters salivating for the spectacle the upcoming trial was certain to create. The journalists had been hand-picked by Hunter, including the Associated Press reporter and the New York *Herald* correspondent, Gallagher, who soon became Old Brown's ally.[20]

Having already made up their minds about the past events, the reporters often were more interested in Brown's frequent speeches during the trial than the evidence or other witnesses' testimony. When asked the day of the preliminary examination if he would accept the aid of Faulkner and Botts, Brown appealed to Gallagher and the other reporters in the courtroom. He reiterated his request for counsel who would defend his rights to a fair trial.[21] Down came the gavel as the presiding magistrate issued peremptory orders that "the press should not publish detailed testimony, as it would render the getting of a jury before the Circuit Court impossible."[22] Faulkner also expressed a desire not to serve as counsel because he had been among those men who had subdued Brown's party at Harper's Ferry. He was requested to remain at least until the closure of the preliminary examination.[23]

The preliminary examination moved quickly. Eight witnesses, seven of whom had been hostages at Harper's Ferry, were called to testify about the capture of the residents, the occupation of the armory, the battle, the casualties of the fight, the rebels' professed philosophies and purpose, and the treatment of the hostages. By 5 p.m., the prisoners had been remanded for trial and brought before the grand jury.[24] Court reassembled at 10 a.m., October 26. According to one press account:

> The prisoners were brought in, accompanied by a body of armed men. Cannon were stationed in front of the Court House and an armed guard were patrolling around the jail. Brown looked something better and his eyes were not so much swollen. Stevens had to be supported, and reclined on a mattress on the floor of the court room — evidently unable to sit. He has the appearance of a dying man, breathing with great difficulty. The prisoners were compelled to stand during the indictment, but it was with difficulty, Stevens being held upright by two bailiffs.[25]

At noon the Grand Jury reported a "true bill" against each of the prisoners, whom they declared "evil-minded and traitorous persons . . . not having the fear of God before their eyes, but being moved by the false and malignant counsel of other evil and traitorous persons, and the instigations of the devil."[26] Faulkner had already departed, and the court appointed Thomas C. Green, mayor of Charlestown, to hear the indictments, along with Botts, who decided to remain on the case. The five prisoners were charged with confederating to make rebellion against Virginia; conspiring to induce slave insurrections; and committing murder upon four men.[27]

The prisoners' pleas of not guilty surprised no one, and Hunter readily agreed to requests for separate trials. This way, he could try Brown first. At this point, Botts reiterated Brown's earlier plea for a two- or three-day delay to heal from his wounds.[28] Hunter objected vehemently, fearful of another uprising as well as an attempt to rescue the prisoners. Following testimony from the prison physician that Brown was physically able to stand trial (in fact, Brown could not stand at all, and throughout the trial was not seated with the defense counsels but lay in a cot instead), Judge Parker ruled that Brown's trial should begin immediately.[29]

For slavery supporters, this was probably the worse tactical decision the State could have made. The excitement and sentiments about the case were already extremely passionate. A wiser alternative would have been to delay the trial until attitudes calmed. The spectacle of wounded prisoners on trial for their lives when they seemed too weak to defend themselves elicited sympathy and support from journalists and citizens throughout the North. Even those who had been outraged by Brown's actions at Harper's Ferry were equally affected by the description of a haggard Brown, weak from unhealed wounds, having to attend his trial while lying on a cot.[30] Northern editors hastened to point out how swiftly slavery supporters were willing to move, trampling moral rights and human dignity to maintain their way of life.

Immediately after the raid, reactions among the press had been decidedly mixed on the events at Harper's Ferry. Most editors could not determine if Brown was a madman driven insane by his cause or a martyr motivated by his beliefs. Abolitionist editor William Lloyd Garrison was repulsed by Brown's violent actions and professed his opposition to the raid.[31] Similarly, New York *Tribune* editor Horace Greeley, who was among those mentioned by Democratic pro-slavery newspapers in the North as being culpable for Brown's deeds, fully expected the prisoners to pay for their crimes: "The prisoners in fact have no defence, and their case will probably be speedily disposed of."[32]

Later, Greeley and the *Tribune's* tone changed considerably as Brown was repeatedly denied delay requests because of his health or to prepare a complete defense against such serious charges. During the trial, for example, the *Tribune* wrote that authorities wanted "a full five-act tragedy. . . It is a pretty scheme — a scheme worthy of Virginia . . . ."[33]

Feelings quickly shifted in Brown's favor. Each day of the trial brought more instances in which newspapers depicted the entire process as unfair. It was difficult not to notice how the trial was beginning to take a toll on Brown. During the afternoon session on October 26, Brown, who had declared himself unable to rise from his bed, was carried into the courtroom on a cot. Most of the time he lay quietly with his eyes closed and the covers pulled up close to his chin.[34]

Daily dispatches from Hunter's "authorized" group of journalists revealed numerous surprises for the readers. Brown's dissatisfaction with his counsel, the prosecuting attorney's personal bias in the case, and the concern over the consequences of the outcome provided constant conflicts to be reported. Most carried full transcripts of each day's testimony. On October 27, the first full day of testimony and opening arguments, Brown's attorney attempted to enter an insanity plea despite Brown's protestations. Such a move would have defeated Old Osawatomie's plan to put slavery on trial. Consequently, before the judge or the prosecution could respond, Brown raised himself up in bed and remarked, "I will add, if the Court will allow me, that I look upon it [insanity plea] as a miserable artifice and pretext of those who ought to take a different course in regard to me, if they took any at all, and I view it with contempt more than otherwise."[35]

It was obvious Brown felt that he'd get a fairer trial — or at least a trial that martyred him and furthered his cause — if he had counsel who could be trusted to understand his motivation. It was not surprising when, after several disparaging comments in court against his attorneys, both Botts and Green demanded to be dismissed from the case. Brown, who certainly had vast experience in explaining, and defending, himself, now had what he wanted — himself as a client. Yet this was just the beginning of the most significant day of the trial. According to Associated Press reports, it was a damaging day to Brown, but one wonders how his predicament could have been worse.

The same day Botts and Green resigned, John Cook was captured. A member of Brown's force at Harper's Ferry, Cook was brought to the jail, loudly blaming his involvement in the incident entirely on Brown. Brown, Cook told anyone within hailing distance, was a Piped Piper in complete control of his minions. The defense was dealt yet another significant blow when the prosecution entered as evidence the Constitution and Ordinance of the Provisional Government for the area Brown had intended to free through his ill-advised resurrection. This damning evidence had been written by the old man himself. In addition, a large bundle of letters and papers from other abolitionists thought to be involved in the planning of the raid was admitted into evidence. But there was more. Testimony from some of the hostages — particularly Henry Hunter, the prosecutor's son — about the murder of one of the hostages increased spectators' hostile sentiments.[36]

And still the day was not done. A young Boston attorney arrived at the trial, not to participate but to report details back to northern abolitionist leaders. Beyond spying for Brown supporters such as Wendell Phillips and John Andrew, George H. Hoyt was to arrange for Brown's escape. Except Brown didn't want to escape. He wanted to stay; he wanted the story to grow; and he wanted to die. Said Brown: "I am worth now infinitely more to die than to live."[37]

Although Hoyt stayed, observed, and visited Brown in his jail cell, the old man was as tough-minded with friend as foe. He would not be deterred.

The following day the arrival of Brown's northern counsel, Samuel Chilton of Washington and Henry Griswold of Cleveland, did not provide the relief Brown expected. Since the attorneys based their case on the legalities of the indictment, the case in Brown's defense was inordinately swift. Following a break for Sunday, both sides concluded arguments on Monday, October 31, at 1:30 p.m., and the jury retired.

After deliberating for 45 minutes, the jury returned. Spectators filled the courtroom, pressing against the railings, out through the hall and beyond the doors. Like an early morning fog in a West Virginia hollow, a stillness blanketed the room. Brown sat up in bed to hear the verdict: guilty, guilty on all counts. Guilty of treason, guilty of conspiring and advising with slaves and others to rebel, guilty of murder in the first degree. Then he laid down quietly and said nothing.

Two days later, Judge Parker sentenced Brown while the jury retired for deliberation in Coppic's trial. It had been assumed that all the prisoners would be condemned and executed on the same day. Brown, then, was surprised when asked if he wished to say why sentence should not be passed. The old man rose from his seat near his counsel, rested his hands lightly on the table, and issued his last words to the public. He said, in part:

> I deny every thing but what I have all along admitted — the design on my part to free the slaves.... I believe to have interfered as I have done, as I have always freely admitted I have done, in behalf of His despised poor, was not wrong, but right. Now, if it is deemed necessary that I should forfeit my life for the furtherance of the ends of justice, and mingle my blood further with the blood of my children, and with the blood of millions in this slave country whose rights are disregarded by wicked, cruel, and unjust enactments — I submit: so let it be done...[38]

Despite an overflow crowd in the courtroom, there was complete silence during Brown's speech. And then the judge sentenced Brown to be hanged on Friday, December 2. One man applauded but was quickly suppressed. Brown, who had remained silent throughout, was taken back to his cell. Meanwhile, after an hour of deliberation the jury found Coppic guilty on all counts.[39]

The remaining days of Brown's life were spent writing letters to family and friends.[40] Newspapers were rife with speculation over whether Brown would remain in custody long enough to hang. Again, fear ran rampant in the South while the reason for that apprehension quietly wrote his will.[41] By the time his execution day arrived, the old man had been imprisoned in the Charlestown jail for 40 days. He had entertained numerous journalists in his cell during that period, particularly during his last days. Correspondents filled northern and southern newspapers with accounts of these visits and those of others who came to console Brown. And the media event continued to grow.

On the day of his execution, however, Brown was alone. No dispatches were to be sent out without prior approval from authorities. Charlestown officials had limited access into the city, and many northern editors, feared to be abolitionists planning to rescue Brown, were barred from the event.[42] From 8 a.m. until 10 a.m., military troops arrived and positioned themselves at the site. Lines of pickets and patrols numbering nearly 3,000 soldiers encircled the place of execution for 15 miles, with more than 500 troops posted around the scaffold. Only about 400 citizens were present, along with what few reporters had been allowed to attend the event.[43]

When Brown disembarked at the field, without benefit of clergy, the scaffold and the rope, shipped in from Kentucky, had been made ready. With little delay, Brown was led up the scaffold; the noose was set; the trap door opened; the old man hanged. After swinging for 38 minutes, the body was cut down and delivered to his widow at Harper's Ferry.[44] It was then taken to North Elba, where abolitionist orator Wendell Phillips gave the eulogy. John Brown's body was laid to rest on December 8.[45]

Newspaper accounts included specific details of the execution, along with coverage of meetings and mourning sessions held to honor him. Mourners gathered throughout the United States and Canada — including Montreal, Rochester, New York, Plymouth, Concord, New Hampshire, New Bedford, Albany, and Fitchburg — to remember this most controversial of men.[46] Many editors lauded his death sentence.[47] The Portage, Ohio *Sentinel*, published in Brown's old hometown, viewed the execution as proper penalty for the crimes of one who had always been a "lawbreaker."[48] Others, such as the Baltimore *American,* hoped Virginia might "settle down" after the execution, comparing Brown's death to that "of a Thug, dying by the cord with which he had strangled so many victims."[49]

However, other newspapers like Greeley's *Tribune* provided Brown with the martyr status the anti-slavery movement would need to give impetus to the cause. A particularly large meeting in Boston was detailed in abolitionist newspapers throughout the country. The desk for the speakers was adorned with a likeness of Brown, a cross, a laurel wreath, placards with quotes from Brown, and an "insurrectionary emblem" of a warrior with his foot on a tyrant. The message on the emblem read: SIC SEMPER TYRANNIS ('So be it ever to tyrants.'). The December 9 issue of the *Liberator* declared: "It is no use. Old Brown will have his day. He is the hero of the hour, and fills every ear with the story of his daring, of his fall, and of his fate." The day following his execution, the Springfield *Republican* wrote: "John Brown still lives." Later, Ralph Waldo Emerson wrote that Brown had "made the gallows glorious like the cross."[50]

Other papers simply exploited the entire affair. Frank Leslie's *Illustrated Newspaper,* which pictured elaborate wood carvings of the execution, was, according to the owner, "the most important paper we have yet issued."[51]

The following year, on July 4, 1860, blacks and abolitionists would make a pilgrimage to North Elba to remember Old Brown. He was saluted by such notable journalists as Frederick Douglass, James Redpath, and William Lloyd Garrison as a patriot worthy of the respect of the country's Founding Fathers.[52] The passage of time and impending civil unrest had softened the impressions of many Americans toward Brown and his actions. By literally being tried, convicted, and sentenced in the press, Brown had achieved his ultimate goal of attacking the atrocities of slavery. And even those who had not approved of his actions grudgingly acknowledged his ability to foresee the violent thunderclouds filling the horizon.

Notes

1. New York *Herald,* 26 October 1859; Quoted in Thomas Drew, *The John Brown Invasion: An Authentic History of the Harper's Ferry Tragedy* (Boston: James Campbell, 1859), 25.
2. See, for example, New York *Herald,* 20 October 1859; Cleveland *Weekly Leader,* 26 October 1859; Hartford *Evening Press,* 20 October 1859; *Freedom's Champion* (Atchison City, Kansas), 22 October 1859; New Orleans *Daily Picayune,* 22 October 1859.
3. Benjamin Quarles, ed., *Blacks on John Brown* (Urbana, Ill.: University of Illinois Press,

1972), xiii.
4. Quoted in Truman Nelson, *The Old Man: John Brown at Harper's Ferry The Old Man: John Brown at Harper's Ferry* (New York: Holt, Rinehart & Winston, 1973), 200.
5. New York *Tribune*, 18 October 1859.
6. Oswald Garrison Villard, *John Brown, 1800-1859: A Biography Fifty Years After* (Boston: Houghton Mifflin Co., 1910), 478-479.
7. New York *Times*, 29 October 1859.
8. Baltimore *Patriot*, 18 October 1859; Baltimore *American*, 17 October 1859; Baltimore *Exchange*, 18 October 1859.
9. See Stephen B. Oates, *To Purge This Land with Blood: A Biography of John Brown* (New York: Harper & Row, 1970), 238; Tilden G. Edelstein, *Strange Enthusiasm: A Life of Thomas Wentworth Higginson* (New Haven: Yale University, 1968), 224-225.
10. F.B. Sanborn, *The Life and Letters of John Brown, Liberator of Kansas, and Martyr of Virginia* (Boston: Roberts Brothers, 1891), 12.
11. Bernell Tripp, *Origins of the Black Press in New York, 1829-1849* (Northport, Ala.: Vision Press, 1992), 52-53.
12. Lloyd Chiasson Jr., ed., *The Press in Times of Crisis*, (Westport, Conn.: Greenwood Press, 1995), 69.
13. Baltimore *Patriot*, 17 October 1859; Baltimore *American*, 18 October 1859; Baltimore *Exchange*, 18-19 October 1859.
14. Nelson, *The Old Man: John Brown at Harper's Ferry*, 198.
15. New York *Herald*, 6 December 1859; James Redpath, *The Public Life of Capt. John Brown, with an Auto-Biography of his Childhood and Youth* (Boston: Thayer and Eldridge, 1860), 288.
16. Nelson, *The Old Man: John Brown at Harper's Ferry*, 203.
17. Villard, *John Brown, 1800-1859: A Biography Fifty Years After*, 644.
18. Nelson, *The Old Man: John Brown at Harper's Ferry*, 206, 229.
19. See, for example, New York *Times*, 21 October 1859; New York *Herald*, 20 October 1859; Hartford *Evening Press*, 20 October 1859.
20. Nelson, *The Old Man: John Brown at Harper's Ferry*, 207.
21. Drew, *The John Brown Invasion: An Authentic History of the Harper's Ferry Tragedy*, 26.
22. Associated Press telegraph report. Reprinted in Redpath, *The Public Life of Capt. John Brown, with an Auto-Biography of his Childhood and Youth*, 294.
23. *Ibid.*
24. Redpath, *The Public Life of Capt. John Brown, with an Auto-Biography of his Childhood and Youth*, 298.
25. Reprinted in Redpath, *The Public Life of Capt. John Brown, with an Auto-Biography of his Childhood and Youth*, 301.
26. Drew, *The John Brown Invasion: An Authentic History of the Harper's Ferry Tragedy*, 26.
27. *Ibid.*
28. Redpath, *The Public Life of Capt. John Brown, with an Auto-Biography of his Childhood and Youth*, 300; Drew, *The John Brown Invasion: An Authentic History of the Harper's Ferry Tragedy*, 27; New York *Herald*, 27 October *1859*.
29. *Ibid.*
30. New York *Herald*, 28 October 1859; New York *Times*, 27 October *1859*.
31. *Liberator*, 21 October, 1859.
32. New York *Tribune*, 25 October, 28 October 1859.
33. *Ibid.*, 16 November 1859.
34. *New York Times*, 27 October 1859; Redpath, *The Public Life of Capt. John Brown, with an Auto-Biography of his Childhood and Youth*, 308.

35. *Ibid.*
36. As cited in Richard O. Boyer, *The Legend of John Brown* (New York: Alfred A. Knopf, 1973), 18.
37. New York *Herald*, 29 October 1859; New York *Times*, 29 October 1859.
38. Redpath, *The Public Life of Capt. John Brown, with an Auto-Biography of his Childhood and Youth*, 340-342.
39. *Ibid.*, 342-343.
40. *Ibid.*, 344-372.
41. *Liberator*, 4 November, 25 November 1859; Tallapoosa (Ala.) *Times* and Philadelphia *Christian Observer*, reprinted in New York *Times*, 25 November 1859; New York *Herald*, reprinted in *Liberator*, 18 November 1859.
42. Baltimore *American*, 1 December 1859; New York *Times*, 2 December 1859.
43. *Liberator*, 2 December, 9 December 1859; New York *Times*, 3 December 1859.
44. New York *Times*, 3 December 1859; Associated Press report, reprinted in the New York *Times*, 3 December 1859.
45. Villard, *John Brown, 1800-1859: A Biography Fifty Years After*, 561.
46. *Liberator*, 9 December 1859; New York *Tribune*, 3 December 1859.
47. New York *Herald*, reprinted in *Liberator*, 18 November 1859; Richmond *Enquirer*, reprinted in New York *Times*, 2 December 1859; New York *Observer* and *Central Presbyterian* (Richmond, Va.), reprinted in *Liberator*, 25 November 1859.
48. *Weekly Portage Sentinel*, 7 December 1859.
49. Baltimore *American*, 7 December 1859.
50. Louis L. Snyder and Richard B. Morris, eds., A *Treasury of Great Reporting* (New York: Simon and Schuster, 1962), 124.
51. *Ibid.*, 125.
52. *Liberator*, 27 July 1860.

5

Censorship, Racism, and the Antebellum Press: *Harper's Weekly* Reports Harper's Ferry

Robert C. Kennedy
HarpWeek

The news coverage of John Brown's Raid of 1859, the subsequent trial, and executions, represent "a milestone in the development of American journalism." These events signaled the coming of age for modern field reporting. Never before in American history had so many reporters and illustrators been sent by distant urban newspapers to cover a breaking story.[1]

Reflecting the sectional tensions surrounding issues related to slavery, the Northern press faced considerable censorship and harassment as it tried to report the incident. This censorship continued for the citizens of Virginia in the wake of John Brown's raid. Both the postal service and the press faced increased scrutiny and suppression, similar to the period following the unsuccessful Nat Turner Rebellion in Virginia in 1831.

With the national spotlight focused on the fate of John Brown, and rumors of daring rescue attempts circulating, Virginia authorities clamped down on civil liberties, severely limiting freedom of travel, freedom of the press, and freedom of speech. Governor Henry Wise issued a proclamation, reprinted in *Harper's Weekly*, warning that "strangers" who could not give "a satisfactory account of themselves" would be summarily arrested. Caught in the midst of this repressive atmosphere was a Yankee patent medicine peddler, who, according to the New York *Herald* account excerpted in *Harper's*, was jailed, then expelled from town because his purpose was suspect.[2]

Harper's Weekly reported that several editors of Northern "abolitionist" newspapers were removed from railroad cars or otherwise kept from the scene. Those who successfully reached the destination had to go to great lengths to cover the events. Henry S. Olcott of the New York *Tribune* used Masonic connections to enter Charles Town with the local militia from Petersburg, Virginia. Another *Tribune* reporter, Edward H. House, whose news reports constantly berated the Virginia militia, had to remain incognito during the time he was in Charles Town.

In another proclamation, Governor Wise activated the militia and ordered that certain railroad lines be reserved only for the military. In accordance with those gubernatorial proclamations, the commander of the Virginia militia, General William B. Taliaferro, announced to the public that no "abolitionists or Republicans" would be allowed in the city on the day of the hangings.[3]

For several weeks, *Harper's Weekly* depicted the mounting tensions and fear of violence as the execution date neared. The correspondent of the *American*, quoted by *Harper's*, noted that although the city was not officially under martial law, the military surveillance was so sweeping that it inconvenienced even the local residents. They could not pass through the streets without interrogation or even arrest.[4] Nerves were so on edge that a wayward cow in the dark of night caused a sentinel to fire his rifle and sound the call to arms.[5]

Harper's Weekly further reported that Governor Wise had requested the formal opinion of state Attorney General John Randolph Tucker concerning whether state laws could be used to restrict the postal distribution of "incendiary publications." In his response, Attorney General Tucker made a fine distinction between the transmission of the mails and the publication and circulation of printed material. He advised the governor that while the federal government had authority over distribution, state laws and local ordinances could constitutionally restrict publication and circulation of the offensive material within its jurisdiction.[6]

Harper's Weekly, despite its promise of bringing national and world news into the parlors of America's burgeoning middle-class, avoided highlighting the contentious issues of slavery and sectionalism. Their editorial policy was constrained by both fiscal realities and political beliefs. The newspaper had been an immediate success in establishing a truly national base of subscribers. To discuss, much less to take a firm stand, on the issues of slavery and slavery expansion, would have alienated *Harper's* Southern readers and lost the journal substantial revenues. The conservative politics of the Harper brothers further checked any attempt to publish controversial views on the subject. As Douglas Democrats, they considered both Northern abolitionists and Southern fire-eaters to be unpatriotic, dangerous radicals.7

The far-reaching significance of John Brown's Raid on Harper's Ferry, and the attention it commanded, forced *Harper's Weekly* for the first time to grant slavery and sectionalism a prominent position in its news coverage. The journal reported and commented on John Brown's Raid in three venues: the "Domestic Intelligence" column; David Hunter Strother's series of illustrated articles and cartoons; and the editorial page. Each of these formats offers insight into different aspects of antebellum journalism and the biases and prejudices of the day. The conservative views of the publishers and editors were juxtaposed by Strother's harsh rhetoric—some of the most explicitly racist language to appear in *Harper's Weekly* in the antebellum years.

Coverage began in the October 29, 1859 issue on the editorial page and in the "Domestic Intelligence" column, a weekly feature of news highlights gleaned from papers from around the country. Only major stories received significant space in this column. The editors' decision to devote a substantial portion of the column to the Harper's Ferry Raid placed the story on par with the president's annual message to Congress and the notorious Sickles murder case.

The editors of *Harper's Weekly* made judgments in choosing which journals and sections of news stories to quote in "Domestic Intelligence," and in assigning to this copy their own sub-headings. Much of the twelve weeks of coverage of John Brown's Raid appearing in "Domestic Intelligence" was attributed to the New York *Herald*, a common source for *Harper's Weekly*. Although the *Herald* had a pro-Southern tilt and clamored for Brown's execution, their copy was vetted by *Harper's* to remove most of the overt partisanship. The result was a rather straightforward delineation of the raid, trial, and executions.8

Ironically, the *Herald* citations in "Domestic Intelligence" usually referred to John Brown and his cohorts with the rather elevated designations of "insurrectionists" or "conspirators," while *Harper's* editors used the more pejorative "outlaws" in the sub-headings. In the text of the copy, Brown's quoted or paraphrased statements in the court room, prison interviews, or written correspondence, allowed select portions of his message to reach *Harper's* audience. Overall, the readers of "Domestic Intelligence" received a dichotomous picture of Brown: his age and frailty were emphasized in the correspondent's choice of phrases, yet "Old Brown" was also depicted as a man "of extraordinary nerve" who "bore the impression of the conviction that [his actions were] ... right."9

The extensive coverage of the Harper's Ferry Raid in "Domestic Intelligence" represented an editorial shift away from *Harper's* former reticence toward the issues of slavery and sectionalism. But the November 5 issue, the second week of coverage, was truly precedent-setting. The editors gave the story front page attention with a panoramic illustration of the arsenal and town of Harper's Ferry.10 Even more important, the journal began the first installment of David Hunter Strother's illustrated series on the incident.

Strother, also known by the pen name "Porte Crayon," joined the staff of *Harper's Monthly* in 1852, and was one of its highest paid contributors throughout the decade. As the magazine's first illustrator-writer, his commission allowed him to travel through the South and West, sketching and recording the life of its residents for *Harper's* readers. Strother was from one of the First Families of Virginia, and most of his relatives were slaveholders. Strother's views were both strongly Unionist and anti-abolitionist, fitting in well with the conservative Douglas Democratic position of the Harper brothers.11

Serendipity gave *Harper's* the competitive edge, as Strother was courting a woman in nearby Charles Town when the raid at Harper's Ferry occurred. He was an eyewitness to nearly the entire event, from the skirmish between Brown's men and the militia on October 17 to the executions on December 2.

In contrast to his fellow journalists, Strother, *Harper's* man on the scene, faced no censorship or harassment from state or local authorities. In fact, he enjoyed privileged access to the officials and principals involved, as well as support of a major news outlet. In addition to being a native Virginian and critic of abolitionism, a relative of Strother, Andrew Hunter, served as special prosecutor and Governor Wise's personal representative at Brown's trial.12 Strother was allowed to join Governor Wise and Prosecutor Hunter as they interviewed Brown.

Strother's first article began innocuously enough with an explanation of the location of Harper's Ferry, along with some demographics of the town. He stated that the facts of the unfolding events had been, on the whole, reported accurately. Strother, though, was clearly conscious of the important role language played in influencing the impression readers carried away from a story. He pointed out, for example, what he believed was an important misrepresentation in the terminology chosen by other journalists; a misrepresentation that went to the heart of the affair's morality.

Strother insisted that Brown and his followers be labeled "outlaws" and the incident an "invasion" rather than as "insurgents" and "insurrection," as many reporters had. Although this choice was not explained, Strother would have understood that "insurrection" still resonated with the legitimacy of the American Revolution. Heeding the suggestion, *Harper's Weekly* continued to use the term "outlaws" in their sub headings of "Domestic Intelligence" reports on the trials and sentencing.[13]

As a writer, Strother used the tools of language and perspective to advance his own political and social ideas. In the nearly three page article, Strother's rhetoric underlined the criminality of Brown, his men, and their actions by the consistent use of terms such as "the outlaw chief" and "old felon" to designate Brown, and "outlaws" to refer to his followers. That language was exacerbated by the imagery of animal and uncivilized human brutality in such phrases as "murderous schemes," "savage audacity," "bloody band," "savage game," and "ferocious beast." The fear of many Southerners that a violent slave uprising might one day occur was registered in Strother's dual portrayal of John Brown's Raid as both an evil event and one that was "folly," "intense[ly] sill[y]," and "ludicrous."

Strother's racism was apparent in his textual and pictorial depiction of slaves and free blacks, whom he blatantly labeled "darkeys" and a "good-humored, good-for-nothing, half-monkey race." Strother reassured his white audience that the blacks at Harper's Ferry had neither the foreknowledge of, nor the inclination to join, Brown and his followers. Not only did threats, promises, and persuasion fail to convince the blacks to join Brown, but some openly resisted, including the murdered railroad porter, whose actions Strother called "heroic" and "faithful."

Strother claimed to have interviewed several slaves who had been captured by Brown and his men. The slaves–presented as too frightened to take up weapons and join Brown–were jubilant to be freed from his clutches and jeered at their former captors. The readers were informed that "full evidence" supported the contention that the slaves would have "cheerfully" taken up weapons against Brown and his men, if only the slaves' owners had been present.

Here, Strother attempted to assuage the Southern fear of a violent slave revolt by presenting the slaves as child-like, cowardly when left to their own devices, yet fiercely loyal to their masters. Strother's cartoons reflected those stereotypes and reinforced the message of his text. The image in the reader's mind of the commitment of the entire community to the slave system and plantation hierarchy was completed by the reporter's insistence that the overwhelmingly majority of the militia volunteers who fought to suppress the "invasion" were non-slaveholders.

A class bias was also evident in Strother's reporting. Although more subtle, his depiction of the common whites was similar in key ways to his portrayal of blacks. The volunteer militia, mainly plebeian representatives of the white community, were portrayed as oafish rubes. The "unorganized multitude," as Strother called them, gave "the affair more the character of a great hunting scene than that of a battle." They stood in sharp contrast to the professional officers of the gentry class from the United States Army and Marines.

Under the command of Colonel Robert E. Lee and Lieutenant J. E. B. Stuart, these gentlemen-soldiers seemed to ride in on white horses to save the day. "The quiet and thorough manner in which this delicate business was executed reflects great credit on the officers and men engaged, and is a beautiful exemplification of the immense superiority of trained soldiers over all others." When one of the militia officers was shot, readers were told of his West Point education and his social and economic standing as "a gentleman of fortune, and one of the most esteemed citizens of the county." [14]

In the second illustrated article, Strother shared with *Harper's* readers his impressions of three of Brown's jailed men–Edwin Coppic, Shields Green, and John Copeland. Still concerned that the rhetoric used by journalists reporting the trial created an image that was too sympathetic, Strother stressed that Brown and his men were not housed in "cells," but in "large, well-ventilated, and comfortable" rooms.

In one of the top rooms Coppic, a white man, and Green, a black man, were described as handcuffed together, sharing meals and the same bed. Although men sharing a bed was common in nineteenth century America, the image of a white and black man conjoined in sleep, dining, and every waking moment must have caused no little discomfort to *Harper's* readers. The racism of most Northerners, even of those opposed to slavery, would have caused them to recoil from the social equality implicit in the image.

In accord with Strother's racial stereotyping, Green's illiteracy was noted and he was accused of lying about his age in order to generate sympathy as a victim of youthful naïveté. Copeland was described as "a likely mulatto" and paternalistically contemned as one who "would make a very genteel dining-room servant." The men were characterized as "cowed," "haggard," and "penitent," but Strother remarked that it was impossible to have pity for them.

Strother then proceeded in the second article to give a fictional account of what he stressed was Brown's goal: the overthrow of the federal government "and the Anglo-Saxon race in the South." In the racist reverie that Strother spun, Green was a Member of Congress in Brown's provisional government, while Copeland was a Supreme Court justice. These black men were portrayed as lazy—"snoozing and snoring" on the plantation—and greedy—wanting "the spoils of the conquered territory, confiscated estates, and lucrative offices."

Green was characterized in ostentatious dress—"his fingers stiff with diamond rings, his vest loaded with gold chains and stuffed with jeweled repeaters"—while his servants were drawn from the erstwhile First Families of Virginia. In Strother's version of Brown's utopia, the social hierarchy of the plantation South was inverted, with the bottom rail definitively on top.

Congressman Green was driven to the Supreme Court where a group of Southerners, facing the death penalty for defending their homes and families, begged Justice Copeland for mercy. While a dour General John Brown stood ready to lead the white men to the gallows, Congressman Green, sated with food and drink, suggested that the white men become slaves on his plantation. After hearing Brown bark out the order to march, Green awakened to the terror, then anger, of reality. Strother was known to inject humor into his writing, so he emphasized to readers that this story presented the real dreams "of the fanatical conspirators."15

In contrast to Strother's inflammatory language and unyielding stance, the rhetoric and perspective on the editorial page of *Harper's Weekly* was a great deal more cautious and decorous. The first editorial addressing the "Insurrection at Harper's Ferry," began by registering the astonishment that most Americans purportedly experienced when learning of the event. Had readers relied exclusively on *Harper's Weekly* for national news coverage, they certainly would have been shocked that sectional tensions over slavery could have fueled this event.

The editors identified Brown as a "soldier of fortune" involved in Bleeding Kansas. All but the most radical on the slavery question, the editors attested, abhorred the idea of a slave insurrection and would take up arms to suppress it. Skirting the underlying social questions, the editors chose to establish a negative political association between sympathy for Brown and political power; that is, Republican supporters could expect lower vote totals in the fall elections.[16]

After Brown was found guilty of murder and treason, the editors, in a subsequent lead editorial, asked the question: "Will John Brown Be Hanged?" They believed that Brown had received a fair trial and was guilty, with no extenuating circumstances, of the charges which justly carried the capital penalty. The editors sought, however, to ease sectional tensions as the nation entered a presidential election year, recognizing that political rhetoric could exacerbate existing divisions. They emphasized that Brown's execution would strengthen the abolitionist cause in the North, while a pardon would undermine it. The editors suggested, therefore, that if the South—not the governor, not Virginia, but *the South*—could be merciful without abetting similarly delusional men, then the region would gain much more respect from the North.[17]

Keenly aware of the national and local strains surrounding the executions, *Harper's Weekly* entitled a later editorial "American Conservatism." Though it dealt with no specific issues or events in an explicit manner, the timing of its appearance after the abundant coverage and controversy over John Brown's Raid at Harper's Ferry seems no coincidence.

In part, "American Conservatism" was a classical republican criticism that the spirit of business enterprise had raised unrealistic, even dangerous, expectations in the social realm. "We improve machinery, and forthwith the notion seizes us that we can manufacture a better article in the way of society. We cheapen clocks, and thence conclude that we can reduce the cost of virtue." Emphasizing a clear distinction between philosophical ideals and the actual circumstances of society, the editors concluded by advising caution in regards to social evolution.[18]

George William Curtis, who would later serve as *Harper's Weekly* long-time editor-in-chief (1863-1892), was at the time of the Harper's

Ferry Raid authoring its "Lounger" column, a weekly collection of art and music criticism and social commentary. The liberal Curtis, an anti-slavery advocate, followed the lead of the editors by entitling his commentary in the same issue: "Conservatism." Curtis's perspective and conclusion, however, were very different from that of the editorial writer's.

In the future, Curtis would spend much of his tenure as editorialist excoriating "benighted" conservatism and praising liberalism for its moral goodness and progressive characteristics. In the context of John Brown's Raid, "The Lounger" praised what he termed "genuine" conservatism by essentially redefining it as liberalism or radicalism—that which goes beneath the surface appearances to get to the root of social problems.

Curtis warned that society could not remain static, but must improve in order to be preserved. Whereas the editorial writers denigrated adherence to philosophical ideals, Curtis appealed to moral absolutes and higher law. Both attempted to give their point of view divine sanction: the editorial writer claimed that Providence would correct society's faults over time, while the Unitarian Curtis endorsed an activist Christianity.[19] But Curtis's voice was, at the time, a lone exception in the editorial perspective of *Harper's Weekly*.

Despite the cautious approach that the publishers and editors of *Harper's Weekly* had taken concerning the issues of slavery and sectionalism, they were reprimanded from both sides for their coverage of the Harper's Ferry incident. A few weeks after the executions, an editorial reported that their coverage of Harper's Ferry had piqued the Richmond *Enquirer* to label *Harper's Weekly* "an abolitionist journal." Conversely, *Harper's* reporting had provoked a Milwaukee chapter of the Young Men's Christian Association to cancel its subscription because of the newspaper's "shameful cuts and still more malicious articles on the cause of freedom." In *Harper's* response, the editors defended their coverage as fair-minded, and boasted that the journal could "afford not to be much disturbed by occasional abuse from extremists on either side."[20]

In truth, the brash declarations of the editorial were belied by their decision to quash Strother's final story and sketches of the executions, deeming them too incendiary to publish. The New Orleans *Times-Democrat* reported that Strother, whose vantage point was the foot of the scaffold steps, walked up to the hanging body of Brown and lifted the dead man's cap in order to sketch his face. Previously, *Harper's Weekly* had not hesitated to print explicit illustrations and text of grisly murders, torture, or other sensational topics.

The difference in this case was clearly the ominous ramifications that John Brown's Raid and the executions held for the fate of the Union. It had been primarily Strother's illustrated articles that had roused the ire of both anti-slavery Northerners and pro-slavery Southerners.[21] Instead of running Strother's illustrated article, *Harper's Weekly* relegated coverage to the staid "Domestic Intelligence" column, as it pleaded from its editorial page for national harmony and the quelling of the slavery issue.

Ironically, Strother's rejected article was far milder than his prior work and did not differ greatly in language and structure from the "Domestic Intelligence" report of the execution. The article was more drawn out than the column and it contained occasional barbs against Brown's character, but Strother's conclusion that the execution was an affirmation of the rule of law was in congruence with *Harper's* conservative proclivities.

In addition, the illustration he submitted was a rather innocuous panoramic view of the scaffold and the crowd of militia officers and official guests below it.[22] Nevertheless, the editors judged that a description of the execution in the fine print of the "Domestic Intelligence" column would have less impact and criticism than the personal tone of an illustrated article signed by the man who personified *Harper's* controversial coverage.

The final major address by *Harper's Weekly* of John Brown's Raid at Harper's Ferry came in the lead editorial on December 17, entitled "North and South." The editors labeled the North-South tensions over the slavery issue a massive misunderstanding fomented by vocal, radical minorities in both sections for their own gain. The South had the view that most Northerners sympathized with John Brown and considered him a martyr. The editors proffered that Northern popular opinion, on the contrary, viewed Brown as a criminal who had killed innocent people and was justly punished.

Northerners, on the other hand, thought that the Southern fire-eaters represented typical Southern opinion. *Harper's* assured its audience that those views were only representative of a self-interested minority. In an apostrophe to its Southern readers, *Harper's* delineated the reasons that disunion would hurt the South economically far more than it would the North. The editorial concluded by musing that the gibbet would be a fitting end for the selfish politicians in both sections who, in "pandering to the worst passions of the mob," could "plunge a peaceful and contented people into the horrors of civil war."[23]

During John Brown's raid, trial, and execution, *Harper's Weekly* faced a difficult challenge to their conservative Democratic principles: how to use their coverage to sell newspapers without exacerbating sectional divisions? When Strother appeared on the scene at Charles Town, *Harper's* immediately took advantage of his writing and artistic skills. The journal showcased Strother's racist stories and cartoons for several weeks, allowing *Harper's Weekly* to be competitive in the national newspaper market with their chief rival, *Frank Leslie's Illustrated Newspaper*.

With the execution of Brown and his men, the use of Strother's work as a marketing tool had reached the saturation point. The criticism of *Harper's* coverage, and the heightened sectional tensions surrounding the events, had become too great in the editors' estimation. Their solution was to censor their own writer. In so doing, *Harper's Weekly* appeared to have succeeded in business without contributing to a full-scale destruction of the existing social and political order. Once again, the contentious issues of slavery and sectionalism would virtually vanish from the pages of *Harper's Weekly* until the firing on Fort Sumter.

Notes

1. Boyd B. Stutler, "An Eyewitness Describes the Hanging of John Brown," *American Heritage* (February, 1955), pp. 4-9.
2. Domestic Intelligence," *Harper's Weekly*, November 19, 1859, p. 742 (c. 3-4).
3. Domestic Intelligence," *Harper's Weekly*, December 10, 1859, p. 794 (c.1-3); Boyd B. Stutler, "An Eyewitness Describes the Hanging of John Brown," *American Heritage* (February, 1955), pp. 4-9.
4. "Domestic Intelligence," *Harper's Weekly*, December 10, 1859, p. 794 (c. 1-3); "Domestic Intelligence," *Harper's Weekly*, November 26, 1859, p. 758 (c. 2-4); Boyd B. Stutler, "An Eyewitness Describes the Hanging of John Brown," *American Heritage* (February, 1955), pp. 4-9.
5. "Domestic Intelligence," *Harper's Weekly*, December 3, 1859, pp. 774 (c. 4) - 775(c. 1).
6. "Domestic Intelligence," *Harper's Weekly*, December 10, 1859, p. 794 (c. 1-3).
7. J. Henry Harper, *The House of Harper: A Century of Publishing in Franklin Square* (New York and London: Harper & Brothers, 1912), pp. 177-178. See also, Frank Luther Mott, *A History of American Magazines*, vol. 2 *1850-1865* (Cambridge, Mass.: Harvard University Press, 1938), p. 472; Tyler Anbinder, *Nativism & Slavery: The Northern Know Nothings & the Politics of the 1850s* (New York: Oxford University Press, 1992), pp. 11-13; Jerome Mushkat, "Harper, James," in *The Encyclopedia of New York City*, ed. Kenneth T. Jackson (New Haven: Yale University Press, 1995), p. 528. Elder brother James Harper had been elected mayor of New York City in 1844 on the American Republican ticket, a nativist and reform party. For an example of their conservatism, see the journal's first editorial, "Compromise and Union," *Harper's Weekly*, January 3, 1857, p. 1 (c. 1-4).
8. Thomas C. Leonard, *News for All: America's Coming-of-Age with the Press* (Oxford University Press, 1995), pp. 96-98.
9. *Harper's Weekly*, November 12, 1859, p. 728 (c. 1-4); "Domestic Intelligence," *Harper's*

Weekly, November 5, 1859, pp. 710 (c. 3) - 711 (c. 2); "Domestic Intelligence," *Harper's Weekly*, October 29, 1859, pp. 694 (c. 4) - 695 (c. 4).
10. *Harper's Weekly*, November 5, 1859, p. 705 (c. 1-4).
11. J. Henry Harper, *The House of Harper: A Century of Publishing in Franklin Square* (New York and London: Harper & Brothers, 1912), pp. 88-89; Eugene Exman, *The House of Harper: One Hundred and Fifty Years of Publishing*. New York and London: Harper & Row, 1967, pp. 73, 78; Boyd B. Stutler, "An Eyewitness Describes the Hanging of John Brown," *American Heritage* (February, 1955), pp. 4-9; Frank Luther Mott, *A History of American Magazines*, vol. 2 *1850-1865* (Cambridge, Mass.: Harvard University Press, 1938), pp. 110, 388, 390, 472.
12. Boyd B. Stutler, "An Eyewitness Describes the Hanging of John Brown," *American Heritage* (February, 1955), pp. 4-9.
13. "Domestic Intelligence," *Harper's Weekly*, November 19, 1859, p. 742 (c. 3-4).
14. David Hunter Strother, "The Late Invasion at Harper's Ferry," *Harper's Weekly* (November 5, 1859), pp. 712 (c. 1) - 714 (c. 3). The preceding several paragraphs refer to this source.
15. David Hunter Strother, "The Trial of the Conspirators," *Harper's Weekly*, November 12, 1859, pp. 728 (c. 1) - 729 (c. 1). Strother also claimed that Brown "had entered Virginia of the purpose of making war on the white race, determined to kill all who opposed his views."
16. *Harper's Weekly*, October 29, 1859, p. 690 (c. 3-4).
17. *Harper's Weekly*, November 12, 1859, p. 722 (c. 1-2).
18. American Conservatism," editorial, *Harper's Weekly*, December 3, 1859, p. 770 (c. 3-4).
19. George William Curtis, "The Lounger," *Harper's Weekly*, December 3, 1859, p. 771 (c. 1-2).
20. Our Politics," editorial, *Harper's Weekly*, December 24, 1859, p. 818 (c. 4).
21. Boyd B. Stutler, "An Eyewitness Describes the Hanging of John Brown," *American Heritage* (February, 1955), pp. 4-9. The *Times-Democrat* reported that Lydia Maria Child had requested the sketch of the deceased Brown.
22. Boyd B. Stutler, "An Eyewitness Describes the Hanging of John Brown," *American Heritage* (February, 1955), pp. 4-9; "Domestic Intelligence," *Harper's Weekly*, December 10, 1859, p. 794 (c. 1-3).
23. North and South," editorial, *Harper's Weekly*, December 17, 1859, p. 802 (c. 2-3).

6

Abolitionism at the Crossroads: Lydia Maria Child and the *National Anti-Slavery Standard*, 1841-1843

Leonard Ray Teel
Georgia State University

This paper looks at a two-year period in the career of Lydia Maria Child, an author and editor who was among the first women to take a major leadership role in the abolition movement at a time when women in the movement were excluded from meetings and relegated to supporting roles as fundraisers. Seven years before the convention launched the women's movement, Child demonstrated a steely determination to force men to listen, if not bend, to the views of women. Criticism from men of her two years as editor testified clearly that she made an impression. Though she quit in frustration in 1843, she had become a pioneer advocating responsible roles for women in the movement. She was a harbinger of the women's rights movement of the 1850s which sprang from the abolitionist cause.

* * * * * * * * *

In May 1843, the best known woman author in America and a

leading abolitionist resigned after two difficult years as editor of the *National Anti-Slavery Standard* in New York City. Lydia Maria Child's farewell column mirrored the controversies dividing abolitionists in the early 1840s, roughly halfway between the birth of the movement and the Emancipation Proclamation. Child dealt with argumentative factions seeking to direct the antislavery movement — Nonresistance, Immediatism, New Organization, Third Party, Calvinists, Quakers, Channingites, Henry Clay Whigs, abolitionists, slaveholders, and Democrats, to name the most prominent. As editor, Child endeavored to take a neutral position, to be a moderate among radicals. When she resigned, she insisted that none of "these whirling eddies have [sic], at any time, made me swerve one hair's breadth from the course I had marked out for myself."[1]

Remarkably, she insisted from the outset that she would not edit the *Standard* as a forum for warring factions. Other abolitionist newspapers could serve those polemic needs. She wanted to expand the base of abolitionism to involve the middle class and particularly women. What the movement needed most, she argued, was a "medium of communication with the *people*," a "good *family* newspaper." *Family* was a code word for *women*. By the 1840s, women had learned from the experience of earlier women editors that men suspected any publication directed at women. In 1828 when Sarah Josepha Hale began editing *Ladies' Magazine* she expected that many men likely would not "allow their women-folk to read it."[2] In her first issue Hale stated that "Husbands may rest assured that nothing found on the pages of this publication shall cause her [the wife] to be less assiduous in preparing for his reception or less sincere in welcoming his return."[3]

Child's strategy for widening readership was to expand content. Rather than feeding readers a diet of polemics, she wanted a balanced diet. By providing news, features, literature and such, she said, the *Standard* could make "a calm rational appeal to the people at large, without any particular aim to please abolitionists." Rather than cater to the converted, she wanted to win converts she was certain were there to be awakened if only their attention could be gained with appealing content.[4]

To achieve her vision, Child insisted on complete editorial independence. In doing so, she girded for resistance from that "class of abolitionists" who wanted the *Standard* to be a "controversial and agitating paper." In a message to readers and foes alike, she expression of opinion, from any man, or body of men." In return, she pledged to "work according to my conscience and ability; promising nothing but diligence and fidelity...and equally careful to respect the freedom of others; whether as individuals or as societies."5

She gained her demand for independence in 1841 because of the politics of the moment. The National Anti-Slavery Society, whose leading light was William Lloyd Garrison of the Massachusetts Anti-Slavery Society, was desperate to find a capable editor who was dedicated to the cause and loyal to Garrison's uncompromising ideal of immediate emancipation. The editor also had to be willing to relocate to live in New York City; most of the dedicated abolitionists loyal to Garrison lived in or near Boston. Indeed, Child agreed to edit the *Standard* for only one year, partly because she disliked New York City, but mainly because the job separated her from her husband who did not want to leave Massachusetts.

When the opportunity arose, Child and her husband, David Lee Child, were in a difficult situation. They had been trying to make a living from the poor soil of a farm near the village of Northampton. The desperation of the enterprise and the petty scale of thought there were wearing on her. "I dislike it more and more and more every week I live," she confided to a friend in Boston. Her "roving imagination" was stifled by chores, telling her brother that "these million Lilliputian cords tie down the stoutest Gulliver that ever wrestled in their miserable entanglement." To make matters worse, her father had moved in with them and was in a state of "perpetual restlessness and gloom," enough to "have at times almost driven me crazy." On occasion when David expressed his "sentiment and romance," her father called it "childish folly."6

By contrast with all this, she had been accustomed to Boston and the stimulus of the movement. The abolitionists, drawn together all the more by public animus against their cause, often met late into the night; Garrison early on listed her among the "anti-slavery friends" and observed that she "made some remarks at the ladies' meeting on Wednesday last which manifested that she was as vigorous in spirit as in body." In the backwater of Northampton, her spirit was undernourished. The goals of abolitionism there, she observed, were held hostage while Calvinist and Baptist preachers ranted with "sectarian hate."7

Child deliberately solicited the editorship. At first Garrison offered it to David Child, who had a law degree. Garrison knew that a man would be more acceptable to the national membership and perhaps thought that David would be more effective in New York. But David declined, mainly because he was still dedicated to experimental farming. The Childs had invested their savings in his belief that he could raise sugar beets as a domestic sugar source; they had sold their cozy cottage near Boston that had been a gathering place for their friends so that he could study beet sugar farming in Belgium. He was still determined he could replicate the European success despite the resistance of the poor soil of his farm at Northampton, and despite the burden of their increasing debts. They had borrowed from Lydia's father to buy the farm and David had spent more to invest in European farm machinery.

When David declined, Lydia volunteered. "It was not zeal for the cause, but love for my husband" which urged her to seek the job, she explained. "But since it was necessary for me to be leaving home to be earning somewhat, I am thankful that my work is for the anti-slavery cause." With Garrison's backing, her appointment for one year was approved by the American Anti-Slavery Society. The newspaper's budget was so "precarious" that Child could not afford her own place to stay; the society arranged for her to board in New York in the home of the prominent Quaker philanthropist, Isaac Hopper.[8]

There was little doubt about Child's ability to edit the newspaper. In 1826, she had founded a children's bimonthly magazine, *Juvenile Miscellany*, the first of its kind, which she edited until 1836. Certainly she was an accomplished writer. In 1823 at the age of 21 she published her first novel, and in 1825 a second. She also wrote nonfiction, including a home economics handbook which was translated into French. By 1833 she was the best-known woman writer in America.[9]

Garrison had no doubt that Child was devoted. By 1842 she demonstrated as much commitment, fervor, courage — and sacrifice — as anyone in the movement. Indeed she had become in a sense a martyr to the cause. The turning point had come in 1833 when she published her historical polemic on the race question, *An Appeal in Favor of That Class of Americans Called Africans*. Immediately, the same middle class readers who responded warmly to her novels in the 1820s turned in revulsion in the 1830s. She had committed the unpardonable social act of joining the radicals who smashed the social covenant to keep polite silence about slavery. Child sacrificed popularity, social privilege, and a steady income. Even her access to a private library was revoked.[10]

Her book affronted a polite New England society which, for its own social and economic reasons, had come to terms with slavery. *An Appeal* began by urging unwilling citizens to open their minds on the closed subject. Child spoke as from a pulpit to unconverted sinners. "Reader, I beseech you not to throw down this volume as soon as you have glanced at that title." Child anticipated her audience. "Read it if your prejudices will allow, for the very truth's sake."

She anticipated the "unpopularity" of her subject and the "ridicule and censure" she would receive from the very literary and social circles which had welcomed her after her novels. "It is not in my nature to fear them," she wrote. "Worldly considerations should never stifle the voice of conscience."[11]

Child's thrust was to stimulate discourse, not insurrection. She argued for "the liberty to investigate this subject." Such rationality was nonetheless radical. By 1833 polite society in the North had come to terms with slavery, more or less, but not discussing the situation. Northerners might readily agree that slavery was detestable or even, as she maintained, a national evil. But the dimensions of the slave question and the ramifications of emancipation, playing upon economic and psychological insecurities, channeled social discussion in favor of the status quo and aroused mobs to rout abolitionists from their meeting places and make Garrison fear for his life and liberty, North and South.[12]

Into this demonic, shadowy world, Child had cast the lantern of reason and made Bostonians squint. She argued against accepting the Southern view that "slavery is *unavoidable*" and Southerners' insistence that they would not tolerate any schemes for abolition. She also challenged Northerners who "take the *necessity* of slavery for an unalterable truth, and put down any discussions, however mild and candid, which tend to show that it *may* be done away with safety." "Avoid the subject in Boston, New York and Philadelphia," she wrote, and "we thus strengthen each other's hands in evil....To enlighten public opinion is the best way that has yet been discovered for the removal of national evils." Child's approach, scholars have noted, "merged well with those of the antislavery movement because in the 1830s the Garrisonians saw their primary task as eliminating racism in the minds of the populace while at the same time aiming for the concrete goal of immediate emancipation."[13]

After 1833 Child was one of America's leading women abolitionists. Her zeal and energy helped direct the Boston Female Anti-Slavery Society. In this network, she was adept at fundraising, organizing antislavery fairs which raised as much as $1,000 for Garrison's New England Anti-Slavery Society (which David Child had helped found in 1832). In 1840 she, Maria Weston Chapman of Boston and Lucretia Mott of Philadelphia became the first three women members of the executive board of the American Anti-Slavery Society.14

In 1841 Child's insistence on making the *Standard* a non-partisan publication appealed to Garrison. The previous editor's polemics had created the current vacancy. He was forced to resign after his personal agitation offended members of the Massachusetts slavery society. Child's appointment was attractive also because it gave public credence to Garrison's radical determination to break with tradition and place women in responsible roles.

From the beginning, the editorship troubled her endlessly. The profound and divisive cross-currents of opinion continuously challenged and undermined the absolute editorial independence on which she had insisted. Despite the clear articulation of her views about literary and informative content, male readers especially discounted her concept or never took it seriously.

Child had insisted on editorial independence for another reason. For political reasons Garrison appointed both David and Lydia as co-editors, with the understanding that David was bound to the farm in Northampton most of the year and would have little time for the newspaper. Lydia, in New York City, would edit and direct the newspaper. Some abolitionists assumed that David as co-editor would provide necessary male force and ballast. "I would have wished and supposed," wrote her friend Ellis Gray Loring, "that Mr. Child's name as well as yours would appear as Editor. We need all the strength & influence possible."15

Child allowed the appearance of shared responsibility. She put David's name on the masthead as "assistant editor," in smaller type. Later, after the sugar beet experiment failed, he reported from Washington. She was deeply devoted to David, who remained her lifelong companion and intellectual partner. But after the failure of the farm and his declaration of bankruptcy, David appeared to her to have an "incurable flaw," that of being a misguided idealist. He sought out and dedicated himself to the utopian philosophies of the day — abolitionism being the only one they agreed on. He seemed more comfortable in retreat from society than in confrontation with it. It was David who had drawn Lydia away from Boston to vegetate in misery in Northampton. "To pump water into a sieve for fourteen years," she wrote, "is enough to break the most energetic spirit. I must put a stop to it, or die." On advice, she separated her income from her husband's. Even so, she regretted that the editorship kept them apart while she was in New York. After several months as editor, she lamented to her brother: "My domestic attachments are so strong, and David is always so full of cheerful tenderness, that this separation is dreary indeed."16

For two years, Child fought passionate battles with the various abolitionist factions. She kept determined to steer a neutral course for the *Standard*. From time to time she explained her rationales. First was her commitment to an audience beyond the converted, to women and men who were opposed to slavery but had neither motivation nor information. To this end, she had to defend her regular use of a "large proportion of literary and miscellaneous matter." Because of such features "many might be induced to subscribe for the *Standard*, who would not take an exclusively anti-slavery periodical."17

One of the more remarkable literary features she published weekly were her own city sketches. Each week she turned "wearily aside from the dusty road of reforming duty" to conduct "rambles," exploring some vast expanse or dark corner of New York, then in the early stages of the industrial revolution. She found the city sometimes wonderful and frequently ghastly, raw and untamed, contrasting always with the civility of Boston. She called her sketches "the New York Letters." The New York Letters, she explained

> were inserted upon something of the same principle that the famous Timothy Dexter sent a stock of Bibles to the West Indies, with warming pans to be used for sugar ladles and strainers. No purchaser was allowed to have a pan unless he would buy a Bible also. Thus have I bought some to look candidly at anti-slavery principles by drawing them with the garland of imagination and taste. It was an honest, open trick, and I think may be easily pardoned.18

In her two years as editor, Child wrote almost 100 city sketches. She never admitted to liking much about New York, but she was fascinated with its wild, outrageous contrasts, its characters and situations. The city provoked her sensibilities, often to disgust. By contrast with Boston's rough edges, Manhattan's seaminess was less predictable, ever changing, sometimes shocking. She retained her first impression on arriving "at early dawn, amid fog and drizzling rain, the expiring lamps adding their smoke to the impure air, and close beside us a boat called the 'Fairy Queen,' laden with dead hogs.'" To breath air as yet unsullied by the city, she wrote, she would retreat to the Battery, especially at night.19

The great city's dirty, odorous regions seemed all the uglier in contrast to the opulence of rich New York neighborhoods she was later admitted to because of her position. She felt she saw more people suffering, women and children miserable in abject poverty, all the more poignant against the obvious wealth of the nouveau-riche class of merchants and financiers. New York City's credo, she quickly understood, was to make money. In its seamier sense, it was a gross market energized by greed and raw power. These extremes repelled her sensibilities and attracted her literary instincts. It was as though she had a great need to look deeper into the chasm.[20]

In the weekly Letters she shared her impressions of the characters and situations she discovered in "this great Babylon." She wrote about street musicians, crews of dog-killers with bloody cudgels, a "ragged urchin" selling penny newspapers, an insane asylum, a prison. "More, perhaps, than any other city, except Paris or New Orleans," she wrote

> this is a place of rapid fluctuation and never-ceasing change....The enterprising, the curious, the reckless, and the criminal, flock hither from all quarters of the world, as to a common centre, whence they can diverge at pleasure. Where men are little known, they are imperfectly restrained; therefore, great numbers here live with somewhat of that wild license which prevails in times of pestilence.[21]

Perhaps most reprehensible to an abolitionist was the city's acquiescence with the trafficking in slaves. When the opportunity presented she underscored that issue. She recounted the story of a fugitive slave who had been helped to freedom by Isaac Hopper; Child found the ex-slave's daughter had become a preacher, a "female Whitfield," her voice enthralling a full church. Not far away, slavers still thrived. "There, amid the splendour [sic] of Broadway, sits the blind negro beggar, with horny hand and tattered garments, while opposite him stands the stately mansion of the slave trader, still plying his bloody trade, and laughing to scorn the cobweb laws, through which the strong can break so easily."[22]

A second editorial tenet she reiterated was her opposition to using the paper as a forum for divisive debates. She reasoned that public rancor injured the cause by emphasizing differences rather than unity on the central issue of . Amid such passionate factionalism Child's rationality spoke to deaf ears. Those who did hear misinterpreted or misunderstood her. Not without irony, she observed: "Some complained that the slaveholder was treated too harshly; others, that my reproofs of sin were 'mere child's play.'"[23]

share with readers. This was her understanding that by minimizing coverage of factional disputes she sided, though silence, with the Garrisonians who established the newspaper. Child's policy of avoiding acrimony did not prevent her from publishing information about Garrison's activities and views; this was done indirectly by reprinting dispatches from Garrison's Boston newspaper, *The Liberator*, and by covering news events which often involved Garrison.[24]

Garrison's vision still guided the national movement. By 1841 he was insisting on a strategy of building a moral consensus and avoiding politics. He championed a policy termed Nonresistance — a variation of civil disobedience which dictated non-cooperation with the established government. Nonresistants, he argued, should abstain from participating in a corrupt political system, to the extent that they should abstain from voting.

A turning point had come in 1839. Profound differences over the role of politics led to a schism. The "New Organization" which split from Garrison was led by men who emphasized initiatives in the political arena. Some among them proposed abandoning the cautionary and Democrats. Many of these banded together to form a third party — the Liberty Party — dedicated to abolishing slavery. After 1839, the New Organization expressed its voice in its own newspaper, *The Emancipator.*

Child personally differed with both extremes. She favored neither abstention from voting nor the third party. Yet she strived to keep her personal views out of the paper. "Has a word ever dropped from my editorial pen involving that paper in non-resistance doctrines?" she asked a Philadelphia Quaker six months after she became editor. In letters, however, she noted that the "immense majority of the American [Anti-Slavery] Society, nearly all of them, approve of voting." Those few who advocated Nonresistance, she stated, "have as good a right to their opinions, as anti-bank men have to theirs." As for the third party, the American [Anti-Slavery Society] opposes the Liberty Party, not because it is political *action,* but because it is an organized *party,* and therefore likely to do harm."[25]

Foes on all sides attacked her editorial even-handedness. Advocates of the New Organization complained that she "stood so carefully aloof." Others urged that she "was doing incalculable mischief to the cause, by not attacking new organization; and declared that I made the true-hearted blush." Third-party issues were even more tangled in intrigue. "Many complained," she wrote, "because I calmly stated my reasons for believing complained," she wrote, "because I calmly stated my reasons for believing that a distinct political party would do immeasurable injury to the anti-slavery cause; while others were impatient because I spoke of the 'liberty party' with so much smoothness and courtesy; assuring me that it was absolutely necessary to show up its intrigues, duplicity, and meanness."[26]

* * * * * * * * * *

On the slavery question, the *Standard* offered readers a kaleidoscope of news and views about the abolitionist movement in the North and the status of slavery in the South. Child made the coverage national in scope by reprinting articles from other newspapers, permitting the *Standard* to keep up with slavery issues as far as the western territories. In this way, readers learned about the "black laws" in Ohio, legislation in Kentucky, and the Underground Railway spiriting fugitive slaves from Missouri across the Mississippi to a mission in Quincy, Illinois, and then on toward Canada. Child also published letters from the South, dispatches from Congress, letters from politicians, excerpts from Garrison's *Liberator*, and proceedings of the American Anti-Slavery Society.[27]

When the Society held its eighth convention in 1841, the acrimonious schism was obvious. "The ranks of the abolitionists were thinned and broken, while the obstacles before them were no less formidable than ever," read the "Annual Report" published in the first issue after Child became editor. Despite the setback, the Society's executive committee concluded that

> the cause of human freedom has unquestionably acquired an accelerated program. The public mind at the north has become more familiar with free principles. It daily grows less intolerant [of abolitionists] and proscriptive. Anti-slavery principles have been spread abroad with zeal and faithfulness.[28]

The Society noted that the divisive political wing, which called itself the American and Foreign Anti-Slavery Society, had suffered a setback. A new antislavery convention, held in Western New York, had drawn nearly 600 delegates; its board "repudiated the Third Party Political Scheme, which would involve all the energies of anti-slavery in the vortex of political strife." Momentum was building for a national convention of "abolitionists who are opposed to the identification of the cause with politics...."[29]

Nor were the Garrisonians boasting without merit. The results of the 1840 election had dismayed some of the most fervent political abolitionists. The Liberty Party presidential candidate, James G. Birney, received just 7,054 votes, not even a tenth of the eligible abolitionists. One third party stalwart, Joshua Leavitt, discovered the difficulty of persuading abolitionists to quit the Democrats. Loyalties were such that "it is almost like plucking out a right eye, or off a right arm, for one who has mingled much in party strife and enjoyed the confidence of political associates, to cut loose and pronounce his party corrupt." The election results, Garrison said, were "equally ludicrous and melancholy."30

Despite their differing methods, abolitionists both political and nonpolitical hoped that Congress would act to end slavery and prevent its extension. Since the American Anti-Slavery Society's founding in 1833 it had petitioned Congress to act in the one area under their specific jurisdiction, the District of Columbia. In 1841, Child's *Standard* confirmed that of slavery in the national capital was still a priority. The strategy remained the same: the Society depended upon "friends of bleeding humanity" to "petition Congress." One member of the Society proposed spending $50 to speed a lawsuit to the U.S. Supreme Court "claiming freedom for all persons held as slaves in the District of Columbia." The proposal was referred to the Executive Committee.31

In trusting the tactic of petitions in 1841, the radical political abolitionists might have had cause enough to ridicule the Garrisonians. Congress was considering statehood for Texas, which would extend slavery. The Texas issue became a rallying point for abolitionists of both stripes. Even Garrisonians, despite a ban of political involvement, officially adopted "the practice of interrogating the political candidates of the whig and democratic parties...in regard to their views of the anti-slavery enterprise, and their readiness to assist in promoting it."32

When Winfield Scott, hero of the war in Mexico, seemed a likely presidential candidate for 1844, the *Standard* published his letter responding to questions on the slave issue. Scott equivocated on his personal view toward slavery, holding to a strict interpretation of law. Congress, he wrote, "has no color of authority...for touching the relation of master and slave in a State." In the District of Columbia, however, Scott indicated he was inclined to agree with the abolitionists, but added two major caveats:

> Here, with the consent of owners, or on the payment of "just compensation," Congress may legislate at its discretion. But my conviction is equally strong that, unless it be step by step with the legislature of Virginia and Maryland it would be dangerous to both

dangerous to both races in those states to touch the relation between master and slave within this District.33

Far from the Society's general hope for immediate emancipation, Scott supported gradualism. He gave credence to the view, widely held in the North, that responsibility of ending slavery lay with the masters. He was "persuaded that it is a high moral obligation of masters, and slaveholding States, to employ all means, not incompatible with the safety of both colors, to ameliorate slavery to extermination." Scott said he was gratified "to know that general amelioration has been great and is still progressive." Amelioration was evident because "the race has wonderfully multiplied, compared with anything ever known in barbarous life. The descendants of a few thousands have become many millions—and all, from the first, made acquainted with the arts of civilization, and, above all, brought under the light of the gospel."34

Stinging rebuffs to Scott's equivocations were stacked up under his letter. Child placed Garrison's reply first, reprinted from the *Liberator*. After attacking the general's belief in gradualism and his trust in Southern promises, Garrison assaulted another view that was commonly held in the North — that slaves were not prepared for immediate freedom. "It can never be rational or humane," wrote Garrison, "to enslave those who know not how to provide for their own necessities."35

The mentality of the South's slavemaster class had long been a target of the abolitionists. In 1841, Child published a letter from an abolitionist traveling in South Carolina; the writer purported to understand the behavioral springs of Southern slave owners, or at least what made them resistant to lawful authority and, in that way, supportive of John C. Calhoun's political doctrine of Nullification. The writer, identified only as Delta, traced this strain of belligerence to the extraordinary circumstances in which the slaveowner's children were reared. This tendency

first shows itself in the family. The child, accustomed to unquestioning obedience from the servants to every expression of his will, soon becomes impatient of restraint from its parents, and at an early age practically nullifies every unpleasant requisition.36

Such efforts to plumb the mind of slavery fit with Child's own life's work. Her *Appeal* in 1833 had sought to probe the roots of the slave trade. Nine years later, in July 1842 in New York City, after writing so much about the slave trade, Child met a slaveowner who happened to be in the city. He owned slaves in Florida and Haiti. In her weekly "Letter," she wrote that she found the man "altogether unaccountable" — "as great a puzzle to phrenologists as...to moralists and philosophers." Their conversation had the quality of an angel conversing with a devil:

> Then you have been on the coast of Africa?
>
> Yes, ma'am; I carried on the slave trade several years!
>
> You announce that fact very coolly. Do you know that, in New England, men look upon a slave-trader with as much horror as they do upon a pirate?
>
> Yes; and I am glad of it. They will look upon a slaveholder just so, by and by. Slave trading was very respectable business when I was young. The first merchants in England and America were engaged in it. Some people hide things which they think other people don't like. I never conceal anything.

The slaveowner, who was seventy-six years old, told Child his slaves in Haiti were already free, working land he had bought with money earned from the work of the slaves in Florida. He said he also planned to free his slaves in Florida, but conceded that if he died before he got "all my plans settled in a few years" his heirs "would break my will, I dare say, and my poor niggers would be badly off." Child urged him

> Then manumit them now; and avoid this dreadful risk.
>
> I have thought that all over, ma'am; and I have settled it that I can do more good by keeping them in slavery a few years more. The best we can do in this world is to balance evils judiciously.
>
> But you do not balance wisely. Remember that all the descendant of your slaves, through all coming time, will be affected by your decision.
>
> To do good in the world, we *must* have money. That's the way I reasoned when I carried on the slave trade. It was very profitable then.
>
> And do you have no remorse of conscience, in recollecting that bad business?

The slaver astonished Child by admitting that his father was a Quaker and he still loves Quaker meetings; particularly silent ones, where he says he has planned some of his best bargains. To complete the circle of contradictions, he likes the abolitionists.37

* * * * * * * * *

That summer, she carried on her ramblings and other responsibilities despite falling out of favor with a great number of Garrisonites. Garrison had speculated in the *Liberator* of April 22 that the annual convention of the American Anti-Slavery Society in May would "undoubtedly" discuss "the subject of a repeal of the Union between the North and the South...in order that the people of the North might be induced to reflect upon their debasement, guilt, and danger, in continuing in partnership with heaven-daring oppressors, and thus be led to repentance." The idea of dissolution was amplified in the New York newspapers, stirring hostility against the Society. The "mobs might have sacked the city," Child wrote to Maria Chapman. In self-defense, the Society's executive committee, including Child, issued a circular contradicting Garrison. Disunion would not be on the agenda, they declared. From Boston, Chapman expressed her vexation that the Society was rebuking Garrison. Child justified the circular and called Garrison's imposition of personal views upon the Society "imprudent" and "rash." Although her husband, David, considered the circular a "mistake," Lydia insisted that it was the correct course and underscored her continued devotion to Garrison.[38]

The rupture was only temporary but it served to underscore the difficulties Child faced in steering an independent course with "un-impeded freedom" through the swirling waters of the movement. Was there room for further division within the ranks? She repeated her stance, the same position she held before taking the editorship. "An agitator I am not, and never will be," Child wrote to Chapman

> But whenever the *Standard* becomes the organ of agitation, the adaptation of character to employment will require another editor. For myself, I would like to leave it tomorrow, and accept the propositions of booksellers here; but my attachment to anti slavery principles would lead me to wish to stand by it, so long as the Society were content to have it a good family anti-slavery newspaper, not intended to meet the wants of ultraists, but to gain the ear of the people at large.[39]

Early in 1843, Child envisioned the end of her ordeal. Editorial friction was not the only vexation. Child was perpetually frustrated by the *Standard*'s financial straits and embarrassments. The abolitionist movement from the beginning had been underfunded, dependent on donors' generosity, which deflated during an economic recession. Child had been led to believe that the Society had committed funds to guarantee the *Standard*'s survival. She discovered that she often needed to appeal or beg to pay the printer, who advanced credit at his own risk. Her own salary, which ironically was a central reason for accepting the job, was not always paid as agreed. She was embarrassed because she had little she could give the Isaac Hopper family for their generosity in providing her room and board; she offered babysitting. At one point she had only 37 cents to last three months. Her coat was frayed, which may have helped her in interviewing some of New York's lower classes, but she worried that upper-class New Yorkers might decline an interview.

On the newspaper's business side, the general agent added to her frustrations. From the beginning, she disagreed with John A. Collins over so many aspects of the operation that she wondered how the Society could have shackled her with him. Collins had risen in the ranks as a fundraiser; in 1841 he was sent to England to raise money from British antislavery philanthropists. He associated with altruists in the circle of Harriett Martineau and other "friends of human liberty." On his return, it may have seemed natural to place him with the *Standard* where he could raise funds. If he were there also to provide some masculine ballast for the female editor, the scheme seemed to be sabotaging Child.[40]

Child believed that Collins' obstinacy threatened her independence and undermined her effectiveness. More than once she wrote to friends that the manager's actions so undermined her authority that one of them had to go. "If John A. Collins is to be continued Gen. Agent," she wrote to Maria Chapman, "it will be necessary to change editors....[H]e surrounds me with a circumstance...which wars with my line of policy, and will not mix with it. The *Standard* is a hindrance in his path...and must continue to be while I edit it." The Society had to decide between her and Collins. "My very soul," she declared, "is sick of these perpetual discrepancies [sic]."[41]

The clash of strategies played out in May 1843. Just before the annual convention, she resigned. Her husband had agreed to take over for a time. While her "Farewell" column gave her reasons for leaving, her last "Letter from New York," in May 1843, was positive, hopeful and reminiscent, focusing on the promise of spring and what seemed to be a ritual among New Yorkers in May — moving to new abodes. "I am by temperament averse to frequent changes," she wrote. After the changeover, Lydia stayed with the Hoppers and, at Garrison's request, continued to contribute "Letters from New York." David eventually left the paper and returned to Northampton to farm and do odd jobs while she remained in New York until 1850. She edited two volumes of her Letters, enjoying popularity despite her past, weakening associations with the movement. After 1850, she and David reunited and retreated into farm and village life.[42]

* * * * * * * * *

The role of women in the movement continued to divide abolitionists. Garrison had provoked the question in the 1830s by asserting, against tradition, that women should participate alongside men rather than in separate, supportive female societies. He saw practical reasons for egalitarianism. Child and others in the women's network demonstrated indefatigable energy and commitment matching his own. Certainly the movement, always short of sponsors, benefitted directly from initiatives such as fundraising. After the schism, he felt freer and delegated more responsibilities to women. Nonetheless, women seemed defensive when publishing their views. When a group of Ohio women gathered 177 signatures for abolishing slavery in the District of Columbia, they devoted most of their petition to a defense of women. "An American woman," they wrote in a petition reprinted in the *Standard*, "can have no 'higher and holier duty,' in a temporal point of view, than to understand the liberty of her country, as it stands connected with her other liberties."[43]

Concerning the public role of women as activists, Child was enigmatic. She was a woman in transition, born into the old tradition but seeking a new world. Some characterized her as "one of the most eighteenth-century of the nineteenth-century women reformers." She led a life of contrasts. In the public realm she was profoundly egalitarian. But at home she "held to the post-Revolutionary ideal of the 'Republican mother.'" Though she had no children, she valued her marriage, the role of a helpmate to her husband, and the creation of a home, as more important than a career. After her service on the *Standard*, she gradually withdrew from public life for the most part and eventually joined David in living a quiet village life, tending her garden. Yet that same eighteenth-century spirit, as one scholar noted, stirred her to fight for the freedom to act according to her conscience.[44]

Her ideas anticipated concerns of the feminist movement that came to life in 1848. One of these concerned economic independence. In her personal life, she eventually separated her meager income from her husband's for a time, protecting herself from being drained by his luckless utopian schemes.

Child was also sensitive to publications and utterances which demeaned women. Her exposure to the rhetoric of pro-slavers disposed her to be all the more repelled by stories with sexist language which depreciated or discounted women. "I know full well," she told readers, "that from these subtle and unnoticed influences, more than from any other cause, flows the unclean public sentiment, which degrades woman, and desecrates the sacred sentiment of love and marriage." She refused to publish stories "which tell of countries where they raise 'fine *wine*' and fine *women*,' or where they have 'the handsomest *horses* and the handsomest *wives*.'" Similarly she had "thrown aside all poetry about' tempting lips and voluptuous forms,' all jokes about matrimony and women."[45]

Notes

1. Lydia Maria Child, "Farewell," *National Anti-Slavery Standard*, May 4, 1843, p. 2.
2. Ruth E. Finley, *The Lady of Godey's: Sarah Josepha Hale* (Philadelphia: J.B. Lippincott Co., 1931), p. 39.
3. Sarah Josepha Hale, *Ladies' Magazine* (January 1828), pp. 1-4.
4. *Standard*, May 4, 1841; Lydia Maria Child to Maria Weston Chapman, Jan. 11, 1843, Lydia Maria Child Papers, Ms. A.51, no. 32, Antislavery Collection, Boston Public Library.
5. *Standard*, May 4, 1843.
6. Lydia Maria Child to Ellis Gray Loring, Feb. 9, 1841, Loring Family Papers, Schlesinger Library, Radcliffe College [afterwards LFP,SL,RC]; Lydia Maria Child to Convers Francis, Oct. 20, 1840, Lydia Maria Child Papers, Anti-Slavery Collection, Cornell University (microfiche 9/215), in Lydia Maria Child, *Lydia Maria Child, Selected Letters, 1817-1880*, ed. by Milton Meltzer and Patricia G. Holland (Amherst, Mass.: University of Massachusetts Press, 1982), pp. 133-134.
7. William Lloyd Garrison, *The Letters of William Lloyd Garrison*, ed. by Louis Ruchames (Cambridge, Mass.: The Belknap Press of Harvard University Press, 1971), II: 78; Child to Loring, Feb. 9, 1841, LFP, SL, RC.
8. Lydia Maria Child to Elizabeth C. Pierce, May 27, 1841, in Phillips, *Letters*, p. 42; Lydia Maria Child to Francis Shaw, Meltzer, *Letters*, pp. 141-142.
9. William S. Osborne, *Lydia Maria Child* (Boston: Twayne Publishers, 1980), pp. 10-11; Child, *Appeal*, pp. i-ii.
10. L. Maria Child, *An Appeal in Favor of Americans Called Africans* (New York: Arno Press and The New York Times, 1968) rpt. of 1836 edition (New York: John S. Taylor), pp. i-ii.
11. Child, *Appeal*, p. 3. Her first two novels, *Hobomok* (1823) and *The Rebels* (1825), secured her reputation. In a foreword, James M. McPherson, the Princeton historian, wrote that Mrs. Child "could not rest content with popular acclaim and material success while her country was living a lie." *Ibid.*, p. ii; John F. Hume, *The Abolitionists: Together with Personal Memories of The Struggle for Human Rights, 1830-1864* (New York: AMS Press Inc., 1973), rpt. of 1905 edition (New York: G. P. Putnam's Sons), pp. 30-35.
12. Child, *Appeal*, p. 126. The Georgia legislature offered $5,000 to anyone who will "arrest and prosecute him to conviction *under the laws of that State*." In South Carolina, "an association of gentlemen have likewise offered a large reward for the same object." *Ibid.*, p. 209.
13. Child, *Appeal*, pp. 126, 216; Meltzer, *Letters*, p. xiii.
14. Lydia Maria Child, *Lydia Maria Child, Selected Letters, 1817-1880*, ed. by Milton Meltzer and Patricia G. Holland (Amherst, Mass.: University of Massachusetts Press, 1982), p. xii; Garrison, *Letters*, II: pp. 194, 717.
15. Meltzer, *Letters*, p. 139; Ellis Gray Loring to Lydia Maria Child, April 29, 1841, Ellis Gray Loring Letterbook, Houghton Library, Harvard University.
16. Helene G. Baer, *The Heart is Like Heaven: The Life of Lydia Maria Child* (Philadelphia, 1964), p. 160, cited in Osborne, *Child*, p. 30; Lydia Maria Child to Ellis Gray Loring, June 16, 1843, New York Public Library, cited in Osborne, *Child*, p. 31; Lydia Maria Child to Rev. Convers Francis, Feb. 17, 1842, *Letters of Lydia Maria Child*, ed by Wendell Phillips (Boston: Houghton, Mifflin and Company, 1883), p. 50.
17. *Standard*, May 4, 1843.
18. *Ibid.*
19. Lydia Maria Child, *Letters from New York*, rpt. of 1845 edition (Freeport, N.Y.: Books for Libraries Press, 1970), pp. 2, 17.
20. *Ibid.*, p. 2.
21. *Ibid.*, pp. 68-69.
22. *Ibid.*, pp. 2, 73.

23. *Ibid.*
24. Meltzer, *Letters,* p. 139.
25. Lydia Maria Child to James Miller McKim and Philadelphia Friends, Nov. 24, 1841, Lydia Maria Child Papers, Anti-Slavery Collection, Cornell University (microfiche 12/290), in Meltzer, *Letters,* p. 155. McKim was secretary of the Eastern Pennsylvania Anti-Slavery Society, which published the *Pennsylvania Freeman.* The Pennsylvania Friends considered merging the *Freeman* with the *Standard* but Child's statement of policy discourage that idea. Instead, the *Freeman* was suspended and their subscription lists were combined from 1842-1844, when the *Freeman* resumed publication. Meltzer, *Letters,* p. 153.
26. *Standard,* May 4, 1843.
27. "Pro-Slavery: The Way Abolitionists Manage It," reprinted from the St. Louis, Mo., *Republican,* in *National Anti-Slavery Standard,* May 4, 1843, p. 1. The *Republican* had itself reprinted this letter about the Underground Railway from the Paris, Mo., *Sentinel.*
28. "American Anti-Slavery Society, Annual Report," *National Anti-Slavery Standard,* May 20, 1841, p. 1.
29. *Ibid.*
30. *Ballot Box,* Oct. 20, 1840, and Richard H. Sewell, *Ballots for Freedom: Antislavery Politics in the United States, 1837-1860* (New York, 1976), cited in Hugh Davis, *Joshua Leavitt: Evangelical Abolitionist* (Baton Rouge: Louisiana State University Press, 1990), p. 175.
31. Aileen S. Kraditor, *Means and Ends in AmericanAbolitionism: Garrison and His Critics on Strategy and Tactics, 1834-1850* (New York: Pantheon Books, 1969), p. 5; "The Anniversary," *National Anti-Slavery Standard,* May 20, 1841, p. 1.
32. *Standard,* May 20, 1841.
33. *Ibid.*
34. *Ibid.*
35. *Ibid.*
36. "Selections: Letters from the South," *National Anti-Slavery Standard,* May 20, 1841, p. 1.
37. Lydia Maria Child, "Letter XXIII," *National Anti-Slavery Standard,* July 7, 1842, in Child, *Letters,* pp. 153-159.
38. William Lloyd Garrison to the Executive Committee of the American Anti-Slavery Society, May 9, 1842, in William Lloyd Garrison, *No Union with Slaveholders, 1841-1849,* Vol. III of *The Letters of William Lloyd Garrison* (Cambridge, Mass.: The Belknap Press of Harvard University, 1973), pp. 71-73; Lydia Maria Child to Maria (Weston) Chapman, May 11 [1842] in Meltzer, *Letters,* pp. 175-177.
39. Child to Chapman, May 11 [1842], p. 175.
40. "Annual Report of the American Anti-Slavery Society," *National Anti-Slavery Standard,* May 20, 1841, p. 1.
41. Child to Chapman, [Jan. 1843]. These were the same complaints Child had made to Chapman seven months earlier. Lydia Maria Child to Maria Weston Chapman, June 1842, Ms. A.5.1, no. 33, in Lydia Maria Child Papers, Boston Public Library.
42. Child, *Letters,* pp. 283-287; Meltzer, *Letters,* pp. 199-200, 256.
43. "Women's Political Rights and Duties," [reprinted from the Cadiz, Ohio, *Republican,* January 1841], in the *National Anti-Slavery Standard,* May 13, 1841, p. 1.
44. *Meltzer,* Letters, *pp. xi-xii.*
45. *Standard,* May 4, 1843.

7

"I hear nothing about me now but politics — slavery, and antislavery *ad nauseam*": Paul Hamilton Hayne and the Editorial Policy of *Russell's Magazine* 1857-1860

J. Michael Robertson
University of San Francisco
and *Alton Loftis*

Scholars tend to oversimplify the antebellum Southern mind, assuming a predictability and monotony of thought that is not always the case. Richard Calhoun says this state of affairs developed because of a series of misconceptions, the oldest and most important of which was "the belief that the South had only two preoccupations in the 1840s and the 1850s, slavery and politics, and that these precluded the possibility of Southern objectivity on anything local or Northern."[1] Perhaps more than any Southern periodical, *Russell's Magazine*, the only significant Southern magazine founded in the decade before the war, has been a victim of this misconception. The prevailing image of *Russell's* has been that of a chauvinistic, narrowly sectional journal devoted to the defense of Southern institutions, mainly slavery, and to the expression of Southern ideas. Frank Luther Mott has grouped *Russell's* with such outspokenly Southern periodicals as *Southern Quarterly Review* and *De Bow's Review*, finding it permeated through and through with proslavery arguments making it "ardently sectional beyond anything known to the periodicals of other regions."[2] Mott emphasized the local character of *Russell's*:

> *Russell's* never aspired to be a national periodical. In some respects it was a local Charleston magazine, telling of Charleston culture and Charleston events. The opening of an art gallery in that city, the appearance of Rachel at the Academy of Music there, and the literary activities of Charleston writers furnished themes for many pages. But its aim was to be a magazine for the whole South and to speak with the voice of the South. It was filled with sectional feeling.[3]

One might anticipate such an editorial focus given the time of its publication, 1857-1860, and its place, secession-obsessed Charleston, South Carolina. Several of the planners of the venture strongly favored the Southern movement, and the two chief editors, Paul Hamilton Hayne and William Carlisle, were as much influenced by the emotional currents of the day as young men often are. No full-scale prospectus of *Russell's* was ever drawn up, but the announcement on September 18, 1856, in the *Courier* comes closest to describing the scope of the project: "The essential plan and purpose of the work contemplate the largest catholicity and the amplest freedom of thought, inquiry, and discussion in all matters that touch the Southern mind, genius or destiny." The secessionists took such statements to mean that the new periodical would be vigorously pro-Southern in every way. "Its motto, we trust," opined the Charleston *Mercury*, "will be 'the South, the whole South, and nothing but the South!' So mote it be!"[4]

What has not been shown before is that soon after the magazine was under way, Hayne significantly altered the original editorial policy, making the magazine more literary, less concerned with political and sectional matters, and generally less hostile and abrasive towards Northern men and publications than was the case for most Southern periodicals of the decade.

At the moment of *Russell's* projection in the late summer of 1856, sectional feeling in South Carolina was perhaps more intense than it had been at any time since the Nullification crisis. After the remarkably strong showing of the Republican Party in the presidential election of 1856, in South Carolina both moderates and extremists were agreed that a Republican victory in 1860 would bring disunion.5 Governor James H. Adams expressed the feeling of the extremists in a speech to the South Carolina state legislature on November 24, 1856:

> Slavery and Freesoilism can never be reconciled. Our enemies have been defeated — not vanquished.... The triumph of this geographical party must dissolve the confederacy, unless we are prepared to sink down into a state of acknowledged inferiority. We will act wisely to employ of interval of repose afforded by the late election, in earnest preparation for the inevitable conflict.6

Sectional concerns were not confined to politics, of course. Beginning in the 1830's, sectionalism gradually spread from the halls of the national congress to many areas of intellectual life, including religion, education and literature.7 At about the same time an intolerant attitude toward any criticism of slavery developed throughout the South; Southern editors continued to speak of freedom of thought, but from 1835 on freedom of speech and freedom of the press were virtually dead in all parts of the South except one or two of the border states. After that time, to speak out against slavery, and later against secession, meant immediate loss of political power for the politician. For the newspaper or magazine editor, the risks were much greater.8 By the mid-1850's, there was a whole generation of young Southerners who had never known the meaning of genuine intellectual freedom and who could not remember when sectional distrust and dissension had not played a major role in the thinking of most Southerners.

For magazine editors, it became a standard function to complain against the refusal of Northerners to buy Southern books, against the neglect by Northern textbooks and anthologies of Southern contributions to the national heritage and, after the appearance of *Uncle Tom's Cabin* in 1851, against the distorted picture of Southern society presented in abolitionist propaganda.9 Southerners were urged to stop sending their sons to Northern colleges, to disallow the use of Northern textbooks in Southern schools, to cancel their subscriptions to hostile Yankee journals and newspapers, and most of all, to support the budding efforts of Southern men of letters to provide them with reading matter that would reflect their own beliefs and values.

As the antislavery controversy grew hotter and hotter, the effects on Southern periodicals became more and more pronounced. To some degree nearly all Southern magazines from the 1820's on were sectionally motivated;10 but beginning around 1835, what had been no more than mere healthy sectional pride began to be accompanied by belligerence and hostility towards the Northern states. After 1850, it became difficult, if not virtually impossible, for both Northern and Southern magazinists to avoid discussion of political issues.11 The editorial career of William Gilmore Simms in the late Forties exemplifies the transition that took place among Southern editors. As editor of the *Magnolia* in 1842, Simms expressed a desire to promote literature in the South, but he was careful to emphasize that his policy involved no wish to disparage the literature of other sections. When he launched the *Southern and Western Monthly Magazine and Review* about 30 months later, he indicated that he wanted to give it "a more decided political complexion than was borne by the *Magnolia*, and, if possible, to impress upon it more of those sectional aspects, South and West, which need development quite as much as advocacy."12 During his term as editor of the *Southern Quarterly Review* (1849-1854), by which time he had dedicated himself wholly to the cause of separate nationality for the South, Simms brought sectional matters to the fore, often complaining against the North and urging other Southern editors to follow suit.13

Even those editors who preferred to avoid politics found it necessary to adopt a strong proslavery stand. In 1853, for example, John R. Thompson, who had tried to avoid politics as editor of the *Southern Literary Messenger*, finally committed his magazine totally to the Southern political cause.14 By the mid-fifties, Southern readers were so absorbed by political questions that Simms asserted that every Southern periodical would have to include discussions of politics:

> No periodical will succeed in the South, which does not include the *political* constituent. The mind of the South is active chiefly in the direction of politics. We breakfast on politics, lunch with party, dine with corporation, sup with the wire-pullers, and sleep with bad fellows.... The only reading people of the South are those to whom politics is the bread of life, and all those periodicals which address themselves to the sentimental, the tender, the fanciful, or the merely funny, take but a slender hold upon the public desires.15

In view of the highly charged political and social atmosphere in which the magazine was conceived, it comes as no surprise that *Russell's* began operations firmly committed to a "Southernist" policy and to discussion of the political aspects of the sectional controversy. The magazine's initial editorial stance was passionately pro-Southern. The reception accorded it by the Southern press was chauvinistic in the extreme, which also contributed to the 20th Century image of the magazine as an ardently Southern organ. These and other conditions of the magazine's existence insured that sectional issues would be dealt with by its contributors, and certainly there is enough writing in *Russell's* on sectional topics to make sectionalism an important theme in any study of the periodical. But this emphasis on the narrowest and most partisan elements in *Russell's* editorial stance misrepresents a periodical that in several important ways strove for a balance, a diminution of partisanship. Though it is perhaps difficult for us to appreciate the distinction today, *Russell's* editor Paul Hayne was feeling for a middle way between virulent loathing for the North and all things Northern, and unmanly toleration of what he considered to be the stupidities and inaccuracies about the South he found among Northern journalists, literary or otherwise.

How then to establish that *Russell's* should be understood as something other than a casebook on the uses of literary journalism for propagandistic purposes? Some idea of the degree to which sectionalism defines the magazine can be gained by examining the contributions in terms of bulk. Combining all essays defending slavery and the Southern way of life, all essays and articles on Southern history and culture, all poems and stories using a Southern setting or presenting a distinctively Southern point of view, one arrives at a total volume of about 900 pages, or about 25 percent of the magazine's 3,432 pages. For reasons of health, for six issues Hayne relinquished editorship to William Grayson, a pro-slavery but anti-secession South Carolinian who was more interested in sectional politics, as the contents of the magazine during his time at the magazine indicate. Hayne presided, however, at the magazine's founding and at its demise. During his tenure, sectional materials composed about only one-fifth of the magazine's pages.

Other statistics are also suggestive. Ninety-seven of the 145 essays, articles and other contributions on general subjects deal with completely non-sectional matters; of the 48 remaining, less than one-half treat political topics. Of the 57 book reviews and essays on literary subjects in the regular pages of *Russell's*, less than one-half treat American authors, and these are divided about evenly between Northern and Southern writers; only seven of these contributions concern matters that may be regarded as sectional. In the book notice column, there are more notices of Northern than Southern works. Only 25 percent of the notices deal with works by Southerners, about Southern materials, or about sectional matters; if the numbers edited by Grayson are omitted from the tabulation, the percentage drops to less than 20. Only four percent of all notices contain a strongly sectional point of view or deal with works that have a direct bearing upon sectional and political issues of the day. These would not seem to be very high percentages for a magazine that "aimed to speak with the voice of the South" in the late 1850's.

Neither does Hayne's evolving editorial policy square with the view of *Russell's* as a strictly sectional periodical. Two months before the demise of the magazine, the editor described his official policy with respect to politics.

> It is not the province of the Magazine — at least not in its EDITORIAL department — to touch, however superficially, upon the question of politics.
>
> Although we believe that the SOUTHERN STATES are standing on the verge of a Revolution; although it appears to us, that the elements of strife, discord, and hatred have been heated up to the point of absolute convulsion; — we shall not abandon the line of our original policy by intermeddling with any of the grand national or sectional issues of the day.[16]

Because several of the contributors often defended slavery and touched on sectional matters in the pages of *Russell's*, Mott and other critics have accused Hayne of inconsistency, or at best, of unrealism.[17] However, even if the policy was unrealistic, it should be noted that Hayne succeeded in executing it; although his magazine began operation with a commitment to discuss any and all questions of importance to the Southern mind — literary, political or otherwise — from the first issue onward he declined to comment either as editor or contributor on controversial issues of the day. On some occasions he felt constrained to defend Southern writers against what he believed were prejudiced, unfair attacks by Northern and Southern critics, but he was willing to defend Northern writers for the same reason; whenever such action became necessary, Hayne usually went to considerable lengths to separate sectional feelings and literary judgments. While he was willing to print essays defending slavery written by other men, as for himself he preferred not to indulge in discussions that tended to intensify sectional hostility.

It is also worth noting that those contributors who were willing to engage in sectional discussions, exemplified by William Grayson, usually confined themselves to one main topic in such discussions; nearly the entire thrust of their contributions in this field is directed to one end and one end only — the justification of slavery. The right of the state to secede, the question of extending slavery to the territories, the struggle in Kansas, the platforms of the national political parties, decisions of the federal courts, presidential policies and congressional legislation regarding slavery — all these and other important topics related to the great sectional crisis of the 1850's are nearly always ignored by the *Russell's* corps of contributors. If *Russell's* is to be regarded as representative of Southern opinion, one gathers that the basis for such a reputation must be something other than the breadth and frequency of its attention to the political aspects of sectionalism.

Because sectionalism tends to become a nebulous concept when applied to non-political areas and because it is always a matter of degree, statistics and facts of the kind we have presented here can be misleading. Nonetheless, we believe that they lead to two valid conclusions. First, if the phrase "representative opinion" is taken to mean a full range and variety of opinions that are typical of a specific group at a particular time, then *Russell's Magazine* was not genuinely and truly representative of Southern or even Charleston opinion of the late 1850's. During a period when Southern feelings became more abrasive, bitter and intensely emotional than at any other time in American history, Hayne practiced moderation and calmness most of the time and all of the time tried diligently to avoid issues that involved bitterness and hatred. While most of the newspaper and periodical press of the South was becoming aggressively and insolently hostile to all things Northern, he continued to hope and call for a universal brotherhood of all practitioners and lovers of art and literature, regardless of how impractical or unrealistic such a hope might have been in such turbulent times. Moreover, although *Russell's* affords much discussion of the issue that was most vital to the ante-bellum South (i.e., slavery) several other topics that were important to southerners are seldom touched upon in its pages. Because politics was so important to leading South Carolinians and Southerners in the 1850's, no magazine of the time that sought to avoid "intermeddling" with national political issues can be called a truly representative organ with respect to public opinion.

Second and of equal importance, the same features and aspects of *Russell's* that kept it from becoming fully representative of Southern opinion, along with other qualities, gave it an overall tone that was far more complex than one would expect to find in a journal devoted to defense of the South and promotion of Southern letters. Hayne was eager to do all he could to help foster a distinctively Southern literature, but the appropriation of literary forms for dissemination of propaganda did not appeal to him. Translation of his ideas into editorial practice resulted in a program of regional literature, to be sure, but it was a program that stimulated very little local color writing and hardly any literary defenses of Southern institutions. The scarcity of these kinds of writing in the magazine combined with Hayne's avoidance of politics and his desire to make *Russell's* chiefly a literary magazine led inevitably to an idiosyncratic tone rather than a narrowly chauvinistic point of view. That the magazine was a sectional periodical cannot be gainsaid. But that its editors were incapable of objectivity was infrequently the case.

That the magazine was inordinately preoccupied with slavery and other political questions of particular interest to Southerners at the expense of all other topics is not demonstrable. These topics inevitably found their place in the magazine along with others, but literature — and not only Southern but Northern and British literature — was the primary concern of the journal during most of its life. Some of the chief contributors, Hayne included, often seemed to regard polite literature as a retreat from the troublesome issues of modern life. Even the contributions of some of the most vehement, rabid secessionists dealt only with faraway places and remote times. The conception of literature as a form of escape tended to pull *Russell's* away from the discussion of current problems, whether sectional or otherwise.

After Carlisle's withdrawal from the magazine in its early days, things were left in Hayne's hands. Though an active supporter of secession, he shared one important view with members of the small, politically powerless Unionist party in South Carolina: American party politics, both Northern and Southern, they believed, was too often an exercise in demagoguery and chicanery, and intelligent Southerners devoted far too much of their time and energies to it. Unlike most members of his social class, Hayne did not hold politics in high esteem as a vocation. He conveyed his feelings about politics best in his personal letters. "I hear nothing about me now but politics — slavery, & antislavery ad nauseam," he wrote to Richard Stoddard in 1855 as the public reaction to the Kansas-Nebraska Act mounted. "Fat old gentlemen catch me by the button, & want to know with a fierce look what I think about Nebraska. My days are rendered wretched by such persecution. Who the deuce cares about whether the President cuts the throats of democracy, or the democracy cut his...."[18] Politics was an unpleasant theme, which men of good temper and goodwill would do well to avoid. Literary men especially, he thought, should concern themselves with the universal moral truths and values reflected in all of the world's great literature, not with current political problems. "D—n sectional difficulties," he advised Stoddard on December 15, 1856. "What have we — (I and you) to do with Politics. Many a pretty fellow has been ruined by that accursed trade already. Let it alone. Let it alone —."[19]

Because of his rejection of partisan politics as repugnant to him,

Hayne decided to exclude the subject altogether from the editorial columns of *Russell's*. In rare instances he spoke of politics in the general sense, but characteristically his purpose on such occasions was to protest against the current excessive attention to politics and to point out that politics in America was a low calling. For the inaugural issue of the magazine, Hayne wrote a short editorial on general politics, which expressed his attitude precisely. "One great danger which has threatened our country, from the beginning," he warned, "lies in the ardent, inconsiderate haste with which our young men of talent rush into *politics*." This custom was causing American art and literature to languish, and if some of the young politicians of the country would devote their abilities to these fields, they "might accomplish a world of good." As for politics, "as conducted at present (it) is merely a game," he lamented, and the majority of politicians were interested only in "the promotion of selfish, sectional, personal interest," not the public or national welfare. Hayne made no sectional distinctions, thus implying that Southern politicians were as culpable as Northern ones.[20]

Even when using excerpts from other magazines and from newspapers, Hayne was reluctant to print comments addressed to the sectional controversy. On two occasions he lifted chunks of quotation from the *Saturday Press*, a Northern journal of which he heartily approved because it regarded all American politicians as "an uninteresting species of maniac."[21] The only excerpt from the *Charleston Mercury* dealing directly with politics concerns the baneful effects of excessive preoccupation with politics.[22] As editor, Hayne never touched on the question of slavery, but on a few occasions he was willing to reprint or quote from articles reinforcing the Southern point of view or exposing the hypocrisy of critics of slavery. In the issue for September, 1857, he printed an excerpt from an article in the New York *Sunday Times* by a supposed abolitionist who had reversed his decision. The author professed a love for freedom "as an inalienable possession of mankind" but admitted that upon seeing that "free labor, in the tropics, will *not* pay beside the labor of the slave," he was forced to agree that Northern attempts to coerce the South into emancipation were "something very unwise."[23] In the following month, Hayne quoted a long passage from an article in the *Edinburgh Review* on the cruel tortures used by British government in India against the local populace. He did not see how the "Exeter-Hall philanthropists" could "continue to throw up their eyes in holy horror at their neighbors' enormities" if they read this expose of their own government's inhumane misdeeds.[24]

When a British writer, who had been hospitably treated during a tour of the South, sneered at Southern society and condemned its system of slavery as barbarous and inhumane, Hayne joined the protest, approvingly reprinting a portion of an article in the Knoxville *Southern Citizen* in which the writer was dubbed "the laureate of current cant and balderdash."[25] But the handful of excursions into the field of political or explicitly sectional journalism we have just cited are almost the only ones in the editorial pages of *Russell's*. Hayne readily confessed that the world of literature was large enough to consume all his energies. It was not lack of sympathy for the Southern cause that motivated him; it was simply that after the political loyalties of the magazine had been sufficiently demonstrated in newspaper advertisements and in the inaugural issue, he was content to ignore politics. Inasmuch as he believed that overemphasis on politics was retarding the progress of literature in the South, he spoke out against it as an editor.

If the foregoing is an even-handedness that results from mere fastidious neglect, as a journalist/reviewer Hayne actively labored to play fair, if only to serve as an example for Northern periodicals and newspapers. However much Hayne hoped for a literary awakening in the South, he recognized that no one in America had built a lasting literary reputation without some assistance and approval from the Northern literary establishment. The larger publishing houses and the best and most successful literary magazines were located in the North, after all. What useful purpose would be served by blindly lashing out against all things Northern without making necessary and proper distinctions? Such a practice would only alienate Hayne from the many Northern writers he had cultivated over the years, and as the history of Southern magazine publishing had shown, it probably would not inspire Southern financial support. Besides, Hayne's personal concept of gentlemanly behavior excluded bellicosity and harsh attacks upon other gentlemen only because of honestly held differences of opinion on sectional matters. As long as the writers from sections of the country did not distort the truth or falsely malign the South, Hayne was eager to extend a hand of friendship.

All of these attitudes led Hayne to pursue an editorial course that differed from most Southern editors of the 1840-1860 period. In essence Hayne had two major guidelines that ruled his policy: retain a strong sense of sectionalism but avoid all unnecessary antagonism against the North by overlooking the more offensive abolitionist works, and by emphasizing only the positive aspects of the movement for Southern literary independence while ignoring some of the unpleasant realities that had generated the movement. After the secessionist press repeatedly had indicated that it was expecting the new journal to be provincial and chauvinistic, Hayne issued an announcement that suggested the line he would take:

> ... we propose to offend no one, and least of all to imitate our Northern friends of the (Boston) *Traveler* and (New York) *Times* school, in habitual, rude, and insolent aggressiveness of opinion and assertion. We shall, as a general rule, leave the North and Timbuctoo to take care of themselves ... and do our own land a service in any degree.[26]

In the final analysis, more than 75 percent of Hayne's editorial space was devoted to non-sectional topics: well under 10 percent of the column could be called belligerently sectional, and only about three percent concerns the topic of Southern nationalism. It is worth noting that the most strongly sectional comments are concentrated in the first two issues, before Hayne had assumed complete control of the editorship, and in the issue for January, 1859, at which time he was trying to revive the periodical by means of a sectional appeal. The reason for Hayne's avoidance of these topics is clear: he wanted readers to regard him as a refined editor of a literary magazine, not as a Southern provincial or common journalist. A high-toned, culturally elevated journal had no place for sectional animosities. In his view, Northern sneers at the South were but another form of shallow parochialism. He did not wish to lay himself open to a similar charge by overpraising local products or by vaunting too loudly the Southern cause.

Of course, whenever Hayne saw what he thought were signs of cultural awakening in the South, especially Charleston, he offered encouragement. The lyceum movement, which sprang up in South Carolina in the late 1850's, was one indication that local culture was striving toward a more elevated level. Hayne approved it as a powerful tool for public education and a means by which "narrow local prejudices are removed, and geniality, heartiness and breadth of view (are) imparted to the general thought, and sentiments.[27] By the same token, he called attention to the meetings of scholarly associations and the Carolina Art Association, and to other cultural events in the state, even though this practice sometimes made it seem that *Russell's* was moving into newspaper reporting. Hayne explained his policy in February, 1858. "It falls not within our province to note or chronicle merely local movements, or matters of news, but we may say with strict propriety, devote a portion of our editorial space, to all efforts and enterprises that promise to extend the influence and prevalence, either of pure literature or of high art."28 The statement affords an important clue to Hayne's whole editorial policy: his crusade was not so much for the South as it was for the improvement of culture in the South. Indeed, however strongly he might be attached to his section, he believed that the attainment of cultural refinement automatically meant replacing narrow, provincial standards with the universal values by which all true art and literature were to be judged at last. He was not willing to sacrifice critical objectivity about the current literary situation.

This said, however much Hayne may have wished to minimize discussion of sectional politics in *Russell's*, he was not able to exert a controlling influence beyond his own contributions and the editorial and review columns in the magazine. From the beginning of publication a shortage of contributions compelled him to accept almost anything that was offered; and since the sectional controversy was uppermost in most men's minds, it was inevitable that some contributors would want to express their opinions on current politics. The combination of articles on history, politics and other Southern subjects, numbering 48 altogether, was the single most important factor in creating and sustaining the image of the magazine as narrowly sectional journal.

Even so, in evaluating the political side of *Russell's*, one should note that the total volume of these essays is less than 425 pages, about 10 percent of the total contents of the magazine. Essays motivated by sectional interests appeared in the periodical at a rate of slightly less than two essays for every three issues. The rate is roughly equivalent to that for the *Southern Literary Messenger* in the 1850's, and it does not exceed the rate at which antislavery and anti-Southern articles appeared in the *Atlantic Monthly* during the years 1857-1860. It is much smaller than the rate for such Southern periodicals as the *Southern Quarterly Review*, *De Bow's Review*, *Whitaker's Magazine* and Joseph Addison Turner's *Plantation*, all of which were totally committed to defending the Southern position and disseminating proslavery propaganda in the 1850's.

But regardless of how these facts and statistics may qualify one's final judgment, the fact remains that a large amount of energy was expended in the pages of *Russell's* in defense of the South and slavery. Taken in the aggregate, the articles on sectional matters constitute a significant although not fully comprehensive body of pro-Southern opinion during the last years before the Civil War. One need only compare *Russell's* with such national magazines as *Graham's*, the several themes, albeit an important one. He was glad to print papers that expounded the Southern point of view, but he had no desire to convert *Russell's* into a political organ. One sometimes reads through entire issues of *Russell's* without encountering evidence of sectional feeling.

In conclusion, if *Russell's*, was in fact something other than a journal of narrow sectional interests, the reason is not that Hayne had a deeper understanding of the South's great dilemma (i.e., its infatuation with the cause of slavery that had so fatally entwined itself with the notion of state's rights). His first interest was literature. His first principle, which he maintained with some consistency, was that parochialism was the enemy of art. *Russell's* began with an official commitment to a sectionalist stand but under Hayne's guidance soon abandoned it in search of "the peaceful realms of literature."

However, as Louis Rubin points out, Hayne may have created a false opposition in his vision of hectoring and vulgar politics opposed to the higher stability of literature. In the final analysis, the political fury he would have preferred to ignore crippled the intellectual enterprise into which he poured so many of his hopes. "What the *Russell's* writers suffered most from was a political situation that prevented them from doing what similar literary groups customarily do — grounding their literary interests in a cultural and social position that placed them in a quasi-adversarial relationship with the larger community."[29]

Speaking specifically of Henry Timrod, whose poetry is certainly *Russell's* most lasting contribution to American letters, Rubin suggests:

> What seems obvious in almost everything Timrod wrote for *Russell's* is his general dissatisfaction with the attitudes and tastes of the community. But if so, it does not carry over into a criticism of the social and political arrangements of Charleston and the South. One can only speculate on the extent to which, in a politically less volatile and militant atmosphere, the young professional writers of *Russell's* might have been emboldened, through mutual encouragement, to undertake the radical critique of Southern institutions that, in the situation they found themselves, they showed no sign whatever of wanting to make.[30]

Notes

1. Richard J. Calhoun, "Literary Criticism in Southern Periodicals, 1828-1860" (unpublished Ph.D. dissertation, University of North Carolina, 1959), p. vii.
2. Frank Luther Mott, *A History of Southern Magazines* (Cambridge, Mass., 1957), II, 110, 490.
3. *Ibid.*, II, 489.
4. Oct. 1, 1856.
5. Harold S. Schultz, *Nationalism and Sectionalism in South Carolina, 1852-1860: A Study in the Movement for Southern Independence* (Durham, N.C., 1950), 13-133. Once there was widespread acknowledgment that the success of the antislavery movement would cause disunion, the unconditional secessionists actually worked secretly for the

success of the Republican Party by trying to split the national Democratic Party on the slavery issue. See Schultz, 94.
6. *Journal of the House of Representatives* (Columbia, 1856), 28. Secessionist newspapers also carried numerous predictions of disunion in 1856; see, for example, the *Sumter Watchman*, Oct. 29, 1856, and the *Mercury*, June 19, 1856.
7. Charles S. Sydnor, *The Development of Southern Sectionalism, 1819-1848* (Baton Rouge, 1948), 315-316.
8. Clement Eaton, *The Freedom-of-Thought Struggle in the Old South* (New York, 1964), 87-88, 174, 377.
9. The most significant study of the Southern literary movement of 1830-1860 remains Jay B. Hubbell's "Literary Nationalism in the Old South," *American Studies in Honor of William Kenneth Boyd*, ed., William K. Jackson (Durham, N.C., 1940), 175-220, to which we are indebted for most of our general facts. See also Guy A. Cardwell, "Charleston Periodicals, 1795-1860: A Study in Literary Influences, with a Descriptive Checklist of Seventy-Five Magazines" (unpublished Ph.D. dissertation, University of North Carolina, 1959), 180-203, and Joseph L. King Jr., *Dr. George William Bagby: A Study of Virginian Literature, 1850-1880* (New York, 1927), 31-52.
10. Cardwell, 185.
11. Mott, II, 132. On 131-139 Mott discusses the drift of American periodicals toward political discussion during the 1850's.
12. I (Jan., 1845), 67, quoted by Cardwell, 187-188.
13. Mott, I, 649-650, 725. For a study of the evolution of Simms' attitude, see John W. Hingham, "The Changing Loyalties of William Gilmore Simms, *Journal of Southern History*, IX (May, 1943) 210-223.
14. Robert D. Jacobs, "Campaign for a Southern Literature: The *Southern Literary Messenger*," *Southern Literary Journal*, II (Fall, 1969), 95.
15. *Southern Quarterly Review*, VII, N. S. (April, 1853), 520.
16. "Editor's Table," VI (Jan. 1860), 364.
17. II, 489. See also Fronde Kennedy, letter to Yates Snowden, May 19, 1919 (Snowden Papers, South Caroliniana Library), 132.
18. July 28, 1855, in *A Collection of Hayne Letters*, ed. Daniel M. McKeithan, (Austin, 1944), 9.
19. McKeithan, 22. Hayne evidently was trying to persuade Stoddard that the sectional orientation of *Russell's* need not be a reason for Stoddard to withhold his contributions. Three months earlier he had conceded that the politics of the new magazine would displease Stoddard: "The Politics won't suit you I suppose, but what of that — you are not Politician, but a Poet whose audience is humanity everywhere." (Sept. 17, in McKeithan, 16).
20. I (April, 1857), 88-89. Hayne's only other discussion of general politics in *Russell's* concerns the low level of political journalism in America (III, 1858, 376); in that essay he treats the nation as a whole without making any sectional distinctions.
21. Quoted in "Editor's Table," IV (March, 1859), 562. See also VI (Dec. 1859), 280.
22. VI (Jan., 1860), 371.
23. Quoted in "Editor's Table," I, 560-561.
24. II, 89.
25. III (June, 1858), 276; see also II (Jan., 1858), 367, and VI (Dec., 1859), 278-279.
26. *Mercury*, Dec. 2, 1856.
27. II (March, 1858), 565.
28. II, 467.
29. Louis D. Rubin, Jr., "Simms, Charleston, and the Profession of Letters," in *Long Years of Neglect: The Work and Reputation of William Gilmore Simms*, ed. John Caldwell Guilds (Fayetteville: University of Arkansas Press, 1988), 222.
30. *Ibid.*, 223.

8

The Lion's Roar:
Cassius Clay's *The True American*

Gene Murray
Grambling State University

When the name Cassius Marcellus Clay is mentioned, most people think of the boxer who changed his name to Muhammad Ali and became heavyweight champion of the world. Outside of Kentucky, little is known of the Cassius Marcellus Clay who earned a reputation as a fighter himself in the 1800s. Ironically, the original Clay, son of a wealthy slaveowner, gained the title of "Champion of Liberty" while fighting to free Ali's ancestors some 100 years before Ali was born.

Similarities exist between the two Kentucky-born Cassius Clays. Both men were talkative and could back up their boasts with action. Clay the boxer became known as the "Louisville Lip," and the man for whom he was named was called the "Lion of White Hall." Each was married more than once, and each was widely traveled.

The White Hall part of the first Clay's nickname came from his 30-room estate near Richmond, Ky., where he was born and died. In the intervening 93 years, Clay established himself as an expert bowie-knife fighter, tried his hand at politics, edited an abolitionist newspaper in the midst of slave holders, fought in the Mexican and Civil wars, served as ambassador to Russia, advised President Lincoln to free the slaves, co-founded Berea College, and, at the age of 85, married a 15-year-old.

This paper focuses on 1845-46, when the original Clay was editor of *The True American* of Lexington, Ky., and on events leading to the establishment of the newspaper.

Beginning of the Antislavery Press

From the 1830s through the outbreak of the Civil War, slavery shared top billing with politics in many newspapers. William Lloyd Garrison, who influenced Cassius Clay's abolition views, established the best known and longest lasting antislavery newspaper in 1831. Published in Boston, *The Liberator* was well edited and ordinarily consisted of four pages. Postmaster General Amos Kendall, a former journalist, tried to gag Garrison by allowing his papers to be culled from official mail bags, but Garrison continued to publish. He survived an attempted lynching from an angry mob.[1]

An abolitionist editor who did not escape the mobs was Elijah Lovejoy of the *St. Louis Observer.* In 1833, he founded the *Observer* as a religious newspaper and took up the fight against slavery. St. Louis citizens pressured Lovejoy into moving his press across the Mississippi River to Alton, Ill., in 1835. A mob wrecked the newspaper office and destroyed his press, and two years later another press was dumped into the river. In 1837, while setting up a third press in Alton, Lovejoy declared he would defend his right to publish with his life. He was killed, giving the abolitionist movement its first martyr.[2]

In Kentucky, James G. Birney of Danville in the early 1830s discussed establishing an emancipation newspaper. Danville citizens bought the town's printing press and instructed the postmaster to refuse mailings of abolitionist material. Birney established his *Philanthropist* in Cincinnati in 1835. Mobbed in a free state, Birney escaped with his life but lost his press. [3]

Although Birney was not allowed to set up an abolitionist journal in Danville, the state of Kentucky did not pass any legislation restricting press freedom until 1860.[4]

As opposition to slavery spread throughout the North, Cassius M. Clay thought the time was ripe for Kentucky's first antislavery newspaper in 1845. The son of one of the commonwealth's wealthiest slaveowners sought to bring the battle against slavery to the slaveholders' territory. Although he was asking for gradual emancipation, the explosions which followed were inevitable.

An Emerging Emancipator

Cassius Clay, youngest of seven children of Green and Sally Clay, was born October 9, 1810, in a stately mansion. A native of Virginia, Green Clay came to Kentucky in the 1770s, fought in the American Revolution and settled in Madison County. Kentucky's first deputy surveyor, Green Clay amassed extensive holdings and immersed himself into politics. He passed his love for politics to his son Cassius, who strived but fell short of the political power exerted by his father. After his father's death in 1828, Cassius attended Transylvania University in Lexington for two years. [5]

Discovering Abolitionist Ideas in New England

Clay left Kentucky in 1831 to enter Yale's junior class. In New England, he met poet John Greenleaf Whittier, Julia Ward Howe and Robert Winthrop, but the most influencial person he met was William Lloyd Garrison.[6] Although Clay joined an emancipation society in Kentucky, he wrote:

> When I entered Yale, with my soul full of hatred to slavery, I had never known anything of Garrison. I had never heard an Abolitionist, nor the name hardly, so I went to hear Garrison. As Garrison "dragged out the monster from all his citadels, and left him staffed to the vitals," the arguments were "water to a thirsty wayfarer" to Clay, who wrote: "I resolved, when I had the strength, I would give slavery the death struggle."[7]

Honored by his classmates to deliver the Centennial Oration on Washington's Birthday in 1832, Clay gave his first antislavery speech. In language from the Bible, he called for a rededication to national liberty. He expressed his fear that the Union might some day dissolve.[8] His New England education had given him much more than a degree.

Fighting Slavery in Kentucky

Returning to Kentucky, Clay was a much more determined man than the youth who ventured East. Clay studied law six months at Transylvania. [9] Politics remained in his blood, and he was elected Madison County's representative in the Kentucky General Assembly in 1835 and 1837. During his second term, Clay opposed slavery and angered the slaveholders, especially Robert Wickliffe, father of one of Clay's Yale classmates. Clay and his wife moved from White Hall to Lexington, where he defeated Robert Wickliffe, Jr., for an 1840 General Assembly seat.

In 1840, Clay spoke against slavery at Crab Orchard in Lincoln County, Ky. "The legend goes," wrote Clay, "that I placed a pistol on the buck-board and a Bible by its side, saying: 'For those who obey the rules of right, and the sacred truths of the Christian religion, I appeal to this book; and to those who only recognize the law of force, here is my defense,' laying my hand on the pistol." Despite a death threat, Clay also made an antislavery speech, which he called a signal victory, at Stanford. "If I was victorious in the blue-grass region, the very stronghold of slavery, I might claim as easy triumph elsewhere,"[10] Clay reasoned.

Robert Wickliffe, Sr. began an oratorical battle with Clay on the slavery issue. The "war" ranged from speeches, debates, pamphlets and even an aborted duel. Differences between the men had to be settled on the "field of honor," so they met in Louisville for a duel. Both men fired at 10 paces and missed. The seconds prevented a rematch as Clay suggested, but no apologies were made.

Another episode in the Wickliffe-Clay war was in 1841. During a political speech by Wickliffe Jr. at Russell Cave Spring near Lexington, Clay interrupted. When Clay stood up, Sam Brown from New Orleans struck Clay, and Clay drew his bowie knife. Brown pointed a pistol at Clay, but the knifesman advanced toward his opponent. Although Brown fired at Clay's chest, Clay exhibited his expertise with his weapon, laying open Brown's head, carving off an ear and extracting an eye. Brown's bullet was deflected by a silver case in Clay's pocket. After throwing Brown over a cliff, Clay raised his bloody blade and challenged: "I stand ready to defend the truth." No one took his dare. Somehow Brown survived.[11]

The bowie knife incident gave him notoriety, but Cassius Clay promised his brother he would give top priority to his farm and milling interests. After a year's silence, Cassius surfaced in 1843 to debate the legislature's repeal of the the Negro Law, a slave import restriction. Further importation of slaves would drive out free white laborers, destroy industry and cause "rich fields to grow sterile," argued Clay. He said he fought the slave system, not because he loved the Negro, but because he wanted to assist the white. "If we are for emancipation," he explained, "it is that Kentucky may be virtuous and prosperous." Fellow Kentuckians called him a "nigger lover."12

Words did not halt Clay. Later in 1843, he published in Horace Greeley's *Tribune* a piece entitled "Slavery: The Evil—The Remedy." Greeley reprinted the tract and circulated it as a pamphlet. Clay cited census statistics to show that free states were far ahead of slave states in education and industrialization. He urged gradual emancipation under the law. Clay argued that since the number of nonslaveowners outnumbered the slaveholders in Kentucky, the nonslaveowners could vote for an amendment to change Kentucky's proslavery constitution. By appealing to nonslaveowning whites, Clay hoped to gain support and further his political ambitions.

He predicted an antislavery press could be set up in the 1840s. Before his press became a reality, the 1844 presidential election provided him with more audiences for his antislavery campaign.

Campaigning for Henry Clay in the North

After establishing himself as the creator of the American System and a distinguished statesman, Henry Clay was nominated as the Whig presidential candidate in 1844. He was opposed by James K. Polk, a Tennessee Democrat without a political reputation, and James G. Birney, a former Kentuckian representing the Liberty Party and calling for immediate emancipation. To weaken Birney's chances, the Whigs needed a spokesman to influence antislavery elements. Cassius Clay seemed to be the answer, so Northern Whigs asked him to tour the Northeast on Henry Clay's behalf.

Cassius Clay's reputation as an abolitionist had spread because of his articles in Northern newspapers. In January, 1844, he freed his own slaves, making him acceptable to the Yankees. [13] His reputation with the bowie knife and his willingness to face danger also made him attractive. Being a relative and associate of Henry Clay were additional assets for Cassius. Before leaving for his campaign tour, Cassius made a supposedly nonpartisan speech opposing annexation of Texas. Henry told Cassius he did not agree with Cassius' interpretation of the Texas issue, but he felt Cassius was a greater asset than liability.

As a spokesman for the Whigs, Cassius Clay was a loser. He spoke out against slavery and annexation of Texas, and his candidate lost. He later wrote that abolitionists defeated the "most honest man, next to Lincoln, that ever ran for President."[14] Calling himself a scapegoat and a sacrifice for the Whigs, Cassius Clay did not let the setback hamper his antislavery campaign.

Birth of *The True American*

Although *The True American,* did not appear until June 3, 1845, a notice of the publication appeared in the Lexington *Observer and Reporter* in February, 1845. The newspaper's name was chosen because "the cause of liberty is expansive-*American*: and the American, to fulfill his destiny among men, must be True."[15] Four months after the announcement, the newspaper appeared.

Preparing for mobs

Fearing mob violence, Clay bought a brick building in Lexington and had the outside doors lined with sheet iron to make it fireproof. He ordered two four-pounder cannons, loaded them with shot and placed them in strategic positions where they could be fired at an invading mob. The office was fortified with other weapons, including a keg of powder which Clay would set off to destroy himself and his enemies if all else failed. [16] Clay's precautions were based on his knowledge of what happened to Lovejoy and Birney.

Outlining Lofty Goals

The first issue of *The True American*, a full-sized weekly with four pages, appeared on Tuesday, June 3, 1845. According to its nameplate, it was "Devoted to Universal Liberty; Gradual Emancipation in Kentucky; Literature; Agriculture; the Elevation of Labor, Morally and Politically; Commercial, Intelligence."

Clay argued that 600,000 Kentuckians should not "postpone their true prosperity" in order to satisfy the interests of the 31,000 slaveowners. The slaveholders, he wrote, claimed a title deed through the U.S. Constitution. He also pointed out that the First Amendment and Article 10, Section 7, of the Kentucky Constitution guaranteed freedom of press and opinions. The first editorial page included a four-column attack on slavery.

Presenting Varied Content

The True American's typographical makeup was very similar to other journals published in the 1840s. Seven columns wide by 23 inches long, the paper was printed on Clay's press in Lexington. It included no headlines, but occasional labels appeared over stories. Sometimes woodcuts illustrated advertisements. Subscriptions cost $2.50 annually in advance or $3 if not paid within three months.

The journal had 300 subscribers in Kentucky and 1,700 outside the state.[17] The first issue contained three classified ads. Numerous stories were reprinted from other newspapers.

An early advocate of abolishing the one-crop system, Clay wrote a weekly agricultural column. The paper also printed market reports and local news; but the primary focus was on articles dealing with abolition, both pro and con. Clay's antislavery editorials, which sounded like his speeches, took up most of a page.

Content of the newspaper was not violently radical. Clay's editorials argued that slavery was economically unsound and that nonslaveholders should unite to legally abolish the slave system.

Maintaining "that is property which the law makes property," Clay recognized the legal rights of slaveowners.[18] State and foreign news gradually increased, and new laws were reported.[19]

Directing his emancipation arguments to the free white laborers of Kentucky, Clay had no desire to reach literate blacks. He requested that subscribers furnish written orders when sending a slave for a newspaper. Although he said his material would be harmless if read by slaves, Clay intended his message for whites only. Although his paper was circulated mainly in the North, he hoped to reach the ordinary worker and to inspire him to help form an emancipation political party.[20]

Feuding with Churches

Churches were among objects of Clay's antislavery attacks. He had separated from the church because the church condoned slavery, and he said that some ministers catered to slavery rather than risk losing members and donations from slaveowners. Clay wrote: "Let the Church cleanse itself from the dark stain of slavery."

A report of the General Assembly of the Presbyterian Church, held in May, 1845, and printed in the June 10 issue of *The True American* showed the church was considering the slavery question. The assembly agreed to not denounce slavery because that would be "charging Apostles with conniving with sin." Clay charged the churches lacked courage and were not "clear-sighted."

Feuding with Wickliffe Again

Not only did Clay strike out against slavery and the churches but also against old enemies. In his first issue, Clay printed a letter written by Robert Wickliffe, Sr., in April, 1845, to the Kentucky *Gazette*. Wickliffe warned Kentuckians that if they allowed open advocacy of abolitionism "every Whig organ in the State will openly demand the emancipation of slaves." The Whigs were united with the Northern abolitionists, contended Wickliffe, now a Democrat, and only the Democrats could save the state.

In response, Clay called Wickliffe an "ungrateful monument of the forbearing mercy of the people." Clay argued that 200 free men put more money into the economy than the 70-year-old slaveholder would buy for his 200 slaves. "We stand for the whites; Mr. Wickliffe for the slaves," added Clay. [21]

Clay, however, did give the senior Wickliffe a compliment by reporting on June 17, 1845, that his old enemy had saved a slave from hanging. In a story labeled "Give the Devil His Due," Clay admitted "'Old Duke' has some good traits, among which we do not number the unrelenting steadiness of denunciation with which he pursues a *good-natured* fellow like ourself."

Feuding with Lexington Citizens

Ignoring rumors that action might be taken to silence him, Clay attacked an ultra-conservative slaveowner, former Gov. Thomas Metcalfe. The newspaper ridiculed a Metcalfe speech defending southern slavery. The editor advised Metcalfe to return to his old profession as a stonemason or to sing a "good old song about wife, children and friends."[22] Clay wrote that when the law failed to protect him he would resort to "the pistol and Bowie knife." [23]

The Lexington community was suspicious of Clay because of his friendship with Delia Webster and Calvin Fairbanks, who aided the escape of three slaves in September, 1844.[24] Clay's outbursts did nothing to calm the townspeople's tempers. A group mailed him a note written "in blood or red turnip juice":

> C.M. Clay:
> You are meaner than the autocrats of hell. You may think you can awe and curse the people of Kentucky to your infamous course... Eternal hatred is locked up in the bosoms of braver men, your betters, for you. The hemp is ready for your neck.

> Your life cannot be spared. Plenty thirst for your blood—are determined to have it. It is unknown to you or your friends, if you have any, and in a way you little dream of.
>
> Revengers.

Unruffled by the threat, Clay printed the message in his newspaper.25

An editorial in the August 12 issue of *The True American* set off an emotional powder keg in the city. The anonymous material, written while Clay was home with typhoid fever, concluded:

> But remember, you who dwell in marble palaces—that there are strong arms and fiery hearts and iron spikes in the streets, and panes of glass only between them and the silver plate on the board and the smooth skinned woman on the ottoman. When you have mocked at virtue, and made your honied faith; tremble! For the day of retribution is at hand— and the masses will be avenged.

Lexington slaveowners interpreted the editorial to mean the newspaper was inciting slaves to revolt and murder their masters. *The True American,* through its editorial campaigns, had aided in the defeat of pro-slavery candidates for Congress in the recent August election. With an emancipation rally planned for the next July 4, Clay's newspaper, which was growing in influence, had to be silenced.26

Five men met in a Lexington office on August 14, 1845. After discussing *The True American* editorial, they called a citizens' meeting at the courthouse to discuss persuading Clay to cease publication. Clay appeared at the meeting to answer charges, but the group forced him to leave. A three-man committee presented the group's demands to Clay at his home. The committee told Clay that they had not come with a threat of force but that the safety of his newspaper office and the Lexington community depended upon him. He arose from his sickbed to prepare for an attack. Shortly after his reply was read at the August 15 meeting, the group recessed until Monday, August 18.27

A "battle of handbills" was waged between August 15 and August 18, with Clay issuing four broadsheets and his antagonists publishing the proceedings of their meeting. Clay's second handbill called for a new state constitution with a provision that every female slave born after a certain date should be freed at the age of 21. Also, after 30 years, the state should free the remaining slaves by paying their masters an emancipation fee.28

Handbill No. IV, issued August 18, attempted to explain the controversial editorial of August 12 and stated Clay's willingness to moderate his future language. If his office were not harmed, he would restrict the latitude of discussion of slavery. "You will so act, however, I trust, that this day shall not be one ACCURSED to our county and state," Clay concluded.29

Temporary Suppression

Lexington's leaders did not settle for promises. On August 18 Judge George R. Trotter issued an injunction against *The True American* and Clay, who yielded the office keys. A crowd of 1,200 citizens gathered at the courthouse, where Thomas F. Marshall, a proslavery politician, charged Clay with trying to incite a riot.

Marshall called Clay a trespasser, an invader intending to destroy the foundations of society.30 Marshall said since no law existed preventing the establishment of an abolitionist paper, the people must act outside the law. His speech ended with six resolutions condemning Clay's actions and calling for the appointment of a committee of 60 men to pack up the press of *The True American* and ship it to Cincinnati. Clay's illness prevented him from taking stronger action against his opponents. Editorials and stories in the *Observer and Recorder* boasted that citizens demonstrated self-control in dealing with the antislavery newspaper. They were able to "accomplish their purpose without the slightest damage to property or the effusion of a drop of blood."31

While Lexingtonians were patting themselves on the backs, Northern abolitionists portrayed Clay as a martyr. A Cincinnati writer sang a hymn praising Clay: "He braved a tyrant power with a courage great as the occasion." One abolition editor called the incident an attempted murder, and a writer named Clay the "Champion of Liberty." An orator said Clay's authority came from the "framer of the highest constitution and laws known to man, by the commands of the living and eternal God."32

After recovering from his illness, Clay renewed his fight against the slaveowners. Exactly one month after the suppression, Clay brought charges of riot against the Committee of Sixty. Defense attorneys argued that the slaves had been bolder since *The True American* began publication. Slaves armed with pistols traveled the roads at night, and once they marched loudly past the mayor's house. Based on an old English law, the jury declared Clay's newspaper a nuisance and found the committee not guilty.33

At a meeting at Washington in Mason County on October 13, 1845, resolutions were adopted condemning the character of *The True American* and recommending that a law be passed forbidding antislavery papers in the state. Such a law passed the Kentucky Senate in January, 1846, but was defeated in the house.34

Revival and Death of *The True American*

The voice of *The True American* was temporarily silenced, but the newspaper reappeared on September 30, 1845, bearing a Lexington dateline but printed in Cincinnati. Weekly editions of the revived newspaper appeared regularly, but it was evident that the short suppression had a defeating effect on Clay. Two changes took place: plans to organize an emancipation party were not mentioned, and most of the articles and editorials took a moralistic tone. 35

Issues of the new *True American* were filled with interpretations of the August 18 suppression. The front page of the September 30, 1845 edition was full of sympathetic remarks from Northern editors. Page 2 carried an article labeled "Our Appeal," in which Clay called for "Kentucky and the world" to judge the events of August 18. More of Clay's version of the incident was on the third page, where he charged the committee of stealing his press and the jury of justifying the action.36

Circulation of *The True American* dropped after its suppression, and Clay tried to increase readership by offering the paper to non-slaveholders for half price. The newspaper had been established, Clay explained, to inform non-slaveholders of the oppressive nature of slavery. In his opinion, the Lexington committee suppressed the newspaper because they "saw that, if you once learned your rights, slavery, as you had the power, being five freedmen to one tyrant, would be destroyed."37

Capitalizing on his reputation, Clay spoke in New York City and Philadelphia in early 1846. The January 28 issue of *The True American* gave five and one-half columns of front-page space to the text of Clay's anti-slavery speech in the Broadway Tabernacle and coverage from other newspapers. Speaking before large audiences was a treat to Clay, but he grew tired of the confining task of editing the newspaper. In April, 1846, he wrote that the "daily spreading of one's thoughts before men" was taking its toll on him.

News concerning a possible war with Mexico occupied more space in *The True American*. Bitter toward President Polk, Clay criticized him and editorialized that Texas was annexed for slavery's sake. The President, wrote Clay, was trying to "make it appear that Mexico has declared war against the U.S."[38]

Abruptly in 1846, Clay executed an about face concerning the Mexican War and went to "fall into the ranks, as a private, with my blanket and canteen, giving practical illustration of that equality of privilege among men which I have ever advocated." In a May 20 speech in Lexington, Clay said that he had "both by speech and pen" warned against the war. Left with no alternative, he said, "My country calls for help, and 'right or wrong,' I rally to her standard."

A true friend of his country, said Clay, "not only warns her against evil, but rescues her from the danger of her errors or her crimes."[39]

In a letter to the readers on June 17, 1846, Clay wrote he was forsaking his writing for fighting: Clay joined the "Old Infantry" of Lexington as a private, but he persuaded the company commander to resign and the soldiers to elect him captain.

After Clay left for the war, *The True American* was edited by John C. Vaughan, then a citizen of Ohio. The former assistant editor conducted the paper in a manner similar to Clay—arguing against slavery for economic reasons and chiding ministers for failing to speak out against the "evil." Vaughan attacked old targets such as President Polk, colonization, and Kentucky's lack of jobs because of slavery. On July 15, 1846, Vaughan wrote the paper's main purpose was to promote universal freedom in the public's mind. A free press was necessary to encourage progress and to elevate the working class, Vaughan added.

Quality of the paper did not suffer noticeably after Clay's departure, but *The True American* died on October 21, 1846. It had survived threats from a mob, temporary suppression, a change of location of its printing press, and loss of its editor; but it could not live without financial support. Income from subscriptions and advertising could not keep the paper alive.

In the final issue, Vaughan told readers to regard the discontinuance as a suspension and predicted that another Kentucky paper would soon replace *The True American*. Less than a year later, Vaughan's prediction came true as his Louisville *Examiner* began publication on June 18, 1847. It voiced the emancipation cause until December, 1849, when it, too, died from lack of funds. Cassius Clay was not associated with the paper, but he urged former subscribers to accept the new journal; and unexpired subscriptions to *The True American* were filled with copies of the *Examiner*.40

The life of *The True American* was brief, but in its own way, the newspaper, like its owner, fought valiantly until the end. Would it have lived longer had Clay not gone to the Mexican War? Can a newspaper survive very long when its expenses continue to exceed its revenue? Was Clay promoting emancipation to achieve personal political power? These questions gather conflicting answers.

Clay's Motives and Impact

The impact of a man and his newspaper upon history is hard to evaluate, especially if the man was a paradox and the newspaper was short-lived. Clay struggled for years to convince Kentuckians the economic and moral welfare of the state demanded emancipation. Unlike radical abolitionists in the North, Clay appealed for gradual emancipation through legal means. Since nonslaveowners outnumbered slaveholders by a large majority, he tried to convert the nonslaveowners to his cause. *The True American*, the first antislavery newspaper among Kentucky's slaveholders, was a weapon in Clay's arsenal to fight the slavery "monster in its own den."

Clay did not fit the stereotype into which slaveowners tried to place abolitionists. He was not a Northerner, but a native of the Lexington area. He was not a member of the working class trying to advance his own status, but the son of a wealthy slave-holder. Instead of calling for immediate abolition at any cost because of a "Higher Law," Clay wanted gradual emancipation through a constitutional amendment. He wanted Kentuckians to change their constitution and abolish slavery.

Charges leveled against Clay are that he advocated emancipation to gain political power, he deserted his newspaper to die while he sought military honor, and his actions were inconsistent. Enough evidence can be produced only for the third charge.

If Clay advocated emancipation to gain political power, he certainly did not choose the easy route. Kentucky's bluegrass region was the center of the tobacco plantations and a stronghold for slavery in the antebellum 1800s. Clay, who inherited a considerable number of slaves and wealth, could have gone against his scruples to join the pro-slavery element. A forceful and popular speaker, Clay possibly could have toned down his speeches and could have advanced to the governorship or the U. S. Senate. He was only 25 when he won a General Assembly seat, and he was popular when he withdrew from local politics.

When asked to convert abolitionists from the Liberty Party to win votes for his cousin in 1844, Clay could have suppressed his own feelings about gradual emancipation and annexation. Instead, he spoke his mind and was blamed for the Whig defeat. If he had stifled himself, he could have received a high post in Henry Clay's administration.

On the other hand, Cassius Clay might have felt that slavery would eventually be abolished and that he could become a front-runner, since he had been a longtime opponent of slavery. After his third term in the Kentucky legislature, Clay seemed to have a reverse Midas touch in politics. He had plausible ideas, such as gradual emancipation, internal improvements, crop rotation, and women's suffrage, but he was unable to make these ideas materialize to his benefit. Clay advocated abolition because he felt it was economically unsound, not because he sought high elected office.

Arguments, both pro and con, can be made concerning the charge that Clay deserted *The True American* to die while he chased military glory. Abolitionists charged that Clay sold out to slavery by going to war. Clay justified his actions: "I wished to prove to the people of the South that I warred not upon them but upon Slavery, that a man might hate slavery and denounce tyrants without being an enemy of his country."[41]

Clay, popular among Northern abolitionists, could have made a fund-raising tour of Northern cities to save the newspaper from financial disaster. He left *The True American* in the care of a capable assistant editor who later ran his own antislavery newspaper. Perhaps Clay felt that his patriotism held a higher priority than his antislavery feelings. If a war hero were to advocate abolition, he might gain more support than a mere editor, Clay reasoned. Regardless of Clay's motives, upon his return from the war, he helped form an emancipation political party and later advised President Lincoln to free the slaves. Clay spent his fortune on the abolitionist cause.

That Clay's character was complex is evident. The charge that he was inconsistent is true, but he was consistently inconsistent. He was a fierce fighter with weapons or words and a southern gentlemen who could compliment or complement ladies. He was an abolitionist who wanted gradual, legal emancipation, and for years he was a slaveowner who preached against slavery. Truly, Clay was a

complex, unique antislavery spokesman of the antebellum era.
Clay's newspaper experience indicates that in order for a fledgling newspaper to survive long it must have:

- an adequate steady income from advertisers and subscribers
- a dedicated editor/publisher who will stay on the job, not go running around   the country and even Mexico the way Clay did.
- support from the local community.

Clay seemed to rely heavily on his own fortune to keep the newspaper running. He wanted to speak out against slavery, but he seemed to enjoy the speaking tours more than being tied to a newspaper desk. He gained very little support for the local citizens as he tried to fight slavery in its own den. The large crowd that gathered to watch his press leave Lexington is evidence of that. Perhaps he was fortunate not to suffer the same fate as Lovejoy.

Notes

1. Edwin Emery. *The Press and America*. 3rd ed. Englewood Cliffs, N.J.: Prentice-Hall, Inc., 1972, p. 212.
2. John Vivian. *The Media of Mass Communication*. Needham Heights, Mass.: Allyn and Bacon, 1993, pp. 2-3.
3. Clement Eaton. *Freedom of Thought in the Old South*. Durham, N.C.: Duke University Press, 1940, pp 175-76.
4. Eaton, p.126.
5. Betty Ellison. "The Clays Come to Kentucky," *Kentucky Pioneer*, III, (May, 1972), p. 3.
6. Ellison, p. 4.
7. Cassius M. Clay. *The Life of Cassius Marcellus Clay: Memoirs, Writings, and Speeches.* Cincinnati: J. Fletcher Brennan & Co., 1886., pp. 55-57.
8. Horace Greeley, ed. *The Writings of Cassius Marcellus Clay.* New York: Harper and Brothers, 1848, pp. 43-44.
9. Clay, *Life*, p. 66.
10. Clay, *Life*, pp. 75-77.
11. Clay, *Life,* pp. 82-89.
12. David L. Smiley. *Lion of White Hall*. Madison: University of Wisconsin Press, 1962, p. 56.
13. "Deed of Emancipation, March 14, 1844." Copy in Special Collection, Berea College Library, Berea, Ky.
14. Clay, *Life,* p. 101.
15. Greeley, p. 430.
16. Clay, *Life* p. 107.
17. Ellison, p. 6.
18. *The True American*, June 24, 1845.
19. *The True American*, April 22, 1846.

20. *The True American*, July 1, 1845.
21. *The True American*, June 3, 1845.
22. *The True American,* June 17, 1845.
23. *The True American,* July 1, 1845.
24. Coleman, J. Winston, Jr. "Delia Webster and Calvin Fairbanks," *Filson Club History Quarterly,* XVII (July, 1943), 131-132.
25. *The True American,* June 17, 1845.
26. Cassius M. Clay. *Appeal of Cassius M. Clay to Kentucky and the World.* Boston: J.M. Macomber & N. L. Pratt, 1845, p. 5.
27. *History and Record of the Proceedings of the People of Lexington and its vicinity in the suppression of the "True American,"* from the commencement of the movement on the 14th of August, 1845.
28. Greeley, p. 292-293.
29. Greeley, p. 298-300.
30. Smiley, p. 93.
31. Lexington *Observer and Reporter,* Aug. 20, 1845.
32. Smiley, p. 99-100.
33. Lexington *Observer and Reporter,* Oct. 8, 1845.
34. Louis Miller. *The Crusade Against Slavery, 1830-1860.* New York: Harper and Row, 1960, p. 117.
35. Smiley, 104-105.
36. *The True American*, Sept. 30, 1845.
37. *The True American*, March 11, 1846.
38. *The True American,* June 3, 1846.
39. Greeley, p. 475-76.
40. Clay, *Life,* p. 175.
41. Greeley, p. 486

9

Preserving a Denomination:
The Promotion of Women by
North Carolina's Antebellum Baptist Press

David A. Copeland
Emory & Henry College

In 1832, Baptist minister Thomas Meredith[1] convinced other Baptists in North Carolina that the denomination needed a voice. The ministers at their annual convention agreed. North Carolina Baptists, they believed, would benefit from "a well conducted religious journal"[2] to explain who they were and gave Meredith its approval to begin publication. Meredith, in response to the Convention's sanction, promised "to promote the cause of Religion and Morals, with a special reference, however, to the prosperity of the Denomination, and the important interests and objects of the Convention."[3]

For Tar Heel Baptists the prosperity of the denomination[4] was the key. Surrounded by Methodists, Presbyterians, and Episcopalians all of whom practiced infant baptism, the Baptist concept of believer baptism, which signified a regenerate membership immersed by consent, had to be constantly defended. And although Baptists had grown since the beginning of the century, they were far from being the dominant religious group in the state. In 1840, three-fourths of a million people lived in the North Carolina, and the Baptist State Convention's 1843 minutes stated that only 24,180 of them were Baptists.[5]

Faced with a small, scattered membership in a state that was 98 percent rural and with the fact that nationally the denomination seemed ready to rupture over slavery, Baptists thought that Meredith's press would help bring them prosperity. A newspaper alone, however, could not ensure denominational success. The newspaper had to appeal not only to the male pastors of the denomination, it also had to become a part of families' lives. To be successful in the lives of families, the *Biblical Recorder* had to be an instrument of news, entertainment, and growth for the entire family. And, it had to appeal to women because females represented the majority of the weekly church congregations and served as the central figures in the homes. Meredith's plan was the salvation for Baptists and other evangelical denominations. "Virtuous and patriotic mothers" could be found at the hearth of every home, one writer pointed out in 1834,[6] and Meredith and his colleagues believed the best way to ensure Baptist prosperity was to appeal to this strength of family and religious life. From its inception and through the rest of the antebellum period, especially from the time of Baptists' division North and South to the national division sixteen years later (1845-1861), the *Biblical Recorder* established an agenda that elevated women through an emphasis upon the significance of home and education. In return, the denomination would be preserved. The home, the *Recorder* advocated in 1850, was the place "the Church and State must come for their origin and support," and both depended upon " the virtue of woman."[7]

The emphasis on the role of women in Baptist life takes on even more significance when it is remembered that men held all positions of importance in Baptist hierarchy, as they did as well in other evangelical groups. Although some females such as Martha Shubal Stearns had served as ministers in the past, the general practice of the nineteenth century found men assuming all of the leadership roles within the local church and the denomination. Yet, Baptist hopes of growth and survival, if they had to depend upon the majority of male leadership, were small. That is why the plan to preserve the denomination through women, the home, and the *Biblical Recorder* was vital, and it was successful. By 1880, Baptists were the largest denomination in North Carolina. Before the end of the century, women accounted for 60 percent of the denomination's membership in all of the South.8 In addition, Baptist women put into place the Women's Missionary Union, Southern Baptists' best and most successful way of raising money to support mission efforts.

But this emphasis on women that appeared in the *Biblical Recorder* did more; it helped to foster a desire for an education among women equal to that of men, and it fostered a desire for women's rights. Although women played a secondary role in Southern society, they played the foundational role at home9 and consequently, in the church according to the *Recorder*'s theory of promoting the denomination.

The concept that southern evangelical religion promoted women is not universally accepted, though. Jean Friedman in *The Enclosed Garden* says that until late in the century "southern culture inhibited the formation of women's consciousness, collective identity, and self assertion and at the same time discouraged female asssociation."10 The fact that Southern Baptists refused to seat women at their 1885 convention and even voted to change the name of those attending from "messengers" to "brethren" supports this idea. But the insitutional press of North Carolina Baptists tells a different story. This research seeks to demonstrate that the Baptist press of North Carolina made a conscious effort to strengthen the denomination by promoting the importance of women, their education, and their sphere of influence—the home.

The *Biblical Recorder* was but one of many religious newspapers published in America.11 For that reason, understanding the nature of the religious press in America should help in understanding the *Recorder*'s goals in antebellum North Carolina. That understanding will also point out how religious newspapers fit into American life.

The Growth and Origins of the Religious Press

Papers such as the *Biblical Recorder* did not just materialize; they originated in the revivals, the Great Awakening of the eighteenth century and the Second Great Awakening or the Great Revival, that ushered in the nineteenth. Controversy surrounded the revivals, and controversy spawned the religious press in efforts to define religious traditions and to sustain them against attack. For these reasons in the fervent atmosphere of revival-torn 1740s Boston,12 the religious press was conceived.

The first religious periodical in America was Thomas Prince's *Christian History*, which appeared in 1743. Its purpose was to record the progress of the Great Awakening and its silver-tongued orator, George Whitefield.13 The *Christian History* continued to be published until 1745. Nineteen years later, the first southern religious periodical, the *North Carolina Magazine, or Universal Intelligencer*, was printed in New Bern. The *Universal Intelligencer* was part magazine and part newspaper and was published in 1764 and 1765.[14] Even though Prince had begun the publication of religious periodicals and the *Universal Intelligencer* brought the attempt at religious publications southward, religious newspapers and magazines did not flourish until after the Second Great Awakening.[15] In Georgia, Baptist minister Henry Holcombe responded to the Great Revival and published the *Georgia Analytical Repository* in 1802. Although the paper folded after six issues, it set the agenda for the religious papers that would follow. Benevolent undertakings by religious groups, accounts of revivals, essays on civil government, information on the organization of Georgia Baptists, articles on the arts and sciences, and news of secular importance filled those six issues.[16]

From the time of the *Georgia Analytical Repository* to 1850, countless other religious periodicals sprang into existence and disappeared almost as quickly. Although the revival fervor of the Awakening came to North Carolina in 1801 with a Baptist preacher named Lemuel Burkitt,[17] North Carolinians would not produce a religious paper for another twenty years.[18] The success of the *Biblical Recorder* following its publication in 1833, in comparison with the lack of success of many of North Carolina's secular papers during this period, confirms the fact that religious newspapers competed successfully with the secular press of the day. Because the religious press dealt with issues outside of the religious sphere as well as those within, it could serve as the sole informational outlet for many. Whether or not it served as nobly as the *Presbyterian* of Philadelphia claimed in 1854 is questionable. That religious paper asserted:

> In many cases, the religious newspaper is the only channel of communication with the world at large. Not a few families rely upon it entirely for their secular as well as their religious information.... It is not simply taken up, hastily run over, and then thrown aside for waste paper, it is returned to again and again, until every article, even the advertisements, has been pored over; it passes into the hands of every member of the family, undergoing in each case, perhaps, a similar process. It is referred to in the conversations of friends and neighbors; its opinions and statements are quoted; in fact, it comes at last to be regarded as a sort of living companion, and as an old and reliable friend with some, too, it takes the place of books, where books would seldom or ever reach them.[19]

The *Biblical Recorder* never made such a claim for itself, but Baptists recognized this kind of potential for a denominational newspaper. Meeting together in 1837, Baptists declared, "A religious paper is an organ of general communication for the scattered members of the church, and thus becomes the medium through which her movements may be carried forward. It is here we learn each other's sentiments and compare each other's views."[20] Whether in Convention or in the issues of the *Recorder*, Baptists continued to insist on the importance of the newspaper. "Our state should furnish 3,000 subscriptions," the 1844 State Convention maintained. "Every Baptist family in the State should weekly receive a copy of the Biblical Recorder," the Convention affirmed in 1855. By 1859, the Convention voted "to enlarge the *Recorder* by one column inch on each page and add an additional editor."[21] This progression of events speaks to the success of the *Biblical Recorder* as does Meredith's editorial in January 1850. "We are gratified to be able to state, however, that the circulation of the *Recorder* in North Carolina now, is greater than it has been in any previous period."[22]

The religious newspaper was the product of revival, and the 1850 United States Census listed 191 religious newspapers or periodicals that were being published in the nation.[23] But religious periodicals in the first half of the nineteenth century failed when they dealt solely with the religious. Meredith's approach of dealing with the whole of news, sacred and secular, allowed his type of religious newspaper to succeed. In fact, from 1845-1861, the *Recorder* printed 20 percent more news of secular events than stories of religious news.[24] When the telegraph changed the method of news gathering so that dailies could print news within twenty-four hours of occurrence[25] and when printing presses that could deliver tens of thousands of double-sided printed pages in an hour's time[26] altered the newspaper business in America, the religious press changed, too. It became more of a denominational organ[27] and less of a news source to be embraced by the entire family for all of its news as the *Presbyterian* proclaimed in 1854. As the *Biblical Recorder* followed this trend in the years after the Civil War, it continued to be successful because of the place it etched for itself among the citizenry of North Carolina from 1845-1861, especially females.

For the Prosperity of the Denomination

The *Biblical Recorder*'s emphasis on women and Meredith's subsequent plan for strengthening Baptists through them were not unique. Education, women, and the home increasingly garnered attention in the antebellum period both in and out of the church.[28] Education on the national scene was perceived to be absolutely necessary for the success and survival of the country. Reformers such as Catharine Beecher told Northeners that the education of every American child was "the immediate object which has called us together."[29] Education for males produced a literate class and trained lawyers, doctors, and ministers. It was also seen as the only way to preserve American government.[30] Education for females, besides the fact that it was good in and of itself, produced future wives and mothers.[31]

Following Meredith's and other evangelicals' concept, educated women would be the source of denominational and morals preservation, a great necessity for the welfare of society. As antebellum northern America sped—or perhaps fled—toward large urban centers and an industrialized society, there was only one place that provided safety from the "chaos of the streets," and that was the home. Antebellum America recognized home as a sanctuary from the world, and the home was the sphere of the woman.[32] As society decayed, its salvation lay in the woman and home. "When our land is filled with virtuous and patriotic mothers, then will it be filled with virtuous and patriotic men," wrote the Reverend John S. C. Abbottt[33] *Mother's Monthly Journal* laid the future at woman's feet: "The mother's appropriate sphere and pursuits give her a decided advantage in the great work of laying a foundation of future characters; inculcating those principles and sentiments [that] are to control the destiny of her children in all future time."[34]

Women were, as Cotton Mather had called them more than a century earlier, "The Hidden Ones," those that always supported the minister and the church in a quiet, silent manner. And women were, in Laurel Ulrich's words, the church members who "went to hear the minister preach even when it snowed . . . [and] they never asked to be remembered on earth."[35] In the church, women were always present, always working quietly, always giving without asking to be remembered. For the *Recorder*, women became "the cornerstone of Church and State."[36]

If the *Biblical Recorder* planned to preserve Baptists by promoting women, it had to make sure its pages appealed to a female readership. From the *Biblical Recorder*'s beginnings, Meredith provided articles for women. Each week, the four-page paper devoted one page to poetry, short stories and bits of wisdom. At times these were written by women. In July 1850, Meredith commented on "a beautiful thing from the pen of Mrs. Cornwald Barry Wilson." Wilson's poem, "The

Head and the Heart" followed. These types of articles were directed at a female readership but so were sensational news items as well as articles such as "The Good Wife," which extolled the wife that each day outfitted her husband to face the rigors of the world.37 Because women were so involved in the life of the church, they were probably interested in *Recorder* articles dealing with doctrinal issues and obituaries, including those of women; announcements of ordinations; special sermons; meetings; marriages; and similar notices.38

The *Biblical Recorder* succeeded in its first step of prosperity for the denomination by providing articles that appealed to its female readership. Since women were already in place in the home, promoting their education was the next step. Meredith and subsequent editors through the *Biblical Recorder* advocated education for both sexes. From 1845 to 1861, the *Recorder* repeatedly emphasized female education, something it had begun to push as early as 1835 with other Baptist leaders in the northeastern part of the state. Although the state convention did not provide support for such an institution, local Baptists did and opened Chowan Female Institute in 1848 in Murfreesboro. Coinciding with the opening of the school, the *Recorder* ran a series of articles on female education. In the December 4, 1835, paper, Meredith published a lengthy article on "Female Scholars of the Reformation." The history extolled the intelligence of females who learned the biblical languages and challenged the religious and political leaders of the day on their errors in biblical understanding. Meredith also ran in the same edition the first announcement of the Chowan Female Institute, which promised to offer a variety of courses including grammar, philosophy, logic, algebra, French, and Latin.

The list of courses for Chowan Female Institute and the article on the intellectual women of the Reformation, along with the *Recorder*'s publishing of John Milton's essay advocating equal education for male and female, made it appear that the *Biblical Recorder* advocated equal education for both sexes. That was not, however, the *Recorder*'s purpose. "Female education is highly important as connected with domestic life. It is at home where man passes the largest portion of his time," the *Recorder* noted in 1850. "Intelligence and piety throw the brightest sunshine over private life, and these are the results of female education."39 The Baptist woman's role was preserver of religion, educator of children through home primers and the maintainer of the home—the "cornerstone of Church and State." She needed education to accomplish such lofty goals.40

From 1850 to 1861, the *Recorder* repeatedly emphasized this multifaceted role of the female and the necessity of her education. The 1850 papers ran numerous articles on education and reported on the improvements to the facilities at Chowan saying "it always affords us pleasure to promote its interests." The same edition also directed its readers' attentions to Forestville Female Institute that had opened just minutes from Wake Forest College, the Baptists' school for educating its male clergy.[41] By May, the *Recorder* reported the addition of chemical, astronomical, and philosophical apparatus at Chowan noting that they were "far superior to that of any similar Institution in this State, or, the adjoining States."[42] From April through July, the *Recorder* ran seventeen separate articles on education with about half focusing on female education. On January 6, 1854, the *Biblical Recorder*'s enthusiasm for female education practically leapt from its pages. There were promotions for Metropolitan Female Seminary in Raleigh, Castalia Female Institute, Oxford Female College, and a report of the addition of a library at Chowan. In its report from Chowan, the *Recorder* carried these words: "To woman how invaluable in all the relations, and duties, and trials of life, is an education!"[43]

As the *Biblical Recorder*, North Carolina Baptists, and the South moved toward the division of the Union in 1861, the editors of the newspaper continued to promote education for both sexes, but they also addressed women in other ways. Woven into every edition of the *Recorder* were the stories of the home and virtuous woman. The *Recorder*—as well as other evangelical publications—were helping create a self-confident and more independent southern women in the waning days of the antebellum South.[44]

The articles are too numerous to list: "The Wife," "The Dying Mother," "A Daughter's Devotion," "Home and Woman," "A Mother's Prayer," "What a Prudent Wife Did" are examples of the stories that elevated the role of women and demonstrated the importance of the home. The stories portrayed the female as the "greatest of all earthly gifts, far beyond gold," and declared, "No wife, no home."[45] Taken alone, these articles might lead to the conclusion that the *Biblical Recorder* wanted to keep women in a subservient role, and to some extent, that may be a correct assumption since keeping women in their proper sphere of home where they could properly care for husbands and family was being promoted especially in northern America.[46] But when these articles on service and the importance of woman's sphere—the home—were coupled with the large number of articles promoting education, the results were not demeaning. Woman's sacrifice for home and family was Christlike, and no greater comparison could be made in a Christian environment. A mother's love was unconditional; she would tenderly care for a child, even if that child were born without appendages, one story said.47 The *Recorder*'s greatest praise for women may have come on September 5, 1855, when a front page story, "Female Piety," said, "Such a being is indeed worthy of reverence and admiration of every true and generous heart, and she will command it, even when the light of her beauty is quenched, and the flower of her loveliness is faded."

Just as "Female Piety"48 lifted the female to a pedestal, "Home and Woman," printed November 2, 1850, wrapped woman, the home, and her education into one neat and all-significant package. It is significant because the concept of "home," as portrayed in the rural-oriented *Biblical Recorder*, has been considered as a part of urbanization and the creation of a middle class in the North.49 Meredith, a northerner transplanted into North Carolina as a missionary in 1816, did not seem to know that the agricultural South was different. He thought that North Carolina would have to face the problem in the all-encompassing package of "home" as guided by the educated woman. So as Meredith introduced the tribute, he was paying homage to woman for saving society, church, and perhaps a way of life. He said, "If there has ever been a more touching and eloquent eulogium upon the charms of home, and its dearest treasure, woman, than is contained in the following . . . it has not been our good fortune to meet it." The tribute declared:

> Our homes, what is their cornerstone but the virtue of woman, and on what does social well-being rest but our homes? . . . Are not our hearth-stones guarded by the holy forms of conjugal, filial, and paternal love, the cornerstones of Church and State; more sacred than either, more necessary than both? Let our temples crumble, and our academies decay . . . but spare our homes. . . . Mother is a holy and a peculiar name—this is home; and here is the birth-place of every virtuous impulse, of every sacred thought. Here the Church and the State must come for their origin and their support. Oh, spare our homes!50

The biblical significance of this tribute would not have been missed by the *Recorder*'s readership, male and female. The comparison of woman to the cornerstone carried tremendous scriptural importance. The Synoptic gospels, all quoting Psalm 118, announced that Jesus had "become the head of the corner; this was the Lord's doing, and it is marvelous."51 In Acts, the concept was further expanded. Peter, talking to a crowd, said that Christ was that cornerstone and "there is salvation in no one else."52 The Ephesian letter pointed out that "Christ Jesus himself" was the cornerstone, "in whom the whole structure is joined together and grows into a holy temple in the Lord."53 Christlike importance was being attributed to women and their role in preserving home, society, the church and even humankind.

There can be little doubt of the significance of woman, education, and the home for Baptists in antebellum North Carolina. The female in Baptist life was assuming ever increasing importance. In Baptists' efforts to secure another generation that would accept the tenets of its faith, they looked to the home, the dominion of the female. By promoting women, the *Biblical Recorder* found the way to ensure the success of the denomination. By comparing woman to Christ as the cornerstone, the *Recorder* approved a metaphor that should have elevated females and enhanced their self-esteem. As has been said, the education of females was the necessary ingredient that had to be added to the existing feature of home and woman. The emphasis on education helped to foster a desire among women for an education comparable to or even superior to that of men, and it fostered a desire for women's rights, especially in the denominational sphere where women sought admission to national conventions as equals to men and set up the Women's Missionary Union as a separate, independent entity from the denomination's foreign missions program.

Conclusion

The agenda of the *Biblical Recorder* in antebellum America was the prosperity of the denomination. In a newspaper and a denomination outwardly geared to a patriarchial society, Thomas Meredith and subsequent editors of the *Biblical Recorder* did something seemingly inconsistent—they made sure there were articles in the paper for women. The wealth of stories aimed at females and the home may have been printed to urge men to take more seriously their female counterparts, but it is more likely that the *Recorder*'s editors knew their readership—their female readership—needed to know that women were vital to the success of the denomination and society. Why else would the *Recorder* repeatedly point out that woman was the most treasured, most important asset man and home could find? Why else would the *Recorder* insist that woman was the cornerstone of the home and the home the very cornerstone of church and state? Why else would the *Recorder* insist that women needed an education? Meredith and the editors that followed him knew that Baptists in rural North Carolina centered life around the home. It was there, and not in the local Baptist church, that the denomination would be preserved. The home was woman's sphere, and she and she alone could ensure "the prosperity of the denomination." Why else would the *Recorder* declare, "No wife, no home"?

The *Biblical Recorder*'s efforts to strengthen Baptists through women and the home proved successful as the growth of North Carolina Baptists in the nineteenth century proves.

Reading the *Recorder* rightly suggests that the readership of religious newspapers included a large number of women who passed on religious beliefs to their children—the future of the denomination. For its female readership, these stories emphasized the value of woman, elevating her importance in society and instilling self-esteem and value. Even though they might have to wash, sweep, bake, sew, garden, conceive, give birth, and nurture children, women could see that without their selfless contributions, society would likely crumble. Although this may have been a self-serving concept for the male-dominated denominations and religious press, it still fueled women's involvement in the church and supported their participation in benevolent organizations within the community and nation. And, in the case of North Carolina Baptists, it proved to be the prosperity and salvation of the denomination.

Notes

1. Thomas Meredith came to North Carolina shortly after attaining his M.A. in 1816 from the University of Pennsylvania to serve as a home missionary appointed by the Triennial Convention, the name Baptists gave to their mission society. Meredith quickly assumed a leadership role among Baptists in North Carolina. He moved from Edenton to New Bern and back to Edenton again as he held pastorates in two of the state's most influential towns. Meredith and another northern Baptist who came to North Carolina on mission work, Samuel Wait, saw the need for education among North Carolina Baptists. They knew that a religious periodical could be used to promote their original purposes for coming to the state—missions and education.
2. North Carolina Baptist State Convention, *Proceedings* (1832), 13.
3. *North Carolina Baptist Interpreter* (Edenton), 17 January 1833, 1. This monthly journal was the first edition of what was to become the *Biblical Recorder*, the name used beginning in 1835 and continuing to the present.
4. Denomination refers to a religious group that holds to a certain set of beliefs. Often, the group adheres to a certain creed. The Baptist denomination, however, is one that relies upon believer baptism and the autonomy of the local congregation. Local congregations may be tied together in associations or state or national conventions. The associations and conventions serve to further special interests like missions but do not have any control over the activities of the local congregation. The convention concept among Baptists is further explained in William H. Brackney, "The General Missionary Convention of the Baptist Denomination, 1814-1845: An American Metaphor," *Baptist History and Heritage* 24 (1989): 13-23.
5. U.S. Census Figures in Hugh T. Lefler and Patricia Stanford, *North Carolina*, 2nd ed. (New York: Harcourt Brace Jovanovich, Inc., 1972), 467. Baptist figures from *Minutes*,

Baptist State Convention of North Carolina (Raleigh, 1843).
6. John S. C. Abbott, *The Mother at Home; or, the Principles of Maternal Duty Familiarly Illustrated*, revised and corrected by Daniel Walton (London: John Mason, 1834), 166.
7. *Biblical Recorder*, 2 November 1850.
8. *Baptist Courier*, 14 May 1885.
9. One of the concepts prevalent in America—especially in the North—from 1820-1860 was the concept of the "Cult of True Womanhood." Under the rubrics of this guideline for the ideal woman, women were to concern themselves only with domestic affairs and remain "a hostage of the home." Barbara Welter, *Dimity Convictions. The American Woman in the Nineteenth Century* (Athens: Ohio University Press, 1976), 21-30.
10. Jean Friedman, *The Enclosed Garden* (Chapel Hill: University of North Carolina Press, 1985), xi.
11. Little has been written about the religious press. Religious periodicals are discussed briefly in each of the following three volumes by Frank Luther Mott: *A History of American Magazines, 1741-1850* (Cambridge: Harvard University Press, 1966), 337-342, 369; *A History of American Magazines, 1850-1865* (Cambridge: Harvard University Press, 1967), 61-65; *American Journalism. A History: 1690-1960*, 3rd ed. (New York: The Macmillan Company, 1962), 206, 321, 513. North Carolina religious newspapers are mentioned in Guion Griffis Johnson, *Ante-Bellum North Carolina. A Social History* (Chapel Hill: University of North Carolina Press, 1937). Methodist periodicals are studied in Joanna Bowen Gillespie, "The Emerging Voice of the Methodist Woman: *The Ladies' Repository*, 1841-61," in Russell E. Richey and Kenneth E. Rowe, *Rethinking Methodist History* (Nashville: Kingswood Books, 1985). Sam G. Riley and Gary Selnow, "Southern Magazine Publishing, 1764-1984," *Journalism Quarterly* 64 (1988) discusses the beginning of religious journalism but does not discuss the its subject matter. The best volume on the southern religious press is Henry Smith Stroupe, *The Religious Press in the South Atlantic States, 1802-1865* (Durham: Duke University Press, 1956). Stroupe's work, however, is a bibliographic directory to the newspapers, not a history of them. The *Biblical Recorder* is the topic of Stroupe's M.A. thesis, "History of the *Biblical Recorder*, 1835-1907, As Recorded in Its Files" (M.A. thesis, Wake Forest College, 1937). The thesis makes little mention of the *Recorder*'s agenda of promoting women, and focuses upon the slavery issue during the 1845-1861 period.
12. Boston, in the 1740s, was a city divided on the validity of religious revival. Ministers like Charles Chauncy vehemently opposed the changes in religion that were taking place. Others, like the overzealous James Davenport and New York itinerant Gilbert Tennent, supported revival. From 1740-1745 the Boston clergy argued over the itinerants' call for conversion and their attacks against the established clergy.
13. George Whitefield was an Anglican itinerant preacher who preached in the American colonies on seven different tours from 1739 until his death in 1770. Scholars disagree on the dates of the Great Awakening. Some consider it an event encompassing twenty years, 1730-1750. Others, like Edwin Scott Gausted, *The Great Awakening in New England* (New York: Harper and Brothers, 1957), 57, believed the Great Awakening lasted only two years, from 1740-1742. All, however, credit Whitefield with being the revival's real spark.
14. Sam G. Riley, and Gary Selnow, "Southern Magazine Publishing, 1764-1984," *Journalism Quarterly* 64 (1988): 900.
15. The Second Great Awakening or the Great Revival are the names given the religious revival that erupted as the eighteenth century gave way to the nineteenth century. Preachers like Timothy Dwight stirred revival in the North, but that revival paled in comparison with the religious renewal that grew from the preaching of men like James McGready and Barton W. Stone in the area of Cane Ridge, Kentucky. That revival spread eastward and southward to renew religion that had grown, for the most part, dormant. The Baptists, Methodists and Presbyterians developed into the dominant American denominations with this revival. The Second Great Awakening flourished through camp

meetings and helped spawn interest in missions, morals and temperance in America.
16. Stroupe, *The Religious Press*, 4-5. Stroupe, in his introduction, provides a chronological essay of the development of the Southern religious press. The papers and their publishers are the focus.
17. Lemuel Burkitt and Jesse Read, *A Concise History of the Kehukee Baptist Association from its Original Rise Down to 1803*, revised by Henry L. Burkitt (Philadelphia: Lippincott, Grambo and Company, 1850).
18. Two papers, the *North Carolina Evangelical Intelligencer* and the *North Carolina Telegraph*, failed to gather a following in the state during the 1820s. See Johnson, 801.
19. *Presbyterian* (Philadelphia), 1854, quoted in C. C. Goen, *Broken Churches, Broken Nation. Denominational Schism and the Coming of the American Civil War* (Macon: Mercer University Press, 1985), 36.
20. *Minutes*, Baptist State Convention of North Carolina (Raleigh, 1837), 11.
21. *Minutes*, Baptist State Convention of North Carolina (Raleigh, 1859), 28.
22. *Biblical Recorder* (Raleigh), 5 January 1850. No subscription records exist for the *Recorder*. There is occasional mention of numbers in the Baptist State Convention minutes and in 1870, publisher J. H. Mills mentioned printing 2112 editions.
23. Frank Luther Mott, *A History of American Magazines, 1741-1850* (Cambridge: Harvard University Press, 1966), 342.
24. This figure was obtained by studying the content of the *Recorder* in five-year and quarterly increments beginning in 1845. Each news story was counted, but length did not figure into the count. Important religious stories, especially those on believer baptism, were almost always longer than secular news. The comparison of secular and non-secular news items is as follows: 1845-76 religious, 98 non-religious; 1850-76 religious, 142 non-religious; 1855-111 religious, 82 non-religious; 1860-126 religious, 173 non-religious.
25. Frank Luther Mott, *A History of American Magazines, 1865-1885* (Cambridge: Harvard University Press, 1967), 66.
26. Johnson, 775.
27. Mott, *American Journalism*, 513.
28. During the antebellum period some southern ministers and college presidents realized that women, at least intellectually, were not inferior to men. They began to advocate a more serious and thorough education for females. Anne Firor Scott, *The Southern Lady. From Pedestal to Politics 1830-1930* (Chicago and London: The University of Chicago Press, 1970), 67. In addition, Donald G. Mathews, in *Religion in the Old South*, a treatment of antebellum southern religion, states that Baptist, Methodist, and Presbyterian southern churches constructed their religion and subsequently the entire nature of southern life upon woman, her education, and the home.
29. Catharine E. Beecher, *The Evils Suffered by American Women and American Children: The Causes and the Remedy* (New York: Harper & Brothers, Publishers, 1846), 3.
30. Lawrence A. Cremin, *American Education, the National Experience 1783-1876* (New York: Harper & Row, Publishers, 1980), 103. For a full discussion of sectarian education during this period see 107-147. Jane Turner Censer, *North Carolina Planters and Their Children, 1800-1860* (Baton Rouge and London: Louisiana State University Press, 1984), 43- 44.
31. Censer, 46; Barbara Welter, "The Cult of True Womanhood, 1820-1860," *American Quarterly* 18 (1966): 151-174; Mary P. Ryan, *Cradle of the Middle Class. The Family in Oneida County, New York, 1790-1865* (Cambridge: Cambridge University Press, 1981), 235- 238.
32. Ryan, *Cradle of the Middle Class*, 238; Jeanne Boydston, "The Pastorialization of Housework," in Linda K. Kerber and Jane Sherron De Hart, *Women's America*, 3rd ed. (New York and Oxford: Oxford University Press, 1991), 150-151.
33. John S. C. Abbott, *The Mother at Home; or, the Principles of Maternal Duty Familiarly Illustrated*, revised and corrected by Daniel Walton (London: John Mason, 1834), 166, quoted in Cremin, 65.

34. *Mother's Monthly Journal* (January 1836), 10, quoted in Ryan, 101.
35. Laurel Thatch Ulrich, "Vertuous Women Found. New England Ministerial Literature, 1668-1735," in *Women in American Religion*, Janet Wilson James, ed. (Philadelphia: University of Pennsylvania Press, 1980), 67.
36. *Biblical Recorder* (Raleigh), 2 November 1850.
37. The *Biblical Recorder* (Raleigh), 5 October 1850. Since 1930, journalism scholars have studied readership patterns to determine which gender reads certain types of stories in newspapers. George Gallop, "A Scientific Method for Determining Readership-Interest," *Journalism Quarterly* 7 (1930), 11 discovered that women read serial type stories, obituaries, marriages, births and health columns nearly twice as often as men. These types of articles appeared consistently in the *Recorder*. In addition, a 1978 study, David H. Weaver, and John B. Mauro, "Newspaper Readership Patterns," *Journalism Quarterly* 55 (1978), 87 demonstrated that women preferred service items and human interest stories over men. They even read a large amount of local, state and national stories, crime and accident news, and military information. While these studies are based on twentieth-century newspapers, it is a reasonably safe assumption to say the same held true in the antebellum period, especially given the prominence of women within in the church and the unfolding nature of the religious press.
38. Gallop, 11. Announcements made up just over 16.5 percent of the *Recorder* from 1845-1861. Gallop, in his 1930 readership study, found that the readers of these types of news were made up of a surprising large number of women.
39. *Biblical Recorder* (Raleigh), 5 January 1850.
40. Mathews, 120; James Leloudis, "The *Southern Lady's Companion*, 1847-1854: A Study in the Subversion and Modification of the Southern Model of Women" (Honors thesis, University of North Carolina at Chapel Hill, 1977), 51; Eleanor Wolf Thompson, *Education for Ladies, 1830-1860: Ideas on Education in Magazines for Women* (Morningside Heights, NY: King's Crown Press, 1947), 39.
41. *Biblical Recorder* (Raleigh), 5 January 1850.
42. *Biblical Recorder* (Raleigh), 10 May 1850.
43. *Biblical Recorder* (Raleigh), 6 January 1854.
44. Mathews, 101; Gillespie, 148-149.
45. *Biblical Recorder* (Raleigh), 2 November 1850.
46. See Ann Douglas, *The Feminization of American Culture* (New York: Alfred A. Knopf, 1977), 74; and Welter, *Dimity Convictions*, 41.
47. *Biblical Recorder* (Raleigh), 6 April 1850.
48. "Female Piety" embraces the concept that wherever woman was—and we can assume that where she was was in the home—her devotion to family and God produced a sanctuary of safety for the entire family. Her selfless giving produced a calm and protection; therefore, she was glorified. As Jeanne Boydston explained, the glorification of wife and motherhood lay at the heart of the nineteenth-century belief system. This concept of gender spheres, as Boydston and others call the domain of nineteenth-century women, produced a near universal uplifting of American women. Widely read works of the period like Horace Bushnell's *Views of Christian Nurture* and Heman Humphrey's *Domestic Education* promoted these concepts along with a multitude of other works. Daniel C. Eddy wrote, "Home is woman's throne, where she maintains her royal court, and sways her queenly authority" (Boston, 1857), 23.
49. See Linda K. Kerber and Jane Sherron De Hart, eds., *Women's America*, 3rd ed. (New York and Oxford: Oxford University Press, 1991), 9-22; Ryan, 98-104; Cremin 64-66.
50. *Biblical Recorder*, 5 September 1855.
51. Matthew 21:42; Mark 12:10; Luke 20:17; quoting Psalm 118: 22-23. The same concept is reiterated in Acts 4:11 and 1 Peter 2:6-7.
52. Acts 4:12.
53. Ephesians 2:20-21.

10

Mississippi's Fire-Eating Editor Ethelbert Barksdale and the Election of 1860

Nancy McKenzie Dupont
Loyola University - New Orleans

On January 9, 1861, Mississippi became the second state to secede from the United States of America. This set in motion a series of events that would prove disastrous for Mississippians. Late in life, former governor James Lusk Alcorn described the secession crisis: "(Mississippi) was hurled from its seat of prosperous repose and unquestioned power into the embrace of causeless, cruel, and bloody war."[1] Secession came as a direct response to the election of Abraham Lincoln, which was perceived as a direct threat to slavery. It is appropriate to investigate the role of the newspaper editors in leading Southerners to Civil War. In South Carolina, the leading fire-eater was unquestionably Robert Barnwell Rhett, politician and newspaper editor, who used the forum of his Charleston *Mercury* to lead the call for secession.[2] A vocal fire-eater also emerged in Mississippi in the form of Ethelbert Barksdale, politician and editor of the Jackson *Mississippian*. Barksdale's influence on antebellum journalism in Mississippi was overpowering: "When the paper (the *Mississippian*) roared in Mississippi all the little country papers yelped."[3]

Mississippi voters went to the polls to choose delegates for a constitutional convention on December 20, 1860, the same day that a South Carolina delegation voted unanimously to leave the Union. For 20 days, South Carolina stood alone as the only seceded state while Mississippians debated their own course of action. Mississippi's position on secession at this time was far from clear: only 60 per cent of the voters who cast ballots in the November presidential election went to the polls on December 20.[4] And though the potential convention delegates were not required to state their position on secession, it is clear that true anti-secessionists ran for election in 34 of Mississippi's 60 counties.[5]

How, then, did Mississippi decide to leave the Union? Because the Constitutional Convention followed so closely the November election and because so few voted in the December election, it is apparent that much can be learned from the rhetoric of the 1860 presidential campaign. As an influential newspaper editor, Barksdale's contributions to Mississippi's 1860 decision are considerable.

Barksdale's Life

Barksdale was 35 in 1860. Born in Rutherford County, Tennessee, he had moved to Mississippi during his childhood. He was one year older than his better-known brother, Confederate General William Barksdale, who was killed at Gettysburg on July 3, 1863.[6] Still, Ethelbert Barksdale was notable in his own right. He was hot-tempered with a flair for prose and a yen for conflict. Newspapers, especially during the era of personal journalism, seemed an ideal vocation for him.

At 20, Barksdale began his career by editing the *Yazoo City Democrat*. In 1850, he moved to Jackson and bought a controlling interest in the *Mississippian*.[7] But politics was also his calling: He was a delegate to the 1860 Democratic National Convention in Charleston, a member of the Confederate Congress, and, in 1882 and 1884, he was elected to serve in the U.S. House of Representatives. He served on the platform committees for the Democratic party in 1868, 1870, 1872, and 1880.[8] But for all of his political success, he had many failures: His campaigns to become governor ended without even obtaining a nomination in 1877 and 1881, and he was defeated for the U.S. House in 1890 and for the U.S. Senate in 1892.[9] His contemporaries offer some clues as to why his political ambitions were not realized. Mississippi Civil War hero and politician Reuben Davis wrote:

> Barksdale was the ablest paragraph writer the State has ever afforded. His fault was that he was too caustic and severe. Some of his paragraphs were electric batteries, which produced a shock from which only those victims who were blessed with strong nerves and great recuperative powers could recover. . .He rarely laughed, and there was something in his smile which indicated more of malice than of mirth.[10]

Fellow newspaperman R. H. Henry, who owned and edited the Jackson *Clarion-Ledger*, wrote of Barksdale:

> Major Barksdale had a way of doing things after his own plan with no fear of imitators. He perhaps made more editors and public men mad than any other politician in the state, and rarely was there a reconcilement, for, as a rule, when Barksdale crossed the Rubicon he burnt his bridges behind him.[11]

An account of Barksdale's actions at a political meeting were printed in another newspaper:

> ...Major Barksdale hurled a book and struck Money, who was near the rostrum. The same scene has repeated, violent language meantime having been exchanged.[12]

But at Barksdale's death in Yazoo City, Mississippi, on February 17, 1893, the *Daily Clarion-Ledger* of Jackson reported none of the controversy surrounding his life. The fact that Barksdale had served as editor of that newspaper, in between his various political activities, may have influenced the editorial writer's assessment of Barksdale's contributions: "Love of Mississippi and Democracy was his ruling motive--was the most deeply rooted sentiment in the heart that is now stilled."[13]

Barksdale in 1860

Before becoming one of Mississippi's leading secessionists, Barksdale supported John C. Breckinridge in the presidential campaign of 1860. As early as June 27, 1860, Barksdale was writing about disunion talk and blaming it on the North:

> Wherever any opposition or resistance is made in the South to the aggressions of the

General Government, the cry is immediately raised of "disunion." It does not seem to occur to the aggressors, that *they are disunionists*. Disunion, which follows a perverted Union, is the work of the perverters.[14]

But Breckinridge did not support disunion; his position on Southern rights was weaker than some.[15] Breckinridge fought against the tendency to label him a secessionist; he challenged his enemies to "point out an act, to disclose an utterance, to reveal a thought of mine hostile to the Constitution and the union of the States."[16] It is also surprising that Barksdale had such contempt for Stephen A. Douglas, the Illinois senator who had financial interests in Mississippi.[17] Yet in October 1860, Barksdale's *Mississippian* proclaimed: "How is catastrophe to be averted? It is by giving a united Southern vote for Breckinridge."[18] To understand how Barksdale arrived at such a conclusion, it is necessary to examine his role in the Democratic National Convention at Charleston in April 1860.

The convention was already divided by the time the first gavel fell. The protection of slavery in U.S. territories was the controversy of the day caused by a dual interpretation of the Democratic platform of 1856. Southern Democrats interpreted that platform as protecting territorial slavery, while northern Democrats believed it supported the right of the territory to determine for itself whether slavery would be allowed.[19] The latter became an antebellum buzz-word: "popular sovereignty." Douglas believed that popular sovereignty offered the best chance of compromise between North and South. The Southern delegations went to Charleston anxious to defend what they believed were their rights.

Barksdale was head of the Mississippi Democratic delegation and was selected to present the viewpoints of all southern delegations. He was noticed at the convention and a fellow journalist observed, "He is full of fire and prone to fly off the handle...there is a dangerous glitter in his eye."[20] In his speech, he asked that Democrats take a stand for the principle that only the states could decide on the legality of slavery in a territory while it remained a territory. He asked the convention to:

> ...remove these doubts, to clear away those obstacles to harmony, to blaze out the way that these faithful followers of the Democratic flag must go so plain that even amid the storms of contending factions the faithful advocates of principles may read them inscribed upon its glittering folds.[21]

He concluded with a message directed to the southern states:

...remain firm, be the consequences what they may. Let an abiding faith in the justice and purity of your doctrines, in their efficacy, if carried out, to preserve the equality of the States, guide your counsels in this hour of peril, light up your pathway, and through the storms and darkness conduct you to victory.22

The South needed such a pep talk. When the convention failed to adopt the majority platform committee report, choosing instead the minority popular sovereignty platform of the Douglasites, seven southern delegations including Mississippi walked out of the convention. The rest of the convention adjourned to meet later in Baltimore in June, where Douglas was nominated, but 105 of the delegates were meeting at another location in Baltimore, nominating Breckinridge.23 Before the election in November, yet another party, the Constitutional Union, would be formed with John Bell of Tennessee as their candidate.24 The new party's only platform was to stand on the rights guaranteed in the Constitution.

Backing Breckinridge

Without delay, Barksdale began promoting Breckinridge and defiling Douglas in the *Mississippian*. Each semi-weekly issue contained these words in one of its columns: *For President, John C. Breckinridge of Kentucky*. Barksdale never hesitated to use name calling either in the election campaign or in the days before the Constitutional Convention. In June, he denounced what he called the "Squatter Sovereignty Democrats of the North and South":

> They charge the opposition to Mr. Douglas as an opposition to the Union. Hence, Douglas and the Union are identical. Disunion and his defeat are one. His opponents are traitors, between whom and the Abolitionists the great union saver stands. All this is to be expected.25

Barksdale ended this column with a challenge to both the North and the South:

> The Southern States are engaged in a contest not merely for their rights in our Territories, but for the Constitution and for liberty...If our adversaries think that we can be cowed by words—terrified by denunciation—or made submissive by threats—certainly they ought to use them.26

But how much of Barksdale's writing is in support of Breckinridge and how much is mere emotional verbiage meant to stir up Mississippians to respond to an Abraham Lincoln victory? Barksdale wrote about Lincoln:

> He is an abolitionist in the strictest sense. To prevent his accession to power must now be the great aim and effort of the South, and of all everywhere who would save this Union and uphold its constitution. The possibility (not to say probability) of Lincoln's election renders the question of what shall be the course of the South from now onward, one of the most momentous which a people were ever called upon to decide.27

All the while, he kept the pressure on the Douglas faction:

> We are happy to announce that the Douglas faction in this state is beginning to show signs of walking alone, and like a spoilt child, the first thing it does is to make faces at and strike its nurse who watched over its helpless infancy.28

But in reality, Breckinridge had only one true opponent in Mississippi: John Bell. Unlike South Carolina, which had states' righters as leaders, Mississippi's interest in the 1860 crisis had to do with preserving the status quo. Many old Whig party members still believed that the status quo was best preserved inside the union. The leading secessionists in Mississippi were not the old guard but the younger lawyers and newspaper editors.29 Thus, the Constitutional Union party gained some followers. Barksdale realized this and attacked Bell:

> There is not a single state North in which Mr. Bell's friends pretend that he has half enough strength to carry it. What then is the use of his friends running him in the South?30

But run him in the South they did; both the Natchez *Courier* and the Vicksburg *Whig* endorsed Bell. In contrast to the dour and serious writing of Barksdale, the *Whig* decided to have some fun with the campaign. The newspaper offered in jest to take 12 bets with anyone willing to make them. Among them were: "$500 that Lincoln can't carry 150 strong gin cocktails at one time," and, in a prophetic prediction, "$500 that the Union out lives the disunionists."31 The Whig concluded its joke with a dare: "These are bets to be taken together. We are sick of so much talk. Let us put up some money."32

Conspiracy Theories

Barksdale's public support of Breckingridge was not as great as one might have expected, which may lead one to wonder if the newspaper editor actually wanted a Lincoln victory. Historians have promoted this theory to explain the divisions of loyalties among Southern voters. If they had wanted to defeat Lincoln, why not unite behind one candidate? But such a view disregards the emotions of the day. Historian David Potter writes of these explanations, "They are too rational. The delegates at Charleston and at Baltimore were operating in an atmosphere in which gusts of emotion constantly swept the floor as well as the galleries. In the midst of this turmoil, men took positions which led on to consequences that they did not visualize."33 Mississippi historian Percy Rainwater believes it was "childish nonsense"34 that precipitated secession after the Lincoln election.

> The philosophy of history may, indeed, give one lofty and sublime ideas of human nature; but it annals are filled with the grotesque, the ridiculous, and the vulgar...Amid the existing scenes of bitter conflicts, man's rationalizations are modified, and sometimes prevented, by his emotions.35

Because Barksdale left no personal papers, historians will never know if he was truly supporting a Lincoln candidacy to force the issue on secession. The only evidence of his true feelings is his actions after election day.

The Deed is Done

The final tally of votes in Mississippi on election day 1860 was:

For Breckinridge electors	39,962
For Bell electors	24,693
For Douglas electors	3,597 36

Ironically, Douglas had spent a considerable amount of time campaigning in the South and followed the election returns in the newsroom of the Mobile *Register*.37 He had tried repeatedly to convince the South that it had more protection within the Union than outside of it. On election night, Douglas tried to convince the Mobile newspaper to refrain from calling for a constitutional convention in response to the Lincoln election, but he was not successful.38

In Mississippi, Barksdale was ready for similar action. The headline in the November 14 issue read: "The Deed is Done— Disunion is the Remedy":

> The outrages which abolition fanaticism has continued year by year to heap upon the

South, have at length culminated in the election of Abraham Lincoln and Hannibal Hamlin, avowed Abolitionists, to the Presidency and Vice-Presidency—both bigoted, unscrupulous and cold blooded enemies of the peace and equality of the slaveholding States, and one of the pair strongly marked with the blood of his negro ancestry. . . .Secession is the remedy. Let us take our own rights and institutions in our own keeping. There is safety in no other course.[39]

And he assured his readers there would be no devastating war:

...Why, Lincoln could not control this little establishment of an army against us if he would. Probably one half the number are composed of Southern men, and when the fighting comes they will be found on the side of the South.[40]

In January 1861, the *Mississippian* became a weekly rather than semi-weekly newspaper. No explanation was ever published for this change is production. By August 1861, the writings in the *Mississippian* consisted mostly of lists of wounded and killed Southern soldiers who had joined the cause Barksdale promoted. On September 18, Barksdale's name disappeared from the newspaper and was replaced by two new names: F. T. Cooper and A. N. Kimball, Editors and Proprietors. No explanation was given for the change in ownership. It is possible that Barksdale's participation in the Confederate Congress prevented his continuing work with his newspaper. In 1863, Barksdale paid war's painful price when his brother was killed in battle.

Conclusion

Barksdale's support of Breckinridge may have appeared lukewarm, but it was an important move for his future success. First, because Barksdale spoke so strongly at the Charleston convention and was willing to walk out with his colleagues, his political career was launched; no longer would Barksdale be only a newspaper editor. Second, it allowed him to voice opposition to the Bell and Douglas factions which advocated the South seeking Constitutional protection within the Union; he could lean toward disunion by denouncing the Constitutionalists. Though his intentions during the presidential election may not be clear, it is evident that Barksdale's strong language was against any compromise with the North.

Legal scholar Paul Chevigny has charged that freedom of speech in the South in the days leading up to the Civil War may have been severely compromised.[41] There is much evidence to support this charge, and Ethelbert Barksdale provides one more example of a politically-motivated newspaper editor who was willing to promote his views at the expense of all others. However, the existence of two newspapers (in cotton-producing Adams and Warren counties) willing to support Bell instead of Breckinridge demonstrates that there were options to Barksdale's fire-eating rhetoric. At any time, the people of Mississippi could have decided that Barksdale was wrong.

In his essay, "The Blundering Generation," historian J.G. Randall investigates the reasons why an entire generation of Americans managed to stumble into a bloody war; he contends that none of the explanations for the causes of the Civil War has ever made sense. He points out that very few secession promoters became actual leaders of the Confederacy.[42] Barksdale is an exception to that rule. Barksdale's fiery personality led him into personal and public conflicts all of his life; it was as if he had to be in the middle of the fighting. At the end of Barksdale's life, the Jackson *Clarion-Ledger* said, "It will be the verdict of history that he was predominantly a man for a crisis."[43]

Notes

1. Quoted in Percy Lee Rainwater, *Mississippi: Storm Center of Secession, 1856-1861* (Baton Rouge: Otto Claitor, 1938), 214.
2. See Laura A. White, *Robert Barnwell Rhett: Father of Secession* (New York: Praeger, 1972); and Carl R. Osthaus, *Partisans of the Southern Press: Editorial Spokesmen of the Nineteenth Century* (The University Press of Kentucky, 1994), 69-94.
3. Anonymous statement quoted in William David Sloan, James G. Stovall, and James D. Startt, *The Media in America: A History*, 2nd ed. (Scottsdale, AZ: Publishing Horizons, Inc.)
4. Avery O. Craven, *The Growth of Southern Nationalism, 1848-1861* (Baton Rouge: Louisiana State University Press, 1951), 364.
5. Ralph A. Wooster, "The Secession Convention of the Lower South: A Study of Their Membership" (Ph.D. diss., University of Texas at Austin, 1954).
6. John A. Barksdale, *Barksdale Family History and Genealogy* (Published by the author, 1940), 286.
7. *Daily Clarion-Ledger* (Jackson, MS), 17 February, 1893.
8. *Ibid.*
9. Dunbar Rowland, *Encyclopedia of Mississippi History* (The Southern Historical Publishing Association, 1907),213.
10. Reuben Davis, *Recollections of Mississippi and Mississippians* (Boston and New York: Houghton, Mifflin and Co., 1890), 353.
11. R.H. Henry, *Editors I Have Known Since the Civil War* (New Orleans: Press of E.S. Upton Printing Company, 1922), 94.
12. *Port Gibson Reveille*, 22 July 1891, p. 2, cited in Owen Peterson, "Ethelbert Barksdale in the Democratic National Convention of 1860," *The Journal of Mississippi History* 14 (1952), 264.
13. *Daily Clarion-Ledger* (Jackson, MS), 17 February, 1893, p.3.
14. *Mississippian*, 27 June, 1860, p 1.

15. Frank C. Heck, "John C. Breckinridge in the Crisis of 1860-61," *The Journal of Southern History* 21 (3), (1955), 316.
16. *Ibid.*, 327.
17. The complete story of Douglas's management of two slave-labor Mississippi plantations is found in Anita Clinton, "Stephen Arnold Douglas—His Mississippi Experience," *The Journal of Mississippi History* 50 (June 1988), 56-88.
18. *Mississippian,* 3 October, 1860, 1.
19. Owen Peterson, "Ethelbert Barksdale in the Democratic National Convention of 1860," *The Journal of Mississippi History*, 14 (1952) 258.
20. *Daily Clarion-Ledger*, 23 February, 1893, p. 1, cited in Donald E. Reynolds, *Editors Make War* (Nashville, TN: Vanderbilt University Press, 1966).
21. *Ibid.*, 274.
22. *Ibid.*, 276
23. David M. Potter, *The Impending Crisis, 1848-1861* (New York: Harper and Row, 1976), 413.
24. *Ibid.*, 417.
25. *Mississippian*, 27 June, 1860, p1.
26. *Ibid.*
27. *Mississippian*, 18 July, 1860, p. 1.
28. *Mississippian*, 26 September, 1860, p. 1.
29. Percy Lee Rainwater, "An Analysis of the Secession Controversy in Mississippi, 1854-61," *Mississippi Valley Historical Review* 24 (June 1937-March 1938), 37.
30. *Mississippian*, 3 October, 1860, p. 1.
31. *Vicksburg Whig,* 7 November, 1860, p. 1.
32. *Ibid.*
33. Potter, *Impending Crisis,* 414.
34. Rainwater, "An Analysis," 39.
35. *Ibid.*
36. Rainwater, *Storm Center,* 199.
37. Robert W. Johannsen, "Stephen A. Douglas and the South," *The Journal of Southern History* 33 (1967), 47.
38. *Ibid.*, 48.
39. *Mississippian*, 14 November, 1860, p. 1.
41. Paul Chevigny, *More Speech: Dialogue Rights and Modern Liberty* (Philadelphia: Temple University Press, 1935), 103.
42. J.G. Randall, "The Blundering Generation," *Mississippi Valley Historical Review* 27 (June 1940), 3-28.
43. *Daily Clarion-Ledger* (Jackson, MS) 17 February, 1893, p. 3.

11

Agenda-Setting in Antebellum East Tennessee

S. Kittrell Rushing
University of Tennessee at Chattanooga

East Tennessee during the secession crisis provides an opportunity to explore the use of modern mass communication theories better to understand the historical relationships between a society and its media.

Southern antebellum newspapers are supposed to have exercised a great deal of power during the 1860-1861 secession crisis. Abraham Lincoln and his "Black Republicans" were so despised in the South that neither the party nor Lincoln were on Southern states' ballots. The election contest in the south was between Constitutional Union candidate John Bell and the candidate of the southern splinter of the Democratic Party, John Breckinridge (Stephen Douglas also campaigned in the south but received few votes).

A standard interpretation of the crisis surrounding the two elections is that after Lincoln's election Southern newspapers led the way in altering Southern attitudes toward the Union (Reynolds, 1970).

East Tennessee did not follow willingly into secession athough the region supported neither Lincoln nor the Northern Democratic candidate, Stephen Douglas. The section voted Constitutional Union in 1860 and voted heavily against secession in the election of 1861.

East Tennessee was less dependent on slavery than most of the South, and during the secession crisis, most East Tennesseans apparently saw little future in supporting Southern independence. In the June, 1861, referendum, East Tennesseans voted two to one against secession, and after Tennessee officially seceded, most East Tennesseans rejected the authority of the Southern Confederacy (Bryan, 1988).

The influence of East Tennessee newspapers on public opinion is difficult to gauge 150 years after the fact, but at least two benefits result from the effort. If one applies twentieth century agenda-setting theory to 19th-century press influence a more complete understanding may be achieved of the relationship between the antebellum press and its readership. The second value of looking at the links between a nineteenth century culture and its media is new understandings or appreciations for twentieth century press-culture relationships.

Review of Literature

The majority of nineteenth century newspaper readers knew their editors and generally thought of them as well informed. Country people, especially, trusted the judgment of their community's newspaper editor and accepted editorial slanting as a matter of course.

Small town editors of the nineteenth century often fit easily into twentieth century the definitions of mass communication two-step flow theory. For example, Lazarsfeld, Berelson, and Gaudet hypothesized that ideas flow from print to opinion leaders and from the opinion leaders to less socially or politically involved sections of the population (Lazarsfeld, Berelson, & Gaudet, 1948).

Because nineteenth century editors were close to their readers another fact is significant: the editors shared the people's prejudices and respected their mores (Clark, 1948).

The basic influences which the country papers exerted on local opinion were more personal than formal editorializing. Clark believed that editors were active, engaged members of their communities. They were part of the Southern social system's elite. However, the consequences could be strong when the editors moved in a direction not in keeping with prevailing attitudes and beliefs. Moderate *Chattanooga Gazette* editor James Hood gave up his newspaper and left Chattanooga because, as he remembered it, his "political views were not acceptable to fellow citizens who then "ruled the roost" (McGehee, 1988).

Southern sympathizers accused Knoxville *Whig* publisher William "Parson" Brownlow of treason and libel and threatened him with lashings, tar and feathers, and death. The Parson, a loyal aggressive Unionist, was also a supporter of slavery. As a result he received criticism as well from abolitionists (Humphrey, 1978). Unlike Hood, Brownlow kept publishing until jailed by the Confederates.

Modern readers tend to select information which supports their own point of view (Burns & Peltason, 1968). This is an important observation when one assesses the impact of media. People tend to pay attention to information which supports what they already believe.

Modern research findings seem to support the mutual influence and mutual reinforcement between audiences and their media. Don Reynolds, writing about nineteenth century readers and their media, made observations similar to twentieth century researchers (Reynolds, 1970).

A relationship between voting behavior and editorial slant should be identifiable if a tie existed during the turmoil of the secession crisis between newspapers and audience attitudes and beliefs.

Methodology

Results from the presidential election of 1860 and the secession election of June, 1861, are available for 28 East Tennessee counties. Fairly accurate counts of the number of antebellum newspapers published in East Tennessee exist, and of those newspapers publishing just prior to the crisis some evidence remains of their political slant.

The method used to explore a relationship between East Tennessee newspapers and voting behavior is to compare the number of newspapers in a county, the political slant of the newspapers, and the county's voting behavior.

Relatively few East Tennessee newspapers remain from the years just preceding the outbreak of hostilities. Of those that are preserved, no concrete way exists to determine the actual circulation. However, examination of the existing papers does often reveal the political slant of the editor.

Analysis of Data

According to information available from the Tennessee State Archives 16 newspapers were published in East Tennessee during the secession crisis—1860 and 1861.

Of those East Tennessee newspapers with an identifiable editorial slant, six aligned with the Southern wing of the Democratic Party. Three of the six, *The Chattanooga Advertiser, Chattanooga Reflector* and the *Cleveland Banner,* were located in the southern part of the state. Three of the Democratic papers, *The Knoxville Register, Jonesborough Union,* and *Greeneville Democrat* were in the northern part of the section.

Two of the six East Tennessee Whig papers, *The Chattanooga Gazette* and the *Athens Post,* published in the southern portion of the sector. The other four Whig papers were located in upper East Tennessee. Three, all controlled in some way by the infamous Parson Brownlow, were located in Knoxville (Humphrey, 1978).

Table two is a master listing of East Tennessee counties, the newspapers categorized by editorial slant, and the county by county vote totals for the 1860 presidential election and the 1861 secession vote. The election data is from Verton M. Queener's 1941 article, "The Origin of the Republican Party in East Tennessee."(Queener, 1941).

TABLE 1.
Newspapers and Editorial Slant 1860-1861 and 1860-1861 Vote

County	Whig Papers	Dem Papers	Unknown Slant	Dem Vote 1860	Whig Vote 1860	Secession Vote 1861	Union Vote 1861
Anderson	0	0	0	369	614	97	1276
Bledsoe	0	0	0	215	361	197	500
Blount	0	0	0	633	1261	418	1766
Bradley	0	1	1	1060	710	507	1382
Campbell	0	0	0	291	345	59	1000
Carter	0	0	0	220	839	86	1343
Claiborne	0	0	0	728	614	250	1243
Cocke	0	0	0	487	933	518	1185
Grainger	0	0	0	684	1047	586	1492
Greene	0	1	1	2092	1048	744	2691
Hawkins	0	0	0	1239	1067	908	1460
Hamilton	1	2	0	985	1074	854	1260
Hancock	0	0	0	511	309	279	630
Jefferson	0	0	0	716	1623	603	1987
Johnson	0	0	0	144	508	111	787
Knox	3	1	0	1087	2417	1226	3196
McMinn	1	0	0	1119	986	904	1144
Meigs	0	0	0	609	150	481	267
Marion	0	0	0	403	498	414	600
Monroe	0	0	0	1151	915	1096	774
Morgan	0	0	0	264	165	50	630
Polk	0	0	1	888	396	738	317
Rhea	0	0	0	410	289	360	202
Roane	0	0	0	882	1105	454	1568
Sevier	0	0	0	195	1035	60	1528
Scott	0	0	0	155	252	19	521
Sullivan	0	0	1	1586	358	1586	627
Washington	1	1	0	1398	967	1022	1445
Totals	6	6	4	20521	21886	14627	32821

When the election returns from 1860 are paired with those from 1861 and analyzed using a t-test for paired samples, the 1860 Whig vote for president and the 1861 vote for union are related at a statistically significant level. (t value = -3.63, df = 10, 2-tail prob = .005) (Norusis, 1990).

A similar significant relationship exists between the 1860 Democratic vote and the 1861 vote for secession.

(t value = 2.58, df = 10, 2-tail prob = .027) (Norusis, 1990).

In other words, the data indicate that those who voted Whig tended to vote for Union, those who voted Democratic tended to vote for secession.

However, when one attempts to analyze the presence of newspapers and county vote totals the comparison is more difficult.

TABLE 2.
Democratic Newspapers 1860-1861 and 1860 Democratic Vote

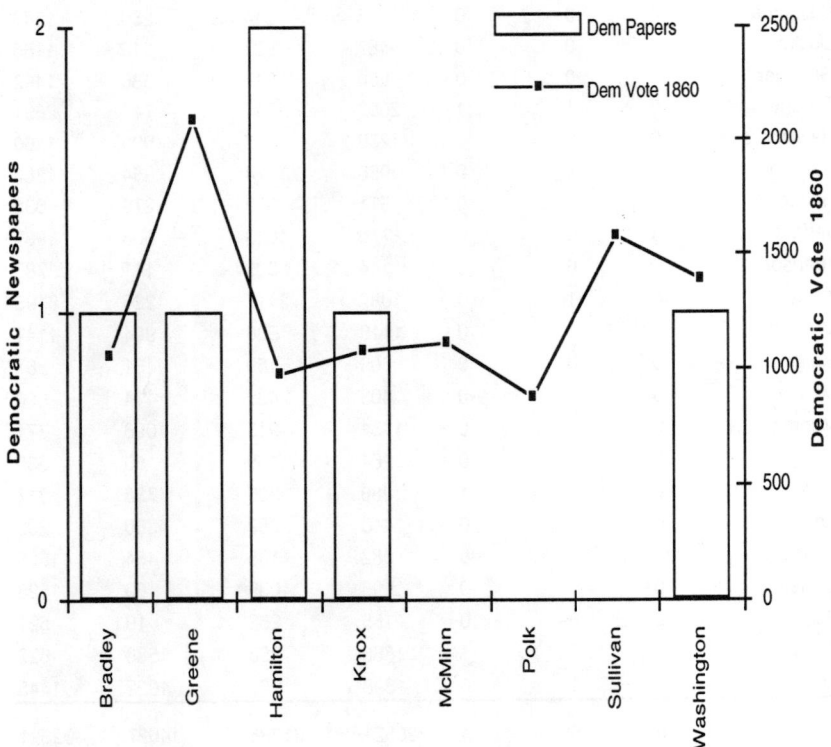

Table 2 portrays the East Tennessee counties in which newspapers published during the crisis. The table contains the number of papers, and the 1860 Democratic vote. Cell values are too low (0 to 2) to undertake meaningful statistical analysis of the relationship; however, visual examination seems to indicate little relationship between the presence of Democratic newspapers and vote totals.

TABLE 3.
Democratic Newspapers 1860-1861 and 1861 Vote for Secession

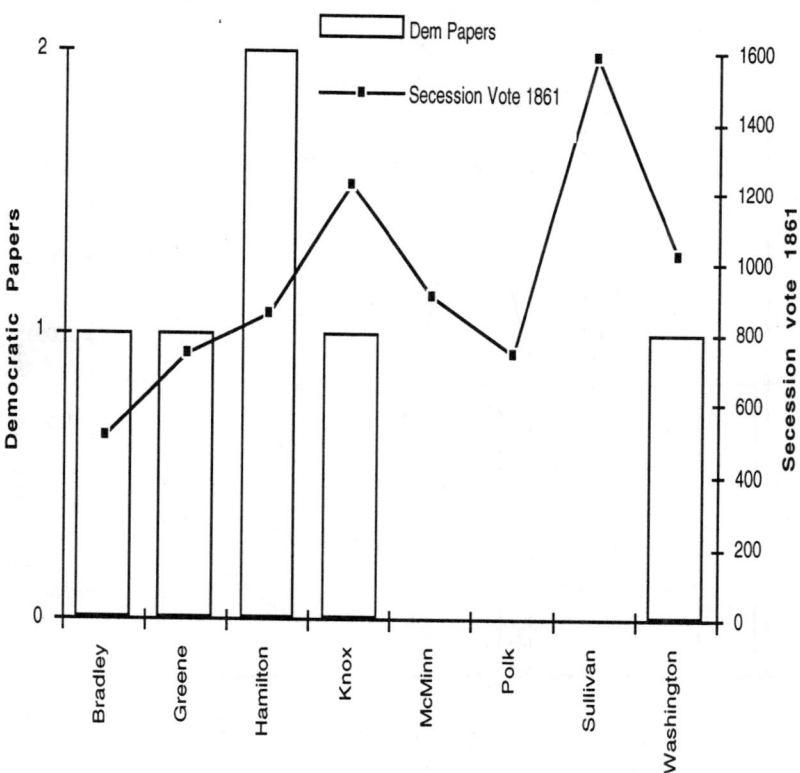

Table 3 compares the 1850-1861 presence of Democratic newspapers and the 1861 secession vote. Once again, little apparent relationship exists between vote totals and the presence of newspapers.

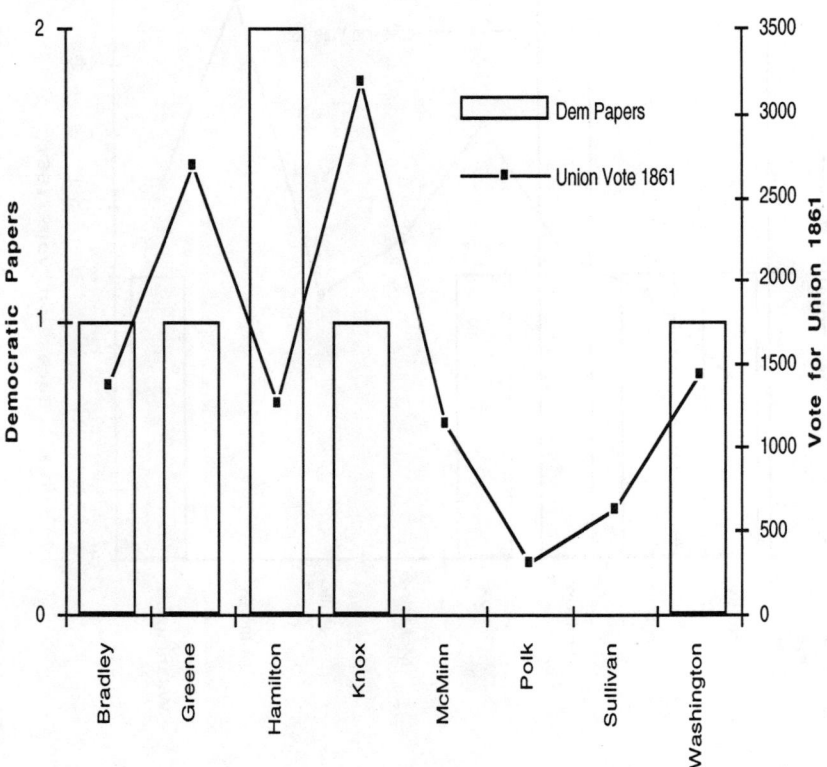

TABLE 4.
Democratic Newspapers 1850-1861 and 1861 Vote for Union

An interesting element of the Table 4 comparison is the low vote for Union in McMinn, Polk, and Sullivan counties. The three are counties without Democratic papers. If the editorial slant of papers generated a heavy impact on public opinion, this graph of Union votes probably should be reversed. In other words, the vote for Union should be higher in counties without Democrat leaning papers and lower in those counties with a Democrat leaning publication. That is not what one finds.

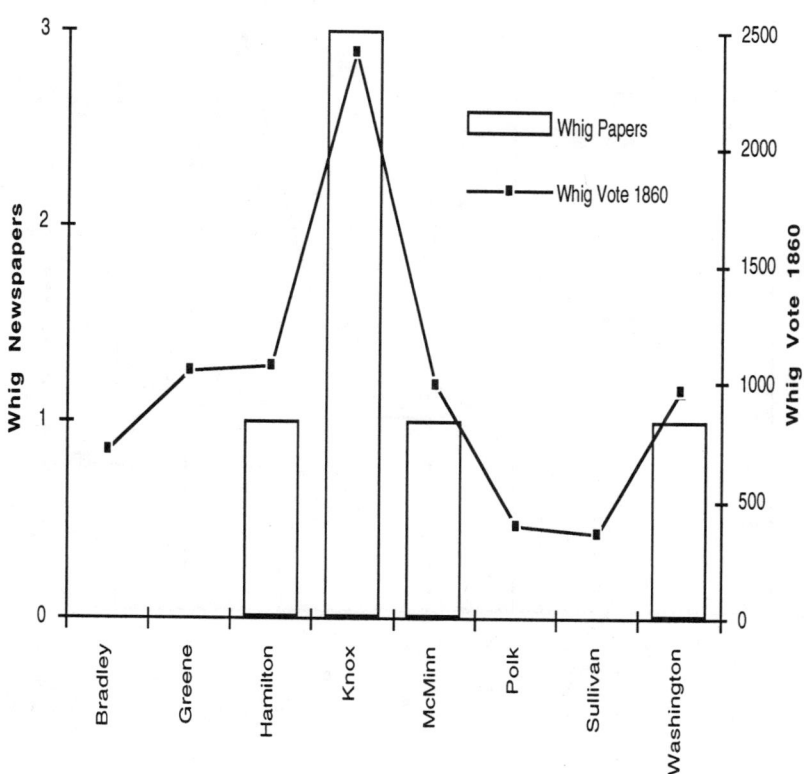

TABLE 5.
Whig Newspapers 1850-1861 and 1860 Whig Vote

The heavily Whig characteristics of Knox county are apparent in Table 5. The table also supports the hypothesis that Whig leaning newspapers would foster a higher Whig vote. The overlay of the 1860 Whig vote over number of newspapers seems, at last, to demonstrate a relationship between newspaper and voting behavior.

Knox county's outspoken newspaper publisher and editor, Parson Brownlow, during the crisis operated at least three newspapers, the

Knoxville Whig, The Knoxville Whig and Independent Journal, and *Brownlow's Tri-Weekly Whig.* The county voted two to one for John Bell, the Constitutional Union (Whig) candidate in the 1860 presidential election. Knox county voters followed in June of the next year by voting overwhelmingly against secession, 3,196 to 1,226.

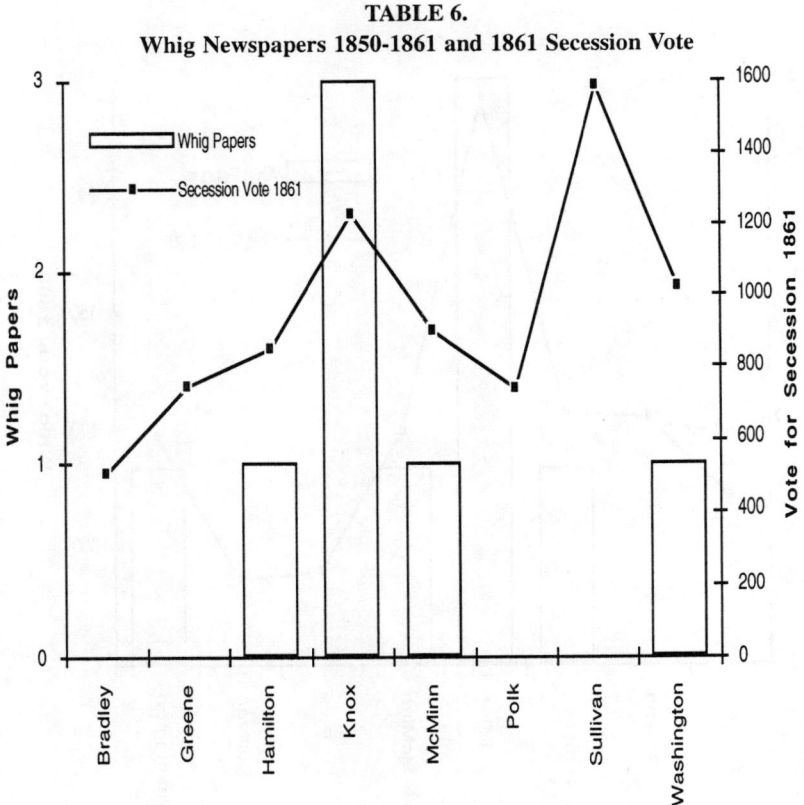

Table 6 illustrates the number of Whig newspapers and the 1861 vote for secession. Some visible relationship seems to exist between the number of newspapers and voting patterns. Interestingly, the direction of the relationship, as was shown earlier in Table 4,

"Democratic Newspapers and Vote for Union," also goes against that which might be expected. Whig newspapers should be related to a lessening of the secession vote. The expectation is not supported by the data illustrated in the tables..

TABLE 7.
Whig Newspapers 1850-1861 and 1861 Vote for Union

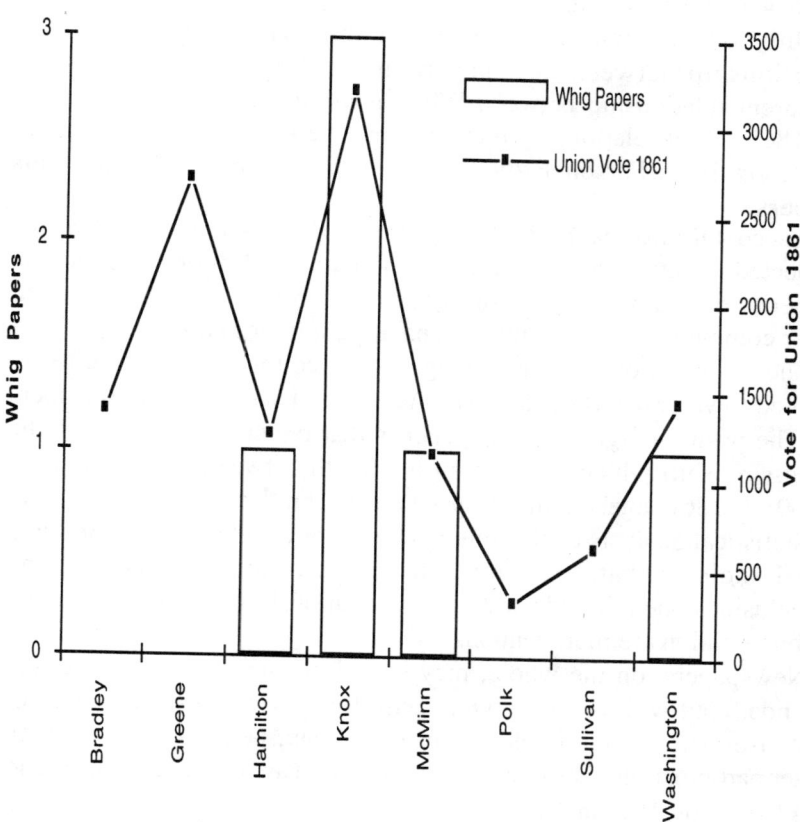

Table 7 illustrates the vote for union and the number of Whig newspapers. This comparison, with the exceptions of Bradley and Greene counties, fits expectations. Voting for the Union seems to be related to the presence of Union supporting newspapers.

Summary and Conclusions

Some visible relationship seems apparent between the presence of newspapers and county election returns. However, the direction of the relationship was not always as one might expect.

For example, counties that voted for the democratic presidential candidates tended to vote for secession. Therefore, if newspapers are directly related to public opinion, the expectation should be that counties with a Democratic newspaper should have a higher proportion of secession votes than counties with Whig newspapers. That was not the case.

Only one comparison closely fit the hypothesis of a direct relationship between newspapers and voting. That fit was the apparent relationship between Whig newspapers and the Whig vote of 1860. That relationship may be more the result of the personality of Knoxville's Parson Brownlow than the editorial content of his papers.

Anecdotal information seems to support the observation that media reflected the attitudes and values of the readers. Editors who had the temerity or courage to publish material not in sync with the views of their community received threats and at least in one case left town.

The influence of a prominent, aggressive editor appears more likely related to voter behavior than was the editorial slant of the newspaper.

The position argued in this paper is that rather than fomenting the secession shift which occurred in the South between the elections of 1860 and 1861, antebellum newspapers at most reflected existing opinion.

Statistical analysis of the vote results from the election of 1860 and 1861 indicate that a relationship between the two existed. The conclusions one might draw about the relationship between media and public opinion are more tenuous.

Newspapers, on the whole, may have lead the discussion, "set the agenda," but with one exception, East Tennessee newspapers did not exercise visibly identifiable power other than, perhaps, to encourage voter participation. The one notable exception are the papers edited and published by Parson Brownlow.

Analysis of 20th-century media influence based on nineteenth century evidence may suggest that twentieth century mass media, although changed dramatically in appearance, reach, and use, continue to reflect public opinion and foment discussion.

However, based on the evidence developed in this paper, one might hypothesize that mass media of the twentieth century, like their antebellum progenitors, probably do not impact dramatically on attitudes and beliefs. Perhaps, the variable of greater influence is the social standing and community acceptance of the editors, publishers, and other real people, community leaders, associated with a publication.

Notes

Bryan, C. F., Jr. (1988). Tories' Amidst Rebels: Confederate Occupation of East Tennessee, 1861-1863,. *East Tennessee Historical Society's Publications,* 60, 3-22.

Burns, J. M., & Peltason, J. W. (1968). *Government by the People.* Englewood Cliffs: Prentice-Hall.

Clark, T. D. (1948). The Country Newspaper: A Factor in Southern Opinion, 1865-1930. *The Journal of Southern History,* XIV(1), 3-33.

Cohen, B. C. (1963). *The Press and Foreign Policy.* Princeton: Princeton University Press.

Humphrey, S. (1978). *"That D——d Brownlow," Being a Saucy & Malicious Description of Fighting Parson William Gannaway Brownlow, Knoxville Editor and Stalwart Unionist Who Rose from a Confederate Jail to become One of the Most Famous Personages in the Nation, Denounced by his Enemies as Vicious and Harsh, Praised by his Friends as Compassionate and Gentle.* Boone, North Carolina: Appalachian Consortium.

Lazarsfeld, P. F., Berelson, B., & Gaudet, H. (1948). *The People's Choice.* New York: Columbia University Press.

McCombs, M. E., & Shaw, D. E. (1972). The Agenda Setting Function of the Mass Media. *Public Opinion Quarterly,* 36(Summer 1972), 176.

McGehee, C. S. (1988). The Property and Faith of the City: Secession and Chattanooga. *East Tennessee Historical Society's Publications,* 60, 23-38.

Norusis, M. J. (1990). *SPSS for Macintosh* (4.01 ed.). Chicago: SPSS Inc.

Queener, V. M. (1941). The Origin of the Republican Party in East Tennessee. *The East Tennessee Historical Society's Publications,* 13, 66-90.

Reynolds, D. E. (1970). *Editors Make War: Southern Newspapers in the Secession Crisis.* Nashville: Vanderbilt University.

12

Between Tradition and Innovation: The Nature of Antebellum News in the *Courant*

Robert Dardenne
University of South Florida-St. Petersburg

Profound influences on American journalism during the period between the 1830s and the Civil War are attributed to the New York penny papers. But the antebellum era was rich in expansion and change that came from many sources. News during the period reflected the modern and some might say revolutionary influences of the Penny Press and the stable and some might say old-fashioned influences of tradition. American journalism did not change overnight, and the combination of modern and traditional influences created a dynamic, colorful, and often unpredictable news environment.

During the period cities in America grappled with effects of urban growth and the beginning of the industrial revolution; newspapers expanded westward and in the urban northeast and an anti-slavery or abolitionist press flourished. From 1830 to 1861 the number of daily newspapers increased from 65 to more than 350, and circulation from 78,000 to 1,478,000 (Sloan, 1991). Total newspapers increased from about 1,200 to 3,000 in roughly the same period (Mott, 1962). While several influential publishers and editors dominate the period, historians cite many reasons for the broad changes and advancements that emerged in content and practice.

Science and technology advanced, the telegraph was introduced in 1844 and the transatlantic cable came in 1858. Hoe improved the rotary press, and while its practical use for journalism didn't come until later the typewriter was further developed during the antebellum period. Public education and the post office improved, numbers of literate readers increased, and journalists became more professional. Transatlantic steamship service commenced in 1838 and later, Congress passed legislation to develop the transcontinental railroad. The Associated Press began in 1848.

The Penny Press, in New York at least, is usually cited as revolutionizing journalism, expanding from an elite to a popular audience, and from a partisan press of issues and opinions to a more commercial, independent press of facts and human interest. Hughes (1968) has said that modern newspapers exist because antebellum newspaper publishers in New York and London "discovered (1) that most human beings, if they could read at all, found it easier to read news than editorial opinion and (2) that the common man would rather be entertained than edified" (p. xxiii). Mott (1962) summarized those publishers' creed in four parts — that common people should know what's happening, abuses in institutions should be exposed, news and not support of class or party should be a paper's first duty, and local and human-interest news is important.

Among major changes conventionally attributed to the Penny Press are the creation of "modern" news through increased local news and coverage of community life, crime, sex, scandals, sports, financial, and meeting news; domination by flamboyant, opinionated, strong-willed publishers and editors; emergence of commercialism that made news a commodity; higher advertising rates, different ways of selling advertising, and emphasis on advertising as the chief source of revenues; emphasis on street sales and delivery; focus on news as opposed to opinion; emergence of departments that separated news from business, and editors from reporters; and a zestful, colorful style of writing. "In effect," Dicken-Garcia (1989, p. 40-41) wrote, "journalism was redefined."

Outside New York, some of these changes were less dramatic. In Hartford, for example, the Penny Press and the telegraph made little immediate difference in the way the *Courant* gathered or presented news, although a "By Telegraph" section offered short, discrete, and often timely items from throughout the country (Dardenne, 1990). In Cincinnati, the telegraph and practices attributed to the

Penny Press prompted no immediate changes, although they hastened commercialization and long-distance communication, both under way before the Penny Press period (Nerone, 1993).

Aspects of modern journalism emerged in the antebellum period, but many journalistic practices in the 1850s reflected an earlier era, which held notions of ethics and truth different from our own. New ideas of journalistic content and practice resided and sometimes clashed with the conventions and traditions of a press from a pre-industrial and basically rural environment.

The antebellum period, pivotal for Hartford's *Courant,* was characterized by *Courant* writers' absolute certainty on most issues, including politics, temperance, moral and social qualities and values, and foreigners and Catholics. Further, news in the *Courant* began to concentrate more on events than issues, and modern notions of boundary, proximity, and timeliness emerged as important. Modern news forms eventually dominated traditional ones. While conscious use of the inverted pyramid did not begin until well after the Civil War, the self-contained, single-article traditional story with beginning, middle, and end gave way to the "story" we now associate with journalism — updated daily and characterized by fact, quotes from authoritative sources, and sensationalism and drama.

Following the *Courant* through the years, one sees that Penny Press and telegraph influences acted in conjunction with other long-term changes and with the transition in 1837 from weekly to daily publication.

II

The Penny Press may have "invented the modern concept of 'news'" (Schudson, 1979), but not all newspapers traveled the high road of reason and impartiality, and developing concepts of ethics and truth were flexible, and at times quite old-fashioned. Papers perpetrated hoaxes and freely stole from one another. The *Times* in 1855 stole the *Herald*'s lead story about the wreck of the steamer Arctic, taking it directly from a covertly obtained copy. The *Times* published first, selling a record number of issues. The journalistic code was a "little crude and raw, and almost anything went" (Berger, 1970, p. 21).

Much antebellum news interested, entertained, and surprised, sometimes playfully, as illustrated in the *Courant's* comments on a *Springfield Republican* article about the murder of Mr. Steer, who had been courting a "grass widow." Her husband, Mr. Butcher, killed Steer, cut the body in pieces, and packed it into a barrel. "Good!" the *Courant* crowed. "We like to see our wide awake neighbors at Springfield taken in sometimes" (April 13, 1855, p. 3). Butchers, the editor gleefully noted, commonly kill steers, cut them up, and pack them in barrels.

The *Courant* maintained such playful qualities since its founding in the 1700s, but did not publish hoaxes as elaborate as those of the New York press, especially the *Sun*'s moon hoax of 1835 (mentioned in most journalism histories, including Mott, 1962, and Sloan, Stovall, & Startt, 1989). Nonetheless, news columns of the 1850s still had room for rumor and speculation as part of the record, indicating that one of the paper's functions was to provide readers with a broad range of information, including that not necessarily factual.

James Gordon Bennett thought newspapers could be the "greatest organ of social life." A newspaper "can send more souls to Heaven, and save more from Hell, than all the churches or chapels in New York—besides making money at the same time" (*Herald*, 1836, quoted in Mott, 1962, p. 232). Samuel Bowles thought the telegraph had made newspapers roughly even in news, so people should expect newspapers to progress in "culture and conscientiousness, in candor and philosophy, in breadth and thoroughness and wisdom, in their treatment of the universal questions of life and civilization ... " (quoted in Wingate, 1970, p. 42.). Henry Raymond thought the press's responsibility was "reform of evils, correction of abuses, the preservation ... of free institutions" (quoted in Wingate, 1970, p. 73). The common mission of the press, was to "elevate humanity" (p. 74).

Throughout its early history, the *Courant's* publishers or editors noted its function was to circulate information to readers who could then make their own truth decisions. In 1855, recognizing a mistake pointed out by the arch-rival *Hartford Times*, the *Courant* reiterated its position: "We say again, as we have said before, that we place such items in our leaded columns to make them more conspicuous, not because we endorse them as true" (May 21, 1855, p. 2).

Often items appeared with tags or even headlines indicating suspicion, doubt, or sarcasm. For example, a brief item said that P.T. Barnum had refused to admit black children in his upcoming baby show merited an "Important, if true" (May 9, 1955, p. 2). It used the same comment the same day for a letter from "a country gentleman" who wrote about the proper feeding to cure a horse of the heaves (May 9, 1955, p. 2). An article branding Hungarian revolutionary hero Lewis Kossuth as a traitor warranted a "For what it is worth," indicating outright doubt. But the *Courant* also used such lines as sarcasm, ridicule, or understatement, as when a Catholic priest was quoted as saying that hell was inside the earth, about 21 miles from its surface. Coming amidst the paper's vicious attacks on Catholics, it was headed, "Alarming Intelligence, If True" (April 13, 1855, p. 2).

The 1830s to the Civil War saw the advent of relatively neutral reporting of facts. Many papers were said to be formally independent of political parties and more or less indifferent to political events (Schudson, 1979). In New York, the *Times*, particularly, promoted a kind of restraint to distinguish itself from the *Herald* and *Tribune*. Raymond wrote that it would be the voice of reason: "We do not mean to write as if we were in a passion, — unless that shall really be the case; and we shall make it a point to get into a passion as rarely as possible" (Quoted in Sloan, Stovall, Startt, 1989, p. 135).

This was not true of all newspapers of the period, and certainly not true in Hartford, which in the 1850s began to more consistently separate news and comment. The paper cannot be said to have embraced neutrality or even impartiality. In fact, in 1855, it might be said the paper was defined by partisanship, often viciously attacking political opponents. Unwavering, partisan political views on issues and people was part of an attitude that emerged in the early 1800s and was reflected in news on many subjects. The mid 1800s was the climax of this attitude, which contrasted with a kind of speculation that emerged in the *Courant* after the Civil War.

The *Courant* exhibited certainty about virtually everything, including politics, morals, general human qualities, and foreigners. Its columns illustrate the attitude hundreds of times, including in a piece attacking a politician editors believed acted badly against a watchman. The politician was

> sullen, stupid, ignorant, narrow-minded, bitter bigot and locofoco partisan, who has been sucking uncle Sam's treasury for years past, whenever he could lay hold of the smallest teat, under the name of Seth Belden — a man recommended by no manly trait whatever, and singled out for patronage, for the double reason of his swinish greed and connection with the *Times* office; if that personification of littleness has any power to feel, he must have writhed in his worm hole as members of all parties commented on his precipitate haste to wreck his malice and ventilate his brief authority on the unoffending faithful watchman. (April 23, 1855, p. 2)

In discussing a political opponent's poetry, the paper said:

> His see-saw, sing-song, wishy-washy rhymes never reached a slipshod mediocrity and

the project of dressing up, in a book bindery, such metrical nonsense for a pecuniary speculation, is a species of fraud, which the laws of good society, not to say, the provisions of the Statute, could not tolerate for a moment ... . Time may possibly improve his manuscripts. Age improves wine. It may improve bad verses .... A man is not often appreciated by his own generation. Hope on, Sir. You may yet find an age of men, heathenish enough to relish very stupid verse. (April 20, 1845, p. 2)

Writers used news and comment to promote by preaching and illustration the values of not only sobriety, but hard work, honesty, economy, and common sense, the traits of good, temperate, God-fearing Connecticut men who supported the paper's political and social philosophy. They favored sound, unchanging government by those fit to govern. The opposition, meanwhile, favoring direct elections by the people, were the great unwashed lower orders, the drinkers and foreigners and Catholics. They sought change, spoke out, and challenged authority. While speaking for the common people, the *Courant* writers often seemed contemptuous of them, particularly if they were Democrats or immigrants. This attitude came out when the paper urged the common people to keep in their places and not emulate their betters, and through "instructional" articles that often told common folk that poverty can be enriching if only they find and learn to love its enriching qualities. *Courant* writers did not trust men, only laws, institutions, and traditions. One, for example, quoted the governor saying that Connecticut citizens "trained from infancy to those habits of subordination which are essential to the enjoyment of rational liberty have generally yielded a cheerful obedience to the laws" (May 8, 1845, p. 2). The *Courant's* journalists apparently wanted a docile, polite, essentially non-ethnic, frugal, temperate underclass.

Immigrants, especially Catholics, were seen as threats to this idealized community and the paper took every advantage throughout the antebellum period to promote its opinions on the matter. One of the more vivid attacks against Catholics came in a lengthy article saying that Negro slavery could not end until the country ended white slavery.

> We have taken more than three millions of the European races within our borders; and a large proportion of these, with a vast number of native Americans, are owned, soul, body and estate, by a foreign slaveholder, who claims the control, not only in time, but for eternity. ... Who ever furnishes the voters, furnishes in fact, the government. Let us not, then (fool) ourselves into the belief that it is all right for the Pope and his priests to send over these Catholic foreigners to control our elections. It is mere suicidal folly; and the Pope and his Priests only chuckle over the greenness of simpletons who can cut their own throats. (April 2, 1855, p. 2)

After protests about the tenor of its comments, the *Courant* summarized its editorial policy on the matter: "Everyone is willing that foreigners and Romanists should ride in the Chariot of American Liberty, but *Americans must drive*" (May 10, 1855, p. 2). The anti-foreigner, anti-Catholic sentiment disappeared from the paper at the Civil War.

Shifts from weekly to daily publication combined with the many other things occurring in the period led to significant changes in the presentation and nature of news. For example, in the *Courant*, the correspondence ambiance was lost, proximity and timeliness became dominant characteristics of news, the inverted pyramid emerged and reports appeared far more than stories, people began to be used more as sources of information, and writers speculated more about the future and oriented content toward fact more than opinion.

III

Letters, essays, comments, articles, and other material received through the mails decreased as newspaper content after the 1830s, when journalists reported more local news. Daily distribution made mailing copies of papers cumbersome. By the middle to late 1850s, the telegraph provided a consistent, timely, and plentiful supply of items of news from throughout the country. This and other new sources of news helped lessen dependence on items from other newspapers and the mails.

Those items, along with the letters from travelers, correspondents, farmers, and others interested in expressing opinions had given the *Courant*, at least, a kind of correspondence ambiance, a forum in which people addressed their concerns, expressed their opinions, and otherwise discussed the issues in what amounted to an informal exchange of letters. Even the items from other newspapers, in this context, seemed more like correspondence than newspaper articles or factual information. *Courant* editors commented on and responded to articles from other papers in editor's notes.

Time in this environment was measured in relation to the letter, which although it might have traveled by swift pony or fast steamer and train, was still something to be opened and leisurely read, and pondered. It is true that news in the earlier decades emphasized issues, and issues perhaps are more conducive to this kind of contemplation. It is also true that weekly publication may have set a more deliberative pace, in which issues could be mulled over and events presented whole, their endings and perhaps some of their consequences already known.

The pace of daily publication was much different. With fewer letters, fewer pieces from other papers, less discussion of issues, and far more coverage of events, or more accurately, the daily unfolding of incomplete events, the paper's ambiance began to change from that of correspondence to one we recognize today as journalism, a faster-paced amalgam of fact, comment, and event.

An evolution in the nature of news in the *Courant* was in part characterized by an increasing importance of proximity as a news value. In 1765 focus had been almost solely on Europe and various powerful commercial and military seagoing centers. The Revolutionary War in 1775 forced the paper to give more consideration to the colonies, but after 1775 interests again shifted to the international. The paper showed little or no special interest in Hartford's people or events. A murder in Kentucky or a storm in South Carolina or an election in Connecticut seemed to have the same prominence. In the early 1800s battles with Democratic foes locally and nationally made editors aware of the *Courant* as a local paper and the city as a source of news.

Then, the Penny Press brought reporters covering more issues and activities, and also solidified and expanded the commercial nature of the press. News sold, and publishers discovered and developed vast audiences for the kind of news and information they offered. As daily editions became commonplace and competition for news among papers increased, sources of cheap and plentiful information became valuable.

For example, police stations and court houses housed virtually unlimited supplies of information that newly tapped audiences found irresistible, and it was free for the taking. Information from and about many other aspects of the community became part of the news starting from the 1830s. Prior to that the *Courant* occasionally published local articles, but without the conscious notion they were valuable because they were local.

The changing local environments including the effects of urban growth and industrialization encouraged the use of local information and news, and as the organization of news within newspapers became institutionalized, not only did local news become more valuable, but proximity became a prominent determinant of news judgment.

IV

Timeliness also became important in virtually every type of story and article, changing dramatically the nature of news and perhaps the concept of story. After the paper began daily publication, it became important that the day's events be covered thoroughly, usually in articles that were part of greater stories that unfolded in subsequent days and weeks. Many of the traditional or self-contained in the 1700s and early 1800s were about unnamed people who may or may not have been real, involved in activities that may have taken place, if at all, years before. By the mid 1800s, the traditional story form appeared less frequently, leaving continuing stories involving real people involved in real events covered in real time. Daily publication, the telegraph, the commercialization of news, the interest in science and scientific method and eventually "fact," and other developments led to the eventual dominance of the inverted pyramid, a more or less rigid form well-suited to a news in which timeliness was a basic value.

The inverted pyramid is a report (described more fully in Dardenne, 1990 & 1993), a straightforward rendering of facts in a variety of lengths and basic forms. The report appeared more frequently after the mid 1800s, although it was the most common form of article throughout the *Courant's* history. The inverted pyramid is not as easy to trace as some theories of origin suggest. In the decades after the telegraph gained wide acceptance as a means of sending news, articles in the "telegraphic news" sections were shorter and more ordered than newspaper articles in previous decades, but evidence in the *Courant* and elsewhere indicates that the inverted pyramid emerged as a consistent, conscious form later (see Mindich, 1993, p. 2-4). Although official dispatches from the War Department during the Civil War and especially during the period of Lincoln's assassination were written in almost perfect inverted pyramid form (Dardenne, 1990, and Mindich, 1993). Edwin M. Stanton, secretary of war during the Lincoln administration, has been credited with if not originating the form at least using it consistently well before it was an established journalistic practice (Mindich, 1993).

Antebellum use of such a form, even after the telegraph, was inconsistent at best. The *Connecticut Courant* (before 1837) and the *Daily Courant* (after 1837), for example, published items that fit the inverted pyramid form, but they lacked consistency and pattern, suggesting they were not conscious constructions. As Mindich (1993) noted, such items, particularly one or two paragraph police articles, naturally fell into inverted pyramid form, often with first sentences greatly resembling the modern-day "lead."

The inverted pyramid proved to be an effective way of delivering facts and information, which, as opposed to opinions and values, became more important in news. The traditional story, however, had its advantages as well. It injected into the news ideas, issues, values, and morals not easily provided in other forms. With traditional story forms, news had many dimensions beyond straight reporting of fact. Some of those dimensions waned during the antebellum period along with the story form itself.

A story in 1855 in the *Courant* is an excellent example of the traditional story in the news. It belongs more to pre-antebellum news in which such stories frequently brought ancient themes and traditional values to *Courant* readers. It involves a plot originated centuries before and repeated several times over the years in the *Courant* alone.

> —At Beloit, on the night of the 23rd ult., the wife of a citizen of that place awoke and saw a man with a dark lantern in the bed-room, and awakened her husband with her screams. As he sprang from the bed the intruder fired at him with a pistol, the ball just missing his head and burying itself in the pillow. Snatching a double-barreled gun from the wall he discharged both barrels at the intruder.—The contents of one barrel entered the man's head and the other his body, killing him instantly. Leaving the body where it fell, the gentleman and his wife proceeded to the nearest neighbor, told him what had happened, and induced him to return with them to his house. But imagine the feelings of the neighbor, himself a man universally esteemed and respected, to recognize in the mangled body of the dead robber, his own son. (May 3, 1855, p. 2)

In other stories, some details are changed, including site of the crime, circumstances surrounding the killing, and relationship of the victim/robber to the people who killed or discovered him. The identity, however, was always a tragic surprise. This format was common among traditional stories of many kinds in that people are rarely or vaguely identified and places were remote or obscure. Among traditional-type stories in the middle 1800s in the *Courant*, hidden or surprise identity plots were most numerous.

These traditional stories, often sketchy with concrete details, taught the power of prayer and faith, the evils of drink and other indulgences, and the strengths and goodness of gentle mothers, hard workers, frugal wives, and general Yankee qualities. They provided information in the form of broad themes — generosity, religious devotion, deception, greed, self-indulgence, benevolence, intemperance. Often stories included God or deity or providence, as in references to victims taken by a merciful God or saved by the hand of providence. The paper used stories as examples of romance and tragedy, good and bad, or acceptable and unacceptable behavior, repeating the themes and often supporting their morals with editorial comment. The diminishing of the traditional story form decreased the paper's range of material it could publish, limited its voice, and dulled its personality.

With the waning of traditional stories and their broad themes, a new kind of story emerged, one in which daily reports, accounts, and other articles formed a completed story, not in one article, but over time. The continuing stories might be said to have elements of some of the themes, but they emphasized events, facts, and actions, usually human.

Other connotations of "story" made it less desirable in a culture flirting with such terms as "science," "fact," and "truth." "Story," used for different forms, never has been fully defined in a journalistic sense. It can also mean fiction and untruth. A "story" as an historic, truthful accounting of the past is a less common meaning than "story" as something made up or created. "Story" can also mean "lie," as when people say "You told me a story" meaning "You told me a lie." The more traditionally storylike the article, the more likely it is to be perceived in this manner.

Also, Munz (1977) noted that it is difficult to write any story without knowing the ending. Many of the stories before 1837, the year the newspaper became a daily, were complete and self-contained. Writers knew endings before they wrote, thereby freeing them to write a story aimed at the ending. When writers worked on daily deadlines, they often had no idea of how an event might turn out; therefore, writing the same kinds of stories was impossible, and the nature of story changed.

Yet, story form may be integral to human understanding (Rockwell, 1974), and certainly proved resilient in news. Journalism kept "story," but without the "fiction" implied by the traditional story form. Articles about events and actions over several days, weeks, or even months, taken as a whole, formed "stories" that delivered facts and other information about those events or actions. And, while continuing stories were usually without broad, traditional themes, they were not without their own influences.

Essentially amoral, they were published for information, presenting a series of facts without obvious lessons to be learned. Moral, social, and cultural instruction diminished with the self-contained story, or changed as it was left to other forms such as columns. Still, the continuous stories had powerful themes — reliance on authority, expertise, and official voice; focus on the individual as embodiment of issues or events; celebration of order through technology and efficient, usually official, organization; truth through accumulation of relatively neutral facts, conflicting claims, and quotes from authorities or experts. The journalistic story and its lessons evolved with the culture and technology. Its morals were no longer obvious, but its facade of objectivity obscured powerful ways of conceiving the world.

V

Hazel Dicken-Garcia (1989) argues that news became more story-like in the specific as time went on because it began to focus more on people rather than issues. Depending on how you define story, her observation holds true for the *Courant*. Beginning in the antebellum period, especially in the Penny Press papers, more news emphasized dramatic and sensational ("human interest") elements, but news "stories" were most often continuing stories of the post 1840s, not traditional stories of the past. Both forms emphasized people, but continuing stories dominated news in ways traditional stories never did.

With sensation and human interest important, events and people took precedence over issues, which were often complex and difficult to grasp. Further, people became more significant to news with the increasing importance of fact, the interview, and attributed news sources. As journalists struggled to capture a more and more illusive reality, "facts" became more important. Journalists began to see people, again, usually authorities or experts, as repositories of easily and cheaply obtainable facts (as well as colorful comments of all kinds). The best way to get facts and comment was by direct questioning; hence, the interview. However, in the *Courant,* people in the news after the antebellum period were often more important for their attribution authority (as a credible source of a quote) than for any value as citizens or even humans.

Further, in the mid 1800s, articles in the *Courant* reflected an increased tendency to cover complicated events through simple anecdotes about people. This practice illustrated the beginnings of an event- rather than issue-centered approach to news and continued into the 20th century. Most often, for example, the complex Kansas-Missouri issues were reduced in the *Courant* to reports and descriptions of often violent incidents.

For much of the period, the *Courant*, was belligerently subjective and its writers had a political stake not only in informing about and reinforcing a political attitude or position, but also in persuading others to take it. Articles attacked and challenged readers, persuaded them to some political position, encouraged involvement, and reported some outrageous position or behavior of the opposition and some courageous or noble action by proponents. Articles throughout the *Courant* were filled with sarcasm, wit, and personality stemming from fervent stands on moral, social, political, and religious issues, from unyielding beliefs. Much of the paper's bright personality, manifest through its news, dimmed as the nature of news in the mid 1800s began to change from advocacy to fact.

Daily publication and the coming of the telegraph helped transform notions of time and proximity in news, resulting in, among other things, speculation about the future. The telegraph gave the illusion of instantaneous news from everywhere. Before, communication was slow and uncertain, leaving people to speculate on what was happening elsewhere and to depend on rumor and infrequent and often contradictory information. Speculation was usually about contemporary events, but after the telegraph and into the 20th century, the enormous amount of speculation in the news focused on the future.

This shift in speculation about the future may have stemmed from a confusion about the present. Journalism and literary criticism have rough parallels. As reality came to be seen as something "utterly unstable, shifting, moving," the notion of "realism" became more confusing (Kahler, 1973, p. 221). Reality became a function of perception, therefore relative. In that sense, news prior to the Civil War reflected a naive view of reality, one in which writers essentially presented to their readers descriptions of a concrete, perhaps unambiguous reality This naive view is in part reflected in the years of the *Courant's* certainty, in which nothing was doubted. Later, certainty gave way to uncertainty, as the past and present gave way to the future. The writer's own descriptions and explanations were no longer acceptable; only facts would do, and facts came to mean information from appropriate sources. The harder reality was to capture, the more writers chased it with facts.

The *Courant's* news in the middle 1800s following the change to daily editions and introduction of the telegraph began to illustrate this greater emphasis on fact. In fact, the telegraph, which wasn't a major part of the paper's news until the 1860s, was identified with fact, at least in the sense that its dispatches were almost always "official" and, as the paper seemed to treat it, truthful versions of events. The telegraphic dispatch stood alone, no matter how many times the same information appeared in other forms in the same paper, or even the same article. It sometimes seemed as though the event did not truly happen unless it was reported officially. Information in one dispatch might be expanded, amended, corrected, or even superseded in a later dispatch in the same column, but the earlier dispatch was left as part of the record.

It is also likely that the paper's more unbiased quest for "truth," also beginning to be seen in the middle 1800s, as well as the telegraph, moderated its excessive rhetoric and story-like narratives, as concise, ordered, fact-laden articles with material attributed to official sources enhanced credibility.

These changes in journalism have enormous impact for the present. Although much newspaper history of this period comes out of New York, many of these significant changes and shifts in news cannot be explained solely by innovations from the Penny Press. The complexities of antebellum news, including the interaction between tradition and change, provide varied and rich explanations for the development and evolution of journalism and its practice today.

Notes

Berger, M. (1970). *The story of The New York Times*, 1851-1951. New York: Simon and Schuster.
Carey, J. (1986) "The dark continent of American journalism," in Mannoff, R.K. and Carey, J. *Reading the News*. New York: Pantheon Books, p. 146-196.
Congdon, C. T. (1869, 1971), *Tribune Essays: Leading Articles Contributed to The New York Tribune from 1857 to 1863*. Freeport, N.Y.: Books for Libraries.
Connecticut Courant, The, (1805, 1815, 1825, 1835). Hartford, Connecticut.
Crouthamel, J. L. (1989). *Bennett's New York Herald and the Rise of the Popular Press*. Syracuse: Syracuse University Press.
Daily Courant, The. (1845, 1855). Hartford, Connecticut.
Dardenne, R. W. (1990). "Newstelling: Story and themes in The Courant of Hartford from 1765 to 1945." Ph.D. dissertation, University of Iowa.
Dardenne, R. W. (1993). "News and other worlds: Observations on news." International Communication Convention, Washington D.C., May 1993.
Dicken-Garcia, H. (1989). *Journalistic standards in Nineteenth Century America*. Madison, Wisc.: University of Wisconsin Press.
Dominick, J. R. (1978). "Crime and law enforcement in the mass media," in C. Winick (Ed.), *Deviance and mass media*. Beverly Hills: Sage Publications.
Greeley, H. (1869, 1971), Introduction, in C. T. Congdon, *Tribune essays: Leading Articles Contributed to The New York Tribune from 1857 to 1863*. Freeport, N.Y.: Books for Libraries.
Hughes, H. M. (1968) *News and the Human Interest Story*. New York: Greenwood Press.
Kahler, E. (1973). *The Inward Turn of the Narrative*. Evanston, Ill.: Northwestern University Press.
Kluger, R. (1986). *The Paper: The LIfe and Death of The New York Herald Tribune*. New York: Alfred A. Knopf.
Lane, R. (1979). *Violent Death in the City, Suicide, Accident, and Murder in Nineteenth-*

century Philadelphia. Cambridge, Mass.: Harvard University Press.

Marzolf, M. T. (1991) *Civilizing Voices: American Press Criticism, 1880-1950.* New York: Longman.

Maverick, A. (1870/1970). *Henry Raymond and The New York Times.* New York: Arno Press and The New York Times.

Mindich, D. T. Z. (1993). Edwin M. Stanton, the inverted pyramid, and information control. *Journalism Monographs,* 140/August.

Mott, F. L. (1962). *American Journalism.* New York: Macmillan.

Munz, P. (1977). *The Shapes of Time.* Middletown, Conn.: Wesleyan University Press.

Nerone, J. C. (1993) "A local history of the early U.S. press: Cincinnati, 1793-1848," in Solomon, W. S. and McChesney, R. W. (Eds.), *Ruthless Criticism.* Minneapolis: University of Minnesota Press, ppg. 38-65.

Rockwell, J. (1974). *Fact in Fiction, the Use of Literature in the Systematic Study of Society.* London: Routledge & Kegan Paul.

Schudson, Michael. (1978) *Discovering the News.* New York: Basic Books.

Sloan, W. D., Stovall, J. C., & Startt, J. D. (1989). *The Media in America: A History.* Worthington, Ohio: Publishing Horizons Inc.

Sloan, W. D. (1991). *Perspectives on Mass Communication History.* Hillsdale, N.J.: Lawrence Erlbaum.

Startt, J. D. and Sloan, W. D. (1994). "The Historical Search for significance," in Startt, J.D. and Sloan, W.D. (Eds.), *The Significance of the Media in American History.* Northport, Ala.: Vision Press, p. 1-15.

Tucher, A. (1994). Froth & scum: *Truth, Beauty, Goodness, and the Ax Murder in America's First Mass Medium.* Chapel Hill: The University of North Carolina Press.

Ward, H. H. (1994). "The media and political values," in Startt and Sloan,*The Significance of the media in American history.,* pp. 129-146.

Wingate, C. F. (Eds.) (1970, reprint of 1875 ed.) *The American Journalists: Views and Interviews on Journalism.* New York: Arno and The New York Times.

II

In Time of War

13

Edwin M. Stanton, the Inverted Pyramid, and Information Control

David Mindich
Saint Michael's College

The whole nation is impressed with the same idea at the same moment. One feeling and impulse are thus created and maintained from the centre of the land to its uttermost extremities.
— James Gordon Bennett[1]

Let a man only tell you his story every morning and evening and at the end of a twelvemonth he will have become your master.
— Edmund Burke[2]

  Until the end of the 19th century, the discourse of storytelling nearly always took a standard form: First, an announcement of the utility or importance of the story, as in the start of the *Iliad*, "Sing, goddess, the anger of Peleus' son Achilleus and its devastation, which puts pains thousandfold upon the Achaians . . ."[3] the penny papers' "By Telegraph!" or the familiar "you'd never believe what I saw at the office." The story teller, having given a promise of astonishment,

---

Previously published in Journalism Monographs, 140/August 1993 (AEJMC).

narrates in chronological order, leaving the surprise, what Aristotle calls "Reversal of the Situation," for last.[4] The New York *Herald's* 1847 story, promising astonishment with the headline, "Terrible Flood in the West," fits this pattern:

> On Friday afternoon strong evidence of a freshet was exhibited, and many had their fears excited. The water began to approach some of the inhabitants in the lower parts of the city....We were aroused from our slumbers by some kind persons...

The reporter withholds what would be the modern "lead" until the final paragraphs: a woman and her six children are missing, the flood swept away $2 million worth of property.[5]

* * * * * * * * * * *

When, as a young man in 1892, Theodore Dreiser entered the world of journalism and the office of the Chicago *Globe*, his editor told him that the first paragraph of a news story must reveal "who, what, how, when, and where," giving away the punch line, or lead, in the beginning.[6] Between 1847 and 1892 someone, or someones, somehow, at sometime, somewhere, did something to change the way newspapers tell stories.

On or about April 15, 1865 the character of newswriting changed. At least that is the date most cited by historians as the first example of a new journalistic style, the "inverted pyramid," a system of ordering facts in descending order of importance. A 1912 textbook describes the inverted pyramid lead as telling "the gist of the news first and the details later."[7] Or, as a modern textbook explains,

> The inverted pyramid form demands that the most important elements of a story be placed at the beginning of the article (or at the wide end of the inverted pyramid) and that the least important information be placed at the end of the article (or at the lower point of the inverted pyramid).[8]

The importance of the inverted pyramid, which supplanted the chronological style of antebellum news writing is difficult to overstate. It is a system that appears to strip a story of everything but the "facts," and changes the way we process news. The new style, as Mitchell Stephens writes, reflects a new age concerned with facts. It is an age with no time to hear a good story: "The essay—perfected by eighteenth-century journalists. . .placed too much emphasis on point of view; there was to be no point of view in the new world of unambiguous fact."[9] Often called "objective" or "straight" newswriting, the inverted pyramid system is a central element of "objectivity." Given the importance of the inverted pyramid, it is surprising that its birth has not been adequately explained.

Although Stephens and others mention and date the development of the inverted pyramid, they do not offer any individuals as singularly important. This article began as a search for the first journalists to write inverted pyramids, but the data all pointed to a surprising conclusion: that the earliest examples of the form may have not been written by journalists, but by Edwin M. Stanton, Abraham Lincoln's Secretary of War.

Stanton has found his way into many histories of American journalism, but always in his notoriety as a press censor. There is another, equally important aspect of Stanton's role in the newspapers of the Civil War period: Stanton as writer. Because Stanton's terse, impersonal dispatches appeared unedited on the front pages of newspapers across the Union, he was widely read throughout the war. This article attempts to reveal Stanton as a writer of inverted pyramids and to reconcile this form with his tight rein on discourse—journalistic and otherwise—during the Civil War period.

First, this article will briefly examine the historical scholarship on the inverted pyramid and reveal Stanton's announcement of Lincoln's assassination as a prototypal inverted pyramid, contrasting it with other reporting. Second, it will examine Stanton's role as a censor, jailer, and controller of information through his unusual style of writing. And finally, it will reveal his effect on reporters and reporting of the Civil War through his daily press releases and will suggest a structural connection between his writing and his other instruments of social control. There seems to be, of course, an irony in the suggestion that Stanton the censor may have also been a progenitor of a modern journalism. But given recent criticism of "objectivity," which suggests an over-reliance on authoritative sources, a governmental source for the inverted pyramid may be less surprising, and in fact fitting.

Civil War Reporting and Lincoln's Assassination

Most journalism historians point to the American Civil War as an era of changing reportage. Stephens writes that the inverted pyramid form was developed by Civil War reporters "rushing to transmit their most newsworthy information over often unreliable telegraph lines."[10] As an example of this kind of reporting, Stephens cites the first dispatch of Lincoln's assassination, written by the famous Associated Press reporter, Lawrence Gobright. Jean Folkerts and Dwight Teeter, in *Voices of a Nation*, suggest that the Civil War saw the rise of the news lead and the beginnings of the inverted pyramid style.[11] Another journalism historian, Robert W. Jones, agrees, stating, "The *'Lead'* Was War-Born." According to Jones, the "news lead or summary introduction," as he calls it, was developed to increase newsstand sales.[12] Jones also cites Lincoln's death as the turning point in the development of the new journalistic style.

Some historians, including Frank L. Mott and Michael Schudson, suggest that the lead was developed after the war. Civil War reporting was more "direct," suggests Mott, but the various dispatches were still organized in chronological order.[13] Whereas Stephens chooses an A.P. dispatch "lead," Mott quotes from an A.P. article that uses a chronological style. Michael Schudson, in *Discovering the News*, questions the importance of the Civil War in the formulation of the inverted pyramid style, and suggests that the first examples appear in the 1870s and 1880s.[14]

Still another textbook suggests that a concentration on facts arose after the Civil War. Michael Emery and Edwin Emery write that the style change was caused by a public wanting to decide issues for itself. A purely "factual" style would allow readers to draw their own conclusions. According to the Emerys, the wire services, telegraph, and competitive market forces all had a role in developing an "objective" style, and that this took place after the Civil War. Like the others, however, Emery uses the coverage of Lincoln's death as an example of journalistic change, citing Gobright's succinct "lead."[15]

Why is the Lincoln assassination so often cited as a significant milestone in journalism? After an extensive, if not conclusive, search of the New York *Tribune*, *Post*, *Sun*, and *Times* for the earliest examples of the inverted pyramid, none was found prior to Lincoln's assassination.[16] Inchoate examples of the inverted pyramid style in the 1840s and 1850s were found in the New York *Herald*, particularly in the one-paragraph police blotter stories, which, by their nature, assert their own factuality (what Daniel Schiller has called a "pattern of objectivity") and include a few of the W's, often the "what" and "when."[17] But it seems that the careful, "objective" ordering of facts into an inverted pyramid style did not appear in the *Herald* until 1865.[18] In a 1987 dissertation, Harlan Stensaas conducted a content analysis of six U.S. dailies and found that the inverted pyramid form was not common until the 1880s and not standard until the turn of the century.[19]

Donald L. Shaw and others have suggested that the rise of the wire services and the telegraph contributed to the development of an "objective" style of writing. In a study of news reports of the antebellum period, Shaw finds that news via telegraph was practically nonexistent before 1847 and rose to eight percent of all stories between 1847 and 1860. This wide dissemination of wire news led to the realization that "facts were more safely marketed than opinion."[20] Shaw's study, however, does not look for the inverted pyramid form. Stensaas's findings suggest inverted pyramids were not widely used in wire and non-wire news until the 1880s. In a separate project, Shaw studied stories about presidential campaigns in Wisconsin dailies from 1852 to 1916 and found that the use of the telegraph had a direct correlation to the emergence of "unbiased" stories. However, Shaw's findings reveal that while "bias" declined in tandem with the rise of the telegraph in 1876, "bias" was highest in 1872, a generation after the first telegraphs were used.[21]

True inverted pyramids written by reporters were probably not, as Jones puts it, "War-Born." None of the above journalism historians, including Jones, cite Civil War examples of inverted pyramid articles. Gobright's account of Lincoln's assassination, which many of the historians cite, occurred a week after Lee's surrender at Appomattox, after all of the war's major battles. Mott and Schudson suggest that the innovations were mainly postwar, and it seems that they are correct. Four years of war reporting, prior to the assassination, were chronological and self-conscious; at the earliest, it seems, the lead was born with the coverage of Lincoln's death.

In his 1869 autobiography, Lawrence Gobright, the Washington agent for the Associated Press, recalls the events of April 14th, 1865. It was late in the evening, and Gobright had just written a tidbit about General Grant missing that night's performance of "Our American Cousin" at Ford's Theatre. As Gobright sat alone in the A.P. telegraph room, puffing on a cigar, he scanned the out-of-town papers for news. Washington was in a celebratory mood that night: the Rebels were defeated and were suing for peace. The South had lost its largest army with Lee's surrender, and Gobright expected a slow night.[22]

Suddenly a friend burst through the door, excited and shouting. Minutes later, Gobright dispatched the following to New York:

WASHINGTON, APRIL 14, 1865
TO THE ASSOCIATED PRESS: THE PRESIDENT WAS SHOT IN A THEATRE
TONIGHT AND PERHAPS MORTALLY WOUNDED.[23]

Although his dispatch is often cited as an early example of a lead, "lead" implies that something is led; Gobright had no other information at hand and was merely telegraphing the sum of his knowledge. He would later write a detailed, chronological account to the dailies.[24]

The same hour found the Secretary of War, Edwin Stanton, dressing for bed when he heard a knock at the door. "Mr. Seward is murdered," was the cry. Suddenly people began pouring into the house, each with a different story. Some were saying that Lincoln, too, was murdered. Stanton found a hack and took it to the house of William Seward, where he found the Secretary of State and his son beaten and unconscious. Blood was everywhere. A doctor was treating the injured men. Stanton then rushed to Ford's and went across the street to a small boarding house where doctors were ministering to Lincoln.[25]

Lincoln lay diagonally across a short bed, his breathing labored and erratic, his face discolored and pained. Soldiers and messengers rushed in and out of the boarding house, and many of the cabinet members stood dumbly around the President, not knowing what to do. Meanwhile, Stanton ordered an unofficial court, with the Chief Justice, the Attorney General, a military shorthand clerk, and representatives from the local police, the military, and the U.S. Marshall's office to gather as much evidence as they could from witnesses.[26] Stanton immediately put the city under martial law, organized squads to capture the assassins, and wired the New York chief of police to "send here immediately three or four of your best detectives."[27] Gideon Welles, the Navy Secretary, wandered into the room, but given the weight of the events, felt "indisposed," and "oppressed... physically" by the crowds.[28]

Charles A. Dana, an assistant Secretary of War, remembered being summoned to the boarding house by Stanton, who

> dictated orders, one after another, which I wrote out and sent swiftly to the telegraph. All these orders were designed to keep the business of the Government in full motion until the crisis should be over. It seemed as if Mr. Stanton thought of everything, and there was a great deal to be thought of that night.... The coolness and clearheadedness of Mr. Stanton under these circumstances were most remarkable.[29]

It was Stanton's ability to manage men and information that allowed him to control events that night. And control he did: "in the next eight hours [following Lincoln's death] the country was run by a dictator....Edwin McMasters Stanton," said one chronicler.30

Gathering and interpreting a daunting amount of data under adverse conditions, Stanton tried to piece together what had happened. At first, he thought that the assassination was part of a massive Southern plot to overthrow the government. But by 1 a.m., less than three hours after Lincoln was shot, Stanton had the names of Booth, Atzerodt and Herold, three of the four conspirators, and was beginning to understand the relatively limited scope of the scheme. Stanton wrote a number of dispatches to be released to the New York dailies, some by his own hand and some by Dana's. Stanton himself wrote the letter that would inform Vice President Andrew Johnson of Lincoln's death.31 Although Dana was an excellent writer (he had been an editor of the New York *Tribune* and would become the editor and part owner of the New York *Sun* after the war), on this night he merely took dictation from his boss, Stanton. Dana wrote: "I remember that one of his first telegrams was to General Dix, the military commander of New York, notifying him of what had happened. No clearer brief account of the tragedy exists to-day than this, written scarcely three hours after the scene in Ford's Theater, on a little stand in the room where, a few feet away, Mr. Lincoln lay dying."32 The first dispatch, sent to the New York papers through General Dix, may very well be one of the first in history.

Stanton's dispatch appeared as the New York *Herald*'s lead story the following morning. The editors shortened the paragraphs, but the contents were unchanged. Below is how the story appeared in the *Herald*:

War Department,

Washington, April 15 - 1:30 A.M.

Major General Dix, New York: -

This evening at about 9:30 P.M., at Ford's Theatre, the President, while sitting in his private box with Mrs. Lincoln, Mrs. Harris and Major Rathburn, was shot by an assassin, who suddenly entered the box and approached behind the president.
The assassin then leaped upon the stage, brandishing a large dagger or knife, and made his escape in the rear of the theatre.
The pistol ball entered the back of the President's head and penetrated nearly through the head. The wound is mortal.
The President has been insensible ever since it was inflicted, and is now dying.
About the same hour an assassin, whether the same or not, entered Mr. Seward's

apartments, and under pretense of having a prescription was shown to the Secretary's sick chamber. The assassin immediately rushed to the bed and inflicted two or three stabs on the throat and two on the face.

It is hoped the wounds may not be mortal. My apprehension is that they will prove fatal.

The nurse alarmed Mr. Frederick Seward, who was in an adjoining room, and he hastened to the door of his father's room, when he met the assassin, who inflicted upon him one or more dangerous wounds. The recovery of Frederick Seward is doubtful. It is not probable that the President will live through the night.

General and his wife were advertised to be at the theatre this evening, but he started to Burlington at six o'clock this evening.

At a Cabinet meeting, at which General Grant was present, the subject of the state of the country was discussed. The President was very cheerful and hopeful, and spoke very kindly of General Lee and others of the confederacy, and of the establishment of government in Virginia.

All the members of the Cabinet except Mr. Seward, are now in attendance upon the President.

I have seen Mr. Seward, but he and Frederick were both unconscious.

EDWIN M. STANTON,
Secretary of War.[33]

Stanton's most thorough biographer, Benjamin P. Thomas, praises Stanton for assembling "a logical narrative of the attacks on Lincoln and Seward from the incoherent accounts he had heard."[34] However, while Stanton deserves praise, the above dispatch is no narrative in the classic, storytelling sense. It doesn't reserve or withhold attention-getting information, nor does it provide a chronological account of events. Rather it is a striking example of an inverted pyramid. Stanton opens with a sentence that conveys the central fact—that the President had been shot. He briefly discusses the particulars and then moves to the assassination of Secretary Seward. Stanton ends with relatively minor points: General Grant's whereabouts, a Cabinet meeting, and the condition of the Sewards.

Stanton's dispatch, while not perfect as a modern news story, is still much closer to the inverted pyramid style than Gobright's longer narrative that followed his initial one-sentence "lead": Gobright begins, "President Lincoln and wife, with other friends, this evening visited Ford's Theatre, for the purpose of witnessing the performance of the 'American Cousin.'"[35] The first eleven paragraphs are written in straight chronological order and it takes the reader four paragraphs of narrative to get to Lincoln's injury. Unlike Stanton, whose aim was to present important facts quickly, Gobright reported events nearly in the order that they occurred. Gobright's chronological report, while perceptive and well wrought, has neither a paradigmatic nor prototypal relation to later inverted pyramids.

Ironically, some of the articles hailed as a new beginning in the history of journalism were written not by reporters but by Stanton. In trying to place an early example of a lead, Jones writes, "the Chicago *Tribune's* noteworthy story began. . .,"[36] and then quotes a dispatch written by Stanton! Jones's argument may be that the papers, in their choice and placement of dispatches, were, in effect, creating a de facto inverted pyramid. However, the papers' choices better support Mott's contention that the press was still operating in chronological structures; dispatches were usually laid out in the order they came in. On April 15th, 1865, it was the War Department, and not the press, that adhered most closely to the new style.

The notion of the inverted pyramid as an "objective" mirror of "reality" is impossible to accept.[37] The "objective" news report is, at best, an earnest self-credulous assertion of its own factuality; at worst, it is a deliberate ordering of "facts" to manipulate public perceptions. Stanton's conveyance of the facts in the above dispatch includes Lincoln's "kindly" stance toward General Lee and "others in the confederacy, and of the establishment of government in Virginia." This information, not centrally important to the assassination itself, may very well have been used to enrage Northerners (by emphasizing Lincoln's benevolence even to traitors) and instruct Southerners of their mistake. In fact, at the final cabinet meeting Lincoln was not especially conciliatory toward the South, and apparently accepted much of Stanton's harsh reconstruction plan.[38] Stanton's "objective" facts are used to mask his personal agenda.

During his tenure as War Secretary, Stanton was fanatical about controlling the dissemination of information. In this attempt to establish a connection between Stanton's controlling and repressive acts and his writing style, it is essential to examine the nature and structure of his attempts to control discourse and attain power through his manipulation of information.

Stanton's Background

By the end of 1861, the U.S. War Department had become corrupt and inefficient, and the House set up a special committee to investigate it. The committee found that the War Department had purchased "rotten blankets, tainted pork, knapsacks that came unglued in the rain, uniforms that fell apart...hundreds of diseased and dying horses— all at exorbitant prices." The committee found "colossal graft" and a "prostitution of public confidence to purposes of individual aggrandizement" under War Secretary Simon Cameron. Lincoln needed a change and picked an unlikely candidate, Edwin McMasters Stanton.[39]

Stanton had a fitting background and temperament for a man who would be at the forefront of a new, "factual" style of newswriting. An extremely ambitious man, he became a lawyer in 1835 (at age 21) and earned early recognition as a skillful rhetorician and a brilliant legal strategist. He shared many of the views of abolitionism (his grandmother had manumitted her dead husband's slaves at the turn of the nineteenth century), but he carefully avoided the sensitive subject. It might have been this trait that attracted Lincoln to Stanton; the President was looking for a War Secretary who could avoid discussion of slavery until strategic issues were settled. In this, Stanton did not disappoint Lincoln. A tight control of utterance was central to Stanton's value to his President.[40]

From his early years as a lawyer, Stanton's chief concern was with minutiae, leading him to find loopholes in the law. The case of a Lisbon, Ohio wagoner, who was accused of damaging a road, is an example. The man had driven his cart uphill with its brakes on, creating deep ruts in the already ill-kept road. Stanton successfully argued that, as the town's ordinance forbade drivers from going *down* the street with their brakes on, his client, going uphill, was innocent.[41]

Stanton's most sensational case was the murder trial of his friend, Daniel Sickles, a New York congressman who discovered that his wife was having a love affair with Washington socialite Philip Barton Key (son of the author of the "The Star Spangled Banner"). Sickles had shot Key dead on a Washington street. Stanton and his associates successfully defended Sickles and were the first in United States history to use the defense of "temporary insanity."[42]

His expertise also brought him fame and a substantial income. Just prior to the Civil War, he was one of the leading lawyers in the United States. In 1859, his last year of private practice, Stanton cleared $40,000. It was then that James Buchanan, in the final year of his presidency, named Stanton as his Attorney General.[43]

Stanton thought Buchanan was becoming too conciliatory to the South, and while he maintained Buchanan's trust, Stanton was also apprising Republican leaders of threats to the Union. Stanton, a Democrat, was able to keep the trust of the President and conservatives back home while secretly planning strategy with radical Republicans in

Edward M. Stanton, the Inverted Pyramid, and Information Control 189

Congress. He was able to accomplish this difficult task only by a careful management of information: during Stanton's tenure as Attorney General, he met with Republican Senator Sumner a few times in complete secrecy; Stanton always understood how quickly a subordinate would take information to a newspaper.[44]

In 1855, when Stanton was working as an attorney on an important patent case, a young lawyer from Illinois was retained to assist him. Stanton and his associates were rude to the man, did not include him in their stratagems, and generally ignored him. The young man sat quietly through the trial and tried to learn as much as he could. The snub would never be forgotten by the man, and when this gangling young attorney from Illinois was elected President in 1860, the insult was still fresh in his memory. If Lincoln resented Stanton, the sentiment was mutually displayed; Stanton, through letters, disclosed his mistrust of the Lincoln administration, which he perceived as corrupted and bureaucratic.[45] If his secret dislike of Lincoln resembled his previous disapproval of Buchanan, it also foreshadowed his surreptitious machinations against General George McClellan and his public wrangling with President Andrew Johnson, who tried to expel Stanton during the time of Johnson's impeachment. Stanton's relationship with his superiors was always complex and often displayed his conspiratorial mind.[46]

When Lincoln had to replace War Secretary Cameron, the powerful Republicans may have remembered Stanton's favors to them and recommended him to Lincoln. But Lincoln may have also considered Stanton's legal expertise, put his personal feelings aside, and picked the man because he would be a discreet and able administrator. As a lifetime civilian, Stanton could offer no military background; however, Stanton's legal expertise would allow him to quickly train himself in military matters.

More than one of Stanton's biographers and many of his contemporaries saw him as a misanthrope. L.A. Whiteley, chief of the *Herald*'s Washington office, wrote to James Gordon Bennett: "Stanton absolutely stinks in the nostrils of the people and the army. His manner has made him offensive to every one who approaches him."[47] It is consistent with Stanton's character that the telegraph was his preferred form of discourse: it is far less personal than the courier system used by many of his colleagues.[48]

It is true that he was often rude to his generals and subordinates, but it may have been Stanton's repugnance that drew Lincoln to him. In a fascinating book, David Bates, a telegrapher during the Civil War, describes the two men closely. He writes, "Lincoln's heart was greater than his head, while Stanton's head was greater than his heart."⁴⁹ Lincoln needed someone to end favoritism in the War Department and he may have thought Stanton's lack of ardor to be the answer; during his secretaryship, Stanton was impeccable in his hiring practices, even denying an appointment (signed by Lincoln!) to his own favorite nephew. His vigilance paid off, saving the Department $17 million in adjusted contracts.⁵⁰

Stanton Takes Control of Discourse in the North

It is strangely fitting that the author of what might be the first inverted pyramid was also one of the most notorious censors of the nineteenth century press: both sides of Stanton reflect his control of information.⁵¹ Henry Villard, of the *Herald* and the *Tribune*, writes in his memoirs about what Stanton did to the War Department: "This change, while of immeasurable benefit to the country, proved a decided disadvantage to my profession; for whereas Cameron was always accessible and communicative—no doubt too much so for the public good—his successor had the doors of the War Department closed to newspaper men."⁵² Not only did Stanton close the doors, he rerouted the telegraphs, created a secret police force, arrested reporters, restricted press passes, and even usurped the authority of his generals.

Stanton was confirmed in January, 1862, at the height of Lincoln's impatience with George McClellan. McClellan, Hamlet-like in his timidity, was constantly stalling for more time and resources. "If General McClellan does not want to use the army," the President said to his war council, "I would like to borrow it for a time."⁵³ McClellan's procrastinations were aided by the his complete control of telegraphic dispatches. Less than two weeks after his appointment, Stanton penned a letter to Lincoln asking for total control of the telegraphs. On the reverse side of Stanton's request is a message, dated the same day, from Lincoln: "The Secretary of War has my authority to exercise his discretion in the matter within mentioned. A. Lincoln." That day, Stanton wrote to Dana, then the editor of the *Tribune*: "The champagne and oysters on the Potomac must be stopped." Two weeks later, Stanton dismantled McClellan's telegraph office and rerouted all lines into the room adjacent to his own.⁵⁴

On the same day he received control of the telegraphs, Stanton also created a new assistant-secretaryship for his trusted friend, Peter

Watson. Watson was put in charge of press releases and the newly formed secret police, his dual role reflecting Stanton's concern with the dissemination of information.55

On February 10th, a reporter for the New York *Herald*, "Dr." Malcolm Ives, told a War Department assistant that the *Herald* expected to hear of all classified and non-classified War Department decisions in advance of the other dailies, and that the newspaper would decide whether to withhold information. He suggested that this was simply the price of the *Herald's* support of the administration. Ives then stormed into Stanton's busy office, saying that as a *Herald* reporter, he had freedom to come and go as he pleased. When Ives went to sleep that night, he was a reporter; the next morning he was a prisoner in Fort McHenry, and an accused Rebel spy.56 Certainly, Ives was guilty of insubordination, but the charge of espionage was clearly an attempt by Stanton to establish power over the powerful press. Two days later, the War Department was given control over all political arrests, and one historian credits Stanton with more than a quarter of a million seizures.57 At one point late in the war, a salesman was caught trying to smuggle $25,000 worth of military goods into the South. Ninety-seven of Baltimore's leading businessmen were implicated by the salesman's receipts; all were promptly arrested by Stanton.58

Although the press almost universally applauded the arrest of Ives (the *Herald's* misfortunes were always widely applauded), they soon began to realize that news gathering would be severely curtailed under Stanton. Newspaper reporters could not send their stories directly to their papers; instead they had to pass through Stanton's office and his censors. Stanton restricted press passes to the front and arrested reporters and telegraphers.59 At one point in the war, a dishonest investor circulated a phony letter, said to be written by Lincoln, to the New York dailies. The sham letter had Lincoln calling for many more troops and practically admitting surrender. Of the papers that had received the letter, only two, the *World* and the *Journal of Commerce*, printed it. Stanton quickly ordered the arrest of their editors. The other dailies considered the imprisonment a violation of first amendment rights. Indeed, Stanton did keep the editors in jail after their innocence was determined, and it was due only to Lincoln's intervention that they were released at all.60 In order to track the source of the hoax, Stanton ordered an investigation of the Independent Telegraph Company, and when its manager refused to surrender its records, Stanton sent agents to telegraph bureaus across the country and jailed the company's entire national staff.61

Stanton's control of telegraphic information extended well beyond the press dispatches. General Grant, who basically liked Stanton, writes in his memoirs about his only wartime disagreement with the War Secretary. Because he had split his field communications in two, Grant asked an army telegrapher to give his cipher to one of Grant's trusted captains. The telegrapher refused. Grant writes,

> Mr. Stanton had taken entire control of the matter of regulating the telegraph and determining how it should be used, and of saying who, and who alone, should have the ciphers. The operators possessed of the ciphers...were practically independent of the commanders whom they were serving immediately under, and had to report to the War Department...all the dispatches which they received or forwarded.... The operator refused [Grant's request] point blank..., stating that his orders from the War Department were not to give it to anybody— the commanding general or any one else.... He said that if he did he would be punished. I told him if he did not he most certainly would be punished. Finally, seeing that punishment was certain if he refused longer to obey my order, and being somewhat remote...from the War Department, he yielded.

When Stanton found out, he promptly relieved the dispatcher, and Grant had to intercede on the man's behalf.62

Reactions to the Secretary's Control

The various impressions of Stanton dichotomize into two distinct groups: those who were hurt by Stanton's restrictions and those who saw their necessity. Gideon Welles, the Navy Secretary, complains in his *Diary* of the difficulty of getting information from Stanton. On many occasions, Welles writes, his ships would show up to battles long finished. Welles interpreted Stanton's control of information as greed: "He wants no general to overtop him, is jealous of others in any position who have influence." 63 William T. Sherman hated Stanton. When Sherman made a provisional peace with Johnston, a Confederate general, days after Lincoln was assassinated, Stanton was furious and sent down Grant to Sherman's command, "to direct operations against the enemy." Then Stanton used his office to send press releases informing the public of Sherman's error and implying that Sherman might help Jefferson Davis escape.64 Stanton may have been injudicious in publishing the story; Sherman was a loyal soldier who, at worst, acted on his own initiative in the absence of specific orders from Washington. But Stanton tolerated no forays into his command, and one of the offshoots of his tenure as a strict press censor is that he used the press so effectively as an instrument of control, as above. In his *Memoirs*, Sherman tells about refusing to shake Stanton's outstretched hand at a parade, although Dana writes it was not offered.65

It is a testament to Stanton's stature that he was often contrasted with Lincoln. They were usually seen as opposites. For example, Grant compares Lincoln's pleasant, yielding, but forceful personality with an odd mixture for Stanton: "He cared nothing for the feelings of others....Mr. Stanton never questioned his own authority....The Secretary was very timid."66 Stanton also lacked Lincoln's waggishness (some say Stanton lacked a sense of humor altogether) as reflected by a participant's observation of a cabinet meeting: "President mentioned [a funny] book. Proposed to read a chapter which he thought very funny. Read it, and seemed to enjoy it very much— the Heads also (except Stanton) of course."67

Stanton's detractors and supporters, while disagreeing on many points, all acknowledge the secretary's "superhuman" energy— Stanton worked fourteen-hour days—and his frantic efforts to consume information and details. It is interesting that Stanton, who conducted business in an aloof style, could display such histrionics over the channels of information. Dana, like Grant, spoke of a kind of timidity, but in Dana's eyes, Stanton was "a very anxious man." This, for Dana, was a good quality; he said this about Stanton while recalling how the secretary took precautions to insure Dana's safety. David Bates, the telegrapher, writes that Stanton often wrote dispatches and releases himself. Bates contrasts the slow, clean and deliberate writing style of Lincoln with that of Stanton, "whose drafts or letters and memoranda were jotted down at a terrific pace, with many erasures and interlineations."68 This attention to detail gave Stanton the "attitude of a man who is always trying to catch a mental train," said one writer.69

Stanton missed a big slow train in his fear of the Rebel ironclad, the Merrimac, which had destroyed or crippled three Union ships in a day and, feared Stanton, would single-handedly destroy Washington and New York. Stanton wanted to dam up the Potomac by sinking sixty canal boats at its mouth and attempted to do so without informing the Navy Secretary, Gideon Welles. An indignant Welles convinced Lincoln to wait until the ironclad was spotted before acting. The Merrimac, in the meantime, was defeated by a Union ship. Steaming down river a few weeks later, Lincoln spotted the barges. "Oh, that is Stanton's navy," said Lincoln. "As useless as the paps of a man to a sucking child. They may be some show to amuse the child, but they are good for nothing for service."70

Stanton told Lincoln repeatedly to stay away from crowds and was always convinced that the President was in danger. When Lincoln visited the fallen Richmond, Stanton warned against exposing "the nation to the consequences of any disaster to yourself."[71] Stanton assigned a guard around Lincoln, who tried for a time to avoid it, only to give in: "If Stanton should learn that you had let me return alone," he joked to his guard, "he would have you court-martialed and shot." Two weeks later, on April 14th, 1865, Stanton told Lincoln not to go to Ford's Theatre. Although the Lincolns invited the Stantons to accompany them that night, Stanton refused, hoping to sway the President.[72]

Stanton's control over the telegraphs made his office the North's nucleus of information, and Lincoln often spent more time in the telegraph office than his own; the President even had a special chair in which he read the daily dispatches.[73] Stanton, in turn, often came late to cabinet meetings, refused to speak if non-cabinet members were present, and would occasionally bypass the meetings completely, speaking directly with Lincoln.[74]

According to James Rhodes, a nineteenth century Lincoln biographer, and Stephen Oates, a recent one, Lincoln considered Stanton an important aide and one of his favorites.[75] Lincoln's fortune was to have a tough secretary "who never questioned his own authority." Lincoln could stand by his secretary when force was needed, and he could stop him when necessary. At Lincoln's final cabinet meeting, on the day he died, he allowed Stanton to present a reconstruction plan more radical than his own, accepting most of it, while letting Navy Secretary Welles and others have their way on some particulars.[76] Lincoln seemed to enjoy his secretary's superciliousness. Once, upon hearing that Stanton had called him a fool, he returned, "Did Stanton call me a fool? Well, I guess I had better go over and see Stanton about this. Stanton is usually right."[77]

Exhausted from his efforts at the War Office, three times Stanton offered Lincoln his resignation, and three times Lincoln rejected it. The last time was at that last cabinet meeting, when Stanton felt his work was done. But Lincoln explained that the work of reconstructing the South was just as important as war, and besides, he told Stanton, "you have been a good friend and a faithful public officer and it is not for you to say when you will no longer be needed here."[78]

Stanton's "War Diary"

Until Lee's surrender in 1865, Grant's 1864 Wilderness campaign was one of the most important maneuvers of the war. Grant and Lincoln agreed that they would not communicate for the duration of the battle, but after a week of silence, Lincoln and Stanton were getting nervous. It was then that a young reporter from the New York *Tribune*, Henry Wing, sent a message to the War Department. Wing had just broken through enemy lines and wanted to send a battle report to his paper. Stanton himself answered the request, telling the reporter to send an account to the War Department and refusing Wing's request for a message to the *Tribune*. When Wing refused these terms, Stanton made a counter-proposal: Wing's immediate arrest.

Just as Stanton made his threat, Lincoln walked into the telegraph office. "Ask him if he will talk with the President," Lincoln told the dispatcher.[79] Wing stated that he wanted to send one hundred words to his newspaper before he answered the President's questions. Lincoln quickly agreed, and did not limit the length of Wing's article, under the condition that Wing report to Washington the next day.

Wing's dispatch begins in a chronological style. Reporting information occurring from a Wednesday to a Friday, Wing begins at the beginning: "The grand Army of the Potomac crossed the Rapidan on Wednesday." Wing takes four paragraphs to describe the events of Wednesday, another six for Thursday's skirmishes, and in the thirteenth paragraph of a fifteen paragraph story, Wing comes to the point: "heavy firing had commenced on our right when I left at 5 o'clock [this morning]....there has been a grand victory."[80] Unreliable telegraph lines and enemy presence did not stop Wing from saving his best material for last.

A dispatch, hastily written in Stanton's hand, was immediately sent to New York:

> A dispatch of the New York *Tribune* reporter just received states that yesterday the Army of the Potomac came in collision with Lee's army in Chancellorsville; that Lee's whole army is there, and that a general battle would take place to-day. After he left the army on his way in, heavy cannonading was heard, showing that the engagement was going on. Burnside reached the field with his forces last night.
>
> EDWIN M. STANTON, Secretary of War.[81]

Stanton's dispatch, as compared with the longer narrative of Wing, is much closer to the inverted pyramid style: informative, terse, factual, detached, and impersonal. Unlike Wing's dispatch, Stanton's doesn't start at the beginning of the action, and avoids all mention of Wednesday's activities. He first discusses the lead (Friday's battle), then he moves to Thursday, and finally, takes a more cautious position than Wing's: Stanton did not echo Wing's announcement of a "grand victory," choosing instead to wait for an "official" word before announcing it (Stanton immediately sent down his assistant, Charles A. Dana, to get official statements).

In the last year of the war, Northerners received most of the important news through Stanton's daily dispatches to General Dix, stationed in New York, who released the dispatches to the New York dailies. Stanton, after getting information from generals, Dana, reporters, deserters, and sick soldiers, would consolidate the information under the heading, "War Diary." He had a journalist's love for "breaking the story," and Gideon Welles, who on rare occasions beat Stanton to the telegraphers, wrote that Stanton "craves to announce all important information."[82] In assessing Stanton's role in creating the new journalistic style, one should remember the prominence of these daily editions of the "War Diary": major battles, especially near the end of the war, were almost always announced by Stanton's dispatches on the front pages of papers across the Union. In fact, the bigger the battle, the more likely Stanton's dispatches would appear on the front page. No other writer in the press or government could boast of such a readership.

It is important to place Stanton's dispatches in the context of the political shift in America from a loose confederation of states to a strong centralized executive branch. "Before the war," said Shelby Foote, "it was said 'the United States are...' It...was thought of as a collection of independent states. After the war it was always 'The United States *is* ...' And that sums up what the war accomplished. It made us an 'is.'"[83] The scope of the Civil War required unity, and Lincoln, in suspending *habeas corpus* and giving his War Secretary a long leash, must have considered that unity is gained by extra-legal and other maneuvers that strengthen executive power. To lead a nation into a non-defensive war, and the bloodiest in its history, Lincoln himself had to appeal to *all* Americans. He did so by surrounding himself with a cabinet of Democrats and ex-rivals for the presidency. He did so by his conciliatory speeches to the South. And he did so by his special relationship with the press.

The relationship of the executive branch with the press changed markedly with Lincoln. Before the 1860s, presidents maintained a semiofficial organ among the Washington newspapers.[84] Lincoln broke with this tradition and relied on a direct appeal to the burgeoning low priced newspapers which, significantly, were asserting their own nonpartisan stances. With less unquestioned newspaper loyalty, Lincoln had to market himself as a president for the whole country—at least the mainly white, male voters—and this marketing included the selling of his rhetoric. The Associated Press, a young organization in the Civil War, has always prided itself on its ability to write "objectively" to different news audiences. Lincoln, too, had to take his words to the market.

The United States Government Printing Office was founded in 1860. Although not widely seen as a major event in the history of the United States, it did have profound implications for journalism, effectively ending partisan printing contracts and hence the party press. Combined with a telegraphic network that allowed for rapid communication from Washington, and the emerging wire services, which delivered a single message to newspapers of all political stripes, the end of the party press forever altered the nonpartisan press as well.

As with most changes, something was gained and something lost with the end of the party press. What was gained was that politicians suddenly had greater audiences, made up of newspapers of all parties, and in turn granted access to journalists. President-Elect Lincoln made his famous trip to Washington from Illinois accompanied by a New York *Herald* reporter. Journalists were granted greater access than they ever received as partisans, but in giving up their partisanship, gave up their partisan voice. Because of this the media were now free from direct political control *and* deeply connected to the actions and operations of the government. When, to use a recent example, aides to President Reagan told television journalists that they could no longer ask questions of the President during meetings with foreign digitaries, the television journalists protested and immediately began a boycott of these meetings, only to give up the boycott within hours. Michael Deaver, Reagan's Deputy Chief of Staff, had predicted that the Administration would win the confrontation with the press: competitive economic forces were too strong to resist covering the nation's most important newsmaker.[85]

This shift from the party-based press organs to a wider dissemination gave the executive branch far greater powers. Stanton's "War Diary" appeared on the front pages, usually in the lead column, often in larger type, in newspapers across the Union. Imagine the effect of these terse statements on news-hungry families of hundreds of thousands of soldiers. Stanton's dispatches were read by the North, and helped to create a shared discourse, which in turn pushed the nation toward what one historian calls an "American federal community," a community sharing a common interest in what Washington says and does.86 "Mr. Stanton sends a cheerful bulletin touching the advance movements of General Grant," wrote a *Herald* editorialist near the end of the war, emphasizing Stanton's role as conveyor.87 That the *Herald* and the other papers would accept freely what "Mr. Stanton sends" speaks to the North's need for authoritative news, especially in the vacuum created by Stanton's censorship, telegraph and press pass restrictions, and jailings. The "War Diary," then, is welcome, even though the dispatch's overt role, the dissemination of information, masks the intentions of suppression, distortion, propaganda, and curtailment of press freedom.

* * * * * * * * *

While not always written in descending order of importance, Stanton's daily dispatch was never chronological, and was always terse. Stanton's biographers suggest that the pressures of the Civil War nearly killed him. For a man so busy, to write a long chronological dispatch would be impossible. Instead, Stanton wrote his "War Diary" in a hurried style. Journalism historians have suggested that the inverted pyramid style best serves people who don't have time to read a narrative. It may be that the style was started by a man with no time to write one.

Although Stanton left no memoirs behind, he did make comments on writing that reflect his stance on clarity and terseness. Dana's dispatches, clear, impersonal, and written from the perspective of an impartial spectator (if there is such a thing) were appreciated by Stanton "for their clearness of narrative and their graphic pictures of the stirring events they describe."88 Stanton loved Lincoln's Gettysburg Address. The speech was not universally hailed at the time, and was terse compared to Edward Everett's two-hour lecture of the same day. "Mr. Lincoln has made a speech of perhaps forty or fifty lines," Stanton told Dana. "Everett's is the speech of a scholar, polished to the last possibility...but Lincoln's speech will be read by a thousand men where one reads Everett's, and will be remembered as long as anybody's speeches are remembered." Stanton's fondness for concision was shared by Dana, who, as an editor, once admonished a particularly gushing reporter, "Hereafter, in sending your reports, please specify the number of the hymn and save telegraph expenses."89

Edward M. Stanton, the Inverted Pyramid, and Information Control 199

Dana, the ex-*Tribune* editor, may have been the freest reporter in the Civil War. With Stanton's restrictions, other reporters had difficulty gathering information; if they learned anything the War Department did not know, they could not send it by telegraph. Dana had no such restrictions. In 1863, Stanton dispatched Dana to provide the government with "semi-official" reports on Grant's movements. As Lincoln balanced allegations of Grant's drunken misconduct with his own realization that "I can't spare this man. He *fights*,"[90] Dana's observations may very well have swayed Lincoln's decision to keep Grant. Dana's dispatches from Vicksburg are detailed, factual, and terse, and in an impartial tone convey the competence of Grant and his men.

Dana's detached style may very well hold a connection between "objective" writing and socio-political repression, the two sides of Stanton. Dana's autobiography seems to include an example of how Dana neglected to report one of General Grant's drinking binges: Grant's steamer was stopped by Union boats who warned Dana of danger ahead. The general was "sick and asleep....too sick to decide" whether to turn back. Dana decided to turn back, and Grant awoke the next morning "fresh as a rose" and not remembering a thing. That Dana did not mention Grant's "sick" episode in his dispatches, which could have resulted in Grant's dismissal, shows how "objective" reporting may be less than honest while still keeping an impersonal and "factual" tone. Dana, the reporter, while asserting facts, had left out some as well.[91]

"Strategic Ritual" of Manipulation

"Objectivity" has been called by one journalism critic, Gaye Tuchman, a "strategic ritual."[92] By this she means that reporters must rely on authoritative quotes and other measures as a defensive gesture, to avoid lawsuits and professional censure. The press, Tuchman says, tends to choose the discourse of power because it is more reliable and verifiable. Stanton's rituals of manipulation also revolved around a central strategic question: How to minimize the damage from unofficial press leaks to the enemy. Stanton's solution was to assert the factuality of his own dispatches while diminishing the importance of all nonauthorative sources.

Stanton's careful control of information was often not enough to stop the South from profiting from the Northern dailies. A New York *Tribune* article announced that "General Sherman would not be heard from about Goldsboro because his supply vessels...were known to be rendezvousing at Morehead City," a fact that Sherman was trying to keep quiet. The *Tribune* editor must have known he had a scoop because he announced his "satisfaction to inform his readers" of the information. Unfortunately for Sherman, Confederate general William J. Hardee was a *Tribune* reader that day and gave Sherman a fight he never forgot. Robert E. Lee was an avid reader of the Northern dailies, and often, much to the amazement of his enemies, anticipated Union moves. Once, he discovered that General Burnside was moving alongside Grant from the pages of the New York *Daily News*. On another occasion, a statement about McClellan's movements, appearing in the Philadelphia *Inquirer*, convinced Lee that a withdrawal from Richmond was a safe move.[93]

Stanton's terse communiqués were the "official" statements that were supposed to be believed. Given the difficulty of getting news, and given the penalties of printing false material, an emphasis on the "official" word could be seen in newspapers across the Union. Similarly, in his "War Diary," Stanton often announced that an "official report" or "official word" had been received by his department.

Another example of the way facts were used to manipulate perceptions is Stanton's dispatch, (an inverted pyramid except for its personal nature) to Lincoln on January 17th, 1865, and sent to the papers, about the battle for and surrender of Fort Fisher. It begins: The rebel flag of Fort Fisher was delivered to me on board the steamer, *Spaulding*, off that place, yesterday morning, Jan. 16, by Major-Gen. Terry.

The dispatch's touching conclusion reminds readers of the cost of victory and why they must keep fighting: On Monday, everything was quiet as a Sabbath day. The dead were being buried and the wounded collected and placed in transports and field hospitals.[94]

That is how the newspaper account ended, but Lincoln's copy ended with a paragraph about Sherman's movements, life in Savannah, and seized Rebel cotton. Of this expunged information only Sherman's movements seem classified, but the news consumers saw none of the material about Savannah and the cotton. Because it has no narrative flow, the inverted pyramid is easier to manipulate than the chronological account; it is easy to delete paragraphs and facts without disturbing the sense of the story. And the Fort Fisher dispatch shows how Stanton was able to omit nonessential facts to convey a different impression of the event.[95]

* * * * * * * * * *

The reports of major battles reflect the stark differences between Stanton's dispatches and those of the reporters. Sherman's march on Atlanta is an excellent example. Stanton's terse, unemotional comminiqué to Dix, "General Sherman's official report of the capture of Atlanta has just been received by this Department...," announces the news. This is followed in the *Tribune*, *Times*, and *Herald* by an Associated Press summary of the celebrations of cities throughout the North. A reporter's article then follows, written chronologically by the newspaper's "Special Correspondent":

> BEFORE ATLANTA, Ga., *Aug. 25, 1864.*
> *Early on the morning of the 18th* [italics mine] the 1st Brigade of this Division, Col. R. H. G. Minty, commanding, with the Second Brigade, Col. Eli Long, now Brigadier General, commanding, were ordered to march rapidly to our right flank...[96]

The story, written on the 25th, begins with events of the 18th. It proceeds in the classic storytelling mode, withholding the most important news until the end.

Another example of the differences between Stanton and reporters can be seen in the coverage of the fall of Richmond, ten days before Lincoln was assassinated. Stanton relied on reports from Abraham Lincoln, who was in Virginia to witness Lee's defeat firsthand. With Lincoln as a reporter and Stanton writing in his anomalous style, the battle for and surrender of Richmond was a great news event. Sometimes Stanton would send along Lincoln's dispatches to the newspapers. Occasionally he would refuse to name his august source:

> To Major General Dix,
> The following telegrams [from the President] announcing the victory won yesterday by Major General Sheridan over Lees army [the enemy's force at Burk's Station] has just been received by this department.
>
> Edwin M. Stanton
> Secretary of War

The above dispatch, with Stanton's deletions in brackets, displays a deliberate attempt to conceal Lincoln as the source of Stanton's information. The words, "from the President," are crossed out, allowing Stanton to announce the "victory" himself.[97] After the fall of Richmond, Stanton received Lincoln's dispatches and, as usual with important information, penned the following dispatches himself:

> Secretary Stanton to General Dix:
> The following telegram from the President, announcing the EVACUATION OF PETERSBURG, and probably of Richmond, has just been received by this department.
> EDWIN M. STANTON,

> Secretary of War
>
> The President's Despatch:
> Hon. Edwin M. Stanton, Secretary of War:—
> This morning Lieut.-Gen. Grant reports Petersburgh evacuated, and he is confident that Richmond also is.
> He is pushing forward to cut off, if possible, the retreating rebel army.
>
> A. Lincoln
>
> Secretary Stanton to General Dix:
> It appears from a dispatch of Gen Weitzel's, just received by this department, that our forces under his command are IN RICHMOND, having taken it at 8:15 this morning.
>
> EDWIN M. STANTON,
> Secretary of War.[98]

The effect of Stanton's dispatches on reporters is evident in their articles on the surrender of Richmond. Stanton's and Lincoln's dispatches were given the lead position in April 4th's New York *Tribune*, followed by a long dispatch by the paper's reporter. The reporter may very well have understood that Lincoln and Stanton's short paragraphs would serve as a lead because he began his story,

> As you doubtless have accounts of the operations in progress here up to yesterday, I will confine myself to a brief synopsis.
>
> The heaviest fighting has been done by the Fifth Corps and Sheridan's Cavalry...[99]

If not *infantilized* by Stanton's monopoly of information, the reporter was at least relegated to telling the non-"authoritative" elements of the story. It is quite apparent that his role in the dissemination of information was reduced to recalling his experience as a participant. But a close reading of Stanton's orchestration of the above news event shows that Lincoln's role was similarly diminished. Stanton writes that "the following telegram from the President, announcing the EVACUATION OF PETERSBURG, and probably of Richmond, has just been received by this department." This usurps Lincoln's role by anticipating Lincoln's news and announcing it before Lincoln does (indeed, the front pages lead with Stanton's dispatch). That Stanton has "received" the news, and that this is important to convey, suggests that it is only with Stanton's release that it becomes "official." This is all similar to the ritual of hierarchical privilege which takes place daily on today's television news shows. Anchors and reporters talk directly into the camera and address the audience directly; interviewees must look not at the audience, but at the reporter, making the person look askance of the camera. In the same way, Stanton gave the privilege of direct transmission to no one but himself.

Conclusion

Given that extensive research and leading historians have not produced Civil War examples of inverted pyramid reports, the theories about the development of the form should be examined further: were there any journalists writing in this style before Stanton? If so, the history books should be revised to include Civil War examples. In any case, Stanton's writing of inverted pyramids at a time when chronological forms were still standard is interesting because of Stanton's special relationship with the press.

The two most widely held theories of the development of the inverted pyramid are 1) that the war and unreliable telegraphs pushed reporters to put their most important news in their first paragraphs; and 2) that wire services, notably the Associated Press, used the inverted pyramid because they had to be impartial. But there is no evidence that the telegraph or the wire services produced a basic shift in the way stories were written until *after* the Civil War. Telegraphs and press agencies may have influenced the form, but as Stensaas and Shaw have found, this probably did not happen until the 1870s or 80s.

Some journalism historians might prefer to see a glorious genesis to the inverted pyramid; it immortalizes valiant Civil War reporters and validates the modern notion of "objectivity." But a repressive, manipulative, authoritative prototype for the "objective" style if not soothing, is revealing. Our modern notion of finding news in a balance of authoritative sound bites and quotes is, in some ways, a reflection of how information, when cleverly managed and manipulated, may be little more than the unquestioned dogmas of authority.100

Stanton "never questioned his authority," said Grant. This is true, and it is precisely this excess of governmental *authority*, blended with the privilege to *author*, that made Stanton so powerful. His role as dictator was a function of his *dictation*. While we consider that the Civil War press was held prisoner to a controlling central *authority*, we might want to remind ourselves how much the modern inverted pyramid form relies on government sources to *author* both sides of a "balanced" story.

It would be hasty to suggest that Stanton developed the inverted pyramid; however, it does appear that he was writing inverted pyramids at a time when most news writing was still chronological and narrative. Stanton's role in the journalism history books needs to be revised, from that of a censor. He was harsh with the press. But he was also among the first to write in a style that would replace narrative with a hierarchical ordering of facts.

Bibliographic Essay

The chief sources for this research are a one-hundred volume compilation of the dispatches of the Civil War commanders, including all Stanton's dispatches to Dix [Department of War, *The War of the Rebellion: A Compilation of the Official Records of the Union and Confederate Armies* (Washington: Government Printing Office, 1884-1900)]; the New York *Herald* and other dailies during the Civil War period; Stanton's papers, held in the Library of Congress; and the War Department's hand-written dispatches in the National Archives.

Diaries and autobiographies from military figures, notably U.S. Grant's *Memoirs and Selected Letters*, edited by Mary Drake McFeely and William S. McFeely, (Washington D.C.: Library of Congress, 1990), the *Memoirs of General W. T. Sherman*, edited by Charles Royster (Washington: Library of Congress, 1990), Charles A. Dana's *Recollections of the Civil War: With the Leaders at Washington and in the Field in the Sixties* (New York: Appleton, 1898), and the voluminous *Diary of Gideon Welles: Secretary of the Navy Under Lincoln and Johnson* (3 volumes. Boston: Houghton Mifflin, 1911) gave the paper greater depth in recent drafts. An exceptional little book by a telegraph clerk in Stanton's office, David H. Bates's *Lincoln in the Telegraph Office* (New York: Century Company, 1907), revealed much about Lincoln, Stanton, and the flavor of the War office.

For Stanton, Benjamin P. Thomas and Harold M. Hyman's *Stanton: The Life and Times of Lincoln's Secretary of War* (New York: Alfred A. Knopf, 1962) was thorough and authoritative.

Notes

1. Quoted in Isaac Clark Pray's *Memoirs of James Gordon Bennett and His Times. By a Journalist* (New York: Stinger and Townsend, 1855), p. 364. Bennett made these remarks in 1845.
2. Quoted in Menahem Blondheim, *News Over the Wires: the Telegraph and the Flow of Public Information in America, 1844-1897* (Cambridge, Mass.: Harvard University Press, 1994), p. 1 and in George S. Merriam, *The Life and Times of Samuel Bowles, In Two Volumes* (New York: Century, 1885), p. 363, Vol. 2.

3. Homer, *The Iliad of Homer*. Trans. by Richard Lattimore. (Chicago: University of Chicago Press, 1951), p. 59.
4. Aristotle, *Aristotle's Poetics*. Trans. S.H. Butcher (New York: Hill and Wang, 1961.), p. 72.
5. The New York *Herald*, 18 January 1847.
6. Michael Schudson, *Discovering the News: A Social History of American Newspapers*. (New York: Basic Books, 1978), p78.
7. Grant M. Hyde, *Newspaper Reporting and Correspondence: A Manual for Reporters, Correspondents, and Students of Newspaper Writing* (New York: D. Appleton and Co., 1912), p. 36.
8. Michael Ryan and James W. Tankard, *Basic News Reporting* (Palo Alto: Mayfield, 1977), p. 102.
9. Stephens, *A History of News*, p. 253.
10. Stephens, *A History of News*, pp. 253-254.
11. Jean Folkerts and Dwight L. Teeter, Jr., *Voices of a Nation: A History of Media in the United States* (New York: Macmillan, 1989), pp. 203-205, 220.
12. Robert W. Jones, *Journalism in the United States* (New York: E. P. Dutton and Co., 1947), p. 322.
13. Frank Luther Mott, p. 330.
14. Schudson, *Discovering the News: A Social History of American Newspapers*, pp. 61-87, especially pp. 66-67.
15. Emery & Emery, *The Press and America*, pp. 160-166, 171, 212-217.
16. Richard Scheer, Mari An Milchman, Pat Mayer, and Tory Shirley researched the *Tribune, Post, Sun,* and *Times,* respectively. In the *Tribune,* the inverted pyramid style was not found in Civil War correspondence nor was it standard by 1870. See especially New York *Tribune,* 1 January 1863, 30 July 1870, and 6 November 1872. The New York *Post, Times* (see 13 October 1853 and 7 November 1864) and *Sun* reporters generally employed a chronological style until the early 1880s. There are some examples of news stories from the New York *Times* at the start of the Civil War that contain some elements of the classic inverted pyramid, but these are either too short, too personal, or too chronological to be judged as full inverted pyramids. Still these stories, written during the siege of Fort Sumpter, contain elements of the inverted pyramid form. See the lead stories in the New York *Times* of April 12, 13, 15, and 16, 1861.
17. For an example, see the *Herald's* "Police Intelligences" of 18 October 1864, which combines the factual, legalistic, and impersonal lead with a chronological story line. Daniel Schiller, in his *Objectivity and the News: The Public and the Rise of Commercial Journalism* (Philadelphia: University of Pennsylvania Press, 1981) looks at the reporting of the *National Police Gazette* of the 1840s and finds a "pattern of objectivity," including an emphasis on reliable sources; however, the stories do not fit the classic inverted pyramid form.
18. Of course, storytellers have always used the "when" and "what" elements. Author, "The Inverted Pyramid in the New York *Herald*" (Unpublished paper, New York University, 1988). For examples see in the *Herald*: "Terrible Flood," 16 January 1847; "Important From Washington," 5 January 1850 ; "Police Intelligence," 22 January 1864; and "Fire in Nashville," 11 June 1865. To say with certainty that there were no inverted pyramids prior to the assassination is impossible. However, that none were found in the *Times, Tribune* and *Herald* is significant, for these were the leading dailies in the country [Louis M. Starr, *Bohemian Brigade: Civil War Newsmen in Action* (New York: Knopf, 1954), p. 11].
19. Harlan Stensaas, *The Objective News Report: A Content Analysis of Selected U.S. Daily Newspapers for [sic] 1865 to 1954* (Dissertation, University of Southern Mississippi. Ann Arbor: University Microfilms International, 1987), p. 57. The six newspapers are the Chicago *Tribune,* the Atlanta *Constitution,* the San Francisco

Examiner, the New Orleans *Times-Picayune,* the New York *Times,* and the New York *Tribune.*
20. Donald L. Shaw, "At the Crossroads: Change and Continuity in American Press News 1820-1860" *Journalism History,* volume 8, number 2 (Summer, 1981), pp. 39-41.
21. Stensaas, *The Objective News Report,* pp. 57, 61; Donald L. Shaw, "News Bias and the Telegraph: a Study of Historical Change" *Journalism Quarterly,* (Spring, 1967), pp. 5-11. " A biased news story," Shaw writes, "was any which had as a referent a presidential or vice-presidential candidate and which contained value statements in such a way that the over-all impression created upon today's reader was a positive or negative feeling toward that referent" (p. 5).
22. Lawrence Gobright, *Recollections of Men and Things at Washington During the Third of a Century* (Philadelphia: Claxton, Remson & Haffelfinger, 1869), pp. 347-8. Oliver Gramling, *AP: The Story of News* (New York: Farrar and Rinehart, 1940), p. 53.
23. The New York *Tribune* and *Herald,* 15 April 1865.
24. Although Gobright's account is not a "modern" news story, it does contain a number of interesting facts. After writing the dispatch, Gobright hurried to the theater to view the scene firsthand and to gather information. Gobright viewed Lincoln's box and described it in a later dispatch: "On an examination of the private box, blood was discovered on the back of the cushioned rocking chair in which the President had been sitting; also on the partition and on the floor. A common single-barrelled pocket pistol was found on the carpet." (New York *Tribune, Times* and *Herald,* April 15, 1865). Gobright also played a significant role that evening: In his autobiography, he tells of finding the murder weapon, refusing to give it to a naval officer, and handing it over to the chief of police (p. 349).
25. Moorfield Storey, "Dickens, Stanton, Sumner, and Storey," *Atlantic Monthly,* volume 145, (1930), pp. 463-465; Gideon Welles, *The Diary of Gideon Welles: Secretary of the Navy Under Lincoln and Johnson,* 3 volumes (Boston: Houghton Mifflin, 1911), vol. 2: pp. 284-5.
26. Stephen B. Oates, *Abraham Lincoln: The Man Behind the Myths* (New York: Harper and Row, 1984), p. 162; Jim Bishop, *The Day Lincoln Was Shot* (New York: Perennial Library, 1955), p. 256.
27. Telegraph, Stanton to "Chief of Police, New York," 15 April 1865, from the War Department files in the National Archives, Washington, D.C.
28. Welles, *Diary,* vol. 2: p. 288.
29. Charles A. Dana, *Recollections of the Civil War: With the Leaders at Washington and in the Field in the Sixties* (New York: D. Appleton & Co., 1898), p. 275.
30. Bishop, *The Day Lincoln Was Shot,* p. 241.
31. Andrew Johnson, *The Papers of Andrew Johnson,* volume 7: 1864-1865, edited by Leroy P. Graf (Knoxville: University of Tennessee Press, 1986), p. 553; National Archives.
32. Dana, *Recollections,* p. 275.
33. The New York *Herald, Times,* and *Tribune,* 15 April 1865; Department of War, *The War of the Rebellion: A Compilation of the Official Records of the Union and Confederate Armies* (Washington: Government Printing Office, 1884-1900), series I, chapter XLVIII, part 3, p. 780.
34. Benjamin P. Thomas and Harold M. Hyman, *Stanton: The Life and Times of Lincoln's Secretary of War* (New York: Alfred A. Knopf, 1962), p. 398.
35. *Herald, Times,* 15 April 1865.
36. Jones, *Journalism in the United States,* p. 332.
37. See especially Schudson's *Discovering the News* and the following article by Robert A. Hackett: "Decline of a Paradigm? Bias and Objectivity in News Media Studies," *Critical Studies in Mass Communication,* volume 1, number 3 (September, 1984), pp. 229-260.

38. Oates, *Abraham Lincoln: The Man Behind the Myths,* 172; Stephen B. Oates, *With Malice Toward None: The Life of Abraham Lincoln* (New York: Harper and Row, 1977), pp. 427-428.
39. Oates, *With Malice,* pp. 276-77.
40. Thomas and Hyman, *Stanton,* pp. 3-4, 145.
41. Thomas and Hyman, *Stanton,* p. 58.
42. Thomas and Hyman, *Stanton,* pp. 83-84.
43. Thomas and Hyman, *Stanton,* pp. 90-91.
44. Thomas and Hyman, *Stanton,* pp. 111-113.
45. Thomas and Hyman, *Stanton,* pp. 63-65, 124.
46. Stanton, however, was unfairly accused in this century of plotting Lincoln's death. For a discussion of the accusation, and a forceful repudiation of it, see Oates, *Abraham Lincoln: The Man Behind the Myths,* pp. 170-177.
47. F.B. Marbut, *News From the Capital: The Story of Washington Reporting* (London: Southern Illinois University Press, 1971), p. 124.
48. I thank Carl Prince for this observation.
49. David H. Bates, *Lincoln in the Telegraph Office* (New York: D. Appleton-Century Company, 1939), p. 389.
50. Oates, *Abraham Lincoln: The Man Behind the Myths,* p. 173.
51. I thank Will McCormack for his suggestions here.
52. Henry Villard, *The Memoirs of Henry Villard, Journalist and Financier, 1835-1900, in Two Volumes,* volume 1 (Boston: Houghton, Mifflin and Co., 1904), p. 339.
53. Geoffrey C. Ward, Ric Burns and Ken Burns, *The Civil War: An Illustrated History* (New York: Knopf, 1990), p. 90.
54. Dana, *Recollections,* p. 5; Stanton Papers, Library of Congress, Washington, D.C.
55. Thomas and Hyman, *Stanton,* p. 152.
56. J. Cutler Andrews, *The North Reports The Civil War* (Pittsburgh: University of Pittsburgh Press, 1955), pp. 56-58; Stanton Papers; *New York Tribune,* 11 February 1862.
57. James Ford Rhodes, *History of the Civil War, 1861-1865,* edited by E. B. Long (New York: Frederick Ungar, 1961), 350; Bishop, *The Day Lincoln Was Shot,* p. 16.
58. Dana, *Recollections,* p. 237.
59. Before Stanton took over, the Treasury and then the State Department were in charge of censorship. According to an 1862 Congressional report, (United States House of Representatives, Judiciary Committee. "Telegraphic Censorship." 37th Congress, 2nd Session: Report 64. March 20, 1862. pp. 1-14), the Administration transferred the responsibility for censorship from the State to the War Department on Februrary 25, 1862. Stanton's censors, according to the report, were more consistant than Secretary of State Seward's, although Stanton, as we shall see, could be severe with those who disobeyed his orders; Starr, *Bohemian Brigade,* p. 95.
60. Thomas and Hyman, *Stanton,* pp. 301-302.
61. Starr, *Bohemian Brigade,* pp. 318-19.
62. U.S. Grant, *Memoirs and Selected Letters,* edited by Mary Drake McFeely and William S. McFeely (Washington D.C.: Library of Congress, 1990), pp. 460-61.
63. Welles, *Diary,* vol. 1: pp. 83, 127-129.
64. William T. Sherman, *Memoirs of General W. T. Sherman,* edited by Charles Royster (Washington: Library of Congress, 1990), pp. 850-854.
65. Sherman, *Memoirs,* p 866; Dana, *Recollections,* pp. 289-290.
66. Grant, *Memoirs,* p. 769.
67. almon P. Chase, *The Diary and Correspondence of Salmon P. Chase* (New York: De Capo Press, 1971), p. 87.
68. Bates, *Lincoln,* p. 282.
69. Bishop, *The Day Lincoln Was Shot,* p. 15.

70. Welles, *Diary*, vol. 1: pp. 65-67.
71. Bishop, *The Day Lincoln Was Shot*, p. 44.
72. Oates, *With Malice*, p. 417.
73. Bates, *Lincoln*, pp. 138-143. Much of Lincoln's important business was conducted in the telegraph office; he wrote the first draft of the Emancipation Proclamation there, and on another occasion, Welles reported finding Lincoln lying on Stanton's couch, reading dispatches (vol. 1: p. 371). On the night of his reelection, Lincoln was at the War Department reading returns.
74. Welles, *Diary*, vol. 1: pp. 319-321.
75. Oates, *With Malice*, p. 409; Rhodes, *History*, p. 196.
76. Oates, *With Malice*, pp. 427-428.
77. Oates, *Abraham Lincoln: The Man Behind the Myths*, p. 174.
78. Oates, *Abraham Lincoln: The Man Behind the Myths*, p. 172.
79. Thomas and Hyman, *Stanton*, p. 300.
80. *The New York Tribune*, 7 May 1864.
81. National Archives; also Department of War, *The War of the Rebellion*, Series I, chapter XLVIII, p. 471.
82. Marbut, *News From the Capital*, p. 127.
83. Ward, Burns, and Burns, *The Civil War*, p. 273.
84. Schudson, *Discovering the News*, p. 65.
85. Daniel Hallin, *The Uncensored War: The Media and Vietnam* (New York: Oxford, 1986), p. 8; Mark Hertsgaard, *On Bended Knee: The Press and the Reagan Presidency* (New York: Schocken Books, 1989), pp. 141-143.
86. I thank Peter Filardo for this observation; Donald L. Shaw, "At the Crossroads," p. 49. One hundred and twenty years after Stanton's "War Diary," the Reagan Administration took the concept to its logical conclusion with a daily "Line of the Day." Although derided by journalists as a "known quantity," the "Line" was still duly reported. [Hertsgaard, *On Bended Knee*, pp. 34-35]
87. New York *Herald*, 1 October 1864.
88. Dana, *Recollections*, p. 152.
89. Starr, *Bohemian Brigade*, p. 16. Civil War reporters occasionally held telegraph lines by sending portions of the Bible until their story was composed.
90. Ward, Burns, and Burns, *The Civil War*, p. 281.
91. Dana, *Recollections*, p. 83.
92. Gaye Tuchman, "Objectivity as Strategic Ritual: An Examination of Newsmen's Notions of Objectivity," *American Journal of Sociology*, volume 77, number 4 (January, 1972).
93. James G. Randall, "The Newspaper Problem in its bearing upon Military Secrecy during the Civil War," *American History*, volume 23, number 2 (January, 1918), pp. 310-312.
94. *New York Times*, 19 January 1865.
95. Department of War, The War of the Rebellion, series I, volume XLVI, Part 2, pp. 155-156.
96. New York *Herald, Tribune and Times*, 4 September 1864; *Tribune*, 5 September 1864.
97. National Archives
98. New York *Times* and *Herald*, 4 April 1865.
99. New York *Tribune*, 4 April 1865.
100. Stensaas found a relationship between the inverted pyramid form and the use of governmental sources (p.67).

14

For Women and the War: A Cultural Analysis of the *Mayflower*, 1861-1864

Janet M. Cramer
University of Minnesota

Those living during the nineteenth century, according to historian Anne Firor Scott, frequently referred to it as "the woman's century."[1] The women's rights movement, which began during this century, reflected and anticipated the social, political and cultural changes of its time. Though traditionally dated to the Seneca Falls convention of 1848, the women's rights movement began when women formed and entered voluntary service organizations as early as the beginning of the century, creating a consciousness of women's public and social capabilities and the resulting need for equal rights for women.[2] Elizabeth Cady Stanton and a handful of Eastern women cemented this nascent awareness of woman's social and political position when they met in Seneca Falls. Linked early on with the abolition effort, the movement progressed with the emergence of local and state groups and some politician's support. But efforts stalled when the Civil War began. Professing loyalty to "the Cause," leaders of these groups agreed to suspend women's rights activity until war's end.[3] There was little activity on an organizational level for women's rights, but women's wartime experiences awakened more women (and men) to their capabilities for civic contribution as they nursed, organized fund raisers and charity drives, took over family businesses, and engaged in other war-related service.

Though a number of periodicals emerged in the 1850s to address the issue of women's rights and to unify the movement, only one woman's rights periodical was published during the Civil War years: the *Mayflower*. This eight-page semimonthly, published in Peru, Indiana, by Lizzie Bunnell, contained articles and editorials designed to continue the woman's rights and communications legacy of Amelia Bloomer's periodical, the *Lily*. Published from 1849 to 1856, the *Lily* began as a temperance journal; later, Bloomer and her columnists advocated dress reform and promoted human rights. According to communications scholar Edward A. Hinck, the *Lily* "laid the foundation for the early woman's rights movement" by exposing social injustice toward women and "reshaping the image of woman in ways that empowered them to act as reformers without violating their traditional roles."4 Bunnell and Dr. Mary Thomas, her associate editor, sought to purchase the *Lily* and resume its circulation after it was discontinued in 1856, but could not come to a satisfactory agreement with its owners. Still, the editors recognized the need for a woman's rights publication, and Bunnell wrote that "with the assurance of their [the *Lily*'s editor and publisher] support and assistance we were induced to undertake the publication of a new paper devoted to their interests."5 Indeed, Bloomer supported the publication of the *Mayflower* and was a frequent contributor.6

Through her publication Bunnell wanted to sustain the woman's rights movement and encourage commitment to the causes of intemperance (the "scourge that blights our homes, desolates our firesides, confiscates our property, and destroys the family relation") and education ("the basis of all rational liberty and equality").7 The publication was short-lived, but its life span coincided with the Civil War years, thus highlighting its importance and significance for research into its content, message, and potential contribution to the woman's rights movement and woman's emerging civic and political identity; thus, this is the purpose of research presented here.

Its obscurity has possibly prevented investigation of the *Mayflower*. Louise Noun notes its significance to the Iowa suffrage movement, as well as Lizzie Bunnell's later contributions to that state's suffrage effort.8 Linda Steiner mentions the *Mayflower* in her overview of woman's rights periodicals, including it in her list of periodicals directed to, and creating, strong-minded women (though she describes the publication as more congenial to "true women" of the time, given what she identifies as its editorial emphasis on "chaste literature, happy homes, purity" — contrary to Bunnell's frequent assertions that the publication stood adamantly for women's equal rights).9 Other than these short references, the *Mayflower* is not represented in any of the literature on the woman's rights press.10

Research on woman's publications focuses primarily on suffrage journals and the more "mainstream" periodicals of the nineteenth century, such as *Godey's Lady Book* and *Ladies' Home Journal*. These works are primarily analyses of the content of various publications, with some examination of the rhetorical and social movement functions of the suffrage press, as well as descriptions of the general characteristics of suffrage publications and the factors that limited their success in terms of circulation and revenue.11 Few examine the notions of womanhood promoted by these periodicals.12

In general, research on women and the press is lacking in treatments of the Civil War press. Yet the war had a significant effect on women's conceptions of themselves and their capabilities. Similar to religious and benevolent involvements earlier in the century and the social reform and suffrage movements at the end of the century, the Civil War provided a means for women to define themselves and their contribution.13 Scott asserts that "wartime experience prepared a generation of women for the great leap forward they were to make in the postwar decades."14 Indeed, Clara Barton, in 1888, said that as a result of the Civil War, "woman was at least fifty years in advance of the normal position which continued peace . . . would have assigned her."15 War-time experiences also propelled later movements, such as the women's missionary societies, as this excerpt from one of their publications indicates: "[T]he efforts of our sex during our late war exhibited, as never before, their latent and unemployed power to plan and labor for great and noble ends."16

Scholars refer to war as a "gendering activity" that demarcates roles based on gender; at the same time, "the physical, social, and economic demands of war simultaneously bring about temporary redefinitions of gender and power relations for specific purposes."17 As historian Elizabeth Leonard argues, "Wars produce abrupt, conscious and concentrated adjustments in the behaviors considered appropriate for men and women and allow for some crossing of gender lines otherwise considered inviolable," and these alterations "have certain long-term consequences for gender redefinition."18

One interrogation of this research, then, will be the articulation of womanhood in the *Mayflower* and how that is conflated with wartime demands.

This paper supplements research by Hazel Dicken-Garcia and Janet Cramer into images of women in mainstream newspapers during the Civil War. Images identified in that study suggest a shift in the conception of woman's role, particularly that the war years were transitional in notions about what was appropriate gender behavior, and that patriotism and women's very public war work were important to such a shift — that is, news items indicated increasing acceptance of women in public activities through the value of patriotism embedded in the coverage of those activities.[19]

Two sets of images were used in that study, one drawn from images of women before the war and the other from images after the war. Antebellum images were woman as ornamental, romanticized, or radical. The ornamental image denotes "proper" women who remain in their domestic sphere and realize their ultimate purpose in serving husband and family. The romanticized image placed women on a moral and spiritual pedestal, claiming that women should dedicate themselves to the highest influence of motherhood. The radical image extended woman's moral strength to wider social concerns, claiming that "women could transform the world from greed, malice, avarice to virtue, justice, morality. But the purpose was to improve the world for men and not woman's lot."[20] Post-war images also focused on woman's moral superiority, exalted motherhood role, and altruistic nature, but added notions of woman's equality with man by natural or divine right.

Dicken-Garcia and Cramer found that while most news items could be classified as straight news — that is, conveying no particular image or idea of womanhood — when items did convey an image it most frequently was the ornamental image, though all four post-war images were also represented. They concluded that news content reflected a transition in conceptions of women and that patriotism was key to that reconceptualization. It is significant that evidence of a transition was found in mainstream papers. Did women's publications echo these sentiments? Particularly, did the *Mayflower*, with its stated purpose of women's rights reflect these themes and the transition they represent?

The purpose of this research is to uncover the *Mayflower*'s role in the construction of woman's civic and political identity through examination of its content and message. This approach to texts — as shapers, reflectors, and conveyers of cultural meanings — is consistent with a cultural studies and discursive approach that seeks to identify how texts convey meanings or shared beliefs.21 Using this approach, texts are situated within the contexts in which they are produced, a form of analysis that takes into account not only the ideas presented in a text through recurring patterns and themes (such as those listed above regarding women's roles), but also links these to wider historical and social structures.22 In addition, analysis of these textual structures is combined with an analysis of the practices of a text's production and reception. Thus, this tripartite approach focuses on the historical context, the product itself and its message, and its reception or the concerns of its readers and their uses of the product.23

The questions guiding research are: 1) What ideas and images of womanhood are promoted in the *Mayflower*? 2) To what extent do these ideas and images convey the themes identified above as ornamental, romanticized, radical, mother, altruistic, equal with men, and morally superior? 3) Are these ideas and images linked to wartime experiences, and if so, how? 4) What were the conditions of the *Mayflower*'s production and did this influence content in any way? and 5) How was the publication received by its readers?24

Images and Ideas of Womanhood

Bunnell, associate editor Thomas, and the writers for the *Mayflower* presented an image of woman that was vigorous, educated, and capable. Moreover, the image of woman is well-rounded, presenting a woman committed to the home and her duties there but unwilling to be circumscribed to a particular sphere, especially due to fashion — that is, to what was culturally acceptable: "We want the woman who dares step out of the paths of fashion, knowing that she will be scoffed at and scorned for so doing. . . . We want men and women who are able to live above [fashion's] law; whose souls worship at Nature's shrine."25 It was natural, then, for women to explore all avenues of interest and development. To that end, the *Mayflower*'s ideal woman was interested in politics and in literature, poetry, and advancement through education. Legislative updates and commentary on legislation were regular features along with serial fiction and poetry. While some articles were critical of the quality of educational institutions for women, the mandate for women's education was clear, as this excerpt illustrates: "Access to better libraries will afford more intellectual entertainment. . . . What sources of happiness will be afforded her then! The mind will revel in joys permanent and lasting. Oh, the exceeding bliss, when ladies shall all be well educated! when they shall take their places among the wise and intelligent!"26

The image presented of womanhood was, in a way, boundless, and it afforded women the opportunity to see themselves as full human beings, capable of any situation and not confined to a particular realm of influence. Clarifying her definition of women's rights, Bunnell wrote, "By 'woman's' rights, we mean those inalienable rights which are God-given and Heaven-implanted in every human soul, but from the free use and exercise of which woman has been debarred by public opinion and unfriendly legislation. We believe that woman's capacity and woman's aspiration, are the only true boundaries of woman's sphere."27 Woman's place in the home was still honored, but it did not represent the limits of woman's role: "We would not say . . . that home is not the *center* of the true woman's sphere . . . but we do say that it is not necessarily its *circumference*."28

Women were considered uniquely influential. But rather than linking this influence to woman's essential nature, the editors argued that only with equal standing in the family and in the community — including social and political life — could a woman exert her influence. Moreover, a woman's ability to beneficially affect others depended on the development of her physical and intellectual attributes. Woman's influence, therefore, was not tied to her essential (moral) nature and in her role as mother (images that were promoted in antebellum years, especially in connection with Puritan reforms and Victorian ideology), but was a special quality honed and developed through education and development of physical stamina and nurtured in a social atmosphere of equal opportunity.29 Though presented as uniquely situated to influence others, women were, above all, presented as equal to men, especially regarding innate capability and talent.

Themes of Womanhood

Equality with man was the most frequent category constituted by the *Mayflower*'s content. Especially when espousing their views on equal rights, Bunnell, Thomas, and other writers based these arguments on woman's essential equality with man, suggesting that when this was realized, not only women but all of society would be enhanced: "We contend that man and woman were created equal, and that when properly united they will assist each other through all the storms of life, conferring together, and cheering and strengthening each other in heart and hand, to make life a pleasure and the world better for their having lived in it."30 In another article, Bunnell asserted that the "machinery of society would run more smoothly" with the "restoration of a just equilibrium."31

Bunnell and her writers drew on the tenets of a United States built on inalienable rights and equality as foundation for their arguments for woman's advancement: "Is one human being created equal in natural rights to other human beings? No true American will deny it, in theory, at least; and this places those who have no sympathy with us at a wonderful disadvantage; and then our social position is such that it leaves no ground for them to stand upon."32 In addition, by noting that women were fulfilling many of the roles men fulfilled before leaving to serve for war, Bunnell, Thomas, and other writers claimed evidence of essential equality, as when Bunnell asserted that "many women know as much about business as their husbands, and some of them more."33

None of the antebellum images of womanhood were found in the *Mayflower*. This finding is consistent with earlier portrayals rejecting a sphere for woman's influence and contribution. All of the antebellum images support a notion of woman as confined to the domestic sphere, or as providing energy and influence to improve a social and political life in which she was not included. Bunnell and Thomas rejected such a conceptualization; therefore, it is not surprising that content in their paper doesn't reflect these images. In fact, they criticized the characterization of women in the mainstream press — particularly in the case of a Chicago *Journal* editor who lauded "noble heroism" and "self-sacrificing patriotism" but flung "a random shot at the agitators of past years, who have been claiming for woman a wider sphere of influence."34

The second most frequent image from the post-war set (but that also reflects antebellum values) was the image of woman as mother. This image was not, however, a way to justify or characterize woman's contributions to social and political life; rather, it was an acknowledgement of woman's opportunity to influence others, linked with the responsibility of cultivating one's intellectual, spiritual, and physical endowments in order to fulfill this role effectively. In other words, rather than presenting motherhood as the ideal role for women and construing women's energies as an extension of this role, Bunnell and her writers presented the role as a fact of some women's lives, and given the requirements of motherhood, women were encouraged to develop themselves as fully as possible: "[T]he mother [trains her child] for moral and christian battles. How, then, can she feel the dignity of her calling, if her mind be uncultivated? How can she discharge her duty to her children and her country?"[35] Such development, of course, served to promote the image of woman that Bunnell favored, especially in connection with the political role she ultimately desired for women.

Other evidence that the motherhood role was not universally and instrumentally lauded were articles that acknowledged that not all women were mothers, nor were all women privileged enough to have the time and energy to educate themselves and serve in social life. The realities of wage-earning women were presented in the pages of the *Mayflower*, often highlighting the contradictions between popular notions of womanhood and the realities: "Not one of the most zealous advocates of woman's rights wishes to see woman neglect her home duties. . . . But let it be remembered that many women are not blessed with homes. . . . Others have children dependent upon them for support. . . .Have these homeless women no sphere of action — no duties?"[36]

With the reconceptualization of the woman as mother image and since antebellum images of womanhood were relatively absent, there isn't evidence of a transition underway in the pages of the *Mayflower*. Instead, the image is already advanced to the point of recognizing, acknowledging, and celebrating woman's equality with man. Informed by this value of equality, *Mayflower* writers did not strongly assert woman's morality or altruistic nature. Women were just as capable of men as being immoral, and the editors did not shirk from printing information about women drunkards in their diatribes against the evils of intemperance.[37] Similarly, altruistic service to others was not construed as woman's primary function nor as rationale for her increased social involvements. While the editors saw opportunities for women in wartime work, as described below, they did not link a woman's nature with this willingness to serve. Rather, they embraced the opportunities that the war provided for women to engage in public work and to be lauded for this "transgression" of a presumed proper sphere.

Wartime Experiences and Influence

Bunnell capitalized on the increased opportunities the war provided women in terms of public service by linking this work with advocacy for equal rights. "The war," she wrote, "is demonstrating the impossibility of always excluding the woman question from politics."[38] She even viewed the changes as "one grand swoop of fate" that could accomplish "what years of effort have failed to bring about."[39] Shortly after the war began, Bunnell began featuring columns titled, "What the War is Doing for Women" and "Women and the War." Francis D. Gage wrote that, because of the war,

> every latent power of woman, so long sleeping, has been aroused to active and vigorous life.... This is what the war is doing for women: teaching the great responsibilities of life; teaching them of their own power; teaching them through suffering to grow strong. The womanhood of our whole nation is being uplifted, and twenty years hence we shall see, not only what this war has done for woman, but what it has done through her, for the race.[40]

The experience of war is not only a story of increased opportunities for women, as content of the *Mayflower* reveals other tensions and competing interests in those years — namely, the abolition effort, divisions between the North and South, and cessation of overt woman's rights activities.

Writers for the *Mayflower* supported abolition efforts. As historians for the woman suffrage movement have noted, the cause of women's rights was linked to abolition efforts. Many women believed that as they fought against injustice toward African Americans they would secure justice for themselves as well. They understood this as an application of the principles of the new Republic of equality for all. They were to be disappointed when legislators passed an amendment guaranteeing suffrage for all *males*. It was "the Negro's hour," and women would have to wait for full enfranchisement. Of course, Bunnell and her writers could not know this. In their support for women's rights, they may have just as strongly promoted abolition sentiment as a cause not only for African Americans but also as a sweeping reform for justice for all: "[W]e only see in this great strife a struggle between freedom and slavery," Bunnell wrote. "We have always regarded slavery as evil and only evil, and that *continually* — let it appear in what form it may — whether it assume the badge of color, capital, social caste, sex, or in whatever other guise it may hide itself." Similarly, Bunnell mused, "It may be easier to wipe out from our statue books the distinctions of *sex*, when we can no longer be pointed to *African* slavery in justification of the stronger ruling over the weaker."[41] Still, when African-American men were voted into the Constitution as full citizens, suffrage supporters were outraged, leading to animosity between the African-American community and, perhaps, to a suffrage movement that was increasingly defined by whiteness and that discriminated against African-American women.

Some articles in the *Mayflower* reflected a growing enmity between

Northern and Southern women. Undoubtedly informed by the wartime experience, these items in the *Mayflower* indicate that Northern women saw Southern women as depraved, indolent, and cruel.42 Such sentiments may have been appropriate — even patriotic — in wartime, but after the war, when women needed to coalesce and fight for suffrage, they encountered deep divisions and mistrust. Southern women were slow to support the national suffrage movement. The controversy over whether suffrage should be sought through a federal amendment or on a state-by-state basis highlighted regional divisions, as Southern women largely favored a states' rights position that probably was influenced by antebellum and wartime sentiment.43 Through their portrayals of Southern women, writers for the *Mayflower* (and readers, through their letters to the editor) may have, in part, fostered (or at least reinforced) future difficulties for the women's rights movement.

The most ominous factor in terms of the success of Bunnell's paper was a wartime moratorium on the women's rights movement. Bunnell began publication of her paper on January 1, 1861. Her intent was to continue the legacy of the *Lily* and provide an organ for the woman's rights movement. Associate editor Thomas had "*confidence* that there was a demand in the *soul* of woman for such a paper," and she believed that with an organ of communication, women could rally and present the Legislature with a "throng" of petitions.44 Tactically, it may have been a propitious time for a woman's rights periodical, and Bunnell's publication may have enjoyed national support and success. She could not have anticipated that when the war began, women's sentiments would turn toward loyalty to "the Cause" and that a distinctly *women's rights* movement would declare a moratorium on itself. The Women's Loyal League, established in 1863, certainly embodied this re-channeling of energies. Though universal suffrage was considered the ultimate aim of this group and may have served, as Scott suggests, as a "covert" method of keeping the women's movement alive, the League devoted itself to abolition lectures and gathering signatures to petitions calling for a constitutional amendment to end slavery.45 As mentioned earlier, a focus on abolition seemed an appropriate cause since women were construed to be linked to African Americans in terms of freedom and justice, and they believed that universal amnesty and suffrage would result from their efforts — but this was not to be the case. So even though Bunnell sought to sustain a purely woman's rights movement, it was, given the realities of wartime, a fated venture.

Conditions of Production

The wartime cessation of women's rights activity was, perhaps, the greatest factor in the *Mayflower*'s demise. But the war brought other difficulties as well, primarily a scarcity of necessary supplies and a drain on family incomes that deemed periodical subscriptions superfluous. These difficulties were insurmountable for a small, burgeoning publication, especially a publication by and for women. As Linda Steiner observes, women begin publications not because it is their occupation or a profitable venture, but because they see it as an "opportunity to work intensively, for no or low pay, with a community of similarly-impassioned women on a cause they find important. . . . They are activists dedicated to bringing forth knowledge to bring about transformation, not neutral observers distributing information commodities."[46] With an emphasis on social change, these publications go against the cultural grain and speak to a limited audience. The limited circulation of these periodicals discourages strong advertiser support, and even if advertisers were available, editor's political sympathies may prevent them from running certain advertisements. Historically, therefore, women's publications have been short-lived, hampered by lack of personnel, income, and readers.

The *Mayflower* was a small, family operation. Though Bunnell was a trained printer and saw this as her livelihood, she assisted the financing of the operation by funneling profits from her "little two-acre 'farm'."[47] Her sister did the typesetting and her father oversaw the business details and handled the mailing; in 1863, Bunnell hired a woman as her compositor to assist with the operation.[48] Though published in Indiana — and therefore outside the Eastern centers of women's political activity — after only six months Bunnell's paper was distributed in 14 Eastern and Midwestern states.[49] She received early support from Amelia Bloomer, Francis D. Gage, and other women's rights leaders in the form of garnering subscriptions and writing articles.[50] Moreover, editors of temperance publications endorsed the *Mayflower*, giving "favorable and flattering notices" to the editors.[51]

By the end of the first year, Bunnell foresaw the difficulty her publication faced. The paper was clear of debt by December 1861, but the wartime economy was "severely felt" by Bunnell and her staff and she felt the *Mayflower* had not "attained as high a literary character as it would have achieved under more favorable circumstances." Bunnell was committed to continue her publication, however, claiming that women needed an organ of their own "wherein the standard bearers of reform may utter their sentiments freely." She continued,

> [N]o reform can expect any success whatever unless it controls a press — an organ for the publication, inculcation and dissemination of its doctrines and purposes. The Woman's Rights reform needs such an organ.... If we are to have such an organ and advocate, it *must be sustained*. It *ought* to be *well* sustained.... [I]t will be cheaper for the woman rights people of the eighteen States over which our circulation now extends, to sustain their organ already established, than it will to establish another at any future time. *Will you do it*? Give us the support which will enable us to keep our boat afloat....[52]

In spite of her plea, support from the women's rights community waned, and by 1863, Bunnell chastised her comrades in the women's rights movement for failing to support her publication.[53] Though she claimed to still receive more submissions than she could publish, Bunnell said these submissions didn't fit with the purpose of the publication. As a result, content in the *Mayflower* shifted to more domestic pieces, fewer pieces written by outside contributors, more reprints and exchanges from other publications, and fewer letters to the editor.

Dwindling support appears to be a chicken and egg question — either lack of support and editorial contributions created a less appealing paper in terms of diversity and strength of content, or a less appealing paper caused a loss of subscribers and support. Given Bunnell's connections with the movement and her dedication to promoting a strong image of women and support of equal rights, the former seems most likely — that is, that without article contributions from respected movement leaders, Bunnell's paper began to lose its cutting edge. This, coupled with the larger social and cultural forces that mitigated against a strong women's rights movement in the 1860s, created a stale climate for Bunnell's editorial mission.

Bunnell's publication was a casualty of war in ways that affected many periodicals of her day. The war made some supplies difficult to procure, especially the turpentine used in the ink, resulting in what Bunnell termed an inferior printed product.[54] Wartime budgets were tight, and though Bunnell's subscription rate was a low fifty cents a year, a tight rein on any nonessential expense could be expected and subscriber revenues may have become lessened as the war continued. Some items in the *Mayflower* indicate that postal interference may have prevented distribution of some copies. Bunnell would report that issues had been mailed on schedule, and that if someone had not received a paper, she could only suspect that they had been intercepted en route. In a play on words, Bunnell assured her readers that "we shall 'continue to publish the paper' for some time yet, but we hope the 'males' will not continue to delay or miscarry it."[55] Postal censorship was not unusual during the war; if Bunnell's paper was confiscated it may have been due to the controversial content in terms of women's rights or a perceived anti-loyal sentiment that the movement came to represent in wartime. Regardless the reason, there is evidence that, in spite of Bunnell's efforts, some subscribers were not receiving regular issues, and this, in turn, may have translated to diminished support for the publication.

Readership/Reception Considerations

By reading letters to the editor and Bunnell's editorials, a picture of the readers of the *Mayflower* emerges. Letters to the editor were apparently profuse and complimentary, and Bunnell was not shy about informing readers of the quantity of letters received (especially if not published) nor about publishing these accolades on occasion.[56] Readers recognized the niche that Bunnell's paper filled and they were enthusiastic about a new women's right organ emerging from the ashes of the *Lily*. Readers engaged with the content, asking follow-up questions regarding a particular article or questioning a position taken. Readers shared Bunnell's political inclinations and often picked up an argument and supported it with their own observations: "[W]oman must think herself made something beside pandering to man's wishes in everything," one reader wrote. "[S]he must look upon herself as . . . man's equal, and not his slave; not put in this world to ornament a man's house . . . but to stand at his side, his equal in everything noble and good. . . ." Bunnell sometimes printed a letter and her response to it in the same column, thus presenting a kind of dialogue between editor and reader.[57] In its inaugural year the *Mayflower* had at least one full page devoted to letters from the editor.

In subsequent years, letters to the editor became less frequent. In addition, Bunnell editorialized that she was not receiving enough submissions that reflected the women's rights mission of the paper. She stepped up her position by revising the prospectus of the *Mayflower* to include more specific information about the women's rights reforms she supported and that the publication was designed to address.[58] Still, she lamented that the women's rights movement was not supporting her paper. Some readers wrote to her saying the *Mayflower* "savors too much of politics," and Bunnell's tone was defensive, but good-natured, when she suggested that some of her more "conservative" readers could "read with their eyes shut" what they didn't appreciate in her columns.59 Therefore, it seems that Bunnell, though devoted to women's rights, addressed an audience increasingly distanced from that issue. Indeed, her readers were full of "deep feeling upon the war question," and Bunnell noted that there "seems to be little disposition to think, speak, read or write of anything else, while the mightiest drama the world has ever beheld is passing before us."60

* * * * * * * * * *

Bunnell's *Mayflower* is unique among women's rights publications precisely because it was published during the Civil War years. Adopting a position that texts reflect and reproduce the culture in which they are embedded, content in the *Mayflower* reveals the beginnings of a divided women's rights movement. Although the viewpoint that woman was equal to man and therefore entitled to full opportunity and expression in the social and political realm was strongly asserted and supported, this conceptualization of womanhood could not be sustained during the war. Ironically, while the war presented increased opportunities for women and apparently made their social and political contributions more acceptable, it is also a fact that full acceptance of women into this realm — that is, the right of suffrage — was not achieved for another sixty years. So while there were very real gains in terms of woman's self-image and increased visibility in the public sphere, it may be, as Leonard suggests, that the gender system of the nineteenth century "demonstrated remarkable rigidity and stability at its core" or exhibited what historian Nina Silber characterized as a "postwar backlash."61 Bunnell, herself, predicted this when she wrote, "The fact is men have rather more than got their hands full with this war, and they welcome woman as a powerful and generous ally [but] . . . when they are done with us, they will turn us over to our former occupations and abuse just as handsomely as ever."62

Still, the predominant image of womanhood presented in the *Mayflower* is of strong, vigorous women who were equal with men — an image made more visible and manifest in wartime service. Due to a lack of support from within the women's rights movement, and other structural and production constraints, the *Mayflower* met an early demise. Though Bunnell's mission was to sustain the women's rights movement, her publication may have served other purposes. By promoting abolition and divisions between Northern and Southern women, Bunnell and her writers reinforced the sentiments that resulted in a divided women's movement after the war. Moreover, such positions may likely have strengthened Northern women's dedication to the cause of the war, supporting Clinton and Silber's observation that Northern and Southern views of gender "contributed to each section's ability to mobilize and sustain the war effort."[63] Therefore, while Bunnell encouraged a particular vision of womanhood, its link to the demands and opportunity of war may have resulted less in support of the women's rights movement and more in support for the war. That is, as women's wartime contributions were lauded and reinforced, Bunnell's *Mayflower* — while seeking to support what became a reluctant, if not nonexistent, women's rights movement — fulfilled a mission more distinctly related to wartime needs.

Notes

1. Anne Firor Scott, *Natural Allies: Women's Associations in American History* (Urbana and Chicago: University of Illinois Press, 1992), 134.
2. See Scott, *Natural Allies*, for an account of the various nineteenth-century women's associations devoted to social and political causes. Historian Sara Evans traces the shift in women's social and political activity to a dramatic increase in the number of voluntary associations in the nineteenth century, saying they "made a powerful impact by redefining the meaning of public and private life." Evans, *Born for Liberty: A History of Women in America* (New York: The Free Press, 1989), 92.
3. Scott, *Natural Allies*, 72; Louise R. Noun, *Strong-Minded Women: The Emergence of the Woman Suffrage Movement in Iowa* (Ames, IA: Iowa State University Press, 1969), 23. Also, an item in the June 1, 1861, issue of the *Mayflower* announcing that the 1861 National Woman's Rights Convention had been "postponed on account of the political excitement now existing," 78. Following the war, members of women's rights organizations were bitter about the primacy given the campaign for black suffrage, and internally the movement splintered over tactics and strategies. See Eleanor Flexner, *Century of Struggle: The Woman's Rights Movement in the United States* (Massachusetts: Harvard University Press, 1975) for a comprehensive overview of the suffrage movement.
4. Edward A. Hinck, "The *Lily*, 1849-1856: From Temperance to Equal Rights," in *A Voice of Their Own: The Woman Suffrage Press, 1840-1910*, ed. Martha M. Solomon (Tuscaloosa, Alabama: The University of Alabama Press, 1991), 46-7.
5. "To Correspondents," *Mayflower* (March 1, 1861), 36.
6. "Letter from Mrs. Amelia Bloomer," *Mayflower* (March 1, 1861), 37. See also "The Shadow," and "Letter from Mrs. Bloomer," *Mayflower* (July 15, 1861), 107, 109.
7. "Prospectus of *The Mayflower*," *Mayflower* (March 1, 1861), 40.
8. Louise Noun, *Strong Minded Women*, 24, 120, 151, 189, 272. Lizzie Bunnell married Dr. S.G.A. Read in 1863 and used the name Lizzie Bunnell Read thereafter. While the periodical is mentioned in the records of the Iowa suffrage organization, Noun found no mention of it in movement records in Indiana, where the *Mayflower* was published. That there are any copies of this publication available for research may be credited to Noun, who discovered thirty-one issues in the attic of an Iowa suffragist. She donated the issues to the Schlesinger Library, Radcliffe College, where they are stored on microfilm.
9. Linda Steiner, "Nineteenth-Century Suffrage Periodicals," in *Ruthless Criticism*, eds. William S. Solomon and Robert W. McChesney (Minneapolis: University of Minnesota

Press, 1993), 78-9. In her dissertation, Steiner describes the *Mayflower* in more detail, acknowledging the editor's intent to "educate and prepare women for their political responsibilities" and on the "significance and responsibilities of women" in the Civil War. See Linda Steiner, "The Woman's Suffrage Press, 1850-1900: A Cultural Analysis" (ph.D. diss., University of Illinois at Urbana-Champaign, 1979), 130-1.
10. Ann Russo and Cheris Kramarae include mention of the *Mayflower* in their edited volume, *The Radical Women's Press of the 1850s*, but it is a brief description listing the *Mayflower*'s purpose as a "semi-monthly devoted to the interests of women" and its editors, Bunnell and Thomas. Ann Russo and Cheris Kramarae, eds., *The Radical Women's Press of the 1850s* (New York and London: Routledge, 1991), 294.
11. For instance, Marion Marzolf, *Up From the Footnote: A History of Women Journalists*; Lynne Masel-Walters, "Their Rights and Nothing More: A History of the *Revolution*, 1868-1870," *Journalism Quarterly* 53 (Summer 1976): 242-51; Lynne Masel-Walters, "A Burning Cloud by Day: The History and Content of the *Woman Journal* [sic]," *Journalism History* 3, no. 4 (Winter 1976-77): 103-10; Lynne Masel-Walters, "To Hustle with the Rowdies: The Organization and Functions of the American Suffrage Press," *Journal of American Culture* 3 (Spring 1980): 167-83; Ann Mather, "A History of Feminist Periodicals, Part I," *Journalism History* 1, no. 3 (Autumn 1974): 82-85; Lana F. Rakow and Cheris Kramarae, eds., *The Revolution in Words, Righting Women 1868-1871* (New York and London: Routledge, 1990); Solomon, ed., *A Voice of Their Own*; Linda Steiner, "The History and Structure of Women's Alternative Media," in *Women Making Meaning*, ed. Lana F. Rakow (New York: Routledge, 1992): 121-43.
12. Exceptions include Helen Damon-Moore, *Magazines for the Millions: Gender and Commerce in the Ladies' Home Journal and the Saturday Evening Post, 1880-1910* (Albany: State University of New York Press, 1994) and Linda Steiner's works, "Nineteenth-Century Suffrage Periodicals: Conceptions of Womanhood and the Press" and "Evolving Rhetorical Strategies/Evolving Identities," in *A Voice of Their Own*, 183-97.
13. Historian Nancy Cott claims that religious activities were "a means used by New England women to define self and find community, two functions that worldly occupations more likely provided for men." *Bonds of Womanhood* (New Haven: Yale University Press, 1975), 138. This "identity formation" aspect of social and civic involvement is, according to some historians, distinctly related to class: Nancy Hewitt thinks women sought to create a social order that reflected the needs and priorities of their respective socioeconomic positions, while Mary Ryan believes women's organizations helped form "middle-class" values and ideals. See Ryan, *Cradle of the Middle Class: The Family in Oneida County, New York, 1790-1865* (New York: Cambridge University Press, 1981), and Hewitt, *Women's Activism and Social Change, Rochester, New York, 1822-1872* (Ithaca, NY: Cornell University Press, 1984).
14. Scott, *Natural Allies*, 59.
15. "Memorial Day Address," 30 May 1888, Clara Barton Papers, Sophia Smith Collection, Smith College, Northampton, Mass., as quoted in Scott, *Natural Allies*, 74.
16. "Appeal to the Ladies of the Methodist Episcopal Church," *Heathen Woman's Friend* (May 1869), 2.
17. Margaret Randolph Higonnet, Jane Jenson, Sonya Michel and Margaret Collins Weitz, eds, *Behind the Lines: Gender and the Two World Wars* (New Haven and London: Yale University Press, 1987), 4-6, 17, as cited in Elizabeth D. Leonard, *Yankee Women: Gender Battles in the Civil War* (New York and London: W. W. Norton and Company, 1994), xxi.
18. Leonard, *Yankee Women*, xxi.
19. Hazel Dicken-Garcia and Janet Cramer, "Images of Women in Civil War Newspapers Leave the "Proper Sphere" (Paper delivered at the Symposium on the 19th-Century Press, the Civil War, and Free Expression, Chattanooga, Tennessee, November 1995), 25-6.
20. Dicken-Garcia and Cramer, "Images of Women in Civil War Newspapers," 12. These

images are drawn from Ronald W. Hogeland, " 'The Female Appendage': Feminine Life-Styles in America, 1820-1860," in *Our American Sisters: Women in American Life and Thought* 2nd edition, eds. Jean E. Friedman and William G. Shade (Boston: Allyn and Bacon, Inc., 1976), 133-48. Post-war images were drawn from Janet Cramer, "Woman as Citizen: An Ideological Analysis of Three Women's Publications, 1900-1910" (Unpublished MA thesis, University of Minnesota, 1994). Historians who have identified these images include Aileen S. Kraditor, *The Ideas of the Woman's Suffrage Movement, 1890-1920* (New York and London: Columbia University Press, 1965); Sheila Rothman, *Woman's Proper Place: A History of Changing Ideals and Practices, 1870 to the Present* (New York: Basic Books, 1978); Sarah Eisenstein, *Give Us Bread But Give Us Roses: Working Women's Consciousness in the United States, 1890 to the First World War* (London, Boston, Melbourne and Henley: Routledge and Kegan Paul, 1983).

21. See James W. Carey, *Communication as Culture: Essays on Media and Society* (Boston: Unwin Hyman, 1988), 43; Lawrence Grossberg, "Strategies of Marxist Cultural Interpretation," in *Critical Perspectives on Media and Society*, eds. Robert K. Avery and David Eason (New York: The Guilford Press, 1991), 134-45; Stuart Hall, "The Rediscovery of 'Ideology': Return of the Repressed in Media Studies," in *Culture, Society and the Media*, eds. Michael Gurevitch, Tony Bennett, James Curran and Janet Woollacott (London and New York: Routledge, 1982), 56-90; Janet Woollacott, "Messages and Meanings," in *Culture, Society and the Media*, 91-112.

22. In addition to the works cited in the above note, see Clifford Christians and James Carey, "The Logic and Aims of Qualitative Research," in *Research Methods in Mass Communication*, 2nd edition, eds. Guido Stempel and Bruce Westley (Englewood Cliffs, NJ: Prentice Hall, 1989), 354-74; John Pauly, "A Beginner's Guide to Doing Qualitative Research in Mass Communication," *Journalism Monographs* 125 (February 1991); Graeme Turner, *British Cultural Studies* (New York and London: Routledge, 1992), 32-3; Teun van Dijk, *New Analysis* (Hillsdale, NJ: Lawrence Erlbaum Associates, Inc., 1988).

23. Norman Fairclough describes this approach in several recent works: *Discourse and Social Change* (Cambridge, Polity Press, 1992); *Media Discourse* (London and New York: Edward Arnold, 1995); *Critical Discourse Analysis* (London and New York: Longman, 1995). An application of this approach may be found in Catherine A. Lutz and Jane L. Collins, *Reading National Geographic* (Chicago: The University of Chicago Press, 1993).

24. Historical studies are obviously limited in terms of reception analysis; however, letters to the editor and editorial responses to criticisms or suggestions received provide some evidence of the readership climate of the *Mayflower*.

25. "What We Want and What We Don't Want," *Mayflower* (July 1, 1862), 101.

26. For example, "Physical and Intellectual Development of Women," *Mayflower* (March 1, 1861), 33; "A Brighter Day for Women," *Mayflower* (June 15, 1861), 89.

27. Woman's Rights," *Mayflower* (May 1, 1861), 68.

28. Woman's Rights," *Mayflower* (May 1, 1861), 68, emphasis in original.

29. This excerpt illustrates: "Being acknowledged as a member of the body politic . . . she would immediately be regarded with increased respect, and her judgment, her intuitions, and her personal character would have more weight in forming the standards of law and equity." See "The Greatest Good of the Greatest Number," *Mayflower* (March 1, 1862), 38.

30. "Woman's Rights," *Mayflower* (June 15, 1861), 95

31. "The Greatest Good of the Greatest Number," *Mayflower* (March 1, 1862), 38.

32. "Equal Rights," *Mayflower* (May 1, 1861), 72.

33. "Woman's Rights in Ohio," *Mayflower* (June 1, 1861), 75.

34. "Women and the War," *Mayflower* (August 1, 1861), 117.

35. "Female Education," *Mayflower* (July 1, 1861), 98.

36. "Woman's Influence," *Mayflower* (September 1, 1862), 130; See also "Is Labor Dishonorable?" *Mayflower* (March 1, 1862), 34.

37. For example, "Drunken Women," *Mayflower* (March 1, 1861), 40.
38. "The Blessings of the War," *Mayflower* (July 15, 1862), 18.
39. *Mayflower* (May 15, 1861), 76.
40. "What the War is Doing for Women," *Mayflower* (December 15, 1861), 185.
41. *Mayflower* (May 15, 1861), 76, 78, emphasis in original.
42. For example, *Mayflower* (March 1, 1862), 34; "The Blessings of the War," *Mayflower* (July 15, 1862), 18.
43. Elna C. Green, *Southern Strategies: Southern Women and the Woman Suffrage Question* (Chapel Hill, NC: The University of North Carolina Press, 1997), 6, 128-31. For divisions between Northern and Southern women regarding racial issues, see Paula Giddings, *When and Where I Enter: The Impact of Black Women on Race and Sex in America* (New York: Morrow, 1984), and Rosalyn Terborg-Penn, "Discrimination Against Afro-American Women in the Woman's Movement, 1830-1920," in *The Afro-American Woman: Struggles and Images*, eds. Sharan Harley and Rosalyn Terborg-Penn (Port Washington, NY: National University Publications, 1978).
44. "To Correspondents," *Mayflower* (March 1, 1861), 36, emphasis in original.
45. Scott, *Natural Allies*, 59, 73. See also Noun, *Strong-Minded Women*, 32, and Mari Jo Buhle and Paul Buhle, eds., *Concise History of Woman Suffrage* (Urbana: University of Illinois Press, 1976), 198. Positions regarding woman suffrage and the abolition effort may be found in Elizabeth Cady Stanton, Susan B. Anthony, and Matilda Joslyn Gage, eds., *The History of Woman Suffrage*, vol. 2 (Rochester, NY: Fowler and Wells, 1881), appendix.
46. Linda Steiner, "The History and Structure of Women's Alternative Media," in *Women Making Meaning*, ed. Lana F. Rakow (New York and London: Routledge, 1992), 124.
47. *Mayflower* (May 1, 1861), 69; "Circular to the Friends and Patrons of the *Mayflower*," *Mayflower* (December 1, 1861), 177.
48. "Editorial Remarks," *Mayflower* (April 15, 1863), 59.
49. "To Non-Subscribers — Specimen Copies," *Mayflower* (June 15, 1861), 92. In this same article, Bunnell indicates that she has the financial means to continue publishing the paper but that the paper should be, "if not profitable, at least self-supporting."
50. The March 1, 1861, issue of the *Mayflower* was sent to "several hundred persons" whose names had been furnished by "Mrs. Bloomer and others" in the hopes of "transferring many of them to [the *Mayflower*'s] subscription books." "Editorial," *Mayflower* (March 1, 1861), 38.
51. "Notices of the Press," *Mayflower* (March 1, 1861), 38.
52. "Circular to the friends and patrons of the *Mayflower*," *Mayflower* (December 1, 1861), 177, emphasis in original.
53. "Just a Little Scolding," *Mayflower* (June 1, 1863), 80.
54. *Mayflower* (May 1, 1863), 66.
55. *Mayflower* (March 1, 1861), 39; *Mayflower* (April 15, 1863), 58.
56. Bunnell informed her readers that not every letter could be printed because she had such a large number. *Mayflower* (March 1, 1861), 38.
57. For example, "A Few Questions Answered," *Mayflower* (September 15, 1861), 140.
58. "Prospectus of the *Mayflower*," *Mayflower* (January 1, 1862).
59. "The War Again," *Mayflower* (September 1, 1862), 132; *Mayflower* (December 15, 1861), 183.
60. *Mayflower* (May 15, 1861), 76.
61. Leonard, *Yankee Women*, 199. Catherine Clinton and Nina Silber, "Epilogue," in *Divided Houses: Gender and the Civil War*, eds. Catherine Clinton and Nina Silber (New York: Oxford University Press, 1992), 338; the authors cite Silber's essay which suggests that "northern men did not emerge from the war with any new acceptance of female activism," 338. See Nina Silber, "Intemperate Men, Spiteful Women, and Jefferson Davis," 283-305.
62. "Women and the War," *Mayflower* (August 1, 1861), 117.
63. Clinton and Silber, "Epilogue," 339.

15

Isaac Leeser and *The Occident*: A Jewish Leader's Response to the Civil War

Barbara Straus Reed
Rutgers University

Isaac Leeser was the "most important and the most influential American Jewish religious leader in the antebellum period."[1] His most lasting contribution was founding the first successful Jewish periodical in this country—The *Occident And American Jewish Advocate*. "Practically every form of Jewish activity which supports American Jewish life today was either established or envisaged by this one man," wrote Bertram W. Korn, historian of American Jewry. "Almost every kind of publication which is essential to Jewish survival was written, translated, or fostered by him."[2] Maxwell Whiteman and Edwin Wolf did not indulge in hyperbole when they wrote: "The years of American Jewish history from 1830 until the close of the Civil War are, in fact, the 'Age of Leeser.'"[3] Thus, it is important to ask, who was Leeser, for what did he stand, and what was his position on the Civil War?

Biographical Sketch

Born in the village of Neuenkirchen in Westphalia on December

12, 1806, Leeser moved to a town nearby when he turned eight, after the death of his mother. He received a traditional but limited formal Jewish education, studying with several traditional Hebrew instructors but not receiving rabbinical ordination. His father died in 1820, which caused a move to the provincial capital city of Muenster. Here he was enrolled at a local Catholic academy to embark on a secular education.[4] Leeser was able to pursue a broad course of studies including mathematics and Latin. Some classes were taught by Jesuit priests. "Their warm acceptance of a young Jewish student helped to create in Leeser a broader hope for mutual understanding between Christians and Jews "[5]

While he studied at the Academy, he also attended the Jewish Institute of Muenster where he came under the influence of Jacob Mordecai, a rabbi who while strictly traditional, could entertain innovations: He was one of the first rabbis to deliver sermons in German; he wrote a polemic against liberal Judaism, yet he adapted and conformed to changes taking place in German Jewish society. While he wrote defenses of Judaism, he endorsed the modernization of Jewish religious pedagogy. In addition, he defended Jewish civil rights, stimulating Leeser to follow suit.

He left the Catholic school when he was about seventeen.[6] In 1824, he emigrated from Central Europe to Richmond, Virginia, to live for almost five years with his uncle, Zalma Rehine, his mother's brother.[7] Rehine arranged for Leeser to study with a private tutor. However, after only ten weeks, the instructor left Richmond to study medicine in Philadelphia. Undaunted, Leeser later entered a private school and studied English for a few months, then learned the ways of a shopkeeper from his uncle. His uncle, who had no children of his own, remained a father figure to Leeser throughout his life and was someone to whom he often turned.[8]

Leeser developed as a religious leader and writer when, in 1828, an individual in Richmond asked him to consider an article in the *London Quarterly Review*, reproaching the Jews as a group, defaming and maligning their ethical and spiritual nature. Subsequently, the article was picked up by a New York newspaper, and he wrote two spirited letters strongly defending his people, which were printed in the *Richmond Whig*. Others noticed!

Leeser was nominated for the position of *hazzan* of Mikveh Israel, or Gathering or Repository of Israel, a congregation in Philadeiphia (*Hazzan* at that time meant lay reader or leader of services, although it has since come to mean cantor or chanter of the liturgy.) He was modest and unsure of himself, but his uncle and many friends prevailed on him to accept, and he consented to serve.9 On September 6, 1829, the members of Mikveh Israel, by a small margin, elected Leeser, then twenty-two, as their *hazzan*. Unfortunately, those opposed remained opposed after the election, causing the novice leader discomfort as he sought to fulfill his new role.10

Philadelphia's first Jewish congregation, Mikveh Israel, was the last established in pre-Revolutionary America. Founded in the 1740s, it did not conduct formal organized worship until 1771, the year the first synagogue opened.11 Most Jews lived in cities in the United States in 1830, almost one third residing in two, New York and Philadelphia.12 The Jews lived as an integral part of the total citizenry, and no government enforced observances: they were left up to the individual. Consequently, most were lax in their observance and in their financial support of the congregation. Mikveh Israel did not get much support as Jewish immigrants drifted away from their faith completely. American Jews, now in an open, free land could neglect religious practices. They violated the Sabbath, many out of economic necessity, but most of them abandoned the ideal of study and worship for picnics, outings, and lounging around at home. Infrequently they attended synagogue, and they intermarried and assimilated.13

Leeser the Leader

It was to this discouraging, unpromising, unsettled Jewish community that Leeser came. From the beginning, Leeser apparently knew American Jewry's need for articulation, communication, education, publication, translation, and unification—a weighty order, indeed. He was a man with new ideas, energy, and the courage to try those ideas. One idea was to preach sermons in English.14 He wrote, he translated, he published; he created the blueprint for, then organized — and in many areas of Jewish religious life. Nothing could keep him from his endeavors, perhaps because no personal distractions entered his life. In 1840, unexpected events propelled him to national prominence.

In that year, the charge of ritual murder was brought against the Jews of Damascus at the insistence of the French consul of that city. He utilized the accusation for political purposes and was actively supported by the Franciscan order. Many Jews were imprisoned and tortured, and of these a number died. In Europe, Sir Moses Monteflore of England and Adolphe Cremieux of France aroused public opinion about the infamous historic lie. In the United States, Leeser organized efforts. He urged President Martin Van Buren to pressure the American consul in Egypt to use his offices to end the injustice and inhumanity toward to the Jews of Damascus; the President's dispatch was the first of its kind from the United States.[15] A brief series of dispatches passed between the United States Minister at Constantinople and the State Department. An order to free all Jews accused of ritual murder was made, as "these accusations were false, pure calumnies and absurd slanders."[16]

The campaign to defend Jewish rights abroad demonstrated to Leeser what the Jewish community could do if it united. He took a broad look at what could be done in America to promote unity. Despite the desires of his congregation, he held much wider interests and commitments to furthering Judaism throughout America. After discussion with friends, he decided to embark on a publishing effort, modeled after those in Europe. It would take the form of a magazine, for Leeser wanted to expand and expound his views to a larger audience than his congregation afforded.

In April 1843, Leeser began publishing a monthly magazine, *The Occident and American Jewish Advocate*, using it as a forum to promote his ideas. "Leeser had to be his own publisher, business manager, proofreader, salesman, and agent."[17] That he was willing and able to assume these extras, in addition to the creative aspect of his work, tells a lot about his character. Leeser's willingness to assume these extra burdens for the benefit of his coreligionists, rather than for personal pecuniary gain, demonstrates his commitment to the Jewish people and to Judaism.

Leeser was always eager to express his opinions to his congregation. This, and continued personal difficulties, caused Leeser's relationship with his congregants to deteriorate. The congregation actually never comprehended who he was. When his contract expired, he made a complete break with his congregation, which he had served for twenty-one years.

He also lost the financial stability steady employment gives. Freed from congregational responsibilities, he immersed himself fully in his publications.[19] He figured the most expedient method of garnering support would be to take up an appeal, face-to-face, by meeting many of his growing number of supporters who lived throughout the country, to promote his main method of earning a living: *The Occident*. He also traveled by railroad through the South and West to urge in person what he wrote about and to bring his work to the attention of the Jewish public.20 From his trip he learned that all the Jewish communities were isolated.21 Few other American leaders were known beyond their local communities. Leeser's journal carried his name and opinions to every Jewish community in North America, the Caribbean, England, and Europe.

Leeser experienced pleasures during his lifetime. Because he never married, Leeser never could encounter the warmth, tenderness, and support a family can give, but he had an extensive "family" of Jewish followers scattered across the country. Those individuals resided in both the North and the South, including Gershom Kursheedt of New Orleans who, with Leeser, was instrumental in having Judah Touro of New Orleans leave more than two hundred thousand dollars to Jewish organizations both in America and in Palestine, and Solomon Nunes Carvalho of Charleston and Baltimore, who contributed to Leeser's magazine over the years. His better educated friends paid deference to him, valued him, sought him out when they needed his assistance in solving problems.22 No Jewish leader in antebellum America received the veneration Leeser did. He fiercely believed in Anglo-Saxon culture and in American political and civil liberties, as his magazine demonstrates. He wrote more than twenty books, and his influence lasted beyond his years. Through his own sagacious view, and the labors of his disciples, can be traced the establishment of many institutions, though he did not live long enough to see the results. Leeser's monthly journal, *The Occident*, became the first instrument to instill a sense of national and cultural belonging to the broadly dispersed Jews in the United States. Surprisingly, it did not devote a great deal of space to the Civil War but rather contained articles that mattered to the Jewish community vis a vis the War Between the States.

Leeser's Views and *The Occident*

The Occident came into being in 1843, and Jews everywhere relied on it alone for six years until the appearance of the first Jewish weekly newspaper, in New York, in 1849. Moreover, the magazine lasted a generation, until 1869, a year following his death. Thus, its contents are available for the entire Civil War period.

In the first issue, Leeser explained the purpose of his publication, whatever could advance the cause of Judaism and promote the true interests of the Jewish people.23 However, most new immigrants did not know or read English at that time. *The Occident* was published for those native-born, British, Dutch, and some Polish Jews. Leeser also fully intended his magazine to be read by non-Jews.[24]

Leeser included in *The Occident* news of every synagogue and Jewish organization in the country that was brought to his attention. The magazine reported on successful programs, experiments and developments in various parts of the country, stimulating other communities to strengthen their own institutions; spread far and wide the names of emerging lay and rabbinical leaders, and brought them into contact with each other; aroused local leaders to look beyond their immediate problems to the more fundamental challenges of Judaism throughout the land; welcomed new congregations, clubs, and newspapers, and sadly and respectfully it commented on the deaths of prominent men and women. Through its pages, Jewish life moved as in a stream, sometimes rising to a swirling, sweeping flow, other times dwindling to a shrinking trickle.

In addition to denunciation and disputation, and the admonition that Jews shut their doors to proselytizers, *The Occident* prescribed new communal institutions as the best defense against Christian missionaries. Jewish schools, hospitals, even a Jewish publication society, would serve to guard the vulnerable and ignorant from missionary snares while building up Jewish knowledge and pride.[25] Leeser intended to reach the younger generation; they constituted his primary target audience, for they were more conversant with English than were their parents.

Leeser opened his pages to contributions from many Jewish leaders from around the country, and prominent Jewish citizens. Speaklng on behalf of their communities, they told of the progress in adapting to life in their new homeland, such as a series by Mordecai Sheftall on the Jews in Savannah and Isidor Bush of St. Louis. These critical analyses of the position of Jews in the United States, of problems that confronted them, and of the means of solving them, were valuable contributions.[26] Sermons came from various "Reverend Doctors" from around the country and from Europe as well.

Leeser and The Civil War

By 1850, an American population of twenty-three million included about fifty thousand Jews. However, America experienced a tripling of its Jewish population in the decade of the fifties, with barely a ten percent increase in its general population. At the end of the decade, Jewish immigrants represented two thirds of the one hundred and fifty thousand Jews.[27] They came from economic deprivation and after revolutionary movements that swept through Europe in the late forties.[28] Most still remained city dwellers, carried over from their days in Europe, where for centuries they were denied land ownership. As a minority group, they were inclined to live in close proximity with others of their persuasion to preserve their customs and ceremonies. By 1860, they had four fraternal orders, foster homes and hospitals, young men's literary societies and associations, philanthropic and social activities, and educational functions through synagogues.

This communal growth spawned a new attempt at unity: a Jewish board representing more than a dozen congregations. The formation of the Board of Delegates of American Israelites found a champion in Isaac Leeser, who urged its growth, resulting in representation from thirty congregations.[29] During the next five years, despite its inability to meet because of the War, the Board's executive committee—and Leeser was a prominent member—dealt with a number of diplomatic problems of Jews in Switzerland, Palestine, and Morocco.

The Civil War presented Leeser with new challenges of leadership. The rising tensions brought with them a great increase in anti-Semitism in both North and South. In the North all Jews were accused of being pro-slavery and suspected of being Copperheads. On December 14, 1860, President James Buchanan proclaimed January 4, 1861, as a National Fast Day to try to mobilize national feeling against the impending break-up of the Union; Leeser referred to it as "a day of penitence."[30] He wrote: "We would earnestly urge on all Israelites to use whatever influence they have on the side of moderation, and not be the means of injury to the State through their joining the violent counsels of the extremes of all parties."[31] He followed with a prayer for the speedy dissipation of "the evil which now appears to impend over this land. . .the torch of war" where men "dip their hands in brother's blood."

Jews throughout the country gathered for worship and prayer. The anti-Semitic accusations began after an Orthodox Rabbi Morris J. Raphall, used the occasion to discuss "The Bible View of Slavery."[32] This sermon aroused more comment and attention than any other sermon ever delivered by an American rabbi or lay leader. The learned Rabbi had settled the matter favoring slavery's proponents. His remarks soon found print in the daily press and were reprinted as a separate pamphlet. The Northerners also blasted the Jews because of the prominence of one Jew, Judah P. Benajmin, in the government of the Confedacy; Benjamin occupied the positions of Secretary of War and Secretary of State in the Confederate government.33

Leeser chose not to preach on National Fast Day, because "we could not have avoided political allusions had we spoken." He regretted that Dr. Raphall had decided to speak on slavery, although he admitted that he agreed with the New York rabbi's conclusions. He wrote,

> Let us, then exhort all our readers not to contribute, by word or deed to extend the excitement which now prevails, so that, should evil befall this land, they may not have cause to accuse themselves to have contributed to the destruction of the temple in which human freedom had dreamed to have found a refuge.35

Moreover, he printed the prayer of the Rev. J. M. Michelbacher of Beth Shalom synagogue in Richmond, Va.

> The present union of these United States is in danger of instant dissolution. Panic and distress prevail throughout the land. Commerce and business are declining, and cannot be carried on under these circumstances. . . . save us from the horrors of anarchy and of civil war.36

Jews were open targets for anti-Semites in the South as well, because the Jewish merchant was sometimes a conspicuous figure in the small Southern towns and as such was often blamed for wartime shortages, high prices, and the failure to obtain adequate supplies for the troops.37

Further, Leeser ran a number of essays by a correspondent identified only as MRM, justifying the idea of slavery. MRM wrote: "It is a great error in the American mind that slavery is a sin in itself, a sin *per se* . . . It is a great error.. that duty calls for the immediate emancipation of all slaves . . . slavery is an essentially beneficent institution, that is a desirable state of society...entitled to perpetuity. "38

The closest that Leeser ever came personally to discussing slavery was an editorial in which he cautioned Southern Jewish merchants against disobeying local regulations concerning commerce with Negro slaves. In late 1860 he wrote, "We have been shown a notice from a committee of vigilance addressed to a Hebrew in a town in Georgia, ordering him 'and his brethren' to quit the place by the 15th of November, alleging as a reason, that they had offended the public sense of propriety by their traffic [by trading with Negroes]. . . ." Significantly, Leeser advised Jews who disagreed with regulations against commercial intercourse with Negroes to move North rather than stir up trouble.39 "Let them go elsewhere, egress is free to them, and this would be the best remedy for them to embrace," he wrote.40 This was in line, Leeser felt, with the traditional view expounded in *The Talmud* that Jews should obey and respect the law of the lands where they live.

While a few Jews, including some leading rabbis, openly opposed slavery and a few others strongly supported it as sanctioned in the *Bible*, most Jews shared the opinions of their non-Jewish neighbors in the regions in which they lived and wanted their leaders and rabbis to keep away from this controversial subject.41 On the moral issue of slavery, Leeser pointed out that in the *Bible* slavery had been considered an exceptional circumstance rather than a normal thing and that the Biblical slave had always been considered a person, not just a piece of property.42 He pointedly warned his coreligionists that "the Jews in the last 1800 years have certainly not tasted much happiness from the principle that one portion of society has been made for perpetual servitude and another are divinely authorized to oppress them."43 Nevertheless, Leeser would have nothing to do with the views of the Abolitionists whom he considered malicious troublemakers. While he believed the "peculiar institution" of the South to be a bad one, he felt that its elimination was best left to basic good sense and good will of the Southerners. Leeser's usually keen sense of justice failed to operate. Leeser's position was consistent with this; he was neither pro-South nor pro-North. He clearly wanted to avoid bloodshed. He fought for the legal rights of the Jews but never concerned himself with the rights of the Negro.44

It appears that Leeser's main concern was not the elimination of slavery but rather the preservation of the Union. The United States was a special country to Leeser because, as was true of his fellow Americans and especially inimigrants, he believed that America was the great experiment to prove for all time to a doubting world that free people could govern themselves successfully. Moreover, he believed that the success of the American mission, the preservation of American democracy, depended not only on natural resources and good laws but even more upon the attitude of American citizens, their respect for each other, and their constant striving for domestic and international peace.

In case of conflict between religion and patriotism, Leeser felt that religion must come first. Therefore, while Jews were entitled to hold office and should be willing and eager to serve, they should not accept positions that would necessitate the breaking of any Jewish laws. For instance, Leeser celebrated American national holidays with enthusiasm, but he refused to participate in a national day of fasting called by President Zachary Taylor because it corresponded with a happy Jewish holiday on which Jews were forbidden to fast.[45] Yet such occasions proved rare; more typically Leeser's religion and his patriotism reinforced each other.

Leeser rarely wrote or spoke about politics in a partisan fashion, deliberately avoiding political comment in *The Occident*, for he believed it to be outside the proper scope of a magazine.

> Our paper has no connection with politics, and we would consider it a degradation.. .were it to leave its proper sphere, that is, to influence, if possible, its readers... and enter on a field of discussion which may be more properly left to those whose business it is to wade into the pool of partizan[sic]warfare.[46]

His own party preferences he considered of no interest to the Jewish community as a whole. Indeed, it appears that throughout his life he disapproved of Jews as a group taking any political position: "In the synagogue and congregational meetings we want Jews; in political matters, only American citizens."[47] For political purposes, Leeser identified Jewish welfare with the general welfare of the United States. All Americans should vote as they each saw fit, being sure, however, that whoever was chosen favor civil liberty,

> for the more the utmost liberties of the subject are left untouched, without interference from political or ecclesiastical chiefs, the more we will be secured in what we most need.. an undisturbed freedom of action by which we can best develop our spiritual and material welfare.[48]

He apparently had conflicts about controversy. On the one hand, he wrote he wanted to "rebuke the spirit of sectarianism which would, if left uncombated, bring disunion in our midst."[49] He also wanted to fill his pages with articles that would be regarded as harmless by "universal consent, if they even fail to please all."[50] At a later time, he wrote,

> The most unpleasant thing connected with journalism is the necessity under which one is placed, from time to time, to admit controversial articles, which, more or less, partake of a personal nature.... People at the same time soon become tired of non-committal editors, who write for years without ever betraying their sentiments....[51]

On the other hand, Leeser admitted: "... as a friend of free discussion, we will not refuse the use of our columns to those who differ from us in their views."[52]

Leeser refused to condemn the Southerner, because he felt that understanding and conciliation rather than condemnation were called for. Despite his unquestioned loyalty to the Union, his basic attitude toward the South remained unchanged throughout the war, and he even praised Southern Jewry for their loyalty to the Confederacy. Leeser's refusal to condemn the South led to an unfortunate but rather interesting misunderstanding with his old friend, lawyer Moses Dropsie, who was one of the organizers of the Republican Party. On one occasion during the war, Dropsie visited Leeser and threatened him, "You better take care of what you say; you are already on the suspected list and you may be compelled to quit the city before long." Alarmed at this threat, Leeser wrote to Mayor Alexander Henry, who assured him that there was no such thing as a "suspected list." The mayor continued, "Your loyalty has never been impugned so far as I am aware."[53] Leeser reported that just the month before lawyer Dropsie had addressed the graduates of the Hebrew Education Society of Philadelphia. In a "patriotic strain" he told them the meaning of the flag, its character, its significance: "He exhorted that children to love the flag, and spoke of the peculiar fitness at the present moment for displaying it, when malcontents in some of the States had cast aside their allegiance to the government which upheld it."[54] Added Leeser, ". . .at present we sicken at the thought of the fratricidal strife in which parties are about to plunge."

The long bitter war which divided the country caused Leeser much personal suffering, as he had close friends on both sides of the conflict. From New Orleans came word to him of "the direful calamity which now sweeps over this once peaceful country and brings sorrow and mourning to many a bereaved heart...let us be humble as we contemplate the extent of the evil which no human forethought or knowledge was able to avert."[55] It hurt Leeser deeply to see the Jewish community which he had tried so hard to unite, torn, as was the whole nation, with hatred and bloodshed. He feared for the strength of the American Union which he loved. Perhaps most important, he feared that even if the war were won, the passions it had evoked would do irreparable damage to the American dream of civil and religious liberty.[56] While he did not pretend to analyze all of its causes, long-range or immediate, he saw the war principally as a failure of Americans to appreciate their good fortune and the practice charity toward one another. He saw it as further evidence that man, however civilized, had great need of God and God's laws. "Let us be humble when we contemplate the extent of the evil which no human forethought or knowledge was able to arrest."[57]

Leeser became involved in incidents defending Jewish rights during the Civil War. First came the fight for the Jewish chaplaincy in the Union Army. In the summer of 1861, Congress passed a law regarding the appointment of chaplains to the Union Army: all chaplains were "to be regularly ordained ministers of some *Christian* [italics in the original] denomination."[58] The failure of Congress to provide for Jewish chaplains was probably a thoughtless act of omission rather than a conscious manifestation of anti-Semitism. However, many Jewish soldiers were serving in the Union Army, and this was perceived as an injustice and a danger to American democracy in general because a particular religious group was excluded from holding a public office.[59] Leeser mounted a campaign to place Jews on equal footing with the others, urging readers to act by signing the draft of a petition, copying it and signing the copy and then giving it to members of both houses of Congress who represent them.[60] Leeser spearheaded a letter-writing project himself. He went directly to the top: to Mr. Lincoln. His letter, which he reprinted in *The Occident*, also had a response from John Jay, dated only two weeks later: The President would appoint a Jewish chaplain if his Board "will designate a proper person for the purpose."[61] In the end, the Union Army had three Jewish chaplains, from Philadelphia, Louisville, and New York, but the first was not appointed until April 1864.[62] The presence of Jewish chaplains helped to prevent secret baptisms of Jewish persons as they lay dying, even of those who were unconscious. Leeser said those Jews would have resisted had they the power of speech or were they otherwise able to prevent it. There was fear, "a hesitancy to confess our religion, for fear of taunt or shame, . . . powerful enough to act as a check on them." Clearly, other examples exist "if we could get free access to the various hospital records."[63]

Probably the most famous issue involving Jews during the Civil War was General Ulysses S. Grant's order: "The Jews, as a class violating every regulation of trade established by the Treasury Department and also departmental orders, are hereby expelled from the department within twenty-four hours from the receipt of this order."[64] These were the words of Order No. 11, issued on December 17, 1862. The result was the Jewish population—men, women and children—were evacuated forcibly from Holly Springs and Oxford, Mississippi, and from Paducah, Kentucky. American Jewry responded with feelings of shock, rage, and pain. Leeser denounced Order No. 11, urging any individual, Jewish or otherwise, guilty of breaking government regulations be punished as an individual. Such a thing as Order 11 was possible, he declared bitterly, because "the parties threatened with such ill usage were not Christians, not even

Negroes, nothing but Jews."[65] Leeser immediately became involved in public protest meetings in Philadelphia; such also took place in Chicago and New York. He also whipped the American press to support him, visiting major newspapers in Philadelphia. The *Public Ledger* responded to his overtures by demanding that the offensive order be cancelled and publishing an irrelevant but well meaning, list of Jewish contributions to civilization. The *Inquirer* refused to print anything about Order 11 at all.[66] President Lincoln, when he was informed of its content, revoked Order 11 immediately under his personal authority as Commander-in-Chief of the United States Armed Forces.

Another battle in which Leeser participated actively during the war was his successful fight to prevent Christianity from being declared the legal religion of the United States. Influenced by the long and bloody Civil War and the emotionalism which surrounded it, a revival of religious activity occurred in the United States during and immediately following the war. A Presbyterian Synod meeting in Pittsburgh in 1864 decided to petition Congress for a constitulonal amendment recognizing Christianity as the official religion. In February 1865, the petition was prepared and presented to Congress.

Leeser sounded the alarm. In issue after issue of *The Occident*, he reiterated the case for complete separation of church and state and pointed out that the religious freedom of all Americans would be endangered if the Presbyterian movement to amend the Constitution was successful. Preferring unified action on a national level whenever possible, Leeser brought the matter to the Board of Delegates of American Israelites. As the Board's spokesman, Leeser then drafted an opposition statement to the proposed amendment. On February 11, 1865, it was introduced to the the Senate and referred to the judiciary committee, where the proposed amendment died. It was this rather than the protest of the Jewish community which prevented the amendment of the Constitution that would have made Christianity the official religion of the Umted States.[67] This action helped to clarify the relationship of church and state in America and by maintaining the rights of one minority group, indirectly benefited all minority groups.

When the war was finally over, Isaac Leeser echoed Lincoln's appeal for conciliation and renewed brotherhood. Yet, he was sickened upon learning what had been destroyed.[68] Speaking in Washington upon the occasion of Lincoln's death, Leeser urged all Americans to honor Lincoln by peaceful labor, not vengeance, directed at quieting the fears of the defeated South and restoring the peace and prosperity of all. Jews especially should "contribute all in your power to the healing of the fratricidal strife."[69] Leeser admitted that after the Presidential assassination, he received all kinds of written material about Lincoln, in English and German, including two Hebrew poems. However, he found it "impossible" to print them.[70]

With Lincoln's death came a description of the Sabbath service following and Leeser's remarks. He said, "Enable [the inhabitants of the country] to heal the breaches which a desolating war has inflicted on the land during four years of severe conflict."[71] And he took pleasure in noting around Thanksgiving time that year, that although defeated in a "gigantic contest," the people of the South had cause for thanksgiving:

> After four years of bloody strife the sword at length is sheathed... war is one of the greatest curses which can afflict any people... With the close of the war which terminated so disastrously to the South... moderate counsels have prevailed, . . . and [there is] not a man who formerly vehemently opposed the Union, but is as honest and firm in the determination to uphold it in all its integrity, and to be faithful without hesitation or mental reservation to the Constitution, under which he is henceforth to live. . .[72]

The closing of the Civil War and the tragedy of Lincoln's death presented the occasion upon which Leeser once again stated his concept of the role of the Jew on the American scene: "to do all in our power to promote the welfare of the country in which our lot is cast...bear the burdens imposed...never offend against the laws. . . ."[73]

Impact and Evaluation

Isaac Leeser visualized the free Jewish community as a part of, rather than separate from, the free American community. Its unique religious and cultural heritage, must, of course, be preserved, but this uniqueness did not prevent the American Jew from being in every sense at the same time an American. Leeser believed that American Jews must defend their rights within the larger community, and he was a leader in defending these rights; but the rights which Leeser spent his lifetime defending he envisioned as being the rights belonging to the Jews as Americans, rather than particularly as Jews. To Leeser, for example, Sabbath observance was an individual, private matter—one not to be legislated. Such laws violated the Bill of Rights with its freedom of religion clause. In battling for religious liberty and complete civil equality for Jews, then, he battled to extend the basic rights of the entire American community. In another instance, the experience of the Jewish community in the chaplaincy struggle was significant, because it confirmed the basic equality of religious groups in the United States. Also, cooperative national action could accomplish much for the Jewish comunity, Leeser again recognized.

Leeser's periodical, *The Occident And American Jewish Advocate*, became the instrument for fostering community identity and Jewish culture. He became a leader in the fight against missionary groups, and governors and judges who vitiated his religion and his people. *The Occident* became a major vehicle to propose, to ensure, and to watch the growth of community institutions. Yet, during the Civil War, circulation suffered because there was no prospect for a large increase in the North because of increased taxation. [74] Nevertheless, the publication helped unify the Jews, widely scattered throughout the continent, and made them aware of each other. While it espoused political neutrality, it also helped to implant Jewish religion and culture, and to connect to Jewish communities worldwide.

The Occident offered a mirror to reflect the age: Every topic of real concern was covered and debated. *The American Jewish Advocate* enabled Leeser to plead for Judaism, to defend the faith in the face of clashing opinions on religious reform that were beginning to tear at the Jewish fabric. It became an important forum for the most important leaders of American Jewry to expound and debate the form Judaism would take in this country.

As noted above, Leeser had spent his first years in America in Virginia. Also, he traveled frequently throughout the South, had many friends and acquaintances there. Unlike some Northerners then, Leeser could not view all Southerners as either sinful or as traitors. In fact, he saw the partisans of both sides as the results of conditioning, environment, and upbringing and urged national tolerance and forbearance by both. Leeser faced the difficult dilemma of a man of divided loyalties, in a day which required undivided allegiance. It was a strange time, a time of growing up and of integration, an age of acceptance and of rejection, a period of involvement in communal affairs and of personal loneliness. Isaac Leeser and his magazine came at a crucial time in the development of America and American Jewry. Both served the community well, giving hope and vitality.

Notes

1. Leeser translated the Hebrew *Bible* into English, organized Jewish "parochial" or all-day schools, and made the English sermon a regular feature of the Sabbath morning service.

It was Leeser who was responsible for the first American Jewish publication society and the first American rabbinical school. Jacob Rader Marcus, *Memoirs of American Jews, 1775-1865,* "Isaac Leeser, American Jewish Missionary," Vol.11 (Philadelphia: The Jewish Publication Society of America, *1955)* p.58. Data about Leeser's life include Henry Englander, "Isaac Leeser," *Yearbook, Central Conference of American Rabbis,* Vol. 28 (1918), pp.213-52, which discusses in detail some of Leeser's convictions and beliefs; Bertram Korn, *Eventful Years and Experiences: Studies in Nineteenth Century American Jewish History,* (Cincinnati, Ohio: American Jewish Archives, 1954) pp.151-213; Marcus, *op. cit.*, pp.58-87, which excerpts reports of his travels to various Jewish communities; Maxwell Whiteman, "Isaac Leeser and the Jews of Philadelphia," *Publication of the American Jewish Historical Society,* Vol. XLVIII (June, 1959), pp.207-44; Maxine Seller, "Isaac Leeser, Architect of the American Jewish Community" (Ph.D. dissertation, University of Pennsylvania, 1965); Naomi Cohen, *Encounter with Emancipation: The German Jews* in the *United States 1830-1914* (Philadelphia: The Jewish Publication Society of America, 1984); Lance J. Sussman, "'Confidence in God': The Life and Preaching of Isaac Leeser (1806-1868)" (Ordination thesis, Hebrew Union College-Jewish Institute of Religion, 1980); Lance J. Sussnian, "Another Look at Isaac Leeser and the First Jewish Translation of the Bible in the United States," *Modern Judaism,* Vol. V (May, 1985), pp.159-90; Lance J. Sussman, "Isaac Leeser and the Protestantization of American Judaism," *American Jewish Archives,* Vol. 38 (April, 1986), pp.1-21, and Mayer Sulzberger, "No Better Jew, No Purer Man: Mayer Sulzberger on Isaac Leeser," *American Jewish Archives,* Vol. 21 (November, 1969), pp.14048.
2. Bertram Wallace Korn, "Isaac Leeser: Centennial Reflections," *American Jewish Archives,* Vol. 19 (November, 1967), p.133.
3. Maxwell Whiteman and Edwin Wolf, *History of Jews of Philadelphia from Colonial Times to the f Jackson* (Philadelphia: The Jewish Publication Society of America, 1957) pp.372-73.
4. Sussman, *op. cit.*, "Another Look . . .," p.160.
5. *Ibid.; The Occident,* Vol. 16, No.10, January 1859, p.485; *Ibid.*, Vol. 13, No.1, April *1855,* p. *39.*
6. Sussman, *op. cit.*, p.161, also Sussman, "Isaac Leeser and . . .", p.7.
7. *The Occident,* Vol. 10, No.1, April 1852, p.23 note.
8. *Ibid.*
9. "Isaac Leeser," by Max Schloessinger, Ph.D., *The Jewish Encyclopedia* (New York: Funk and Wagnalls, 1901), Vol. 7, p.663.
10. To glean Leeser's relation to Mikveh Israel see *A Review of the Late Controversies Between The Rev. Isaac Leeser and The Congregation Mikveh Israel,* pamphlet, Philadelphia (1850), pp.1-17; copy available in New York Public Library, Jewish Division.
11. Whiteman and Wolf,*op. cit.*, p.11.
12. Ira Rosenwaike, *On the Edge of Greatness, a Portrait of American Jewry in the Early National Period* (Cincinnati, Ohio: American Jewish Archives, 1985), pp.30-33, 45, 49. Charleston came next, with 650 Jews in a population of 40,000, followed by Cincinnati's 140 Jews of 25,000 people.
13. *Ibid.*, "Moving Westward," p.232; Hyman B. Grinstein, *The Rise of the Jewish Community of New York, 1654-1860* (Philadelphia: The Jewish Publication Society of America, *1945), pp.14-15.*
14. Sussman, *op. cit.*, "Another Look. . .," p.163.
15. Jacob Ezekiel, "Persecution of the Jews in 1840," *Publication of the American Jewish Historical Society,* No.8 (1900), p.143.
16. Cyrus Adler and Aaron M. Margalith, *With Firmness in the Right, American Diplomatic Action Affecting Jews, 1840-1945* (New York: The American Jewish Committee, 1946), p. 5. The American Minister sent a copy of the order to Washington, expressing his hope that, in the future, it would not be necessary for him to take any steps when the interests of the United States were not immediately affected.

17. Korn, *op. cit.*, "Centennial Reflections," p.134.
18. *The Occident*, Vol. 7, No.7, October 1849, p.377.
19. *The Occident*, Vol. 10, No.11, February 1853, p.535. For seven years he was without a pulpit, but in 1857, some friends convinced leeser to lead another synagogue in Philadelphia, where he remained till his death, February 1, 1868.
20. *Ibid.*, Vol. 10, No.1, April 1852, p.2.
21. *Ibid.*, Vol. 11, No.10, January 1854, pp. 521-22.
22. The collection of some of his letter files, the Leeser Collection, are on deposit at the former Dropsie Annenberg Research Institute, now the Center for Judaic Studies, University of Pennsylvania, Philadelphia. A visit to the collection shows how numerous and widespread were his contacts. Some found themselves to be the only Jews in a territory. After his death his many books were catalogued by Cyrus Adler as a labor of love. In custody at Dropsie College, his extensive collection was under Adler's eye for fifty years. "Leeser was not completely without an heir," wrote Anita L Lebeson, in *Pilgrim People* (New York: Harper and Bros. 1950), p.332.
23. *Ibid.*, Vol.1, No.1, April 1843, p.1; also see *Ibid.*, Vol. 17, No.1, March 31, 1859, p.1, where he states a distinguished physician of Philadelphia urged him on begin his journal: "You have to journalize if you expect to be read."
24. *Ibid.*, Vol.1, No.1, April 1843, p.6.
25. *Ibid.*, Vol.1, No.1, April 1843, pp.43-7; *Ibid.*, Vol. I, No.2, May 1843, pp.100-08; *Ibid.*, Vol.1, No.3, June 1843, pp.145-46; *Ibid.*, Vol.1, No.4, July 1843, pp.183-90; *Ibid.*, Vol. 1, No.6, September 1843, pp. 300-1; *Ibid.*, Vol.1, No.7, October 1843, pp. 350-52; *Ibid.*, Vol.1, No.9, December 1843, p.411; *Ibid.*, Vol.1, No.10, January 1844, pp.511-12; *Ibid.*, Vol.11, No.1, April 1844, p.48; *Ibid.*, Vol. II, No.2, May 1844, p.63; *Ibid.*, Vol.2, No.8, November 1844, pp.387-93; *Ibid.*, Vol.11, No.10, January 1845, p.513; bid., Vol.2, No.11, February 1845, pp.517-27., 561, 605; *Ibid.*, Vol.111, No.1, April 1845, pp. 40-48; *Ibid.*, Vol.111, No.7, October 1845, p.355; *Ibid.*, Vol.111, No.9, Dcecember 1845, p.421; *Ibid.*, Vol. 4, No.3, April 1846, p.165; *Ibid.*, Vol. 4 , No.7, October 1846, pp.351-57; *Ibid.*, Vol.4, No.8, November 1846, pp.404-5; *Ibid.*, Vol. 6, No.9, December 1848, pp.462 ff.; *Ibid.*, Vol. 7, No.2, May 1849, pp.98-103; *Ibid.*, Vol. 7, No.4, July 1849, pp.223-34; *Ibid.*,Vol. 7, No.6, September 1849, p.319; *Ibid.*, Vol. 7, No.7, October 1849, pp.359-66; *Ibid.*, Vol. 7, No.9, Dcecember 1849, p.356; *Ibid.*, Vol. 7, No.10, January *1850*, pp. 481-95; *Ibid.*, Vol. 8, No.1, April 1850, pp.37-42; *Ibid.*, Vol. 8, No.2, May 1850, pp. 90-92; *Ibid.*, Vol. 8, No.5, August, 1850, pp.259-61; *Ibid.*, Vol. 9, No.7, October 1851, pp.356-72; *Ibid.*, Vol.9, No.8, November 1851, pp.422-25; *Ibid.*, Vol.11, No.11, February 1854, pp.541-52; and *Ibid.*, Vol. 14, No.6, September 1856, p.303.
26. The latter essay is reprinted in *American Jewish Archives*, Vol. 18 (November, 1966), pp.155-60.
27. *Ibid.*, Vol. 20, No. 5, August 1862, p.237.
28. Jacob Rader Marcus, *To Count a People: American Jewish Population 1585-1984* (Lanham, MD: University Press of America, 1990).
29. Allan Tarshish, "The Board of Delegates of American Israelites (1859-1878)," *Publication of the American Jewish Historical Society*, Vol. XLIX *(1959)*, pp. 16-22. Also, Rabbi Joseph Buchler, "The Struggle for Unity: Attempts at Union in American Jewish Life, 1654-1868," *American Jewish Archives*, Vol.11, No.1, June 1949, pp.97-122.
30. Printed in *The Occident*, Vol. 18, No.39, December 20, 1860, pp.237-238.
31. *Ibid.*, p.238.
32. Schappes, *op. cit.*, "'Bible View of Slavery,' A Discourse by Rabbi Morris Jacob Raphall, before Congregation Bnai Jeshurun, New York on the National Fast Day, January 4, 1861," pp. 405-18.
33. After the war he escaped to Great Britain to avoid Federal officials' wrath. He became the Queen's counsel, developing an international reputation. See Jacob Rader Marcus, *Memoirs of American* Jews, Vol. 3 (Philadelphia: The Jewish Publication Society,

1955, 1956), pp.241-42. In 1862 Benjamin was censured by the Confederate Congress for failing to send war supplies to Roanoke, resulting in it loss to the Union. Had he complied, however, Norfolk would have been left vulnerable.
34. *The Occident*, Vol. 17, No.43, January 17, 1861, p.259; No.44, January 24, p.268; No.45, January 31, p.274. While leeser would not take a public stand, he substantially agreed with Raphall, differing only on minor points.
35. *Ibid.*, Vol. XVIII, No.43, January 17, 1861, p.1.
36. *Ibid.*, p.260.
37. Henry Feingold, *Zion in America* (New York: Hippocrene Books, Inc.: 1981), p.92.
38. Vol 18, No.43, January 17, 1861, p.259; *Ibid.*, Vol.19, No.8, November 1861, pp.356-366.
39. *Ibid.*,Vol.18, No.33, November 8, 1860, p.197. The town of Thomasville, Georgia, ultimately passed a resolution banishing all its Jewish residents.
40. *Ibid.*
41. Korn, *op. cit.*, *Eventful Years*, pp.43-44.
42. *Ibid.*, Vol.6, No.5, August 1848, p.248.
43. *Ibid.*, Vol. 19, No.7, November 1861, p.365.
44. *The Occident*, Vol. V, No.6, October 1847, pp.520-31; Leeser praised the removal of legal disabilities against non-Christians regarding the law of violence in Maryland, but he ignored the fact that the law still did not grant legal equality to Negroes and mulattoes.
45. Englander, *op. cit.* "Isaac Leeser," p.231.
46. *The Occident*, Vol. XVIII, No.33, November 8, 1860, p.1.
47. *Ibid.*, Vol.12, No.6, October 1854, p.563.
48. *Ibid.*, Vol. XXII, No.6, October 1864, p.531.49. *Ibid.*, Vol. 20, No.1, April 1862, p.6.
50. *Ibid.*
51. *Ibid.*, at least April 1859, no page given as microffim consists of pieces of page only.
52. *Ibid.*, Vol. 17, No.1, March 31, 1859, p.2.
53. Isaac Leeser to Mayor Henry, June 3, 1861, and Mayor Henry to Leeser, June 5, 1861. Leeser Collection, Philadelphia.
54. *The Occident*, Vol. 19, No.3, May 1861, p.92.
55. *Ibid.*, Vol. 20, No.5, August 1862, p.238.
56. *Ibid.*, Vol. 23, No.8, November 1865, p.314.
57. *Ibid.*, Vol. 20, No.1, April 1862, p.28.
58. *Ibid.*, Vol. 19, No.9, December 1861, p.420. The October 1862 issue, p.325, noted the impact of the law on those in Philadelphia.
59. Bertram Korn, "Congressman Clement L. Vallandigham's Championship of the Jewish Chaplaincy in the Civil War," *American Jewish Historical Quarterly*, Vol. LIII, No.2 (December 1963), pp.188-191; *The Occident* Vol. 29, No.6, September 1861, pp.417-420 *Ibid.*, Vol.20, No.4, July 1862, pp.236-237.
60. *Ibid.*, Vol. 29, No.9, December 1861, p.419.
61. *Ibid.*, Vol. 20, No.7, October 1862, p.325-327.
62. *Ibid.*. Vol. 23, No.5, August 1865, pp.234-235.
63. *Ibid.*, Vol. 23, No.7, October 1865, pp, 294-295.
64. Schappes, *Documentary History*, *op. cit.*, pp.472-425, "Revoking General Grant's Order No. 11."
65. *The Occident*, Vol. 30; No.6, September 1862, p.493.
66. *Ibid.*, pp.497, 501.
67. Lebeson, *Pilgrim People*, *op. cit.*, pp.325-326; *The Occident*, Vol. 21, No.?, 1863.
68. For example, *Ibid.*, Vol. 23, No.3, June 1865, p.142, reports that a synagogue in South Carolina was burned, along with eight Torah scrolls.
69. *Ibid.*, Vol. 23, No.3, June 1865, p.164.
70. *Ibid.*, Vol. 23, No.6, September 1865, p.286.
71. *Ibid.*, Vol. 23, No.2, May 1865, p.85.
72. *Ibid.*, Vol. 23, No. 11, February 1866, pp.462-468.
73. *Ibid...*,Vol. 23, No.4, July 1865, p.168.
74. *Ibid...*,Vol. 20, No.1, April 1862, p.1.

16

The Albany Patriot, 1861-1865: Struggling to Publish and Struggling to Remain Optimistic

Ford Risley
Pennsylvania State University

In mid-May 1864 Union and Confederate armies prepared to meet on the battlefield near Resaca, Georgia. Some 250 miles south in the small offices of the *Albany Patriot*, J. W. Fears and F. Hienan struggled to get out the weekly newspaper without their only help, a sixteen-year-old boy who was away attending his father's funeral. But not even the lack of help could sour their mood. In an editorial Fears wrote, "Never since the commencement of the war, have the prospects of the Confederate states appeared so permanently cheerful and brilliant." Hienan cited as proof recent Confederate victories in Louisiana, Arkansas, Tennessee, and North Carolina. What he failed to mention was that General William T. Sherman's 100,000 Union troops had been camped near the north Georgia border for months and had just begun their campaign to take Atlanta and the rest of the state out of the war.[1]

The *Patriot's* creed in 1864 was "Our Country's Independence," but a more appropriate one probably would have been: "Struggling to Publish and Struggling to Remain Optimistic." Over the course of the Civil War, the little weekly endured a change in ownership, suspension for two years, sickness and death among employees, as well as repeated financial and personnel worries.[2] Yet in spite of all its problems, the *Patriot* tirelessly promoted the Southern cause and consistently remained optimistic about the Confederacy's chances of winning —right up until the end of the war.[3]

Early Days

The *Patriot* was established in 1844 by Nelson Tift, the same man who founded the town near the banks of the Flint River. That year, Albany had a population of 700 and included two churches, the Baptist and Methodist, one hotel, five stores, one drug store, ten lawyers, eight doctors, and a few mechanics. Tift owned the *Patriot* until 1858 when he sold it to A. J. McCarthy, another local man.[4]

By 1860, Albany had grown to a population of 1,618.[5] And under McCarthy's direction, the *Patriot* became a militantly Democratic newspaper that spoke out forcefully for Southern rights. The *Patriot* joined many other newspapers in Georgia, and throughout the South, in calling for secession from the Union.[26] Early in 1860 the *Patriot* declared, "We might as well sing Psalms over the dead carcass of a buzzard, as to appeal to the Union for rights and justice, with any hope of success, so long as we remain in the Union."[7] Later that year, as the talk of war increased, the *Patriot* promised to insure with a postage stamp every Southerner killed in fighting with the North.[8] When Confederate troops captured Fort Sumter in April 1861 the *Patriot* reveled in the news.[9]

Once the war began, the *Patriot* proudly trumpeted the Southern cause. The journal heaped great praise on the Confederate Army and its leaders after every battle and skirmish. Even everyday matters were a way for the newspaper to proclaim the Southern way of life was superior. In an editorial, the *Patriot* noted that a local woman had brought by the office a cabbage weighing seven and one-half pounds. The newspaper declared it "the finest cabbage we ever saw" and added, "[I]t speaks this in regard to Southern independence — that in all things we can compete with the North and generally surpass them."[10]

At the beginning of the war, the *Patriot* was published as a broadsheet. In the June 6, 1861 issue the paper announced it was switching to a smaller seven-inch by nine-inch size as an experiment.[11] By present day standards, the *Patriot's* format was dull and monotonous. It contained no photographs, no cartoons, and no illustrations except for those accompanying ads. The banner headline had been introduced in the 1850s, but like most newspapers in the state, the *Patriot* stuck with the old one-column head. The same story might appear for several days depending on the amount of new news. Advertisements ran for weeks or even months with no changes except their position on a page.

Most issues of the *Patriot* had four pages. Page one contained mostly war news clipped from other newspapers, both South and North. Page two was devoted to editorials, letters to the editor, poetry, and a smattering of local news items, while page three had telegraphic news and legal notices. Page four contained advertising almost exclusively.

Outwardly the *Patriot* appeared to be a financially successful sheet. Advertisements were plentiful in most issues, and some weeks the entire front page was devoted to advertising. No subscription figures are available, but a minimum estimate would put the number at 350.[12]

As 1862 began, however, cracks began appearing in the *Patriot's* operation. The paper failed to publish an issue the first week of the new year after the printing foreman unexpectedly quit to go back to farming. By early January, McCarthy had hired the former editor of the *Griffin Independent South*, Colonel A. P. Burr, to take charge of the printing office. The first issue of 1862 was published January 9.[13]

The journal also was apparently experiencing financial problems. In the January 9 issue, McCarthy complained that far too many subscribers had past-due bills. He pleaded for prompt payment. "The accounts are not large," McCarthy wrote in an editorial note, "but they are many, and when summed up amount to many thousands."[14] The *Patriot* published an issue January 16, 1862, but for unknown reasons the newspaper stopped appearing sometime after that date. No explanation was offered for why the *Patriot* was suspending publication.[15]

New Ownership

With the January 21, 1864 issue McCarthy announced he had sold the *Patriot* to Fears, a former resident of Albany who had moved to Macon. In a "Valedictory," McCarthy did not mention any of the *Patriot's* past problems, nor did he offer any explanation for why he was giving up the newspaper. He did, however, take one last opportunity to extol the important mission of the press in promoting the Southern cause.16 Fears, apparently a man of some wealth, operated a plantation and owned a dry goods store in Macon.17 But there was no indication he had any experience in publishing. In a "Salutatory" in the same January 21 issue, Fears wrote that he had turned over publishing of the paper to two printers, Hienan and Wm. F. Walker, war veterans who had been injured at the Battle of Shiloh.18

Hienan and Walker declared the weekly would be impartial in its editorial comments noting, "We will recognize no friend or foe but our country's." In a plea for community support — and obviously in need of money — the new publishers wrote, "Send us your names, advertisements, job work, and the CASH." And even though the first issue under their operation was late appearing, the two men declared that the days of the newspaper missing an issue were over. They wrote, "Hereafter, we assure you, there will be no napping or lagging about this establishment."19

Some six weeks later, however, the *Patriot* was late publishing once again. The reason: co-publisher Walker died from head injuries he received in the war. Walker was 28 years old and had been married only six months. In an editorial eulogy, the *Patriot* described him as "steady, persevering and industrious in business, and kind, affable and upright in social life. With his death, "the community lost a faithful servant and good citizen, and we a genial associate and friend."20

Later that month, Hienan announced that the *Patriot's* subscription rates were increasing from two dollars annually to five dollars for six months and ten dollars for a year. He said the increase was justified in light of the increased cost of other goods in Albany and was, in fact, far smaller percentage-wise. Seeking community support, the publisher wrote: "We make this advance in our rates, not to extort or hoard up money, but simply to make an honest living. We hope the public will sustain us, and we will serve them faithfully in return."21 The higher subscription rates also were needed because advertising in the *Patriot* had fallen off. Whereas early in the war the *Patriot* averaged two to three pages of advertising per issue, by 1864 that figure had dropped to one page — and some weeks was even less. The few ads that appeared in 1864 generally were found on page four and sometimes page three.

Among the most frequent advertisers in the *Patriot* in 1864 were the Albany House, druggist I. E. Welch, and the Albany Book Store. Most weeks the newspaper also carried the schedules of the Central, Macon & Western, and South-Western railroads. Advertisements for rental properties and slave auctions appeared regularly as well as notices reporting lost or found horses and mules. Occasionally subscribers even advertised for a mate. The following advertisement appeared in an 1864 issue of the *Patriot* with an address for any reader who wanted to reply:

TO WHOM IT MAY CONCERN

A gentlemen of good character, some attainment and tolerably good looking, aged 25 years, desires, sincerely, to open a correspondence with some young lady who wishes to marry. To suit him, she must be between the ages of 16 and 25, intelligent, kind, modest and gentle in disposition, and must be free of the pernicious habit of using snuff. He has been wounded in the war, but not enough as to injure either his appearance or general health, or in any way impairing him physically or mentally.[22]

As most weekly newspapers in the nineteenth century, the *Patriot* supplemented its income through commercial job work. No records are available to indicate how successful the *Patriot's* job shop was. But the newspaper boasted that it could handle everything from the "neatest and most fashionable" full sheet posters to "elegant" visiting cards.[23] The material shortages suffered by the press also were evident on the pages of the *Patriot* as almost every week the newspaper carried an advertisement offering fifteen cents per pound for cotton and linen rags needed to make the paper used by the newspaper. The rags were essential for printing, the *Patriot* declared: "We hope the people of this county will save their Rags if for no other motive than to insure the paper's continuance."[24]

With Walker gone, Hienan published the *Patriot* with only the help of George Woods, the sixteen-year-old boy who lost his father in 1864. The small staff meant that illnesses and other problems sometimes kept the *Patriot* from being published on time. For example, one issue in 1864 was delayed when the publisher came down with a chill and fever just before the newspaper was going to press. In an editorial note, he wrote that he was still languid and weak but recovering thanks to the "well-known skill of Dr. Jennings."[25] Later in the year, Hienan apparently lost the services of young Woods. That, along with mechanical problems with the printing press, caused the delay of two issues.[26]

Reporting the War

Despite all its problems, the *Patriot* remained optimistic about Confederate fortunes in 1864. The spring brought new confidence in the outcome of the war — even as the Union Army posed a grave threat to Georgia. In an editorial entitled "Hopeful and Bright," the newspaper boasted that the prospects of the South winning independence were cheering. While Confederate soldiers were in good spirits and the ranks of the army swelled, the *Patriot* claimed that the North was having trouble recruiting soldiers for its army. In fact, the newspaper proclaimed, the only thing that could keep the South from winning the war was a poor harvest. To that end, the *Patriot* urged the farmers of south Georgia to push their farms to the utmost capacity.[27] A month later, with fighting in Georgia increasing, the newspaper made its boast that the Confederacy's prospects had never been brighter.[28]

The *Patriot* could not entirely forget about the problems facing the South — and south Georgia. In one editorial, the newspaper noted that President Jefferson Davis had proclaimed April 8 as a day for fasting and prayer. But it hastened to add: "Owing to the scarcity of provisions, it will not be difficult to extract a compliance with the first injunction in this section."[29]

Yet these bouts of pessimism were brief. In May, editor Fears traveled to nearby Andersonville Prison for a view of the place that he correctly predicted was destined to become either "famous or infamous." The hamlet of Andersonville, Fears noted, was little more than a water tank, a depot, and a whiskey mill, which was closed. It was overshadowed by the enormous compound nearby which held the "captured heroes of yankeedom." The enclosure, built near the slope of two hills, was scattered with small huts, lean-tos and other structures to ward off the weather. Yet the weather was still taking its toll on prisoners, an appropriate fate, in the view of Fears who expressed no concern about the wretched conditions of the camp. The mortality rate at Andersonville averaged thirty-five a day, he noted, and twenty-two prisoners had died the day before. They would be buried, like all others, "without coffin or shroud" in a large field near the stockade, Fears wrote.[30]

The telegraph and news clipped from other newspapers were the two chief sources of war news for the *Patriot*. Like most weeklies in the South, the *Patriot* did not have the financial resources to keep a full-time correspondent in the field reporting the war. But in June, editor Fears traveled to the Georgia front with the Battlefield Relief Society to see the fighting firsthand. In correspondence from Marietta, outside Atlanta, he described a town where the effects of war were visible everywhere. Using the byline "F" Fears wrote, "Through the city may be seen night and day trains of wagons, cavalrymen, horses, cattle, sheep, wounded men on litters . . . and often ambulances coming in from the front with the groaning and dying." The Marietta Hotel was one vast hospital and the nearby park was covered with the sick and suffering.[31] Probably because

Fears apparently had no access to Confederate officers, the story contained little news of the fighting that had taken place at nearby Kennesaw Mountain. But that did not stop Fears from expressing the utmost confidence that Confederate forces could keep Sherman's army out of Atlanta. He predicted correctly that after the fighting at Kennesaw Mountain General Johnston's army would take up a position on the Chattahoochee River just outsideAtlanta. Then with the bravado that so often characterized the *Patriot*, Fears wrote, ". . . but below that, if Sherman attempts to go, his fate will be defeat, if not annihilation."32

The *Patriot* continued to praise the strategy of General Johnston, even as the Union Army was getting dangerously close to Atlanta. The word retreat was rarely used in these accounts; instead the *Patriot* called it "retrograde movement." In a June editorial the newspaper asked for patience by readers, despite the steady backward march of Johnston's army through north Georgia. The *Patriot* said the general was simply "maneuvering for position" and "saving his men." In fact, the newspaper proclaimed, Johnston's "movement from Dalton to Aaltoona [sic] surpasses the world in strategy."33 A month later, with Sherman's army just across the Chattahoochee River from Atlanta, the *Patriot* was still boasting of Johnston's achievement. The newspaper said: "Gen. Johnston has immortalized himself in his retreat from Dalton. No living man could have retreated an army the size of Johnston's, a distance of seventy-five miles, and kept the confidence. . . of his men as he has done."34

Other News

News of the war unquestionably dominated the pages of the *Patriot*. And with no editorial staff except Fears, the newspaper was hard pressed to carry much local reporting. But the *Patriot* tried to record at least some of the everyday events taking place in Albany. The weather, crops, and social events occasionally were noted on the pages of the *Patriot*. Sometimes these came in the form of brief and humorous editorial notes. In one issue, editor Fears lamented his poor luck on a recent fishing trip. The editor also described a barbecue he attended on a Saturday in July. The dinner, held near the banks of the Flint River, was a splendid affair with plenty of good food including a couple of roasted goats. One of the goats, the editor noted humorously, bore a "striking resemblance" to his own missing animal. However, since the goat already had been carved and offered to the guests, he wrote, "we concluded to remain silent."35 In another small note, the *Patriot* described the summer weather and its effect on the south Georgia's pesky insect population.

> Thus far August has been rainy, salubrious, and pleasant. The nights are cool, and mosquitoes, flees [sic] and bed-bugs have been less jubilant in their nocturnal feasts over their unconscious victims. We have no fear now of any kind of vermin, save the yankees.36

A more serious problem was the increasingly high prices charged by merchants in Albany. The newspaper said it had refrained from complaining each week in the hopes these business operators would become ashamed of themselves and lower their prices. But merchants had not done so. The *Patriot* complained that the price of bacon was one dollar more per pound than that charged in Macon, Columbus, or Savannah. It went on to say, "we know of no reason to justify this system of extortion only that our non-producing citizens have quietly submitted to it."37

Social news also was taking place inside the offices of the *Patriot*. In the fall, editor Fears was married. In a brief editorial note carried published in November, he announced he was back on the job after a brief period away from the *Patriot*. Fears wrote:

> We thank the publisher for discharging our duty during our absence. He announced us captured recently; it is true we are in captivity, but it is such as every man covets, who has wits about him. We would say to all in a state of singleness to go and get captured in the same way and live as our creator designed we should.38

Struggling to Remain Optimistic

As the fighting in the state dragged on, the *Patriot's* sources for news became less and less reliable. Telegraphic accounts from Georgia had all but stopped. In an August issue the newspaper admitted it had little real news of the war. The *Patriot* printed the rumor that in fighting near Macon, Confederate forces had killed or wounded 1,500 of the enemy while not losing a single man. But even this was too much for the optimistic sheet to believe: "This we consider as presuming too far upon our credulty [sic], and we put it down as one of the numerous canards, circulated to prop the drooping spirits of the despondent."39 When real news was in short supply, the *Patriot* occasionally turned to its "more expert and reliable medium," known as Grapevine. This correspondent, the paper sarcastically noted in one issue,

> extends from this city to Johnston's army, thence through Sherman's line, into Lee's camp, then, dodging the myriads of Grant, it follows the Potomac into Washington, and there is not a movement made by either General, a speech made in the Yankee Congress, or a joke perpetrated by the Ape, that is not learnedly discussed the following evening

in front of the post office in this city.40

In the first issue of September, the *Patriot* reported that Atlanta had fallen to the Union Army. The newspaper did not gloss over the significance of the loss, bluntly calling it a "disaster." But the *Patriot* refused to place blame on Confederate troops and its leaders; instead it claimed the sole reason for the fall of the Gate City was the superior size of the Union forces. The newspaper reported incorrectly that Sherman's army had been reinforced with 50,000 new troops since the Battle of Kennesaw Mountain, while the Confederate Army had added only 15,000 new men. The *Patriot* also refused to place blame on the new commander of Confederate forces, General John B. Hood, saying that he had done "all a good General and brave man could do."41 In fact, the paper easily transferred the confidence it had placed in Johnston to Hood.

During this same period the impact of the fighting in Georgia increasingly, was felt in Albany. In one issue, the weekly noted that Albany no longer was the quiet little community it had been only a couple of months earlier. Most noticeable were the numerous hospitals that had been established in the city. Although no patients had arrived, surgeons and attendants were setting up practices. Refugees from the fighting also had begun arriving in Albany. Many had to live in train boxcars because no other accommodations were available.42

By late-September, the *Patriot* was struggling mightily to find anything encouraging in the news from Georgia. In an editorial bearing the headline "What of the Night?" the journal said that not since the opening of the war had the Confederacy's existence been so imperiled. "We confess that we can perceive nothing calculated to dispel the clouds of disaster, which are daily towering around us," Fears wrote.43 By this point, the *Patriot* had changed its opinion of General Hood's command. It said Georgia's fate was sealed if Hood remained in control of Confederate forces in the state. The only thing that could save Georgia was "an experienced General with 30,000 reinforcements." But the newspaper held out hope that the government in Richmond would come to the aid of Georgia. In the meantime, the *Patriot* said in a plea to readers, "it behoves [sic] us to contribute our whole energies to the same end."44

By November, telegraphic news from the state had been lost and many of the newspapers north of Albany had shut down or moved out of the state. So the *Patriot* again turned to "Grapevine" for news. But even the rumor mill could not be sure of General Sherman's next target after Union forces captured Milledgeville, the state's capital. Likewise, the paper could report little news from nearby Macon because the city's daily newspapers had packed up and fled. The *Patriot* once again called on the Confederate government in Richmond to restore General Johnston to his command. In its view, Johnston was the "only competent and fit man to save our State and remedy the many palpable blunders already made in this military department."[45]

In the first edition of 1865, the *Patriot* admitted that the news recently had been "anything but cheering." The paper noted the capture of Savannah and the abandonment of the state by Confederate forces. Still, the *Patriot* called on Georgians to stand by the Southern cause and continue supporting the Confederate Army.[46] In that same issue, publisher Hienan recounted the trying year the weekly had gone through, beginning with the death of his co-publisher. He complained that half of the paper's subscribers had outstanding debts, making it impossible for the *Patriot* to pay many of its creditors. But the days of the free ride were over. The newspaper would suspend publishing for a week while he personally called on subscribers with past-due bills. This time, Hienan wrote, he would take no excuses.[47]

The *Patriot* managed to continue publishing even as the fate of the Confederacy was slipping away. Then in April 1865 the journal was forced to acknowledge that General Robert E. Lee's army had "capitulated" to Union forces at Appomattox, Virginia. The *Patriot* remained defiant, however, and never once used the word "surrender" in the account. The paper refused to attribute defeat to Northern superiority or military prowess, instead placing blame on the general apathy of the South. True to its nature, the *Patriot* concluded the account of Appomattox with this proclamation: "We are yet unconquered, and until the sword of the enemy is at our throats, we upbraid our fellow citizens for their recent nefarious conduct. God help our country."[48]

Conclusion

The *Patriot* continued publishing until 1866 when it closed for good. The struggle had ended. Seen from a late twentieth century viewpoint, the disparity between what appeared on the pages of the *Patriot* and what was taking place on the war's battlefields is obvious. Yet it should be remembered that the *Patriot* was giving its readers a distinctly Southern viewpoint of the Civil War. Like many of its readers, the newspaper fervently believed in the Confederate cause.

In this respect, it accurately reflected the public opinion of the times in south Georgia. Perhaps more easily appreciated are the difficulties the *Patriot* endured in simply putting out a newspaper. Beset with problems, the little weekly still managed to serve its readers in south Georgia as best it could. In a war with so many casualties, that was no small accomplishment.

Notes

1. "The Prospects," *Albany Patriot*, 12 May 1864. p. 2. For an account of the Battle of Resaca, see Philip Secrist, "Resaca: A Moment of Truth," *Atlanta Historical Journal* (Spring 1978): 8-43.
2. Virtually every newspaper in Georgia suspended publishing at times and a total of fifty-three ceased publishing entirely during the war. T. Conn Bryan, *Confederate Georgia* (Athens, University of Georgia Press, 1953), 207. For a sketchy picture of the state's newspapers during the war, see Rabun Lee Brantley, *Georgia Journalism of the Civil War Period* (Nashville: George Peabody College, 1929).
3. For background on the tendency of the press in the South to try and preserve public morale by being optimistic, see Alan Bussell, "The Atlanta Daily Intelligencer Cover Sherman's March," *Journalism quarterly* 51 (1974): 405-410; and J. Cutler Andrews, "The Confederate Press and Public Morale," *Journal of Southern History* (1966): 455-465. No studies have examined how the weekly press sought to preserve morale.
4. "Albany," *The Georgia Review* 9 (April 1950): 30-42. As the war began, the *Patriot* competed with two other newspapers in the town, the *Albany News* and the *Albany Journal*. No known copies of either publication exist and little is known about either one. The *Journal* died early in 1861 and the *News* published irregularly during the war. See Brantley, *Georgia Journalism*, 26 and 38.
5. U.S. Census Bureau, *Population of the United States in 1860* (Washington: Government Printing Office, 1864), 74.
6. See generally Donald E. Reynolds, *Editors Make War* (Nashville: Vanderbilt University Press, 1966).
7. *Albany Patriot*, 1 March 1860, p. 2.
8. *Albany Patriot*, 15 November 1860, p. 2.
9. *Albany Patriot*, 18 April 1861, p. 2.
10. "Thanks," *Albany Patriot*, 9 January, 1862, p. 2.
11. *Albany Patriot*, 6 June 1861, p. 2. This "experiment" lasted until November 1864 when the new publisher said he was switching back to a broadsheet format. Although the publisher said he preferred the smaller folio size, the format was too "unwieldy" when printing. "A Change," *Albany Patriot* 3 November 1864, p. 2.
12. According to the 4 January 1865 issue, the *Patriot* had 350 subscribers in 1864. Given the far better economic conditions in 1861, it is safe to believe the newspaper had at least that many subscribers.
13. "To Our Readers," *Albany Patriot*, 9 January 1864, p. 2.
14. *Albany Patriot*, 9 January 1864, p. 2.
15. When the *Patriot* resumed publishing, the new publishers alluded to past problems in securing experienced printers to put out the newspaper. Most likely this was the cause for the *Patriot* suspending publication. "Salutatory," *Albany Patriot*, 21 January 1864, p. 2.
16. "Valedictory," *Albany Patriot*, 21 January 1864, p. 2.
17. Advertisements for the dry good store owned by Fears appeared regularly in the *Patriot* after he purchased the newspaper.
18. "Salutatory," *Albany Patriot*, 21 January 1864, p. 2.

19. "Hear Us for Our Case," *Albany Patriot*, 21 January 1864, p. 2. Hienan later wrote that they had only a "bundle of paper and about $50" with which to start the newspaper back up. "End of Volume Eighteen," *Albany Patriot*, 4 January 1865, p. 2.
20. "Death of Wm. F. Walker," *Albany Patriot*, 3 March 1864, p. 2.
21. "Increase of Rates," *Albany Patriot*, 24 March 1864, p. 2.
The increase was in line with the new rates adopted at the annual Convention of Publishers and Editors of Weekly Newspapers which met at Milledgeville, Georgia March 2, 1864. *Albany Patriot* 10 March 1864, p. 2.
22. *Albany Patriot*, 7 April 1864, p. 2.
23. *Albany Patriot*, 3 March 1864, p. 2.
24. *Albany Patriot*, 3 March 1864, p. 2. For the problem of paper and other material shortages experienced by Southern newspapers, see Mary Elizabeth Massey. *Ersatz in the Confederacy*. (Columbia: University of South Carolina Press, 1952).
25. *Albany Patriot*, 8 September 1864, p. 2.
26. "Cause of Delay," *AlbanyPatriot*, 27 October 1864, p. 2.
27. "Hopeful and Bright" *AlbanyPatriot*, 7 April 1864, p. 2.
28. "The Prospects," *Albany Patriot*, 12 May 1864, p. 2. For the importance of public morale to the Confederate cause, see Kenneth M. Stampp, "The Southern Road to Appomattox" in *The Imperiled Union. Essays on the Background of the Civil War* (New York: Oxford University Press, 1980); and Richard E. Beringer, Herman Hattaway, Archer Jones, and William N. Still, Jr. *Why the South Lost the Civil War* (Athens: University of Georgia Press, 1986).
29. *Albany Patriot*, 7 April 1864, p. 2.
30. "Our Trip to Andersonville," *Albany Patriot*, 19 May 1864, p. 2. For more on Andersonville, see Ovid Futch, *History of Andersonville Prison* (Gainesville: University of Florida Press, 1968).
31. "Editorial Correspondence," *Albany Patriot*, 30 June 1864, p. 2.
32. *Albany Patriot*, 30 June 1864, p. 2. Two good recent accounts of the Battle of Kennesaw Mountain can be found in Charles Royster, *The Destructive War: William Tecumseh Sherman, Stonewall Jackson and the Americans* (New York: Alfred A. Knopf, 1991); and Albert Castel, *Decision in the West: The Atlanta Campaign* (Lawrence: University of Kansas Press, 1992).
33. "Georgia Front," *Albany Patriot*, 9 June 1864, p. 2.
34. "Georgia Front," *Albany Patriot*, 13 July 1864: 2. The newspaper's support of the general put it in the "Johnston school," those who supported the general's conduct of the campaign. This contrasts with the "Hood school" which viewed the retreat as a demoralizing disaster. Richard M. McMurray, "Confederate Morale in Atlanta Campaign of 1864," *Georgia Historical Quarterly* (Summer 1970): 226-243.
35. "The Barbecue," *Albany Patriot*, 7 July 1864, p. 2.
36. *Albany Patriot* 4 August 1864, p. 2.
37. "Albany Market," *Albany, Patriot* 12 May 1864, p. 2. For more on the problem of speculation and profiteering, see Bryan, *Confederate Georgia*, 60-62.
38. "At Our Post," *Albany Patriot*, 10 November 1864, p. 2.
39. "The News," *Albany Patriot*, 4 August 1864, p. 2.
40. "Grape-Vine in Albany," *Albany Patriot*, 23 June 1864, p. 2.
41. "Atlanta Taken," *Albany Patriot*, 8 September 1864, p. 2.
42. *Albany Patriot*, 29 September 1864, p. 2.
43. *Albany Patriot*, 22 September 1864, p.2.
44. *Ibid*.
45. "The News," *Albany Patriot*, 25 November 1864, p. 2.
46. "End of Volume Eighteen," *Albany Patriot*, 4 January 1865, p. 2.
47. *Ibid*.
48. "The News," *Albany Patriot*, 27 April 1865, p. 2.

17

Images of Women in Civil War Newspapers: Leave the "Proper Sphere"

Hazel Dicken-Garcia and Janet M. Cramer
University of Minnesota

Scholarship on gender in America usually notes serious regression in women's rights during formation of the new nation.[1] Among developments cited, professionalization of law incorporated the notion of marital unity, which interpreted a wife as part of a husband's existence, and systemizing of laws accompanied the emergence of the modern family that emphasized different roles for men and women as well as women's moral superiority—all of which reinforced women's lowered status by "freezing" law at the nadir of women's rights.[2] During the same period, the developing "cult of true womanhood" meant, in the words of Barbara Welter, "a woman judged herself and was judged by her husband, her neighbors and society" by "four cardinal virtues—piety, purity, submissiveness and domesticity."[3] Women were seen as emotional, delicate, physically inferior, and morally superior,[4] and even independent businesswomen were judged by such attributes and behaved accordingly.[5]

This paper about images of women during the Civil War addresses broad questions about conditions and impetus for change in gender roles. Wars have been treated as particularly significant in reshaping gender systems, but what exactly in wartime conditions prompts such shifts? The thesis here is that specific values, such as patriotism, become propelling forces. The purpose of this research, then, was to examine Civil War news coverage for images of women, shifts in images, and the relevance of patriotism to any changes found.

Wars bring "abrupt, conscious, and concentrated adjustments in the behaviors considered appropriate for men and women and allow for some crossing of gender lines otherwise considered inviolable," Elizabeth Leonard argues, citing scholars who have called war a "*gendering* activity, one that ritually marks the gender of all members of a society...."[6] In other words, "war instantly demarcates, on the basis of sex, the theoretical position, role, and function of each individual in society." Men, thus, become "soldiers and warmakers," and women "serve passively at home as the one for whom the war is fought." At the same time, "the physical, social, and economic demands of war simultaneously bring about temporary redefinitions of gender and power relations for specific purposes."[7]

These conclusions have come generally from studies of World War I, World War II, and, to a lesser extent, the American Revolution. Less attention has focused on how the Civil War influenced women's history, although regarded as significant for women, who may have been more deeply involved in that crisis than any war engaging America.[8] Evidence suggests that resistance to women's rights hardened in the years just before the war and was reflected and reinforced in the press.[9] One reporter wrote that goals women sought "would set the world by the ears, make confusion worse confounded, demoralize and degrade from their high sphere and noble destiny women of all respectable and useful classes, and prove a monstrous injury to all mankind."[10] Yet the war demanded everyone's assistance, and women gave wholeheartedly, garnering praise for unconventional and very public behavior. How did society accommodate to such unconventional gender behavior, and what was the impact?

Women and the Civil War: A Brief Review

Women's Civil War activities represent a paradox regarding gender. On the one hand, women were to remain apart from public affairs. Even such hospital work as nursing, later stereotyped as a "woman's profession," was (despite the fame of Florence Nightingale) regarded as unacceptable for women when the war began.[11] A view prevailed that men's activities belonged in the public sphere while women belonged in the private—the home—and the term "proper sphere" had long been current as if all knew what it meant. Drew Gilpin Faust quotes a *Confederate Baptist* item during the Civil War, for example, that women might give valuable assistance in hospitals if they remained "in their proper sphere" and did not seek to "direct or control the physician."[12] The paradox is that, despite such notions, women's activities, especially as spies, scouts and soldiers, exceeded what might be expected a century later. Mary Elizabeth Massey estimated that 400 women served in both Northern and Southern armies as soldiers; many others followed husbands, sons and fathers to the front, and a substantial number served as couriers and spies.[13] Leonard says approximately 20,000 women provided medical services to the North while another 3,200 worked for the Union Army under Superintendent of Nurses Dorothea Dix, and many cooked and did laundry for husbands' regiments. On the home front, women organized to support the war effort and maintained husbands' businesses, engaging in such work as management and bookkeeping while maintaining homes.[14] Women entered into public events during the war, often creating events, such as the bread riots and the "battle of handkerchiefs" in the South in 1862 and 1863.[15]

Massey called the Civil War a turning point in the history of American women.[16] Lyde Cullen Sizer says that such activities as spying changed gender convention because they took women out of the "private sphere"—the home—and implicitly rejected any "traditionally established set of values for women."[17] Criticizing assumptions in the work of some historians that "abnormal" wartime gender behaviors revert afterwards to pre-war status because war disrupts normal activities, Leonard asserts that women's war work shifted some boundaries of acceptable behavior between women and men—regardless of the amount of resistance.[18] George Rable says the war from the beginning "strained traditional definitions of gender by testing long-established customs in the fiery furnace of social revolution."[19] Mary P. Ryan wrote that the war complicated and significantly expanded women's political roles,[20] and Faust says it brought "both reassertion and reconsideration of gender assumptions" and "stimulated especially significant examination and discussion of women's appropriate relationship to war—and thus to society in general."[21] The war "required an extraordinary level" of participation by women, and they ceased to see themselves as passive. Experiences of Southern women, particularly, "shattered ... the myth of the male as protector," while women, in general, began "to form new expectations for themselves...."[22]

Although scholarship about women generally emphasizes the white middle class, study of the Civil War must consider differences between North and South, black and white, free and slave. Leeann Whites says many Southern women filled a role not required of Northern women—as symbolic mother of slave children. Southern women, in general, seized the rare opportunity to assert "independence" as war propelled "domestic labor into the public arena," and used it to claim more equality.[23]

Women, especially in the South where resources were so scarce, had to be persuaded to the cause, according to Faust, who found a discourse emerged to create a "hegemonic ideology of female patriotism and sacrifice."[24] Greatness of sharing with all other women the sacrifice of men to battle—emphasizing sacrifice as good in itself—was central to the discourse, which Faust says originated so early in the war that it was prescriptive. It was "intended to direct southern women, to outline appropriate behavior in the abruptly altered wartime situation," and its "flattery" and "honorific nature" were "central to its rhetorical force."[25] The first discussions in Southern media stressed women's "accustomed spiritual role," wartime suffering as an "honored undertaking," and patriotism as including responsibility for morale. The discourse subtly redefined women's role from actively nurturing family to stoically sacrificing family. One newspaper item said women had a "glorious privilege" to "contribute to the Cause by offering their men"; and their reward would be "satisfaction of participation in the birth of a new nation."[26] Scholars say Southern white women generally had fewer choices than Northern white women,[27] and black women had even fewer choices. But black women offered help as soon as "contrabands" (slaves who fled to Union camps) appeared. They taught former slaves and,[28] after the War Department authorized black soldiers, prepared food and clothing and wrote letters for soldiers, made flags, and helped recruit. Mary Ann Shadd Cary, the only woman officially commissioned as a recruiting agent, worked in Connecticut and Indiana, and one source says she recruited also in Massachusetts.[29]

Harriet Jacobs went to Washington, D.C., in early 1862 to report on conditions of contrabands and wrote in August one of the first accounts of freed slaves. She stayed to nurse the sick, distribute clothes and help people find jobs, and as contrabands grew to an estimated 10,000 a year later, she and her daughter organized sewing circles and schools and assisted former slaves in finding their voice. "I wanted the colored men to learn the time had come when it was their privilege to have something to say," she wrote, adding, "I think it has a good effect upon these people to convince them their own race can do something for their elevation. It inspires them with confidence to help each other."30

Elizabeth Keckley prompted the "colored church" in Washington to organize in August 1862 to help freed people and continued organizing and fund-raising as she traveled with Mary Todd Lincoln. Sojourner Truth, defying a state law barring blacks from entering Indiana, was arrested several times as she held rallies across the state. She wrote of traveling under an armed guard and advocating "free speech with more zeal than ever before."31

From May 1862, Harriet Tubman taught freedwomen on the Sea Islands to do soldiers' laundry and become self-supporting, built a washhouse with her earnings, nursed soldiers and contrabands at the army hospital, and then, at the request of an army officer, went to nurse soldiers in Fernandina, Fla. As a Union spy, Tubman also led, under Col. James Montgomery of the Second South Carolina volunteers, a group of black river pilots on numerous expeditions to scout cotton warehouses, ammunition depots, and slaves to be freed. Newspapers reported Montgomery's most famous raid, up the Combahee River in June 1863, as "under the guidance of a black woman." Tubman continued spying in the South until May 1864, and, in March 1865, went to James River, Va., to work in hospitals.32

Dorothy Sterling says a study of thirty black teachers of freedpeople in the 1860s shows all except Mary S. Peake, the first black woman teacher of former slaves, were northern-born, single, childless, middle class. Most were in their twenties with above-average education, and most had taught before going South. Peake, who started a school in Hampton, Va., in 1861—a month after Confederate forces left— was in her late 30s, married and had a seven-year-old daughter.33 Women teachers were paid $10 per month, men teachers started at $25 per month.34

Methodology: Identifying Women's Roles and Images in Press Reports

Given attitudes about women's sphere, the need for everyone in the war, and women's unprecedented activities, did notions about women's "proper sphere" change during the Civil War? If so, what propelled change? Was patriotism the driving force? Such questions prompted study of newspaper content—treated here as a "text" reflecting the prevailing social attitudes of the environment in which it was created—for evidence of a shift in gender roles and relevance of patriotism during the Civil War.

How would adjustment occur between the need for women to aid the war and hardened attitudes about women's "proper sphere?" *Patriotism* was expected to propel that adjustment—and stretch gender roles in the process. That is, a sense of patriotic duty prompted women to action they might not consider ordinarily. Further, leaders likely invoked patriotism to a) call on women for assistance, b) justify "abnormal" gender behavior in behalf of the "cause," and c) applaud useful activities that fell outside women's customary role. Changes in images of women would occur ultimately because wartime needs would lead to acceptance of public activity by women and legitimize other behaviors not acceptable before the war.

Since cultural values, attitudes, mores and customs change over time, it was assumed that gender roles and images of women changed during the century and that images embedded in newspapers reflect prevailing views for the time and place created. Thus, images of women were expected to differ across the century, and, if wars transform gender roles, some shift might be discernible during the war.

Civil War events involving women were identified in secondary sources and the New York *Times* index. Of special interest were reports of President-Elect Abraham Lincoln's 1861 trip to Washington, bread riots in the South and draft riots in the North in 1863. Additional items found during research were also analyzed.

Two sets of images identified by historians as typical of early and late nineteenth century were used to classify newspaper content. Antebellum images were drawn from Ronald Hogeland's synthesis, particularly of Janet James' work. Specifically, images of middle and upper class women from 1820 to 1860, which Hogeland called lifestyle patterns, are: woman as *ornamental, romanticized, evangelic* and *radical:*

1. The *ornamental* signified "proper" wives whose purpose was to please men and handle all the domestic work to free husbands to fulfill roles in public life. Women were taught their involvement in

public affairs was against God's will, although they could do charity work so long as they stayed in the background.

2. The *romanticized* image revered women, made them the center of life, embodiments of patriotism, Christianity and motherhood, responsible for perpetuating national morality. In this moralistic, sentimental image, women were society's only suitable moral agents and should dedicate themselves to the home because, through motherhood, they had the highest influence. In the belief that proper moral education of children produced moral adults and a moral nation, women were to make home a sanctuary from "worldly distractions."

3. The *evangelic* image was confined to reformists. Reformers believed reform required all available human resources and therefore was suitable activity for women—but women could not hold positions of authority or study for the ministry.

4. The *radical* image was based on beliefs that public life needed women's moral strength, that women could transform the world from greed, malice, avarice to virtue, justice, morality. But the purpose was to improve the world for men and not woman's lot.[35]

Images from 1860 to approximately 1910 were drawn from Janet Cramer's study, which named four that historians have identified. These are self-explanatory: Woman as mother, morally superior, altruistic, and as equal to man by natural or divine right.[36]

Newspaper items were first classified as 1) containing gender images or 2) straight news, 3) showing women engaged in, or being encouraged to engage in, public activity, and 4) showing the relevance of patriotism to women's activities. Second, statements tied to the subject as women (for example, the "fair sex," "weaker sex," waving of handkerchiefs), were recorded according to the eight images named above (woman as ornamental, romanticized, evangelical, radical, mother, morally superior, altruistic, or equal to man). These were not mutually exclusive, and some news articles had more than one image. Items with no gender-specific reference apart from simple identification were classified as straight news. The following item about spy Belle Boyd illustrates:

> Miss Belle Boyd was serenaded in Knoxville, Tenn., a few evenings ago, by the Florida Brass Band, and being loudly called for by the crowd, she appeared at a window and made the following laconic response: Gentlemen: Like Gen. Johnston, I can fight, but cannot make speeches. You have my heartfelt thanks for your

compliment.37

More than 100 news items about women in 65 issues of five newspapers from 1861, 1862, 1863 and early 1865, plus items quoted in secondary sources from an additional ten newspapers, were studied.

Findings

To summarize findings before proceeding to examples: One antebellum image stood out, but evidence suggests shifts in the conception of woman's role, particularly that the war years were transitional, and that the value of patriotism and women's very public war work propelled shifts. First, most items (66) were classified as straight news, indicating women were treated as newsworthy, which, in itself, may indicate changing notions about their role. Second, nearly as many items (54) showed women engaged in, or being encouraged to engage in, public activity—indicating visibility, acceptance, reinforcement—and ultimately 'nudging' women into the public sphere.

Third, only one image from the set identified for early America appeared while all four late 19th-century images appeared—but the former was pervasive while the latter four were infrequent. The five of the eight images found are, in order of frequency: ornamental (32), altruistic (24), equal (23), mother (6), and morally superior (4). (Absence of the evangelical and reformer images is not surprising since they relate to movements ending by the Civil War.)[38] Woman as romanticized was not found, but this image seems to overlap with the late nineteenth-century images of woman as mother and morally superior—the two least frequent (6 and 4, respectively)—and perhaps a transition to the latter preceded the Civil War. Fourth, woman as altruistic (24) and as equal (23) appeared more often than expected—suggesting that the war years were indeed transitional in conceptions of women. Finally, patriotism figured explicitly in many items (34), but probably implicitly underlay many others.

These findings are elaborated below with attention first to straight news and images, followed by patriotism and public activity.

I. Straight News

Examples of straight news are reports of women's aid organizations, women's attendance at certain functions, presence at the New York draft riots and even participation in the bread riots. Straight reporting seemed to predominate in coverage of Anna Dickinson, the orator paid as much for speeches during the war as the highest paid male orator, Henry Ward Beecher. Nineteen when the war began, Dickinson roused audiences such that Republican leaders believed that her speeches swung some key state elections and suggested she address the House of Representatives. Some, objecting to a woman speaking in Congress, recommended renting a hall. Dickinson refused to speak if not in the House of Representatives and became the first woman to address Congress--Jan. 16, 1864--charging Congressmen admission and giving proceeds to the National Freedmen's Relief Bureau.[39]

The coverage of Dickinson, in fact, may exemplify shifting gender images, for woman as altruistic often appears; in other instances, she seems represented as equal with men; in still others, she is treated as able to get away with things because a woman. For example, one item said Dickinson, "presuming upon her sex, will boldly utter sentiments in condemnation of men and measures, the utterance of which by one of the sterner sex might . . . subject him to some little inconvenience";[40] and another said some who denounced her views "regretted that such sentiments should find a refuge from a storm of indignation protected ... by calico and crinoline."[41] Finally, the opposition newspapers tended to ridicule her.

II. Images

The image found most in the newspaper content studied was woman as "ornamental" (32 of 99 images recorded)—genteel, imparting support by cheerfully being visible—and associated with the private sphere. Although women quickly mobilized to aid the war effort following the firing on Fort Sumter in 1861,[42] the press continued to reflect them as in the home, expressing patriotism through watching husbands, sons, brothers, fathers, go off to war. Women's role was to support, inspire; and they were to find satisfaction and purpose in doing so.

1. Woman as ornamental

Reports of President-Elect Abraham Lincoln's 1861 visit to New York referred to women as enthusiastically waving handkerchiefs and lending a "peculiar and beautiful brilliancy to the scene."[43]

"Ladies'" presence, with numerous references to their beauty and enthusiasm, seems to have been important to note here—as if advertising (and perhaps "teaching") women's support of the war. Similar stories in Southern newspapers are exemplified by a report about a New Orleans military march that "The stands have been reserved for the ladies, who will doubtless repair in great numbers to see the brilliant pageant."[44] Other articles referred to "fashionable belles of Charleston," how "their delicate hands waved wildly,"[45] and called them "delicate creatures" who were "elegantly clad."[46] A letter from "Many Ladies" conveys their agreement with intimations in the Charleston *Courier*'s report of a military display regarding the importance of the presence of a large number of women:

> We fully agree with you in your communication of the military display ... and the appearance ... of so large a number of ladies ... is well calculated to inspire our gallant soldiers with ardor in the cause of the defence of their country ... for none are more fully impressed with the truth, that "none but the brave deserve the fair," than those who are ready to imperil life and honor in defence of home, sweet home, and all that is comprised in that word.[47]

Another letter reminded women of "the glorious privilege ... of testifying [their] gratitude to the military hero [Beauregard] of this glorious revolution," and urged them "to give a testimony of respect to the hero who is made His instrument to rescue us from the oppressor's rod and the despot's tyranny."[48]

2. Woman as altruistic

That woman as altruistic was the second most frequent image found is not surprising when one reflects that much reported women's activities had to do with serving the public good or was intertwined with patriotism. This image's frequency, however, strongly suggests a transition underway in notions of gender roles.

One report of women's public activity that intertwined notions of altruism and patriotism said, "When the history of this war shall be written, there will be no brighter page than that which will record the deeds performed by the heroic and self-sacrificing women, who have been ministering angels of mercy to the sick and wounded soldiers."[49] Another article reported a woman appointed to the rank of army major for her nursing service, and another in the same newspaper repeated a resolution from the Confederate Congress praising the "patriotic women of the Confederacy for the energy, real and untiring devotion ... in furnishing voluntary contributions to our soldiers in the field, and in various military hospitals throughout the country."[50] An army nurse described her work, admonishing any who might think of nursing as no more than "administering a spoonful of wine," or "bathing an officer's temples with a sponge." These activities "require no sacrifice of feeling," she wrote, while a nurse must enter repulsive conditions and, even though a "highly educated lady accustomed to every indulgence that wealth can furnish," she may be found "with disordered hair, hoopless . . . bespattered with blood, coal smut and grease, forgetting every feeling but the one of seeking and helping the most wretched and neglected."[51]

3. Woman as equal with man

Equality is the only "new" image identified for the late nineteenth century. Although a familiar argument in antebellum America and, indeed, embodied in annual women's rights conventions, equality was in no way an accepted image,[52] and nothing in the "cult of true womanhood" suggests equality of the sexes.

The frequency then of the image in Civil War newspapers surprises at first blush. But it is important to stress that, even though women's wartime work was valued and praised, and some received distinction (Dickinson, Dix, and those who served in combat and as spies), newspaper coverage studied reflects no general image of women's equality with men. The image appeared in several isolated sentences in a series of articles otherwise replete with imagery of women as ornamental. Such juxtaposition in itself of two opposed images suggests transition underway. That series and coverage of Dickinson account for virtually all such images found.

A series of articles in the New York *Times*, advocating equality for women in the workplace, specifically through arguments for just wages and sufficient training and education for work outside the home,[53] rarely referred to the war, but women's wartime activities likely prompted both the discussion and the expressions about equality. For example, an early 1864 article, titled "Female Education for the Better Classes," asserted that "There is no question that women's faculties . . . are as useful to the world, and, in some instances, as 'marketable' as the masculine," and used women's war activities as support: "This war has given a remarkable instance of how much value the labor of thoroughly trained women can be. . . ."54 This argument, although not directly related to war news, might not have occurred had not women's wartime activities become so visible.

4. Woman as mother

As mentioned earlier, images of woman as morally superior and as mother were rare. But they were strong when stated. Two brief examples seem sufficient to illustrate:

> In these riots the women have been the leaders; and that fact alone proves absolute hunger must have been the cause of them. Women do not get up street riots, break open provision shops, and pillage bakeries and flour stores from political sympathies, nor from resentment against high prices. When their children are in peril of starvation, they become capable of anything. Nothing short of that extremity can have provoked the demonstrations....55

5. Woman as morally superior

"An American Woman" invoked not only the home to be protected, but the sacredness of the home as she pleaded through a letter to an editor for Northern soldiers to regard even Southern homes as "sacred altars." Seeking to infuse the men with moral standards of conduct, she wrote, "Forget not the weakness of women and the tenderness of childhood! Let your *bravery* be mixed with *gentleness*, your *ardor* with *sobriety!* Let no dastardly act taint the honor of a single man!"56

III. Patriotism

Gender constructions were often merged with the notion of woman's patriotism. For example, after noting the multitudes of "bright-eyed ladies, who smiled and waved and huzzaed with as much enthusiasm . . . as the ruder specimens of humanity who surged by them on foot," one reporter of Lincoln's 1861 trip to New York wrote that the president-elect "thought if there are as many brave men as there are fair women in the city, Newark would be a difficult city to take."57

In effect, patriotism seemed assigned to nearly every wartime activity of women whether sacrifice, inspiration, involvement in relief efforts, nursing, or even rebellion. Women who waved Confederate flags as chaos erupted during the surrender of New

Orleans were praised for patriotism, for example,58 and reference to women's patriotism appear in reports of early war rallies, such as the following:

> If there could be any doubt of their feeling, the waving of banners from roofs and windows ... the spots of color which gleamed from many a badge on patriotic bosoms ... showed that a flame of patriotism blazed with an intense heat through them all.59

An example from Southern newspapers, which also labeled women's behavior as patriotic, is an article about "a patriotic lady" who, upon hearing her husband had been mortally wounded in combat, wished her sons were old enough to take his place.60 Mothers, "with tears of joyous pride half blinding them, helped to buckle on the accoutrements of their sons, and kissed them as they went forth to battle,"61 and an account, suggesting that military zeal created eagerness to enlist, referred to influence of mothers and sweethearts who "yielded up cheerfully—not without tears, it may be, but still cheerfully"— the men who left for the battlefront.62 An article described a "patriotic mother" accompanying her son to a gun store, purchasing the best weapons and other items for him, and saying, "This, my son, is all that I can do. I have given you up to serve your country, and may God go with you—it is all a mother can do."63 In addition, newspapers praised monetary sacrifice as patriotic; daughters and wives in both the North and the South suffered financial losses of wage-earning husbands and fathers gone to war and still donated money to organizations, which the papers reported.64

Woman's patriotism was often equated with sacrifice, an image that blends with woman as altruistic, and these examples, in fact, highlight a recurring theme not only of women sacrificing *for,* but also sacrificing *of* their men, feelings and money.

IV. Women in the Public Sphere

Whether women covered in newspapers were engaging in public activity or not, the very coverage made all women more public. Women's wartime activities made them more newsworthy, more visible, and more public—which had consequences. Newspapers reveal a shift to accommodate women's increased public activity as such reports helped create an ideology over time of women's patriotism characterized by waiting, sacrifice, service and moral infusion of responsibility in husbands and sons. Women's aid societies, church clubs and other organizations assisted the war effort—engaging women more in public work than normally acceptable because it was compatible with the notion of women as "caretakers."

Discussion

The findings here are preliminary, of course, since the items and newspapers studied are insufficient to support generalizations. The extent to which changes in images, and gender roles, may have preceded the Civil War needs study. Further, nearly all items read for this study came from 1861-1863, most from Northern newspapers, and much more evidence is required to adequately support claims about change across the war. Still, the findings are very suggestive and bear further consideration.

Some surprising findings included: 1) more coverage of women than expected; 2) more straight news than expected—that is, coverage that betrayed no particular treatment due to the subject being woman, and 3) underlying attitudes that women could get away with things men could not.

Among limitations of this research, the analysis did not take into account that images about women in Civil War newspapers may have been aberrant. In other words, efforts may have been made to "construct" certain images and create an ideology promoting women's support of the war effort. Faust, cited above, reported on such discourse in Southern newspapers, in fact. This could mean images found were born of wartime crisis and did not prevail. In fact, newspapers studied here reveal what seem to be purposeful references to women's behavior—such as sacrifice and service to others—as distinctly patriotic activity, suggesting a temporary construction of appropriate gender behavior in time of war.

Another limitation is that images used for analysis are not perfect types; further, some of the terms may be different ways of labeling the same images that persisted over time. For example, two images from the late nineteenth century, woman as mother and as morally superior, seem encompassed by woman as *romanticized* from images identified for early America; and the notion of woman as altruistic in the late nineteenth century seems to encompass *evangelical* and *radical* images. However, no images (defined for analytical purposes or found in newspapers) are perfect types, and, despite possible overlapping, these were useful mechanisms for examining recorded language.

Conclusions

Although only suggestive, images found in 65 issues of five Civil War newspapers (plus ten additional newspapers quoted in secondary sources) indicate increasing acceptance of women in public activities. These images also indicate that the value of patriotism, embedded in coverage of women, made such activity acceptable for a society unaccustomed to such gender behavior. The antebellum notion of woman's proper role as primarily in the private sphere—serving the home as dutiful wife and devoted mother—prevailed but was weakening. The war created a way for women to enter the public sphere, primarily through providing care, but also through direct involvement as spies, soldiers, prisoners of war and in filling jobs left vacant by enlisting men.

The belief that woman's true nature was expressed in service to others thus opened the door for public activity through nursing and relief work and expanded the notion of women as altruistic—an image that persisted and abetted women's increased public activity after the war. Altruism—work for social good—is by its nature public. Further, praise for altruism made women visible, and that visibility was extended, reinforced, and ultimately perpetuated through press coverage.

Perhaps calling women's work patriotic made it acceptable in the public sphere—despite contradictory expectations—and press coverage reinforced and perpetuated such changed notions. Indeed, it appears that the need to define women's work as patriotic created opportunities for shifts in their activity and in perceptions of its importance.

In any event, women were unlikely to revert to the purely private sphere, and they were also unlikely to suffer severe ostracism for public activity after the war. Although some sentiment remained, no doubt, about women's "proper sphere," their wartime work, which heightened visibility and appreciation for what they could contribute outside the home, seems to have substantially eroded that sentiment.

Notes

1. Janet Wilson James, *Changing Ideas about Women in the United States, 1776-1825*, (New York & London: Garland Publishing, Inc., 1981); Jean E. Friedman, William G.

Shade, Mary Jane Capozzoli, eds., *Our American Sisters: Women in American Life and Thought*, 4th ed. (Lexington, Mass., & Toronto: D. C. Heath and Co., 1987), especially chapters by Gerda Lerner (125-137), Nancy F. Cott (138-168), Linda K. Kerber (96112) and Ellen Carol Dubois (230-255). See also Linda K. Kerber, "'I Have Don ... Much to Carrey on the Warr': Women and the Shaping of Republican Ideology after the American Revolution," *Journal of Women's History* 1:3 (Winter 1990): 231-243.
2. Jeanine Halva-Neubauer, "The Legal Status of U.S. Women, 1783-1848" (History 5381, Department of History, University of Minnesota, 1986), 1-4. Sources important to Halva-Neubauer's summary include: Jamil Zainaldin, *Law in Antebellum Society: Legal Change and Economic Expansion* (New York: Alfred Knopf, 1983); Joan Hoff Wilson, "Are Women Citizens," in *Sexism and the Law: A Study of Male Beliefs and Legal Bias in Britain and the United States* (New York: Free Press, 1978); Lawrence Friedman, *A History of American Law* 2nd. ed. (New York: Simon and Schuster, 1985); and Carroll Smith-Rosenberg, "Beauty, the Beast, and the Militant Woman: A Case Study in Sex Roles and Social Stress in Jacksonian America," *American Quarterly* 23 (1971), 562-584.
3. Barbara Welter, "The Cult of True Womanhood," *American Quarterly* 18 (Summer 1966): 152
4. Halva-Neubauer, 3-4.
5. Lucy Eldersveld Murphy, "Business Ladies: Midwestern Women and Enterprise, 1850-1880," *Journal of Women's History* 3:1 (Spring 1991), 65-89; Loren Schweninger, "Property owning Free African-American Women in the South, 1800-1870," *Journal of Women's History* 1:3 (Winter 1990), 13-43.
6. Elizabeth D. Leonard, *Yankee Women: Gender Battles in the Civil War* (New York and London: W.W. Norton & Co., 1994), xx-xxi; 212n27. See Margaret Randolph Higonnet, Jane Jenson, Sonya Michel and Margaret Collins Weitz, eds. *Behind the Lines: Gender and the Two World Wars* (New Haven and London: Yale University Press,1987), 4-7.
7. Leonard, 212n27.
8. *Ibid.*, xv-xvi.
9. Gary L. Bunker, "Antebellum Caricature and Woman's Sphere," *Journal of Women's History* 3:3 (Winter 1992): 6.
10. Elizabeth Cady Stanton, Susan B. Anthony and Matilda Joslyn Gage, *History of Women Suffrage* 6 vols. (Rochester: Charles Mann, 1887), 4:292-293.
11. Mary Elizabeth Massey, *Women in the Civil War.* Lincoln: University of Nebraska Press, 1966), 43-44.
12. Drew Gilpin Faust, "Altars of Sacrifice: Confederate Women and the Narratives of War," in Catherine Clinton and Nina Silber, eds., *Divided Houses—Gender and the Civil War* (Oxford and New York: Oxford University Press, 1992), 185.
13. Massey, 65-86. See also Penny Colman, *Spies! Women in the Civil War* (Cincinnati: Betterway Books, 1992); Lynn Cullen Sizer, "Acting Her Part: Narratives of Union Women Spies," in Clinton and Silber, *op. cit.*, 114-133.
14. Leonard, xvii; Jane E. Schultz, "Race, Gender, and Bureaucracy: Civil War Army Nurses and the Pension Bureau," *Journal of Women's History* 6:2 (Summer 1994), 45, estimates 18,000 women worked in Union military hospitals for six to 12 dollars per month.
15. Clinton and Silber, 144. Ryan, 143-152; see, for example, the following items in *The New York Times*, "Bread Riot in Richmond," April 8, 1863; "Bread Riot in Raleigh, N.C.," April 19, 1863; "Famine at the South," April 20, 1863; "A Mob of Ladies," April 21, 1863; "A Woman's Riot at Milledgeville, Ga.," April 26, 1863; "Gen. Butler Defends his Famous Order," *New York Tribune*, July 16, 1862; "The Richmond riot....," *Charleston Daily Courier*, April 9, 1863.
16. Jean V. Berlin, "Introduction to the Bison Book Edition," viii.

17. Clinton and Silber, *op. cit.*, 117.
18. Leonard, xxi.
19. George Rable, "'Missing in Action': Women of the Confederacy," in Clinton and Silber, *op. cit.*, 135.
20. Mary P. Ryan, *Women in Public: Between Banners and Ballots, 1825-1880* (Baltimore and London: The Johns Hopkins University Press, 1990), 142.
21. Clinton and Silber, *op. cit.*, 171.
22. *Ibid.*, 137-144.
23. Leeann Whites, "The Civil War as a Crisis in Gender," in Clinton and Silber, eds., *Divided Houses,* 5-16. An important article on differences is Gerda Lerner, "Reconceptualizing Differences Among Women," *Journal of Women's History* 2:3 (Winter, 1990): 106-122.
24. Clinton and Silber, *op. cit.*, 172.
25. *Ibid.*, 172-174.
26. *Ibid.*, 177-179.
27. Massey, *op. cit.*, 19-22.
28. Dorothy Sterling, ed., *We Are Your Sisters: Black Women in the Nineteenth Century* (New York: W. W. Norton & Co., 1984), 237; 245; 256; Schultz, 47.
29. *Ibid.*, 256-258.
30. *Ibid.*, 245-248.
31. *Ibid.*, 248-253.
32. *Ibid.*, 258-161.
33. *Ibid.*, 261-263.
34. *Ibid.*, 265.
35. Ronald W. Hogeland, "'The Female Appendage': Feminine Life-Styles in America, 1820-1860," in Jean E. Friedman and William G. Shade, eds., *Our American Sisters: Women in American Life and Thought* 2nd ed. (Boston: Allyn and Bacon, Inc., 1976): 133-148.
36. Janet Cramer, "Woman As Citizen: An Ideological Analysis of Three Women's Publications, 1900-1930" (Unpublished MA thesis, University of Minnesota, 1994), 77. Historians who have identified these images include Aileen S. Kraditor, *The Ideas of the Woman's Suffrage Movement,* 1890-1920. New York and London: Columbia University Press, 1965; Shelia Rothman, *Woman's Proper Place: A History of Changing Ideals and Practices, 1870 to the Present.* New York: Basic Books, 1978; Sarah Eisenstein, *Give Us Bread But Give Us Roses, Working Women's Consciousness in the United States, 1890 to the First World War.* London, Boston, Melbourne and Henley: Routledge and Kegan Paul, 1983.
37. *New York Times,* Feb. 24, 1863.
38. Henry Steele Commager, *Era of Reform, 1830-1860.* New York: Van Nostrand Reinhold, 1960; Sweet, William Warren, *Revivalism in America: Its Origin, Growth and Influence.* New York: Charles Scribner's Sons, 1944.
39. Giraud Chester, *Embattled Maiden* (New York: G. P. Putman's Sons, 1951), 45-78.
40. Chester, 37, quoting the *Providence Press.*
41. Chester, 32.
42. *New York Times,* April 25, 1861.
43. "The President-Elect En Route," *New York Tribune,* Feb. 20, 1861; Feb. 22, 1861.
44. *New Orleans Times-Picayune,* Feb. 22, 1861.
45. *New York Times,* April 21, 1863 (quoting Southern newspapers).
46. *New York Times,* April 26, 1863 (quoting Southern newspapers).
47. *Charleston Courier,* Aug. 15, 1861.
48. *Charleston Courier,* Aug. 19, 1861.
49. *New York Tribune,* May 16, 1862.
50. *New Orleans Times-Picayune,* April 25, 1865.

51. *New York Tribune*, May 16, 1862.
52. Judith Wellman, "The Seneca Falls Women's Rights Convention: A Study of Social Networks," *Journal of Women's History* 3:1 (Spring 1991), 9-37; Eleanor Flexner, *Century of Struggle: The Woman's Rights Movement in the United States* rev. ed. (Cambridge and London: The Belknap Press of Harvard University Press, 1975), 9; 71-102.
53. *New York Times*, Nov. 15, 18, 21, 22, 26; Dec. 6, 12, 1863.
54. *New York Times*, Jan. 17, 1864.
55. *New York Times*, April 20, 1863.
56. *New York Times,* April 20, 1861.
57. *New York Times,* Feb. 22, 1861.
58. *New York Times*, May 18, 1862.
59. *New York Tribune,* April 20, 1861.
60. *Richmond Daily Dispatch*, April 8, 1863.
61. *New York Times*, April 20, 1861.
62. *New York Tribune*, April 20, 1861.
63. *New York Tribune,* April 29, 1861.
64. See, for example, the *Charleston Courier*, April 25, 1862, and May 16, 1862.

18

Two Men, Two Minds: An Examination of the Editorial Commentary of Two Georgia Editors During Sherman's March to the Sea

Debra Reddin van Tuyll
Augusta State University

Sherman's march to the sea presented Georgia newspaper men with their biggest story of the war: marauding invaders pillaging and burning through the mid-section of the state. As would be expected, these editors jumped on the story, scrambling for information from any source and reporting any information they could lay their hands on. The three most common sources included two of the same ones newspapers had relied on throughout history: newspaper exchanges and eye witness accounts. A third source used in the Civil War was the news service. Of course, one would expect the paper's politics to be evident in what stories were used and what stories were neglected. Interestingly enough, this was not so for most newspapers in Georgia. Those who were fully behind the idea of a Southern victory and those who were convinced that it was time to lay down the swords and talk peace, for the most part, were amazingly similar in their news reporting. However, there was a divergence in the content and tone of their editorials. This paper will look at how two Georgia newspapers, the *Augusta Chronicle* and the *Macon Telegraph*, covered the march as a news story, and what the papers' editors were saying in their editorial columns. Their papers were chosen for this study because almost all copies of the papers were available from the time period of Sherman's march and subsequent capture of Savannah, Mid-November through December 22 when Sherman sent his famous telegram to President Abraham Lincoln.

The Editors

A consideration of a paper's news judgment and editorial stance must begin with the editors, for they were the ones who determined story selection and make editorial opinions.[1] "Editors carefully selected news that reflected their own view points."[2] Carl Osthaus, in his book about the partisan Southern press, observed that newspapers of 19th century were characterized by personal journalism. Colorful "personalities" dominated the papers of the day which were still partisan and which were devoted to politics and quarrels. Until the 20th century, many Southern newspapers were run by a single editor who dominated every aspect of the paper.[3] This was certainly true for the *Augusta Chronicle* and the *Macon Telegraph*, although the editors of the *Chronicle* and the *Telegraph* could not have been more different from one another.

Henry Lynden Flash, editor of the *Macon Telegraph*, could have been the poster boy for what today is considered the stereotypical Southern aristocratic gentleman. Flash looked to the past for guidance on how to conduct not only his own life, but the affairs of the nation as well. Reared in New Orleans and Mobile, Flash read Sir Walter Scott, wrote romantic poetriy and served in the Confederate cavalry under Wheeler and Hardee. That he was committed to traditional Southern values and attitudes is obvious from his poetry. On the other hand, Nathan Morse, the *Chronicle*'s editor, was a Northerner who had come South earlier in the war. Morse was able to view the conflict between North and South with a pragmatic eye. He had none of the emotional entanglements with Southern honor and traditions which blinded Flash to the dire reality of the Confederate situation in the fall of 1864.

Nathan Morse, editor of the *Chronicle*, came to Augusta early in the war. He was employed at the paper prior to its November 1862 sale to Thomas Chichester of Augusta and Wellington Stevenson of Charleston. The two new owners agreed to give Morse one-half the paper's annual profits for running it, and a year later, the men sold Morse 1/3 the stock, making him an equal partner.[4] He later bought out his partners with, some say, money borrowed from Georgia governor Joeseph Brown with the intent of making the *Chronicle* the mouthpiece of the Confederate Peace Movement,[5] though Charles C. Jones, Jr. says the money came from Henry Moore.[6] Chichester and Stevenson gave Morse a free hand in running the newspaper.[7]

A Yankee by birth, Morse had been editor of the Bridgeport, Conncecticut *Republican Farmer* when the war broke out. Even from the beginning of the Civil War, he advocated an early peace, and his pro-peace stance led to his newspaper's office being mobbed by a bunch of angry Abolitionists.[8] It was after this that Morse moved to Augusta.

Morse was described as "a man who quite evidently could strut sitting down" and who had a round face with bright, protuberant eyes that made him look quite boyish. His "disposition was that of good-humored selfishness, but he affected the Western Bill style of deportment to a great extent." He loved weapons, and was especially fond of a huge revolver and a bowie knife.[9]

In their 1960 history of the *Augusta Chronicle*, Bell and Crabbe devoted and entire chapter to Morse, which they titled "Nathan Morse, Turncoat Editor." As was obvious from the title, they found little to like about the Yankee editor; they wrote that there was little good about Morse other than a "spurious, self-proclaimed love for Dixie and a recognizable ability with the pen." They went on to write that "this displaced Yankee soon revealed himself to be thoroughly despicable and absolutely lacking in any lasting loyalty."

Early on, Morse editorially supported the war effort. He even went so far as to seek scapegoat for Confederate defeats. However, according to John E. Talmadge, after Vicksburg and Gettysburg, Morse's editorial stance changed, and he became abusive of the Confederate government.[10] During the occupation of Atlanta and the March to the Sea, Morse took to writing editorials that called for a negotiated peace.

It is this "changed" Morse, of course, to whom Bell and Crabbe refer to as a "turncoat." But they are not the only writers to take

Morse to task for his editorials. Even during the war, the *Chronicle* was often accused of being disloyal.[11] In 1951, Louis Turner Griffith, in his book *Georgia Journalism 1763-1950*, accused Morse of being the only newspaper editor in Georgia who sought to hasten the fall of the Confederacy.[12] However, the dates of Bell and Crabbe's and Griffith and Talmadge's words are significant here. In the 1950s and 1960s, the South was embroiled in the civil rights movement, and the Cold War was at its peak. Many writers of those days used their work, in a sense, to "refight" the War Between the States, and anyone, living or dead, who dared criticize Jefferson Davis or the Confederacy or any of its generals was automatically labeled a "turncoat," or, at the very least, viewed with deep suspicion. It should be noted that Griffith and Talmadge went so far as to state that, during a time of war, a newspaper should be an aim of the state, blindly generating whatever propaganda is dictated to it by government so as to buck-up the public so it will continue to support the war. While even today many Americans would agree with Griffith and Talmadge, most journalists would argue that their role as watchdogs on government is redoubled in time of war.

During war, a journalist such as Morse has the responsibility to lead the debate about government conduct and to present information to the readers so that they may interpret and find meaning in current events. Morse was quite consistent in this; even before leaving Conncecticut, he was an advocate of peace. He came to Augusta, watched the Confederacy's situation deteriorate to the point where, by the fall of Atlanta in September 1864, there was no rational hope for a Confederate victory, and this is what he told his readers. And he was right.

Perhaps because Morse was an outsider, a Yankee by birth, he was better able to actually see and assess the Confederacy's position after Vicksburg and Gettysburg. Morse, because he wasn't a Southerner, could look at the situation objectively, as any great journalist should (though, of course, objectivity was not a wide-spread journalistic tenant at that point in history); his pride and love for his homeland weren't at stake, as they were for Southern-born editors.

Far less information is available about Henry Lynden Flash, the *Macon Telegraph*'s editor during the period covering Sherman's march. Flash bought the *Telegraph* from Joseph Clisby and began publishing the paper on September 19, 1864. Prior to buying the *Telegraph*, Flash had been editor of the Macon *Daily Confederate*, which he merged with the *Telegraph*.[13] Perhaps the biggest change

Flash made upon acquiring the paper was his alteration in the *Telegraph's* appearance of the newspaper: he changed the banner from an ornately illustrated, outlined text font to a very stark modern font (along the lines of Bodoni).

Flash was a former Confederate cavalry officer, having served with both Hardee and Wheeler prior to November 1863.[14] Sometime after the Army of Tennessee fell back to Dalton, Georgia, Flash resigned his commission and came to Macon to visit his brother who was a refugee from New Orleans. While visiting Macon, Flash went to work for L. F. M. Andrews as assistant editor of the *Daily Confederate*. He later bought the paper, though the date of the purchase is not known.[15]

Flash was apparently a poet of some note; Joel C. Harris wrote an article about him for *The Countryman*'s June 14, 1864 edition, and he is also mentioned in James W. Davidson's *The Living Writers of the South* which was published in 1869.

Flash was described as "a man with keen piercing eyes and a strongly marked Roman nose."[16] He was probably born in the West Indies in 1835 and immigrated with his family to New Orleans at an early age. He attended Georgetown College in Washington, D.C., but actually graduated from college in Kentucky. Probably from Transylvania or Centre. After graduation, he worked for awhile at the Mobile *Register*. Before the war, he had owned a produce business in Galverton, though he freely admitted to being more interested in writing poetry than in selling produce. Produce and newspaper work were, for Flash, a day job that supported his poetry writing, and he had poems published in publications such as the New Orleans *Delta*, *Peterson's Magazine* and the, then, very popular *Home Journal*.[17]

In 1857, Flash went to Europe and spent 10 months in Florence, "which, according to Joel Chandler Harris, 'did not tend to decrease the poet's zeal for the cause of Love and Romanticism.'"[18] This experience may well be what led Flash to come home and join Hardee's staff— in spite of the fact that he was related to the famous English abolitionist William Wilberforce.[19]

Being a stereotypical, romantic Southerner, Flash could not conceive of the Confederacy ever giving up in its rebellion, nor could he accept the fact that, by the fall of 1864, the Confederacy was near defeat. Instead, he, unlike Morse, turned away from reality and did his best to build up the spirits of Maconites.

Flash and Morse were two very different men; Morse was the practical Yankee, very firmly grounded in reality while Flash was the romantic cavalier, riding off on the mists of poetry to chase dragons on tilt at windmills. He was a Southerner by birth, and he had served in the Confederate cavalry. He had mites in his eyes with regard to the progress of the war. The rather significant differences in these two men led, as one might imagine, to significant differences in their editorializing about Sherman's campaign through middle Georgia.

A common topic was editorials designed to build the spirits of readers and to garner their continued support for the war effort. According to Wilken, Flash used these techniques to encourage Macon residents' support for continued fighting. They were:

1) He tried to make the readers feel guilty for their shortcomings.
2) He tried to arouse the reader's hatred of the Yankees.
3) He exaggerated hopes for ultimate Confederate victory.[20]

Flash reminded his readers of how little they had suffered compared to Virginians, or compared to what the Scots had suffered at the hands of the English.[21] Morse, who was not above a little boosterism himself, in a November 22 editorial, held Virginians up as an example of how to bear suffering nobly. "For nearly four years she has borne the brunt of this terrific contest, and yet she is unsubdued; she stands erect and defiant."[22] On November 21, Flash published a call to action for all Georgians, telling them it was "a thousand times more glorious to die in defense of your homes than to barely surrender them without an effort to the contrary....display the valor of the Romans, and the sun will soon shine brightly again where so late was darkness and gloom."[23] Further down, Flash writes that if Georgians don't "come down upon Sherman like wolves and sheepfold, they are unworthy of themselves. Fight him in the front, fight him on the flank, fight him in the rear. Remove everything valuable from his path and throw every obstruction in his way."[24]

Morse was equally eloquent in the November 22 editorial mentioned earlier when he wrote,

> Yet we should meet his formidable invasion as becomes a people worthy to be free -- calmly and courageously, and with an unfaltering trust in that benign Providence which has heretofore smiled upon our cause. There should be no panic, no despondency, no shirking from duty. The patriot in this hour of public calamity, rising about all fear and agitation, should address himself with cool courage and resolution to the sacred and indispensable duty of defending his country. There is strength, there is success in that calm determination which meets danger with an unquailing heart. In all the great exigencies of life it is this that insures success, that enables men to triumph over difficulties seeming insurmountable.[25]

He goes on to quote Patrick Henry, telling his readers "we should be ready to exclaim, 'Better to do die as freemen than live as slaves;' and 'Give me liberty or give me death.'" On the topic of freedom, Morse could be as romantic as Flash.

Both editors spent much of their commentary assessing Sherman's chances of successfully marching through Georgia after cutting off his lines of supply and communication, an unheard of action by a military commander. On November 30, Flash said in his editorial that he was certain Sherman's move would result in the destruction and demoralization of his troops.[26] Flash said that at the end of the March, all Sherman would have to show for it would be the total destruction of Georgia, which, he predicted, would unite Southerners even more against the Yankees (he was right about that, of course, but he neglected to consider what the destruction of Georgia would mean to the Confederacy strategically). Flash, misguidedly, believed that Sherman's abandonment of Atlanta was "an open confession of weakness" by the Federal commander. The *Telegraph* editor wrote, "That he (Sherman) is a fugitive is proven by his avoiding Macon and his apparent intention to leave Augusta unmolested....The devastation of our homes, the destroyer of our property, the Attila of the West, seeks sanctuary." (By this point, Sherman's troops who had feinted toward Macon, and battled with Confederate cavalry at the nearby town of Griswold, had already turned back toward Milledgeville and beyond).

Chronicle editor Morse had, much earlier in November, written an editorial in which he predicted Sherman's march. On November 13, a day before Sherman's first troops even left Atlanta, Morse wrote that, now that the Northern general had captured Atlanta, his safety lay in flight (*Chronicle*, Nov. 13).[27] This editorial ran four days before the Chronicle's first story announcing that Sherman's forces were on the move. Actually, on the 17th, the *Chronicle* ran several stories about Sherman's movements, and one bears repeating: A traveler arriving from Atlanta told the *Chronicle* about a woman of his acquaintance who lived outside of Atlanta and needed to get into Atlanta to conduct some business. She knew she'd never be allowed into the city because she was white (Sherman was, at that point, evacuating all Atlanta residents), and the city was then being evacuated. So she boiled up some walnut shells and dyed her hands and face so she would appear to be a mulatto. While in Atlanta, the woman heard from Federal troops that they would be leaving soon and that their route would be first Macon and then

Augusta.[28]

Morse, like Flash, also said that Sherman's march had united Georgians. This, Morse belived, would strengthen the Confederate military. Morse wrote that with each of Sherman's victories, Confederate will to win increased (which is probably true, but it takes more than will to win a war) and, he predicts, this will be the undoing of Sherman. "We can and will defeat him, let him take what course he may."[29] Of course, there was one problem with Morse's point, and Flash unknowingly identified it on December 16 when he reprinted an editorial from the Memphis *Appeal* which complained that Sherman's troops wouldn't stand still for a fair, open battle.[30] Sherman's cavalry, commanded by West Point graduate Judson Kilpatrick, effectively screened the ground troops from all but insignificant interference from the few thousand Confederate troops (mostly militia) in Georgia at that time. "While the infantry foraged freely and carried out their work of destruction with a little enemy interference, the Federal cavalry fought eleven days between November 15 and December 4."[31]

Another frequent editorial topic, at least for Morse, was where Sherman was going. Flash also dealt with this topic, but he did so primarily in his news pages. One explanation for this difference may be that Macon dealt with Sherman early in the campaign; Maconites knew he'd been there already. Augusta was one of the frequently suggested destinations for Sherman's troops, and since the town had two strategically important installations (a Confederate arsenal and a Confederate powderworks), it was a likely target. It is only logical that Augustans would be interested in reading about where Sherman was headed and how likely it was he was headed their way.

On November 25, Morse made one of his few wrong guesses about Sherman's destination.[32] On that day, Morse predicted Sherman would not go to Savannah because that's where the northern press was saying he was headed. He thought it more likely that Sherman was going to Brunswick, Georgia, or Beaufort, South Carolina. Morse did admit that Savannah was a remote possibility. However, this is an important editorial for another reason as well. In this editorial Morse predicted that Sherman was not coming to Augusta. Morse wrote:

> Although the Northern press has hinted that Sherman might attempt to march to Charleston by way of Augusta, recent developments we think show very clearly that such is not his

design. If this were his route, he would not be diverging from it so widely. He would have advanced directly upon Augusta. He would not have spent all this time moving with his whole force on the Control road, and so far out of his direct road."[33]

Also in this editorial, Morse addressed the necessity of stopping Sherman before he reached either Beaufort, Brunswick or Savannah. Morse wrote that the North would have a fatal advantage over the South if Sherman were allowed to reach any of these potential bases in that, from his new base, Sherman could send harrassing expeditions all over the country.[34] Morse pointed out:

> The people should know that by timely energy on their parts to prevent him from gaining an advantage, they will save themselves from infinite trouble and danger hereafter. Now is the time, if ever, to defend their homes, their families and their all against future invasion and devastation. By defeating Sherman now, they will make themselves secure hereafter.[35]

Four days later, an exasperated Morse was complaining that Sherman had been trying to "mystify our military authorities through the use of divided forces which were harnassing both Macon and Augusta,"[36] while bodies of cavalry have been dashing about, cutting railroads and doing other mischief. He referred to Sherman in the editorial as "An Artful dodger." Morse acknowledged that all Sherman's subterfuge was for one purpose: to conceal his ultimate destination. Morse went on to point out, though, that it was only a matter of time until Sherman had to commit to one destination or another.

Further on in this editorial, Morse says it looks like Sherman is headed toward the Savannah river, though that conclusion was not certain. "Until he shall get out of the triangle in which he has been maneuvered since he left Atlanta, we can infer nothing with certainty from any of his movements, as to his ultimate course." The editorial pointed out the need for vigilance since Sherman's movements were at the moment, unpredictable. Morse says he doesn't think Augusta will be attacked, but, it could be, he says, because of the city's strategic importance.[37] (*Chronicle*, Nov. 29).

By December 4, Morse was certain of Sherman's destination: Savannah. He drew this conclusion based on Sherman's capture of Millen. Morse thought Sherman's plan might be to join up with Federal General Foster at Grahamville. Foster had been sending up signal rockets and balloons with calcium lights for several days, the Chronicle reported. Morse believed that if Sherman made it to

Grahamville, he would effectively cut off Savannah from reinforcements from Augusta and other places. Morse predicted Sherman would not risk a battle before reaching Savannah because he was low on supplies. Morse wrote that he believed the "military genius and talent" of the Southern generals who had come to Georgia to repulse Sherman, Beauregard, Bragg and Smith, was sufficient to do the job.[38] That could well be true; unfortunately, however, generals must have troops with which to wage war, and these generals were essentially troopless.

Like Morse, Flash addressed Sherman's destination early in the campaign, and he drew a different conclusion; he believed Sherman was going to Savannah (*Telegraph,* Nov. 26, 1864).[39] He stuck with that conclusion.

While Morse was busy worrying about whether Sherman was heading toward Augusta, Flash was busy nullifying Sherman in his editorial columns. About the worst the *Chronicle* ever called Sherman was "an artful dodger" (while this is no direct evidence to prove it, one might speculate that Morse had a respect for Sherman's generalship and audacity which kept him from stooping to meanspirited attacks). Flash, however, was vicious in his attacks.

On December 5, Flash wrote that it would be difficult to assign Sherman his appropriate place in history. Flash wrote

> His generalship will be lost in the second of his infamy, and the brilliancy of his military genius eclipsed in the darkness of his cold and heathen cruelties....Who would have believed that in the 19th century a monster would rise up in the shape of a man, whose acts should shock all humanity and startle Christendom with their atrocities.[40]

Flash went on in that editorial to accuse the Yankees of preferring genocide to low taxes and custom with the South.

Later that month, Flash told his readers that Sherman was subject to "fits" of insanity and that the Northern general had once been confined to an asylum. Flash declared Sherman "deranged."[41] As mentioned previously, Flash also referred to Sherman as Atilla of the North.

An issue unrelated to the Sherman campaign got frequent consideration. That issue was freedom of the press from government censorship, and the discussion grew out of Jefferson Davis' proposal to lift the exemption of newspaper employees from conscription.

Morse strongly believed Davis' plan was nothing more than a sneaky way to silence the Southern press; he felt Davis would use his new power to draft newspaper editors to get rid of those who were not towing the Davis line. While he did not use the term "censorship," it is clear that Morse saw Davis' play as an attempt to control the Confederate press.[42] Perhaps Morse's most eloquent statement on the topic appeared on Christmas Day in 1864. Morse begins the editorial with a collection of quotations by famous men that address the topic of press freedom. Included among the quotations are the following:

> "The experience of the English nation demonstrates, as indeed does the experience of every civilized people, that without a free Press, no Government can long remain free."
> —David Hume

> "The Press should be untrammelled."
> —Henry Clay

Following these quotations, Morse says that "the wise men" (his quotation marks) of the present day seemed to believe they knew more than the wise men he quoted in the editorial. Without saying so, he made it clear that they did not. Concluding the editorial, Morse wrote that Confederate leaders were saying, with the threatened repeal of the exemption, that the South must give up freedom of the press to win the rebellion. While, again, Morse did not say so in so many words, his implication was clear: Some principles, and press freedom was one, are more important than winning a war (although, according to Talmadge, Morse once broke a strike at the *Chronicle* by getting some of his printers conscripted into the Confederate army).[43] It is exactly this attitude for which Talmadge and Griffith take Morse to task. They wrote in their 1951 history of Georgia journalism that, during time of war, a newspaper should be an arm of the state, blithely producing whatever propaganda is necessary to buck up the public will to win the war (Griffith and Talmadge 66). Two years later Talmadge again addressed this topic, and he admitted then that Morse was allowed to continue publishing his criticisms of Davis and the Confederate government because, "the military might of Sherman and the peace efforts of Brown and Stephens had completely broken Georgia's fighting spirit. Also out of that answer emerges the reminder that Morse was, after all, largely echoing the arguments of the still popular vice president and governor."[44] This may explain why Davis' proposal failed.

While Flash was far more of a "fire-eater" than a Union man, he too saw Davis' proposal as a potential threat to press freedom. On

December 2, the Macon *Telegraph* reprinted an editorial from the Mobile *Press Advertiser and Register* which contended that "An attack on the press is an attack on freedom for all."[45] On December 5, a letter to the editor in the *Telegraph* said that it was folly to suppose an editor can "act fearlessly and independently and can point out errors by those in power if he is to be harassed by conditions and placed under the supervision of a censor." The letter continued: "A detailed press! Shades of Jefferson! We have indeed fallen upon strange times. Could such things be, it would require no great stretch of imagination to suppose ourselves in Russia."[46]

These letters and editorials are important not only for the glimpse they give into the issues of the day but also for the view they give of editorial attitudes toward press freedom among Confederate journalists. For even so ardent a Southern supporter such as Flash, Davis' proposal to draft newspaper employees was too much. These men's attitudes sound almost contemporary; they have much in common with today's thinking on government intervention in publishing. Prior to the Vietnam War, the common 20th century journalistic practice had been to work with the U.S. government to underestimate casualties or downplay other aspects of wars that might have a negative influence on the public's support for the war. Since Vietnam, the American press has been more diligent in digging out the truth and questioning government statements and policy, as did Morse and Flash (and many of their fellow Georgia editors whose writings are not addressed in this paper).

Perhaps the most important issue addressed by these editors was the question of peace. Morse editorialized about peace often during Sherman's Georgia campaign, and the topic appeared frequently in his news columns. His editorials were in reference to Davis' appointment of peace commissioner to meet with Lincoln. His editorials were consistent calls for a negotiated peace. In late December, Morse's editorials on peace took something of a turn when he coupled arguments for peace with commentary on Jefferson Davis' appointment of peace commissioner to meet with Lincoln. In a December 22 editorial, Morse argues for a negotiated peace, and criticizes other Southern editors who, he says, consider peace to be a forbidden theme. "The peace of our torn and bleeding country is too sacred and important a subject to be dismissed at the bidding of any man....The miseries and calamities inflicted upon our suffering people, by a war almost unexampled in its horrors, appeal pathetically to the heart of every true and enlightened patriot to seek by all honorable methods to arrest its ravages."[47] Morse went on to praise Davis for appointing the commissioner. "No harm can result from negotiation," Morse wrote, "And it is highly probable that when once commenced, the war will never be renewed. We can well afford to take the chances of an effort to settle the conflict by diplomacy."[48] Unfortunately, Davis' appointment of the peace commissioner was too little too late.[49]

Unlike Morse, Flash did not really address the issue of peace head-on. Instead, he went to great lengths to bolster the spirits of Macon residents by reassuring them that all hope of a Confederate victory was not lost.[50] Of course, on that same day, he ran another commentary in which he admitted that the fall of Savannah was eminent and asked, then what? Flash thought that Sherman would not merely sit in Savannah but would move on, possibly to Augusta (*Telegraph*, Dec. 21 b).[51]

Wilken wrote that Flash's attempts to rekindle the fighting spirit in Macon were in vain because "for prerequisite to restoration of the Confederate war spirit was faith in the Confederate government itself, something which fewer and fewer Southerners had as conditions steadily worsened at the front and at home."[52] If this were true of Georgians living in Macon in the fall of 1864, it would also have been true of Georgians living elsewhere. Perhaps this lack of fighting spirit explains why Morse's calls for peace and criticism of the Confederate government were apparently at least tolerated, if not agreed with, by Augustans. Historians of the mid-20th century have roundly declaimed against the Yankee-born editor's "turncoat" stance and have particularly criticized him for daring to question Davis' policies. However, there is no evidence that the people living in Augusta, or other parts of the state either, ever jobbed the paper or attempted to burn it down or in any other way attack Morse for holding opinions that were far away from the norm. In fact, Morse's opinion that it was time to settle the war with a peace agreement may well have been more in step with common opinion than was the fire-eater position of editors like Flash who were hanging on to the ideal of a negotiated peace which would leave the Confederacy an Independent Country, fully recognized by the United States. By the fall of 1864, realistically, there was no possibility of that ever happening. Morse realized this. He had both eyes open and a firm grasp of reality. Flash, even with his service in the Confederate military, was still looking at the war as a romantic clash between the forces of good and evil; this is apparent by his liking of Sherman to a monster and his use of the epithet "Attilla of the North," for the union general. Even in the 19th century, when journalistic practices and standards were so different from today's, the journalist who best served his or her community is the one who has a keen standard of truthfulness, a firm grounding in reality and an outstanding analytical ability. The best editorial writer is one who succinctly identifies the problems besetting a community and suggests a realistic solution to those problems. Morse, for all his foibles, did meet these criteria. He was, in many ways, the forerunner of the 20th century journalist. He was detached from the story. He preferred to love the South, but he was not of the South. Flash was hindered in serving his community for at least two reasons. First, he was bred in the South, if not born there, and his attachment to and love for the region is apparent in his writing, both journalistic and poetry. When one is consumed by a passion to protect home and hearth, one is not likely to view ones strategic position realistically; it's human nature to believe that your desire to repulse the enemy is sufficient to accomplish the fact. Oftentimes, it is not. Secondly, Flash was a romantic. He was, from all accounts, the Southern male on whom all the stereotypes are based; he was Ashley Wilkes. He wrote really schmaltzy poetry, he fought for his cause and he did all within his power as a newspaper owner to keep the flames of patriotism and commitment to the war effort burning in his readers. It is clear that, of the two, Morse's editorials undoubtedly served his readers better than did Flash's because they painted a clear picture of the direness of the Confederacy's situation, and they suggested the only true solution: peace.

Notes

1. Reynolds, Donald E. *Editors Make War: Southern Newspapers in the Secession Crisis.* Vanderbilt Univ. Press: Nashville. 1966, viii.
2. *Ibid.*, ix.
3. Osthaus, Carl A. *Partisans of the Southern Press : Editorial Spokesmen of the Nineteenth Century.* Lexington: The University of Kentucky Press. 1994, 1.
4. Talmadge, John E. "Peace-Movement Activities in Civil War Georgia." *Georgia Review.* Summer 1953, 193.
5. *Ibid.*, 196-97.
6. Jones, Charles C. *A Memorial History of Augusta, Ga.* Syracuse: D. Nasib & Co. Publishers. 1890, 280-81.
7. Bell, Earl L. and Kenneth C. Crabbe. *The Augusta Chronicle: Indomitable Voice of Dixie. 1785-1960.* Athens: UGA Press. 1960, 65.
8. Talmadge, 193.

9. Belle and Crabbe, 66.
10. Talmadge, 193
11. Andrews, J. Cutler. *The South Repents the Civil War.* Princeton Univ. Press. Princeton 1970, 492.
12. Griffith, Louis T. *Georgia Journalism 1763-1950.* University of Georgia Press. Athens 1951, 85.
13. Wilken, William Herbert. "As the Telegraph Saw It: A Study of the Editorial Policy of the Macon Daily Telegraph (And Confederate), 1860 - 1865." Master's Thesis: Emory University. 1964.
14. *Ibid*
15. *Ibid.,* 15.
16. *Ibid.*
17. *Ibid.,* 16.
18. *Ibid.,* 16.
19. *Ibid.*
20. *Ibid.,* 67.
21. *Ibid.*
22. *Augusta Chronicle.* "Up the Road." Nov. 17, 1864.
23. *Macon Telegraph.* "To the Rescue." Nov. 21, 1864.
24. *Macon Telegraph.* "The Situation." Nov. 21, 1864.
25. *Augusta Chronicle.* "The Duty of the Hour." Nov. 17, 1864.
26. *Macon Teletrph.* No title. Nov. 30, 1864,
27. *Augusta Chronicle.* "The Front." Nov. 13, 1864.
28. *Augusta Chronicle.* "From Up the Road." Nov. 17, 1864.
29. *Augusta Chronicle.* "The Effect." Dec. 8, 1864.
30. *Macon Telegraph.* "Will Sherman Be Allowed to Escape?" Dec. 16, 1864.
31. Rowell, John W. *Yankee Cavalrymen: Through the Civil War With the Ninth Pennsylvania Cavalry.* Knoxville: UT Press. 1971.
32. *Augusta Chronicle.* No Title. Nov. 25, 1864.
33. *Ibid.*
34. *Ibid.*
35. *Ibid.*
36. *Augusta Chronicle.* "The Situation." Nov. 29, 1864.
37. *Ibid.*
38. *Augusta Chronicle..* No Title. Dec. 4, 1864,
39. *Macon Telegraph.* No Title. Nov. 26, 1864.
40. *Macon Telegraph.* "Sherman's Place in History," Dec. 5, 1864.
41. *Macon Telegraph.* "Sherman the Lunatic," Dec. 13, 1864.
42. *Augusta Chronicle.* "Dodging the Issue," Dec. 9, 1864.
43. Talmadge, 202.
44. *Ibid.,* 201-202.
45. *Macon Telegraph.* "The Duty." Dec. 2, 1864,
46. *Macon Telegraph.* "Independence of the Press." Dec. 5, 1864.
47. *Augusta Chronicle.* "Peace." Dec. 22, 1864,
48. *Ibid.*
49. Catton, Bruce. *Never Call Retreat.* Gander City: Double Day & Co. 1965, 419-430.
50. *Macon Telegraph.* "The Loss and Gain." Dec. 20, 1864,
51. *Macon Telegraph.* "Sherman's Campaign Developing," Dec. 20, 1864.
52. Wilken, 74.

19

The Paradox of Samuel Medary, Copperhead Newspaper Publisher

Reed W. Smith
Georgia Southern University

Following his death in 1864, *The Nevada Gazette* editorialized, "When Sam Medary died one of the devil's own children went home to his father's house."[1] But in 1932, Ohio State University inducted him into its Journalism Hall of Fame. These two incidents point up the quandary of assessing the Civil War publisher of *The (Columbus, Ohio,) Crisis*, Samuel A. Medary. The epitaph was written by a Republican newspaper, which attacked his political activities, while the award focused on Medary's journalistic achievements. This paper will evaluate the appropriateness of the conflicting sentiments.

Much has been written about Medary, but troubling questions remain unanswered. Why, when lesser opposition publishers were being harassed and jailed, was he able to continue publishing *The Crisis* during much of the war? Why, although he eventually was arrested for conspiracy, was he never tried? And did he merely employ the First Amendment to defend his questionable position, or did he somehow have a better recognition of its purpose than his contemporaries?

II

Medary operated his newspaper during the most difficult period in American history. The Civil War created a situation in which the priorities of winning the conflict and of preserving constitutional civil liberties clashed. In the years preceding the war, newspaper publishers had become so influential, individualistic and affluent that they rejected any form of regulation. Most papers were partisan; they made no pretense of objectivity. Publishers were politicians first and newspapermen second. One historian observed of the era: "The newspaper editor was, in fact, lord and master of a considerable group of loyal disciples."[2] It was a common practice for newspapers, when aligned with a losing political party, to criticize the winning party's leaders and policies, whether they were proving successful or not.

From the beginning of the Civil War Northern newspaper reporters traveled unrestrained with Union troops. Through the use of telegraph lines they were able to transmit bulletins from the front to their editors in a timely manner. However, it was soon discovered that the Confederacy was learning of troop movements and battle plans by intercepting telegraph messages. At the same time, in the border states of Kentucky and Maryland, Southern sympathizers attempted to convince the people of those states to secede, as Tennessee and Virginia had done. These two situations made a war zone out of more than just those areas where military battles were taking place. To deal with these problems, President Abraham Lincoln took unprecedented steps to restrict the flow of information and deal with dissenters.

Recognizing the difficulties a rebellion or invasion could cause in the exercise of effective government, the framers of the U.S. Constitution had authorized suspension of the "writ of Habeas corpus." Lincoln was the first president to exercise this option. He censored the transmittal of news by restricting the flow of messages of a military nature over the nation's telegraph lines. In the border states, the president discouraged secession by having outspoken dissenters arrested and held in jail without trial. Press historian Robert Harper says these actions caused the Constitution to be strained until "it threatened to crack."[3] Lincoln's efforts to maintain security set up an untenable relationship between the constitutionally-guaranteed freedoms of speech and the press and the federal government. The highly partisan press not only chose sides concerning Lincoln's drastic policies, but quickly reacted to the perceived threats to its rights to report and editorialize on the conduct of the war. This led to a war being fought by the North on two fronts: against the

Confederacy and within the Union. Edwin and Michael Emery observe, "One of the serious problems of the war was how to keep the public properly informed without giving aid and comfort to the enemy."[4] The difficulty was exacerbated when numerous Northern newspapers, including Medary's, not only kept the public informed but, in addition, severely criticized Lincoln's policies. In January 1863, Lincoln said he feared "'the fire in the rear'—meaning the Democracy, especially at the Northwest—more than our military chances."[2] Several historians note that publishers more viciously attacked Lincoln during the war than they have any other U.S. president.

Opposition newspapers were especially prevalent in the Midwestern states of Ohio, Indiana, Wisconsin and Illinois. They included, the *Detroit Free Press*, the *Chicago Times*, *The (Cincinnati) Enquirer*, the *Dayton Daily Empire*, *The (Lacrosse, Wisconsin) Democrat*, *The (Indianapolis) Sentinel* and *The (Columbus) Crisis*. Many individuals in the Midwest strongly disagreed with the reasons for fighting a war, and later with the operation of the military effort. They said they were Peace Democrats, but Republicans referred to them as "Copperheads," an analogy to the North American snake, which gives no warning of its attack. Peace Democratic newspapers reflected this dissenting line of opinion. Later, when the administration took steps to quell the opposition, the publishers responded by charging that their press freedom was being threatened.

In most Northern cities during the Civil War, there were at least two newspapers that clearly opposed each other along political lines. In Columbus, the Republican *Ohio State Journal* supported Lincoln's and Ohio Governor David Tod's pro-war policies. It also carried on a quarrel in print with the disagreeable opposition newspaper in town, Medary's *Crisis*.

III

Ohio historian Eugene Roseboom writes, "Of those whose reputations rest upon their newspaper careers, the name of Samuel Medary undoubtedly should rank near the top."[6] What this statement does not mention is that much of this sizable reputation was earned prior to the Civil War. In the eyes of fellow Peace Democratic editors, Medary's reputation grew during the war years, but in the eyes of his opponents, between 1861 and 1864 he detracted from his substantial record.

Medary came to Ohio from Pennsylvania in the 1820s. He initially was a school teacher, but he soon became involved in local politics. In 1828, he and future U.S. Senator Thomas Morris started publishing *The Ohio Sun* in Batavia. The two men said they began the newspaper to perpetuate the legacy of Thomas Jefferson, and to help elect Andrew Jackson to the presidency.

As a Jefferson disciple, Medary believed an individual's rights were supreme to those of government, and they should remain unrestrained. He saw Jackson as the ideal statesman and the first "People's President." For the rest of his life, Medary identified himself with the Jacksonian, states rights point of view. His stated purpose, in publishing *The Sun*, was to be "unawed by the influence of the rich, the great, or the noble, the people must be heard and their rights protected."[7] Medary foresaw that the growth of a centralized federal government, which characterized the Civil War period, would diminish state's rights and bring into question civil liberties. Upon his death, *The Sun* eulogized that Medary's "greatest anxiety seemed to arise from the fear that he would outlive constitutional law."[8]

In 1834, Medary won election to the Ohio House of Representatives and two years later to the Ohio Senate. Beginning in 1837, and continuing for the next ten years, he held the post of State Supervisor of Public Printing, a post he attained because Democratic friends controlled the legislature. In 1837, he also had become publisher of the *Ohio Statesman*, the state Democratic organ. Holding the two positions concurrently allowed him to allocate state printing contracts as well as to control state Democratic communications.[9] He published the *Statesman* for a total of seventeen years, between 1837 and 1857.

By 1856, Medary had risen to the top of the Ohio Democratic party and had gained the title of "The Old Wheelhorse of Ohio Politics." He was a large man, with a full gray beard and a strong command of the English language. He was popular, not only as a publisher, but also as a public speaker. Respected, stubborn and stern, he played the role of the experienced, elder statesman. Ohio politicians characterized him as "a vigorous partisan. . . . The bitterest of his political foes conceded his ability."[10] Roseboom writes that Medary seemed at times to be almost the "dictator of the Democratic party" in Ohio. The only hitch in his political career occurred in 1854, when a squabble in the state party cost him a cabinet seat he dearly desired in the Pierce administration.

Medary was instrumental in the national Democratic party's

nomination of James Buchanan for the presidency in 1856. After Buchanan's election, the new president appointed Medary to the governorships of the Minnesota, and then the Kansas territory. In this latter position, Medary attempted, but failed to defuse the efforts of abolitionist John Brown. In 1860, the Democratic national convention split because of Southern states' threats to withdraw from the Union and made Republican victory a foregone conclusion. With the subsequent presidential victory by the Republicans, Medary was out of a job and returned to Ohio to try to stop the impending war.

IV

On the last day of January 1861, at age fifty-nine, Medary began publishing *The Crisis*, an undertaking that would thrust him into the three most controversial years of his life.[2] He set up business at the corner of Gay and High Streets in Columbus, one block from the state Capitol. The first issue of his new paper appeared forty-two days after South Carolina seceded from the Union and two months before the first shots were fired on Fort Sumter. In the first edition, Medary wrote, "*The Crisis* will fully and thoroughly sift the great issues that hang like a cloud over our common country." He believed determined publishers could head off the war, and hoped "fraternal feeling and discussion" could reunite the Union.[12]

Medary proceeded to say *The Crisis* would "work for a 'peaceable solution,' war on Republicanism, and try to save the country from politicians."[13] He believed the common man favored compromise over war, but that the Union was offering no opportunity for such men to be heard; he intended to help them have their say. Medary saw the disintegration of the United States as threatening the very structure of American society and viewed it as his task to help re-establish it. Critics speculated that Medary began *The Crisis* to make money from the conflict, but there is little evidence to support the claim. *The Crisis* carried limited advertising; its main source of income came from $2 yearly subscriptions. Although Medary boasted that *The Crisis* attained the largest circulation among the Peace Democratic press, he never released circulation figures. Press historian Osman Hooper writes that Medary "was not out to make money, but to advocate a cause."[14]

A typical *Crisis* was eight pages long and featured writing by Medary, letters from supporters and stories reprinted from other Peace Democrat papers. Medary alone composed each week's *Crisis*, and refused to use a wire service or reporters. He put out *The Crisis* "with scissors, a paste pot, and a pen filled with venom," according to the *Ohio Press in the Civil War*.[15] He was not, of course, impartial, but in the words of another historian, "There is no indication that he ever falsified a report or garbled a public document."[16] It was possible for a reader to tell where the document ended and interpretation began.

Initially, Medary used his newspaper to argue for peace "at any cost," and he thought this aim necessitated drastic rhetoric. In February 1861, he asserted that if the North went to war with the South, "The West [including Ohio] would set up for themselves or ally with the South."[17] After the major battles of the war began, he urged that Northern troops be withdrawn from Southern soil. Medary argued the war could not be won and compromise with the South was the only way to preserve American society. He faulted abolitionists for being the cause of the conflict and labeled their agenda as synonymous with that of Republicans. Medary blamed Northern industrialists with fostering a myth that the only way to settle the differences between the North and the South was with war. He believed New England business interests, in particular, were attempting to expand their influence across the continent through a conspiracy with Union politicians. He charged that the federal government's economic policies "enriched the manufacturer at the expense of Western farmers and workingmen."[18]

In March 1861, Lincoln assumed office and Medary began writing of his disdain for the new president. He considered Lincoln a "very ordinary individual," and asserted that the wrong man was in Washington because Lincoln had been elected by a minority of the voters.[19] After reviewing Lincoln's inaugural address, Medary wrote: "The message gives the president too much elbow room—to steer for any port. I will judge the new president by what he does rather than what he says."[20]

In April 1861, the Ohio Legislature passed a $1 million excise tax to help finance the war. This action, along with Lincoln's efforts to suppress opposition within the Union, increased Medary's indignation. Soon after the start of the war, Lincoln instituted martial law throughout the North. Although it would take two years for Congress to officially confirm his authority to take this action, 14,000 arrests were made between 1861 and 1863.[21] Medary saw simultaneous attempts to censor speech and the press as intrusions on the Constitution as well as on state and civil rights. He had harsh words for members of the press, such as New York's Horace Greeley, who supported administration policies. At one point, Medary wrote that he had "discovered" that Greeley was the real president, and Lincoln was subservient to him.[22] Contrary to Lincoln's "house divided" sentiments, Medary believed the nation could survive "half-free and half-slave." As the war dragged on, his writing reflected a man whose sympathies, although initially grounded in politics, later became a personal vendetta against the president.

In many ways, the activities of the Lincoln administration made Medary's task simpler. Arbitrary arrests, censorship, corruption within the White House, conscription and inept battle performance by Union generals gave the Peace Democrats grist to grind. An 1863 *Crisis* editorial read, in part: "Lincoln is running our country to perdition . . . everybody not crazy with 'negro on the brain' knows and knows it well."[23] Such statements made it clear where Medary stood on slavery. Press historian Robert Harper says Medary was the only publisher in the North who consistently referred to members of the Negro race as "niggers." Medary did not think slavery was worth fighting over or could be legally determined by the national government. He reasoned that since the states existed before the federal government, it was up to individual states to deal with slavery. Furthermore, Medary charged that, under the Constitution, the federal government had no jurisdiction in mandating that slaves be granted citizenship. He wrote, "The negro was never intended to be the equal of the white man."[24]

As with most Peace Democrats, the underside of Medary's concern with slavery stemmed from his fear that the influx of blacks into the white labor market would reduce white employment opportunities. On March 5, 1862, he wrote, "Now what would be the poor white man's condition in this state with thousands of wooly heads to compete with?" The following January, when Lincoln made the Emancipation Proclamation official, Medary called the president "a half-witted usurper" and proclaimed: "The moment is frightful."[25]

Regarding the war, Medary wrote that he opposed it because "in a country based on public opinion it cannot accomplish the end desired. . . . It is entailing a debt and bringing misery on the people disproportionate to the benefits."[26] He made it clear his quarrel was not with those who had been forced to fight—they were patriotic—but he condemned the officers and politicians for theft and fraud in orchestrating the war. Nevertheless, his son, Charles, served as an artillery officer in the Union army. In the pages of *The Crisis*, Medary reprinted accounts of the major battles and listed the names of Ohioans killed or missing in action. He referred to Ohio soldiers as "our boys" and praised them for their bravery, albeit under duress.

By 1862, Medary's assessment was that the first year of the war had been "a year of blood and plunder, of carnage of conflagration ... of falsehood and corruption ... of defeat, desolation and death."[27] He charged that Lincoln "ought to be impeached, either for violating the Constitution or for incompetence and idiocy."[28] Throughout the war, he did not veer from his opinion that the administration had not shown good cause for continuance of the costly struggle.

Within the first year of its existence, Medary called *The Crisis* "one of the most influential voices for those in the Copperhead movement."[29] Several historians have supported his claim. *The Crisis* quickly became "the most restless and outspoken newspaper during the Civil War, and increased in circulation at a remarkable rate," according to historian Henry Hubbart.[30] This popularity, coupled with Lincoln's pragmatic approach to civilian threats to the Union, served as fuel for Medary's radical fire. As a result, an evolution in Medary's editorials became evident. As the war moved into its second full year, *The Crisis* evolved from its campaign for peace to an ongoing defense of dissident Northerners' constitutional liberties. With each new presidential move, Medary's belief that the president intended to rob Americans of their civil rights was strengthened.

V

Although Peace Democratic activity was prominent throughout the Midwestern states, in no state was it more visible or led by more capable men than in Ohio. Among its members were: former Senator and publisher of the *Chillicothe Advertiser*, William Allen; former Senator George Pugh; past *Dayton Empire* editor and former congressman Clement Vallandigham; Dr. Edson Olds; future vice-presidential candidate George Pendleton; and Medary. Their rallying cry was: "The Union as it was, the Constitution as it is."[31] The Midwest was fertile ground for this movement for several reasons. Many of the people living in these states were Irish and German immigrants or transplanted Southerners. These farmers, white laborers and former neighbors of slavery, were universally opposed to Abolition. They clung to traditional convictions and resisted the elimination of established, sectional boundaries. Many midwesterners blamed the economic downturn of 1860-61 on New

England businessmen. They particularly feared that a stronger, more centralized government would rob them of their independent lifestyle. Many saw Lincoln's usurpation of constitutional law as a sure sign that the Republicans would eventually elevate Lincoln to the position of "U.S. dictator."

In addition, many Peace Democrats had strong pacifist-religious ties. They disputed the concept of war as an option for settling differences, and many refused to take up arms. Medary had been raised a Quaker. But he had parted company with his family's affiliation long before the war, and he did not justify his activities with religious platitudes. However, on political grounds, his opinions were consistent with those of other pacifists who lived in Ohio during the Civil War.[32]

Initially, Ohio had oversubscribed Lincoln's first call for volunteers in 1861, but in the early days of the war, while the North searched for victories, casualties mounted. Ohio units were especially hard hit, and before the end of the war more Ohio soldiers would be killed than from any other Northern state. The growing casualty lists and incomplete Union victories led to widespread anti-war protests. Desertions became an increasing problem as the war progressed, and eventually bounties and a draft were necessary to maintain enlistments. Peace Democrats became especially volatile after the enactment of conscription in 1863, which Medary labeled "a monstrous enormity."[33]

Throughout the war, Peace Democrats urged Ohioans not to enlist or, if they had, to desert. They asserted that Union soldiers had a right to reject the cause of those who betrayed "white civilization." Eleven Ohioans, including Dr. Olds, served prison sentences for obstructing recruiting efforts. The imprisonments allowed Medary to depict the men as martyrs for free speech. He used the pages of *The Crisis* to sanction and give voice to the incarcerated resistors. While in prison, *The Crisis* printed their letters so they could indirectly correspond with loyal supporters.

The Peace Democrats gained strength as a result of the 1862 general elections. Much of Ohio, Indiana, Illinois, and half of Wisconsin elected "peace" candidates. Medary called it "the greatest revolution since the election of Jackson."[34] After their success, the Peace Democrats became more aggressive and visible; their campaign reached its pinnacle in the spring of 1863. The war continued to bring mixed results for the administration, and following the issuance of the Emancipation Proclamation, the Peace Democrats sought an accommodation with the Confederacy. But they found that their pleas for peace were as unpopular in the South as they were in the North.

Meanwhile, the tide turned against the Peace Democrats almost as quickly as it crested. Congress had passed the Treason Act in 1862, which was a veiled version of the Alien and Sedition Acts of 1798. Using the act as ammunition, in April 1863 General Ambrose Burnside began a campaign in the Midwest to put an end to the Peace Democrats' crusade. Burnside had been the overly aggressive Union commander during the Union's costly defeat at Fredricksburg. Shortly thereafter, Lincoln reassigned him to command the Department of the Ohio; his jurisdiction included all of the states bordering the Ohio River. Burnside took it upon himself to aggressively enforce the Treason Act. In April 1863, he issued General Order No. 38, in which he said, "The habit of declaring sympathy for the enemy will no longer be tolerated. . . . Persons committing such offenses will be subject to military procedures."35 The order effectively stripped Midwest civilians of their right to trials in civil courts for the duration of the war. Burnside thus set himself up to determine the difference between criticism and treason and to decide when a publisher was giving aid and comfort to the enemy. Medary was outraged. In *The Crisis* he insisted, "We claim the right to discuss public matters . . . and as a conductor of the public press, to give our interpretation of the law."36

Vallandigham became Burnside's first target. The outspoken Dayton resident was the most visible and impulsive Peace Democrat. He boasted that he wanted to test the order by making himself a public martyr for freedom of speech. Medary saw Vallandigham as the Peace Democrats' unofficial leader, who could eventually lead the party to Northern political conquest. But, although they shared party affiliation, the men's tactics were dissimilar. Vallandigham was an aggressive and confrontational firebrand, who inspired impetuous action. Medary was a political theoretician, a man of words, who maintained throughout his life that the nation's direction could be altered at the ballot box. In May 1863, Union troops arrested Vallandigham for challenging Burnside's order. The seizure set up the most celebrated civil liberties case of the war. Medary called the arrest "a great blunder" and warned that "civil war might visit the Midwest if rights were trampled upon any more."37 Vallandigham was tried in Cincinnati, found guilty, and taken to Boston to serve a prison term, but Lincoln, realizing that Burnside had overstepped his authority, had Vallandigham sent to the Confederacy. Eventually, with the assistance of Confederate troops, Vallandigham made his way to Canada.

Another 1863 Burnside target was the Chicago *Times'* Peace Democratic publisher Wilbur Storey. Storey had summed up the temperament of his opposition, by saying, "It is a newspaper's duty to print the news and raise hell."[38] In June, Burnside's troops barred the doors to the *Times*, but under pressure from the Illinois legislature and a bipartisan group of publishers, within days Lincoln ordered Burnside's order revoked.

In the fall of 1863, Medary presided over the Ohio Peace Democrat's state convention and spearheaded Vallandigham's nomination for Governor. At the same time he petitioned Lincoln to allow the exile to return to the buckeye state but was denied. In the pages of *The Crisis*, however, Vallandigham campaigned for governor, while remaining in Canada. A *Crisis* editorial read, "Mr. Vallandigham . . . approaches the executive chair of Ohio with peace and order on his banner."[39] But Medary's attempts to get Vallandigham elected were futile. He lost the election by over 100,000 votes and Lincoln sent a telegram to the new governor, John Brough, that read, "Glory to God in the highest; Ohio has saved the Union."[40] Vallandigham's defeat reflected the declining fortunes of all Peace Democrats.

VI

Because of Union military and Republican electoral victories, the appeal of the Peace Democratic movement diminished by late 1863. *The Crisis* was denied mail circulation in several Northern states and was in financial difficulty.[41] Although he did not intend to get rich from his paper, it was becoming increasingly necessary for him to dip into his own savings to keep the paper afloat. In January 1864, Medary appealed to subscribers: "We throw ourselves on the generous support of our readers."[42] But other events would soon revitalize *The Crisis*.

The ideological battle between the Peace Democrats and Unionists was escalating into violence. In 1864, five Ohio peace papers were attacked by super-patriotic groups. *The Crisis* suffered two such occurrences. On March 5, a group of 200 soldiers from Camp Chase, near Columbus, attacked the paper's office. Fortunately for Medary, *The Crisis* was printed at another location, and there were no presses to destroy. He placed the property loss at $600 to $800 but did not blame the soldiers. He said they merely had been influenced by abolitionist civilians, "too cowardly to own their complicity."[43] Medary was in Cincinnati at the time of the incident, but when he returned the following day, he was accorded a hero's parade by a crowd of approximately 1,000 supporters. Two weeks later, there was a second attempt by a civilian mob to destroy *The Crisis*' office. A fire was set, and the outside of the building sustained some damage, but neither incident prevented Medary from publishing his weekly. Both attacks were instigated by Unionists who believed *The Crisis* was both lengthening the war and costing more Union soldiers their lives.

Nevertheless, the affairs primarily succeeded in helping Medary attain the status of "press freedom martyr." "These acts of violence served to make *The Crisis* more popular than ever," according to press historian Osman Hooper, "and gained new friends for its harassed editor."[44] It also helped improve the paper's financial situation. Soon afterward, although Medary increased the cost of yearly subscriptions from $2.00 to $3.00, he announced that circulation had increased markedly.

By 1864, for all intents and purposes, however the peace movement was dead in Ohio. With many of its proponents either in jail or having moved west, it had lost most of its influence. Medary, however, refused to accept defeat. In March, he continued to write:

> Let us go to work for the campaign of 1864 . . . for state's rights . . . for white men's liberty—for freedom of speech . . . for freedom of the press . . . for peace, unity, good and liberty.[45]

Despite his continued public influence, Medary had fallen out of favor within the upper ranks of his own party. His attempts to get a peace plank in the 1864 presidential platform of former-Union General George McClellan were rebuffed by the now more conservative mainline Democrats. Likewise, Medary failed to receive enough votes from fellow Ohioans to attain a delegate seat to the Democratic National Convention in Chicago. As a result, he editorialized against the ticket of McClelland and Pendleton, which he viewed as too moderate.

An intriguing aspect of Medary's wartime undertaking is that he got away with his brand of social protest for so long. Finally, however, his notoriousness caught up with him. On May 20, 1864, a federal grand jury in Cincinnati indicted him for conspiracy, and charged him with being a member of a subversive pro-Southern group that attempted to free Confederate soldiers from the penitentiary in Columbus. There was no concrete evidence that Medary either belonged to or supported the under-taking, but at this point in the war many Unionists were not interested in differentiating between actual treason and appearance of such activity. During the course of the war Medary's editorials had generated an extensive personal enemy's list.

Predictably, several Republic editors wrote that the arrest was overdue, while peace publishers came to his defense. One called Medary "a brave and indomitable journalist." Another said the charge of conspiracy "was outrageous and preposterous."[46] In *The Crisis*, Medary wrote: "Against all this we have what force an independent press could bring to bear. . . . If a man cannot read a paper in favor of peace . . . what can he read?"[47] Before he could test the strength of the First Amendment in the courts, however, the confrontation was defused.

Medary was released on bond and a trial date was set for six months later, in October 1864. Peace Democratic publisher Washington McLean, of the *Cincinnati Enquirer*, paid the $3000 bond because he saw the case as an opportunity to see dissident press opinion vindicated. Back in Columbus, Medary wrote of his arrest, "It is too vile a business to spend breath over. It is just the thing . . . to try to injure our paper."[48] Medary never got his day in court to fulfill his martyrdom, however. He collapsed in August, while giving a speech on the Franklin County Court House steps and died November 7, the night before Lincoln's re-election. The cause of death remains unknown, but foul play was not suspected. Medary had been suffering from exhaustion and depression for over a year, and it was speculated that his heart finally gave out. A *Cincinnati Enquirer* obituary read: "A great and distinguished man . . . whose name had become a household word—has fallen in Ohio."[49]

VII

Historians have had difficulty considering Samuel Medary "the politician" separately from Medary "the journalist." By the time he died, the publisher had attained the status among some as "one of the vilest scoundrels that ever lived."[50] For most, his questionable political record during the war clouded his contributions to the field of journalism. Politically, Medary was a victim of his allegiances. Civil War historian Eric Cardinal observes: "He belonged to one of the most misunderstood political parties in American history."[51] On the surface, Medary's desire for peace seemed honorable, but underneath, his sentiments and means for achieving a settlement were misguided, outdated and unclear. He was a Populist. Consistent with this line of nineteenth century thinking, he opposed any actions that would diminish individual or states' rights. He opposed the termination of slavery and sectionalism, on purely economic grounds. He feared that emancipation would throw whites out of work, and that a more unified Union would impose Eastern, industrialized control on the agrarian Midwest. The most obvious problem for the Peace Democrats was that they never offered a viable alternative plan for peace. Medary was adept at being a squeaky wheel, but his only alternative to civil war was to stop the fighting and let the South continue as a separate entity. By the time he started proposing it, this option was past being palatable.

More importantly, however, Medary's case focuses several issues relating to the conduct of war by a democracy versus the right to dissent. The molders of the Constitution made no provision for handling a robust and free press during a period of civil strife. In the 1860s, press dissent was not a new phenomenon in the United States. During the Revolutionary War, after the Patriots or "dissenters" won, they wrote their own definition of justice and treason. But by the time of the War of 1812 and the Mexican-American War, dissenters were labeled traitors. The Civil War was no different. Although Lincoln took steps which, at the least, bent the spirit of the law, history has treated him with high regard. For him, winning the war exonerated his methods.

In the final analysis, an unanswered question about this case is: If Medary had lived to be tried, would his case have vindicated Peace Democrat's journalistic tactics, as his supporters hoped it would? The answer is probably not. But a case can be made that at the time of his death Medary's activities had already raised the degree to which journalists could disagree with their government.

There is some question whether Medary would have been tried if he had lived. The fact that his trial date was delayed so many months indicates that there was concern about whether Burnside's last challenge to the opposition press during the war would be sustained. It can be speculated that the previous embarrassments to the federal government in the Vallandigham and *Chicago Times*' cases had an impact on the slowness with which the administration dealt with Medary. Even more interestingly, why, although he was widely recognized as the most influential Peace Democratic publisher, did it take so long for the Union to get around to prosecuting Medary?

Dating back to publication of *The Ohio Sun*, Medary demonstrated a lifelong commitment to the cause of freedom of the press. The fact that he was able to write confrontational sentiments in *The Crisis* during the war, and was never arrested for his sentiments, seem to demonstrate that what he was fighting for was already protecting his ability to do so. Therefore, although Medary's campaign for peace and sectionalism was a failure, to a greater degree his journalistic battle was useful. It can be argued that Medary, however misguided, helped redefine the outer limits of press dissent in America. Unfortunately, whether the press should remain unrestrained when the safety of the nation is in question raised issues that remain unanswered.

It also is possible to surmise that Medary had an impact on the Lincoln administration's attempts to quell disloyalty in the North. Medary's unrelenting questioning of the tactics prompted the federal government to temper its aggressive restraint of opposition. This became obvious when the president, at the height of his confrontation with the Peace Democratic press, said:

> Must a government of necessity be too strong for the liberties of its people, or too weak to maintain its own existence? Must I shoot a simple-minded boy who deserts, while I must not touch a hair of a wily agitator who induces him to desert?[52]

Historian Richard Hofstadter says men such as Medary, although unpopular, are invaluable in a democracy. Medary played the role of a provocateur, just as abolitionist Wendell Phillips did. In citing Phillips' words, Hofstadter says, "The work of the agitator . . . consists chiefly in talk; he is the counterweight of sloth and indifference."[53] The service Medary provided was not lost on *The Crisis*' loyal readers. In a letter representative of many he received during the war, the writer thanked Medary, "Wherever there is wrong in the conduct of public business, you are prompt to point it out . . . it is good to have a watchman on the heights."[54]

This study has attempted to show why it has been difficult to affix Samuel Medary's place in journalism history. It is easy to see why some considered him a champion for press freedom, while others cursed his political agenda. Medary sincerely believed he was performing the duties that nineteenth century American newspapermen were supposed to render. That his activities were considered treasonous by some astonished him. He failed to understand that during such an emotional crisis as the Civil War, the majority of the Northern population would not tolerate his flagrant opposition journalism.

In the years following the war, American politics and journalism changed dramatically. The expanded influence of the federal government, development of wire services and popularity of objective journalism reduced the influence of partisan newspaper publishers. But in 1937, biographer Helen Dorn wrote of Medary: "One thing is for certain, he died for a principle . . . in the hope that he might prevent destruction of the Union he loved so well."[55] The Union was never the same after the Civil War, but neither was this country's understanding of the extent to which the First Amendment protected opposition commentary. Because Abraham Lincoln recognized that it was his duty, as upholder of the Constitution, to allow opposition editors to oppose federal policies, Medary helped redefine the limits of press dissent in this country.

Notes

1. Medary's successor as editor of *The Crisis* reprinted this quote from *The Nevada Gazette*, with an editorial defending Medary. *The Crisis*, January 25, 1865.
2. Helen P. Dorn, "Samuel Medary—Journalist and Politician, 1801-1864," *The Ohio Archaeological and Historical Quarterly* 53 (1944): 15.
3. Robert S. Harper, *Lincoln and the Press* (New York: McGraw-Hill Book Company, Inc., 1951), x.
4. Edwin Emery and Michael Emery, *The Press and America: An Interpretative History of the Mass Media*, 5th ed. (Englewood Cliffs, New Jersey: Prentice-Hall, Inc., 1984), 195.
5. James M. McPherson, *The Oxford University History of the United States*, Vol. IV: *Battle Cry of Freedom, The Civil War Era* (New York: Oxford University Press, 1988), 591.
6. Eugene H. Roseboom, *A History of the State of Ohio*, Vol. IV: *The Civil War Era, 1850-1873* (Columbus, Ohio: Ohio State Archaeological and Historical Society, 1944), 199.
7. *The Ohio Sun*, June 23, 1828, quoted in Dorn, 15.
8. Osman C. Hooper, "The Crisis and the Man, An Episode in Civil War Journalism," *Ohio State University Journalism Series*, Vol. I (Columbus, Ohio: The Ohio State University Press, 1929), 33.
9. Medary's position as Supervisor of Public Printing gave him control over state legislative printing contracts, which were typically allocated to local newspaper publishers; usually, on the basis of political favoritism.
10. Hooper, 9.
11. Medary did not mention why he called his paper *The Crisis*; but it can be surmised that the title bore a relationship to his feelings toward the war. In his editorials, he repeatedly referred to the Civil War as "the crisis."
12. *The Crisis*, March 7, 1861.
13. Ibid.
14. Hooper, 20.
15. Robert S. Harper, *The Ohio Press in the Civil War* (Columbus, Ohio: Ohio State

The Paradox of Samuel Medary   307

University Press, 1964), 4.
16. Hooper, 33.
17. *The Crisis*, February 7, 1861.
18. *The Crisis*, January 31, 1861.
19. *The Crisis*, March 14, 1861.
20. Ibid.
21. George Brown Tindall, *America: A Narrative History*, 2nd ed. (New York: W.W. Norton Co., 1988), 679.
22. *The Crisis*, August 19, 1863.
23. *The Crisis*, January 27, 1864.
24. *The Crisis*, March 5, 1862.
25. *The Crisis*, January 7, 1863.
26. *The Crisis*, October 16, 1863.
27. *The Crisis*, December 31, 1862.
28. Medary regularly devoted space in *The Crisis* to criticizing the president for causing the war. A typical emotional sentiment from September 16, 1863, read, "Mr. Lincoln called out immense armies and plunged the country into an immense civil war, such as the world never before witnessed—drenching the peaceful fields with human blood, involving the people in debts untold and incalculable—disturbing the interests of the civilized world."
29. *The Crisis*, March 11, 1863.
30. Henry Clyde Hubbart, *The Older Middle West 1840-1880: Its Social, Economic and Political Life and Sectional Tendencies Before, during and After the Civil War* (New York: Russell & Russell, 1963), 149.
31. Justin E. Walsh, *To Print the News and Raise Hell: A Biography of Wilbur F. Storey* (Durham, North Carolina: University of North Carolina Press, 1968), 170.
32. This characterization is summarized from the first chapter of Frank L. Klement, *The Copperheads in the Middle West* (Chicago: The University of Chicago Press, 1960), 1-39. Prior to the Civil War, Peace Democrats had been known as Progressive Western Democrats.
33. *The Crisis*, March 20, 1863.
34. George W. Knepper, *Ohio and Its People* (Kent, Ohio: Kent State University Press, 1989), 236.
35. Roseboom, 411.
36. *The Crisis*, June 1, 1863.
37. Medary used instances such as this to link with and expound upon his disdain for Northern authorities. In *The Crisis*, he charged, "Vallandigham is under arrest as a traitor. (Ohio) Governor Tod is still at large. Judge ye of the Government that so judges men!" Ibid., June 1, 1863.
38. Walsh, 3.
39. *The Crisis*, September 16, 1863. In addition, Vallandigham campaign letters appeared in the July 22, August 12, September 31 and October 21 edition of *The Crisis*.
40. Knepper, 245. Vallandigham returned to Ohio in 1864, but his political power base was gone and he turned to the practice of law. In 1871, while trying a case, he accidentally shot himself to death.
41. Harper, *The Ohio Press in the Civil War*, 9.
42. *The Crisis*, January 6, 1864.
43. *Ibid*, March 11, 1863.
44. Hooper 32.
45. *The Crisis*, March 16, 1864.
46. The former comment originated in the New York *Metropolitan Record*, while the latter appeared in the New York *Freeman's Journal*. They are quoted in Harper, *Lincoln and the Press*, 341.

47. *The Crisis*, June 1, 1864.
48. *Ibid.*
49. *The Cincinnati Enquirer*, November 8, 1864.
50. Harper, *Lincoln and the Press*, 342.
51. Eric J. Cardinal, "The Ohio Democracy and The Crisis of Disunion, 1860-1861," *Ohio History*, Vol. 86 (Winter 1977): 19.
52. Klement, 323.
53. Richard Hofstadter, *The American Political Tradition, and the Men Who Made It* (New York: Alfred A. Knopf, Inc., 1948), 138.
54. *The Crisis*, September 16, 1863.
55. Dorn, 37. Also see Thalman Krumm Jr., "The Gethsemane Factor: A Historical Portrait of Samuel Medary of Ohio and an Analysis of the Rhetorical Dilemma of his *Crisis* years, 1861-1864" (Ph.D. diss., Ohio State University, 1978). He notes, "For Medary and Lincoln the issue was the same: Save the Union. The question was which one?"

20

Picturing the News: Frank Leslie and the Origins of American Pictorial Journalism

William E. Huntzicker
Minneapolis Free-lance Writer

Since he was a child, Henry Carter wanted to be an artist. Born March 29, 1821, the son of a glove manufacturer in Ipswich, Suffolk, England, Carter loved drawing and wood carving, but his father called him impractical and insisted that he assume a leadership position in the family's business. While working at his father's manufactory, Carter became fascinated with silversmiths in the factory, noting their tools and how they were used. Eventually, he collected enough engraver's tools to teach himself engraving and to begin working at it.

Unwittingly, his family cooperated by sending the young man to London for more business experience. But London afforded young Henry Carter opportunities to study both the theory and the practice of the trade he loved. Combining his business acumen with his art, Carter submitted sketches to London magazines. Fearing discovery by his father, he created a professional name: Frank Leslie.

When young Carter saw the pioneer pictorial weekly *Illustrated*

Copyright ©1995

London News, founded by Herbert Ingram in 1842, he knew what he wanted to do. He deserted the family business and worked his way up to superintendent of the new magazine's engraving department. Along the way, he learned every aspect of the trade, including the system of controlling light-and-shade on wood engravings for printing — a process he would later introduce to the United States. With his background and a new name, Henry Carter would start the first successful American news picture magazine, *Frank Leslie's Illustrated Newspaper*, and create the role of pictures in the news.[1]

Creating U.S. Illustrated Publications

In London, Carter proved to his father that an artist could make a decent living, but he saw a larger, untapped market for illustrated journalism across the Atlantic. At 27, Carter landed in New York with the goal of creating a national *Illustrated London News* in the United States. Frank Leslie wanted to add pictures to newspapers.[2]

Even though photography began in the 1830s, the technology for publishing photographs on the printing press didn't develop for another half century with the creation of the halftone. In the 1840s and 1850s, newspapers and magazines depended upon engravers, who carved pictures by hand in wood blocks for the printing press. But Carter had no money when he arrived in the United States. He convinced promoter P.T. Barnum to hire him to produce illustrated programs to accompany the celebrated tour of European singer Jenny Lind in 1850. When Boston publisher Frederick Gleason founded *Gleason's Pictorial Drawing-Room Companion* in 1851, Leslie was one of the few experienced wood engravers in the United States so he joined this first American publication to copy the *Illustrated London News*. *Gleason's,* a 16-page illustrated folio, used wood engravings to print on one side —eight pages — of each large sheet used to create each issue. The pictures covered such timeless subjects as travel, natural history, sculpture, ships, military scenes, and moral or religious themes. *Gleason's* showed little interest in illustrated news, and Leslie left the staff after less than a year, but many other writers, illustrators and publishers started at *Gleason's.*

Engraver T.W. Strong soon followed with the *Illustrated American News* using a similar formula but adding cheap fiction, popular poetry and many more illustrations. From Leslie's perspective, Strong's publication had a major difference: it added pictures to news. But labor-intensive hand-carved engravings took too much time. The experiment lasted six months, but Barnum with partners H.D. Beach and A.E. Beach revived it. Leslie worked as an illustrator-engraver for Barnum and Beaches' *Illustrated News* in 1853, and, after Leslie turned down Barnum's invitation to manage the publication, the showman sold it to Gleason.

Newspapers, such as James Gordon Bennett's *New York Herald*, had run occasional news pictures, but the process was too slow and too expensive to become a standard part of routine daily news. The most dramatic reproduction of news pictures came when Bennett devoted the entire first page and part of the second to illustrations of the funeral of former President Andrew Jackson in 1845. And long-running advertisements occasionally sported illustrations. Otherwise, newspaper illustration relied upon standardized graphic illustrations, such as pointing fingers, ships (for shipping notices), trains (for railroad schedules), a running person (for ads for runaways slaves, wives and children) and items offered for sale like houses, hats, horses, and patent medicine.3

Building Leslie's Empire

Leslie claimed he could succeed with news pictures where the others failed. But first he would have to build the capital and his own printing plant to do news successfully. And he had learned American marketing by working with Barnum. In 1854, Leslie began his own publishing firm with the *Gazette of Fashion,* and the following year he published his first book, *Frank Leslie's Portfolio of Fancy Needlework* written by dime novelist Ann Stephens. Although the book carried the Stringer & Townsend imprint, its success encouraged Leslie to do book publishing business himself. The success of *Gazette of Fashion*'s formula of women's topics and miscellany exceeded expectations and, at the end of the first year, Leslie wrote that the magazine's success paid for a new steam press. He added four pages to each monthly issue in 1855, increased the price to 30 cents in 1856, and added four more pages in 1857. The publication was superseded by *Frank Leslie's New Family Magazine* in September 1857, by *Frank Leslie's Monthly* in April 1860, and by *Frank Leslie's Lady's Magazine* from February 1863 through December 1882. The *Gazette*'s early success generated enough capital for Leslie to purchase the failing *New York Journal of Romance,* which published fiction. To this publication, Leslie added illustration and miscellany to create *Frank Leslie's New York Journal of Romance, General Literature, Science and Art*, which appeared in January 1855.

Leslie's in-house engraving department and presses designed for pictorial work gave him an advantage with both price and the quality of illustrations. Although the *Journal* depended as much upon illustration as his later publications, the early issues reveal the formula on which Leslie built an empire. Typically, the first page begins with the monthly installment of a long-running, continuing story. Throughout each magazine, contemporary and historical anecdotes preach morals, evoke chuckles, describe exotic behavior, and convey simple nonsense.

After six months, the *Journal* reported that its success "has astonish-ed even ourselves." Leslie exhibited his self-importance gained from the *Illustrated London News* and his penchant for overstatement from P.T. Barnum. "Since the NEW YORK JOURNAL passed into the hands of FRANK LESLIE, it has contained one-third more reading matter than it did before." The *Journal* now "contains more reading matter, and of a higher class, than any work of the country, perhaps of the world. To this is added more engravings, and of a superior quality, than any work illustrated after a like fashion can give for the price, as the best artists are employed, always under the publisher's own supervision."[4] At least the last statement is true. "Mr. Leslie, who was himself a first-class engraver, was severe in his judgment of my work," artist Joseph Becker recalled nearly 50 years later. "I have to thank him, however, for the exacting standard he set up for me. It made me toil harder and more carefully."[5]

Getting into News

Leslie's, his leading publication, still followed a typical magazine formula. His second preface reported that the *Journal*'s first year had been "a prosperous one beyond our most sanguine expectations." The *Journal* ran only a few full-page illustrations, it contained a monthly news summary. Even though events were outdated, the *Journal* illustrated scenes from war-torn Sebastopol cities. Relief maps put readers at the scene without depicting specific events, which could be outdated at publication time. Leslie's *Journal* also provided biographical sketches accompanying engraved portraits of famous people.[6]

But Leslie wanted what Richard Kimball described as "exact

illustrations of the current events of the day, and in this way to make them a prime agent in the instruction of the people."7 Leslie promised *Journal* readers his new paper would be more important than the one they were reading. "In the course of a few weeks will be issued from this office a Pictorial Weekly Newspaper, so superior to anything of the kind that has been heretofore presented in the United States, that we have the assurance of a paying circulation from the commencement."8 With the *Journal* and *Gazette,* Leslie drew together the literary, artistic and mechanical talent to support his news weekly of the stature of *Illustrated London News.*

Because of the earlier failed attempts, Leslie's first issue outlined his chances for success, clearly differentiating his *Frank Leslie's Illustrated Newspaper* new publication from earlier failures. The *Republic* failed for lack of experienced wood engravers, late news, and too few, although good, illustrations. Gleason's paper and Strong's sold for six cents. And their illustrations were also too late to provide credible coverage of news events. Barnum and Beach lacked supplies, artists, engravers, and proper wood, Leslie said. And they depended upon foreign supplies of bolts, screws, and blocks. Proper presses also had to be obtained.

The first issue of *Frank Leslie's Illustrated Newspaper* appeared December 15, 1855. The cover illustration of Kane's expedition to the Arctic portended many expeditions that would be chronicled over the years, including Perry's to the Orient and Livingstone's to Africa. Leslie himself would sponsor expeditions across the continent to the West Coast and to Alaska. *Frank Leslie's Illustrated Newspaper* was printed on a single sheet and cut and folded to make 16 pages. Illustrations appeared on only one side of the original sheet, thus on Pages 1, 4-5, 8-9, 12-13, and 16 of the tabloid-size newspaper. Despite the pretensions, the 10-cent small folio contained long, serial fiction and miscellaneous material similar to that which appeared in his *Journal.*

Leslie invented a mass-production process to allow his engraving department to complete illustrations overnight for major events. With his process, an artist drew an illustration on the wood block for the printing press. He then cut the block into as many as 32 separate squares for a full-page illustration, and different engravers carved different parts of the scene. When they all finished, they bolted the block together. Previously, one or two engravers would complete an entire scene over several days. With this division of labor, engravers could finish an entire full-page illustration overnight — a savings of several weeks' time. Sometimes the seams showed in white in the final pictures. Occasionally, Leslie took illustrations to extremes by producing large fold-out engravings nearly two by three feet in 1856 and 1857.

But the *Illustrated Newspaper* was so expensive to produce that the publication often teetered on the verge of bankruptcy. A large, expensive staff turned out timely stories and illustrations, but pressures for such news didn't occur every week.

Then came competition in 1857. Seeing Leslie's potential, the Harper publishing company, which had been established longer with its monthly magazine since 1850, jumped into the weekly news business. Leslie said *Harper's Weekly* was successful because, as part of a major publishing empire, its publishers could afford to run it at a loss. Leslie said he created his many different publications to support the weekly; the economies of scale helped him keep prices low to reach the mass audience he needed. Unlike *Harper's*, Leslie could not afford to run his illustrated newspaper at a loss; he had invested heavily in news.

Tabloid Journalism

Leslie soon found another means for ensuring his weekly's success: sensationalism.

This discovery followed a visit to a secret donor who had helped Leslie in times of financial stress. Once when business had been dull, he had called upon his donor three times, Leslie told an employee. "On the third visit he handed me the desired sum, saying, in a kind tone, 'Leslie, don't you think you had better give it up?' It was the severest shock I ever received. ... A few mornings after this incident, I awoke and heard the newsboys crying a shocking murder of a dentist that stirred all New York, and which, by the mystery surrounding it and the proceedings which followed, became a *cause celebre*. So great was the excitement, that it required a force of policemen to keep the multitude from the house. I seized upon this incident. I caused exact illustrations to be made of the minutest detail, and to be published immediately. The sales of the *Newspaper* rose enormously, and when the excitement subsided, enough new purchasers stuck by it to put the paper beyond any fear of failure."[9]

Three issues of *Frank Leslie's Illustrated Newspaper* covered the murder with detailed illustrations and, if Leslie is to be believed, his paper was saved from bankruptcy by this one dramatic news event.

Leslie also provided illustrated detail of current events, such as the inauguration of President Buchanan the following month, at a time of growing demand for news about the sectional crises. Leslie also drew readers with illustrations of street scenes, everyday life, and technological innovations, such as railroad building and laying of the Atlantic cable. The novelty of having current events illustrated contributed to its success.

Leslie faced a pivotal year both professionally and personally in 1857. Despite his professed high hopes for his *Journal,* Leslie sold it at a profit and created *Frank Leslie's Illustrirte Zeitung,* a German-language version of his *Illustrated Newspaper.* The year marked a national depression and the creation of Leslie's major rival, *Harper's Weekly.* In response, Leslie held his price at six cents a copy or $2 a year, and, he claimed, circulation soared to 164,000 before the war. Yet the financial crisis created hardships, and Leslie may have laid off employees.

But more pleasant, personal news came from Albany, where a special act of the New York Legislature legally changed Henry Carter's name to Frank Leslie. In the same year, Leslie gave his original ladies' publication a facelift. With the appearance of *Frank Leslie's New Family Magazine* in September, "Frank Leslie's Gazette of Fashion" became a 16-page supplement at the end of the 25-cent, 80-page quarto.

Discarding the original *Gazette* formula, Leslie extolled himself as arbiter of the public taste. "We do not flatter ourselves when we say, that the MONTHLY GAZETTE OF FASHION has long been known and acknowledged as the highest and only reliable authority in matters of taste and artistic elegance known in the United States; and encouraged by this appreciation, we are determined that no effort shall be spared on our part to make it, in its new form, still more worthy of the high position it occupies, until it is considered not only a desideratum, but a necessity in every family with any pretensions to cultivation and refinement." The magazine promoted itself as a guide to "the art of dressing" and the "art of shopping."[10]

All Leslie magazines contained miscellany, humor and short anecdotes, and anecdotal storytelling often led longer articles. The *New Family Magazine* carried an article on learned humorists which opened with Dr. Johnson: "Mrs. B— desired Dr. Johnson to give his opinion of a new work she has just written, adding that, if it would not do, she begged him to tell her, for she had other *irons in the fire,* and in case of its not being likely to succeed she could bring out something else. 'Then,' said the doctor, after having turned over a few of the leaves, 'I advise you, madam, to put it where your *other irons are.*'" Some subjects appear in the magazine only because they made interesting illustrations. For example, "The Antiquities of Strasbourg" showed two animal illustrations: one of six large rats whose tails are connected and the other of five cats in the same predicament.

Ordinary people sent pictures to the illustrated publications. In 1860, Leslie published a "notice to photographers" thanking them for their help but asking them to provide a context for their pictures.

> We shall be much obliged to our photographic friends if they will write in pencil the name and description on the back of each picture, together with their own name and address. This notice is rendered necessary from the fact that so many photographs are sent to us from our friends throughout the country without one word of explanatory matter, they giving us credit for being *en rapport* with everything that transpires or exists in all parts of the United States. The columns of our paper prove that we are up to the times in almost everything which occurs of public importance throughout the world, still we are not so ubiquitous but that something may occur beyond the circuit of our far-reaching information. To save labor and insure accuracy, description and names (as above indicated) should *in all cases*, accompany all photographic pictures or sketches.[11]

This emphasis on illustration was underscored as late as 1883 in an article on the Leslie enterprise in the *Popular Monthly*. "The stories required by *Frank Leslie*'s should consist of from 2,500 to 3,500 words, and should be full of action and incident, so as to give opportunity for making effective pictures," the report said. Magazines "made" pictures, even as they added halftone-reproductions in the 1880s.

Investigative Reporting

In the spring of 1858, Leslie became a pioneer muckraker and investigative reporter with a series that became known as "the swill-milk horrors." Cows in the dairies that supplied New York City were fed refuse from distilleries, and cows became so sick that sores developed all over their bodies. Even as their tails rotted off, the cows were still milked. This "swill milk" business had become so powerful that even *Leslie*'s exposés failed to get reform from the City Council.

So Leslie dug in against corrupt city fathers. "For the midnight assassin," he wrote, "we have the rope and the gallows; for the robber, the penitentiary; but for those who murder our children by the thousands we have neither reprobation nor punishment." When the Board of Health issued a reassuring report, *Leslie's* responded: "Every one of these cows has a vote!" The newspaper hired detectives to follow milk wagons, noting the addresses at which the milk was left. Then it published a warning to the buyers that they were feeding poisoned milk to their children.12

Leslie sought to prove that illustrations would increase his impact on public opinion. In one picture, Leslie and his artist-reporter are shown with health officials at the scene of a cow dissection done as part of the health department's investigation. The attacks finally forced a formal city inquiry, but it too yielded a reassuring report. City politicians were too close to the dairies and distilleries. In response, the paper printed a cartoon showing three aldermen whitewashing a stump-tailed cow—the illustration a logo for the campaign.

Leslie began attacking an ever larger group — police, aldermen, health officers, and the mayor. Finally, the mayor asked the New York Academy of Medicine to make a real investigation that found Leslie's attacks justified. But the legislature took another two years to outlaw the sale of milk from cows fed on distillery waste.

Reviewing the subject several years later, the *American Medical Times* said that Leslie's reports, as horrible as they were, fell short of the truth. The report said: "Unmoved by threats, by legal prosecutions, and by attempts at actual violence, Mr. Leslie week after week gave such graphic illustrations of the revolting state of things at these swill-milk yards, that the public was aroused, and the nefarious business broken up for many years. For his action in this, he received a public testimonial."13 The success of the swill milk campaign allowed Leslie to convert his publication into more of a newspaper. He reduced space for humorous articles, gossip, cartoons, literary illustrations and borrowings to make more room for contemporary events, such as the great prize fight in England between Tom Sayers and John C. Heenan, a native of Troy, N.Y., known as the Benicia Boy because he first boxed in Benicia, California.14

Although boxing was illegal in many states, Leslie spared no expense in covering the fight. Chief artist Albert Berghaus and staff writer Augustus Rawlings went to England to cover the Heenan-Sayers fight. Twenty-four hours after the fight a few miles from London, Berghaus and Rawlings had an extra edition available on London streets, impressing the British with their speed. The pair then hurried aboard a ship with the plates and some completed pages.

Leslie's crew produced additional engravings on ship and had the pictures ready for publication when they landed in New York. Their fight edition of May 12, 1860, sold a claimed record 347,000 copies in New York.

Illustrating the Civil War

Frank Leslie's Illustrated Newspaper produced dramatic pictures of John Brown's raid on Harper's Ferry and its aftermath. After secession, Leslie placed correspondents in both North and South, asking soldiers in both armies to send sketches from which engravings could be made. In the process, he created a solid pictorial history of the Civil War. He issued extras for big events and carried many full- and double-page action pictures of battle scenes. At one time, he had twelve correspondents at the front. He claimed to have more than 80 artists working on sketches and to have published nearly 300,000 Civil War pictures. And he published books based on this coverage.

Three major illustrated newspapers — *Harper's Weekly*, *Frank Leslie's Illustrated Newspaper*, and the *New York Illustrated News* — competed in a national market. Competitiveness begat timeliness. The weeklies generally advanced dated each issue by one week. Leslie's illustrations and reports generally appeared on the New York streets one week after an event occurred, even though the publication's date may indicate a longer delay. The date on the front of the newspaper was one week after the publication appeared on the street.[15]

During the war, the news weeklies hired "special artists," illustrator/reporters who sent back both written and artistic sketches from the field. These artist-reporters observed details, sketched them quickly, and reported them for the paper back home. In New York, other artists redrew the pictures on a wood block sent to the engravers who would then cut away the wood around the second artist's lines. Of course, artists in the field seldom saw the final redrawn sketches until they were actually published. And changes could be made along the way, including the addition of signatures by the second artist or engraver. Of course, this situation often created tension between artists in the field and those in New York, even though some moved between the two roles.

Many factors affected an illustration's content. Like many newspaper engravers, Berghaus was better at drawing architecture than people and his illustrations, even of current events, often emphasized scene over action. The engraving process also favored the simplicity of setting over people. In the heat of battle, illustrators could miss details about a scene so they sometimes visited scenes before events to sketch details and backgrounds to before action took place. Sometimes artists depicted events without ever seeing them. Credible artists at least interviewed participants to get some factual basis for their scenes.[16]

Historians have noted the importance of newspapers and correspondents during the Civil War.[17] Similarly, the special artists found newspapers among their topics of life in camp. To accompany an illustration "Arrival of the News-Boy," *Leslie's* artist Edwin Forbes told the story of two mounted news boys he once encountered on the trail. Later he encountered the two boys again but here they told a story of being captured by Confederates but released with their horses as poor boys. Special artists, like other newspaper correspondents, conveyed much of their information through anecdotes.[18]

Correspondents and special artists could not see all the action they depicted. Writing thirty years after the war, *Leslie's* artist Edwin Forbes began his illustrated memoir with an anecdote about himself and another reporter: "My friend and I mutually agreed that our situation was becoming rather more interesting, and that however much we might desire newspaper information, discretion was the better part of valor; so we made for the rear." When the battle ended, Forbes said, "hundreds lay dead and wounded, and the dying were praying for the relief that death only brings. What had been accomplished we had to go to headquarters to learn, but the details of its doing were too plain for misunderstanding and far too terrible for any forgetting."[19]

Forbes described the correspondents' duties as "to gather all facts, rumors and matters of interest pertaining to army life, to keep informed of descriptions. During the winter a correspondent's work was easily accomplished; he gathered what information he could of contemplated movements, picked up camp-gossip and incidents, and reported the deaths of soldiers who died in hospitals. But when the spring note of preparation sounded for the army to gird itself up and prepare for a coming campaign, the correspondent as well as the soldier was aroused into active duty."[20]

Looking back from the comfort of three decades of memory, Forbes contributed to the heroic image of the Civil War correspondent. Like soldiers, correspondents saw action and Forbes describes the work of one correspondent with whom he witnessed a cavalry skirmish. After their escape from the thick of battle, the two reporters headed for the field hospitals for lists of wounded, then back to the battle field to witness the burials.

> Making haste then to temporary headquarters in a grove, my newspaper friend sat down upon a stump to write an account of the battle. He interviewed as many as possible of the officers and men who had taken part in the engagement, and, industriously writing all through the evening by the light of a camp-fire in front of the general's tent, he finished his story by midnight. ... although he had been at it since daybreak, his work was not done, for he mounted his horse and visited the hospitals to obtain a final checking of his lists of the names of the dead and wounded. This work was completed by two o'clock in the morning, when he made his way through the sleeping army to deliver his material to the manager, to be forwarded to the home-office by special messenger.

> A correspondent was often compelled to carry his own dispatches to the nearest post or telegraph station, and would ride at break-neck speed to be the first to deliver the intelligence and "get a beat" on other correspondents. Duty often took them through dangerous guerrilla country, and on many occasions they barely escaped. Quite a number of the brave, bright fellows lost their lives on the battle-field, others returned home with shattered health, and a large number were captured and confined in Southern prisons. The smoothly-written, crisp columns that appeared in the newspapers were no criterion of the dangers that their writers were exposed to; and while tributes are paid to gallant leaders and courageous soldiers, the bravery and endurance of the newspaper correspondents should not be forgotten, nor their work unappreciated. For four long years the feverish interest of the nation hung upon their words, and, aside from the official documents and reports, the most valuable material of the history of these times is to be found in the work done by these alert, hardy and heroic soldiers of the pen.21

Artists and engravers often used photographs as a credible picture source, and some published illustrations that reflected the photographic realism. And publications often ran credit lines, such as "photographed by Brady," even though photographs had to be traced or redrawn. Even with competition from photography, engravers sometimes depended upon dubious sources for their illustrations. They created scenes from mere descriptions in letters from soldiers and adventurers, sometimes picturing events and places they had never seen.

The case of A.R. Waud also shows how artists moved around in their careers. Like Leslie, Alfred Rudolph Waud (pronounced Wode) was born into an old English family. After studying art and working as a scene painter for London theaters, he sailed for the United States, arriving in New York in 1850. Failing to get work in a theater, Waud moved to Boston where he learned to draw on wood blocks for engravers of books and periodicals. During the 1850s, he produced sketches for several publications in Boston and New York, including Barnum and Beach's. His earliest surviving sketches of New England, New York, and Washington date back to 1851. He encouraged his younger brother, architect William Waud, to join him in the United States.22

In 1860 William Waud joined *Frank Leslie's Illustrated Newspaper* while Alfred Waud went to work for *New York Illustrated News*, the No. 3 among illustrated newspapers. In May 1861 the *News* announced that Alfred Waud would sketch "the interesting and important events of the war." He did, but he drew them mostly for *Harper's Weekly*, where began in early 1862.

Unlike many of his colleagues, Alf Waud spent most of his time in the field instead of a New York studio. Waud sent first-person accounts of his battlefield experiences along with his sketches, which often received full front-page or double-truck inside display. He scored a number of exclusives as he followed the Army of the Potomac from Bull Run to Appomattox, where he sketched the moment of Lee's surrender. By one count, he published 344 Civil War illustrations in the *News* and *Harper's*, making him the most prolific of the special artists during the Civil War. Unlike those of other special artists, Waud's original sketches are preserved in the Library of Congress.

Editing Pictures

Even when the front-line "special artists" sent back sketches which became the basis for engravings, the New York office could alter the sketches just as a biased editor might rewrite a reporter's story. Some changes reflected the needs of the medium. Scenes depicted in photographs were simplified. For example, *Harper's* scenes of Antietam, based on photographs by Mathew Brady, contained fewer bodies than those in the original photos. The simplification could have resulted from the engravers' need to work with simple designs. But it also reflects the magazine's desire not to damage the nation's morale.

A concern for the sensibilities of the audience is unmistakable in the reproduction of an Alfred Waud sketch of an Army field hospital depicting a leg amputation. The published illustration showed the victim turned around on the operating table so that his head was visible rather than the original sketch of a gruesome, blood-drenched stump from which the leg had been removed.

Hundreds of thousands of Americans read the illustrated magazines weekly. The special artists and reporters provided succinct, tightly written copy around strong illustrations. They often chose a story on the basis of the picture with it. Many Americans formed their impressions of the Civil War from reading and viewing such publications as *Harper's Weekly* and *Frank Leslie's Illustrated Newspaper.*

And the Leslie described in his publications could have been one of the characters in the popular fiction that filled his pages.[23] A former employee described him as gracious and genial to employees, down to the "humblest of boys." He never uttered a profane or coarse or intemperate expression. "In the many years of our intimate personal intercourse, in the midst of pressing affairs ... I never heard from Frank Leslie's lips an expression which might not be uttered in the presence of the most delicate and refined woman," Kimball wrote. Leslie entertained foreign diplomats and other international celebrities at his Saratoga retreat, but he continued to be in touch with common people. In short, Leslie was the archetype of the American self-made man. "Unlike his great rivals, the Harpers, who were four brothers, strong in will, energetic in action, united in purpose and native to the country," Kimball wrote, "he came alone, a young man, from a foreign soil, without means and without friends, and built up a business the like of which the world had never seen."[24]

Frank Leslie helped create the myth of the virtuous individualist at the head of a large media conglomerate. In 1905 artist Joseph Becker, who had run the publication's art department for half of its 50 years, recalled that Frank Leslie's motto was "Never shoot over the heads of the people." As a result, journalism historian Frank Luther Mott writes, his weekly newspaper "was never profound and seldom very stimulating; but it was nearly always passably amusing, and in its earlier years especially it presented a vivid and lively picture of the American scene."[25]

Leslie took hundreds of thousands of Americans to places they had never been before. The technology for reproducing photographs in magazines and newspapers wasn't invented until Leslie's death. During his lifetime, Leslie provided the most earthy realism — sometimes more imagined than real — available in his day.

Notes

1. The Leslie publishing house wrote about its founder on several occasions, including "Frank Leslie," *Frank Leslie's Sunday Magazine* 7:369-72, 373; "Frank Leslie," *Publishers' Weekly* XVII:13 (Jan. 17, 1880): 43; *Frank Leslie's Popular Monthly* XLVII:1 (November 1898). 109, 113-114; "The Frank Leslie Publishing House," *Frank Leslie's Illustrated Newspaper* LVI:1435 (March 24, 1883): 81; (July 16, 1881, Oct. 8, 1881): 82; "The Home of Illustrated Literature," *Frank Leslie's Popular Monthly* XVI:2 (August 1883): 129-138, 140, 141; Richard B. Kimball, "Frank Leslie," *Frank Leslie's Popular Monthly* IX:3 (March 1880): 258-263, with illustrations on 257, 265, 268. Most of the same article appears as "Frank Leslie," *Frank Leslie's Illustrated Newspaper,* Jan. 24, 1880, 382 and cover illustration.
2. The most useful biographical information on Frank Leslie has been done by author Madeleine B. Stern, who wrote *Purple Passage: The Life of Mrs. Frank Leslie* (Norman, Okla, 1953). See also Stern's "The Frank Leslie Publishing House." *Antiquarian Bookman* VII:24 (June 16, 1951): 1973-1975; *Publishers for Mass Entertainment in Nineteenth Century America* (Boston, 1980): 180-189; *Imprints on History: Book Publishers and American Frontiers* (Bloomington, 1956); "The Leslies of Publishers' Row," *Publishers' Weekly,* CLII:15 (Oct. 11, 1947) B233-7; "Mrs. Leslie Goes West," *Quarterly News Letter*, The Book Club of California, XXIV:4 (Fall 1959): 77-80; "Mrs. Frank Leslie: New York's Last Bohemian," *New York History* (January 1948). See also William E. Huntzicker, "Frank Leslie," *Dictionary of Literary Biography, 79, American Magazine Journalists 1850-1900* (Detroit, 1989): 209-222.
3. *The New York Herald,* June 25, 1845.
4. Comments appear over the index to the first volume (six months) of *Frank Leslie's New York Journal of Romance, General Literature, Science and Art* in summer 1855.
5. Becker, Joseph. "An Artist's Interesting Recollections of Leslie's Weekly," *Leslie's Weekly* CI:2623 (Dec. 14, 1905). 570.
6. An excellent discussion of the early years of Leslie's weekly magazine is Budd Leslie Gambee Jr., *Frank Leslie and His Illustrated Newspaper 1855-1860* (Ann Arbor, 1964). Reprint of the first chapters of Budd Leslie Gambee Jr., *Frank Leslie's Illustrated Newspaper 1855-1860: Artistic and Technical Operations of a Pioneer Pictorial News Weekly in America,* Ph.D. dissertation, University of Michigan, 1963.
7. Richard B. Kimball, "Frank Leslie," *Frank Leslie's Popular Monthly* IX:3 (March 1880): 258-263. Quotation from p. 259.
8. Preface over the second volume (first year) of *Frank Leslie's New York Journal of Romance, General Literature, Science and Art.*
9. Kimball, 259.
10. *Frank Leslie's New Family Magazine* I:1 (September 1857).
11. *Frank Leslie's Illustrated Newspaper,* Dec. 15, 1860, p. 50.
12. *Frank Leslie's Illustrated Newspaper,* May 8, 1858; May 15, 1858; Frank Luther Mott, *A History of American Magazines,* II, 1850-1865 (Cambridge, Mass., 1938): 456-458.
13. *American Medical Times,* IV, (May 17, 1862).
14. Budd Leslie Gambee Jr., *Frank Leslie and His Illustrated Newspaper 1855-1860* (University of Michigan Department of Library Science, 1964). Reprint of the first chapters of Budd Leslie Gambee Jr., *Frank Leslie's Illustrated Newspaper 1855-1860: Artistic and Technical Operations of a Pioneer Pictorial News Weekly in America,* Ph.D. dissertation, University of Michigan, 1963 (Ann Arbor: University Microfilms, Inc., 1963).
15. W. Fletcher Thompson, Jr., *The Image of War: The Pictorial Reporting of the American Civil War* (New York, 1960).
16. Theodore R. Davis, "How a Battle Is Sketched," *St. Nicholas* 16:9 (July 1889). 661-

668.
17. The classic studies include: J. Cutler Andrews, *The North Reports the Civil War* (Pittsburgh, 1955); J. Cutler Andrews, *The South Reports the Civil War* (Pittsburgh, 1985); Louis M. Starr, *Bohemian Brigade: Civil War Newsmen in Action* (New York, 1954), Bernard A. Weisberger, *Reporters for the Union* (Boston, 1953).
18. Edwin Forbes, *Thirty Years After: An Artist's Memoir of the Civil War* (Baton Rouge, La., 1993 [1890]): 133-135.
19. Forbes, 1-2.
20. Forbes, 82.
21. Forbes, 82-83.
22. A.R. Waud's work is discussed in Frederic E. Ray, *Alfred R. Waud: Civil War Artist* (New York, 1974). The book includes a discussion of the *Harper's Weekly* field-hospital example that illustrates the difference between the original sketch and the final publication.
23. Although the name *Frank Leslie* is associated with the founder of pictorial journalism in America, two people actually used the name and neither was born with it. Upon Leslie's death in 1880, his widow Miriam legally took the name Frank Leslie and saved his by then ailing empire from bankruptcy.
24. Kimball.
25. Becker, 570; Mott, 465.

21

Jewish Press Coverage of an Anti-Semitic Act: Grant's Order No. 11

Barbara Straus Reed
Rutgers University

With the beginning of the Civil War, 150,000 of 31 million Americans were Jewish. At least two-thirds of these were immigrants, and during the war another 50,000 arrived. Nearly all immigrant Jews had come to taste the nectar of freedom, long denied to them in their native lands. During the Civil War era, Jews resided in both the North and the South. The contributions of Jewish soldiers who fought in the Civil War have largely gone unnoticed. Between 1861 and 1865, approximately 9-10,000 Jews served in the Union Army while some 1,800 - 2,000 fought for the Confederacy.[1] From the initial firing at Fort Sumter to Appomatox, seven received the Congressional Medal of Honor for acts of valor. Many had recently immigrated to the U.S.; they were just beginning to adjust to their new country when war divided the nation. Some Jewish soldiers experienced blatant religious discrimination.[2]

The Americanization of the immigrants proceeded, always accompanied by attempts to convert Jews to Christianity, as Jews organized social activities, synagogue life, literary assodations, and philanthropic entities. The sole interagency instruments were Jewish publications. Of those engaged in Jewish journalism during this period, the two most prominent voices belonged to Isaac Leeser[3] of Philadelphia and Isaac Mayer Wise[4] of Cincinnati. Another prominent voice heard and heeded was that of Samuel Myer Isaacs of *The Jewish Messenger*. The purpose of this paper is to determine coverage by the Jewish press of Executive Order No.11, issued by General Ulysses S. Grant on December 17, 1862. Thus, it is important to ask for what did these editors stand in the Civil War, at least by looking at one issue, and how did they cover that issue, Grant's Order?

The Facts

The most pronounced incident of anti-Semitism in the Civil War, Order #11, resulted from the controversy over illegal trade. Even in the midst of war, Northern and Southern businessmen relied upon one another for the sale of goods. The need for cotton in the North was great, and Southerners often lacked items such as salt, flour and shoes. Private businessmen and soldiers from opposite sides frequently exchanged these items even though both governments had officially banned trade with the enemy. General Grant was determined to put an end to these practices. He issued regulations which made it difficult for merchants to obtain permits for legal trade. Despite his efforts, illegal trade continued to flourish. Jews were soon entangled in the controversy. Several prominent traders who defied Grant's orders were Jewish. Union officers often used the word "Jew" to describe anyone engaged in trade. When his own father approached Grant with two Jewish friends, merchants who were seeking permits, the General became furious, according to one source.[5]

On December 17, 1862, he issued #11 which mandated the expulsion of all Jews from the Department of Tennessee. His savage order read: "the Jews, as a class violating every regulation of trade established by the Treasury Department and also department orders, are hereby expelled from the department within twenty-four hours from receipt of this order. Post commanders will see that all of this class of people be furnished passes and required to leave, and any one returning after such notification will be arrested and held in confinement until an opportunity occurs of sending them out as prisoners, unless furnished with permit from headquarters. No passes will be given these people to visit headquarters for the purpose of making personal application for trade permits."[6] This anti-Jewish attitude embodied in the Order erupted explosively. When Lincoln learned of Order #11, he rescinded it, noting that many Jews were serving bravely in the (Union) army.

Leeser and *The Occident*

Historians recognize: "The years of American Jewish history from 1830 until the close of the Civil War are, in fact, the 'Age of Leeser.'"7 Leeser's most lasting contribution was founding the first successful Jewish periodical in this country-The *Occident And American Jewish Advocate*.8 It came into being in 1843, went to a national audience, and even reached a modest number of persons abroad. Jews relied on Leeser's magazine, which lasted a generation, until 1869, a year following his death.

The price of *The Occident And American Jewish Advocate*, three dollars per year.9 From the first, Leeser decided to go into magazine publishing because it provided another vehicle of instruction to American Jews. *The Occident And American Jewish Advocate* reflected the aims of its editor. It defended Judaism from a variety of attacks, both inside and outside the community.

The Jewish arrivals from Europe found America's diversity and freedom refreshing and intoxicating. Jewish immigrants drifted away from their faith completely. They violated the Sabbath, many out of economic necessity, but most of them abandoned the ideal of study and worship for picnics, outings, and lounging around at home.10 It was clear to many that a new form of Judaism was needed in the new land.

From 1844 until its demise in 1869, *The Occident* became the intellectual and spiritual arena for a fight about a new form of Judaism. The American Jew was not some monolithic creature. Many joined the new Reform movement, which took its cues from newcomers who had been exposed to modifications in German-speaking Central Europe. To them, simply put, Reform was a revolt against the unquestioning authority of the past. The concept of absolute revelation (by God to Moses) no longer held sway. They did not believe in a personal messiah, although they did subscribe to a messianic era of brotherhood and peace. Instead of hallowing the Sabbath, they believed in celebrating the day of rest and communal gatherings on Sunday, the day observed by the majority.

Agitation for reform soon grew into an organized movement with a formal program and militant leadership. Yet, the Orthodox remained powerful, and their attacks on the Reformers had an impact on Leeser. (Nasty remarks by Dr. Morris Raphall, rabbi of the Elm Street Congregation of New York and essentially the leading Orthodox rabbi in America, found Leeser chiming in with disparaging remarks.) For years *The Occident*, and its arch-rival *The Israelite,* Wise's paper, reflected opposite ideas on Judaism, ideas which seemed destined not to meet, like railroad tracks paralleling into the distance. Leeser never abandoned his efforts to adapt traditional Judaism to American culture. A modern Orthodox Jew, he emphasized the fundamental beliefs of Judaism more than the observance of the commandments.

Leeser, the Civil War, and Grant's Order

While he did not pretend to analyze all of its causes, long-range or immediate, he saw the war principally as a failure of Americans to appreciate their good fortune and to practice charity toward one another. He saw it as further evidence that man, however civilized, had great need of God and God's laws. "Let us be humble when we contemplate the extent of the evil which no human forethought or knowledge was able to arrest."[11]

Leeser ran an item about cotton speculation in Tennessee under the headline "Illiberal Comments," in December of 1862.[12] Because his magazine appeared in the first week of the month, one knew this was weeks before Grant's Order. A Colonel Marsh of the Union Army issued an order for clearing the camp of all Jews at Jackson, TN. Leeser quoted from a daily, unnamed, saying he had "tried to fight the same battle again and again without producing any perceptible abatement of the inveterate disease of illiberality which affects the great public at large." He pointed out that all virtues are not necessarily Christian, that all "roguery" is not necessarily Jewish. Moreover, he protested "against the vulgar practice of holding up Jewish people as peculiarly guilty of offences in which so many of their neighbors join them, even assuming that they be guilty." As for cotton speculators, he asked if Jews alone had been guilty of the crime of buying the raw material "in a manner to depreciate the paper-issues of the Government of this country?"

Leeser suggested that other than Jews were cotton speculators. "Why call them *Jews?*" [italics in the original]. It is the intention to censure by implication all Jews and insinuate one cannot expect anything better from such persons, necessarily dishonest. All the while Christians, on the other hand, never can be guilty of such crimes. Moreover, Leeser picked up a familiar theme, in saying that people should drop the expression "a Christian country," which the U.S. is not. "The majority of the people are Christians, at least nominally so; but this does not affect the Constitution, and should not influence legislation."

Leeser then quoted from the *Providence Journal*, a story originally run in the *New York Tribune*, with the headline: "Cotton Speculators by Army Officers." Written by a Memphis correspondent of the *Tribune*, the report noted:

> Cotton that is worth $250 a bale in St. Louis is either taken from the owners without compensation, or at from $25 to $50 a bale, for one hundred miles above and below Helena. Steamboats, under government contract, are sent on expeditions in search of cotton with a military force, provided with wagons for hauling it, but all the cotton obtained goes to enrich officers or speculators, and very little, if any of it, is placed to the credit of the government."13

The next report was in the February 1863 issue.14 Titled "Persecution," the report combined factual reportage with personal opinion. After all, the present crisis brought Jews

> unpleasantly before the public...has made us feel that notwithstanding the boasted progress of the age, we are still in bondage, yes.. .and have yet to dread the decrees of those in power, who are not restrained by any feeling of humanity and justice from inflicting injury on us.15

Leeser did not carry anything about the crisis in the January *Occident*. Why no mention occurred in the January issue remains unknown; perhaps activity on his part to have the order revoked prevented him from writing about the situation in sufficient depth to run an article.

He noted that Lincoln ordered the Army's commander-in-chief General H.W. Halleck to revoke the order. Yet he pointed out the problems with Congress. The Senator from Kentucky, Lazarus Powell, sought to bring the matter before the Senate on January 5, Leeser reported, and four days later called up a resolution censuring Grant's Order. Despite Lincoln's revoking the order, Powell said he wished the resolution to be passed to show the Senate's opinion about the order, "leveled against a class of our citizens." Senator Clark of New Hampshire, however, thought the order wrong but would not censure Grant, in the field, unless he could be heard from, and he moved to postpone the resolution indefinitely. The resolution was tabled, with 30 voting yea, 7 nay.

Leeser's report continued with the House of Representatives, with Representative Pendleton of Ohio introducing a preamble and saying that Grant had caused "peaceable citizens and residents [i]n the said department to be expelled.. .without any other proof than they were members of a certain religious denomination." He resolved that Grant's order deserved "the sternest condemnation" of the House and the President. But the result was to table the resolution, 56 yeas to 53 nays. Wrote Leeser, "it requires not a word from us to fire the heart of every Israelite with indignation that these things could be done in free America."[16] At the same time, one should note that quoting the proceedings verbatim allowed readers to read the words of Powell and Pendleton, which may have brought comfort to some.

Later, Leeser posed what would have occurred had Lincoln not revoked the order, noting it would have gone into effect long before congressmen found it "convenient or compatible with public safety," to inquire if the situation was true. He noted that Jews would have scattered in all directions, abandoning their homes and business, their synagogues and "the graves of those dear to them, to the tender mercies of a lawless soldiery."[17] He called for a condemnation for the majority in Congress because of "their disregard of their obligations as conservators of the rights of the people, which ought to be safe under the guarantees of the constitution." Leeser wrote to the *Philadelphia Public ledger*, which printed his remarks under the headline, "Are Israelites Slaves?" He queried:

> Will not the enlightened and the brave patriots and friends of liberty, of all creeds, unite with us Israelites to put down incipient tyranny, which sooner or later will seek, unless checked, a wider field than is afforded by the small numbers of our race in the Union?[18]

Leeser went on to quote from the *Washington Chronicle,* whose editor was the Secretary of the Senate. Leeser was incredulous that this could have occurred "in this age and in the United States." He then printed the full order, so that readers could see "that bigotry is not confined to Russia, or to the Roman States."[19] *The Chronicle* said that Grant had never been guilty of "wanton tyranny or cruelty," and that he probably had a good reason to issue the order. Its editor berated the Jews, "the scavengers and the pioneers of commerce." The state of the cotton trade in Tennessee "attracted swarms of Jews to Memphis, Columbus, Jackson and other centres of the cotton region," he wrote, as quoted in *The Occident*.

In addition, the *Chronicle* editor suggested that Jews:

> ...hawk notions, cigars, and fruit about the camps; they sell whisky to the soldiers;...they are...abusing...for purposes of smuggling and communicating with the enemy...; they receive stolen goods...the Jewish peddlers who set up...stalls where in army makes a halt...purchase immunity and toleration from each side, by giving the information they possess about military movements on the other.[20]

Leeser commented that no system of laws will destroy "the spirit of persecution." He complained that the editors of the daily press were "singularly silent" as "the matter did not concern them, of course, the parties threatened...were not Christians, not even negroes[sic], nothing but Jews!-nothing but Jews!- and these, every one knows, are enemies of Christ and his apostles." Thus, a little religious prejudice begot a little persecution, and Leeser painfully wrote: "...we are conscious in every fibre of our heart that the world does not love us..."21

He cautioned that vigilance was needed to arouse "the liberal of all classes" to the danger of the Constitution being violated. He noted that two men in Washington replied to the "scandalous piece" in the *Chronicle*, and he reprinted those letters. One man called the order "unjust and tyrannical, as well as illegal."22 He condemned the editor for writing: "Jews have been always notorious for their fondness for illegitimate trading, or at least unusual modes of making money" and posited that this behavior resulting in depriving Jews "of admission into social and political or commercial circles" amounted to unjust slanders "by prejudiced and unprincipled people." The writer, W.B. Hackenburg, admitted he was a member of "the Israelitish faith" and wanted to show that "Jews as a race are not the degraded ones the editor of the *Chronicle* represents them to be, are sensitive to a wrong, and are willing to justify themselves whenever it may be inflicted." The letter appeared in the *Washington Star*, January 7, 1862.23

The second letter also takes exception to Grant's conduct and that of the *Chronicle* editor:

> Crime, the lust of power, and the covetous desire after gain is confined to no sect, to no country; and why we, at this day of emancipation and disenthrolment, should be visited by those time-despised prejudices that have disgraced the past, as a matter of serious regret and dire apprehension.24

The letter writer pointed out that Jews have been in "every regiment, division, and corps of the various armies of the Republic...attesting with their life their devotion to the good cause of union and liberty."25 The writer, S. Wolf, whose letter was printed in the *Washington Chronicle* January 8, concluded: "For it matters not whether the American Senate or the press do us justice: History will--for the dark ages have passed.. ..My hope is in a verdict from the good common sense of the American people...."

Leeser told his readers that his letter printed in the *Ledger* was also personally carried to the *Philadelphia Inquirer;* to no avail as they could not find room for it. He said he would not "go about begging for a corner in any general publication" and used *The Occident* but recognized it might do some good but "not to the great extent . . .if inserted in a paper of extensive circulation "26

Leeser then printed his entire entry for the *Ledger*, which ran to four pages in *The Occident* and was signed An Indignant Israelite. The headline: "Are Israelites Slaves?"27 "If some Jews have sinned, name them, call them before a military tribunal or civil court, punish them to the full. ..but not as Jews."28 He then castigated Lincoln:

> The President could do no less than disapprove of an act he has himself no authority even under the 'war power' to commit; but he ought to have accompanied the dissent with such a declaration as would have restrained forever all the subordinates of the government, of whatever degree, from offending so in future... the personal, civil, and religious privileges shall not be infringed on, as has been done, by men who hold the whole region, where they have command, in absolute subjection... 29

Leeser then questioned how the Methodists or Baptists would feel if accorded similar treatment by Presbyterians or Catholics. Such a scenario as Leeser described could occur, he wrote, "if the wrongs over which we now complain be not promptly rebuked and their recurrence rendered impossible."30

The *Ledger*, he reported, in contrast with the *Inquirer*, promptly printed the remarks and wrote an editorial about the Jews, condemning Grant's Order but "in subdued language." Leeser also republished the *Ledger* editorial, of January 13, 1863, which asked if only Jews had acted as speculators, he answered,

> We think not. There are thousands of other speculators and traitors daily in communication with the enemy. There are certain army officers, certain cavalry colonels, who have been suspected very strongly of holding those communications with the enemy. ...is it right to inveigh against a dass, or against a sect, for the faults of individuals' (the) order issued no doubt thoughtlessly by one of our Generals....in this country,...they have been conceded equal rights, they become increasingly reliable. There are some of the most highly intelligent, educated, conscientious and patriotic men among them.31

Leeser noted that no redress would be open to those expelled, who had incurred expenses needlessly and had to take time to prepare to move. He hoped that the space he had used to air the "merits of the case" might help those Jews who live in remote areas, who are not "ashamed of their faith and descent" to speak up.32

The next month, Leeser continued his "Persecution. No.11" and blasted Grant who "has not shown himself fit to be the leader of *freemen* (italics in the original).. ...A simple revocation of a military order.. is no pledge that it may not be renewed at the first fitting occasion...."33 He felt aggrieved and concerned that an "unruly mob" could be aroused to go against "a small minority who are distinguished by their religious sentiments, especially as so many among them are natives of foreign climes." He cautioned his readers to retire from public view for safety sake, "until the danger be passed." 34

From *The Jewish Messenger,* he reprinted Powell's remarks, commending the President and General Halleck for "countermanding such an outrageous, and unconstitutional, and inhuman order."35 Powell reported that the Jews of Paducah, numbering thirty men, had to leave their homes and businesses, and that Jewish women and children were expelled, too. Only two women who were ill remained. He said: "Jews in Paducah had at no time been engaged in trade within the active lines of General Grant," and he called for a resolution to "let General Grant and all other military commanders know that they are not too encroach on the rights and privileges of the peaceable loyal citizens of the country."

As if he had read Leeser's words of the previous month, Powell remarked that Grant could have expelled the Baptists, Methodists, Episcopalians or Catholics, as a class, as to have expelled Jews, noting that two of the expelled Jews had served in the Union army. He said: "...while I commend him [Grant] for his gallant conduct, I must censure him for this most atrocious and illegal order. It is inhuman and monstrous." Powell asked that the resolution actually be a preamble to the statement revoking the order, a resolution of censure by the Senate.36

In sum, Leeser believed that American Jews must defend their rights within the larger community, and he was a leader in defending these rights; but the rights which Leeser defended he envisioned as being the rights belonging to the Jews as Americans, rather than particularly as Jews. His battle for religious liberty and complete civil equality for Jews in America was at the same time a battle to extend the basic rights of the entire American community.

Wise and *The Israelite*

Isaac Mayer Wise in 1845, visited Frankfurt from his native Bohemia and attended the second of three great Reform rabbinical conferences held in Germany between 1844 and 1846, and later introduced to the Jews in America the reforms approved at this conference.37 Wise became a rabbi in Albany, New York. He realized he could achieve reform, change, through a publication.

Many Jews in America were estranged from their religious heritage, and Wise perceived the best kind of Judaism in this country would be one free from some of the demands of tradition. Jewish immigrants needed unity, Wise thought. Unity would assist the Jewish immigrants in adapting to the new land, while increasing their resistance to making concessions to the majority culture. It would also help them to remain a distinctive ethnic and religious group and to perpetuate Judaism.

Leeser, sympathetic with the concept of a union, placed *The Occident* at Wise's disposal. As Wise campaigned, he alienated different factions opposed to him; eventually he lost interest in Jewish affairs on the national level and wrote little for *The Occident,* and until November 1849, his work did not appear in print. Then he shifted his attention to *The Asmonean,* the first Jewish weekly, based in New York, which ran until 1858. Wise accepted the invitation of Robert Lyon, editor and publisher *The Asmonean,* to contribute regularly. Wise wrote in the *Reminiscences,* "I lacked the mechanical perfection which one gains only through practice. I had to work till twelve o'clock almost every night."[38] For eighteen months he contributed many articles to *The Asmonean,* until shortly before he moved to Cincinnati.

In May of 1854, a month after assuming a rabbinical position in Cincinnati, Wise decided to establish a Jewish weekly. Subscribers to *The Israelite,* which arrived via mail, paid three dollars per annum, in advance. Advertising and subscriptions hardly covered the cost of publication, and financial problems plagued him for years. One of the reasons was that fully two thirds of the Jews in America were unable to read English.[39]

To Wise it was not only a religious paper; it had a higher function to perform as well: "...the duty of a Jewish organ is to instruct the people, to inform them in what is legally permitted, to disperse the clouds of inveterate prejudices...." Wise always stood ready to defend Judaism; obvious anti-Semites drew his instant reaction.

Wise. the Civil War and Grant's Order

Wise assisted the war effort. He reported when a spontaneous meeting took place to raise money for the war and to create a company of Israelites for the Union; this he reprinted from the *Chicago Tribune.*[41] He printed letters of patriotic fervor on the part of Jews, and included the fact that Jewish women were making an American flag to be presented to a regiment in Syracuse, N.Y.[42] He printed poetry, such as "The Soldier's Evening Thoughts."[43]

Wise carried a news report from the *Cincinnati Gazette.* A Colonel J.V. DuBois of Holly Springs, Miss. issued a General Order addressed to all "cotton speculators, Jews and other vagrants" to leave within twenty-four hours or be "put to duty in the Intrenchments."44 Wise responded with an editorial questioning the mention of Jews in the order, which, he noted, was against the laws of the U.S.

> ...by what right were they expelled and particularly mentioned? Which law of the U.S. confers such authority on any person? Which act of congress gives military commanders the right to defy the laws of the land, maltreat and insult loyal and peaceable citizens because A, B or C harbors prejudices against a certain class of people? It is ...a violation of the soldier's oath, a misconstruction of his duty, and a dangerous precedent...45

Wise also noted that other Jews were treated badly by the provost marshal of Nashville "and elsewhere.-We are told that every provost marshal down South does in this respect as he pleases, and no superior officer interferes. We are told that it is prejudice with some and avarice with others...." He then complained of living under "arbitrary whims of large and small military chiefs." His solution asked all Jewish men maltreated because of their faith to make affidavits before a proper authority; these would be collected and sent to Lincoln. "If we do not help ourselves, nobody will. We have no member of congress now to watch these things, no particular friend in the cabinet, no hand at the public press," he recognized. He lamented that Jewish soldiers had returned from service bemoaning the prejudices encountered "in higher quarters."

In an attempt to show he was taking action of some kind, Wise told his readers that he would send the issue of *The Israelite* to "the President, Mr. Stanton, Generals Halleck, Rosecrans, Grant and Cortis," with the hope that they would attend to the subject. He also ran a scathing editorial from *The New York Times,* titled "Military Marauding—The Evil," which never mentioned the Jews, curiously, but which called on other organs of opinion in America to raise their editorial voices "against [the Order] and demand its correction." *The Times* suggested that a "thirst for plunder and the lust of domination" caused the wrong.46

On January 2, 1863, Wise followed with a blast titled: "The Outrages in Major-General Rosecrans Army." Like Leeser, Wise protested, and stated that in any other country, such as Turkey, Russia, Austria or Morocco, everyone would be upset and indignant that the military behaved in this way toward the Jews—but not here, not now. He recounted that Grant's Order was issued in Holly Springs; and a Mr. Silberman of Chicago was arrested because he doubted the genuineness of the order, was kept imprisoned overnight, and not released until noon the next day. "Jewish citizens who had resided in Holly Springs for years... were obliged to leave," he reported. The way to leave was on foot; they could not be accommodated that day by train as they were civilians. Thus, they walked to Memphis. Wise condemned this "outrage without a precedent in American history," a phrase he would use frequently.[47]

Again, he asked every person illegally treated to obtain an affidavit made before a justice of the peace or a notary public or published in other papers to send such notices to him, including those other publications.

In Nashville, the chief of police accused the Jews of smuggling. Are all Jews smugglers? Wise asked.

> I sir, am a Jew who did not smuggle, if I come to Nashville, I , nevertheless, must go to the office of the inquisition and sign a pledge *never* (italics in the original) to return....Who is responsible for these high-handed outrages....? General Rosecrans must be able to tell us....[48]

He then condemned Grant's order and explained why it had been created: Jews spoiled the market by selling too cheaply. The cotton speculators learned "they could not get rich fast enough on account of that competition, and the Jews must go to make room to patriotic speculators and valorious companions." He harkened to his readers:

> ... you have been outraged, your rights as men and citizens trampled into the dust, your honor disgraced, as a class you have officially been degraded!
> It is your duty, the duty of self defence, your duty first to bring this matter clearly before the president of the United States and demand redress. . . .[49]

He cautioned that the Jew as a nationality treated with impunity meant that other nationalities, such as Germans, Irish, Dutch or French, could be treated in the same way the next day. And if Jews as a religious community were so handled, what would prevent like treatment of Catholics, Unitarians, Universalists or any other denomination? he wondered in print. Comparing liberty to a wounded woman--each group representing limbs, bones, muscles, nerves, veins, intestines, heart and soul--the whole body must feel the pain and be protected against more serious injuries. Thus, freedom for comparative groups made Wise's case for the Jews compelling. Moreover, he probably would need and want their help when he spoke to officials in the federal government.

As with other Jewish editors of the period, Wise placed the main issues of the war outside his purview, becoming righteous and indignant when the rights or honor of Jews were touched, particularly when anti-Semitic accusations were rendered and particularly when Grant issued his notorious order expelling Jews from areas under his command. The Jews were singled out in Grant's order because they were a scapegoat.

For Wise, extensive coverage of Grant's Order began with the issue of January 2, 1863. First, a Mr. Gotthelf of Louisville mailed local papers to give more evidence of Grant's expelling Jews from his lines. It quoted from the *Democrat,* the *Louisville Journal,* and the *Christian Advocate,* the last of which attempted to explain the "alleged reason" for the order: "the continual keeping up of a contraband traffic, and of furnishing contraband news to the rebels--by the Jews, as a class." Wise was annoyed that the *Advocate* offered no comments in support of the Jews.50

Again in that issue, under "General Grant's Order," Wise reported on the steps taken to meet with Lincoln to discuss Grant. A committee of four went to Washington, Wise among them, as a delegation, and Wise decided not to report on what occurred for the present. In Cincinnati, where thousands of Jews resided, Wise castigated the local press for not coming to the aid of the Jews and lashing out about Grant's Order. "Shame on such a press!" said the editor. He then identified the *Enquirer* and the *Volksfreund* as the only two which condemned the Order.

Then followed the *Enquirer* article. Titled "Wrong Done a Class of Citizens by General Grant," it said that military officers had a monopoly on the cotton trade in parts of the South where they were in command, and made fortunes for themselves and for relatives. Also, military officers granted permits to "certain persons only to buy cotton; and those officers would receive a percentage on the cotton purchased as a price for the permit....The more we reflect on the order, the more we dislike it. Its injustice is gross and flagrant."51

Under "Letter From the Editor," Wise recounted his journey to Washington: the Cincinnati and Louisville delegation arrived too late. Lincoln had rescinded the order. Still they met with the President for thirty minutes.

> Having expressed our thanks for the promptness and dispatch in revoking Gen. Grant's order, the President gave utterance to his surprise that Gen. Grant should have issued so ridiculous an order, and added--to condemn a class is, to say the least, to wrong the good with the bad. I do not like to hear a class or nationality condemned on account of a few sinners.' The President... fully illustrated to us and convinced us that he knows of no distinction between Jew and Gentile, that he feels no prejudice against any nationality, and that he by no means will allow that a citizen in any wise [sic] be wronged on account of his place of birth or religious confession.52

Wise also reported his frustration with Congress, disappointed a resolution could not pass the Congress. He said one congressman would have made "a brilliant effort to vindicate" the rights and expose a general who committed a gross outrage on "gentlemen of color." He referred readers to letters in the Washington papers, regarding Grant and the Jews, and one especially from the *Daily Morning Chronicle.* "It is a sensible letter," he commented.

Wise concluded with a letter to the editor of *The Israelite* from New York, saying Grant should apologize or he should be dismissed from the service, as he "is not worthy of being an officer in our army." The letter came from Ferdinand Levy, captain of Company II, the Independent Battalion of the New York Volunteers.53

From the *Indianapolis Sentinel* came a letter from "S.M." of Indianapolis, who asserted that he knew quartermasters who received five to twenty percent "on every dollar's worth of merchandise contracted for by them."54 The alpha and omega of the Jews' offense, the letter stated, is that some Jews desire to trade legitimately on the army's route, "where our more greedy Yankee Christian traders don't think it worth their while to waste their *peculiar talents* (italics in the original). S.M. wanted to know when the government would discover and "ferret out the real authors of our public calamities?"

Wise learned from the Eastern papers that the President's countermand of Grant's Order was sent West via telegraph. He then recounted briefly Mr. Powell's statement for a resolution. He then reprinted from the *Washington Chronicle* the letter from S. Wolf of Washington, as had Leeser.55

The editor in Cincinnati had lost interest in the Grant Order controversy, promising not to write anything more of it. In a lengthy editorial, he recapped what had occurred, first recalling the order of Colonel DuBois, and finding "no body appeared to care." Wise wrote he learned of Grant's Order December 27, from two gentlemen from Holly Springs, Miss., and he said he showed several influential men he knew papers documenting what was occurring; but they expressed no interest. He wrote to Secretary Stanton and awaited a reply. With the intention of going to Philadelphia (possibly to meet with Leeser), Baltimore (where radical Rabbi David Einhorn resided) and New York (possibly to see Rabbi Isaacs), Wise learned from the Philadelphia papers that the order had been revoked. In meeting Lincoln, he discovered neither he nor Halleck had believed Grant issued the Order, until the official document reached them.

Following was a recap of Senator Powell and Representative Pendleton's remarks in Congress with their futile attempts to pass resolutions in their respective houses. Wrote Wise, resolutions in their respective houses. Wrote Wise,

> The censure of Grant was a solemn duty of the men chosen by the people to watch vigilantly over our rights; but no, party first. We are by no means satisfied with the result; but we have no means to press our complaints beyond the highest authorities. Citizens thinking as we do, should meet and adopt resolutions of censure to their representatives in congress who neglected our cause, the pain and simple cause of justice.[56]

He had in his possession legal affidavits "by men of undoubted integrity who were in Grant's army," testifying that a Jew never was arrested, tried, or punished for any misdemeanor during their term in service, three months and longer. Moreover, wrote Wise, Colonel Fox, formerly a law partner of Lincoln, testified to the same facts and claimed to have been in a position to observe behavior of the Jews, and never found anything wrong.

Thus, Wise dismissed the "dry and disgusting subject," believing that he would never again revisit it.[57] Yet, in the next issue, he wrote again about Grant's Order. The *Cincinnati Commercial* ran a note in which a man stated that Grant had received orders from Washington to exile the Jews from his department. Wise noted this was corroborated by a friend, who saw the identical order from Washington. Wise suggested: "the fault lies in the Washington atmosphere."[58] Wise called for an investigation, as he understood that the President and General Halleck did not know about the Order for seventeen days, when a private citizen informed them. And there the editor rested, but again, the *Commercial* printed a story that upset him.

"The Jews of New Orleans" and the rest of the South, "ought to be exterminated" because they were running a blockade, and "are at the bottom of every new villainy." These words came from an Associated Press dispatch. Wise reported the foundation of the dispatch: three Jews were found smuggling letters and medicines to the enemy. Cried *The Times,* those who are offending should be punished, but speaking on such sweeping terms is not justified. "We are sick of this sort of business. We have no doubt there are a great many Jews engaged in smuggling, and there are just as many Gentiles." The *Enquirer* rose to the Jews' defense:

> If the Jews are successful in profitable operations, it is because they are enterprising, ready to encounter the risks incident to them, and know how to use the proper applications.... Constant efforts are being made to excite current prejudices to the point of religious enmity against the Jews have been found a feasible place to begin; ...we do not thank the Associated Press for this species of information. It is not news. It is not in the province--It is not put forth for a good purpose.--And the fabricator of it is not fit for the place he occupies.[59]

The editorial continued that Yankees could not compete with the old, established Jewish families, settled in New Orleans and on the shores of Lake Ponchartrain, whose ancestors resided there under the Spanish Monarchy. The Jewish men possess rare business ability, wealth, and character. Therefore, they were unbeatable when it came to cotton, sugar, and other items of the planters, and that was the "secret of this miserable, mischievously-intended dispatch."

It must have pleased Wise that several papers came to the aid of his fellow Jews. However, he fought alone rather than as a team player. He tended not to act in consort, and had he been willing to unite with the Board of Delegates of American Israelites, perhaps more could have been accomplished.

Isaacs, the Civil War, and Grant's Order

The most balanced coverage of Grant's Order, in the context of Jews in America during the Civil War came from a scrappy little New York paper, *The Jewish Messenger,* put together by Rabbi S.M. Isaacs and his son, Myer S. Isaacs, from 1857 until the dawn of the new century. The rabbi was Orthodox, had come from Holland, and was interested in uniting the far-flung Jewish community.

From the beginning of the war, *The Messenger* promoted meeting the needs of the Jewish soldiers serving the Union. It spoke highly, for example, of a Dr. Fischel's mission of visiting several hospitals and camps with the Department of the Potomac, and his presence was appreciated. He asked that some small prayer and psalm books be sent for distribution. This appeal went through the Board of Delegates of American Israelites, an association of non-Reform synagogues, who organized in 1859 but met intermittently because of the war. Unfortunately, a later *Messenger* reports that Fischell's activities lasted but three months, as the Board ran out of funding for his worthy program. When Jewish soldiers died, they were buried near the field of battle, often in unmarked graves.[60]

The Messenger also ran articies by soldiers in the field, some of whom were identified, while others remained anonymous. The first of a series of eight "Sketches from the Seat of War" ran in January 1862.[61] These sketches described the lives of soldiers, mostly as Americans. Thus, readers could gain a sense of life on the battlefields, camp life to the raw recruit, the patriotism experienced by the men.[62]

The fourth sketch, however, noted the involvement of Jewish soldiers. The soldier spoke of at least 5,000 Jewish soldiers, one of every hundred soldiers; at least five Jewish colonels and as many soldiers. The soldier spoke of at least 5,000 Jewish soldiers, one of every hundred soldiers; at least five Jewish colonels and as many lieutenant colonels, majors, captains, lieutenants and quartermasters among the volunteer regiments, but in the regular army, he knew of no Jew holding a rank higher than captain. Some Jewish officers and privates had told him that they had participated in the Crimean, Hungarian and Italian wars. Also, some Jewish soldiers had suggested forming into separate regiments, but such an idea was "disapproved of by wiser heads." The soldier found such was unnecessary as "we are quite satisfied to fight without Christian comrades for one cause, one country, and THE UNION" (caps in original).[63] The correspondent left for Washington and the South and discontinued his messages; he never resumed them. In another letter, from a Joseph C. Levi, Jews were encouraged to visit the soldiers in their tents at camp.[64]

Moreover, *The Messenger* promoted a Jewish Soldiers' Sanitary and Relief Fund, at the behest of a soldier known as "Semi-occasional." The idea was to insure the comfort, improve the chances of recovery of patients. Synagogues were asked to make appeals for the fund at holiday times.[65] The paper also campaigned for a rest for Jewish soldiers on the Jewish Sabbath, requesting that they receive "immunity from guard duty. ..exemption from all labor that is not strictly necessary"; of course, they would be excluded from provisions of observing the Sunday order recently issued by the President as Commander-in-Chief of the Army and Navy.[66]

The Messenger was the only paper of the three that regularly reported on the attacks on the Jewish name in local newspapers. Whenever someone committed a crime or was arrested for a "disloyal practices," if he were a Jew, that would be prominently noted--in headlines, ledes, and cutlines. For example, David Yulee, a senator from Florida in favor of secession: *The New York Times* printed that his "Jew heart did not get all it craved that he urged the secession of Florida--and like the base Judean, threw away a pearl richer than all his tribe." *The Messenger* wrote that Yulee's faith was singled out because he happened to be a Jew.[67] The *Evening Post* came under attack, too, for misusing the Jewish name, and the editor wrote:

> These attacks on the Jewish name are becoming unendurable. The pen appears to be almost useless in recalling the intolerant writers for the press and equally intolerant speakers, to a sense of the injustice they are doing to a quiet and respectable portion of the community who do no man wrong, and whose only offence is that they worship *one* (italics in the original) God in the way their conscience tells them to be right.[68]

Throughout the period of Grant's Order and its repercussions, *The Messenger* hammered away at newspapers which showed no concerns for the feelings of the Jewish community, suggesting Jews are dishonest, immoral, and irreligious. The *Commercial Advertiser* was one; Associated Press was another. "It is about time this annoying practice of correspondents and newsmongers were stopped," *The Messenger* stated.[69] "How could you expect a Jew quartermaster to be honest?" wrote a correspondent of a "pious periodical."

> Why must these news collectors persist in singling us out for special mention under all conceivable circumstances? We are not ambitious of this distinction. We are, as a community, quiet, law-abiding and patriotic citizens. That there are "black sheep" among us reflects no peculiar discredit on our body; there are "black sheep" of all shades of political and religious belief. Yet why compel us then, to bear the unpleasant burden of individual shortcoming charged to our national account? why must these newspaper writers embrace every opportunity of showing their ethnographic ignorance? Because we are Jews, we do not, therefore, cease to be Americans, Englishmen, or Germans...[70]

Indeed, despite the blatant problems with the press and with the image of the Jew held by some members of the society, *The Messenger* called upon Jews to call themselves "Jews," not "Hebrews" or "Israelites," because they should identify with those who suffered martyrdom and persecutions for the sake of their religion. "Prove by your character and career, that being a Jew, need not detract from a man's work, but rather renders him still more worthy of respect."[71] It is reasonable to hypothesize that such an appellation was unpopular at the time.

The paper did a column on the meaning of independence, for individuals and groups, and pointed to problems with the concept of independence. It was a column signed "M." and probably referred to Myer S. Isaacs.[72] Also, it ran the first column about a Jewish vote, and wrote against it, as Jews are not to be "led by the nose." The phrase was "simply ridiculous," as other groups such as Methodists or Episcopalians did not receive special appeals to their prejudices or fears.[73] Another column addressed the need for self-respect, and suggested those lacking it would say to the Editor they knew how the Jews would vote, that they would vote as a unit.

Against this background came reports of Grant, first noted in the Dec. 5, 1862 issue. A correspondent known as J.C.C. reported that Grant had ordered no more "jayhawking," or wholesale plundering, of the countryside; no more pillaging without restraint. Grant sought to prevent such outrageous conduct by issuing an order assessing the Division Brigade Regiment or Company to which the "depredation" is traced, to the amount of damage done the property. Wrote J.C.C., "Jayhawking has increased to such an alarming extent that it has become necessary to use some decisive and vigorous measures to put it down and it is to be hoped that this last plan of Gen. Grant will succeed."74

Isaacs carried the information of Colonel DuBois in Holly Springs and his order in the same issue date that Wise had. It was but a one-half column story in *The Messenger* but conveyed the news succinctly. Isaacs asked:

> Does this include the Jewish officers and privates in Col. Dubois command--for they must certainly be found in the regiments composing it...Does it refer to the many Israelites who from the very first so gallantly distinguished themselves under Cols. Solomon, Bernstein and Stiefel--have formed no inconsiderable portion of the Western forces? ...hundreds [of Jewish soldiers] more of these same Jews, whom Dubois desires to exclude from his "post," were maimed and bled in defence of their beloved Union....While the conflict for the restoration of the Union is still in progress, why must these little post commandants be permitted to promulgate their proclamations and orders, casting odium on a class of citizens second to none for genuine patriotism and devotion to country.75

In the next issue, the Isaacs' note that Colonel Dubois, commander of Holly Springs, Miss., "has been exerting himself so strenuously in the 'purification' of his post from the 'Jews.. ...trading on the miseries of their country,' that he forgot the mission.. .of defending his country's flag...." Isaacs snickered in print: "A fellow who makes extraordinary professions of offended sanctity is not always a good soldier or military commandant. ..Gen. Halleck better invite him to retire into private life."76

Grant's Order bore the headline "Another 'General Order'" and referred to the debacle at Holly Springs. *The Messenger* waited until the January 9, 1863, issue, printed the entire order, as did the other publications, and noted in a separate story that Halleck revoked the order on the day it was received at headquarters.77 Wrote Isaacs: "Gen. Grant doubtless experiences a feeling of unmitigated disgust and abhorrence for these characters....Why single out... .the Israelites residing within his lines?.. .The course of Gen. Grant has excited intense indignation....

The next week carried a lead editorial noting Grant had not atoned for the insult, and Congress had failed to enact a resolution to condemn the order; both caused increased indignation. Moreover, no reparations had been offered to those affected by the order. Grant had declined to apologize, but he was a "marked man" and the paper announced that once peace was restored, the Jewish community would receive "full and complete satisfaction." Isaacs noted that Jews needed to maintain self-respect and respect in the eyes of others and had to protest; but he asked Jews to "exercise a little patience.." The editorial also told readers that they must understand that the Board of Delegates, "and that alone," speaks for American Jews.[78] Isaacs showed leadership by imploring Jews to stand up to newspapers and politicians who hold up the Jewish name to contempt. "...no ghetto is needed here.. we can stand side by side with men of intelligence, of scientific knowledge, of taste, and be not ashamed." In other words, they should take the "high road" and strive to present the Jews as rational: "..thus inspired, no petty assault of ignorance or fanaticism can injure us, can reach us." It was the only publication under study that printed the General's words in revoking Order 11, in a subsequent order.

The same page has another editorial comment about the *Sunday Mercury,* a New York paper, which accused Jews of "indignation mass meetings" and arming themselves "to resist further interference with" their rights. The irate editor wrote, "Gen. Grant is effectually 'squelched'; there let him rest, for the present... But for goodness sake, let him alone, and don't accuse the Jewish community of treason and want of common sense, all in a breath."

The same issue carried the full resolution regarding Grant's Order passed by the Board of Delegates.[79] While it condemned Order 11, it praised Halleck for the "promptitude" with which he revoked it.[80]

Ironically, *The Messenger* carried the editorial on Grant's order from the Philadelphia *Public Ledger,* reproduced by Leeser as well, where it was a local response to that rabbi's letter. *The Messenger* noted that the Washington *Daily Globe* republished *The Messenger* editorial titled "Another General Order."

As a just footnote, J.C.C. wrote about how he went around Grant, because when he applied for a leave of absence, it was denied; so "one of U.S. Grant's 'as a class' friends was speeding homeward"; via a circuitous route he had obtained a leave ("how is nobody's business").[81]

Conclusion

The Jewish editors covered the Grant's Order episode fully and defensively, for the most part. They all editorialized against the spirit and content of the Order, and often criticized mainstream press coverage of it, and the Jewish community by extension. It is important to recognize the milieu in which the Order was made, nationally as well as locally in the Department of Tennessee. This atmosphere singled out Jews in many respects and created such a negative image that a Marsh, a DuBois or a Grant probably thought nobody would bother to notice the implications of their acts.

It was a time when the American Jewish community was far from influential; the influence of Jews over the entire country was slight. A few families were highly respected, but the rank and file exercised but little perceptible influence. Most new immigrants did not know or read English at that time. The papers were published for those native-born, British, Dutch, some Polish Jews, and, the young people newly arrived who had learned a modicum of English.

During the war, the Jewish press editors realized American Jewry needed to achieve a feeling of shared experience and expectation, of laboring in the present and confronting the future. They all wanted to secure the survival of the Jewish community, according to each editor's vision of what that community should be.

To compare, all were strong editors, honest crusaders. They struck out boldly but with a sense of responsibility. Isaacs found himself tempered by events and individuals around him. He would advocate, but he would also instruct, guide. Wise lacked the earnestness of Leeser; nor was he a scholar, but he and Isaacs sensed the needs of the members of the fledgling Jewish community.

To attract readers, each editor wrote in the vernacular, directly, plainly, and, with Wise and Isaacs, in a warm, friendly manner. They all tried to create a favorable climate, determined to speak, argue and persuade on the one hand, but to seek to reach the widest possible audience on the other. Their articles and editorials attest to their passionate belief in reason, liberty, and progress as well as a hatred of any institution—indeed, the military—standing in their way.

Wise and Leeser used their respective publications as their soap box, their platform. Their weekly or monthly interpretations of Jewish thought reflected their plans for Judaism in America. Isaacs, by contrast, was more encompassing, opening his pages to others involved in the Civil War, trying to unite readers by having them acquiesce to whatever position the Board of Delegates might take.

The editors personified tough values firmly held: integrity, uprightness, and straightforward morality. Their major concern was with the Union. Were America to be divided, it may not retain the liberties it held to as Europeans could encroach and build empires. The Union idea came first, and their feelings as Jews played an important part. Nevertheless, despite the anti-Semitic act of Lincoln's general, the Jewish population continued to grow, to 300,000 by the 1880s. That in itself suggests that the freedom of America was thought to be far more crucial than the occasional problem one minority group encountered during those years.

Notes

1. One scholar notes that 1,500 Jews enlisted in the Confederate military, while between 6,500-7,000 donned Federal uniforms; the year he cites is 1861. Mel Young, *Someone Should Say Kaddish* (Lanham, MD: University Press of America, 1991, p. 3).
2. For example, the absence of Jewish clergy and religious services made it difficult for Jews to practice their faith.
3. It was he who was responsible for the first American Jewish publication society, the first American rabbinical school, and the first association of congregations, the Board of Delegates of American Israelites. Leeser translated the Hebrew Bible into English, organized Jewish "parochial" or all-day schools, and made the English sermon a regular feature of the Sabbath morning service. Jacob Rader Marcus, *Memoirs of American Jews, 1775-1865,* "Isaac Leeser, American Jewish Missionary," Vol.11 (Philadelphia: The Jewish Publication Society of America, 1955) p.58. Data about Leeser's life include Henry Englander, "Isaac Leeser," *Yearbook, Central Conference of American Rabbis,* Vol.25, 1918, pp.213-52, which discusses in detail some of Leeser's convictions and beliefs; Bertram Korn, *Eventful Years and Experiences* (Cincinnati, Ohio: American Jewish Archives, 1954) pp.151-213; Marcus, *op. cit.,* pp.58-87, which excerpts reports of his travels to various Jewish communities; Maxwell Whiteman, "Isaac Leeser and the Jews of Philadelphia," *Publication of the American Jewish Historical Society,* Vol.48, June 1959, pp.207-44; Maxine Seller, "Isaac Leeser, Architect of the American Jewish Community" Ph.D. dissertation, University of Pennsylvania, 1965); Naomi Cohen, *Encoumer with Emancipation, The German Jews in the United States 1830-1914* (Philadelphia: The Jewish Publication Society of America, 1984); Lance J. Sussman, "'Confidence in God': The Life and Preaching of Isaac Leeser (1806-1868)" (Ordination thesis, Hebrew Union College-Jewish Institute of Religion, 1980); Lance 3. Sussman, "Another Look at Isaac Leeser and the First Jewish Translation of the Bible in the United States," *Modern Judaism,* Vol.5, May 1985, pp.159-90; Lance 3. Sussman, "Isaac Leeser and the Protestantization of American Judaism," *American Jewish Archives,* Vol.38, April 1986, pp.1-21, and Mayer Sulzberger, "No Better Jew, No Purer Man: Mayer Sulzberger on Isaac Leeser," *American Jewish Archives,* Vol. 21, November 1969, pp.140-48.
4. Biographical information on Wise abounds. His own *Reminiscences* (Cincinnati, Ohio: Leo Wise & Co., 1901) appeared soon after his death. The longest biography of Wise was written by his grandson, Max Benjamin May, *Isaac Mayer Wise-Founder of American Judaism, A Biography* (New York: G.P. Putnam's Sons, 1916). A short biography is included in David Philipson and Louis Grossman, eds., *Selected Writings of Isaac Mayer Wise* (Cincinnati, Ohio:The Robert Clarke Company, 1900; reissued by Arno Press and The New York Times, 1969. Joseph H. Gumbiner wrote *Isaac Mayer Wise, Pioneer of American Judaism* (New York: Union of American Hebrew Congregations, 1959) for high school students. Articles on Wise appear regularly (partial listing): "After 100 years, Isaac Mayer Wise in the West," *American Jewish Archives,* Vol.6, January 1954, pp.14-15; Melvin Weinman, "The Attitude of Isaac Mayer Wise toward Zionism and Palestine," *American Jewish Archives,* Vol.3, January 1951, pp.3-23; Martin Ryback, "The East-West Conflict in American Reform Judaism," *American Jewish Archives,* Vol.4, January 1952, pp.3-25; Sefton D. Temkin, "Isaac Mayer Wise and the Civil War," *American Jewish Archives,* Vol.15, November 1963, pp.120-42; Joseph Gutmann, "Watchman on an American Rhine: New Light on Isaac M. Wise," *American Jewish Archives,* Vol.5, October 1958, pp.135-44; and Isaac Mayer Wise, "World of My Books," translated by Albert Friedlander, *American Jewish*

Archives, Vol.6, June 1954, pp.10747. Perhaps the best treatment of Wise as rabbi, teacher, and guiding spirit of Reform is the two-volume Sefton Temkin biography, *Isaac Mayer Wise,* (Ph.D. dissertation, Hebrew Union College, Cincinnati, Ohio, 1964).

5. See Bruce Catton, *Grant Moves South* (Boston: Little, Brown, 1960), pp. 352-54.
6. See John Y. Simon, ed., *The Papers of Ulysses S. Grant* (Carbondale: Southern Illinois University Press, 1967-), vol. 7, pp. 50-56.
7. Maxwell Whiteman and Edwin Wolf, *The History of the Jews of Philadelphia from Colonial T mes to the Age of Jackson* (Philadelphia: The Jewish Publication Society of America, 1957) pp. 372-73.
8. Bertram Wallace Korn, "Isaac Leeser: Centennial Reflections," *American Jewish Archives,* Vol. 19, November 1967, p.133.
9. *Ibid.,* Vol.1, No.1, April 1843, p.6. However, Leeser would not honor a subscription for less than a year and refused to sell copies singly.
10. Schappes, *op. cit.,* "Moving Westward," p.232. Hyman B. Grinstein, *The Rise of the Jewish Community of New York, 1654-1860* (Philadelphia: The Jewish Publication Society of America, *1945*), pp.14-15.
11. *Ibid.* Vol. XX, No.1, April 1862, p.28.
12. *Ibid.,* Vol. XX, No.9, December 1862, pp.405-10.
13. *Ibid.,*p.410.
14. *Ibid.,* Vol. XX, No.11, February 1863, p.481 ff.
15. *Ibid.,* p.487.
16. *Ibid.,* p.489.
17. *Ibid.,* p.490.
18. *Ibid.*
19. *Ibid.,* p.491.
20. *Ibid.,* p.493.
21. *Ibid.*
22. *Ibid.,* p.494.
23. *Ibid.,* p.496.
24. *Ibid.*
25. *Ibid.,* p.497.
26. *Ibid.*
27. *Ibid.,* pp. 497-501.
28. *Ibid.,* p.499.
29. *Ibid.,* p.500.
30. *Ibid.,* p.501.
31. *Ibid.,* pp. 501-2.
32. *Ibid.,* p.503.
33. *Ibid.,* Vol. XX, No.12, March 1863, p.543.
34. *Ibid.,* p.544.
35. *Ibid.*
36. *Ibid.,* pp. 546-47.
37. At the Frankfurt conference, the principal topics of debate were the necessity for the retention of Hebrew in public services; prayers for the return to Palestine; the observance of the custom of calling to the pulpit men to read parts of the Scripture; and the introduction of the organ into the synagogue. All leaders of Reform Judaism in Germany discussed these questions. See Israel Knox, *Rabbi in America: The Story of Isaac M. Wise* (Boston and Toronto: Little, Brown and Co., 1957), pp.13-21.
38. Wise, *Reminiscences, op. cit.,* p.207. See also pp.200-01; see also Philipson and Grossman, *op. cit.,* p.41.
39. Wise, *Reminiscences, op. cit..,* p.268.
40. *The Israelite,* Vol.11, *No.5,* August 10, 1855, p.36.

41. *Ibid.*, Vol.9, No.9, August 29, 1862. p.67.
42. For example, *Ibid.*, August 19, 1862. p. 83. He reprinted Dr. S. Deutsch's remarks to a war meeting there in *Ibid.*, Vol.9, No. 15, pp. 116-17.
43. *Ibid.*, Vol.9, No.27, January 9, 1863, p.209.
44. *Ibid.*, Vol.9, No.25, December 26, 1862, p. 184. Although papers were beginning to respond to Grant at this time, the DuBois order made the Grant pronouncement seem like part of the same notion, scapegoating the Jews still further.
45. *Ibid.*
46. *Ibid.*
47. *Ibid.*, Vol.9, No.26, January 2, 1863, p.202.
48. *Ibid.*
49. *Ibid.*
50. *Ibid.*, Vol.9, No.27, January 9, 1863, p. 210.
51. *Ibid.*, p.212.
52. *Ibid.*, Vol.9, No.28, January 16, 1863, p.218.
53. *Ibid.*
54. *Ibid.*, p.219.
55. *Ibid.*, p.220.
56. *Ibid.*, p.229.
57. *Ibid.*
58. *Ibid.*, Vol.9, No.30, January 30, 1863, p.236.
59. *Ibid.*, Vol.9, No.33, February 20, 1863, p.258.
60. *The Jewish Messenger*, Vol.11, No.1, January 10, 1862, *p.3; Ibid.*, No. 18, May 16, 1862, *p. 144.* About Fischell, *Ibid.*, Vol.12, No.15, October 8, 1862, p.116. About the graves, *Ibid.*, No.20, May 30, 1862, p.161.
61. They ran in *Ibid.*, Vol. 11, No.2, January 17, 1862, p. 12; *Ibid.*, No.3, January 24, 1862, pp.22-23; *Ibid.*, No.4, January 31, 1862, p.31-32; *Ibid.*, No.5, February 7, 1862, p. 41; *Ibid.*, No.6, February 14, 1862, pp. 46-7; *Ibid.*, No.7, February 21, 1862, pp.54-55; *Ibid.*, No.8, February 28, 1862, p.63; and *Ibid.*, No.9, March 7, 1862, p.73.
62. Wrote JCL, in *The Messenger* of July 11, 1862, p. 14: "...it is the pride of the members of the Regiment to do their duty as soldiers and men. Irrespective of their dress or what may be said of their responsibility which has been placed upon them!"
63. *Ibid.*, p.41.
64. *Ibid.*, No.11, March 21, 1862, p.88; *Ibid.*, No.23, June 20, 1862, p.185.
65. *Ibid.*, Vol. 12, No. 15, October 8, 1862, p. 114, 116.
66. *Ibid.*, Vol.12, No.21, Nov.21, 1862, p.157.
67. *Ibid.* p.88.
68. *Ibid.*, No.13, April 4, 1862, pp. 1O3~O4. See also *Ibid.*, Vol.12, No.21, November 21,1862, p. 157, about the "scribblers for the press."
69. *Ibid.*, Vol. 12, No.24, December 19, 1862, p.188.
70. *Ibid.*, p. 189.
71. *Ibid.*, No.7, February 21, 1862, p.57; also see No.13, April 4, 1862, p. *104.*
72. *Ibid.*, Vol. 11, No 5, February 7, 1862, p.39.
73. *Ibid.*, Vol.12, No.18, November 7, 1862, p.139.
74. *Ibid.*, Vol. 12, No.22, December 5, 1862, p. 170. (How ironic!)
75. *Ibid.*, Vol.12, No.25, December 26, 1862, p. 196-97.
76. *Ibid.*, Vol. 13, No. 1, January 2, 1863, p.3.
77. *Ibid.*, Vol. 134, No.2, January 9, 1863, p. 12.
78. *Ibid.*, Vol. 13, No.3, January 16, 1863, p.20.
79. *Ibid.*, p.21
80. *Ibid.*, p.22.
81. *Ibid.*, Vol. 13, No. 16, April 24, 1863, p.135.

22

Visibility of Women in Newspaper Advertisements During the Civil War

Hazel Dicken-Garcia
University of Minnesota

A line of inquiry since the 1960s has increasingly addressed images in media content with interest in their meaning and implications for 1) those represented in them, 2) those receiving them—particularly children and young people—and for 3) cumulative effects on culture as a whole. While not ignoring overt, intended messages this line of scholarship has probed primarily the latent, unintended messages imparted. Latent messages may overshadow overt messages, and an assumption is that they can, in recurring patterns over time, entrench attitudes and expectations, affecting norms and behavior. Researchers have examined images of Native Americans and African Americans, for example, but most attention seems to have focused on portrayals of women, while advertising media seem to have received most scrutiny.[1]

Study of images has generally dealt with contemporary media. Little research has looked at images over time, their historical development and relevance to culture. How might cultural strains or issues of today be related to images recurring in media over time, for example? What images or portrayals of women appear in media across American history, and how might those have been shaped and reshaped—and in relation to what contexts? How have dominant images developed and endured? And how do images from the past relate to present-day attitudes about women and gender roles?

This paper about advertising in Civil War newspapers rests on an assumption that newspapers, the main advertising vehicle across the 19th century, may reveal much about development and perpetuation of images of women in media. The 1860 U. S. Census shows just over 4,000 periodicals published in northern states and 844 in the states that became the Confederacy. Publishing was more affected by the war in southern states than in northern states, and some differences in advertisements in northern and southern newspapers are probably due to these two facts.

This paper is part of a larger study of images of women during the Civil War, addressing broad questions about conditions and impetus for change in gender roles. Broader questions of particular interest here include: What is the history of newspaper editors' recognition of women as part of the audience? Particularly, when did newspaper advertising target women as decision makers about purchases. What images of women has newspaper advertising conveyed across time? The theoretical framework and methods reported earlier in a segment about images in newspaper coverage of women's public activities apply here and thus require brief reiteration.[2]

Women's Civil War activities represent a paradox regarding gender. In early 19th-century America, the developing "cult of true womanhood" meant, in the words of Barbara Welter, "a woman judged herself and was judged by her husband, her neighbors and society" by four cardinal virtues—piety, purity, submissiveness and domesticity.[3] Thus, at the time of the Civil War, women were to remain apart from public affairs; however, they engaged in activities beyond what might be expected a century later. Estimates of up to 400 women served as soldiers, and many others accompanied husbands, sons and fathers and did cooking and laundry for their regiments; several served as couriers and spies; approximately 20,000 provided medical services for the North while another 3,200 worked for the Union Army under Superintendent of Nurses, Dorothea Dix.

At home, women organized support for the war and maintained husbands' businesses, carrying out management and bookkeeping work while maintaining homes. Women engaged in public activities, often creating events, such as the bread riots and the "battle of handkerchiefs" in the South in 1862 and 1863.[4]

Because cultural values, attitudes, mores and customs change over time, it was assumed that gender roles and images of women changed during the century and that images embedded in media reflect prevailing attitudes and norms for the time and place created. Thus, this research about images of women in Civil War era media seeks to identify any image shifts and whether patriotism may be related.

Scholars have discussed wars as significant in reshaping gender systems but rarely addressed what wartime conditions propel such changes. The thesis here is that specific values, such as patriotism, become propelling forces. Patriotism may have propelled adjustment between the need for women to aid the war effort and the hardened attitudes about their "proper sphere." That is, a sense of patriotic duty may have prompted women to action they might not have ordinarily considered. Further, leaders likely invoked patriotism to a) call for women's help, b) justify "abnormal" gender behavior in behalf of the cause, and c) applaud women's helpful acts that fell outside their customary role.

Wars "allow for some crossing of gender lines otherwise considered inviolable," historian Elizabeth Leonard has argued, citing scholars who have called war a *"gendering activity...that ritually marks the gender of all members of society."* In other words, "war instantly demarcates, on the basis of sex, the theoretical position, role, and function of each individual in society," as men become "soldiers and warmakers" while women "serve passively at home as the ones for whom the war is fought"; and war's "physical, social, and economic demands" "simultaneously bring about temporary redefinitions of gender and power relations for specific purposes."[5]

Scholarship generally emphasizes the white middle class, but black women offered help as soon as "contrabands" (slaves who fled to Union camps) appeared. They taught former slaves and, after the War Department authorized black soldiers, prepared food and clothing and wrote letters for soldiers, made flags and helped recruit.[6] The war "required an extraordinary level" of participation by women, and they ceased to see themselves as passive, Drew Gilpin Faust argues, particularly Southern women, for whom the war "shattered...the myth of the male as protector"; in general, women began "to form new expectations for themselves...."7

This part of the research focuses on advertising, so it is useful to briefly locate Civil War era advertising and the relevance of gender historically. Regarding American advertising, it is generally accepted that the most profound developments as known today came in the last two decades of the 19th century, principally after 1880, and that those developments created the consumer society.8 Although a relatively small part of the gross national product as late as 1850, advertising grew phenomenally by 1900. For example, periodical income from advertising rose from $9.6 million in 1866-67 to $39.1 million in 1880 to $71.2 million in 1890 to $95.8 million in 1900. In 1847, eleven million advertisements appeared in fewer than 2,000 American periodicals; by 1897, there were 350 million advertisements in nearly 20,000 periodicals then published in America. In 1888, only one general advertiser bought large amounts of space, but by 1898, ten general advertisers (representing 155 companies) were buying large amounts of space. In 1898, 2,583 advertisers were using general circulation periodicals (nearly four/fifths of those were in six states—N.Y., Mass., Mich., Ill., Pa., Ohio).9 Patent medicine, with "individual expenditures running up to $700,000 a year" by the 1890s, was the biggest general advertiser in the nineteenth-century, accounting for more than half of the advertising in many newspapers before 1865 and skyrocketing after 1865 as war-related injuries and illnesses fed a patent medicine craze through the 1890s.10

Advertising agents first appeared in the 1840s and numbered approximately 20 in New York plus 20 more around the nation by the beginning of the Civil War. George Rowell, who began the system of buying space in bulk by annual contract and then retailing it to advertisers, began a newspaper directory in 1869 and in 1888 began *Printer's Ink,* a house organ that has been called the greatest single influence for spreading information about advertising and improving its methods.11 Agate type was the standard, and newspaper advertisements averaged four column inches (that is, one column wide by four inches deep). By 1918, the average newspaper advertisement was four times that size. A deep-seated and generally unspoken notion that advertising was somehow demeaning perhaps accounted for most publishers refusing advertisements in large type as late as the 1860s and 1870s.

Most magazine editors, for example, were reluctant to publish advertisements, although some editors did so early on, and scholars say magazine advertising as common practice dates from around

1890. Generally, by the 1870s, it was common for magazine editors to limit the amount of advertising (exemplified as early as 1847 by *Youth's Companion*), and most refused advertisements until late in the century. For example, *Harpers Magazine* editors rejected Howe Sewing Machine Company's offer of $18,000 for a full back-cover advertisement. The *Atlantic Monthly*, which began publishing in 1857, first included advertisements in 1860—but they were few and very small.[12]

Cyrus H. K. Curtis has been called the first magazine editor to show unqualified respect for advertisements (as early as the 1870s and 1880s) and the first to solicit for advertising and to carry full-page advertisements—which, went from approximately one fifth of advertising in magazines before 1890 to one half by 1920. Curtis exceeded all others in building the importance of advertising as a financial basis for magazines; an advertisement solicitor for the Philadelphia *Press* in 1878, he edited *Scribner's (Century) Monthly* and later made the *Ladies Home Journal* the largest circulation periodical in America after 1890.[13]

Developments in advertising in the last two decades of the 19th century shaped an institution that changed society—leading to what is now called the consumer society. Among developments were changes in advertising *content, nature, purpose, form, source*. Up to the 1880s, for the most part, advertisements gave simple facts, without using psychological appeals. But content changed from matter-of-fact statements to emphasis on product qualities and appeals to emotions, senses, cultural values. The nature of advertising shifted from presentation of mere information to techniques of persuasion to techniques of exerting influence on consumer habits; the content changed from specifics of the product to lyrical appeals to consumer desires, from capitalizing on existing needs to "creating" wants and desires in people's minds.

An *Atlantic Monthly* article in 1903 by psychologist Walter Dill Scott epitomizes the changed trend. Called "The Psychology of Advertising," it read, in part:

> How many advertisers describe a piano so vividly that the reader can hear it? How many food products are described so that a reader can taste the food? How many describe an undergarment so that the reader can feel the pleasant contact with his body? Many advertisers seem to have never thought of this, and make no attempt at such description.[14]

In the same year, Scott published a book on psychology in

advertising, which, according to Frank Presbry, marked the beginning of the study of the psychological appeal of advertising.

The purpose of advertising changed then from conveying factual information to persuading people to buy, and the form changed from dry lines of small, dull type to inclusion of display, color, jingles, slogans, music, photos—appeals to emotions and human interest. In fact, the 1890s have been called the great jingle period in advertising. Examples of slogans that began at the time include "It floats" and "99 and 44/100% pure" (for ivory soap) and the likening of Prudential Insurance Co. to the Rock of Gibralter, etc. Trademark brand names registered in the 1890s include Eastman Kodak, Sears Roebuck, Quaker Oats, American Express Travelers Checques, Remingington Typewriter, Shredded Wheat Company.[15]

The source of advertising changed as market emphasis shifted from local to national. Previously, retailers had bought from manufacturers and sold by their own means. The emphasis was on local markets, and brand names were of little consequence. However, in the 1880s, four companies began brand advertising on a large scale—Ivory Soap, Pear's Soap, Sapolio, Royal Baking Power. As all grew rapidly, other companies began to imitate the brand-name model of advertising, and soon nationally known brand names and trademarks dominated. N.W. Ayer & Son advertising agency got advertisements from only retailers and people selling directly to the public in the 1870s and 1880s, but by 1890 these were replaced by manufacturers' advertisements. By the 1890s, then, national producer/manufacturer advertising dominated, and distributor advertising was secondary.[16]

Of particular interest in this research was whether "commercialization of gender," came earlier than 1880. Helen Damon-Moore has asserted that the last two decades of the 19th century saw the commercialization of gender and the gendering of commerce via advertisements.[17] As commercial markets rapidly expanded, creating needs for expanding advertising, commercial discourse shifted from "conceptualizing potential buyers as 'customers' to describing them as 'consumers.'" Advertisers, needing to personalize messages, sought a gendered audience and targeted women. Damon-Moore used data from two magazines, *Ladies Home Journal* and *Saturday Evening Post*, to illustrate her thesis, which may be summed up by the following:

> Producers, advertisers, and readers therefore colluded in the creation and development of a gendered commercial discourse and a commercial gender discourse. All parties believed at the time that they were striking a satisfactory bargain: producers and advertisers

made a great deal of money, female readers gained some autonomy and control of the family purse strings, and male readers retained their privileged status.

Damon-Moore says the development has shaped gender expectations to the present day, explaining that, even though women now work outside the home, they "continue to bear the major brunt of the work done inside the home, and continue to be defined by what they buy. And men are locked into the provider role...."

Women's role as consumer meant not only that consumers were women, but also that women were consumers. Women since the turn of the century have been defined in the media largely in terms of this aspect of their role, portrayed as buying and using most of the products in the home for the good of the family and to improve themselves.[18]

Other scholars, of course, have observed earlier advertising appeals to women, but Damon-Moore's thesis provoked deeper questions about gender in advertising. For example, what can advertising reveal about the history of gender roles? How is the history of gender roles in America related to gender images in advertising?

Method

As a reminder to readers, the larger research project asks: Given attitudes about women's sphere at the time of the Civil War, plus the need for everyone to assist during the war and women's unprecedented activities, did notions about women's "proper sphere" change, and, if so, what propelled the change? The primary interest was, therefore, whether newspaper advertisements might reveal changing notions of gender roles. Related interests were the degree to which women seemed to be recognized as part of the newspaper audience and as exercising purchasing power. (Damon-Moore focused on only magazines; this paper focuses on only newspapers).

Two sets of images identified by scholars as typical of early and late nineteenth century guide the study of Civil War era media content. Antebellum images, drawn from Ronald Hogeland's synthesis, particularly of Janet James' work, refer to middle and upper class women from 1820 to 1860; the images, which Hogeland called lifestyle patterns, are: woman as *ornamental, romanticized, evangelic* and *radical*.

1. *Ornamental* signified "proper" wives whose purpose was to please men and

handle domestic work to free husbands to fulfill public roles. Women were taught their involvement in public matters was against God's will, except charity work so long as they remained in the background.

2. *Romanticized* images revered women, made them the center of life—embodiments of patriotism, Christianity and motherhood—responsible for perpetuating national morality. In this moralistic, sentimental image, women were society's only suitable moral agents and must devote themselves to the home because, through motherhood, they had the greatest influence. In the belief that proper moral education of children produced moral adults and a moral nation, women were to make the home a sanctuary from "worldly distractions."

3. *Evangelic* images were confined to reformists. Reformers believed reform required all available human resources and was thus suitable activity for women—but women could not hold positions of authority or study for the ministry.

4. *Radical* images reflected beliefs that public life needed women's moral strength, that women could transform the world from greed, malice, avarice to virtue, justice, morality; but the purpose was to improve the world for men—not to change women's lot.[19]

Images from approximately 1860 to 1910 were drawn from Janet Cramer's study that distilled four identified by historians that are self-explanatory: woman as mother, morally superior (to men), altruistic, and as equal to man by natural or divine right.[20]

The examination of advertisements in Civil War newspapers focused on how advertising related to women: Did depictions of, or references to, women in the advertisements reflect these images? And, if so, did one kind of image predominate? Did advertisements or references to women in advertisements convey images of them as belonging more to the private than public sphere? Is there evidence of a transition in views about gender roles—from, for example, the notion of women as belonging entirely in the private sphere to more acceptance of women as public beings?

The research design calls for examining advertisements in a dozen newspapers from across the nation at two points in each year of the war. Newspapers from different regions were selected to allow for discerning any regional differences. To try to acount for differences in advertising "seasons," January, April, July, October, and December issues of newspapers were studied. Every advertisement in each issue selected for study was counted and then each advertisement having any relevance to women was recorded. (Appended charts show these results.)

Visibility of Women in Newspaper Advertisements   357

No advertisements were found with images comparable to what would be seen or expected in advertising today. So, advertisements were grouped in the following categories, which were designed to correspond roughly to the images outlined above (discussed further below):

I. Advertisements seeking women
    for domestic work
    non-domestic work
    other

II. Advertisements by women
    seeking domestic work
    seeking nondomestic work
    advertising their own businesses, and other

III. Advertisements targeting women as consumers
    aimed at women in general
    directly addressing women

IV. Advertisements featuring women

Domestic work means situations that cast women in the roles of cook, laundress, chambermaid, caring for children, cleaning, etc., for these correspond to women's work in the "proper sphere." In many cases, it was not possible to distinguish whether advertisers were seeking women for such work in a business or in a family home, but, while women working outside the home is significant, the overriding image here is the gender role reflected. This advertisement from the July 1, 1861, *Cincinnati Commercial* exemplifies those seeking women for domestic work:

> Wanted—A GOOD GIRL.—One who understands waiting on the table. Must bring good recommendation from former place. Apply at No. 160 Plum street.

Advertisements were classified as seeking women for nondomestic work only if the copy showed clearly that they were sought to work in a capacity other than traditional "housework" kinds of jobs. The following from the July 1, 1864, *Cincinnati Commercial* illustrates (although one might argue this belongs in the domestic category):

> WANTED—200 GIRLS—Some to learn to run Singer's sewing machines and others for different parts of the work on Government pants. A good hand can make from

$1.00 to $1.25 per day. Wages paid every Monday afternoon. Union Hall, 38 East Fifth street, fifth story.

The same standard (identified above) applied also to advertisements placed by women. An accompanying page here copied from the *New York Times* shows advertisements placed by women seeking work—all of which are domestic.

Advertisements signed by women who were clearly in charge of, or had "executive" kinds of roles in, a company, business or independent occupational pursuit, were classified in the category of women advertising their own businesses. The following, from the *New York Tribune*, April 1, 1861, illustrates this category:

THE MISSES WALKER will REOPEN their DAY SCHOOL for YOUNG LADIES, no. 132 Madison-ave., Wednesday, Sept. 18.

Other advertisements by women that fit this category included one seeking information about an accident involving her husband, one informing that a stray ox had been found on her property, one publicizing a lost cow, and one involving an estate sale.

To adhere to a strict standard set to avoid ambiguity about whether an advertisement aimed at women, the broad category of advertisements aimed at women was subdivided into a) those aimed generally at women and 2) those directly addressing women. To be included in the broad category (aimed at women), an ad had to clearly mention women or be about items that women, unquestionably, would use. The ad on the next page illustrates. The conservative standard, no doubt, omits many advertisments aimed at women, but one cannot doubt that this advertisement aimed at women. (A cautious conclusion was that all advertisements with ample white space probably aimed at women, but those were included in the category only if they met the standard noted above.)

Table 1
Advertisements in the *New York Times*

Date	Totals	Concerning Women
January 1, 1861	271	44
June 1, 1861	418	80
January 1, 1864	421	29
April 1, 1864	329	36
GRAND TOTALS	1439	189

Table 2
Advertisements in the *Richmond Dispatch*

Date	Total	Concerning Women
July 1, 1861	156	12
December 2, 1861	264	09
July 1, 1864	09	00
December 1, 1864	144	21
GRAND TOTALS	599	42

The category of advertisements directly addressing women seems self-explanatory: Many advertisements began with a salutation, "Ladies," for example, and the following, from the Oct. 1, 1861, *New York Tribune* illustrates:

> Mothers! Mothers!! Mothers!!! An old nurse for children. Don't fail to procure Mrs. WINSLOW'S SOOTHING SYRUP for Children Teething. It has no equal on earth.
> . . .

The category "advertisements featuring women" included those referring to women. Examples are books for sale that were written by women, plays about women and ads featuring women actresses. The following from the Dec. 1, 1874, *Cincinnati Commercial* is another kind that features women:

> **WANTED—AGENTS**—For the Nurse and Spy, one of the most interesting and exciting books ever published, embracing the adventures of a woman in the Union army, as a nurse, scout and spy; giving a most vivid inner picture of the war. Just the book the people want. Send for Circulars. **JONES BROS. 7 CO.**, Publishers, Pennsylvania.

The subcategories named "other" under Roman numeral I included advertisements from men (mostly soldiers) seeking women correspondents. Under Roman numeral II, similarly, at least one such advertisement from a 16-year-old girl was found in the Dec. 1, 1864, *Cincinnati Commercial*:

> **WANTED—CORRESPONDENCE**—A patriotic girl of sweet sixteen, wants to correspond with some of Uncle Sam's nephews. Object, fun, love and pasttime. Direct to E. H., New Dover Post-Office, Union County, Ohio.

This paper reports on advertisements in seven of the newspapers selected to study. Because newspaper advertisements did not change often during this period, examining one day at each of the two points in a year seemed sufficient to capture the kind of information sought.

1) *New York Tribune*, April 1 and Oct. 1, 1861; April 1 and Oct. 1, 1864.
2) *Cincinnati Commercial*, July 1 and Dec. 2, 1861; July 1 and Dec. 1, 1864.
3) *Charleston Mercury*, April 1 and Oct. 1, 1861; April 1, 1864; Oct. 1, 1864.
4) *Charleston Daily Courier*, Jan. 3 and June 1, 1861; and Jan. 1, 1864; June 1, 1864.
5) *Richmond Dispatch*, July 1 and December 2, 1861; July 1 and December 1, 1864.
6) *Richmond Enquirer*, January 1 and June 4, 1861; Jan. 1 and June 3, 1864.
7) *New York Times*, Jan. 1 and June 1, 1861; Jan. 1 and April 1, 1864.[21]

Generally, advertisements were grouped under headings, which were better organized in some newspapers than in others but did not vary greatly. For example, headings in the *Cincinnati Commercial* included: "Groceries," "Banking," "Removal," "Legal," "Oil Portraits," "Engraving," "Painting, etc.," "Pianos." *New York Times* headings, perhaps the most organized, numbered 22—ranging from "Situations Wanted: Females" and "Situations Wanted: Males" to "Furnished Houses to Let," "Boarding and Lodging," "Country Board," "Houses and Rooms Wanted," "Teachers," "Summer Resorts," "Financial," "Medical," "Astrology," and "Auction Sales."

Southern newspaper advertisements were less clearly labeled via columns, and, among Southern newspapers studied, the *Charleston Mercury* and *Richmond Dispatch* had the best organized advertisements. One column in the *Charleston Mercury*, for example, had a few advertisements under headings such as "Books and Stationery," "Miscellaneous," "Toys," "Confectionary," "Hats, Caps &c—Wholesale and Retail," and "Furnishing Goods—Wholesale and Retail." Another column labeled "Charleston Business Directory" included five headings for groceries, carpeting, jewelry, millinery, and druggists. The *Richmond Dispatch* had eight headings for auction sales, runaways, real estate, amusements, personals, and "For Rent," "Amusements," and "Special Notices."

A sampling of advertising costs showed that ads in the *Cincinnati Commercial* were charged seventy-five cents per each insertion of ten lines (eighty words); those under "Business Notices" were charged ninety cents per line; those under "Special Notices" were charged $1.50 per square. Those in the "Wanted," "For Rent," and "For Sale" columns were charged ninety-five cents per each insertion of five lines (forty words or less). A statement in the *Cincinnati Commercial,* July 1, 1864, said that display advertisements were "charged at the above rates in proportion to the amount of space occupied." That newspaper subscription sold for $9.00 per year or $4.00 per six months. The *New York Tribune,* April 1, 1861, p. 1, advertised twelve and one-half cents for city delivery, $4.00 per year by mail or $3.00 for six months. Advertisements in the weekly *Tribune* were charged $1.25 per line per insertion, and no ad appeared for less than $5. The *Richmond Enquirer* announced, Jan. 1, 1861, fees for ads of twenty-five cents per line and subscriptions at $7.00 per year. The *Charleston Courier,* according to a notice in the June 1, 1861, issue, sold for $10.00 per year; the weekly sold for $5.00 (3?) per month. Advertisements were sixty-five cents per square (12 lines or less) per each insertion. The Jan. 1, 1864, issue, p. 1, advertised the daily newspaper at $15. per six months; the tri-weekly sold for $8. for six months. Advertisements sold for $3.00 for each insertion of one square (12 lines or less). (For the sake of brevity, historical background about the newspapers is omitted from this paper.)

Findings

In general, at least traces of "gendering of commerce" appeared by the time of the Civil War. Women were subjects, as well as authors, of advertisements. Generally, women were more visible in the advertisements, and there were more advertisements by women, than expected.

Gender and Advertising Development

Regarding the relevance of gender to advertising development, especially when and how women became subjects, authors, and targets of advertising, classifications of male and female help-wanted advertisements show women clearly were targets of advertising. Advertisements sought women for work, targeted women as consumers, and featured women.

However, the percentage of advertisements relating to women was comparatively small—and far smaller in Southern than in Northern newspapers. (Generally, this could relate purely to the fact that

Table 3
Classification of Advertisements in the *Richmond Dispatch*

Category	1861	1864	Totals
I. Seeking women			
for domestic work	10	4	14
for non-domestic work	1	0	1
II. By women			
seeking domestic work	0	0	0
seeking non-domestic work	2	0	2
advertising own business	0	6	6
III. Targeting women as consumers			
aimed at women	5	1	6
addressing women directly	0	2	2
IV. Mentioning/featuring women	3	8	11
TOTALS	21	21	42

Table 4
Advertisements in the *Richmond Enquirer*

Category	1861	1864	Totals
I. Seeking women			
for domestic work	0	1	1
for nondomestic work	3	0	3
II. By women			
seeking domestic work	0	0	0
seeking nondomestic work	1	0	1
own business	2	0	2
III. Targeting women			
aimed at women	3	1	4
addressing women	0	1	1
IV. Featuring women	3	0	3
TOTALS	12	3	15

Table 5
Advertisements in the *Richmond Enquirer*

Date	Totals	Concerning Women
January 1, 1861	119	08
June 4, 1861	504	04
January 1, 1864	069	03
June 3, 1864	313	00
TOTALS	1005	15

Table 6
Advertisements in the *New York Times*

Category	1861	1864	Totals
I. Seeking women			
for domestic work	7	7	14
for non-domestic work	0	0	0
II. By Women			
seeking domestic work	54	17	71
seeking nondomestic work	1	2	3
advertising own business	6	2	8
III. Targeting women			
aimed at women	36	26	62
addressing women directly	2	1	3
IV. Features	18	10	28
TOTALS	124	65	189

Table 7
Advertisements in the *New York Tribune*

Category	1861	1864	Totals
I. Seeking women			
for domestic work	0	2	2
for non-domestic work	2	1	3
II. By women			
seeking domestic work	28	0	28
seeking nondomestic work	1	0	1
advertising own business	10	15	25
other	1	1	2
III. Targeting women as consumers			
aimed at women	39	24	63
addressing women directly	2	1	1
IV. Featuring women	12	11	23
TOTALS	95	55	150

Table 8
Advertisements in the *New York Tribune*

Date	Total	Concerning women
April 1, 1861	240	47
October 1, 1861	243	48
TOTAL	483	95
April 1, 1964	250	24
October 1, 1861	165	31
TOTAL	415	55
GRAND TOTALS	898	150

Table 9
Advertisements in the *Cincinnati Commercial*

Category	1861	1864	Totals
1. Seeking women			
for domestic work	1	19	20
for nondomestic work		6	6
for correspondence		16	16
II. By women			
seeking domestic work	4	11	15
seeking nondomestic work		1	1
advertising own business	5	11	16
other			
seeks boarding		1	1
lost cow		1	1
estate sale		1	1
wants correspondent		1	1
stray ox	1		1
III. Targeting women as consumers			
aimed at women	20	17	37
addressing women directly	1		1
IV Featuring women	2	15	17
TOTALS	34	100	134

Table 10
Advertisements in the *Cincinnati Commercial*

Date	Total	Concerning women
July 1, 1861	128	19
Dec. 1, 1861	147	15
TOTAL	238	34
July 1, 1964	306	44
Dec. 1, 1861	331	56
TOTAL	637	100
GRAND TOTALS	875	134

Table 11
Advertisements in the *Charleston Mercury*

Category	1861	1864	Totals
I. Seeking women			
for domestic work	5	2	7
for nondomestic work	0	0	0
II. By women			
seeking domestic work	4	1	5
seeking nondomestic work	1	0	1
III. Targeting women as consumers			
aimed at women	6	1	7
addressing women directly	1	0	1
IV Featuring women	6	0	6
TOTALS	26	5	31

Table 12
Advertisements in the *Charleston Mercury*

Date	Total	Concerning Women
April 1, 1861	145	10
October 1, 1861	267	16
April 1, 1864	64	2
October 1, 1864	81	3
TOTALS	557	31

Table 13
Advertisements in the *Charleston Courier*

Category	1861	1864	Totals
I. Seeking women			
for domestic work	6	2	8
for nondomestic work	0	1	1
II. By women			
seeking domestic work	2	0	2
seeking nondomestic work	0	0	0
advertising own business	2	2	4
III. Targeting women as consumers			
aimed at women	2	0	12
addressing women directly	0	0	0
IV. Mentioning/featuring women	6	3	9
GRAND TOTALS	28	8	36

Table 14
Advertisements in the *Charleston Courier*

Date	Total	Concerning Women
Jan. 3, 1861	263	21
June 1, 1861	106	7
Jan. 1, 1864	62	6
June 1, 1864	85	2
TOTALS	516	36

Table 15
Summary Images of Women Reflected in Advertisements in Seven Newspapers on Two Dates in 1861 and 1864

Newspaper	Seeking women for domestic work	Women seeking domestic work	Targeting women for nondomestic work	Seeking women nondomestic work	Women seeking advertising own businesses	By women
Cincinnati Commercial	20	15	38	6	1	16
Charleston Courier	8	2	12	1	0	4
Charleston Mercury	7	5	8	0	1	4
N.Y. Times	14	71	65	0	1	4
N.Y. Tribune	2	28	66	3	1	25
Richmond Dispatch	14	0	8	1	2	6
Richmond Enquirer	1	0	5	3	1	2
TOTALS	66	121	202	14	9	65

Southern newspapers had fewer advertisements.) The largest one-day total of advertisements in a newspaper among those examined was 421 in the *New York Times* on January 1, 1864; 29 of those related to women. (See Table 1). The smallest one-day total was nine in the *Richmond Dispatch* on July 1, 1864—of which none related to women. (See Table 2). The newspapers ranked as follows for totals of advertising calculated for all dates examined:

	Grand Totals	Concerning Women
New York Times	1439	189
Richmond Enquirer	1005	15
New York Tribune.	898	150
Cincinnati Commercial.	875	134
Richmond Dispatch	599	42

Charleston Mercury	557	31
Charleston Courier	516	36

(Note rank order from most to fewest relating to women: *N.Y. Times, New York Tribune, Cincinnati Commercial, Richmond Dispatch, Charleston Courier, Charleston Mercury,* and *Richmond Enquirer.*)

Proper vs. Public Sphere Images

The sets of pre- and post-Civil War images developed for the research design described above could not be applied directly to advertising copy as to the news copy. Rather, an entire advertisement was categorized as representing conceptions of women as either belonging to the private sphere (home gender roles) or not. Rare was the advertisement that might be construed as representing a conception of women as commonly belonging in the public sphere.

No advertisement relating to women was found that could be identified as appealing to patriotism. Even soldiers seeking correspondence with women seemed to be looking for "proper" wives. An ad, although not from a soldier, from the *Cincinnati Commercial,* Dec. 1, 1864, is typical of these:

> **WANTED** CORRESPONDENCE— By a medical gentleman in good practice (aged thirty-three) with some young lady or widow, between the age of sixteen and twenty-five, with a view to matrimony. She must be of small size and pretty, with blue eyes and light complexion, and must understand vocal music. It is immaterial whether rich or poor. As I am in earnest, a photo of the lady must be enclosed in notes addressed to DOCTOR, Cincinnati Post-office, stating where an interview may be had.

A few advertisements about women's war-related activities were too cut-and-dried to be interpreted as making patriotic appeals. An example from the *New York Tribune,* April 1, 1864, page 3, is an advertisement of the "CHILDREN'S DEPARTMENT of the METROPOLITAN FAIR for the benefit of the U.S. Sanitary Commission," for which five of nine executive committee members were women.

In the category of women advertising their own businesses, the vast majority fell generally into three kinds: women who ran schools or were principals; women astrologers; women offering medical services. A few advertisements by women sought boarders, and a few publicized businesses that provided servants. Ads for women astrologers were relatively common, usually long, and riddled with images of women belonging to the proper sphere. A long ad in the July 1, 1861, *Cincinnati Commercial*, with much white space, begins:

> LOOK OUT! GOOD NEWS FOR ALL!
> The never failing MADAME RAPHAEL is the best, she succeed when others have failed. All who are in trouble—all who have been unfortunate—all whose fond hopes have been disappointed, crushed and blasted by false promises and deceit; all who have been deceived and trifled with; all fly to her for advice and satisfaction; all who are in doubts of the affections of those they love, consult her to relieve and satisfy their minds.
>
> IN LOVE AFFAIRS SHE NEVER FAILS
>
> She has the secret of winning the affections of the opposite sex.
> She shows you the
>
> LIKENESS OF YOUR FUTURE WIFE OR HUSBAND
>
> or absent friend. She guides the single to happy marriage, and makes the married happy. Her aid and advice has been solicited in innumerable instances and the result has ALWAYS been the means of securing
>
> A SPEEDY AND HAPPY MARRIAGE.

The advertisement calls her the "greatest Astrologist of the nineteenth century" and advises that "ladies" need not be timid or fearful about her.

Advertisements that targeted women as consumers/buyers obviously showed recognition of women as newspaper readers and as purchasers of goods. Some of those, however, seem unlikely to appeal to women. For example, in the *Cincinnati Commercial*, July 1, 1861, one "doctor" announced, "Women having derangements peculiar to their sex are invited to call for relief," and another announced, "Females having derangements peculiar to their sex are invited to call and be relieved. The French Periodical Drops, an invaluable remedy for irregularities, & c., of females, can be had of Drs. H & W."

Advertisements overwhelmingly cast women in domestic roles. Only the Richmond newspapers show as few as half or less of total advertisements concerning women fitting the domestic category: in the *Dispatch*, 14 of 42 concern domestic work and 8 target women as consumers, while 1 of 15 in the *Enquirer* concern domestic work and 5 target women as consumers. (See Tables 3, 4 and 5).

The ratio in other newspapers is more typical. Of the 189 ads relating to women on the dates in both years studied in the *New York*

Times, 85 concerned domestic work and 65 targeted women as consumers (Table 6). Of the 150 *New York Tribune* ads, 30 concerned domestic work and 66 targeted women as consumers (Tables 7 and 8). Of 134 ads relating to women in both years examined in the *Cincinnati Commercial*, 35 had to do with domestic work and 55 targeted women as consumers (Tables 9 and 10). The figures for the Charleston newspapers are: 10 of 29 *Mercury* ads concern domestic work and 8 target women as consumers, while 10 of 34 *Courier* advertisements concern domestic work and 12 target women as consumers (Tables 11-14).

In sum, traditional notions of gender (that is, images of women as tied to the private sphere) are represented by categories of 1) advertisements seeking women for domestic work, 2) women seeking domestic work, and 3) advertisements aimed at women. Of 5,889 advertisements tabulated for all dates and all seven newspapers, 567 concern women; the total for these combined categories—that is, representing traditional notions of gender—is 389.

The kinds of advertisements represented by the remaining categories—4) those seeking women for non-domestic work, 5) women seeking non-domestic work and 6) women advertising their own businesses—might be conservatively interpreted as suggesting images of women as not limited to the proper sphere alone. The total for those combined categories is 88. (The category of advertisements featuring women has been omitted in this tabulation because of an impression that they generally fit neither sphere; study of a few tended to confirm this, and so the total in that category was not individually scrutinized for images.) Table 15 summarizes these overall findings.

While white women were more visible in the advertisements than expected, women of color were hardly visible at all. A total of 20 advertisements clearly referred to women of color and all concerned slaves. Five categories were: for sale; for hire; wanted for specific work; stolen; rewards for missing slaves. Advertisements seeking black women for specific work included nurse for infant, cook, washer, "Lady's Maid." These 20 ads were found only in the Southern newspapers, specifically the two Richmond and two Charleston newspapers.

In conclusion, then, advertisements in the Civil War newspapers studied targeted women as consumers. The predominant image tied women to the private sphere, but a few advertisements showed white women in other roles that may be interpreted as perhaps moving toward—if not in—the public sphere.

Notes

1. Meike Ceulemans and Guido Fauconnier, *Mass Media: The Image, Role, and Social Condition of Women*. Report no. 84. Paris UNESCO, 1979; A. E. Courtenoy and T. W. Whipple, *Sex Stereotyping in Advertising*. Lexington, Mass.: Lexington Books, 1983; Merle Curti, "The Changing Concept of Human Nature in the Literature of American Advertising," *Business Review History* 41 (1967); J. Dominick and G. Rauch, "The Image of Women in Network TV Commercials," *Journal of Broadcasting* 16:3 (1974); Stuart Ewen, *All Consuming Images: The Politics of Style in Contemporary Culture* (New York: Basic Books, 1988); Erving Goffman, *Gender Advertisements*. New York: Harper and Row, 1979; Sut Jhally, *The Codes of Advertising* (New York: St. Martin's Press, 1987); F. T. Marquez, "Advertising Content: Persuasion, Information or Intimidation?" *Journalism Quarterly* 54:3 (1977); J. Sissors, "Another Look at the Question: Does Advertising Affect Values?" *Journal of Advertising* 7:3 (1978); M. Venkatesan and J. Losco, "Women in Magazine Ads, 1959-1971," *Journal of Advertising Research* 15 (1975); Rosalind Williams, *Dream Worlds* (Berkeley and Los Angeles, University of California Press, 1982); Lawrence Wortzel and John Frisbie, "Women's Role Portrayal Preferences in Advertisements: An Empirical Study," *Journal of Marketing* 28 (1978).
2. Hazel Dicken-Garcia and Janet Cramer, "Images of Women in Civil War Newspapers Leave the 'Proper Sphere,'" presented to the Symposium on the 19th Century Press, the Civil War, and Free Expression, Chattanooga, TN, November, 1995.
3. Barbara Welter, "The Cult of True Womanhood," *American Quarterly* 18 (Summer 1966): 152.
4. Mary Elizabeth Massey, *Women in the Civil War* (Lincoln: University of Nebraska Press, 1966), 43-44, 65-86; Leonard,xvii; Jane E. Schultz, "Race, Gender, and Bureaucracy: Civil War Army Nurses and the Pension Bureau," *Journal of Women's History* 6:2 (Summer 1994); 45; Catherine Clinton and Nina Silber, eds, *Divided Houses—Gender and the Civil War* (Oxford and New York: Oxford University Press, 1992),185, 144; Mary P. Ryan, *Women in Public: Between Banners and Ballots, 1825-1880*. (Baltimore and London: The Johns Hopkins University Press, 1990), 143-152; see also Penny Colman, *Spies! Women in the Civil War* (Cincinnati: Betterway Books, 1992; Lynn Cullen Sizer, "Acting Her Part: Narratives of Union Women Spies," in Clinton and Silber, op cit., 114-133.
5. Elizabeth D. Leonard, *Yankee Women: Gender Battles in the Civil War* (New York and London: W.W. Norton & Co., 1994, xx-xxi; 212n27. See also Margaret Randolph Higonnet, Jane Jenson, Sonya Michel and Margaret Collins Weitz, eds. *Behind the Lines: Gender and the Two World Wars* (New Haven and London: Yale University Press, 1987), 4-7.
6. Dorothy Sterling, ed.*We Are Your Sisters: Black Women in the Nineteenth Century* (New York: W.W. Norton & Co., 1984), 237, 245-248;256-258; Schultz, "Race, Gender, and Bureaucracy....," *Journal of Women's History* 6:2 (Summer 1994): 47.
7. Faust, "Altars of Sacrifice: Confederate Women and the Narratives of War," in Clinton and Silber, 171; 137-144.
8. William Leiss, Stephen Kline and Sut Jhally, *Social Communication in Advertising* (New York: Routledge, 1990; Scarborough, Canada: Nelson Canada, 1990): 49-90.
9. Frank Presbry, *History & Development of Advertising* (Garden City, N.Y.: Doubleday & Co., Inc., 1929), 210, 360-364, 590-591.
10. Presbry, 290-291; 364.
11. Ralph M. Hower, *The History or an Advertising Agency: N.W. Ayer & Son at Work, 1869- 1949* (Cambridge: Harvard University Press, 1949): 1-11; Presbry, 261-266; 278-279; 319-323.

12. Presbry, 466; 457; Leiss, Kline, and Sut Jhally, 99-101; Ellery Sedgwick, "The Atlantic Monthly," in Edward E. Chielens, ed. *American Literary Magazines* (New York, Westport, Conn., and London: Greenwood, 1986): 50-57; Frank Luther Mott, *A History of American Magazines* Vol. 2 (1850-1865) (Cambridge: Harvard University Press, 1957): 27-45.
13. Presbry, 466-471; 479-484; Damon-Moore, 15-28.
14. Presbry, 443.
15. Presbry, 380.
16. Presbry, 337, 339, 342-344.
17. Helen Damon-Moore, *Magazines for the Millions: Gender and Commerce in the Ladies' Home Journal and the Saturday Evening Post, 1880-1910* (Albany: State University of New York, 1994).
18. Damon-Moore, 12.
19. Ronald W. Hogeland, 'The Female Appendage': Feminine Life-Styles in America, 1820-1860," in Jean E. Friedman and William G. Shade, eds., *Our American Sisters: Women in American Life and Thought* 2nd ed. (Boston: Allyn and Bacon, Inc, 1976), 133-148.
20. Janet Cramer, "Woman As Citizen: An Ideological Analysis of Three Women's Publications, 1900-1909," MA Thesis, University of Minnesota, 1994, p. 77; Historians identifying these images include Aileen S. Kraditor, *The Ideas of the Woman's Suffrage Movement, 1890-1920* (New York and London: Columbia University Press, 1965); Shelia Rothman, *Woman's Proper Place: A History of Changing Ideals and Practices, 1870 to the Present* (New York: Basic Books, 1978; Sarah Eisenstein, *Give us Bread But Gives Roses, Working Women's Consciousness in the United States, 1890 to the First World War* (London, Boston, Melbourne and Henley: Routledge and Kegan Paul, 1983).
21. Additional newspapers to be examined are: The *Daily Alta Californian,* New Orleans *Times-Picayune,* Baltimore *Sun, Liberator,* Missouri *Republican* and the New York *Metropolitan Record.*

23

Samuel Chester Reid, Jr.: Confederate Correspondent, 1861-1864

Lisa M. Daigle
Georgia State University

When the Civil War started in 1861, Southern newspapers covered events substantially, providing opportunities for journalists to become field correspondents. Following the Northern or Southern armies for usually one or two newspapers, these men risked their lives to report everything they witnessed. In the South, one such traveling correspondent was Samuel Chester Reid, Jr. He was employed by seven different newspapers throughout the War, an unusual accomplishment. Reid, older than his fellow colleagues, established a reputation as a successful, yet troublesome, reporter for the Southern cause. This reporter, still virtually unknown today, made a solid contribution to the field of journalism by writing enthusiastic and entertaining articles for his readers both at home and in the field.

Reporting the Civil War: Sam Who?

Southern newspapers were popular in 1860, but they did not have the same circulation as their Northern counterparts. "Alabama's annual per capita circulation in 1860 was fourteen [%],...Georgia's, twenty-three [%],...Tennessee's, twelve [%]....;" Northern papers in New York had eighty-four and Pennsylvania, forty-one.[1] The daily edition of the Richmond *Dispatch*, one of the most successful Southern papers, had a circulation of approximately 3,000, and its neighbor, the *Mercury*, had only 550 paid subscriptions. No Southern paper ever sold as many as 10,000 copies of any single edition; the great majority numbered their readers by the hundreds rather than the thousands.[2] Southern newspapers rose in popularity after the War started, for they provided vital accounts of events."Despite their limited circulation, Southern journals were extremely important sources of information."[3] This increasing popularity provided greater opportunities for the field correspondent looking to make a career in journalism, in both the North and the South.

Nearly every Southern newspaper of any size used volunteer correspondents, including officers and enlisted men, to report news from the army and the battlefield. The larger newspapers also employed "special correspondents" of their own.[4] Samuel C. Reid, Jr. was a "special correspondent," working for seven different Southern newspapers throughout the War.

Reid was already 43 years old when the War started, which made him older than most of his fellow colleagues. Few field reporters had the "staying power to follow the armies throughout the War. If bullets, illness, or ennui did not get them, they were expelled, captured, drafted, or simply worn out."[5] Reid was one of these few who had the stamina and perseverance to stay with his chosen career until 1864, when illness finally caused his retirement.[6]

Field correspondents of the Civil War weathered hard conditions along with the soldiers. Often the reporters had a "ragamuffin appearance" from their hardships.[7] Reid was no exception. Aside from the obvious problems a reporter would face following an army into battle, there were usually difficulties with sending in reports as well. On numerous occasions Reid reported the telegraph lines being down or that he was unable to get his dispatches out for lack of sufficient services.

Reid Begins

Reporters during this time were not honored for their work. "It often seemed that appreciation for the correspondent's trade and their daring was confined to the pages of the newspapers themselves."[8] Their dedication to their craft and the subsequent satisfaction their work brought them, not money or fame, was their reward for their accomplishments, especially within the South.

Samuel Chester Reid, Jr.: Confederate Correspondent 375

The compensation for reporting was meager. Yet due to his popularity and determination, Reid managed to make more than a modest living. For his correspondence to the New Orleans *Picayune* in 1862, Reid received twenty five dollars a week, which was a common fee. By 1863, Reid was receiving four times that amount from the Mobile *Tribune*, which included a supplementary allowance for horse feed. His payments from three newspapers amounted to approximately $12,000 during the first two and a half years of the War.9

Correspondents generally did not work for more than two papers at once; in 1862, Reid was reporting for three papers. He had been working of the New Orleans Daily *Picayune* before the War started, and when the first shots were fired, Reid decided to continue his work with the *Picayune* as a roving correspondent. While working for that paper, he also reported for the Mobile Daily *Advertiser and Register* and the Memphis Daily *Appeal*. He did not submit the same letters to all three papers, but wrote separate wires and letters for each paper from the battlefront. In contrast, some reporters would send the same dispatches to each paper they were working for, if they were covering the same events for more than one newspaper at the same time.

After New Orleans fell to Union troops, Reid subsequently quit working for the *Picayune*. By 1863, he was sending dispatches to the Chattanooga Daily *Rebel* and the Montgomery Daily *Advertiser*. After leaving the Mobile *Advertiser* that same year, he started working for its competitor, the Mobile Daily *Tribune*. At the end of 1863, he was also corresponding for the Atlanta Daily *Intelligencer*. Not only did Reid continue to submit different wires to all these papers, he used different pseudonyms in each paper.

While working for either Southern or Northern newspapers, it was customary for correspondents to use pseudonyms in lieu of their names.10 In 1861, Reid was known to the *Picayune* as "Ora;" starting on March 28, 1862, Reid changed to writing as "Sparta" in that paper. For his reports to the Montgomery *Advertiser* he kept writing as "Ora" and for the Atlanta *Intelligencer* he used "290." Before 1862, he usually signed his letters with either "S.C.R." at times or used simply an "R" or an "S." Other letters or telegrams, presumably written in haste, were left unsigned.

First Excitement

Throughout his career, Reid enjoyed the freedom of his job. Many of his letters or telegrams detailed his enthusiasm. While traveling to Memphis, Tennessee in 1861, he sent one of his very first letters to the *Picayune* that stated: "The woods and green fields once more! What a cheering and refreshing sight to a denizen of New Orleans, who has been cooped up by the surrounding of brick walls!"[11] It is evident in this letter that Reid was looking forward to becoming a roaming correspondent. His letters in 1862 retained this initial excitement, elaborating on his experiences while traveling with the Tennessee army:

> I expect my tour will be full of adventure and incident,.... We shall have a fine moon to cross the mountains by, and as we are just entering the glorious autumnal month of October, when the rich foliage of varied green,...changes to all the variegated exquisite hues of the rainbow, I anticipate enjoying some glorious landscape views of woodland and mountain scenery. East Tennessee is the Switzerland of America, and presents views of river, mountain and valley scenery not excelled by any in the world.[12]

Throughout the War, despite the atrocities he witnessed, his retained in each letter both his love for the countryside he traveled through and his passion for his work.

Entertaining Anecdotes

Reid frequently used humor to entertain his readers. He usually made the Northern armies and President Lincoln the subjects of his jests. In one letter to the *Picayune*, he included "a good story on Old Abe, which is too good to keep, and is no doubt true, as it comes from a very high authority."[13] This story gives an account of how a Mr. Abe Enlow, "a sharp, wirey chap,...always up to mean tricks," presumed to be Abraham Lincoln, pilfered a saddle that did not belong to him. This Enlow fellow then ran away from Kentucky to a log cabin in Illinois, where he changed his name in order to escape justice. This story continues, illustrating Reid's feelings for Lincoln:

> There is no one who has become lower since Abe Enlow has become a traitor President, under the stolen name Abe Lincoln. But we all said at the time that the boy who stole Jim Craycroft's saddle would never come to any good end....There can be no doubt, after this authority, as to who Abe Lincoln is. I wish this to take its chance on reaching you, but if any of Old Abe's get hold of it, it will be sure to miscarry.[14]

Reid usually included a humorous story, much like this one, in his letters.

Samuel Chester Reid, Jr.: Confederate Correspondent

Reid attributed a number of these anecdotes and facts to "high authority." This "authority" might have been a "gentleman" that had passed through where he had been staying, or, as in the Lincoln story, to "a highly respectable old lady of this county."[15] In his letters, he would attribute facts whenever possible, yet these attributions did not usually have names attached to them:

> A gentleman who came through from Clarksville, Tenn., reports that all the Federal troops had left there two weeks ago, being the rear of Buell's column. When they left the citizens gave three cheers, which so exasperated the Feds that they threatened to shell the town if the indignity was repeated.[16]

Reid frequently attributed his stories, anecdotes, and most of the facts that he had not seen personally. Yet these attributions were usually nameless people he presumably came into contact with during his travels.

Reid was not only critical of the Northern army and its government; he was critical of all "Yankees," even if they were found as far south as Atlanta, Georgia. For example, in 1862, Reid went to Atlanta to confer with Editor J. Henly Smith of the Atlanta Daily *Confederacy* about the possibility of corresponding for that paper. Smith did not hire Reid; Reid found he did not care for the city. He detected a "slight perceptible odor of Yankeedom" within it. He was obsessed by the fear that the "Gate City" was "alive with Yankee spies."[17] Reid subsequently did not work for an Atlanta paper until his correspondence with the *Intelligencer* in the fall of 1863. Interesting to note, his dispatches to this paper were not as consistent, nor as detailed, as those letters and telegrams he sent to other newspapers.

The Patriot

Reid's letters were often optimistic, showing the solid Southern spirit of the time. In 1861, he traveled to Kentucky to cover their then possible secession from the Union. His letters described his perception of the people and their "general uprising."[18] He found that "secession fever" was "at its height."[19] He described the events in his usual eloquent detail, showing both their fervor and his own:

> The true men of Kentucky are rising, and are determined to free themselves from the Lincoln oligarchy. A spirit of true patriotism and the wildest enthusiasm is spreading itself all over the Southern portion of the State.[20]

This style of writing, which was detailed but did not attempt to cover his own enthusiasm or opinions, was a permanent feature in Reid's articles throughout his writing career.

In another letter to the Memphis Daily *Appeal*, for example, he further describes Kentucky's Southern patriotism, and subsequently his own:

> I have been several days in this so called neutral city, that is, if neutrality means to be all on one side. The Union flag, as they call it, alone floats over the market places and Main Street. It is not the old form of the American flag with the stars running in parallel lines, but with the stars forming a circle, making them link hands...as children do in the play of "Oats, sweet beans, and barley grow," and to my mind pretty much on the same principle. In the old flag...,the lines themselves plainly demand "State Rights.". . . There is no question of the fact but that a large majority of the true general people of Kentucky are in favor of the Southern Confederacy, and when the revolution takes place, which may be daily looked for, it will prove it.[21]

Letters like these, in which this reporter's opinions were clearly defined, were common in both Southern and Northern newspapers. Many reporters did not mask their true feelings in their writings, and Reid was not different from his fellow colleagues.

In most of his letters, Reid rarely hid his patriotic feelings for, and belief in, the South and its causes. One critic notes that the "Southern press chose to accentuate the negative opinions" of Southerners towards the North.[22] However, Southern patriotism in Southern newspapers reflected the sentiment not only of their reporters, but of their readers. Only when reporting failures by the Southern army did Reid's strong beliefs make his accounts questionable. In every instance of this kind, the Southern army "fell back," or used "retrograde movement;" hardly ever were Southern troops "retreating." Yet, Reid was reflecting the opinions of his readers as well as his own opinions.

Countless journals of citizens and soldiers alike describe their loyalty to the South and also their fears of the North. An example of Southern patriotism can be found in the letters of a woman to the Mobile *Register*: "We have left our families, friends and relatives to come here for the purpose of defending our country,...I will just say that our boys are Dixie's own children and are now waiting and praying for marching orders."[23] Support for the Southern cause in the South was not hard to find.

According to Reid, even Northern soldiers were supportive of the Southern cause:

> In a conversations with a number of prisoners from Iowa, Wisconsin, and Illinois, whom I brought in from the battle-field of Shiloh, they admitted that they had been deceived – said that so far as they were personally concerned they had fought their last battle against us, and that they would never take up arms again against a people fighting

for the liberties of their institutions and their independence.24

Granted, prisoners of war would support their captors in most cases; yet, Reid, in his accounts, was not only reflecting his own opinions of the War, but also those of his readers. His readers, Southerners, did support the Southern side of the War. Those at home read the papers to keep abreast of the happenings of the War. He did not only keep these readers at home in mind, but also wrote for the soldier in the field, for their morale was one of his main concerns.

Reid's letters often showed this staunch support of the Southern army. In one report, he contrasted the "just" goals of the Southern soldier and the "tyranny" of their Northern opponents:

> When the wearied soldier, at the tap of the drum, stretches himself at night upon his blanket on the tented field, it is but natural that he should ponder on the issues of the war which has induced him to take up arms in his country's cause. When he reflects that the terrible resort to a bloody strife is forced upon us in defense of our national security and honor; for the preservation of our precious institutions; in the sacred cause of public security, which makes all wars defensive – then it is he becomes nerved for the conflict, and free is a firm reliance in the triumphant (?) of its justice and holiness. Then it is that he feels each morning's reveille is but the overture of our onward daily march towards the accomplishment of a glorious independence.25

In the following paragraph, he continues with a telling portrait of the North:

> On the other hand, no enthusiasm, no fire of patriotism, no glow of the great principle of justice stirs the breast of the brutal hired mercenary who enlists under a tyrant to enslave and subjugate millions of people, to violate their rights, and destroy their institutions secured to them under the common constitution of their country. In justice, fraud and falsehood marked the very threshold of the abolition Government. When Lincoln prevaricated with our commissioners, who went to Washington for the preservation of the peace of the land; when in violation of his word and honor he reinforced Fort Sumter, he determined on a bloody, cruel war. From that moment, a military despotism was established over civil authority, and made to triumph over the constitution of the land.26

His contrasts here of the Southern and Northern soldier delineate a common Southern belief about both the Southern army and the War. Reid used his words to bolster his own feelings, but he also kept his readers in mind, no matter which side of the War his readers may have been on. He was attempting to support both the soldier in the field and those left at home.

Support for the Mothers and the Soldiers

As mentioned, Reid supported the South's desire for independence and individual state's rights. His opinions, however, were not only confined to exclusive Southern motives or cares. Often, he reminded his Southern readers exactly *why* their boys were fighting in this war:

> Justice was denied our citizens at home and abroad. Corruption crept into the national councils, sharpened party animosity, and stifled the rights and liberties of the people. Ambitious political leaders seized upon the favorable moment to usurp the powers of Government, and overturn our institutions. The spirit of the South, irritated to madness, rushed with a wild enthusiasm to the defense of their rights, and civil war has followed.[27]

In many of his dispatches, Reid repeated why the South was fighting against the North, reminding his readers why their sons were dying, and why they must keep the faith in their cause. In doing this, he sustained his support of both those at home and the soldier on the battlefield.

Like many Southern correspondents, Reid was angered by some conditions the Southern army, and especially its lower ranking soldiers and thus himself, were forced to bear. While traveling with these soldiers, he remarked on the inadequacies he witnessed:

> I left Corinth this afternoon...in an ambulance of the 4th Louisiana, having been disappointed in the horse promised me, and it being impossible to obtain another at any price....The road is very rough..., with numerous mud holes, and occasional swamps. To make the trip interesting and diversified, we had a miserable, windbroken, balky, spavined C. S. horse, which some speculating horse jockey had swindled the Government to pay no doubt $250 for. If the villain, and others of the same kidney, had thought for a moment that such a horse was to be used for hauling wounded men from the battlefield, and knowing that he was unfit for service, his conscience would have been troubled with a severe attack of neuralgia. We broke down several times...[28]

Adequate transportation was important to Reid, for he believed it was absolutely necessary in order to report the war. However, he did not usually find sufficient means to get from battle to battle.

While Reid was unhappy with the conditions forced upon the soldiers and himself, he praised the medical care for soldiers:

> I visited the hospital of this regiment...to see how the sick were cared for....I must confess I was rather unprepared to see the cleanliness, comfort, neatness and care which attended the building throughout.[29]

This comment was uncommon in reports from the War; most correspondents, especially Southern reporters, wrote of the inadequate medical treatment soldiers received. Yet Reid usually did find some small "good" to include in his reports from the field, even if it was only a brief mention of the weather. His positive support shined through in most of his writings.

Reid vs. Rumor

Reid despised rumors and tried to dispel them in his writings whenever possible. Circulating camp rumors were common, and he would try to break them by showing either the humor in them or their inaccuracy. For example, in one letter to the *Picayune*, he states:

> There are any quantity of rumors in camp this morning, made up to suit inquiries, of whome there are always a large stock on hand, and the least pretence for a report from the enemy is magnified into immense and exaggerated proportions. For instance, it was a current report that our advance forces had captured yesterday at Monterey,...six of the enemy's artillery pieces, and any quantity of mules – all of which was entirely false. Again, it was said the enemy had advanced last night with a force of 15,000 on Pea Ridge, on the road from Hambury, to this point, and that an engagement would take place to-day. To those who are posted, these rumors afford much amusement, in watching the thermometer of expectation rise and fall with our troops.30

Reid believed that rumors were detrimental to the reporting of the War. He thought that they would always prove to be false, "as all camp rumors generally do."31 When made aware of a rumor, he reported what he knew as the truth, doing his best to do so as accurately as possible. Yet his opinions of these truths, at times, showed more of his personal opinions than accuracy. Reid also believed the circulation of any rumor was bad for morale and therefore bad for the soldier.

Whereas Reid supported the soldiers and their trials, he faulted the higher ranking officers. He did not like the "political jugglery and wire working" by which he saw ambitious soldiers using to obtain higher rank within the army.32 He felt this had a demoralizing effect on the men.

Unlike some of his fellow correspondents, Reid had prior military experience, having served as a Deputy Marshal and as a member of the Texas Rangers during the Mexican War.33 This prior experience gave him an understanding of battles from a military point of view and an edge over his colleagues. It did not, however, give him an innate ability to get along well with his military colleagues of high rank.

Reid had problems when dealing with the higher ranking officers, especially with General Bragg. Reid had a good relationship with the General until he reported on the battle of Shiloh. Bragg did not agree with Reid's dispatch. Reid discovered this a few days after his report was published, when he went to see the General. Bragg stated his displeasure quite adamantly. His complaint was that his name was not in the reports of the battle, "...it would seem, so far as the newspapers were concerned, that I was not in the battle at all!"34 Reid professed that he had done justice to Bragg in his reports, and he had. Reid did mention General Bragg's name in his accounts, when it was appropriate to do so.

Continuing Troubles with the Generals

Beginning March 25th, 1862, Reid wrote two columns from Corinth, one entitled "From the Seat of War" for the New Orleans *Picayune*, and another for the Mobile Daily *Advertiser and Register* entitled the "Latest from Corinth." It was within these columns that Reid's troubles with military officials increased: "It was whispered about the camp that the misbehavior of a single correspondent, Sam Reid...had provoked Beauregard's wrath."35 Apparently, Beauregard was angered by a dispatch by Reid that was sent to the *Appeal*, which stated: "a general engagement is expected tomorrow. Our whole army marched out this evening."36 Reid's report also alluded to Beauregard's abortive advance of that day, which failed to defeat Pope's corps at Farmington. This report angered Beauregard quite a bit.

In his accounts from Corinth, Reid did not try to appease General Bragg or Beauregard, or any other high ranking officials, by including them often in his reports. Reid did include General Bragg when it was possible, and when it was necessary to his story.37 His accounts were similar to each other, and Reid did not leave Bragg out of an event he was involved in:

> This movement of the enemy is for the purpose of flanking Chattanooga, and compelling General Bragg to abandon that almost impregnable position. Whether he will be successful or not, cannot yet be determined.38

However, Reid's hostility towards Bragg, and his personal disapproval of Bragg's actions, was also included in his accounts as well:

> Little doubt can be entertained that the enemy have Chattanooga. That strong and

Samuel Chester Reid, Jr.: Confederate Correspondent 383

important position was evacuated without a blow from Gen. Bragg; because it is said Rosecrans had again "flanked" him, and he was compelled to make a further retreat into Georgia, or fight in a position where complete victory alone could save his army from destruction or captivity.39

Reid reported what he witnessed, and did not cover his opinions, even when discretion may have been better advised.

Due to Reid's growing dislike for Bragg, Mobile *Register* editor John Forsyth directed that none of his letters or dispatches should go to press until Forsyth himself had inspected them.40 Forsyth and Bragg were close friends. Reid did not agree with this new policy, and in March accepted an offer of new employment with the *Register's* competitor, the Mobile Daily *Tribune*.41 That following June, one of Bragg's officers arrested Reid in Tennessee for going into Shelbyville without a pass. Reid was ordered to leave town by two the next afternoon. A cavalry commander of Bragg's, Major General Joseph Wheeler, interceded with Bragg for Reid's sake, and he was allowed to stay with the army. He continued with the army in Tennessee until August. His reports in the newspapers made no comment of this close call nor any other personal events with other officers until the fall of 1862.

At the end of August, 1862, Reid applied for permission to accompany Bragg's invasion march into Kentucky. Reid discovered that Bragg had issued a general order on August 20th stating that "no person not properly connected with this army will be permitted to accompany it – whenever found within the lines, they will be arrested and confined."42 Reid, curious to know whether this order applied directly to him, wrote Bragg a personal letter on August 22nd. No written reply was issued. On August 25th, Reid was notified that Bragg had ordered him personally to leave the army and Chattanooga. Reid printed an expose of Bragg's personal discrimination against him to the Charleston *Mercury*, and it appeared in the September 26th issue. Reid did not try to publish this appeal in the Mobile *Advertiser*, for, as was noted, the editor, John Forsyth, was a close friend of Bragg's.43

The Question of Accuracy

Reid's retellings of the actual battles have been criticized as well as praised. One critic states that in his telegrams, Reid made no attempts to identify any of the Union corps or division commanders.44 In most of his telegrams, Reid did not give incredibly detailed accounts, but he did report Northern losses, captured prisoners, and the identities of Northern commanders, when that information was available to him:

> Lieutenant Colonel { }art's cavalry, belonging to Col. J. Smith's Georgia Legion, have just returned from the Cumberland mountains. They encountered Colonel Cliff's brigade of renegade Tennesseeans near Jameston, when a desperate fight took place. Fifty of the enemy were killed outright, and we took twenty prisoners and thirty horses, without loss on our side.
>
> Col. Cliff is among the prisoners. Ora.[45]

Unlike his telegrams, his letters were more descriptive of the battles, and included more information concerning both sides:

> I leave here to-morrow morning for the celebrated Cumberland Gap, en route for the "dark and bloody ground." It appears..., that on the day previous, Gen. Bragg had demanded the surrender of Louisville, Bull Nelson being in command; Nelson refused, and gave notice to all the women and children to leave.... Gen. Kerby Smith's column had taken position so as to hold Buell's forces in check, whose advance had reached Glasgow, where, it is reported, a small force of our troops had been captured. If this be true, it cannot be long before Kentucky's soil shall once again become reddened by the carnage of the battlefield.[46]

Reid was intending to speak to Southern readers about the state of the Southern army; therefore his articles focused on the Southern rather than the Northern army.

In reporting the battle of Chickamauga in 1863, Reid did make some mistakes. He incorrectly gave the time of the breakup of the enemy's right and center as "about 5 o'clock" and presented a rather confused version of what happened after that. He also misrepresented the direction of the enemy's troop movement.[47] "The statistics Reid used in reporting the battle were in some instances approximately correct, but in others considerably wide off the mark."[48] Yet, he quoted from General Bragg's own reports of the battle. The first news of the battle to pass over the wires was an official dispatch from General Bragg himself, telegraphed from Ringgold.

Much of the information that was misrepresented about Chickamauga was a product of the telegraphic reporting of the battle. Reid was not the only one who made mistakes; others like the Press Association, who first reported that battle took place on Peavine Creek rather than the Chickamauga, and fellow correspondent Peter Alexander, who asserted that the Confederates had captured forty thousand prisoners, were also to blame for misrepresentations regarding the battle.[49]

Despite telegraphic inaccuracies, Reid reported the battle of

Chickamauga with objectivity and care. He researched his story, taking details from battle accounts released by the army and from personal accounts of soldiers present at the battle. His battle story was approximately 10,000 words and has been regarded as the "most complete and informing Confederate newspaper account."[50] In order to create this account, Reid had to overcome many trials, not only with army officials; yet he created an admirable account of the battle.

Most of problems Reid surpassed were traveling concerns, common to many roving correspondents. For example, on his way to Chickamauga, Reid stopped in Savannah and had trouble finding transportation to Ringgold. Unable to buy a horse for less than $1,000, he was still in Tunnel Hill on Sunday, and was unable to locate transportation or anyone to approve his dispatches. He finally reached Chickamauga the next evening, after walking nine miles from the railroad station at Ringgold.[51] His account of the battle of Chickamauga, "which he worked on for nearly two weeks," and which first appeared in print in the Mobile *Tribune*, was later published in pamphlet form ("The Great Battle of Chickamauga") in November, 1863.[52]

Censorship and the Roving Reporter

Despite his problems with the military, and his subsequent problems surrounding the censorship of his dispatches by Forsyth, Reid did believe that censorship was acceptable when reporting actual occurrences or concerns during the War. For example, he felt that reporting the specific movements of troops was absolutely unacceptable:

> Great dissatisfaction is produced at headquarters by imprudent correspondents and others, mentioning the movements of our Generals and other matters, there-by giving the cue to the enemy for obtaining information of our movements and designs. It cannot be repeated too often, and should be kept before the people, that in the present revolutionary struggle, every man of the Confederacy should act as if the whole responsibility of achieving our independence rested upon him. Let every one be governed by this principle, exert every means in his power to effect it, use reflection, prudence and caution, and keep up eternal vigilance.[53]

Yet Reid did not always follow his own eloquent advice. On numerous occasions, he would report the Southern army's exact activities, if not their whereabouts:

> For the last few days, there has been the greatest activity prevailing in all the departments of our army, and especially in the medical department, which is the

surest indication that a battle is at hand.[54]

In many instances, he also reported the army's location, but not only the Southern army's: "Our army advanced to within five miles of the enemy's lines. Their camp is three miles from the Tennessee river, at Pittsburg."[55] However, he did give hints as to what was next in the Southern army's plans:

> ...the battle must certainly take place to-morrow by the advancing of one or the other party.
>
> Most probably it will be commenced by us.[56]

These descriptions were usually found in Reid's letters, which were published several days after the actual events had occurred and thus created no danger, but in a few instances, he did include details like the previously mentioned, in his immediate telegrams.

In either letters or, at times in telegrams, Reid did not only give hints to the Southern army's possible plans, but would also report what he thought the enemy's plans were going to be:

> The enemy is still coquetting on the Tennessee river, making a demonstration at one point to-day, and another to-morrow. It is evident from their movements that they are trying to surprise us at some point, from which they wish to call off our attention from the fact that the enemy is making every possible effort to cross from the Missouri side to the Tennessee side of the Mississippi river, would indicate their intention of trying to effect a junction with the Tennessee river column of their troops in their assault on Memphis, while their Nashville column, the head of which is now within striking distance at Columbia, would be ready to attach us in the rear, and get possession, if possible, of the Charleston road.[57]

In one telegraphed account, Reid even went so far as to tell how the enemy should attack, if they meant to be successful:

> Their only hope is – when they shall attempt this point – to attack us in the rear by the Blandville and Mayfield roads, and attempt to outflank us. The road to Blandville is a little east of it, about eighteen miles from Columbus and 8 miles east-south-east-from Cairo. Mayfield is about twenty-eight miles east-north-east from here ant two to five miles east-south-east from Cairo.[58]

Nevertheless, despite these few questionable dispatches, Reid's accounts were accurate and detailed, even if they at times contradicted his own beliefs in moderate censorship. He gave accounts of what he saw and felt, all of which were strong, if opinionated and slanted.

Samuel Chester Reid, Jr. was a dedicated reporter, showing the Southern side of the Civil War with great conviction and care. Some of his reports may not have been completely accurate, nor unbiased, but they were accounts that clearly gave definition to the Southern voice in the newspapers that employed him. His was a strong voice, intended to speak to the reader fighting in the field or waiting at home. He reached more readers than many of his colleagues by reporting for seven different papers throughout the course of the War. Unlike some associates, he took the time to create different, although similar, letters to each newspaper. Like most journalists, he angered some and pleased others. Yet his work entertained and informed his public, during a time of war and atrocity, thus making a solid contribution to the field of journalism history.

Notes

1. Donald E. Reynolds. *Editors Make War: Southern Newspapers in the Secession Crisis.* (Nashville: Vanderbilt University Press, 1966). p. 5.
2. *Ibid.* p. 4.
3. *Ibid.* p. 5.
4. J. Cutler Andrews. *The South Reports the Civil War.* (New Jersey: Princeton University Press, 1970). pp. 47-48.
5. Louis M. Starr. *Reporting the Civil War: The Bohemian Brigade in Action, 1861-65.* (New York: Collier Books, 1954). p. 134.
6. Reid later died from tuberculosis, in 1865.
7. John. F. Marszalek. *Sherman's Other War: The General and the Civil War Press.* (Memphis: Memphis State University Press, 1981). p. 39.
8. *Ibid.*
9. *Ibid.*
10. *Ibid.* p. 49.
11. "Trip tp Memphis," *New Orleans Picayune,* August 15, 1861. p.1.
12. "Our Army Correspondence," *Memphis Daily Advertiser and Register,* October 3, 1862. p.1.
13. "Letter From Kentucky," *New Orleans Picayune,* September 4, 1861. p.2.
14. *Ibid.*
15. *Ibid.*
16. "Letters From the Seat of War," *New Orleans Picayune,* April 6, 1862. p.1.
17. Andrews. p. 234.
18. "News By Telegraph," *Moblie Daily Advertiser and Register,* September 13, 1862. p.2.
19. "Letter From Kentucky," *New Orleans Picayune,* September 4, 1861. p.2.
20. *Ibid.*
21. "Letter From Kentucky," *Memphis Daily Appeal,* September 5, 1861. p.1.
22. Reynolds, p.157.
23. William Stanley Hoole. *Confederate Norfolk: The Letters of a Virginia Lady to the Mobile Register, 1861-1862.* (Alabama: Confederate Publishing Company, 1984). p.11.
24. *Memphis Appeal,* April 30, 1862. p.1.
25. "Letters From the Seat of War," *New Orleans Picayune,* April 6, 1862. p.1.

26. *Ibid.*
27. *Ibid.*
28. "From the Seat of War," *New Orleans Picayune*, April 10, 1862. p.1.
29. "Letter From Columbus," *New Orleans Picayune*, February 16, 1862. p.1.
30. "From the Seat of War," *New Orleans Picayune*, March 30, 1862. p.1.
31. "Letters From the Seat of War," *New Orleans Picayune*, April 6, 1862. p.1.
32. "From the Seat of War," *New Orleans Picayune*, March 30, 1862. p.2.
33. *Ibid.* pp. 137-138.
34. Andrews. pp. 146-147.
35. *Ibid.* p.156.
36. "Affairs in Tennessee," *Memphis Daily Appeal*, May 22, 1862. p.1.
37. See the *New Orelans Picayune* and the *Mobile Daily Advertiser and Register* from March through May, 1863.
38. "Affairs in Tennessee," *Memphis Daily Appeal*, September 18, 1863. p.1.
39. "From Tennessee: Entry of Yankee Army Into Knoxville," *Memphis Daily Appeal*, September 19, 1863. p.1.
40. Andrews. p. 341.
41. *Ibid.*
42. Andrews. p. 236.
43. Donald E. Reynolds. *Editors I Have Known.* (Nashville: Vanderbuilt University Press, 1966). p. 78.
44. Andrews, pp. 354-356.
45. "Brilliant Cavalry Reconnaissance in East Tenneessee," *Mobile Daily Advertiser and Register*, September 20, 1862. p.1.
46. "Our Army Correspondence: Letter From East Tenneessee," *Mobile Daily Advertiser and Register*, October 3, 1862. p.1.
47. "The Battle — Its Progress and Results," *Memphis Daily Appeal*, September 23, 1863. p.2.
48. Andrews. p. 355.
49. *Ibid.* pp. 354-355.
50. *Ibid.*
51. *Mobile Daily Tribune*, as citied in Andrews, p. 352.
52. Andrews, p.354.
53. "Letters From the Seat of War," *New Orleans Picayune*, April 6, 1862. p.1.
54. *Ibid.*
55. "From the Seat of War," *New Orleans Picayune*, April 8, 1862. p.1.
56. *Ibid.*
57. "From the Seat of War," *New Orleans Picayune*, March 28, 1982. p.1.
58. "Telegraphed: Exciting News," *New Orleans Picayune*, February 18, 1862. p.2.

24

Devil to Clown:
News Coverage of the Capture of Jefferson Davis

Robert Dardenne
University of South Florida-St. Petersburg

April and May of 1865 were eventful months in American history. On April 3, the Confederates evacuated Richmond; on the 9th, Lee surrendered to Grant at Appomattox; on the 14th (Good Friday), John Wilkes Booth assassinated President Lincoln at Ford's Theater in Washington; on the 26th, Booth was tracked down to a barn in Virginia and killed by a sergeant, who was quoted as saying, "Calling on God to execute justice, I fired" (some accounts say Booth killed himself); and on April 10, in no doubt the least of all these events, Jefferson Davis was captured at Irwinville, Ga.

Perhaps because it is the least of these and many events leading to that date in 1865, little has been said of Davis' capture and its coverage by the press. But that coverage not only tells us about news and newspapers of 1865, it reveals flaws we recognize in modern times after frenzied bursts of coverage of some emotional event. Coverage of Davis' capture illustrates how the press fuels speculation by reporting misinformation and rumor and even creating stories, inflames public passions about conspiracy, and allows its emotional involvement to lead it to seek justice and perhaps vengeance.

Davis' flight and capture in many papers, the *Hartford Courant*, for example, was covered in a frenzy of emotion, speculation, and frustration. Davis was seen almost solely in terms of April's events, especially the assassination of Lincoln. Reporters and editors at the Courant and other newspapers refused to believe that Lincoln's death was not plotted by Davis and promised time and again to provide evidence to that effect.

Although the evidence never came, Davis was portrayed as satanic — a monstrous assassin, cowardly assassination plotter, looter of banks, and common thief. From the assassination of Lincoln until after the capture of Davis, news reports and comments went from flatly accusing Davis of the assassination and other planned atrocities to speculating the extent of his involvement, for they offered no doubt that he was involved in all of it. For about two weeks at the end of April and the beginning of May, news reports provided wildly varying estimates about how many people traveled with the escaping Davis and how much "stolen" money they carried. But the intense emotion and hatred could not be sustained.

Perhaps the reading public did not see Davis as the devil portrayed by the press or, at the end of a long and devastating war and after the assassination of their president, people grew tired of the bitterness. In the end, rather than treat him as a devil, editors and reporters resorted to portraying him as a clown, a leader fallen so low that he was captured sneaking out of camp in petticoats and crinoline, an insult aimed directly at his manhood and character and one gleefully reported throughout the country. That little of what was reported was true (or that much was exaggerated) emphasizes the danger — then and now — of news organizations so caught up in the events and people they are covering, so caught up, in this case, in rumors and speculations of conspiracy and the need for justice or vengeance that they create their own story, missing the one playing out before them.

Lincoln's Assassination

In April 1865 the fall of Richmond and Petersburg prompted great celebrations, and, in the *Hartford Courant*, for example overshadowed coverage of the surrender at Appomattox. But the Confederate evacuation of Richmond on the 3rd and Lee's surrender to Grant at

Appomattox Courthouse on the 9th were themselves overshadowed by press coverage of Lincoln's assassination on the 14th. The assassination was perhaps the biggest story in most northern newspapers up to this point — a sympathetic, beloved president killed shortly after the moment of his greatest triumph, and killed, or so several newspapers thought and promoted vigorously, by a hated enemy.

Papers throughout the country covered the Lincoln assassination as their political proclivities dictated. Often they blamed the South, slavery, and/or Davis for the murder at the same time they canonized Lincoln. The Courant provided a typical example.

> Slavery murdered ... Lincoln ... in the blossom and flush of life, ... the full harvest of glory and renoun (sic) which would have been due to him, unreaped. So excellent a man, tender as a child, with a heart overflowing with kindness and good will even to his foes, a man enchanted with peace and its enjoyments and shrinking instinctively from war and bloodshed, has been the victim of a tragedy almost unparalleled in human history. He was, too, so just and benevolent a ruler .... (April 17, 1865, page 2)

Washington D.C.'s *National Intelligencer* also argued that the assassination naturally followed from rebellion, one of its "legitimate fruits." One article claimed that the "first impression" is that of "deep indignation against the author of the rebellion and its participants and sympathizers" (April 17, p.2, col. 2). The next day, the paper, terming the assassination part of a conspiracy to inflame passions and confuse the loyal, noted that investigations "are yet to disclose the extend of the roots of what now appears to be a well-concerted Conspiracy" (April 18, p. 1, col. 2).

The *New York Times* said the assassination was "the logical and legitimate ending" of slavery, the "legitimate crowning of a whole system of crimes and atrocities," all of which have been part of "one great and consistent whole" (April 20, p. 4, col. 4). It was a crime, which, in "dishonor, cowardice and atrocity, is almost without a parallel in history," the "base assassination of the purest public man of his day" (April 27, p. 4, col. 3).

Amid assassination coverage, the *National Intelligencer* was a voice of reason. If Davis and other Rebel leaders were behind the assassination, it assured readers that "appropriate punishment will follow the crime." The writer thought it "needless to anticipate here; to write inflammatory language or to speak it. Justice will be done, and let that suffice" (April 20, p.2, col. 1). In the South, the *New Orleans Picayune* also discussed the issue calmly. Using information gathered "From Southern Papers" it hoped the assassination wasn't "perpetrated by a Southerner, whom its very barbarity would disgrace. ... We deem the independence of the South eminently desirable, but never dreamed that it was to be achieved by assassins" (April 28, p. 1, col. 7).

In mid May, the paper along with many others in the country, reported that a judge and eventually President Johnson had said that documents conclusively linked Davis to the assassination. A "Letter From New York" on May 17 speculated that for the president to issue such a statement, offering a reward for the capture of Davis and others, the evidence must be strong (May 17, p. 1, col. 4). Many papers reported that authorities were compiling conclusive evidence to prove Davis's involvement in the conspiracy. These accusations were widely reported throughout the North and South. Many papers, including the *Courant*, promised indisputable and damning evidence to tie Davis to the assassination, even that Davis planned it. Despite a multitude of such references and many writers' reliance on the suspected evidence to condemn Davis as the ringleader in the assassination, no evidence ever surfaced. Still, *The Times, Courant* and other papers, using this "evidence" and a myriad other speculations to support their belief that Davis and other Rebel leaders assassinated Lincoln, didn't moderate their language in calling for the strictest possible punishment:

> Cruel, vindictive, bloodthirsty, he used his power to the last with the malice of a fiend. Disappointments aggravated his ferocity, defeat intensified the malignancy of his venom .... A braggart and a coward, he leaves by the back door between two days. According to the tenor of advertisements for runaway negroes, he was last seen at Charlotte, N.C., in an extremely dilapidated condition.... Friendless and homeless, staggering under mountains of crime, and chagrined by the failure of his plans, he can turn in no direction for peace and safety. His experience illustrates the curses pronounced by God on the wicked. Few ever waded more deeply into crime, or met more overwhelming retribution. He will perish unpitied, unwept, unsung. Linked with the names of Benedict Arnold and Aaron Burr, the name of Jefferson Davis will go down to posterity. (*Hartford Courant,* April 14, page 2)

A few days later, the paper said he had done enough to "convince the more humane, that the rope and the axe must not be cheated of its lawful prey." Further, the article said, "Woe and bitter anguish are in store for the guilty instigators of this 'foul and most unnatural' murder" (April 17, p. 2).

New York Times editors, before the assassination, argued that the "toad-spotted traitor" Jefferson Davis had to be hanged (April 14, p.2) for his participation in the war, and the assassination only strengthened that belief. Quite specific about perceived connections between southern leaders and the assassination, it condemned Rebel leaders as it mentioned rumors and speculations that had intensified near the end of the war.

> Every possible atrocity appertains to this rebellion. There is nothing whatever that its leaders have scrupled at. Wholesale massacres and torturings, wholesale starvation of prisoners, firing of great cities, piracies of the cruelest kind, persecution of the most hideous character and of vast extent and finally assassination in high places — whatever is inhuman, whatever is brutal, whatever is fiendish, these men have resorted to. They will leave behind names so black, and the memory of deeds so infamous that the execration of the slaveholders' rebellion will be eternal. (April 17, p. 1, col. 2)

In may, *The Times* decided the government should spare no efforts to capture Davis and that he and the "leading traitors should die the most disgraceful death known to our civilization — death on the gallows." Further, Booth should be buried as an outcast, and all Rebel leaders should be "consigned to infamy" by something "especially disgraceful" (May 1, p. 4, col. 2). The *Chicago Tribune* was also blunt. Declaring that Davis decreed the assassination and Booth carried it out, an article, "Davis the Assassin," said

> Davis must die the death of a dog; with these and other kindred revelations lighting up his ghastly form, no spot on earth can hide him. His own bloodhounds even, now released from his control, would trash out the demon and tear him to shreds should union men give up the chance. (April. 20, p. 4)

Finally, on April 19, with rhetoric pretty much at its peak, the *Courant* wrote the inevitable:

> And thus, on Good Friday, the anniversary of that other memorable tragedy, when the Lord of glory was slain by the people he had come to save, how the hellish machinations of the rebels, resulted in the murder of him who, in spite of the reviling and obloquy they have heaped upon him, has never written or uttered one word of malice toward them, but has even shown himself their unswerving friend.... (April 19, 1865, page 2)

With Lincoln as Jesus and the Rebels as the people who killed him, these articles in the *Courant, The Times,* and the *Chicago Tribune* represent the most concentrated rhetoric against the Rebels, blaming them for the death of Lincoln and calling for the death of Davis and other leaders. It all came within a week of Lincoln's death. It is not the last of such rhetoric or accusations, but after this release of emotion, with the exception of Lincoln's funeral, the paper turned from concentrating on the Lincoln death, to the search for his killer, which ended with Booth's death.

This coverage alone was a fascinating glimpse into the journalistic and perhaps the American psyche. It says something of the eventual treatment of Davis as well. It seemed important that Booth suffer. Many papers reported that Sergeant Corbett's bullet was too good for the assassin, who should have died a more horrible death. Even so, further accounts in the *Courant* and other papers noted that his particular wound would cause terrible suffering, and that in fact he endured pain almost commensurate with his foul deed. But this burst of coverage died out quickly as papers turned their attention to other matters, including the capture of Davis, the last vestige of the war and, many felt, the assassination.

Davis's Flight

Some psychic part of the Civil War ended for many newspapers on May 10, 1865, in an encampment near Irwinville, Ga. That's when Union troops captured Jefferson Davis, the man whom newspapers for weeks had portrayed as the devil incarnate. And just as speculation had fueled newspaper stories about his involvement in the assassination, speculation fueled stories about his escape and capture. Unfortunately for Davis, the press had worked itself into a frenzy about his involvement with Lincoln's death and seemed obsessed with details of his escape, especially in the speculations that he was carrying vast amounts of gold.

All the threads in the accounts of his escape are difficult to follow in one paper, but impossible in several of them. Each day the *Courant,* for example, reported where he was, often what he was doing and who was with him, his plans and likely destination, and the amount of money or gold he and his entourage carried. The accounts in the *Courant* alone varied impossibly from day to day and never mentioned the sources of information. Nor did they ever correct the previous day's information. Coverage of Davis's attempted escape was a kind of zany, picaresque miscellany of fact and fantasy that had little or no respect for time, space, or reason.

In the papers studied, only the *National Intelligencer* mentioned the contradictions, and that in a sentence preceding yet another bit of "positive information" about his movements. "Many contradictory and wholly unreliable reports concerning the whereabouts of Jeff. Davis at certain times named have found their way into Northern journals" (May 2, p. 1, col. 6), the *Intelligencer* admitted in "Jeff Davis's Flight." That was an incredible understatement.

Over the month or so of the *Courant*'s coverage of the search for Davis, the paper reported him in one location after another from Virginia to Florida to Texas, and believed him to have done everything from raising a huge army in Texas to continue the fight from Mexico to buying a house in Cuba. The *Courant* alone had him covering thousands of miles, in various guises and modes of transportation, with various numbers of backers and amounts of money. The money provides a vivid illustration of this form of speculative news. Just in April, Davis was reported to be in Macon, Ga., with $160,000 of gold in a Savannah bank, to have crossed the Mississippi River, or to have gone to Trans-Mississippi or Europe with $500,000, to have escaped to Mexico or be moving from Goldsboro with six to thirteen million dollars, and finally, in no particular location with $100,000. In May, he was in Greensboro, N.C., with "considerable quantities" of gold (May 8, 1865, page 2), or in Powelton, Hancock County, Ga. Also in May, a $100,000 reward, to be taken from the gold Davis had with him, was offered. One article after the capture said Davis had $100,000 with him, but the May 22 article said he and his whole party had only $8,000 among them.

Of the papers studied, the *National Intelligencer* appeared the most temperate in all its coverage of the end of the war, the assassination, and the killing of Booth. Its coverage of Davis didn't reach fever pitch, but the paper reported frequently his supposed whereabouts. On April 17, the *Intelligencer* and most papers accurately reported him in Danville, Va., where he had issued a letter more than a week before Lincoln was killed saying the Confederacy would never concede to its enemy. On the 24th, Davis had left Danville and was heading to Greensboro, N.C., but if "hard pushed" he'd go to Texas to raise an army and make another stand (April 24, p. 3, col. 3).

The next day, Davis was reported to have a half a million in specie and had gone either to "the Trans-Mississippi Department or Europe" (April 25, p. 2, col. 3). On the 28th and 29th the paper began to assure readers that their information was good. He was reported — corroborated by "authentic intelligence" from a "trustworthy source" (April 29, p. 2, col. 4) — with Johnson's army at Hillsboro, from which he went by rail to Greensboro, where he planned to leave by horseback through Columbia, S.C., to the far South. For once, the paper reported it didn't know if he carried gold. It was, however, "confidently believed" that he'd try to leave the country and "currently reported" that he'd already started for Mexico (April 28, p. 2, col. 6).

By May 2, the paper admitted that previous reports in "Northern journals" were unreliable, but that its own "last positive information" was that Davis had passed through Charlotte on his way South on April 23rd, but since then nothing had been heard from him. Then the article provided a lengthy speculation on what he might do, deciding that he'd try to go to Cuba "in some small vessel or fishing boat from a point on the Florida coast." The article credited "rumor" with placing

> a heavy sum to his bank account in Havana, and if a tithe of the amount be on actual deposit, he will endeavor to obtain it on his way to Europe. So also he is said to be carrying fabulous sums in specie, forcibly extracted from the vaults of Richmond banks. The latter story probably has little foundation in fact. Specie is too heavy for easy and rapid transportation. Its possession would be known to hundreds of persons, and might lead to his detention, robbery or assassination. He can scarcely entertain a wild hope to escape through Wilson's lines to the Mississippi with such an encumbrance, and would find equal difficulty in getting across to Cuba. (May 2, p. 1, col. 6)

On May 4, the paper reported what many other papers reported, that two men had offered $20,000 toward a half a million dollar reward for Davis's capture. Meanwhile the paper still couldn't decide if he was carrying gold. The May 4 paper reported him in Yorkville, with eleven wagons "supposed to contain specie" (May 4, p. 3, col. 3). The next day a letter writer said it was doubtful Davis could be caught because he'd get out of Florida on a little schooner to Nasseau or Havana, or cross the Mississippi and get to Galveston or the Rio Grande. The writer said estimates of gold are from $300,000 to three million dollars, which would likely be taken from him by his own bodyguards or embittered Rebels. But in the same paper, an article reported that Davis had lost all his gold — only $200,000 — in a burning train. For once, a source was provided for this information, a "Colonel Clark," whose "truthfulness is not doubted by any" (May 5, p. 3, col. 4).

Still Davis could not be put to rest. On the 6th the *Intelligencer* decided that Davis could get to Texas and seek a partnership with Maximilian "in the hope that the two moribund institutions — the tattering empire and the collapsed rebellion — may make common cause, and at least secure a decent burial" (May 6, p.2, col. 1). Two days later the paper used a piece from the *Richmond Whig* that said it is unlikely that Davis had any gold at all. The information now is that Davis can't get to Trans-Mississippi and perhaps got out with some Florida blockade runner. Yet, the writer thinks that if "recent information" about Yorkville is right, that Davis is making poor time (May 8, p. 2, col. 3). Mercifully, the *Intelligencer*'s last report on the hunt for Davis, on the next page of the same paper, had Mosby following Davis toward Texas. After Davis was captured, however, the paper printed a letter from the *Savannah Herald* saying Davis had built a house in Liverpool, England, in which he would live were he forced out of the country. The *Herald* editor appended a statement saying the information "may or may not be true" (May 23, p. 3, col. 1).

The *New York Times* had many of the same locations as the *Courant* and the *Intelligencer*. Additionally, however, *The Times* had him in Augusta, Ga., on April 23, and reported that not only did he have the plundered gold from Richmond banks but also large sums of previous accumulations. On April 28, the paper reported that Davis had from $6 million to $13 million. On May 4, *The Times* reported that a passenger recognized Davis on a train to Charlottesville, but realizing that soldiers had cut off the train, Davis escaped. The paper also reported him in Yorkville and Greensboro, where he had to sleep in his cars for three days because residents feared letting him in their dwellings. Finally *The Times*, which probably was as accurate as any of the papers covering Davis, put him in Washington, Ga., and then Arvelton, Hancock County, Ga.

The *Chicago Tribune* and the *New Orleans Picayune* had much the same information as the other papers. The *Tribune* said Davis wanted to found a Trans-Mississippi Confederacy, and variously reported him in Macon, Ashboro, and Cherow, besides the more usual places. He was also reported to have between $3 million and $6 million in gold. Early in the chase, the *Picayune* reported him at Macon with $160,000 in gold and speculated he might try to make a deal with a Northern general to escape to Mexico or Europe. The *Picayune*'s last report on the chase was that Davis had about $300,000 in gold with him and that he had arranged for the ironclad ram Stonewall to enter an East Coast inlet and carry him to safety.

In the end, none of the wilder speculations were true. Robert W. Winston (1930), said Davis had made his way slowly to Greensboro, N.C., by April 10; to Charlotte by April 19; and to Abbeville and Washington, Ga., by May 3. He was captured at Irwinville, Ga., a week later. Winston and many other historians noted that Davis had little money with him and that all the money from Richmond had been legally and properly distributed.

Davis's Capture

The most curious thing about Davis's capture was not rumors and speculations about his whereabouts and the gold he allegedly plundered and carried with him, but the widely disseminated rumors about the circumstances of his arrest. Ironically, they were reminiscent of a similar incident that happened to Abraham Lincoln on the way to his inauguration four years earlier. In each case, the press reported, devastatingly, that the men were dressed in women's clothing to escape detection. Papers used the rumors and reports about Davis to ridicule and even punish. It satisfied a sense of vengeance, much as did the revealing of names and addresses of people accused of being happy, or not unhappy enough, at Lincoln's death. The publication of their names sometimes brought mobs to their homes or businesses, and some were harmed and even killed. Davis's capture seemed to make the journalists giddy. They couldn't get enough of the story of Davis in petticoats and crinoline. Many reports and rumors no doubt originated from the same military and other sources, and were similar through the coverage of several newspapers. But papers included imaginative descriptions, detail, direct quotes, and embellishments of their own.

The *Courant*'s coverage was fairly extensive, as its reports included much of what other papers published. The first report, on May 15, said Davis tried to "escape to the woods in his wife's petticoats, but the sight of his boots betrayed the cheat. ... Comedy and tragedy go hand-in-hand. The late rebel president in petticoats!" (May 15, p. 2). Another *Courant* article claimed that a soldier went to the tent meeting a partially dressed Mrs. Davis who asked that the ladies be allowed to finish dressing.

> Presently there appeared at the door an ostensibly old lady with a basket on her arm, escorted by Mrs. Davis and her sister: "Please let my old mother go to the spring to get some water to wash in," said Mrs. Jeff. in a pleading tone. "It strikes me that your mother wears very big boots," said the guard, as he hoisted the old lady's dress with his sabre and discovered a pair of No. 13 calfskins, and "whiskers, too," said the sergeant, as he pulled a hood from the face and lo! Jeff Davis stood before them. (May 22, p. 2)

The Washington D.C. *Intelligencer* and *The New York Times* reported much the same scenario, but with different quotes and other details.

An *Intelligencer* report originating with the military said Davis was endeavoring to escape in "his wife's clothes" after he heard gunfire, which warned him of approaching soldiers.

> He hastily put on one of his wife's dresses and started for the woods, closely pursued by our men, who at first thought him a woman, but seeing his boots while running, suspected his sex at once.
>
> The chase was a short one and the Rebel President was soon brought to bay. He brandished a bowie-knife of elegant pattern, and showed signs of battle, but yielded promptly to the persuasion of the Colt's revolvers without compelling the men to fire. . . .
>
> Mrs. Davis remarked to Col. Harden, after the excitement was over, that the men had better not provoke the President, or he might hurt some of them. (May 15, p. 3, col. 4)

The *New Orleans Picayune* reported similarly that Davis had "hastily put on one of his wife's dresses" (May 20, p. 1, col. 7). The *New York Times*, calling Davis "the petticoat hero," also said (in "DAVIS TAKEN!") he drew a bowie knife but relented when "one of our boys presented a revolver, muzzle first, at the Lord of Chivalry (in petticoats) and Jeff, in the language of lesser rogues, 'came down'" (May 13, p. 4, col. 1). Later, in "Davis & Co.," it reported that he had on his wife's clothing, a hood over his face, and a bucket on his arm. It said his wife asked that her "poor old mother" be allowed to get some water, but an alert guard spotted the boots. The *Times* account was detailed.

> It appears that, during the fighting, Mrs. Davis had arrayed her husband in her own dress, put on him her hood and tied her scarf about his head so as to conceal his face completely. When thus disguised the late President of the Confederacy bore a decided resemblance to an old woman. Mrs. Davis took one of his arms and Mrs. Davis's sister the other, and thus, apparently supporting the tattering steps of the old lady, attempted to make away from the scene of conflict into a neighboring swamp.
> Four of Pritchard's men stopped the two however, when a piteous appeal was made to them by the pseudo-daughter to allow them to conduct their poor old mother out of the range of the bullets. One of the soldiers promptly replied that he 'couldn't see it — that they were after Jeff. Davis, he was here somewhere, and they meant to have him.' ... [H]e took off the hood, and instead of an old lady, found the well-known features of Jeff. Davis beneath it. (May 21, p. 1, col. 2, 3)

The *Chicago Tribune* on May 15 unfavorably compared Davis to Lincoln, extensively discussed his cowardice, and emphasized his capture in a woman's dress and crinoline. Another article, similar to that of the *Courant*, said he was captured in petticoats, betrayed by his boots. On the 23rd, the paper, in "Full Particulars of the Capture of the Old Lady," again repeated much of what the *Courant* and other papers had reported. In part, that Davis was "betrayed by his whiskers and No. 13 boots" and that Mrs. Davis tried to pass him off as her "old mother."

Several of the papers became more playful after the capture. The *Tribune* reported that the secretary of war had promised to loan the Chicago Fair the dress and shirt worn by Davis at the time of his capture. The paper also offered a Page 1 illustration of Davis in petticoats, illustrating what he looked like at his capture (May 20, p. 1). The *Courant* reported that two Chicago men were after Davis's frock for the Northwestern Fair, and "a lady" wrote on May 24 that tax problems could be solved if Davis could be exhibited in a cage. "Let Barnum do it. Then let him meditate on his crimes, or hang him" (May 24, p. 2). Another woman made a hangman's rope of South Carolina hemp and forwarded to Washington. "The maker of the rope wishes to have it speedily used" (May 26, p. 2). The paper reported that Davis fought and kicked when put into irons, and that he was encased in a "living tomb" — two rooms, with guards inside and out, and not allowed to speak to anyone (May 27, p. 2).

Several of the papers seemed to have dropped the issue of the money after the capture. The *Courant,* which commented as much as any paper during the chase about the money Davis carried, never decided how much it was, although none of the post-capture figures remotely approached the paper's earlier estimations. After the capture, articles claimed he had from $8,000 to $100,000. The smaller figure was the last one reported, on May 22. Davis, in a book he eventually wrote about the Confederacy, dismissed the money issue in a sentence: "A silly story had got abroad that it was a treasure-train" (Davis, 1958, p. 701).

And, of the several papers examined, only one admitted that Davis may not have been wearing a dress after all. The *Times,* despite its continued insistence that Davis be executed, reprinted an article from The *Macon Telegraph* describing the capture. It differed from most of the other accounts in that it described Davis's actions as honorable and said he was well treated and treated others well. The *Times* noted, "It will be observed that this report says nothing of Davis putting on his wife's clothes and attempting to escape in that disguise" (May 25, p. 8). A May 26 *Times* article reported that Davis was captured in a "waterproof cloak and shawl," not his wife's dress. It said the cloak was worn as "sort of a shirt" (p. 5).

Conclusions

These last *Times* articles probably got closer to the truth, but by that time, cartoonists and writers had worked the dress stories too much for more accurate stories to be very influential. Some people believe that Davis was captured in women's clothes, but most historians don't. Still, combing histories and accounts of the Davis capture is similar to perusing the newspapers of the day. They all agree that he was captured, that he was in the tent with Mrs. Davis before walking toward a wooded area in an attempt to escape, and that he was clothed. Beyond that, details vary.

History has the perspective that journalism lacks, but it often comes from the same human sources. And human witness is affected by all the selective processes that theorists say makes people unique or that contributes to social construction of reality. Historians and others offering accounts of the Davis capture are often less speculative and sensationalistic than the press accounts; for example, they don't dress Davis in hoop skirts and crinoline. It is clear that both historical and journalistic accounts rely on what people said happened, and to that extent they are both speculative. Perhaps speculation is so prominent in both history and journalism because facts are so difficult, if not impossible, to establish.

Based on just the sources used for this paper, the most likely scenario is that Davis, wearing a gray suit, slept in the tent with his wife the night before his capture. He stayed the night because he heard that Confederate renegades had attacked several parties in the area and he thought he might be of some influence if they confronted his group. Gunfire awoke him in the early, misty (if not rainy) morning. Discovering it was federal troops, he determined (and perhaps his wife urged him) to try to escape. His horse was a short distance away, toward a wooded area. Once he decided to go, he grabbed a raglan, a sleeveless water-proof coat, thinking it was his, but, in fact, it was his wife's, although the two had few differences. As he stepped out of the tent, his wife, to protect him from the dampness and cold, threw a shawl over his head and shoulders. He was captured moments later as he walked toward his horse. Soldiers apparently broke open various trunks and among the spoils was one of Mrs. Davis's hoop skirts.

Most historical accounts of the capture vary only in detail from this sequence of events and in most the wording is the same or quite similar to that offered by Jefferson Davis in his books on the Confederacy.

> As it was quite dark in the tent I picked up what was supposed to be my "raglan," a water-proof, light overcoat, without sleeves; it was subsequently found to be my wife's, so very like my own as to be mistaken for it. As I started, my wife thoughtfully threw over my head and shoulders a shawl. (Davis, 1958, p. 701)

Robert Winston (1930), Cass Canfield (c1978), Clement Eaton (1977), Hudson Strode (1955-56), Allen Tate (1929), and William C. Davis (1991) all said he was captured in a raglan and a shawl. E.B. Long and Barbara Long (1971) said it was a "waterproof raincoat" and shawl; John William Jones (1890), a waterproof cloak or robe and a shawl; Armisted C. Gordon (1918), a waterproof cloak; and Edward A. Pollard (1869) and Robert Penn Warren (1980), a shawl. Francis Trevelyan Miller's photographic account of the war (1912) depicted him in what "he wore when he was captured." The picture showed him in a velvet-collared coat to above the knees, pants, and high black boots. Some accounts from the 1800s gave some credence to the dress story (McClure, 1994/1878), although at least one says the petticoats were a newspaper invention.

In his "The American Conflict: A History of the Great Rebellion," Horace Greeley provided the following account of Davis's capture from a statement by Lt. C.E.L. Stuart. It is similar to Davis's account, and it corrected the press coverage of petticoats and crinoline, but embellished some of the detail.

> In a moment, she caught an idea — a woman's idea — and, as quickly as women in an emergency execute their designs, it was done. He slept in a wrapper — a loose one. It was yet around him. This she fastened, ere he was aware of it, and then bidding his adieu, urged him to go to the spring, a short distance off, where his horses and arms were .... As he was leaving the door, followed by a servant with a water-bucket, Miss Howell flung a shawl over his head. There was no time to remove it without exposure and embarrassment; and as he had not far to go, he ran the chance exactly as it was devised for him. In these two articles consisted the woman's attire of which so much nonsense has been spoken and written .... No bonnet, no gown, no petticoats, no crinoline — nothing of these. (1856, p. 756)

Some history book accounts mention newspapers directly or indirectly, usually blaming them for spreading the "dress" story. Guy Lee Carlton (1903) said the woman's apparel story was "cowardly" and "proved to be a deliberate fabrication" (p. 406). It seems clear that several things were newspaper fabrications, either deliberate or as part of rumor and speculation, which, at the time, were often considered part of the record of the day. Although darker motives were suggested for why the press created and continued to disseminate, sometimes gleefully, the descriptions and illustrations of Davis dressed as a woman.

John William Jones in an admittedly pro-Davis memorial volume, reprinted an undated article from the *Maine Argus* and excerpts from a speech made after Davis's death, each originating from participants in the capture. James H. Parker said in the *Argus*, "when it was known he was certainly taken, some newspaper correspondent — I knew his name at the time — fabricated the story about his disguise in old woman's dress" (Jones, 1890, 401-402). In the speech, T.H. Peabody said, "The story of the 'hoop skirt, sun bonnet and calico wrapper' had no real existence, and was started in the fertile brain of the reporters and in the illustrated papers of the day" (Jones, 1890, 404). Armistead C. Gordon (1918) said the "mendacious and silly story" was originated by "a sensational newspaper correspondent, through Wilson's official report to Stanton of May 14, in which he stated he had derived it from his captors ... " (p. 253). Hudson Strode (1955-56) said the North, remembering the treatment its papers gave Lincoln for entering Washington disguised for his first inauguration

> wished to attach a worse humiliation to Davis. It was some time after that the fiction was concocted and used to hold the ex-President of the Confederacy up to national ridicule. The story of Davis attempting to escape in woman's dress, carrying bags of gold, was intended as propaganda to inflame the credulous mob, not the intelligent Northerner. He was to be pictured in cartoons running through bush and briar in cumbrous hoop skirt. One would draw him cavorting in hoops, while melodramatically brandishing a dagger. The great Barnum would present him to the public in mocking tableaux. (p. 222)

And Jones (1890) said near the end of the century it "seems hard to get Northern writers even now to refrain from the sensational slanders which were manufactured at the time" (p. 401).

Parker, in his *Argus* article, said although he thought Davis deserved all the contempt that could be put upon him, he spoke out against the falsehood that Davis was dressed in women's clothes because he would "never perpetuate a falsehood that by any means would become history" (401-402). Despite Corporal Parker's intentions, the dress incident, indeed, has become part of history. It may all have originated with a single newspaper correspondent, perhaps from one of the New York papers. But it took only a little time to be disseminated throughout the country, North and South, and it lives today in history books, works of fiction, and memoirs, including one by writer and poet Robert Penn Warren, who, somewhat sympathetic to Davis, also noted that the incident took on even further life when it, "staged as a comic skit, was to enrich P. T. Barnum and flatter the hearts of patriots" (1980, p, 71).

While illustrating newspapers' use of speculation and rumor, it also illustrates the news media's power to define an incident, issue, or person. Davis was defined in the press about as negatively as he could be. While much of the venom came after Lincoln's assassination, The *New York Times*, for example, from 1863 to the end of the war, as quoted in Craven (c1987), depicted Davis

> as a murderer, a cruel slaveholder whose servants all ran away, a liar, a boaster, a fanatic, a confessed failure, a hater, a political adventurer, a supporter of outcasts and outlaws, a drunkard, an atrocious misrepresenter, an assassin, an incendiary, a criminal who was gratified by the assassination of Lincoln, a henpecked husband, a man so shameless that he would try to escape by disguising himself as a woman, a supporter of murder plots, an insubordinant soldier, an unwholesome sleeper, and a malingerer. (p. xiv)

The *Courant* also directly attacked Davis's character, but it was more rhetorical and less sustained than The *Times*' attacks. For example, one *Courant* article said he was "ungrateful to friends, cruel to enemies, ambitious, implacable and bloodthirsty" and, finally, "hunted down like a mad dog" (May 16, p. 2). The *Intelligencer* was far more forgiving, saying he was "proud, firm, adroit, willful, purposeful," playing "boldly and ably and bravely for a mean, pitiful stake." He lost it, however, like "an adventurer," not a hero or statesman, and he wasted lives in the process (May 15, p. 3, col. 4). The *Chicago Tribune* called him a "traitor, knave and a coward" (May 15, p. 1, col. 4).

These characterizations, constantly repeated, essentially defined Davis for much of the country and, to some extent, defined and continue to define how he is seen in history. 1860s' newspapers, as today's, often didn't "correct" exaggerated and even mistaken accounts. They frequently supplemented one rumor or mistake with another. Impressions linger, sometimes for years or even decades. The perjury of the people that accused Davis of participation in Lincoln's assassination had nothing of the play and passion of the speculations and rumors that Davis was responsible for Lincoln's death. The evidence that Davis and his entourage carried no stolen millions looted from Richmond banks was, in fact, not mentioned by many papers, despite the weeks of pre-capture rumor and speculation about ever-increasing amounts of gold. And few papers corrected the mistaken impressions that he had been captured in petticoats.

Federal troops captured Davis and took him to Fortress Monroe. Despite certainty in scores of Northern and other papers that Davis somehow participated in the Lincoln assassination, the case fell apart immediately as his chief accusers admitted to making up the story. The attempted prosecution of Davis for other crimes, including treason, was complex and feeble, although lengthy, and in early 1869 the case was dismissed altogether. Surviving ill health caused in part by his imprisonment, he lived twenty more years, dying Dec. 6, 1889, in New Orleans.

Davis continues to be a source of fascination today, as evidenced in part by several sites on the World Wide Web. He is used by some as a symbol for historical and contemporary mistreatment of the South, southerners, and southern culture at the hands of a biased North that refuses to forgive Davis and all southerners for their Civil War era actions (McWhiney, 1997).

What is clear from the Davis story is that not so much has changed. The press still gets caught up in the emotions of big stories, especially those that involve war, assassination, and major triumphs or tragedies. While the press cannot be held responsible for all opinions about and attitudes toward Davis, then or now, its story of Davis's capture, fueled by emotion and revenge, consisted of speculation and rumor that laid a foundation for much of what has been since thought and written about the Confederate president.

Notes

Canfield, C. (1978). *The iron will of Jefferson Davis*. New York: Harcourt Brace Jovanovich.
Craven, J. J. (1987). *"Fiction distorting fact": The prison life (of Jefferson Davis)*. Macon, Ga.: Mercer University Press.
Davis, J. (1958) *Rise and fall of the Confederate government*, Vol. 2. New York: Thomas Yoseloff/Sagimore Press.
Davis, W. C. (1991). *Jefferson Davis: The man and his hour*. New York: HarperCollins Publishers.
Eaton, C. (1977). *Jefferson Davis*. New York: The Free Press.Gordon, Armistead Churchill (1918). *Jefferson Davis*. New York: C. Scribner's Sons.
Greeley, H. (1866). *The American conflict: A history of the great rebellion*, Vol. II, Hartford: O.C. Case & Co.
Jones, J. W. (1890). *The Davis memorial volume; or, our dead president, Jefferson Davis, and the world's tribute to his memory*. Richmond, Va.: B.F. Johnson.
Lee, G.C. (1903). *The true history of the Civil War*. Philadelphia: J. Lippencott.
Long, E.B. and Long, B. (1971). *The Civil War day by day, an almanac, 1861-1865*.

Garden City, N.Y.: Doubleday & Co. Inc.
McClure, Alexander Kelly (Ed.) (1994). *The annals of the Civil War / written by leading participants North and South.* New York: Da Capo Press.
McWhiney, G. (1997) "Jefferson Davis: Our greatest American hero." A speech, as published on the WWW: http://www.pointsouth.com/csanet/ greatmen/davis/davis.htm.
Miller, F. T., (Ed.) (1912). *The photographic history of the Civil War,* vol. 9. N.Y.: The Review of Reviews Co.
Pollard, E. A. (1869). *Life of Jefferson Davis: With a secret history of the Southern Confederacy ... .* Philadelphia, Pa.: National Publishing Company.
Strode, H. (1955-56). *Jefferson Davis.* New York: Harcourt, Brace.
Tate, A. (1929). *Jefferson Davis: his rise and fall, a biographical narrative.* New York: Minton, Balch & Company.
Warren, R. P. (1980). *Jefferson Davis gets his citizenship back.* Lexington, Ky.: University of Kentucky Press.
Werstein, I. (1959). *Abraham Lincoln versus Jefferson Davis.* New York: Crowell.
Winston, R. W. (1930). *High stakes and hair triggers: The life of Jefferson Davis.* New York: Henry Holt and Co.

NEWSPAPERS
Chicago Tribune, Chicago, Ill., April and May, 1865.
National Intelligencer, Washington, D.C., April and May, 1865.
The New York Times, New York, N. Y., April and May, 1865.
New Orleans Picayune, New Orleans, La., April and May, 1865.
Yorkville Enquirer, Yorkville, S.C., April and May, 1865.
Hartford Courant, Hartford, Conn, April and May, 1865.

WEBSITES
The Papers of Jefferson Davis Home Page: http://www.ruf.rice.edu/~pjdavis/sdp.htm
The Jefferson Davis Memorial Home Page: http://www.pointsouth.com/csanet/greatmen/davis/davis.htm

25

Journalistic Impedimenta: William Tecumseh Sherman and Free Expression

John Glen
Principia College

"A cat in hell without claws is nothing compared to a reporter in Sherman's army."
Elias Smith, Reporter
New York *Herald*

Essential elements of a free democratic republic may undergo direct frontal assaults during a civil war. The right of habeas corpus can, under the correct circumstances, be abridged. The executive branch of the government might raise, equip and engage thousands of armed volunteers in battle without the consent of Congress. Amazingly enough, in the midst of the uncivil war in America, a Presidential election actually took place. Also, as every American knows (or should know) the Bill of Rights guarantees that "Congress shall make no law.. .abridging the freedom of speech, or of the press..." The framers of that document did not mean to infer that these rights could or should be set aside for the duration of a war. William Tecumseh Sherman held the opposite view. Sherman felt that a victorious war could be conducted only by professional soldiers unhampered by the damaging interference of a civilian press. Any society which encourages a free press, especially during civil war, clearly will face challenges to the safeguards of that freedom. This paper will examine Sherman's relations with the Forth Estate over the period 1861-1865 and attempt to conclude why his feelings were so bellicose.

The problem was essentially one of "high tech." Just as the Napoleonic tactics of the general officers often did not keep pace with the sophisticated weaponry (i.e. rifled muskets) of the era; so the advent of the modern printing press, telegraph and railroad made this the beginning of the information age. Newspaper reporters still "getting the story" now put the lives of the men in uniforms at risk since "the story" could now be so widely and rapidly disseminated.

By way of example, the *New York Times* reported on 17 July 1861 that "the army in Virginia today took up the line of march for Richmond via Fairfax and Manassas. The force starting out today was fully fifty thousand strong."[1]

When the enemy is informed of the other side's strength and route of movement, it gives that enemy a decided advantage and amounts to military intelligence. Whoever disseminates that intelligence to the enemy could, by definition, be labeled a spy. In this case that amounts to the newspaper.

Four days after the *Times* published the report above, Sherman led his brigade forward at Manassas, Virginia, and drove the rebels from Matthews Hill to Henry House Hill. At that point Sherman's force encountered Confederate General Thomas Jackson's brigade "standing like a stonewall." The Federal advance was stalled and soon in full retreat. Sherman wrote, "I have read of retreats before, have seen the noise and confusion of crowds of men at fires and shipwrecks, but nothing like this. It was as disgraceful as words can portray."[2]

Tecumseh Sherman was born on 8 Feb. 1820 in Lancaster, Ohio. Sherman's father, Judge Charles Sherman, died when the boy was 9, and Tecumseh was parceled out to the home of famous politician, Thomas Ewing, a close friend of Judge Sherman's. Sherman's first name of William was added when he was baptized into Catholicism on St. William's Day. Only five other cadets finished ahead of Sherman in the United States Military Academy's class of 1840. While many Civil War officers gained a chance to get "on-the-job training" during the Mexican War, Sherman spent 1846-1848 on recruitment duty in Pittsburgh, Pennsylvania, and Zanesville, Ohio.[3]

In 1850 Sherman married Ellen Ewing, thereby making Thomas Ewing both his foster-father as well as his new father-in-law. Three years later he resigned his army commission for unsuccessful careers in banking, law, business and education. Although he remained a strong Union man, his impressionable years spent in the company of many Southerners at West Point had left him with much sympathy for Dixie.

In 1860 he became the first superintendent of the newly established Louisiana State Seminary, but the appointment was short-lived. He resigned in1861 to command a brigade in Irvin McDowell's Army of the Potomac when Louisiana seceded from the Union.[4]

For the two weeks following what Sherman labeled the "shameless flight of the armed mob" at Manassas, Sherman expected to be discharged along with the other leaders. Instead, he was promoted to brigadier general of volunteers and ordered to become second-in-command to Brigadier General Robert Anderson, hero of Ft. Sumter, then in Kentucky. [5]

Sherman gives historians a glimpse of his views on professionalism when he wrote, "I never did like to serve with volunteers, because instead of being governed, they govern... The volunteers, with their unbridled will are killing hogs, cattle, and taking hay and wheat, all calculated to turn the people against us."[6]

Anderson soon resigned his post, leaving the Department of the Cumberland under Sherman's control. Horace Greeley's *New York Tribune*, a staunchly pro-Republican paper "but as independently cantankerous as its famous editor,"[7] reported on October, 1861, "General Sherman now has at least twenty thousand men in the various camps between this city and Green River, and reinforcements arrive almost daily." The paper then went on to name the reinforcing units. Sherman expected Albert Sydney Johnston, whom he called "a real general" to attack at any time. "Had he done so, he could have walked into Louisville, and the vital part of the population would have hailed him as a deliverer."[8]

At about the same time Sherman received notice by telegraph that the Secretary of War, Simon Cameron, would pay him a visit as he returned from St. Louis to Washington, D.C. At the lunch meeting at Sherman's residence, the Galt House, the Secretary asked the General, matter-of-factly, how things were going. Sherman responded that things were going poorly, "as bad as bad could be."[9] Cameron thereupon asked Sherman to be more specific, "Now General Sherman, tell us of your troubles." Sherman was hesitant but Cameron insisted and attempted to reassure the recalcitrant general. "These are all my friends, all members of my family, and you may speak your mind freely and without restraint."[10] included in the Secretary's "family" was reporter Samuel Willarson of the *New York Tribune,* who was not identified to Sherman as a reporter, and who was allowed to sit in on the discussion of Kentucky's military situation.[11]

Sherman first told Cameron that he needed sixty thousand troops to clear Kentucky of insurgents and two hundred thousand to go on the offensive. Apparently Cameron misunderstood and thought Sherman was asking for two hundred thousand men in order to keep Kentucky from seceding. "Great God, where are they to come from?" questioned Cameron. The Secretary promised reinforcements but clearly felt the number absurd.[12]

The report of Cameron's trip was published in the *Tribune* on 30 Oct. It contained the so-called "Exhibit No.14" which explained the Union army strength in Kentucky in detail. Additionally, it contained an account of the Sherman-Cameron meeting, concluding that Sherman's manpower requests were ridiculous.[13] There is also evidence that Cameron regarded Sherman as "unbalanced" following their conference. Professor J. Cutler Andrews asserts that the press was "watching for a chance to discredit their red-headed tormentor," and calls the entire scenario an example of "the press campaign against Sherman."[14] Professor John F. Marszalek feels the incident to have been the turning point in the newspaper treatment of Sherman. He wrote, "criticism now began to appear where previously there had been mostly praise."[15]

Sherman felt terribly embarrassed when he read about the incident. He continued to complain to Washington about the size of his force in relation to the rebels. Andrews calls him "obsessed" with the idea that he was vastly outnumbered.[16] For three successive days he telegraphed McClellan demanding assistance, reinforcements, suggesting a retreat from Kentucky and castigating both Kentuckians and the administration for their indifference. He wrote Ellen that "the idea of going down in history with a fame such as threatens me nearly makes me crazy, indeed I may be so now."[17] McClellan, concerned over Sherman's ability to command, sent Colonel Thomas M. Key to speak to Sherman. Key's report advised McClellan that "Sherman's mind was too unsteady for command."[18] Assistant Secretary of War Thomas Scott put it more bluntly saying, "Sherman's gone in the head, he's loony."[19] Sherman was ordered to St. Louis to report to General Henry W. Halleck while Don Carlos Buell replaced him in Kentucky.

Sherman took a twenty-day leave to go home to Lancaster, Ohio, in December, 1861. His recovery suffered a setback upon reading the *Cincinnati Commercial* headline, which proclaimed "General William T. Sherman Insane." The article went on to state that Sherman, while commanding in Kentucky had gone "stark mad," and that he had been relieved when commanders became aware of his mental imbalance. The *Commercial* article concluded with, "it seems providential that the country has not to mourn the loss of an army through the loss of the mind of a general into whose hands was committed the vast responsibility of the command in Kentucky." Newspapers all over the country picked up the story. *Frank Leslie's Illustrated* wrote: "General Sherman, who lately commanded in Kentucky, is said to be insane. It is charitable to think so."[20]

Professor Marszalek suggested a possible motive for the vindictiveness of the press. "What better way to get rid of an anti-press general than by capitalizing on his eccentricities and accuse him of insanity?"[21] If the newspapers were plotting Sherman's complete elimination from the war they failed. Following impassioned personal pleas to President Lincoln by Ellen Sherman and Thomas Ewing, Sherman was returned to "light duty" about one month prior to seeing combat again at Shiloh.

At Shiloh it was Ulysses Grant who bore the brunt of the reporters' wrath, and Sherman's daring and bravery brought him into a far better light. Halleck's dispatches to Washington included the following: "It is the unanimous opinion here that Brigadier General William Tecumseh Sherman saved the fortune of the day on the sixth and contributed largely to the glorious victory on the seventh."[22]

Whitelaw Reid, famous reporter for the *Cincinnati Gazette*, and one who had promoted the insanity charges earlier, now praised the General's battlefield activities. "Whatever might be his faults or neglects . . . no one could accuse him of lack of gallantry and energy when the attack was made on his raw division."[23]

Rather than enjoy his new-found acclaim from the press, Sherman instead lashed out at the reporters for their treatment of Grant, his close friend. Sherman called newspapermen the "most contemptible race of men that existed, cowardly, cringing, hanging around, gathering their material out of the most polluted sources."[24] Sometime later he wrote Ellen regarding his journalistic adversaries calling them "dirty newspaper scribblers who have the impudence of Satan." He warned that if any reporters entered his camp they would be arrested, charged with spying, "tried by court martial and if possible shot or hung."[25] Referring to Shiloh, he is alleged to have responded proudly, "Grant stood by me when I was crazy, and I stood by him when he was drunk."26

As part of a reorganization effort, Sherman was next assigned as military governor of Memphis, Tennessee. There he was to continue to be confrontational with the press. Although Memphis had been held by the Union since June, 1862, her newspapers were openly sympathetic to the southern cause. Most defiant was the *Memphis Appeal*, which soon left town but continued to publish from its new home in Grenada, Mississippi. Without fanfare Sherman informed local editors that they would be held strictly accountable for any printed stories which Sherman felt were detrimental to the war effort. However, since Memphis was not an army camp, reporters were readily assimilated into the civilian populace and Sherman's efforts to control them were thus hampered.27

In August, 1862, Sherman received an order he could obey with glee: arrest a reporter! Grant ordered the imprisonment of the *Chicago Times* Memphis correspondent Warren P. Isham (who was also brother-in-law of the *Times'* editor, Wilbur Storey). Isham's crime was authorship of an article Grant felt was both "false in fact and mischievous in character."28 "Sherman arrested Isham with obvious delight," recounts Dr. Marszalek.29 Isham spent the next 90 days incarcerated in Illinois. Sherman wrote Grant he was pleased to punish a reporter since he "regarded all these newspaper harpies as spies, and they should be punished as such. "30

Later that same month Sherman had the editor/publisher of the *Union Appeal,* Samuel Sawyer, arrested for "false and libelous publication." Marszalek argues that this arrest was motivated not by the publication of military secrets but rather a personal attack on the press in general and this newspaperman in particular, and as such clearly violated the First Amendment. Sawyer's malicious article was critical of the conduct of some Union soldiers. Sherman's defense was that a published report such as Sawyer's was detrimental to overall morale. "Any criticism of the war aided the enemy," argued Sherman.31

In December, 1862, Grant and Sherman met near Oxford, Mississippi, to plan an assault on the rebel stronghold at Vicksburg. Grant, Sherman, and General Nathaniel Banks were to make coordinated attacks on the bastion with Sherman's effort concentrated on the enemy right near an area called Chickasaw Bayou. 32 The coordinated attacks of Grant and Banks were anything but that, and Sherman's force was repulsed when he made what amounted to a solo thrust.

In order to insure what Sherman felt were his best chances for success, he issued General Order No.8 which forbade civilians (except the transport crews) from accompanying the army. Anyone writing anything for publication about the effort would be arrested with the charge of spying. Initially the reporters were incredulous, but Sherman was adamant. Unfortunately for Sherman his ban on reporters was violated and accounts of the failure at Chickasaw Bayou appeared in print on 12 Jan 1863: "General Sherman's repulse was complete."33 The reporters were, of course, unaware of the three-pronged plan and thus placed full blame on Sherman. The insanity charge even resurfaced. *New York Times* correspondent Franc B. Wilkie editorialized:

> Had the commanding General W. T. Sherman and his staff spent half the time and enterprise in the legitimate operations of their present undertaking, that they have in bullying correspondents, overhauling mailbags and prying into private correspondence, the country would not now have the shame of knowing that we have lately experienced one of the greatest and most disgraceful defeats of the war.34

The next day Wilkie added that Sherman had "insane ambition."35

Wilkie was not alone in his crimination of Sherman's Chickasaw Bayou fiasco. The *New York Herald* correspondent Thomas W. Knox was also journalistically critical. Sherman's staff intercepted Knox's reports of the debacle. Knox found out about this intrusion into his mail, angrily rewrote his dispatches, took an army steamer to Cairo, Illinois, and filed the report without further interference. Knox again made mention of the insanity claim and called for Sherman's dismissal. Irritated by the criticism, Sherman wrote his brother John:

> Now, to every army and almost every general a newspaper reporter goes along, filling up our transports, swelling our trains, reporting our progress, guessing at places, picking up dropped expressions, inciting jealousy and discontent, and doing infinite mischief...36

Sherman called Knox to task once the newspaperman returned from Cairo. His explanation infuriated Sherman all the more. "Of course, General Sherman, I had no feeling against you personally, but you are regarded as the enemy of our set, and we must in self-defense write you down."37

Sherman wrote Senator Ewing in February:

> ... I am catching balls and bullets in front and curses and malediction of the

nonthinking herd behind. The Newspapers declare me their inveterate Enemy and openly say they will write me down. In writing me down are they not writing the Cause and the Country down?. . . No matter how rapidly we move, our enemy has notice in advance. To them more than any other cause do I trace the many failures that attend our army... Never had an enemy a better corps of spies than our army carries along, paid, transported, and fed by the United States.38

At about the same time as the Vicksburg failure, Sherman was replaced by Major General John McClernand. Apparently this commander change was political in nature and was at Lincoln's behest, not as a result of the Vicksburg defeat. Reporters were as elated as Sherman was downcast. The general decided to retaliate. He ordered Knox court-martialled. By so doing he was attempting to silence the entire press corps since it was obvious that Wilkie or virtually any other antagonistic reporter could just as easily been chosen. Sherman wrote Admiral David Dixon Porter that he was simply attempting to "establish the principle that such people cannot attend our armies, in violation of our orders, defy us by publishing their garbled statements and defaming officers who are doing their best."39 (One wonders if he was referring to himself as one of the officers doing his best?)

Knox's trial began in February, 1863, at Young's Point, Louisiana, Sherman's base camp. The correspondent was charged with: 1) Giving intelligence to the enemy; 2) Being a spy; and 3) Disobedience of an order. Knox pleaded not guilty to all three. Sherman was the prosecution's only witness and indeed its entire case. Knox's attorney, Lt. Col. W. B. Woods, argued his client's innocence due to the fact that he had a pass signed by General Grant which authorized him to travel with the army and report on its activities, and therefore could not be in violation of Sherman's order. Knox wrote his own final argument which Woods read to the court. After four days of deliberation, the court found Knox not guilty of charges one and two but guilty of disobeying an order, with punishment being expulsion from the lines of the Army of Tennessee and ordered not to return. 40

The *New York Herald,* an occasional favorite of Lincoln's, immediately appealed the sentence. The President agreed to countermand the punishment on the condition that Grant agreed. He did not. Grant advised Knox that his only recourse was to get Sherman's consent to stay among the soldiers. Knox wrote Sherman, "I should be pleased to receive your assent in the present subject matter..." and expressed "regret at the want of harmony between portions of the Army and the Press."41 Sherman's response was less than cordial:

> Come with sword or musket in your hand, prepared to share with us our fate, in sunshine and storm, in prosperity and adversity, in plenty and scarcity and I will welcome you as brother and associate. But come as you now do expecting me to ally the honor and reputation of my country and my fellow soldiers with you, as the representative of the press, which you yourself say makes so slight a difference between truth and falsehood, and my answer is, Never.

The incidents outlined above are by no means the extent of the Sherman press battles. More strife occurred in Memphis, during the siege of Vicksburg, and during the campaign from Chattanooga to Atlanta to Savannah where Sherman successfully blacked out news coverage. When Sherman entered Atlanta in early September, 1864, the press was jubilant. It was a masterful success politically and virtually reassured Abraham Lincoln's reelection that November. Sherman was again roasted by the press during his surrender negotiations with Joseph E. Johnston. By and large, however, once he began his string of successful crusades, the battles with the press ebbed to a near trickle. Sherman wrote his half-brother Phil Ewing: "I still threaten the newspapermen with instant death as spies and they give me a wide berth. They manage to go along, but not in that dictatorial way they used to. They are meek and humble enough..."42

Sherman believed that any war news, no matter how trivial, aided the enemy, and therefore none at all should appear in print. He believed further that total censorship was consistent with waging war effectively.43 He wrote, "Napoleon himself would have been defeated with a free press."44 He labeled reporters the "buzzards of the press" and made every effort to exclude them from his army.45 Whenever he was in trouble, the actual culprit was the reporters. He wrote in his Memoirs:

> Yet so greedy are the people at large for war news, that it is doubtful whether any army commander can exclude all reporters, without bringing down on himself a clamor that may imperil his own safety. Time and moderation must bring a just solution to this modern difficulty. 46

Some historians have labeled Sherman the first "modern" warrior. His "march to the sea" did include elements of total war, that is to say, of more than one professional army doing battle with a second. In the Atlanta to Savannah campaign Sherman urged his soldiers to "forage liberally off the land" and attempted to bring civilians and their will to contest this war into the conflict. Perhaps then in his nearly four-year battle with the press, he saw military professionalism being challenged by correspondents who were free to do their job in a way that at times made his more difficult. And while it is true that in wartime, First Amendment rights can be and are restricted in a manner not permitted in peacetime, the really confusing thing is that Sherman advocated eliminating one of the basic freedoms that made up the Federal government for which he fought.

Interestingly enough, however, current authors James L. McDonough in *Hell Before Night,* and Wiley Sword in *Shiloh, Bloody Shiloh* are both critical of Sherman during that engagement. Further, Col. Thomas Worthington, one of Sherman's regimental commanders was so severely critical that Sherman retaliated by having him court-martialed![47]

- Sawyer was released on $1,000 bail and any trial or result thereof is unknown according to Dr. Marszalek.[48]
- Wilkie also libeled Sherman adjutant Col. J. H. Hammond with a threatened duel the result. Cooler heads apparently prevailed and mediation was the result instead of bloodshed.[49]
- Knox moved on to the Eastern theater of the war and reported on numerous other engagements including Gettysburg. Knox's court-martial is the only recorded one of a newsman in American history.[50] Sherman omits the episode from his Memoirs.

Notes

1. AHM, Aug.'87, 25.
2. Sherman, William T. *Memoirs of William T. Sherman*, 2 vols. (New York: Norton, 1987), 151.
3. Marszalek, John F. *Sherman's Other War.* (Memphis: Memphis State University Press, 1981), 26.
4. AHM, Aug.'87, 25.
5. Sherman, 193.
6. AHM, Aug.'87, 26.
7. _____. *The Fate of Liberty.* (New York: Oxford University Press, 1991), 107.
8. Sherman, Vol. 1, 200.
9. *Ibid.*, 201.
10. *Ibid.,* 202.
11. *Ibid.*
12. *Ibid.*, 161.
13. AHM, Aug.'87, 27.
14. Andrews, J. Cutler. *The North Reports the Civil War.* (Pittsburge: University of Pittsburgh Press, 1955), 116.
15 Marszalek, 60.
16. Andrews, 116.
17. Marszalek, 61.

18. *Ibid.,* 62
19. *Ibid.*
20. Sherman, 166.
21. Marszalek, 70.
22. AHM, Aug. '87, 29.
23. Marszalek, 77.
24. *Ibid.*, 79.
25. *Ibid,* 81.
26. AHM, Aug.'87,27.
27. Marszalek, 94-101.
28. *Ibid.*, 103.
29 *Ibid,* 104.
30. *Ibid.*
31. *Ibid,* 105.
32. Sherman, Vol. 1, 284-296.
33. Marszalek, 119.
34. *Ibid.*, 121.
35 *Ibid.,* 122.
36. Andrews, 378.
37. Andrews, 379.
38. AHM, Aug. '87, 31.
39. Marszalek, 129.
40. Andrews, 380-382; Marsazlek, 136-139.
41. AHM, Aug. '87, 34.
42. AHM, Aug. '87, 41.
43. Marszalek, 147.
44. *Ibid,* 140.
45. *Ibid.,* 139.
46. AHM, Aug. '87, 41.
47. Marszalek, 92.
48. Marszalek, 104.
49. *Ibid.*, 122-123.
50. *Ibid.*, 146.

26

The Role of the First Lady and the Media: A Preliminary Case Study of *New York Times* Coverage of Mary Todd Lincoln, 1861-1865

Katherine E. Roberts
University of Minnesota

Americans have been ambivalent about how U.S. presidents' wives have defined the role of First Lady. Although the position has the potential to become an important part of a presidential administration, cultural constraints historically have only allowed the presidents' wives to assist with ceremonial head-of-state duties, thereby limiting them to the seemingly non-political role of "first hostess."[1] But the duties associated with this role have not remained consistent over the years. While each person who comes into the position will likely be expected to live up to somewhat different standards than those who were there before them, they cannot escape the experiences of their predecessors. For example, even though the debate surrounding Hillary Clinton today may result from her own actions, the origins of such controversy can be found in the experiences of earlier First Ladies.[2] Even though the position changes as public opinion about women's societal status evolves, the First Ladyship is, in the words of Barbara Burrell, "a cultural tradition that has developed over time and gradually has become an institutionalized part of the government"[3] Thus, while the duties and responsibilities of a U.S. president's wife have never been concretely outlined in a job description and so are subject to change as administrations come and go, the position is still one of the most traditional public posts women have occupied in the United States.[4]

The purpose of this paper is to discuss coverage in one newspaper about one First Lady who served during a time of crisis and transition in American society—the Civil War 1861-1865. One might expect some change in the images reflected in press coverage about the First Lady during such a crisis and transition time in American society. Common beliefs today about womanhood are similar to those in the 19th century in that the press and public tend to question the "idea of a First Lady openly engaging in the affairs of the state," according to Barbara Burrell. She adds, "The public is still skittish about the idea of a First Lady who is more involved in substance than ceremony."[5] Such expectations and beliefs about the First Lady's role have evolved from different sources and become accepted in American society. One source is through images emphasized in news reports about women. To gain insight into how the media portrayals function in society, one needs to look at the history of press treatment of First Ladies.

When Mary Todd Lincoln took her place in the White House, the position had been defined more or less as a part of the private and proper women's sphere. But her experiences are especially significant because she seems to have been the first First Lady that challenged the private-sphere role her predecessors had perpetuated. "Through her four years at Washington Mary Lincoln inhabited both the male sphere of public affairs and the female's secluded habitat,"[6] according to Bess Furman. Although she did not initially intend to enter the public sphere, two factors made this unavoidable: her personality and the time period during which she lived at the White House. Both factors tended to make her the subject of much criticism, and she received much press attention. Examining the press coverage of her, especially what she was criticized and praised for, may reveal something about what was then expected of the First Lady.

To better understand the news reports about Mary Todd Lincoln, one needs to understand how her experiences in the White House differed from experiences of those who had come before her, for such factors influenced how she was portrayed in the nation's newspapers.

Historical Background

Women in the White House in early America did not lead particularly public lives, and so the coverage of them was similar to that which American women generally received—next to none—until the late 1860s. This adhered to the "time-honored premise that a lady's name appeared in the newspaper only three times in her life: birth, marriage and death."[7] During the early years the presidency was not seen as the influential branch of government it is today, so less attention focused on presidential matters, especially those that were non-political. Most of the political control, and thus the public's interest, lay with the legislative branch. Congress generally possessed more power than the president regarding major policy decisions. But this changed as Abraham Lincoln dealt with the circumstances of the Civil War. Lincoln became the first U.S. president to fully assert executive independence, and as the source of power shifted from one branch to the other, so did the attention of the media.

Lincoln respected and understood the press and appointed influential journalists to posts in his administration, including several *New York Tribune* reporters; and he named editor Charles A. Dana Secretary of War. These journalists were expected to cultivate the beliefs of those who were reading the publications for which they worked.[8]

In 1860, American journalism did not rest on clearly-articulated common ideas and ideals about what journalism should be. Journalism in 1860 did not reflect a sharp divide between facts and values, and objective reporting as now known did not become a norm until much later. Although early partisan journalists publicized and openly criticized an opposition administration's accomplishments, journalists by 1860 had begun to make claims of political independence and autonomy. As the concept of news was increasingly re-defined in the penny press era, newspapers gave less attention to commerce and politics and more attention to various aspects of social life. Intense rivalry over news developed among newspapers, and, according to Michael Schudson, "any event, no matter how apparently trivial, might qualify for print in a newspaper."[9]

This development can be seen in reportage of Mary Todd Lincoln. In the years before she moved into the White House "not even the Springfield newspapers would have 'wasted a line' on her movements"[10] but, as William Howard Russell, a reporter for the

Times of London, wrote after the Lincolns' first official reception, "[I]f she but drives down Pennsylvania Avenue, the electric wire thrills with the news to every hamlet of the Union which has a newspaper; and fortunate is the correspondent who in a special dispatch, can give authentic particulars of her destination and dress."[11]

Thus, by the 1860s the press focused more on the president and also on his wife. In earlier years, the press would likely have pretty much ignored Mary Todd Lincoln because she belonged in the private sphere. While doing research for her 1928 biography of Mary Todd Lincoln, one historian observed that the wives of many early American statesmen were not written about. "They were just wives and that was all."[12] This is especially true of most First Ladies, who remained "shadowy private persons during their tenure in the White House" and avoided any political or public involvement.[13] According to historian Jean Baker, Anna Harrison opposed her husband's political career; Margaret Taylor tried to avoid the Washington scene; Abigail Fillmore spent her time organizing the library in the White House's private quarters; and Sarah Polk despised ceremonial and social engagements. As a result, these women projected an image of the First Lady as passive and non-assertive.[14]

Their actions fit common assumptions of the time about women's place in society and did not present a threat to women's traditional role in the private sphere. The division of society into public and private realms is a socially determined construct, arising from assumptions that men are naturally stronger, superior to and more rational than women, who are the weaker, intellectually inferior and emotionally unstable sex. These assumptions make it seem logical that women would be incapable of political participation, especially since it was assumed they were controlled by emotion rather than reason.[15] First Ladies were in a position where the dividing lines were unclear between the private domain of wife, homemaker, and mother and the public realm of power and influence; but the belief that "women's demands are always excessive, women's anger is terrifying and women's power is not containable"[16] prevailed. This made any woman's ambition for individual achievement an undesirable quality.[17]

But Mary Todd Lincoln received much press coverage, although most members of the media did not allow her to stray very far from that private sphere, the "Dolly Madison stereotype" that former First Ladies had followed.[18] Since reporters quickly noted behavior that varied from that ideal, Mrs. Lincoln had virtually no freedom in the role of the president's wife. Reporters "followed her on wild shopping expeditions . . . exaggerated political meddling, distorted innocent flirtations and libelously insinuated that she was a confederate spy,"[19] according to historian Justin Turner.

Because the role of the First Lady had historically been passive, Mary Todd Lincoln not only broke new ground; she challenged traditions. She took an active part in her husband's work, and this meant some changes in the White House. She was a much more public figure than First Ladies before her. Through her marriage she had "become public property"; she had not purposely selected her public status, but soon after Lincoln was elected president, newspaper correspondents began to seek her out. "Overnight Mary Todd Lincoln made herself a celebrity, closely watched by under-employed Washington based newspaper correspondents who found the president's wife good copy during military campaigns,"[20] according to Jean Baker. William Howard Russell, the *London Times* reporter, observed, "Her smiles and frowns became a matter of consequence to the whole American world."[21] Historian Margaret Leech said that Mrs. Lincoln received more publicity in daily papers during the first year in the White House than the president.[22] Although partially to blame for her celebrity status because she attempted to re-define the First Lady role, she did not believe women should be involved in the public sphere—not even herself.

Despite unprecedented publicity from a large and aggressive press corp, she remained ambivalent about her public status; although she enjoyed the "masculine world" of politics, she directed her energies within the "female domain" and "looked after her husband and children, managed the household, and entertained guests,"[23] according to Gerry Van Der Heuvel. Indicative of her conventional views about women, (holding "a nice home, a loving husband and a precious child" as her ideal), a letter to the editor of the *New York Herald* in 1861 expresses her desire to be located in the private sphere: "My own nature is very sensitive; have always tried to secure the best wishes of all, with whom through life I have been associated. No one is as little desirous of newspaper notoriety as my own inoffensive self."[24] But because of the public nature of that household, her domestic activities were often considered newsworthy. Eventually, she sought publicity—thinking perhaps that it would solidify and demonstrate the importance of her role. It is said she greatly enjoyed her position as the wife of a public personality and desired fame, but she ultimately got more publicity than she wanted.[25]

Facets of Mary Todd Lincoln were in direct conflict and her actions often contradicted her words. She was annoyed with reports of her ambitiousness because "interference" in public affairs made her appear strong-minded, and that was the last thing "a lady" wished to be. Yet she often was bold and demanding in what were considered "masculine indulgences" of the public sphere.26 According to Bess Furman, "There was a wrenching opposition between what she had to do as Mary Todd Lincoln and what she believed 19th-century ladies should do."27 An internal conflict between her adherence to conventional ideas about "female reticence" and her need for acknowledgment becomes especially apparent in how she set out to parallel her husband's accomplishments in the political sphere with her work in the domestic sphere.28

Mary Todd Lincoln had her own vision of an agenda for herself when she went to the White House. According to Baker, she intended to *become* the "First Lady" and was more at home with her 'exalted station' than most of her predecessors."29 One historian wrote that she woke up especially early the day after the inauguration to get on with the duties of the president's wife.30 Her goal was to "make her mark as the first hostess of the land."31 By January of 1862 she had "redecorated the White House, modified the forms of presidential entertaining, outfitted herself like a queen, participated in patronage decisions, reviewed the troops and visited hospitals."32 According to one biographer, it was likely that she was a better manager of domestic affairs of the White House, a more congenial hostess and more compassionate first lady, than many of her contemporaries would acknowledge.33

From the time she was a young woman, she was considered to be a "high spirited, intelligent, unusually well-educated" individual who "delighted in the 'unladylike' game of politics."34 But the American public did not appreciate these traits in a woman, especially in a First Lady. According to Furman, she had a "natural flair for spirited and quotable conversation, driving ambition and passion for pretty clothes,"35 qualities that brought criticism from the Washington elite social crowd, where most of the men were politicians who either opposed Lincoln's policies or often disagreed with his decisions. She had to face the "aristocratic airs" of Washington's social leaders, whose first target was her dress. In a letter, she wrote, "The people scrutinize every article I wear with a heightened curiosity. The very fact of having grown up in the West subjects me to more searching observation."36

During this time period, "dress for social display had thus been built up psychologically to the point where it was an evil as devastating for women as drink was for men."37 She started to use dress to protect herself from the criticism and, in fact, used dress as one of her chief social weapons. But this strategy backfired by bringing much criticism of the expenses she incurred.[38] As Furman observed, "Unluckily, Mary Todd Lincoln had arrived in Washington at precisely the moment Americans demanded strict economy from their officials."[39] Because of this, "few Americans seem to respect this First Lady's purpose of representing her country through high standards of elegance and fashion."[40]

All parties could criticize her many actions outside the definition of "true womanhood." Most women of her generation disliked entertaining and, because they were undereducated and lacked knowledge of public affairs, had little to say to men. Mary Todd Lincoln, however, considered keeping an eye on her husband's political interests as one of her duties as a First Lady. Because it was well known that she had little regard for most of the men her husband appointed, her interest in political matters was of great concern to the Republicans. Most probably did not care for her influence on the appointment of cabinet members and other positions. Many politicians also labeled her a southern sympathizer because some of her relatives were fighting for the Confederacy. In fact, according to Gerry Van Der Heuvel, "Mrs. Lincoln's alleged treasonable activities were often readily believed and so prevalent that the Joint Committee on Conduct of War held a secret session on the topic."[41]

Mary Todd Lincoln basically disobeyed every "rule" expected of 19th-century ladies, especially First Ladies who, as their husbands represented the nation, were presumed to represent American womanhood. Because of her political interests and spending habits, she was seen as lacking the proper self-control of the pious female. Much criticism came from men who "preferred females of incontestable docility and who were shocked at this one's interest in the public world."[42] Women's lives were assumed to belong to a realm entirely outside of politics, and the involvement of First Ladies in such matters enjoins the two domains of public and private life—which could dramatically alter ideas about gender roles.

Even though she was "well bred," well educated, and had the skills and intelligence to meet normal expectations and challenges of her position, Mary Todd Lincoln was "caught in the undertow of animosity within her husband's administration as well as hostilities of a divided land."[43] She was an open target of criticism for many groups, "broken aristocrats, southern sympathizers, disgruntled office seekers, and gossips," who focused attacks on this new social leader in the capital.[44] This resulted in a subtle ostracism by Washington social and political leaders and ultimately brought abuse via the press.

Method

Because there seemed to have been an overwhelmingly negative attitude in both the general press and public toward Mary Todd Lincoln, one might assume all newspapers would present images of her as a woman who did not follow the cultural norms of the 1860s. This assumption led to the following research questions:

* How was the First Lady's role defined in the press content?

* What images of the First Lady appear in news coverage?

* To what extent did these images conform to the prevailing notions of women's proper or acceptable behavior during the period under investigation?

One area of specific interest here is how society viewed women during the period under study. One way to identify such cultural values and attitudes is to discover gender roles and images of women embedded in newspaper coverage. It is assumed that these will reflect the prevailing views for the time and place they were created.[45]

Writing style is also important because it has clear social and ideological implications to the extent that it indicates the reporter's opinion about the news actors or events.[46] This type of analysis may reveal what a First Lady's responsibilities and duties were expected to be as well as how a person in this position was expected to act.

The *New York Times* was selected for study because it was known even then as a reputable paper and became during the Civil War era one of the outstanding dailies of its time with its "reasonable, penetrating and thorough reportage."[47] While the *New York Times* was considered a publication for the masses, Henry J. Raymond didn't like it to be grouped with penny papers of the day and criticized the sensationalism of the *New York Sun* and *New York Herald* and the "whimsy" of the *New York Tribune*. Raymond's contribution was the development of reasonable decency in public reporting, and some scholars describe the *New York Times* at the time as "invariably fair in tone, if not in content."[48] Even while he was deeply involved in politics, they say, he proclaimed a "strongly objective non-partisanship in his paper."[49] Before he started the *Times* he gained a reputation as a budding politician — he was elected to the state assembly in 1849 and was speaker in 1851, became in 1863 the chairman of the Republican National Committee, one of the key political positions in the nation, and managed Lincoln's 1864 campaign. Raymond was initially critical of Lincoln's administration; yet when the war began, he became one of the staunchest Lincoln defenders.

All 19 articles referenced in the *New York Times* index under Mary Todd Lincoln's name from March 1861 (Lincoln's inauguration) through June 1865 (when she moved out of the White House) were studied. Both the type and tone of coverage were noted. In analyzing the content, particular attention was given to what types of events and issues were selected, excluded and emphasized. These events and issues were located through secondary sources.

It is assumed that images and attitudes reflected in these articles indicate what types of activities were acceptable for the president's wife and what character traits were most appealing in a First Lady; some relationship was expected to be identifiable between the message in the text and the social and cultural values and attitudes that prevailed at that time. For example, repetition of a theme could indicate the contemporary limits of the First Lady's role and the expectations about her place in society.

The first part of the analysis focused on what Mary Todd Lincoln was praised or supported for and what she was criticized or given disapproval for. The reasoning was that activities for which she received positive coverage would likely be seen as what should be part of the First Lady's duties, while negative coverage would suggest what were acceptable actions for a First Lady.

Positive and negative coverage was defined by tone and wording. Articles in these categories were either explicitly supportive (stating compliments on her fashion sense or recognition of her skill as a hostess, for example) or explicitly critical (including disapproval of her actions after Lincoln's death, for example). The coverage that seemed indifferent, in that it simply reported Mary Todd Lincoln's involvement in an event, was categorized as "neutral."

Findings

In general, the *New York Times* coverage defined the role of the First Lady as restricted to activities in the household domain. The overwhelming number of images of Mary Todd Lincoln as being politically and publicly passive, yet domestically and privately active, supports this role definition and conforms to the proper sphere ideal that prevailed during the Civil War era.

The analysis revealed one explicitly negative article, five positive articles and 13 that seemed indifferent in tone. It was expected that *New York Times* articles would convey critical commentary similar to that found in other papers during the same time period. The *New York Times* coverage was not as antagonistic toward the First Lady as that in the other daily papers. Taking the history of the *New York Times* and its founder into consideration, the positive coverage of Mary Todd Lincoln makes sense. Actually, the *Times* was communicating the same message conveyed in other publications of the day, and that was that the president's wife should exhibit characteristics of "true womanhood" and be located in the private and proper sphere in society. The assumption that the *Times* coverage would be as critical as that in other prominent publications can lead to a view that everything that Mary Todd Lincoln did fell within the proper sphere. Thus, during that time period, any news reports about a woman in the public realm might be considered negative. Since Raymond was a staunch supporter of Lincoln, he probably tended to place Mary Todd Lincoln in a positive light (knowing that this would in turn reflect well on her husband).

While the focus of this study was on *New York Times* coverage of Mary Todd Lincoln, secondary sources about coverage in the other newspapers from 1861 to 1865 were also examined. A brief analysis of these sources' messages is relevant to understanding the *New York Times*' positive reportage about this particular First Lady.

Definition of the First Lady's Role

The main role that both the *New York Times* and the general press indicated for the First Lady was to support the president. This required that the president's wife either participate in or refrain from certain activities. The degree to which the First Lady can partake in politics or deviate from her sphere depends on the perceived effect these activities are expected to have on her husband's life. Thus, the First Lady's role is defined by how her activities are linked to her husband's goals or pursuits. During this time, both the *New York Times* and the general press indicated that her minimal political participation and an emphasis on the household duties would best further the president's career.

Data showing what the press criticized and praised Mary Todd Lincoln for suggests what was then expected of a First Lady. Strong criticism of Mrs. Lincoln indicated just how far the president's wife could acceptably venture into the public sphere. For example, according to Justin Turner, "Some of the most influential newspapers in the land had published malicious allusions to Mrs. Lincoln's southern antecedents, her lack of indiscretion, her unseemly interest in her husband's' appointments."50 This communicates the message that the First Lady should stay out of politics and remain in her private sphere of true womanhood.

This point is also made in the *New York Times* coverage that praised her involvement in hostess, domestic-type duties and activities. During the inaugural ball, a *New York Times* reporter wrote, "She stood near her husband with dignity and ease. Self-possession, under such circumstances, one would not naturally expect, but it was there. Had the mistress of the White House been born and bred at Washington, accustomed from childhood to the surroundings of the most prominent positions, she could not have exhibited outwardly less anxiety, less embarrassment, or mere savoir faire."51 Although these activities could have been considered outside of the proper sphere they were acceptable because they were associated with support for Lincoln. While the general press could have given this event negative coverage, the impact would be the same as that of the *New York Times* in defining the role of the First Lady.

Images of Mary Todd Lincoln

Although the general press and the *New York Times* coverage seems to have defined the same role for the First Lady, the images reflected of Mary Todd Lincoln were opposite. The *New York Times* conveyed one image of her, but the general press seems to have conveyed another, if the secondary sources are accurate. Most of the coverage studied in the *New York Times* focused on reports of her appearance ("Mrs. Lincoln wore a simple wreath of white flowers in her hair and was dressed with elegance")52, hostess role ("He privately presented to Mrs. Lincoln a splendid blanket as a New Year's offering")53 and relationship with Lincoln ("President and Mrs. Lincoln gave a ball . . . . President and Mrs. Lincoln requested the honor").54 This type of coverage creates an image of Mary Todd Lincoln as a dependent, passive, and supportive wife.

The general press, however, according to secondary sources, portrayed her as an extravagant, socially inept, demanding woman. As suggested earlier, Mary Todd Lincoln was subjected to more press scrutiny than any former First Lady. The most prominent area by far for criticism was her alleged extravagance. Most articles found in this research had to do with her shopping trips. Some reporters went so far as to actually reconstruct a story of a shopping trip that they did not personally witness. Newspapers reported at length each time she traveled to New York and purchased anything. This presented the nation and world with a picture of a First Lady who partook in a "mad frenzy of buying, oblivious to the hardships and suffering of the war."55 One New York correspondent even followed her from store to store and talked with the clerks. He noted how much she spent for what and also reported:

> 'Mrs. President Lincoln,' as the ladies call her, was shopping to a considerable extent in the city in the early part of the week. She has evidently no comprehension that Jeff. Davis will make good his threat to occupy the White House in July for she is spending thousands and thousands of dollars for articles of luxurious taste in the household the way that it would be very preposterous for her to use out in her rural home in Illinois.56

In the spring of 1864 her extravagance became a matter of great public concern when a *New York Herald* reporter called one of her New York visits a "business trip" and portrayed her as a woman who had nothing better to do than shop while the nation was at war. The article's tone is illustrated by the sentences: "From the early morning hours until late in the evening, Mrs. Lincoln ransacked the treasures of the Broadway dry goods stores."57

Mary Todd Lincoln attempted to change the negative image early in her second year in the White House. Because of the war, she dispensed with the official White House dinners and condensed all of the official gatherings into one. Concerned that too many people would show up, she announced the reception was by invitation only. As a result, the press labeled the event a "private party" and criticized her for its exclusiveness. She responded by opening the event to everyone, and, although the reception was considered a great success, she was then denounced for her extravagance because of the number of people who ended up attending the event.

This account demonstrates antagonism toward this First Lady. By publicizing these events and occurrences in such a manner, the press distorted news about Mary Todd Lincoln and limited how the general public viewed her. This suggests the power of the media in shaping an image through tone and type of coverage.

Images of Proper Behavior

The *New York Times* provided an overwhelming amount of images of Mary Todd Lincoln as conforming to the prevailing notions of what was acceptable behavior for women in those times. This illusion of Mary Todd's total adherence to the proper sphere was accomplished by reports—

1. of occurrences and activities that could actually be located in that sphere;
2. that legitimized questionable activities by Mary Todd Lincoln by associating them with one or more characteristic of "true womanhood" (dependence, weakness, frailty);
3. that omitted occurrences that deviated from standards of acceptability.

The first news report of the new administration set the standard for the way Mary Todd Lincoln was covered throughout her tenure as First Lady. The guidelines for subsequent coverage were outlined in an article on the inaugural ball and reception.

> Mrs. Lincoln has three characteristics which given to an American woman, will sustain her under any circumstances and enable her to bear up against any pressure. They are common sense, self confidence, and tact; all of which to a remarkable extent, are hers. In addition to those, she has a naturally pleasing manner, an open heart and a working brain.... I take pleasure in recording the fact that Mrs. Lincoln is eminently qualified for her position... and will show to her country women and to Washington society in particular, that she can, as did Mrs. Polk, adorn as well as sustain the responsible place which she has been called to fill.[58]

From this point until Lincoln's death, the *New York Times* coverage was shaped by methods of selection, association and omission that ensured Mary Todd Lincoln "lived up" to these standards. What follows is a discussion of these methods.

1. Selection.

The type of events the *New York Times* editor saw as newsworthy in relation to the First Lady reveals that he carefully selected events and issues to report that were socially acceptable and well within a woman's proper sphere. Most of the coverage dealt with her involvement in social events, family affairs, or otherwise female-oriented activities. The selected events were reported in a neutral or positive light.

One common theme was the emphasis on the hostess function. These accounts focused on not only Mary Todd Lincoln's attire, but also emphasized the mere fact that she attended a ball or reception considered the "great event of the season." Much of the reportage was quite trivial in that it dealt solely with whom she appeared ("on the arm of Ex-Gov. Newell"), what she wore ("Her dress will commend itself in all who admire simple elegance"), when she arrived ("Shortly after 10 o'clock Mrs. Lincoln appeared"), when she left ("She withdrew about 12 o'clock"), and so on.[59] The majority of the accounts merely emphasized she was there and never reported what she did. In fact, she was never depicted as the "actor"; instead she always was a spectator or—when gifts were presented to her—a recipient.

Although some articles discussed her weaknesses, the weaknesses were always acceptable for women, such as frailty or irrationality, and thus were not criticisms of the First Lady. These characteristics had come to be expected of her gender and therefore were accepted as normal.

2. Association

Weakness is also emphasized in news accounts when her activities did not clearly fall into the proper sphere. Two weaknesses most commonly associated with the female gender were used to sanction the president's wife's involvement in various activities. One of those weaknesses derives from the assumption that women are prone to illnesses of all sorts. This was used as an explanation for why she was unable to fulfill her duties. One account mentions "complaints that the wife of the president is not as accessible as she should be and that she has only taken one or two airings on the beach since she arrived," and goes on to state that "both ladies and gentlemen who have taken the pains to obtain introductions have fallen short in their efforts to pay their respects." While this excerpt by itself could be considered somewhat critical, any negative aspect was countered by an "excuse" for this behavior: "Thus far Mrs. Lincoln appears to have adhered to her intention of maintaining as much privacy as possible during her visit, which has been undertaken much more for the benefit of her health than for the sake of seeing or being seen at a fashionable watering place."[60]

The second weakness was her dependency on her husband. While it is understandable that her husband's name would often be mentioned with hers, such as when they hosted a reception or went on vacation together, it is notable that Lincoln's name continued to be used as if he must guide her even after his death. One example is when she announced the city she had chosen to reside in:

> [I]t is the purpose of Mrs. Lincoln to make this city (Chicago) her future home . . . the President declared to some . . . that after he had laid aside the cares of his great office and retired to private life, it was his intention to spend the remainder of his days in Chicago. He had commissioned one of our citizens to look about . . . to secure the refuge of a comfortable residence.[61]

A later article continued this theme, stating that, "Mrs. Lincoln, instead of being compelled to break up house-keeping, can live in the manner which would have been suited to the tastes and habits of Mr. Lincoln."[62] This implies that she was not capable of making her own independent decision and was expected to continue to rely on what might have been her late husband's opinion.

When she was commended for any accomplishments, usually the president was also mentioned. This is demonstrated in the lack of credit given to her in a *Times* article about her organization of the White House balls and receptions; instead, the article credited both her and her husband for an event's success. "Mr. and Mrs. L sustained the fatigue of the day with remarkable ease and with no evil results, we congratulate alike them and our country that the first reception given by the present occupants of the White House was so eminently popular, successful and complete in all essential particulars."[63] Commending her alone would have indicated that she had influence and power over a public event, and that did not fit properly in the private sphere notion.

3. Omission

The third method that shaped the *New York Times* coverage of Mary Todd Lincoln demonstrates that a lot can be said by omission. The *Times* did not report accounts that criticized the First Lady while Lincoln was still alive. Though other editors often gave lengthy accounts of her extravagances or southern connections, the *New York Times* editor avoided publishing such criticisms. Thus, coverage tended to depict the First Lady in a manner that would lead a reader to believe her behavior never deviated from the proper sphere and women's traditional role.

Perhaps the rationale for this is best revealed in coverage after the president's assassination. Lincoln was to be buried in Springfield, Ill., where a monument in his memory was also to be placed, but Mary Todd Lincoln insisted he be laid to rest in Oak Ridge Cemetery, outside of town. While the town considered the late Lincoln to be civic property, she did not agree. Although alone in her crusade, she seems to have seen it as her prerogative as the president's widow to decide his burial place. In taking this stance she placed herself in the public sphere. The article blamed Mary Todd Lincoln for controversy and noted how the city made numerous attempts "to reconcile the unfortunate difference."[64]

The article continues that the majority of the town favored a certain location for Lincoln's burial, but "To this place, however, it is understood Mrs. Lincoln is unalterably opposed. She refuses ever to allow Mr. Lincoln's remains to be placed there. The reason given by her friends is that some relatives of hers, with whom she has not been for some time on speaking terms, reside on the adjoining property."[65] This makes her seem silly and irrational. What seems to have been a kind of code of silence about some matters concerning Mary Todd Lincoln before Lincoln's death was no longer politically expedient for *New York Times* coverage. Both the tone and wording of a news report about Lincoln's monument and burial site indicate criticism of Mary Todd Lincoln.

Before the assassination, most *New York Times* coverage about Mary Todd Lincoln was indifferent or somewhat supportive, yet this did not accurately reflect the types of activities she was involved in or even the attitude toward what she was doing. The *New York Times* editor seems to have manipulated the type and tone of the coverage so that it reflected an image of a First Lady that the public had come to expect: a passive, dependent, supportive woman who happened to be married to the president. Her role as First Lady as defined by the *New York Times* articles was the same as the role of most women in the 19th century—to provide support for the men in their lives.

Mary Todd Lincoln was criticized in one publication as too aggressive, yet praised in another because she was aggressive in a way that was allowable because the aggression was linked to the proper sphere. Both accounts are detrimental because they suggest the limit of the First Lady's activities is the private sphere.

Conclusion

This study of images of Mary Todd Lincoln and the role of First Lady rests on 19 *New York Times* news reports from 1861 to 1865 that indicated that the First Lady's role was to be wholly supportive of her husband. Images of Mary Todd Lincoln were as a passive, dependent woman, a woman that conformed her actions to the perceived proper behaviors of the day.

The perpetuation of such a "proper image" of the First Lady means that role, as a model of what women should be and how they should act, is very restrictive for the nation as a whole. The significance of media emphasis on gender myths is that it distorts reality—and, in this kind of case, does so on a very broad scale. According to Betty Houchin Winfield: "The media, purveyor of dominant social values, are ambivalent at best about such independence in both first ladies and women generally."[66] When press coverage provides readers with an image of a First Lady who has settled for a secondary role in society, that role's acceptability may be enhanced and thus perpetuated as others attempt to conform to this proper sphere of womanhood.

Such a pattern of perpetuation of this ideal has been noted in the development of the role of the First Lady itself. It seems that First Lady standards have not evolved much because Hillary Clinton is still expected to fulfill the traditional "first lady responsibilities." As Winfield states: "Whether as mirror of American social values or monitor of traditional roles, the press expects stereotypical political wife standards of the first lady. When those "norms" are absent, the mass media generally react negatively, especially to female political power."[67] When Hillary Clinton was asked in 1992 whether she had changed the pattern for First Ladies, she responded, "I don't think there should be a pattern . . . . Everybody should be permitted to be who they are."[68] Yet the question is; will "who they are" be the image that is communicated to the public?

Notes

1. Barbara Burrell, *Public Opinion, the First Ladyship, and Hillary Rodham Clinton* (New York: Garland Publishing, Inc., 1997) 139.
2. Lewis Gould, "There's History to the Role of First Lady," *The Quill* March 1996: 29.
3. Burrell, 140.
4. Burrell, 3.
5. Burrell, 4.
6. Bess Furman, *White House Profile: A Social History of the White House, its occupants and its festivities* (Indianapolis: Bobbs-Merrill Company, Inc., 1951) 181.
7. Gerry Van Der Heuvel, *Crowns of Thorns and Glory—Mary Todd Lincoln and Varina Howell Davis: The Two First Ladies of the Civil War* (New York: E.P. Dutton, 1988) 264.
8. Louis W. Koenig, *The Chief Executive: Revised Edition* (New York: Harcourt, Brace & World, Inc., 1968) 201.
9. Michael Schudson, *Discovering the News: A Social History of American Newspapers* (United States: BasicBooks, 1978) 28.
10. Heuvel, 91.
11. Heuvel, 91.
12. Honore Willsie Morrow, *Mary Todd Lincoln: An Appreciation of the Wife of Abraham Lincoln* (New York: William Morrow & Company, 1928) 8.
13. Jean Baker, *Mary Todd Lincoln* (New York: W.W. Norton & Company, 1987) 178.
14. Baker, 179
15. Burrell, 9.
16. Caryl Rivers, *Slick Spins and Fractured Facts: How Cultural Myths Distort the News* (New York: Columbia University Press, 1996) 51.
17. Barbara Welter, *Dimity Convictions: The American Woman in the Nineteenth Century* (Athens: Ohio University Press, 1976) 4.
18. Justin G. Turner and Linda Levitt Turner, *Mary Todd Lincoln: Her Life and Letters* (New York: Alfred A. Knopf, 1972) xvii.
19. Turner xvii.

20. Baker 180.
21. Baker, 179.
22. Heuvel, 119.
23. Heuvel, 116.
24. Furman, 180.
25. Turner, 35.
26. Furman, 204.
27. *Ibid.*, 181.
28. *Ibid.*,180.
29. Baker, 178.
30. Heuvel, 84.
31. Furman, 196.
32. Baker, 205.
33. Heuvel, 265.
34. Turner, xv.
35. Furman, 171.
36. Heuvel, 144.
37. Furman, 174.
38. Furman, 174.
39. Furman, 185.
40. Furman, 193.
41. Heuvel, 141.
42. Furman, 180.
43. Heuvel, 263.
43. Heuvel, 114.
44 Carl Sandburg, *Mary Lincoln: Wife and Widow* (New York: Harcourt, Brace and Company, 1932) 86.
45. Hazel Dicken-Garcia and Janet Cramer, "Images of Women in Civil War Newspapers Leave the Proper Sphere," University of Minnesota, August 1995: 5.
46. Jensen, 115.
47 Michael Emery and Edwin Emery, *The Press and America: An Interpretive History of the Mass Media* (Boston: Allyn and Bacon, 1996) 134.
48. Emery, 109.
49. Emery, 109.
50. Turner, 79.
51. "The Republican Court," *New York Times*, 11 March 1861, 1:4.
52. "From Long Branch," *New York Times*, 24 August 1861, 4:6.
53. "New Year's Day at the Capital," *New York Times*, 3 January 1862, 5:1.
54. "Jenkins at the White House," *New York Times*, 9 February 1862, 4:5.
55. Heuvel, 119.
56. Turner, 88.
57. Turner, 162.
58. "The Republican Court," *New York Times*, 11 March 1861, 1:4.
59. "From Long Branch," *New York Times*, 24 August 1861, 4:6.
60 "From Long Branch," *New York Times*, 23 August 1861, 5:2.
61. "The President's Widow," *New York Times*, 30 April 1865, 6:3.
62. "Letters of Administration...," *New York Times*, 21 June 1865, 4:5.
63. "The Republican Court," *New York Times*, 11 March 1861, 1:4.
64. "The Lincoln Monument," *New York Times*, 16 June 1865, 1:4.
65. "The Lincoln Monument," *New York Times*, 16 June 1865, 1:4.
66. Betty Houchin Winfield, " 'Madame President' — Understanding a New Kind of First Lady," *Media Studies Journal* (Spring 1994) 71.
67. Winfield, 61.
68. Burrell, 145.

27

Journalists First, Rebels Second: An Examination of Editorial Reaction to the President's Proposed Conscription of Newspapermen

Debra Reddin van Tuyll
Augusta State University

On 7 November 1864, President Jefferson Davis opened the new session of the Confederate Congress with a speech that provoked howls of protest by Southern newspaper editors. In this speech, Davis asked Congress for further revisions to the conscription laws. Tinkering with the laws of conscription was nothing new for Congress; it had done so several times previously. Indeed, only five days after adopting the original statute in April 1862, the Congress began to work out a system of exemptions,[1] a system which would later be a cause of the Confederacy's critical manpower shortage after the fall of Atlanta. The exemptions were also the genesis of the Confederate press' villification of President Davis in the fall of 1864.[2] This was nothing new; even the exemption question in 1862 had been so divisive that it raised opposition to Davis that lasted throughout the war.[3]

In his speech that November, Davis asked the Congress for recision of the draft exemption which certain classes of professions, including newspaper employees, had enjoyed since 1862. This was but one of Davis' several mistakes at the end of the war (though it may have been an honest mistake since the exemptions had been unpopular ever since their adoption[4]) which were to weaken Confederate morale and fighting spirit; indeed, only about six weeks later, Davis's good friend W. N. Pendleton, a Virginia clergyman and soldier, would write to him that he needed to do something to "acquire stronger hold on the public heart."[5]

Pendleton went on to advise Davis that "injurious censure . . . attaches to operations that prove unfortunate. Personally you may disregard such censure, but officially and representatively you have not that liberty. Confidence reposed in you by the country is one element of our strength."[6] Even the most inept politician ought to have realized the mistake of taking on the press in the Confederacy's darkest hour. For as seasoned a politician and military leader as Davis, it should have been, in the vernacular, a "no-brainer," a fact recognized by at least one 19th century Georgia historian who wrote of Davis, "He had many of the requirements of his terrific position. . . . But he was not the man as a whole for it. . . . He was a man of stubborn prejudices and a jagged temper. The diplomacy of statesmanship he knew not at all. He had a large faculty of making enemies."[7] Indeed, Davis had faced opposition throughout the war from certain government officials (Brown and Confederate Vice President Alexander Stephens, both of whom had criticized the first draft law in 1862,[8] were the main two) and newspapers in Georgia , as well as in and North Carolina.[9] This would not have been a new experience for him, yet it seems he was not one to learn from experience. One of Davis' biographers attributes his failure at adequately running the home front for the ultimate collapse of the Confederacy.[10]

The problem between Davis and the press was not so much his proposal to draft editors as the second part of his plan: to detail some editors back to their newspapers while sending others to the front. There is little evidence to support the editors' interpretations of Davis' intentions, really only the fact that he made the suggestion that editors be conscripted and detailed according to need. However, Rep. Henry S. Foote of Tennessee certainly saw Davis' proposal as an attempt at manipulation, and the very next day, he proposed a resolution in the Confederate Congress that would have stopped any attempt to draft editors.[11] In Davis' history of the Civil War, he claimed his primary objective in the fall of 1864 was merely to get men into the Confederate army. He believed all he needed to defeat the Union was enough men to destroy the railroads between Atlanta and Chattanooga so that Sherman's campaign "would be blighted, his capture of Atlanta would become a barren victory, and he would probably be compelled to make a retreat."[12] Clement Eaton's 1977 biography of Jefferson Davis contains an extensive chapter on the president's relationship with the press, but it makes no mention of an attempt by Davis to manipulate the press.

Nevertheless, it is clear how the journalists could have concluded that the president was trying to manipulate a feisty and adversarial press. If military commanders were in charge of deciding which editors went to the front and which stayed home and ran the newspapers, it seems obvious that it would be the troublesome editors who would be sent off to fight.

Consequently, many Confederate editors received Davis' proposal poorly, though some, the *Charleston Daily Courier*, the *Augusta Constitutionalist* and the *Savannah Republican*, for example, gave scant coverage to the speech. It should be noted here that many of the articles mentioned in this paper were found as reprints in Georgia, Virginia or South Carolina newspapers of the day. While the paper will examine the reactions of the Southern press generally, emphasis will be placed upon the reaction of Georgia newspapers because, at the time of Davis' speech, Sherman's forces occupied Atlanta, and the Union general's raid across the state was just about to begin (his speech was on 7 November, and the first of Sherman's men left Atlanta on 14 November). One might expect Georgia newspapers to support any measure that could perhaps repel the occupying enemy army back from whence it came, but this was not the case. Before dealing with the press's reaction to Davis' proposal, it is first necessary to consider why the Confederate Army needed more men.

The need for more men was actually abundantly clear. By the fall of 1864, the Confederate Army was all but decimated. Death, disease and desertion had reduced Confederate forces by between 100,000 and 200,000.[13] Earlier that fall, in a 23 September speech at Macon, Davis had estimated that two-thirds of the Confederate army was absent from duty.[14] In Georgia, the situation was particularly grave. Gen. William T. Sherman's Army of the Tennessee occupied Atlanta, and the Confederate Gen. John B. Hood's force had been unable to repulse the enemy. So Hood, in consultation with Confederate leaders, decided a little artifice might work to pull Sherman out of the city. The Confederate general took his troops and headed north into Tennessee with the hope that Sherman would evacuate Atlanta to protect his supply and communication lines that reached back to Chattanooga.

Unfortunately for the Rebels, this was a major miscalculation; in fact, Civil War historian Bruce Catton called it a "strategy of despair, verging on the wholly fantastic."[15] Pendleton also pointed to Hood's campaign as being partly to blame for the public's dissatisfaction with Davis: "Just as other reverses have been, this added to the depressing affect of disasters . . . has provided a considerable sinking of the public's heart."[16] Hood's campaign failed because Sherman did not take the bait, choosing instead to take off across Georgia on his infamous "March to the Sea." But because of Hood's evacuation, Georgia was left only with the protection of Gen. Joseph Wheeler's 5,000-man cavalry that Gen. P. G. T. Beauregard had ordered to Georgia upon Hood's evacuation. Wheeler's 5,000 horsemen faced 60,000 Union infantrymen and 6,000 Union cavalrymen. Not even the Georgia militia remained in the field; after the fall of Atlanta, Georgia Gov. Joseph Brown sent all the state's militiamen home to tend their farms.[17] Compounding the Confederacy's manpower problem generally, after the fall of Atlanta, Lincoln called for an additional 500,000 Union recruits.[18]

Davis' solution for the relief of Georgia and the replenishment of the Confederate Army was to revise the conscription laws. The draft laws, which were a source of contention between the individual states and the Confederate central government anyway,[19] had been revised periodically throughout the war; earlier in 1864, for example, the provision that draftees might purchase substitutes to serve in their place had been abolished.[20] In his 7 November 1864 speech, when Davis renewed his call for revocation of the exemption of certain classes of professionals to be exempt from the draft,[21] he was repeating a recommendation he had made earlier that year. On 17 February 1864, Congress, upon Davis' recommendation, had already removed about half the exemptions to service which had previously existed.[22] Davis' rationale for recommending even more exemptions that November was this:

> The exemption from military duty now accorded by law to all persons engaged in certain specified pursuits or professions is shown by experience to be unwise, nor is it believed to be defensible in theory. The defense of home, family and country is universally recognized as the paramount political duty of every member of society. . . . No pursuit nor position should relieve anyone who is able to do active duty from enrollment in the army, unless his function or services are more useful to the defense of his country in another sphere. But it is manifest that this cannot be the case with entire

classes.[23]

One might expect, given the desperation of the situation in the Confederacy generally, and in Georgia particularly, that the usually patriotic Southern press would have supported any attempt to remedy the manpower shortage. This was not entirely the case; some newspapermen did respond to the need. In fact, some new militia units were formed to resist Sherman. In Augusta, all newpaper editors and their printers, with the notable exception of the infamous *Augusta Chronicle*, met on Nov. 21 "for the purpose of organizing themselves into a military company for the local defense." They named their new company the Augusta Press Guards, sent a telegram to Sen. B. H. Hill in Richmond to announce their unit's "readiness for the conflict," and then, "After some little convivilaity in which several toasts were drank, and all enjoying themselves hugely the meeting adjourned, and we doubt not should the enemy make his appearance in this vicinity the 'August Press Guards' will be found reporting ready for duty (emphasis theirs)."[24]

Despite this symbolic act of defiance by a handfull of journalists, and despite the desperation of Georgia's situation, that state's editors were, with some exceptions, loud in their criticism of Davis' proposal. The most strident voice was Nathan Morse, the *Augusta Chronicle* editor, who, in the six weeks between Davis' speech and the fall of Savannah, published more than 20 articles criticizing the president's proposal (The count is closer to 30, if one counts each of the reprinted articles singly rather than counting each day's selections as only one "compiled" story). In the same period, the *Macon Telegraph* and the *Southern Watchman* each published only six articles. Figures for the other daily papers in Georgia are unreliable because few copies remain, or, as in the case of the *Columbus Enquirer*, they are so badly damaged as to be virtually unreadable.

At the same time as editors were responding to Davis, the state's major story of the war was unfolding, Sherman's March to the Sea. The attention given to that story, in all the Georgia papers, by far eclipsed that given to President Davis' troubles. If Morse published 20 to 30 stories on the free press issue, he easily published five or even ten times as many articles and editorials about Sherman's six week-long campaign. The same is true for these other editors as well; by far the dominant story of the period was Sherman's March to the Sea.

For Morse, the main point of debate on the free press issue was that drafting editors into the Army was tantamount to despotism and an infringement of the people's constitutional rights. On 12 November 1864, the same day he ran Davis' speech, Morse published one of the few editorials on this topic that he wrote himself (a large proportion of his editoials on the topic he clipped from other Confederate papers). Interestingly, he saw the proposal to draft editors as an issue not only for the press, but for the public as well; Morse and other editors, sounding very much like 20th century editorial writers, clearly believed any infringement of press rights was an infringement of the public's rights, and they called on the people to oppose the plan. In one editorial, Morse quoted former President Andrew Jackson saying that nothing, not even civil war, would justify a government's "official interference with the freedom of speech or of the press," and he called for Confederate citizens to let Richmond know they would not stand for any tampering with the press:

> The people are the power. They will sustain a free and independent press. Let the latter do its duty . . . and at once crush out the hydra-headed monster — military despotism — that has reared its crested head at Richmond. It is very evident that efforts will be made at the present Congress to deprive the people of their few remaining liberties. Let the people notify their representatives that they must oppose any further movement infringing upon their rights. Let the press itself speak out boldly and defiantly.[25]

Other editors echoed Morse's point. On 2 December, Henry Lynden Flash, editor of the *Macon Telegraph* and a former Confederate officer, published an editorial from a Richmond correspondent, P. W. Alexander, which maintained, "The newspaper press is the organ of the aggregate intellect of a people. It is the mightiest power on the face of God's earth." Alexander went on to state that an attack on the press is an attack on the freedom for all. The *Montgomery Appeal* called on Davis to remember that his oath of office required him to defend the Confederate Constitution, and then went on to note, ". . .without a free and independent press to guard and protect them, the liberties of the people will soon be undermined and swallowed up."[26]

The *Camden* (S.C.) *Daily Journal* echoed this sentiment with an editorial on Nov. 23. It predicted that if Davis' proposal passed, the south would turn into a "bowling desert." The press, the paper continued, "is a war power and no professional journalist in the land feels the slightest gratitude for his exemption." The *Charleston Mercury*, one of Davis' most bitter critics, in its first original editorial on the subject (prior to this editorial, it had been using reprints from other newspapers) took a libertarian approach to the question; the paper cited the First Amendment and asks, "Could language be plainer or more conclusive?"27 On 26 November, the paper goes even further in stating, ". . . even a licentious press is far less evil that a press that is enslaved because both sides may be heard in the former case, but not the later. . . . An enslaved press must be evil; for an enslaved press suppresses truth."

Perhaps the most heated point of contention was Davis' proposal that Confederate authorities be given the power to "detail" editors. In other words, editors would be drafted into the Confederate army and then "assigned" the duty of producing newspapers. Most of the writers who addressed this point were unanimous, and quite modern, in their analysis of the problem with a detailed press: a journalist must be independent to do his/her job properly; he cannot owe allegiance to anyone or anything other than the people. The *Macon Telegraph*'s Flash believed that some of the classes of professions who faced a loss of their exemptions could function well as Army personnel, but not journalists: "A shoemaker, a tanner or a blacksmith can perform his duties as well when detailed as when exempt, but the very life and soul of the press is freedom. So impressed were the wise men who framed the Constitution that they expressly declared in that instrument that 'Congress should pass no law limiting the freedom of the press (sic).' "28

John H. Christy, editor of the *Southern Watchman* out of Athens, Ga., reprinted an article from the *Richmond Enquirer* which also addressed this point. The writer of this article contended that, "The Press is not a 'class,' it is an institution. . . . Neither shoemaking, nor tanning, nor blacksmithing, nor milling, nor any of the 'classes' with which the President has connected the Press have any constitutional recognition." The article goes on to conclude that the first step toward despotism will have been taken in the South when the press is under the control of "Executive details."29 The *Montgomery Mail* scoffed, " . . . no thoroughly independent man would accept a detail to edit a newspaper."30 The *Richmond Enquirer* agreed when its editors wrote, "For sixty years the *Richmond Enquirer* has existed a newspaper, free, unbought, unpurchasable and never shall it exist otherwise with [sic] our consent."31

The theme of despotism was a common one in the Confederate press. Many of the articles reprinted in the *Augusta Chronicle* address this point. The *Montgomery Mail, Richmond Whig, Raleigh Progress,*

Macon Intelligencer and *Charleston Mercury* each leveled charges of despotism against Davis. The *Raleigh Progress* went so far as to proclaim that if the South was to have a military dictator, they would just as soon have Abraham Lincoln as their leader. Adding insult to injury, the *Progress* continued: "We have no hesitation in saying that if our authorities had been zealous in prosecuting the war against the common enemy as they have been passing and executing laws to oppress, distress and divide their own citizens, the military situation would have been much better than it is."[32]

Southern editors found other reasons to object to Davis' proposal as well. For example, Flash noted another problem with giving Confederate authorities the right to draft editors; he maintained that it would be quite easy for an officer who had been criticized by a particular editor to draft that journalist and send him to the front. And, along with the *Southern Watchman*'s Christy, Flash noted that there were very few newspapermen in the Confederacy, too few to be of any great service to the cause. On this point, he was absolutely right; by February 1865, just four months after Davis' speech, 123 editors and 683 newspaper employees had exemptions from the Confederate Army.[33] Consequently, Flash argued, if journalists were to be drafted, then their papers should all be shut down. "Given them a Free Press or none at all," he wrote.[34] Christy took a darker view, arguing that if Southern editors were drafted, subjugation of the South would follow within six months.[35] Of course, even without this legislation, the South was subjugated in five months, anyway.

The Southern editors were not Davis' only opponents on this measure. Two days after Davis' speech, on 7 November, Rep. Henry S. Foote of Tennessee introduced a resolution to the Confederate House calling on that body to disapprove the president's request[36] a measure which the *Richmond Enquirer* believed had been a mistake not to pass immediately[37] (the paper made it clear, however, that they were critical only of the effect of the president's measure, not the president himself). Foote denied introducing the resolution to curry favor with the press, claiming that, indeed, he had denounced the press more than anyone else in the House. The measure was sent to the House Military Affairs Committee for consideration.[38]

And, as he could always be counted upon to do, Georgia Gov. Joseph Brown also objected to Davis' proposal[39], and went so far as to prepare a speech on the topic to be given at a joint session of the Georgia Legislature. The speech was never given, due to the capture of Millegeville, Georgia's capital at the time, by Sherman's advancing army.40 However, the speech was reprinted in virtually every Georgia newspaper.

It should be noted that even in this crisis, not all editors were against Davis. The *Richmond Sentinel*, for example, in a story signed "Franklin," spoke out against exemptions for the press. This story contended that there were many exempted so-called editors who "are unable to write a grammatical paragraph and have no more to do with editing their papers than the horses in their stables."41 The editors, according to Franklin, pay others to write for them. "And herein the inquiry naturally arises, how far the liberty of the press is secured by an arrangement of this kind," he continued.

The *Raleigh Progress* estimated that three Confederate newspapers did not oppose Davis' proposal,42 but it does not name the three. This study has identified three newspapers which, while perhaps not supporting Davis, at least did not openly criticize his call for the draft of editors. Those three papers are the *Savannah Republican*, the *Augusta Constitutionalist* and the *Charleston Daily Courier*.

Interestingly, the *Savannah Republican*, for which approximately one-half to two-thirds of the papers from the period survived, published nothing on this issue, at least not in the remaining issues. Nor did the *Charleston Daily Courier* publish much of anything beyond a wire story about the speech on 8 November, the day after the speech had been given. This was followed up with publication of the full text of the speech on 11 November. However, that was the extent of the Charleston paper's coverage. Perhaps it should be noted that the *Courier* ran no editorials on any topic in this period.

The *Constitutionalist*, whose owner was a noted Davis supporter, did make a few comments on the issue. On 8 November, it ran the same wire summary of the speech that several other papers had used. On 10 November, the paper ran a reprint of an editorial from the *Augusta Register* (formerly the *Atlanta Register*) which, while not addressing the conscription issue, was staunch in its support of Davis:

> When the choice is the patriot and statesman, Jefferson Davis, or the Brutes, the tyrant, the Abolitionist, Abraham Lincoln, we admit we are for the former. When the choice is between the acts of the Southern administration and those of the vile Northern despotism, covered with infamy, falsehood, bribery and corruption, we are proud to take sides with the former.43

The *Constitutionalist* goes on to "cordially and unequivocally endorse every word of paragraph." The paper's editors liken people who oppose Davis to those "men who denied the Savior because he came from Nazareth." In the single editorial the paper runs specifically dealing with Davis' 7 November speech, absolutely no mention is made of the conscription of editors, though the paper does mention Davis' proposal to draft slaves into the Army; interestingly, the paper neither criticizes nor praises the president for this proposal.

In one issue of the *Constitutionalist,* a letter to the editor from a retired newspaper editor addressed the issue in a very different manner from the rest of the Georgia press.44 The former editor states that he is an ardent supporter of a free press; however, he sees the editors' objections to being drafted not as standing up for a valued principle but as cowardice, pure and simple: ". . . 'freedom of the press' is a nobler and a higher thing than a shield from a conscript officer. . . . Its essence is of a loftier nature than exemption from military service. The bulwarks and buttresses that support it, are not 'bomb proofs' and hiding places for skulking soldiers." This former journalist went on to argue that the price of his colleagues' objections is disunity, which could cost the South the war:

> If there be danger of a despotism, or a tyranny, or a destruction of our liberties, it is not to be found in the too long delayed routing out from their nests of all exempt persons of fighting age, be they editors or executioners, printers or planters, money-makers or mechanics — but from another source, to which I fear some of my heretofore conferes (sic) are unconsciously contributing, by their uncharitable fault-finding with the President, more than they are aware. The danger is division, want of unity or purpose and of effort, a momentary forgetfulness that nothing can be so valuable to us now, as military success — in other words, that everything sinks into insignificance compared with the great question whether we shall whip this fight.

Revolution, he continued, puts all rights at risk:

> Any people who go into revolution do, in the very nature of the thing, put into peril public and private liberty — place at hazard every valuable right possessed by man for the simple reason that, once engaged in the conflict, once interest and judgment put aside and passion substituted instead, the arbitrament of the sword consented in place of the arbitrament of reason -- to make good the revolution, to be successful in the conflict, to whip the fight, becomes in interest paramount to all others. All rights, all privileges, all franchises, all prerogatives, are paralyzed, are put in abeyance, are as if they never had existence, until the fight is whipped, and the revolution is a success — for it is not in human nature, as revealed by history, that rebels, or those who unsuccessfully attempt revolution, should be allowed to retain any of these rights, privileges, franchises or prerogatives, after the conflict is over and the heel of the conqueror is on their necks, except such poor pittance of existence as will enable them to crawl into dishonored graves, leaving to their children an inheritance of opprobrium and disgrace.45

This letter to the editor is interesting for at least two reasons. First, it so deftly predicted the future of the South following the Civil War. Secondly, the reasoning is much closer to what one might expect out of Southern newspapers at the time. The papers, up to this point, had worked hard to keep up Southern morale, to fan the fighting fire. And, indeed, Confederate editors continued throughout Sherman's campaign, and even after the fall of Savannah, to publish articles predicting a Southern victory and articles obviously aimed at building Southern morale. It is curious that, at the same time, these editors were publishing such divisive commentaries on the events of the war and the Confederate government's lawmaking activities. One explanation is that these editors took their responsibilities as journalists seriously. While press standards had not developed to any significant degree at this period, there certainly is anecdotal evidence presented in these Confederate papers that 19th century Southern journalists were cognizant of the press' responsibility to keep the public informed on the issues of the day. Commentary on those issues may have been, as it is today, a different matter with a different set of standards.

Ultimately, this issue, like so many political fracases, resulted in much newspaper space being filled and much gnashing of teeth, but very little else. When Davis gave his speech, the Confederacy was already falling apart. The Union armies advancing through Georgia shut down or caused many of Davis' newspaper opponents to flee; in Virginia, the military situation forced the Confederate Congress to deal with more pressing issues, and, of course, the war ended only a scant five months after Davis' speech. However, the episode does give us an interesting glimpse into editorial and — to a lesser degree — political attitudes of the day toward the issue of freedom of the press. In sum, it should be remembered that these 19th century editors had two major and quite contemporary-sounding objections to being drafted: the loss of their independence, which they believed was necessary if they were to adequately cover the war for their readers, and the resultant loss of liberty for all Confederate citizens, not just the press. They were, it seems, journalists first, Rebels second.

Notes

1. Moore, Albert Burton. *Conscription and Conflict In the Confederacy.* New York: Macmillan Co. 1924: 52-53. According to Moore, the exemptions were designed to establish two classes of Southerners: the fighters and the producers. He says Congress

created these two classes because of the needs to maintain government through the war and to preserve a healthy national life (that is, so that there was someone at home raising the corn, building the guns and educating the children). The 1862 law exempted the Confederate Congress; members of state legislatures, clerks of the officers of the state and Confederate governments; postmen; ferrymen on post routes; pilots and others engaged in river or rail transportation; telegraph operators; ministers; iron, furnace and foundry workers; printers and editors of newspapers; academics and university presidents; teachers with more than 20 students or teachers of handicapped students; hospital superintendents; nurses who work in hospitals; pharmacists; and wool and cotton factory employees. OR Series IV, Vol. I, 1081.
2. According to Moore, this was not the first time in the war an attempt had been made to remove journalists' exemption, but in the past, such attempts had been attributed to Congress, and it had been Congress who newspapers had criticized rather than Davis. See page 66 for his discussion.
3. Strode, Hudson. *Jefferson Davis: Confederate Hero*. New York: Harcourt, Brace and Co. 1959: 238.
4. *Ibid.*, 63.
5. Letter from W. N. Pendleton to Jefferson Davis, December 26, 1864. Jefferson Davis, 1808-1889 Collection. Special Collections Department, Robert W. Woodruff Library, Emory University.
6. *Ibid.*
7. Avery, I.W. *The History of the State of Georgia from 1850 to 1881*. New York: Brown and Derby, Publishers. 1881:293.
8. Nevins, Allan. *The Statemanship of the Civil War*. New York: Macmillan. 1953:26. In fact, Brown and Davis had begun the war on friendly terms, but it was the president's determination to enforce the conscription laws that led to his estrangement from arch-states righter Brown. See Eaton, 221.
9. Schaff, Morris. *Jefferson Davis: His Life and Personality*. Boston: John W. Luce & Co. 1922:198.
10. Eaton, Clement. *Jefferson Davis*. New York: Macmillan Publishers. 1977:196.
11. *Richmond Sentinel*, 10 November 1864. It is doubtful that anyone took Foote's resolution seriously; according to Eaton, Foote opposed Davis on just about everything, even going so far on one occasion as to propose that Davis be deposed and Lee installed as dictator. Eventually, Foote was expelled from the house for his obnoxious behavior. See Eaton, 215-216.
12. Davis, Jefferson. The Rise and Fall of the Confederate Government. Vol. 2. New York: D. Appleton & Co. 1881:565.
13. Catton, Bruce. *Never Call Retreat*. Garden City, N.Y.: Doubleday & Co., Inc. 1965:396.
14. Avery, 292.
15. Catton, 408.
16. Pendleton letter to Davis.
17. Cox, Jacob D. *The March to the Sea, Franklin and Nashville*. New York: Charles Scribner's Sons. 1882: 6.
18. Moore, Albert Burton. *Conscription and Conflict in the Confederacy*. New York: Macmillan Co. 1924: 320.
19. Moore, 303-304.
20. Moore, 305.
21. *Augusta Chronicle*, 12 November 1864 and *Macon Telegraph*, 14 November 1864.
22. Moore, 83.
23. Rowland, Dunbar, ed. *Jefferson Davis: Constitutionalist. His Letters, Papers and Speeches*. Jackson, Miss: Mississippi Department of Archives and History. 1923:392.
24. *Augusta Constitutionalist*, 22 November 1864

25. *Augusta Chronicle*, 12 November 1864.
26. *Augusta Chronicle*, 25 November 1864.
27. *Charleston Mercury*, 23 November 1864.
28. *Macon Telegraph*, 15 November 1864.
29. *Southern Watchman*, 6 December 1864.
30. *Augusta Chronicle*, 23 November 1864.
31. *Richmond Enquirer*, 9 November 1864
32. *Augusta Chronicle*, 23 November 1864.
33. Eaton, Clement. *Jefferson Davis*. New York: Macmillan Publishers. 1977:13.
34. *Macon Telegraph*, 15 November 1864.
35. *Southern Watchman*, 16 November 1864.
36. *Southern Watchman*, 30 November 1864.
37. *Richmond Enquirer*, 10 November 1864.
38. *Macon Telegraph*, 18 November 1864.
39. The animosity was so great between Brown and Davis that in Davis' history of the Civil War, he makes absolutely no mention of Brown by name, either in the text or in the index. William T. Sherman, by contrast, is mentioned on 12 occasions by name in the book. On the one occasion when a reference to Brown is made, Davis refers to him merely as "the governor of Georgia."
40. *Southern Watchman*, 6 December 1864.
41. *Richmond Sentinel*, 25 November 1864.
42. *Augusta Chronicle*, 23 November 1864.
43. *Augusta Constitutionalist*, 10 November 1864.
44. *Augusta Constitutionalist*, 7 December 1864.
45. *Augusta Constitutionalist*, 7 December 1864.

28

Isaac Mayer Wise, *The Israelite*, and the Civil War

Barbara Straus Reed
Rutgers University

Isaac Mayer Wise was a prolific writer and founded a popular weekly, *The Israelite*, an English-Jewish newspaper. He entered upon a career chiefly directed toward the organization of American Jewry and soon became one of the outstanding Jewish religious leaders in America. Wise was easily the most distinguished organizer and leader of American Reform Jewry. He died in Cincinnati, March 26, 1900.

Born on March 29, 1819, Wise was twenty-three when he passed his rabbinical examinations.[1] He married Therese Bloch; their marriage endured for the next thirty years, and they had ten children.[2] In 1845, while visiting Frankfurt, Wise attended the second of three great Reform rabbinical conferences held in Germany between 1844 and 1846, and later introduced to the Jews in America the reforms approved at this conference.[3] Wise left home and family in Bohemia to breathe in a free atmosphere.[4] It took sixty-three days for the Wises to cross the ocean in a sailing vessel filled with smallpox victims. Wise met with Dr. Max Lilienthal, who served as chief rabbi of three Orthodox congregations, among others.[5]

Wise became rabbi in Albany, New York.[6] He wrote two lectures about Reform and saw one published in *The Occident* and *American*

Jewish Advocate.[7] *The Occident* was the only Jewish magazine, a monthly, at the time; Wise realized he could achieve change through a publication. Many Jews in America were estranged from their religious heritage, and Wise perceived the best kind of Judaism in this country would be one free from some of the demands of tradition.

Wise the Journalist

On invitation, Wise responded to articles written by a young clergyman, identified as M.R. Miller, who claimed that the foundation of Judaism lay in Christian mysticism, and not long after that, Wise contributed several articles.[8] Wise also sought to bring about a union of American Jews in 1848.[9] Unity would assist the Jewish immigrants in adapting to the new land, Wise thought, while increasing their resistance to making concessions to the majority culture. It would also help them to remain a distinctive ethnic and religious group and to perpetuate Judaism.

The Occident was placed at Wise's disposal.[10] As Wise campaigned, he alienated different factions opposed to him; eventually he lost interest in Jewish affairs on the national level and wrote little for *The Occident*, and until November 1849, his work did not appear in print. Then he shifted his attention to *The Asmonean*, the first Jewish weekly newspaper.[11] Unexpectedly, Wise received an offer to create a "department" in the columns of *The Asmonean,* to be called "Theology and Philosophy."[12] Wise's first column appeared on September 10, 1852.[13] He sought to satisfy his audience by tailoring his style and content within their range of comprehension and the news of the time. He said that he had written "simply, democratically, popularly and thoughtfully."[14]

For eighteen months he contributed many articles to *The Asmonean*. His last contribution in *The Asmonean* appeared April 5, *1853*. A week later, he announced that due to his move to Cincinnati he could not continue his weekly articles.[15]

Wise in Cincinnati

Cincinnati was the pioneer city of the West.[16] In 1840 the census figures showed a population of 46,338, growing 149 per cent to 114,435 by 1850.[17] Cincinnati was a predominantly German city. Many who had fled Europe predisposed to ideas of progress did not fear change and innovation.[18] They possessed a high cultural level, and the Jews among them were acculturated to their European neighbors. The result was a significant slowing of the process of

Americanization of the Jews. In the history of Cincinnati's Jewish community, the initial group came from England, and the immigrants arrived between 1820 and 1830; with them came a few Dutch and French Jews.19

K'hillah K'dosha Bene Yeshurun (KKBY), or Holy Congregation of the Sons of Israel, brought the Wise family to Cincinnati. From the start the congregation accepted his ideas for reform of the synagogue, so the goal of creating a palatable Judaism for Jews seemed within reach, at least in Cincinnati. An articulate voice to speak to the larger public of Jewry had yet to be established. *The Israelite,* Isaac Mayer Wise's paper, became that voice.

Before Wise left for Cincinnati, he had inquired of his friends whether they would subscribe to a Jewish weekly which he intended to establish. After receiving encouraging replies, he decided to continue his journalistic activities. On the way to Cincinnati, he traveled through Syracuse and Rochester, and he also probably stopped in New York City where he acquired Hebrew types from someone who had printed the shortlived German-language paper, *Israels Herold,* another publication to which Wise had contributed.

In May of 1854, a month after assuming the Cincinnati position, Wise decided to establish a Jewish weekly and had to fmd a publisher. Charles F. Schmidt, a book and job printer and publisher of a German daily, became publisher, with the promise that Wise "would make good all losses at the end of the first year."21 His German-language evening paper, *Der Deutsche Republicaner* (spelled with a "c" rather than a "k" on the masthead of the paper), in existence since September 1842, espoused principles of the Whig party, to which Wise belonged.22

Now Wise could establish a paper, in English, with a few Hebrew typefaces to give it the flavor he desired. Next came the prospectus, notifying the community of the forthcoming publication; announcing Wise's name and what he stood for, describing the direction Wise would take: the kinds of comment he entertained, and the role the weekly would, play in the Jewish community. He promised "a fearless organ."23

There was no doubt about the choice of "Israelite" for the name of Wise's paper. The connotations of the word "Jew" emotionally, orally, and intellectually, did not make Wise—and many other Jews—happy. Indeed, Wise sought to withdraw as far as possible from the painful and belittling connection. On the other hand, "Israelite" was pure, a new term for Jews in a new land. The non-Jewish community would see this term as identifying a different kind of Jew, a modern Jew.

However, the paper met with indifference from the area surrounding Cincinnati, and few replied; "still fewer from other cities" responded.24 He wrote, "Shortly thereafter I visited.. where about ten Jewish families lived.... Seven of them declared they could not read English; one said that a Jewish paper was a useless commodity, and two subscribed."25 Wise remained undaunted. Later, as an editor, he would make many journeys, for the practice of railroads included issuing passes to newspaper editors, thereby allowing him to promote his publication and also made him aware of concerns of Jews outside Cincinnati.

He and Schmidt had the first paper ready for distribution on Friday, July 14, 1854. The first issue bore the date July 15, 5614, A.M., 1854 A.C., a Sabbath; thus, the first typographical error appeared.27 The date of Volume I, No. 2, was a Friday, and from then on, every Friday afternoon saw a new issue of *The Israelite*.

Subscribers to *The Israelite*, which arrived via mail, paid three dollars per annum, in advance. Wise developed advertising rates on a sliding scale.28 Various individuals undertook the task of acting as agents for *The Israelite*: these people collected subscription money and forwarded it to Wise. However, this hardly covered the cost of publication, and financial problems due to lack of subscribers plagued him for years. One of the reasons was that fully two-thirds of the Jews in America were unable to read English.29 Furthermore, Wise was troubled that: "Frivolity and indifference were the order of the day, and in the cities atheism and hatred of all religion were rampant among Germans."30 He believed that this attitude and behavior influenced newly arrived Jews as well.

Subtitled "A Weekly Periodical, devoted to the Religion, History and literature of the Israelites," *The Israelite* attested to Wise's writing ability and excellent use of English, even though he was self-taught.31 In fact, Wise began to familiarize himself with the English language while in Bohemia.32 Wise wrote and edited everything in the early issues by force of circumstance: Original written contributions promised by friends never materialized.

Wise, who had a sense of history, recognized the need to preserve records and urged secretaries to report results of public meetings, elections, and other transactions, because they "...will be valuable to ...see how Judaism has been planted in this western continent, and how the pioneer societies struggled, worked and triumphed."33 The idea of receiving articles from well-known people was important to impress readers that a *national* Jewish weekly had been launched. Wise reached a large audience through his paper and exercised far-reaching influence, for he edited and published the energetic weekly for the Jewish community across the nation. Wise's product seemed lively and sociable, the articles unpolished. The general physical appearance of Wise's paper was 11 inches wide, 15 and 1/4th inches long.

Debits and Credits

Wise's publishing enterprises appeared to have cost him dearly in money. He lost six hundred dollars on *The Israelite* during the first year, although the losses had been guaranteed.34 Schmidt lost enough on *The Israelite* during the first year to force a change of publisher. However, Wise did not display any signs of financial problems in the contents of the paper. He wrote, "We have learned, that *The Israelite* is a popular and much read journal, not one line of it escapes the notice of our readers, the hearts of our people are with us. . . ."35

Wise and his brother-in-law, Edward Bloch, set up as printers and publishers, bought type and presses, and started business with debts of three-thousand dollars.36 Bloch and Company eventually occupied an entire five-story building, east of Walnut Street, 32 West Sixth Street, "well adapted to large and increasing business. In addition to printing for Wise's output, Bloch undertook job printing. *The Israelite* took on a more interesting look with headlines in new, decorative type.38 Thus, with no hint of the financial troubles, he began the first number of the second volume of *The Israelite* on a note of exultation:

> The progress of *The Israelite* during the first year of its existence has no precedent in the history of journalism. The causes of the brilliant success are manifold. There is the known zeal and unabated enthusiasm of its editor on behalf of Judaism and the nation professing it... *The Israelite* . . . is fully and truly what it pleads to be. . . .
> None we are sure will ever succeed in silencing our voice, frightening us away from the field of sacred action, changing our garment before the eyes of the community, or shaking our confidence in the good sense of our people, the uprightness and fidelity of our friends, and the sacredness and godliness of our cause.39

Wise sought new readers continually.40 Residents of other areas, "having other business," consented to serve Wise's purposes as well as canvass for the paper. Wise also acknowledged that subscribers, too, acted as agents. Beginning with the October 23, 1857, issue, he ran a listing of agents from thirteen cities and towns, from Boston to San Francisco to New Orleans, on the front page. Another method

Wise used to encourage readership was to boast of a large circulation. At the end of the first year, he claimed to have more than 1,500 subscribers; at the end of the third year, ten-thousand readers, certainly a bandwagon approach to gain circulation!

A look at Wise's subscription lists printed in his paper shows a wide geographical dispersion, reflecting settlements of Jews. Cincinnati, a wholesale center for the South as well as the Middle West, served as a spot for Jewish merchants to visit regularly, to purchase goods for their stores and their families which they could not procure in their areas. When these merchants came to visit, they probably placed some out-of-town advertisements in *The Israelite*. The newspaper office stood as the place to buy advertisements as well as subscriptions. Those subscribers received receipts on the spot and were not mentioned in the paper, for there was no need to do so. Wise used his listing of subscribers as a way of giving receipts without having to send separate missives, thereby saving postal costs. Indeed, his journalistic effort operated on a shoestring. He noted the name and city of the subscriber and sum received, in case there was some discrepancy. Mostly those from out-of-town who had mailed in subscriptions were noted, and sometimes *The Israelite* only printed the names of repeat subscribers. Therefore, few local subscribers' names showed up. Nevertheless *The Israelite* was circulated to a large number of settlement points. Certainly many subscribers who never had their names published in the paper, such as those who renewed subscriptions at the same time as they paid for an ad. Clearly *The Israelite* also had a large pass-along rate, probably four or five households per issue.

In addition to the new type and perhaps new readers, Bloch and Company redesigned the publication, beginning with Vol. IV, No.1, July 10, 1857. The paper measured 11 and 3/4ths inches wide and 19 inches long and thus took on a more vertical makeup.

Wise also received assistance from a strong ally. Rabbi Max Lilienthal had been corresponding editor of *The Israelite*, since September 15, 1854, Vol.1, No.10. Another Cincinnati congregation needed a rabbi, and, in May of 1855, acting upon Wise's recommendation, they elected Lilienthal to the pulpit. With his arrival, a most remarkable relationship began between the two, which lasted until Lilienthal's death in 1862.[42] He became associate editor with the July 27, 1855, issue, Vol.11, No.3.

The Israelite reported news from both the local and non-local Jewish community, which enabled Jews throughout the country to feel a sense of belonging to something larger than their own neighborhood or regional settlement. These briefs noted reforms taking place in Jewish congregations throughout the country, issues of injustice and persecution abroad, and notices about famous Jews' travels, books, and the like. Wise saw the connection between peoplehood and religion which combine to form Judaism. He reported on synagogue consecrations in new settlements, the establishment of Jewish hospitals, benevolent-aid societies, orphanages, and schools for the poor. Philanthropy of all kinds offered another way to express ethnic identity and contributed to the survival of isolated Jewish communities. Included in his paper, too, was poetry, sermons, theological discussions, and segments of novels, the last written to stir Jewish patriotism, feelings of Jewish identity.[43] In his *Reminiscences*, Wise disclosed the need to arouse Jewish pride in Jewish history. He recognized the need to educate his readers on Jewish subjects. Historical sketches, biblical criticism, Talmudic and philosophical expositions, discussions of ancient traditions—all found a place in *The Israelite*.

Hard news stories ran from a paragraph as in announcing the sermon schedule, to more than one column for meetings to discuss Reform or to galvanize people to act. Wise carried obituaries and marriage notices about people living throughout the country. He printed resolutions from congregations thanking him or others for services rendered. He carried news of alterations of the English oaths bill and of other legislated injustices. Much correspondence in the weekly dealt with Reform, opposition to statements in sermons he printed, praise for his writing and actions, and defense of Judaism and the Jews from attacks by Christian and American newspapers.

Editorially, *The Israelite* came out fighting. Wise used the paper to disseminate his ideas and views on a wide variety of topics of special concern to him and his readers. Wise was a religious liberal and a Jeffersonian. He took special pride in living in America, the land of freedom, and stood up to every opponent he recognized. Above all, Wise wanted to ward off all attacks directed against Jews, whether intentionally or unwittingly, and to present Judaism in its true form.

Zion College and Unity

In the second issue of *The Israelite* Wise began to project another venture close to his heart.[44] Wise wanted a seminary to train rabbis, and he wanted Jewish congregations to form a union, because he knew that the seminary would be viable only as long as it served the needs of those congregations.[45] *The Israelite* announced that two hundred members had enrolled in the Zion Collegiate Association, and that it would increase to four hundred.[46] Wise assumed formal leadership when he was elected President.[47] Free scholarships, an examination of pupils, and the opening of the course of instruction three days later were announced.[48] Wise soon learned of his blunder in pushing too quickly. In a lengthy statement the New York Association declared, "We are excluded from acting, and we do not consider consistent with our dignity and position to continue our labors under the auspices under which we have been appointed. Wise had pledged to his supporters in New York that they would have a say in the proposed institution, but he had forgotten them. Support for the college outside Cincinnati evaporated. The college was near collapse by the beginning of 1856.

Minhag America

Wise was still ahead of his time. His travels made him conscious of the chaos in ritual and perceived the need for a minhag America, or American rite. Undaunted, Wise went forward with his proposed "book of common prayer for the Jews of America."[50] *Minhag America*, translated by Isaac M. Wise, appeared in 1857.[51] Attacks on *Minhag America* came from *The Asmonean* and *The Occident*.[52]

Wise replied to the attacks in *The Israelite*. The incensed editor wrote with a sharp pen. Wise understood better than his critics what the new Americans wanted. Publishing a heavy tome could take the theological world in Germany by storm, but in America a lighter touch was needed. For Wise, the book represented the union of American Jewry—under *his* leadership, of course!

Wise and the Civil War

Wise was in Cincinnati during the Civil War, and Cincinnati was considered a border between free and slave-holding states. Moreover, the area surrounding Cincinnati was part of the "Underground Roilroad" through which slaves were taken to Canada and liberated. Attempts to arrest slaves and return them under the Fugitive Slave Law even resulted in riots in Cincinnati and environs.

Indeed, Cincinnati was embroiled in controversy before the Civil

War began. A half-dozen years earlier, the Whigs split over slavery. In fact, Salmon P. Chase led a Free Soil movement; from this sprang the Ohio Republican Patty, in July 1855. Chase suggested Wise attach himself to the Republican Party, rather than working for a religious idea within a relatively narrow circle, but Wise, who apparently sat at the table at which the party was created, declined.53

Also, Wise congratulated Stephen A. Douglas for his successful Illinois state campaign; he even noted Douglas's claims to run for President in 1860. Wise offered Douglas his paper's support, and suggested it would be transformed into a daily. Douglas, however, did not respond. Thus, Wise had lost hope for Zion College and an association of rabbis; he turned to the thought of embarking on support of various political causes via a daily paper. Clearly, his role as rabbi of a congregation and editor of a Jewish weekly confined him somewhat. In the election of 1858, one candidate from Cincinnati was a minister, and Wise projected himself—at least in fantasy—into the arena, to be the first rabbi to campaign for election to Congress.

Wise, however, found himself doing political preaching and was put on notice by the board of his congregation that he make no more political allusions in sermons. Wise declared in the *Israelite* in an article titled "No Political Preaching," that "Not one single word have we, as yet, said in the pulpit on the politics of the day. Fifteen years we have preached in this country...we never said one word on politics." 54

Wise took the position of remaining neutral during the election of November 1860. Indeed, he predicted peace: "The republicans have turned lamkins, tender and innocent, immaculate and bashful. . . .They are as tame and obliging now as the peasant the first time in the city. . . .The same thing. ..is the case in the extreme south with fire eaters, seceders and political circus riders."55

He seemed to be seeking reconciliation between the North and South and stated that the two sides would "cool down" before the end of the year.56 He held this to be the case because "people care very little for abstract ideas, extreme views, or false conceptions of honor when their material interests are neglected or even ruined."57 Further, he was so convinced that secession would not occur that he asked for payment for *The Israelite* to be sent from any state in the Union.58

When South Carolina seceded, Wise wrote a long editorial, in which he said,

The fanatics in both sections of the country succeeded in destroying the most admirable fabric of government. Under the pretext of progress and liberty, state rights and personal freedom they have made the beginning of destroying the proud structure of liberty to which all good men looked with hope and satisfaction.[59]

Wise sounded relatively neutral, but his editorial then proceeds with words against the Abolitionists.

Demagogues who sought office at any price, red Republicans and habitual revolutionists who feed on excitement and civil wars, German atheism and American Puritanism who know no limits to their fanaticism, visionary philanthropists and wicked preachers who have that religion which is most suitable to their congregations, speculators in property, stock jobbers and usurers whose God is Mammon, thoughtless multitudes and hired criers in the South and North succeeded in breaking down the fortress of liberty, the great bulwark of our best hopes.[60]

Wise was pessimistic. "Either the Republican party must be killed off forever by constitutional guarantees to the South, to make an end forever to this vexing slavery question or the Union must be dissolved." He observed that the three-quarters of the states needed were not to be had. "Because we have too many demagogues and fantasist [sic] therefore we maintain this Union is as good as dissolved."[61]

Wise, the eternal optimist, turned prophet on the occasion of the Jewish New Year:

The year 1861 must witness either the end of the Republican party or the dissolution of the Union. The Republicans know this very well and talk quite freely of the final and perpetual separation of the North and South. All their maneuvers [sic] are intended to that point They want neither war nor coercion nor compromises. Separation is their final object. They maintain their object of Abolition can best be achieved by the separated of the South from the North.[62]

When President James Buchanan called upon all religious people to observe a day of fasting and prayer on January 4, 1861, *The Israelite* sarcastically referred to Buchanan's actions, describing him as one of the main agents of spreading calamity and as being possessed of "hatred and feeling of vengeance."[63] At the same time, on the very same page, there appeared an announcement of a special service for Friday morning, January 4, at the Lodge Street synagogue, where the "Rev. Doctors Wise and Lilienthal" would preach.

Some concern must have been expressed for they used another synagogue, and the "No Political Preaching" article declaring not to use the pulpit for political messages caused him to admit, "for that very reason refused to preach the fourth of January last, in order not to violate our principle."64 Yet Wise was aware of the uglier side of politics as practiced in America, for he wrote,

> Politics in this country means money, material interest, and no more. The leaders of all parties are office-seekers or office-holders. They hold or seek offices, not in order to benefit the community, but to benefit themselves....
>
> Land speculators, who bought large tracts of land in Kansas, exercized every sort of influence to make her a free state, in order to increase the price of land. Other speculators...exercized all their influence in order to make a slave state of Kansas, in order to direct the current of migration to such states or territories where they possessed land, so as to dispose of it at improved rates. Slave holders favor the extension of slavery because it increased their wealth, and land speculators oppose it because they find their present account by it. Politics and money are synonymous, however holy, exalted or lofty these things may appear to the myriads of honest men who are dragged along by party leaders...
>
> Politics is a business, and in many instances a mean business, which requires more cheat and falsehood than a vulgar scoundrel would practice. Philosiphize over it as you please...it remains a vulgar business...with which we are fairly disgusted on account of its dishonesty and violence.65

To Wise then, the issues wrenching the American republic just prior to the Civil War and the national day of prayer suggest they were not issues worth fighting—and dying—for the Negro, Free Soil or the extension of slavery to the territories, the right of secession or the indissolubility of the Union, seem to be equal to controversies over the spoils of office or the granting of land to a railway, to Wise. Wise did not regard slavery as an issue, it seems; nor did he endorse the Abolitionists.66 On the other hand, he opposed Rabbi Morris Raphall's biblical justification of slavery: "...among all nonsense imposed on the Bible the greatest is to suppose the Negroes are the descendants of Ham, and the curse of Noah is applicable to them."67 Yet though he contested the view that Negro slavery was supported by scriptural texts, he did not feel strongly about the issue of slavery. Yes, he was against it, and openly so after the Emancipation Proclamation. His major concern was with the Union. Were America to be divided, it may not retain the liberties it held to and Europeans could encroach and build empires. The Union idea came first, even if it was blemished by Negro servitude. Thus, if he had to perpetuate slavery to prevent secession, so be it.

It was not only his living in a border area of the nation that accounts for Wise's reticence, but also his feeling as a Jew played a part. Wise "was essentially a middle-of-the-road man, not only in religion, but also in politics. The only exception was where politics touched Jewish emancipation and liberty. Then he was an implacable extremist and demanded immediate change."68 Wise supported the federal and state constitutions; he considered them the crowning glories of the republic. Massachusetts, the center for Abolitionists, also was anti-alien, specifically anti-Irish. However, what immigrant would feel secure in such an atmosphere? So Abolitionists were hypocrites in Wise's view, for in Massachusetts in 1859, they adopted a law requiring aliens to have seven years' residence and naturalization to qualify for holding public office.69 His view reflects an intense dislike of enacting distinctions between different sections of the population. He also saw in the Abolitionists not men who wanted to grant liberty to slaves, but men who wanted to interfere with the liberty of the states, lumping them together with those who would restrict the liquor, traffic, enforce Sunday observance, and somehow make Christianity a legally established religion. Somehow, the Protestant clergy who supported abolition disproportionately came under the Jewish editor's attack.

> Who in the world could act worse, more extravagant and reckless in this crisis than Protestant priests did? From the very start of the unfortunate difficulties the consequences of which we now suffer so severely, the Protestant priests threw the firebrand of abolitionism into the very heart of this country...There was not a Protestant paper in existence that had not weekly an abolitionist tirade. There was scarcely a sermon preached without a touch at least of the "existing evil." You know who made Jefferson Davis and the rebellion? The priests did and their whiners and howlers in the press. The whole host of priests would rather see this country crushed and crippled than discard their fanaticism or give up their political influence.70

He very much felt they were the cause of the war:

> Under the pretext of philanthropy, the everlasting slavery question has been made the text point of almost every sermon. This more than anything else has been instrumental in [bringing on] this war... Had the clergymen excluded politics from the pulpit... I for one believe we should not have experienced this war.71

Later, Wise compared the current situation with that of Moses, showing how the Jews could oppose slavery.72 Yet, Wise could not maintain it "absolutely unjust"to purchase slaves, "or rather their labor, place them under the protection of the law, and secure them the benefit of civilized society and their sustenance for their labor."73 Thus he was able to rationalize not getting involved in abolition. But a more important reason was Wise's concern for what splitting the

Union might do.

Wise deplored secession: "this is the most terrible blow the cause of humanity is likely to suffer in the year 1861," he wrote, as the crisis built. Yet he acknowledged that the right to secede was there, "Force will not hold together this Union; it was cemented by liberty and can stand only by the affections of the people...Force and liberty are antagonistic. Either must fall to the ground."74 By March of the next year, an anti-Semitic attack on Judah P. Benjamin by Senator Henry Wilson of Massachusetts had irritated Wise to the point where he considered secession more favorably.75 It was another instance of his associating Abolitionism with attempts to Christianize the Constitution.

Wise wrote shortly after the fall of Fort Sumter to Confederate forces, under a headline, "Silence, our policy":

> We are the servant of peace, not of war. Hitherto we thought fit to say something on public affairs, and it was our ardent hope to assist those who wished to prevent civil war, but we wasted our words. What can we say now? Shall we lament and weep like Jeremiah over a state of things too sad and too threatening to be looked upon with indifference? We would only be laughed at... or probably abused for discouraging the sentiment. Or should we choose sides with one of the parties? We cannot, not only because we abhor the idea of war, but also we have dear friends and near relations, beloved brethren and kinsmen in either section of the country, that our heart bleeds on thinking of their distress. . . .
> Therefore, silence must henceforth be our policy, silence on all the questions of the day, until a spirit of conciliation shall move the hearts of millions to a better understanding of the blessings of peace, freedom, and union. . . .76

He encountered problems with the breaking out of the war, because subscribers to *The Israelite* lived in the South and became cut off from the paper, and because many in the North canceled their subscriptions. In June of 1861, he lamented that the postmaster-general's stopping mall to seceding states was unconstitutional.77

He also encountered problems with accusations by the Rev. Moncure D. Conway, who accused him of not supporting the Union cause and of unfair motives. Wise responded that he never preached on politics.78 As the weeks and months rolled by, with only the barest suggestion of war penetrating the columns of *The Israelite*, Wise avoided the topic in his reflections, written for the New Year 5622 and twelve months later.79 In fact, he may have been ambivalent. For example, "Should this war result in an entire restoration of this union to its former majesty and integrity . . ." 80; the reprinting "as somewhat of a curiosity" of a form of prayer for the Confederacy introduced by the Rev. Dr. Bernard Illowy into some synagogues of the South[81]; and an editorial headed "To preachers," commending the vacant pulpit at Charleston, S.C.[82]

In his July fourth sermon of 1863, reprinted in his paper, Wise lamented the war and desolation that had overtaken the country, but was careful not to fault one party or the other. The past years of the country he found to be a link each of a long chain of prosperity without precedent in history. Wealth, however, had led them to "an insane, corruptive and demoralising luxury." They had danced madly around the golden calf and therefore stood disgraced before the civilized world.[83] Undoubtedly his observations during this time were influenced by the sadness of the destruction of the war, and there probably was a question in his mind about whether the Union, which meant so very much to him, could survive the conflict

As with other Jewish editors of the period, Wise placed the main issues of the war outside his purview, but he became righteous and indignant when the rights or honor of Jews were touched: when anti-Semitic accusations were rendered; when Congress failed to grant Jews the right to have Army chaplains; or when General Ulysses Grant issued his notorious General Order No.11 expelling Jews from areas under his command. The Jews were singled out in Grant's order because they were a scapegoat. Later, Wise wrote that he was convinced that "The noise against the Jews at that time was a stratagem to cover the huge swindles practised on Uncle Sam's purse."[84] Indeed, Wise did not overlook the problems Grant created as General Grant when he ran for President.

Wise, who had adamantly refused to talk politics, became involved in September 1863. He was nominated for state senator, on a Saturday and so he was not present — and received 280 votes out of a possible 312. "Dr. Wise is a gentleman of learning and accomplishments— and is well known as an estimable Hebrew rabbi of this city. He would make an excellent Senator," wrote the *Daily Enquirer*.[85] While Wise must have been pleased, for members of his congregation the news of the nomination caused concern. The synagogue Board met and unanimously came to a decision, which they communicated to Wise.

> Rev. Sir—By unanimous desire of the Board of Trustees of K. K. Bene Jeshurun, I am instructed to communicate to you that the subject of your nomination as State Senator by a Convention held at Carthage, on the 5th inst., has been fully deliberated upon.
>
> The Board feels greatly honoured by this demonstration of confidence bestowed upon you; they are also well aware of your sincere attachments to our common country;

nevertheless, as it is an established law with us that our minister should be present in the synagogue whenever divine service is held, and also, your services otherwise being indispensably necessary in our congregation, as well as in the scholastic department, you are hereby politely but most emphatically requested to decline the said nomination at once.

With due regard, I have the honor to be, Rev. Sir, your obedient servant, Fred. Eichberg, Sec'y of the K.K. Holy Congregation Bene Jeshuren.

The sharp words "emphatically" and "at once" suggest the Board's urgency and strength of conviction.

Moreover, at the same time, the board of directors of the religious school addressed Wise, enclosing a resolution they had Passed that day. The language is even stronger:

The Rev. Dr. Wise is engaged as school superintendent, with a fixed salary attached, and the duties of the superintendent are such as to require his attendance almost daily at the school.

Resolved, that we remonstrate to the acceptance, by the Rev. Dr. Wise of the above named nomination.

Resolved, that we desire the Rev. Dr. Wise to decline the nomination, and for particular reason, that the duties and obligations due to our Institute are paramount to any other engagements.[86]

Wise replied to the communications, in part saying

I beg leave to state that the duties I owe to the congregation and the school are prior to those of any other office to which I might be elected hereafter; therefore, as long as I am not dispensed of the first, I cannot enter upon any other. As you maintain you cannot dispense with my humble services for the time I might be obliged to spend at the Capital of the State, and the law of the congregation especially ordains it so, I certainly feel obliged to decline a nomination so honourably tendered, not withstanding my private opinion, that I might render some services to my country, not altogether unessential, especially as those who nominated me know well my sincere attachment to this country and government. God will save the Union and the Constitution; liberty and justice for all, without my active co-operation, being, after all, without any political aspirations—only an humble individual. [87]

Certainly, this contrasts with the tone of the editor of *The Israelite*. His denial of political ambitions and his expression of belief in the Union call attention to what he professes to disavow. Some hints or leaks of the proceedings may have been given to the press. The evening paper, the *Daily Times*, published the correspondence, and the *Daily Enquirer* appeared with the following announcement:

> The Rev. Dr. Wise has been forced, by outside pressure, to decline the democratic nomination for State Senator. Had his name been on the other ticket, the Shoddy Contractors who have been so busy in pulling the wires to produce this result, would have been contented to let it remain. The names of these Shoddy Contractors do not appear on the record, but they are known nevertheless.[88]

Evaluation

Wise represented as personal an editor as Horace Greeley, who may have been his role model. The two men met in New York not long after Wise arrived in America and later exchanged letters, intermittently, over the years. Indeed, Stoddard's words on Greeley apply to Wise as well.

> He had a gospel to preach; it was the neediest gospel of the time, and his chosen pulpit was a newspaper.... it was to be a platform from which he would speak to and for the people. There was much to be done in their behalf. . . [89]

To compare, both were brilliant editors, honest crusaders. However, Greeley moved on to other causes when one collapsed and faded; the role model clamored for something new, but when it failed he abandoned friends and allies to move onto another cause. Wise, to the contrary, struck out boldly but with a sense of responsibility. He found himself tempered by events and individuals around him. He would advocate, but he would also instruct. More importantly, he would compromise and improvise in both religious principles and practices. In the end he bested Greeley.

Through his weekly newspaper, whose readership stretched from coast to coast and throughout the Middle West, Wise made himself a well-known rabbi in America. He wanted to interpret Judaism in ways that bore directly on contemporary life. Judaism, he seemed to feel, was a religion for all times. He did not want it to stay hooked on outworn pegs of ritual for ritual's sake. His *Israelite* enabled him to carry his opinions throughout the land, thereby propelling him to national attention in the Jewish community. Wise saw an opportunity to help build that community.

To attract readers, Wise wrote in the vernacular, directly, plainly, and in a warm, friendly manner. Readers of *The Israelite* shared Wise's every feeling. He invited their empathy. Wise became the interpreter of Jewish thought to his reading public, writing as if he were conversing with his readers. He knew that he had to reach and communicate with readers of various types.

Wise's newspaper articles attest to his passionate belief in reason, liberty, and progress as well as a hatred of any institution standing in their way.

In conclusion, Wise used *The Israelite* as his soap box, his platform. His weekly interpretations of Jewish thought reflected his plans for Judaism in America, and the Civil War presented a distraction for him from that goal. He remained relatively uninvolved, this immigrant from Austria, who lived in a state with a slavery ban, and so did not deal directly with the institution of slavery. Indeed, he lived in a city very much connected with the South, so much so that he declined to assume moral superiority or to take the high road. From his perspective, the United States was fine as it was, emphasizing freedom, so he found it unnecessary to depart from the status quo and interfere.

Notes

1. Controversy exists about whether he received *s'micha*, or ordination, which allowed him to call himself "rabbi"; "rabbi" also means teacher.
2. One daughter, Effie, married Adolph Ochs, later owner of *The New York Times*.
3. At the Frankfurt conference, the principal topics of debate were the necessity for the retention of Hebrew in public services; prayers for the return to Palestine; the observance of the custom of calling to the pulpit men to read parts of the Scripture; and the introduction of the organ into the synagogue. All leaders of Reform Judaism in Germany discussed these questions. See Israel Knox, *Rabbi in America: The Story of Isaac M. Wise* (Boston and Toronto: Little, Brown and Co., *1957*), pp.13-21.
4. Biographical information on Wise abounds. His own *Reminiscences* (Cincinnati, Ohio: Leo Wise & Co., 1901) appeared soon after his death. The longest biography of Wise was written by his grandson, Max Benjamin May, *Isaac Mayer Wise—Founder of American Judaism. A Biography* (New York: G.P. Putnam's Sons, 1916). A short biography is included in David Philipson and Louis Grossman, eds., *Selected Writings of Isaac Mayer Wise* (Cincinnati, Ohio: The Robert Clarke Company, 1900; reissued ed. by Arno Press and The *New York Times*, 1969). His influence on Reform is gleaned from the *Year Book* of the Central Conference of American Rabbis; especially when he was president, 1889-1900; as well as the *Procedings* of the Union of American Hebrew Congregations. Joseph H. Gumbiner wrote *Isaac Mayer Wise, Pioneer of American Judaism* (New York: Union of American Hebrew Congregations, 1959) for high school students. Articles on Wise appeared regularly (partial listing): "After 100 years, Isaac Mayer Wise in the West," *American Jewish Archives*, Vol. VI (January, 1954), pp.14-15; Melvin Weinman, "The Attitude of Isaac Mayer Wise toward Zionism and Palestine," *American Jewish Archives*, Vol. III (January, 1951), pp.3-23; Martin Ryback, "The East-West Conflict in American Reform Judaism," *American Jewish Archives*, Vol. IV (January, 1952), pp.3-25; Sefton D. Temkin, "Isaac Mayer Wise and the Civil War," *American Jewish Archives*, Vol. XV (November, 1963), pp. 120A2; Joseph Gutmann, "Watchman on an American Rhine: New Light on Isaac M. Wise," *American Jewish Archives*, Vol. X (October, 1958) pp.135-44; and Isaac Mayer Wise, "World of My Books," translated by Albert Friedlander, *American Jewish Archives*, Vol. VI (June, 1954), pp.107-47. Perhaps the best treatment of Wise as rabbi, teacher, and guiding spirit of Reform is the two-volume Sefton Temkin biography, *Isaac Mayer Wise*, (unpublished Ph.D. dissertation, Hebrew Union College, Cincinnati, Ohio, 1964).

5. Isaac Mayer Wise, *Reminiscences,* translated and edited by David Philipson (Cincinnati, Ohio: Leo Wise & Co., 1901), p.25. The German original, *Reminscenzen*, began appearing in *Die Deborah* on July 3, 1894.
6. May, *op. cit.*, p.47.
7. Wise, *Reminiscences. op. cit., pp.55-56; The Occident*, Vol. V, No.2, May 1847, pp.109-10 and *ibid.*, Vol. V, No.3, June 1847, p.158.
8. The first of five articles under this title appeared in *The Occident*, Vol. VI, June 1848, p.133. Wise incorrectly referred to them as "Reason and Faith" in his *Reminiscences, op cit.,* pp.78-80.
9. Wise, *Reminiscences. op. cit.*, pp.85-86.
10. See *The Occident*, Vol. VI, No.7, October 1848, p.314. Others, including laymen, issued calls for union, *Ibid.*, p.321; Vol. IV, No.6, September 1846, p.308. Also see Maxine S. Seller, "Isaac Leeser's View on the Restoration of a Jewish Palestine," *American Jewish History Quarterly*, Vol. LVIII (September, 1968), pp.118-35.
11. *The Asmonean*, Vol.1, No.3, November 9, 1849, p.17.
12. Wise, *Reminiscences,op. cit.,* pp.200-01; see also Phllipson and Grossman, *op. cit.*, p. 41.Wise remained in touch with her through the years, and she gave him guidance with pieces in *The Israelite*, as Wise revealed in his *Reminiscences*, pp.3 1& 17.
13. *The Asmonean*, Vol. VI, No.21, September 10, 1852, p.199.
14. Wise, "World of My Books," *op.cit.*, p.15.
15. *The Asmonean*, Vol. VII, No.25, April 12, 1853, p.195.
16. Charles Frederic Goss, *Cincinnati: The Queen City, 1788-1912,* VoL II (Chicago, Illinois: The S.J. Clarke Publishing Co., 1912), p.21; Jack Cronin, "Cincinnati," *Museum Echoes* (Columbus, Ohio: Ohio State Archaelogical and Historical Society), Vol. XXVI, No.2, Serial No. 286 (February 1953), p.12.
17. Cronin, *op cit.* By contrast, Cleveland was a town of 17,034 in 1850.
18. Bertram Wallace Korn, *Eventful Years and Experiences: Studies in Nineteenth Century American Jewish History* (Cincinnati, Ohio: American Jewish Archives, 1954), p.1.
19. A significant portait of the first Jews of Cincinnati, their subsequent settlement and development of religious organizations appeared in *The Occident*, Vol.1, No.11, February 1844, pp. 547-50.Written by Joseph Jonas, the first Jew in the city, the history commenced in March 1817, when Cincinnati's population stood at 6,000, and Jonas was the sole Jew.
20. Wise, *Reminiscences. op. cit..* cit, p.266.
21. *Ibid.*
22. Henry John Groen, "A History of the German-American Newspapers of Cincinnati Before 1860," (Ph.D. dissertation, Ohio State University, 1944).
23. Wise, *Reminiscences. op. cit.,* p.267.
24. *Ibid.*, p.268.
25 *Ibid.*
26. Letter circa 1875 from Dr. Solomon H. Sonnensehein of St. Louis to Wise, American Jewish Archives, Cincinnati, Ohio. The letter confirms that Wise possessed such a pass at that time.
27. The year 5614 referred to the beginning of the world according to Jewish reckoning by going back to *The Bible*; A.M. is Latin, ano mundi. or the year of the world; A.C. is After Christ, or according to the Christian calendar.
28. *Ibid.*, p.8. "One square" for a one-time insertion ran $0.75; if it ran two times, $1; one month, $1.50; six months, $4; one year, $6. Display advertisements cost 50 per cent more than the above rates.
29. Wise, *Reminiscences. op. cit,* p.268.
30. *Ibid.*, p.271.
31. *Ibid.*, p.265.
32. Isaac Mayer Wise, "The World of My Books," translated and annotated by Albert H.

Friedlander, *American Jewish Archives,* Vol. VI, 1954, pp. 107-8. "Meine Buechereri" ("The World of My Books") began appearing in Wise's German-language Cincinnati newspaper *Die Deborah,* on September 17, 1896.
33. *The Israelite,* Vol.1, No.1, July 15, 1854, p.8.
34. Wise, "World of My Books," *op. cit.*, p.19.
35. *The Israelite,* Vol.1, No.52, July 6, 1855, p.412.
36. Wise, *Reminiscences. op. cit.*, p.292.
37. *The Israelite,* Vol. IV, No.17, October 30, 1857, pp.129, 132.
38. See for example, "The Fatal Secret," heading for a chapter of a novel, *The Israelite,* Vol. V, No.5, August, 8, 1858, p.33.
39. *Ibid.,* Vol.11, No.1, July 13, *1855,* p.4.
40. *Ibid.,* Vol.1, No.9, September 8, 1854; *Ibid.*, Vol.1, No.10 September 12, 1854; *Ibid.*, Vol.1, No.29, January 26, *1855,* p.228; *Ibid.*, Vol.1, No.34, March 2, *1855,* p.268; and and *Ibid.m* Vol. IV, No.19, November 13, 1857, p.145.
41. *Ibid.,* Vol. IV, No.16, p.113; *Ibid.*, Vol. III, No.5, August 8,1856, p.36; and *Ibid*, Vol.111, No.6, August 15, 1856, p.46.
42. May, *op. cit.*, p.163.
43. Wise, *Reminiscences. op. cit*, p.270.
44. *The Israelite,* Vol.1, No.2, July 21, 1854, p.12.
45. In 1873 he formed the Union of Hebrew Congregations. Two years later he founded Hebrew Union College and in 1889, founded the Central Conference of American Rabbis, an organization uniting America's Reform rabbis.
46. *The Israelite,* Vol I, No.21, December 1, 1854, p.164.
47. *Ibid.,* Vol II, No.14, October 12, 1855, p.108.
48. *Ibid.*, Vol.II, No.19, November 16, 1855, p.156.
49. Reprinted from *The Asmonean* of November 2, 1855, in *The Israelite,* Vol.11, No.19, November 16, 1855, p.156.
50. It was used by congregations in the United States for almost forty years.
51. The second part of the book did not appear for almost ten years. Wise announced its completion in *The Israelite,* July 20, 1866.
52. *The Asmonean,* Vol. XVI, No.20, August 28, 1857, p.156; *The Occident,* Vol. XV, August 1857, p.242.
53. Wise, *Reminiscences,* p.327.
54. *The Israelite,* Vol. VII, No.30, February 1, 1861, p. 244.
55. *Ibid.*, Vol. VII, No.21, November 30, 1860, p.172.
56. *Ibid.*
57. *Ibid.*
58. *Ibid.*
59. *Ibid.*, Vol. VII, No.25, December 28, 1860, p.205.
60. *Ibid.*
61. *Ibid.*
62. *Ibid.* Vol. VII, No.26, January 4, 1861, p.212.
63. *Ibid.,* Vol. VII, No.25, December 28, 1860, p.206.
64. *Ibid.* Vol. VII, No.30, February 1, 1861, p.244.
65. *Ibid.*
66. May, *op. cit.*, p., 243.
67. *The Israelite,* Vol. VII, No.28, January 18, 1861, p.230.
68. Jacob R. Marcus, "The Americanization of Isaac Mayer Wise," in *Studies in American Jewish History, Studies and Addresses* (Cincinnati: Hebrew Union College Press, 1969), p.185.
69. *The Israelite,* Vol.11, No.29, January 25, 1861, p.238.
70. *Ibid.*, Vol. VII, Vol.21, November 30, 1860, p.173; No.23, December 14, 1860, p.188; No.25, December 28, 1860, p.205; No.30, February 1, 1861, p.244; No. 36, March 15,

1861, p.292; No.47, May 31, 1861, p.381; Vol. VIII, No.15, October 18, 1861, p. 124; No.29, January 24, 1862, p.236.
71. *Ibid.*, Vol X, No.3, July 31, 1863, p.36.
72. *Ibid.*, Vol XI, No.24, December 23, 1864, p.204.
73. *Ibid.*, Vol. XI, No.23, December 16, 1864, p.196.
74. *Ibid*, Vol. VII, No.25, December 28, 1860, pp.205-206.
75. *Ibid.*, Vol. VII, No.37, March 22, 1861, p.386; ibid., Vol. IX, No.33, February 22, 1863, p. 356.
76. *Ibid.*, Vol. VII, No.41, April 19, 1861, p.344.
77. *Ibid.*, Vol. VII, *No.50,* June 14, 1861, p.396.
78. *Ibid.*, Vol. VII, No.47, May 31, 1861, p.380. In the latter issue, he also alluded to the interruption in production caused by the proclamation of martial law in Cincinnati.
79. Ibid., Vol. VIII, No.8, September 6, 1861, p.76; *ibid*, Vol. IX, No. 11, September 26, 1862, p.92.
80. *Ibid.*, Vol. VIII, No.32, February 14 1862, p.269.
81. *Ibid.*, p.263.
82. *Ibid.,* Vol. VIII, No.35, March 7, 1862, p.285.
83. *Ibid.*, Vol. X, No.2, July 10, 1863, p.12.
84. *Ibid.*, Vol XV, No.5, August 4, 1868, p.4.
85. Cincinnati *Enquirer*, September 6, 1863, p.3.
86. Cincinnati *Daily Times*, September 10, 1863, p.3, quoting minute books of the Talmud Yelodim Institute.
87. Minute Book, Talmud Yelodim Institute.
88. Cincinnati *Daily Enquirer*, September 11, 1863, p.2.
89. Henry Luther Stoddard, *Horace Greeley, Printer, Editor, Crusader* (New York: G.P. Putnam and Sons, 1946), p. 59.

III

Reconstructing a Nation

29

Republican Newspapers and Freedom of the Press in the Reconstruction South, 1865-1877

Richard H. Abbott
Eastern Michigan University

Discussions of freedom of the press customarily center on the way governments repress, censor, or in other ways interfere with newspaper operations. This discussion should also include consideration of restraints on newspapers created by hostile, and in some cases violent, opposition from the most powerful elements of the society in which these newspapers operate. In the case of the Reconstruction South, antagonism toward the Republican party was so strong that most of its newspapers could not obtain enough subscriptions or advertising to survive, and hence they became dependent on printing contracts provided by federal, state, and local governments. Largely due to this patronage, during the years from 1865-1877 almost four hundred Republican party papers appeared in the ex-Confederate states, as compared to around nine hundred and seventy Democratic sheets, giving the Republicans 29% of the total for those years.[1] When federal subsidies ended, and as Republicans in the South lost control of state and local governments, their party newspapers, deprived of patronage, all but disappeared. From the perspective of Southern Republicans, then, government, rather than threatening freedom of the press, was the only means of sustaining it.

In the 19th century the American two-party system relied heavily on newspapers. Editors transmitted party doctrine to their readers, refuted the positions of their political opponents, rallied support for their party during elections, and sought to convert the uncommitted. Campaigns were frequently in progress, and papers sold candidates space in their papers, printed their handbills, and published news of national, state, and local party conventions and platforms.[2] In the South editors played an even more important role in politics than they did in the North. By 1860 74% of the nation's newspapers reported a political affiliation, but in the South, the figure rose to 83%.[3] Newspapers provided the only mass medium for the South, which lacked the publishing houses, magazines, lyceums, libraries, and schools that were growing more common in the North. For most Southerners, reading a local newspaper was the only way to obtain information from the larger world outside their community. Thus newspaper editors could play a powerful role in influencing public opinion.[4] In such an environment, if the Republican party was to become competitive with the Democrats, they would have to build a viable party press.

In the 19th century it was customary for the party which controlled federal, state, and local governments to reward its journalistic supporters with patronage and deny it to its opponents. As late as 1880, according to S. D. N. North's report in the Tenth Census, the struggle for official advertising was "constant and intense" in many cities and counties.[5] During the years of Reconstruction, the Republican and Democratic parties in the North were pretty evenly matched, and advertising and subscriptions provided income for publishers of both parties. Hence the presence or absence of government patronage, while important and even crucial for individual papers, did not determine the fate of either party's entire press. In the South during Reconstruction, although some Democratic newspapers closed when deprived of this patronage, the party's press as a whole not only survived but expanded. For the Republicans, however, governmental patronage was essential for the development of a South-wide party press, for the hostile reception they received there made it very difficult for the party's publishers to find other sources of revenue to support their papers.

By 1860 the white South had become a defensive, closed society that did not tolerate dissent from the prevailing commitment to slavery, white supremacy, and state rights. As tensions over slavery brought the nation to the verge of civil war, Southern editors played a critical role in uniting their readers against outside threats. This intolerance of dissent continued to characterize the Southern press from the 1850's through the 1870s. Sidney Andrews, a Northern journalist who travelled through the South after the Civil War, found that the region's papers were "all local in character, and most of them are intensely Southern in tone; while as sources of general information, and particularly of political information, they are beneath notice." Democratic newspapers played an important role in undermining the Republican party regimes that emerged in Southern states after the war.[6] As one historian has observed, the Southern editor, more than anyone else, "implanted the idea that the South could maintain its regional integrity only through the predominance of the Democratic party."[7]

The opposition of white editors in the South to the Republican party was not surprising. When the party was organized in the 1850s, it represented the sectional interest of the North; it criticized Southern domination of the federal government, and called for an end to slavery expansion and for legislation that would serve Northern economic interests. After the secession of eleven Southern states, the Republicans led the way in conducting a war to keep them in the Union, and eventually freed the slaves, made them citizens, and gave African-American males the right to vote. With the support of these ex-slaves, the Republican party organized in every state of the former Confederacy and Republican newspapers began to emerge across the South to promote the party's welfare and recruit members.[8]

Since the Republicans depended heavily on the black vote, subscriptions for their newspapers were hard to build; most of the freedmen were either illiterate or too poor to buy a paper. When an acquaintance asked a white Republican editor in North Carolina why he was giving up his paper, the editor replied, "Do you think I'm a d—d fool, to print a paper for a party that can't read?"[9] Although most whites shunned the party, Republicans eagerly courted them, for they knew a party and a press relying only on blacks was doomed.

In their pursuit of white support, Republican journalists faced immense problems that did not confront their counterparts in the North, where the Republican party was seen as a legitimate and necessary political institution. In the South most whites regarded the Republican party as an alien presence brought by outsiders into their midst. Hence they denied it legitimacy, and they denied the state and local governments the Republicans established legitimacy as well.10 As Republican journals began to appear within the South, local newspapermen refused to recognize the new editors as members of the journalistic fraternity, and instead treated them with contempt. Scornfully they rejected offers to exchange newspapers with Republican publishers. One editor claimed he was insulted by the suggestion and would feel degraded even to read such offensive sheets. The editor of the Panola, Mississippi *Star* refused to exchange with the Republican Memphis *Post*, stating that he had no wish to "encourage the circulation of incendiary documents." Conservative editors derided Republican publications as "nigger papers"; in Richmond, the Republican *New Nation* was known as the "New Nigger Nation"; the editor of the Richmond *Examiner* referred to it as "this stinking nuisance." In Alabama the editor of the Democratic Tuscaloosa *Monitor* referred to the Demopolis *Southern Republican* "as the Demopolis Negro Noserag," while the editor of a Mississippi paper characterised the Vicksburg *Weekly Republican* as a "filthy, slimy, sinking, negro-equality, negro-loving, white man-hating, hate-engendering organ of perjured scoundrels."11

Publishers of Republican sheets often complained that they and their families were treated as outcasts by members of the local social elite. A number of editors said they had trouble hiring a staff because other newspapers urged prospective employees not to work for them, and those who did accept employment faced the same social ostracism their employer experienced. Republican editors complained that their political opponents sought to drive away white subscribers by urging other whites to ostracize such readers, or to fire them if they were their employers. According to the editor of the San Antonio *Express*, subscribers to his newspaper tried to sneak it out of their postoffices "like thieves carrying plunder", and the editor of the Vicksburg *Daily Times* complained that newsboys distributing his papers had to conceal them under their coats. Albion Tourgee of the Greensboro *Union Register* claimed that posters advertising his paper were torn down.12 Those who were willing to subscribe to Republican papers were not always sure of receiving them, for a number of editors complained that Southern postmasters and railroad workers interfered with the delivery of their papers.13

Republican publishers had a hard time attracting advertisements from local businessmen who shared in the common determination not to countenance Republican journals or journalists. On occasions when a

Republican proprietor took over an existing newspaper, local businessmen quickly moved their ads to other sheets. This could happen if a newspaper proprietor switched loyalties; when E.M. Pughe, publisher of the Augusta *Daily Press*, decided to support the Republican administration in Georgia he lost advertising which he failed to regain after recanting and going back to the Democrats. He had to close his paper. Businessmen who did choose to advertise in Republican papers faced not only social ostracism but the threat of economic sanction. The *Richmond Whig* published the names of the city's three merchants who advertised in the Republican *New Nation*, clearly hoping that its readers would boycott them. According to Whitelaw Reid, a Northern journalist who toured the South shortly after the war, "to secure a profitable business, a [newspaper]man must either sink politics altogether, or fall into the old habit of pandering to the prejudices of those with whom he traded."[14]

If social ostracism and economic sanctions failed to eliminate Republican editors, their opponents sometimes resorted to violence. Physical attacks on newspapermen were by no means uncommon in the antebellum South, but there were many more instances in the reconstruction years, and their victims were almost always Republicans, not Democrats. Many Republican editors reported receiving threats, and a number of them were beaten with pistols, canes, or whips, often wielded by rival editors. On several occasions angry mobs, or sometimes individuals, killed Republican newspapermen. Sometimes the intended victim had enough warning to escape his assailant, but his newspaper office might be damaged or destroyed. At least a dozen newspaper offices burned to the ground during Reconstruction.[15]

Such ostracism, intimidation, and violence shocked and angered Republican editors. To a man they protested against the violation of press freedom. Edward M. Cheney of the *Florida Union*, noting that he had received threats against his life, declared that "the time has passed, even in the South, when free speech can be suppressed by violence or when a free press can be muzzled by force." According to the editor of the Newbern *Daily Times*, "the denouncing of men for honest differences of opinion either in politics or religion is a species of the intolerance and persecution of the dark ages." Another Republican editor described the spirit of intolerance in the South thusly: "Born of ignorance, bigotry and littleness of soul, it endeavors to proscribe thought, stifle speech and bring the world to a level with its own meanness."[16]

Embattled Republican journalists understood that the political culture of the South would have to change if their party was to gain a foothold and their newspapers an audience there. Southerners had to become more tolerant of diverse points of view, particularly of those opposed to their own. As the Republican editor of the Jacksonville *New South* observed, untrammeled debate between opposing political parties was necessary if democratic institutions were to function. As early as 1856, when Republicans in Wheeling, Virginia met to organize their party in that state, they called for a free speech and press. Following the war, Northern Republicans also recognized the importance of establishing freedom of expression in the South. The Republican National Committee, noting that the party's positions were not welcome in the former Confederacy, expressed the hope that free thought, speech and press would develop there.[17]

Southern Republican editors believed freedom of speech and press was necessary not only to safeguard their own party's interests, but to advance the welfare of the section as a whole. They believed that intolerance and closed-mindedness had retarded Southern development. According to the editor of the Savannah *Daily Herald*, if the antebellum South had enjoyed a free speech and press, slavery could not have endured and there would have been no civil war. Unless Southerners could freely discuss social, political, and economic issues without fear of violent retribution, these editors argued, the section would stagnate, deprived of the stimulation of fresh and innovative ideas which they thought their party would present. The party's Congressional Committee stated that the campaign to build a Southern Republican party was "but a continuation of the war...it is no longer the shock of armies, but the conflict of ideas." To help win that contest, Republicans had to secure free and open discussion in the South.[18]

Until the white South became more tolerant of dissenting views, however, Republican editors, deprived of much income from advertising and subscriptions, came to rely heavily on government support.[19] Lucien Eaton, editor of the Memphis *Post*, told his brother that it was "an absolute impossibility for a Republican daily to live in Memphis without such political favoritism as we have had." The Republican editor of the Austin, Texas *Daily State Journal* echoed this comment, asserting that because of the lack of local advertisements and subscriptions, "if a creditable daily is wanted at the capital it must, to a great extent, be sustained by the State." The editor of the McMinnville, Tennessee *Enterprise*, observing that local legal advertising was the main support of rural weeklies like his, bemoaned the fact that county officials placed their announcements in Democratic papers.[20]

Republican federal officeholders were aware of the importance of subsidizing their party's press. During the Civil War U. S. Army officers and Treasury agents published military announcements and legal advertisements in columns of fledgling Republican newspapers in the occupied South. In 1867 General John Pope, who commanded the military district including Georgia, Florida, and Alabama, ordered state and local governments in his jurisdiction to place their official notices in papers that did not oppose reconstruction. This order effectively diverted printing patronage from Democratic papers to the few Republican sheets in the three states, and led to a great outcry from the former, who condemned Pope for infringing on freedom of the press. Pope's successor, General George Meade, subsequently modified the order.[21]

In 1867 the Republican Congress also made federal patronage available to the Southern Republican press by identifying two "loyal" newspapers in each state to publish U. S. laws, treaties, and official advertisements. Edward M. McPherson, the federal official whose responsibility it was to identify these papers, was soon deluged with appeals from eager editors from across the South. Although the payments were not large, averaging around $1,000 per session of Congress, the possibility of obtaining a federal printing contract seems to be at least one reason why so many Republican papers emerged in the ex-Confederate states in 1867.[22]

This federal assistance generally went to urban dailies, and while it proved important to the papers that received it, federal patronage alone could not sustain them and was of no assistance to the Republican country weeklies that began to appear. Consequently local Republican papers turned to the newly-elected Republican state governments for support. These administrations followed antebellum precedents in naming a leading Republican publisher as official printer for the state who became responsible for producing bound volumes of legislative debates, laws, supreme court reports, and the like. In addition, a number of Republican regimes provided for publishing state laws, resolutions, announcements, and proclamations in party newspapers.[23] City and county governments and state circuit and district courts also published ordinances, documents, and notices in local newspapers; this was a significant source of newspaper income, and some states authorized the governor to identify papers to publish these local notices.[24] Thus newspapers could accumulate revenue from a variety of sources; the Memphis Morning *Post,* for instance, proudly stated that it was the official U.S. journal, the official state journal for western Tennessee, the official journal of Shelby county, and the official journal for the board of education of the city of Memphis.25

On the basis of sheer numbers, the Republican press during Reconstruction appeared to do quite well, as the figure of almost four hundred papers from 1867-1877 attests. These numbers, however, are deceiving. The Republican papers could not match the survival rates of their Democratic counterparts; two thirds of them lasted two years or less, compared to only twenty-five per cent of the Democratic sheets. Republicans had only seventeen per cent of the party newspapers that lasted five years or more. Nor were Republican newspapers evenly distributed across the South. The least effective predictor of party newspaper strength was state population. Florida, which in 1870 was the smallest Southern state with a population of only 176,000, had nineteen Republican papers, a total similar to that in Georgia and Virginia, each of which had almost 1.2 million inhabitants. Louisiana, with a population of 717,000, had the highest number of Republican papers of any state, sixty-three. There was also little relationship between the number of Republican voters in a state and the size of its party press. The 1872 election, which was the most peaceful during the Reconstruction period, saw the maximum number of votes cast by the Republicans. The states with the most Republican newspapers, Mississippi, Louisiana, Texas, and Arkansas, ranked sixth, seventh, ninth, and tenth, respectively, in the number of Republican voters. The four states which cast the most Republican votes in 1872 were towards the bottom of the list of state-wide Republican newspaper totals.

The most important condition affecting the number of Republican papers in each state was the amount of state and local printing patronage available to them. The numbers of Republican newspapers in a given state rose when they gained access to governmental patronage, and fell when they lost this assistance. The states which provided the least amount of patronage had the fewest newspapers; states with the largest number of Republican papers, Arkansas, Louisiana, Mississippi, and Texas, made more state and local printing available to the party press. The reason Louisiana had more Republican newspapers than any other Southern state was because its legislature had the most liberal system of awarding patronage.26

Congress ended federal printing subsidies in 1875. In the South, as Democrats reclaimed control of one state after another, Republican newspapers lost access to state and local printing. By 1880, four years after the last Republican regime had ended in the South, the number of Republican papers there had fallen to forty-four, giving them less than seven per cent of the total partisan newspapers in the South; Democratic journals outnumbered them 13-1. Republican papers survived only in certain sections of the former Confederacy, most notably in the hilly or mountainous regions of North Carolina, Tennessee, and Arkansas which had harbored a significant number of white Unionists during the Civil War who later became Republicans, and in some the larger cities of the South, where they could find enough businessmen and subscribers to keep them going.

Ironically, the very patronage that sustained Republican newspapers in the South also contributed to their demise. Party editors were desperate for this assistance, and the competition among them for government printing exacerbated, and in some cases caused, factional conflict that weakened Republican organizations.27 Heavy reliance on this patronage also left Republican administrations open to the charge that they spent printing funds recklessly and extravagantly, increasing the size of the states' debts and hence the burdens on taxpayers. There was much truth to this accusation, especially in Louisiana and South Carolina. During one three-year period, the Republican administration in the former state spent 1.5 million dollars on printing; in South Carolina, the total cost of state printing from 1868-1876 was over 1.3 million dollars.28 The Republican press, and in turn the Republican regimes that sustained it, faced a dilemma they never could resolve. Bereft of the sources of support normally available to newspapers, Republican journalists had to rely on governmental patronage; in turn, this patronage contributed to their downfall.

In the North the Republican press remained very much in the mainstream, but in the South it became a marginal, or perhaps an alternative press, comparable to African-American, Socialist, Communist, or other minority publications in U. S. history. Regional and racial hostilities directed against the Southern Republican press had been so great that only government patronage could sustain it. Without that patronage, Southerners, black and white, lacked the opportunity available in the North to read about and to debate competing political views and principles. Freedom of thought, speech, and expression in the South remained restricted to parameters set by the dominant Democratic party and its press.

Notes

1. The basic source I used for determining the number of Republican and Democratic papers in the South during Reconstruction was *Rowell's American Newspaper Directory*, which first appeared in 1869 and annually thereafter. I developed a list of Republican party papers that existed prior to Rowell's directory by using a number of sources, including the papers themselves, which often mentioned other Republican papers, and the large secondary literature that is available on the Republican party in the South during the Reconstruction years. My reading of Republican party papers after 1869 also helped me identify party journals that did not appear in Rowell In addition, some papers which were not identified as Republican in Rowell, or which listed themselves as impartial or non-partisan, turned out upon examination to be Republican.
2. Culver H. Smith, *The Press, Politics, and Patronage: The American Government's Use of Newspapers 1789-1875*, xi, 12-13, 19, 22, 42, 60, 70; William E. Gienapp, "'Politics Seem to Enter into Everything': Political Culture in the North, 1840-1860", in Gienapp, et. al., eds., Essays on American Antebellum Politics, 1840-1860" (College Station, Texas, 1982), 41-42.
3. Donald E. Reynolds, *Editors Make War: Southern Newspapers in the Secession Crisis* (Nashville, 1966), 5.
4. *Ibid.*, vii, 5, 9-10; Michael Perman, *Reunion Without Compromise: The South and Reconstruction, 1865-1868* (Cambridge, 1973), 352-53; Thomas Clark, *The Southern Country Editor* (Gloucester, Mass, repr., 1964), 23.
5. S. D. N. North, *History and Present Condition of the Newspapers and Periodical Press of the United States*(Washington, 1884), 87.
6. Carl Osthaus, *Partisans of the Southern Press (Lexington, Ky., 1994)*, 10; Sidney Andrews, *The South Since the War* (New York, repr., 1969), 389; Clark, *The Southern Country Editor*, 169, 178-79; Hodding Cotter, *Their Words Were Bullets: The Southern Press in War, Reconstruction and Peace*"(Athens, Ga., 1969), 42-47.
7. Clark, *The Southern Country Editor*, 22.
8. On the efforts of the Republicans to build their party in the South, a process which antedated the Civil War, see Richard H. Abbott, *The Republican Party and the South, 1855-1877* (Chapel Hill, N. C., 1986).
9. E. Merton Coulter, *The South During Reconstruction, 1865-1877* (Baton Rouge, La, 1947), 288.
10. Eric Foner, *Reconstruction: America's Unfinished Revolution, 1863-1877* (New York, 1988), 346; Otto Olsen, "North Carolina: An Incongruous Presence", in Olsen, ed., *Reconstruction and Redemption in the South* (Baton Rouge, 1980), 156-97; Ted Tunnell, *Crucible of Reconstruction: War, Radicalism and Race in Louisiana, 1862-1877* (Baton Rouge, 1984), 5-6, 172. For a stimulating discussion of the Republicans and the problem of legitimacy, see Lawrence N. Powell, "Southern Republicanism During Reconstruction: the Contradictions of State and Party Formation" (unpublished paper, annual meeting of Organization of American Historians, 1984).
11. Augusta *National Republican*, Feb. 19, 1868; Griffin *American Union*, Aug. 18, 1867; Frank B. Williams, "John Eaton, Jr., Editor, Politician, and School Administrator, 1865-1870," *Tennessee Historical Quarterly*, 10 (Dec., 1951), 293; Richmond *New Nation*, Aug. 16, 1866; *Richmond Examiner* quoted in Memphis *Morning Post*, Apr. 18, 1866; Leslie Winston Smith, "Richmond During Presidential Reconstruction, 1865-1867," (Unpublished Ph. D. dissertation, University of Virginia, 1974), 123; Demopolis Southern Republican, Oct. 18, 20, 1869; Vicksburg Weekly Republican, Mar. 3, 1868.
12. Williamsburg *Gazette*, July 1, 1869; Augusta *Weekly Loyal Georgian*, Aug. 24, 1867; John E. Bryant to J. F. Long [draft, 1868], Bryant papers, Duke University; Demopolis *Southern Republican*, Oct. 26, 1870; Macon *American Union*, Dec. 5, 1872; San Antonio *Express*, Mar. 13, 1868; Vicksburg *Daily Times*, Oct. 28, 1871; Otto Olsen, Carpetbagger's

Crusade: The Life of Albion Winegar Tourgee (Baltimore, 1965), 67.
13. Mobile *Nationalist*, Feb. 1, 1866, Mar. 7, 1867; Griffin *American Union*, Sept. 13, 1867; Harrisonburg *American Union*, May 11, 1867; *Daily Mississippi Pilot*, Jan. 13, 17, 1871; Atlanta *Daily Opinion*, Nov. 23, Dec. 10, 1867; *Atlanta New Era*, Feb. 10, 1869; Knoxville *Whig*, Mar. 18, 1868; Jacksonville *Florida Union*, Oct. 24, 1868; Vicksburg *Weekly Republican*, Mar. 10, Sept. 13, 1868.
14. Mobile *Nationalist*, Dec. 27, 1866; Rutherford *Star*, Aug. 29, 1868; Griffin *American Union*, Nov. 1, 1867; *Woodville Republican*, Oct. 9, 1869; Augusta *Daily Press*, Apr. 18, 1869; Whitelaw Reid, *After the War: A Tour of the Southern States, 1865-1866* (New York, repr., 1965), 235.
15. Memphis Morning *Post*, Mar. 25, 1868; John Hayes to Nathaniel Banks, Feb. 5, 1867, Banks Papers, Library of Congress; Atlanta Daily New Era, Apr. 10, 1868, Feb. 24, 1870; New Bern Daily Republican, Nov. 29, Dec. 1, 1868; James W. Garner, *Reconstruction in Mississippi* (Gloucester, Mass., repr., 1964), 349; Jerrell H. Shofner, *Nor is it Over Yet: Florida in the Era of Reconstruction, 1863-1877* (Gainesville, Fla., 1974), 192; Columbus *Press*, June 6, 1874, Apr. 9, 1875; Fredericksburg Ledger, Oct. 30, 1874; Demopolis *Southern Republican*, Dec. 7, 21, 1870.
16. Virtually every Republican paper contained editorials condemning Southern intolerance. For the quotations, see *Florida Union*, Sept. 30, 1868; New *Bern Daily Times* quoted in Raleigh Carolina Era, Oct. 26, 1871; Demopolis Southern Republican, Aug. 31, 1871.
17. Jacksonville *New South*, Mar. 27, 1875; Richard Lowe, "The Republican Party in Antebellum Virginia, 1856-1860", *Virginia Magazine of History and Biography*. 81 (1973), 265; New York *Daily Tribune*, May 17, 1867.
18. Savannah *Daily Herald*, Apr. 16, 1865; Philadelphia *Press*, July 22, 1867; Washington *Daily Morning Chronicle*, May 18, 1867; New York *Post*, quoted in Atlanta Daily New Era, Apr. 21, 1868.
19. A glance at most Republican newspapers will reveal that they published very few advertisements from local businessmen; Republican editors often complained of that fact. A few Republican papers, particularly in cities, were able to gain enough subscriptions and advertisements to survive for a number of years, even without patronage, but most could not. Circulation figures published in *Rowell's American Newspaper Directory* do not show that Republican papers had significantly lower numbers than their Democratic counterparts. These figures, however, are highly suspect. Rowell did not require publishers to submit documentation for their circulation claims until 1879. See Carolyn Stewart Dyer, "Census Manuscripts and Circulation Data for Mid-19th Century Newspapers," *Journalism History*, VII (Summer 1980), 47. In two cases I have been able to compare the circulation figures that a publisher gave to Rowell with numbers the same editor revealed in personal correspondence. In 1869 Lucien Eaton, publisher of the *Memphis Post*, told his brother that the paper's weekly edition had around 250 subscribers; Rowell's directory did not give circulation figures for this paper for 1869, but the following year (the year the paper closed) it listed the *Post's* circulation at 1,500. In 1872 the publisher of the Lexington, Mississippi *Advertiser* told the chairman of the Republican National Committee that his paper had less than 150 subscribers; that year Rowell credited the paper with 360. See Walter J. Fraser, Jr., "Lucien Bonaparte Eaton: Politics and the Memphis, 1867-1869", West Tennessee Historical Society Papers, XX (1966), 22 n. 9; O. S. Lee to W. E. Chandler, Aug. 18, 1872, Chandler Mss, Library of Congress.
20. Williams, "John Eaton, Jr.", 295; Austin *Daily State Journal*, May 12, 1870; The McMinnville *Enterprise*, June 27, 1867.
21. Richard H. Abbott, "The Civil War Origins of the Southern Republican Press", *Civil War History,* XLIII (1997), 41-45, 50-55; James E. Sefton, The United States Army and Reconstruction, 1865-1877" (Baton Rouge, 1967), 55-56, 148-52; C. Mildred Thompson, *Reconstruction in Georgia: Economic, Social, Political, 1865-1872* (New

York, 1915), 177, 347; Shofner, Nor is it Over Yet, 162.
22. Smith, *The Press, Politics, and Patronage*, 238-39; Abbott, *Republican Party in the South*, 92.
23. See, e.g., Richard H. Abbott, "The Republican Party Press in Georgia, 1867-1874," *The Journal of Southern History*, LXI (Nov. 1995), 744; Laws of the State of Florida...1868" (Tallahassee, 1869), 161; Public Laws of the State of North Carolina...1868-1869" (Raleigh, 1869), 618; Robert H. Woody, *Republican Newspapers of South Carolina*. (Charlottesville, Va., 1936), 50.
24. Charles W. Ramsdell, *Reconstruction in Texas* (New York, 1910), 299; Acts of the General Assembly of Arkansas...1868 (Little Rock, 1869), 42-43; Ella Lonn, *Reconstruction in Louisiana After 1868* (New York, 1918), 86-87.
25. Memphis *Morning Post*, Jan. 2, 1868.
26. In Louisiana, the legislature arranged to publish the journals of each house in fifteen parish newspapers; in addition, the legislature named Republican papers to publish all parochial and judiciary advertisements in the parishes in which they were located. See Francis Byers Harris, "Henry Clay Warmoth, Reconstruction Governor of Louisiana," *Louisiana Historical Quarterly*, 30 (1947), 554-55.
27. For an example of this competition in one state, see Abbott, *"The Republican Party Press in Reconstruction Georgia,"* 725-60.
28. For South Carolina, see Robert H. Woody, *Republican Newspapers of South Carolina* (Charlottesville, Va., 1936), 48-56; for Louisiana, see Ella Lonn, *Reconstruction in Louisiana after 1868* (Gloucester, Mass., repr., 1967), 31, 86-87, and Joe Gray Taylor, *Louisiana Reconstructed, 1863-1877* (Baton Rouge, 1974), 198-99.

30

Suffrage for Freedmen:
The Specter of *Dred Scott*

Kenneth Rystrom
Virginia Polytechnic Institute and State University

"In the opinion of the Court, the legislation and histories of the times, and the language of the Declaration of Independence, show, that neither the class of persons who had been imported as slaves, nor their descendants, whether they had become free or not, were then acknowledged as a part of the people, nor intended to be included in the general words used in that memorable instrument."
—Chief Justice Roger B. Taney, for the majority,
in *Dred Scott v. Sanford* (1857)

"Slavery as an institution tolerated by law would, it is true, have disappeared from our country, but there would remain a power in the states, by sinister legislation, to interfere with the full enjoyment of the blessings of freedom. . . ."
—Justice John M. Harlan, dissenting,
in *Plessy v. Ferguson* (1896)

In 1857 the U.S. Supreme Court ruled that Dred Scott could not sue for his freedom in the courts of the United States because he was not a citizen, and that he was not a citizen because he was black and a slave. After the Civil War, Congress and the required number of states approved constitutional amendments freeing the slaves, guaranteeing them equal rights, and assuring them of the right to vote. But, as Justice John M. Harlan's dissenting opinion foresaw in the *Dred Scott* case, an end to slavery would not necessarily guarantee "the full enjoyment of the blessings of freedom."

The newly freed slaves quickly found that out as the nation moved from Civil War to a Reconstruction that was supposed to bring together North and South, black and white, in a mutual commitment to equal rights for all.

The editors of conservative Southern newspapers had other ideas. In their eyes, the freeing of the slaves did not settle the question of what political rights, if any, should be granted to the freedmen. Freedom did not necessarily mean citizenship, much less suffrage. In every way they could think of, conservative Southerners tried to exclude the freedmen from the political process or, failing that, to control their votes.

An examination of editorials published in Southern newspapers during this period suggests that the strategies adopted by the conservatives went through five phases, reflecting changes in the editors' perception of the likelihood that the freedmen would attain meaningful political power.

The Five Phases:

1. Southern editors assumed that freedom did not mean suffrage for the freedmen (1865 and early 1866).

2. Southern editors recognized that the Radical Republicans intended to impose freedmen suffrage on their states (1866 and 1867).

3. Southern editors realized that the freedmen would get the vote (1867 and 1868).

4. The freedmen began voting and winning elections (1868 and 1869).

5. The white conservatives began winning elections again (1869 and 1870).

In brief, the stands taken by the editors generally were as follows:

Stage 1. Immediately after the Civil War, conservative Southern editors acknowledged that the slaves had been freed, but they did not expect that they would be citizens or voters. In this stage even newspaper editors who later supported the Radical Republican cause did not take on the cause of votes for freedmen. Only the handful of African-American newspapers supported suffrage.

Stage 2. When it became clear that the Radical Republicans meant to

impose freedmen suffrage on the Southern states, the white conservative newspapers tended to adopt one or more of three arguments:
- that the newly freed slaves were inherently incapable of voting responsibly
- that proposals giving freedmen the vote were intended only as a means by which the Radicals and the North could punish and control the South
- that, if voting was inevitable, the freedmen should be educated and prepared to exercise the franchise.

The Radical Republican and African-American press generally expressed in confidence in the ability of freedmen to exercise the franchise responsibly.

Stage 3. When it became clear that the freedmen would get the vote, the conservative editors followed two widely divergent paths:
- that (as during the previous period) the freedmen were ignorant, incompetent, incapable of exercising the vote; that suffrage would result in dire consequences
- that white conservatives should woo, or threaten, the African-American voters in an attempt to convince them that their best political interests lay with voting with their former masters.

The Radical editors during this period continued to express confidence in the freedmen's capacity for the franchise, but they added a warning to freedmen against conservative efforts to mislead, threaten, and punish them.

Stage 4. Once the freedmen began voting, largely for Radical Republican candidates, the conservative editors usually took one of two stands:
- that efforts still should continue toward gaining the understanding, sympathy, and support of the freedmen; that, through wooing or threatening, the freedmen eventually would come to see that their true interests lay with the whites
- that freedmen suffrage was certain to lead to horrible results for the Southern states and for the nation—so horrible, in fact, that scandals might produce a backlash that would lead to the restoration of conservative governments.

African-American and Radical Republican newspapers generally were heartened by the freedmen's support for the Radical cause and by the results of the elections. They continued to express confidence in the freedmen as citizens and voters.

Stage 5. Near the end of the study period, when white conservatives began to win an occasional election, the conservative editors tended to make one or both of two points:
- that at least a number of freedmen had seen the light, recognizing that their true friends lay among white conservatives rather than among the

Radical carpetbaggers – that the election results represented long-overdue justice for the conservative cause and a proper putting in their place of the freedmen and the Radicals for daring to think that there might be a place for them in the white man's government.

The Radical Republican and African-American newspapers included in this study, at least those available on microfilm in this study, did not comment on these elections.

Stage 1: Freedmen Suffrage Seen as Non-Issue

At the end of the Civil War the attitude of most conservative Southern editors toward giving the vote to the freedmen was summarized by the *Louisville Journal*: The newspaper acknowledged that some Northern radicals were urging President Johnson and Congress to impose "negro suffrage" on the Southern states, but it expressed confidence that they would not succeed and equal confidence that the matter would be left to the states to decide. As for the states, "[t]here are questions of tremendous practical importance [facing them], but negro suffrage is not one of them." The writer added: "We have no idea . . . that negro voting is to be made an issue in any general election."[1]

The Northerners' efforts to impose "negro suffrage" were generally viewed as (in the words of the *Richmond Whig*) "flagrant hypocrisy." When "this subject of negro suffrage and negro equality" is "brought home to them, the [Northerners] scornfully reject [it]," the *Whig* said.[2] According to the *Louisville Journal*, the Northern radicals, "ultra as they are, . . . do not all insist, and indeed they are not all of them willing, that negro suffrage shall be established in their own States."[3]

The *Raleigh Sentinel* assured its readers that, at the state level, while delegates seeking election to a constitutional convention would accept "abolition of slavery in place of further conflict and blood, . . . none would accept suffrage" for the freedmen. "They will all recognize the principle that *this is a white man's country*."[4]

As for the freedmen, the *Memphis Avalanche* said that the "negro himself has shown no anxiety for the privilege of voting, and in this he has ignorantly shown a wise policy, for the moment he aspires to office, that moment will his downfall commence."[5]

In an editorial titled "That 'Moses,'" the *Memphis Appeal* stated that, "[i]f the right to vote is to the negroes of to-day the equivalent to the entrance of the Jews upon the promised land, remember that the latter wandered forty years before they were found worthy the fulfillment [*sic*] of the promise. So that gun's spiked."[6]

The *Huntsville Advocate* urged its readers to recognize the freedman's new "legal rights," but "political rights" were different: "He has been granted the former–not the latter."7

The *Livingston Journal* summarized the opinions of most conservative Southern editors at this point in Reconstruction: "This is a white man's government, made by white men, for the benefit of white men, to be administered by white men, and nobody else, forever."8

Even *Brownlow's Knoxville Whig*, a Republican supporter, made it clear that, in Tennessee, suffrage for freedmen was not a real issue. A *Whig* editorial accused several state legislators of "falsehood and duplicity" when they "excused themselves for having voted against the Franchise Law . . . on the ground that efforts were made to *force negro suffrage upon them..*" Noting that freedmen suffrage was not connected to the proposed law, the *Whig* charged the offending lawmakers with taking "advantage of the prejudices of the people against negro suffrage."9

As late as September 1866 another newspaper that later would support the Radical Republicans, the Raleigh *Standard*, recognized that "[o]ur people are opposed to . . . negro suffrage."10

Even editors of the African-American *Loyal Georgian* seemed to be willing to accept citizenship without suffrage for freedmen. Noting that "[t]he Northern people now demand that the freedmen shall have all the rights of citizens, except the right to vote and to sit in the jury box," an editorial in the newspaper said that, if the Southern people would yield to this demand, "we believe that the difficulty might be settled, the Southern Republicans admitted to Congress and the South once more prosper, not as of yore, but as it never dreamed of prospering."11

Not all the African-American press, however, exhibited the *Loyal Georgian's* minimal concern over suffrage for the freedmen.

The *Colored Tennessean* saw the "question of manhood suffrage as a simple one." Arguing that the freedmen deserved their full rights as citizens, an editorial "warn[ed] the country of a fact borne out by all history. . . .[:] A people can be kept in complete bondage much easier than be retained in partial bondage." It added: "Delay it [suffrage], let it be a bone of contention for years to come, something for demagogues to play with, and trouble will most likely result."12

Stage 2: Freedmen Suffrage as a Serious Threat

As it became increasingly evident that suffrage for the freedmen was being seriously proposed by the Radical Republicans, conservative white editors generally adopted one or more of three arguments:

–that the freedmen were unqualified to exercise the right of suffrage responsibly because of inherent deficiencies

–that the Radical Republicans had no real interest in giving the vote to

African-Americans, as witness the way the North treated them; that the Radical Republicans were using the " negro suffrage" only as means to punish and destroy the Southern states

–that, if the freedmen were going to be voters, they should be given education and guidance in their new duties.

Inherent Deficiencies

Among the newspapers that questioned the inherent ability of the freedman to participate fully as a citizen, one of the most adamant stands was taken by the *Memphis Avalanche*. Directing its editorial vehemence toward the Northerners, the *Avalanche* declared: "You have liberated him, but the blood in which you have baptized him no more fit [*sic*] him to become a freeman than the Pharisee, plunged into the waves of the Jordan, came forth a Christian."13 The editorial continued:

> The sword has rescued the negro from bondage, but it cannot confer on him the capacity for self-government . . . .He knows nothing of the calm and enlarged wisdom, the moral courage, the self-denial and self-command without which liberty and franchise is a ferocious and remorseless demon. While the unclear spirit lives without the negro, liberty to him is a curse instead of a blessing.

The *Memphis Appeal* saw "['the negro'] as no more fit . . . to vote than to be the director of an orchestra."14 It described "negro suffrage [as] a putrid poison in all the veins and arteries of the commonwealth. . . a deadly miasma, penetrating every where, and diseasing the whole body of the State."15 The freedmen were seen as "a mass of creatures . . . inferior in intellect and capacity, . . . easily misled and deluded, and . . . cheaply bought and bribed."16

The *Richmond Dispatch* saw the freedmen as the victims of deception (what it called "humbugging the negro") by Northerners intent on winning black votes. "Poor Africans!" the *Dispatch* said. "There is a day of bitter repentance in store for them–the day when they are undeceived, as they surely will be!"17 Before that day came, however, the *Dispatch* expected the freedmen, under the "drilling" of "the most baneful and dangerous organization that ever entered this State" (the Union League), to "[vote] as one man," a combination "disastrous to the public peace and safety."18

A Way to Control and Punish the South

Some of the editors were as intent on discrediting Northern motives as they were African-American capabilities.

The *Arkansas Gazette* accused the Northern radicals of seeking the ballot for the freedman not "to advance his welfare, . . . but simply to gratify a malignant hate against the white men of the South, and to use him as an instrument to perpetuate their own power."19 (The *Gazette* expressed confidence, however, that "there are not a few of the blacks of sufficient intellect to discover" this deception.)

No despotism, no intensity of hate, with all its devilish ingenuities of malice," the *Memphis Appeal* said, "has until now resorted to such a refinement of vindictive vengeance."20

The *Charleston Mercury* recommended that the white citizen "do nothing" in response to imposition of an alien government: "Let him stay away from the polls . . . and leave to the United States military and the negroes to make and carry on *their* government of South Carolina."21 The *Mercury* said that those who had passed the Reconstruction acts and "put over us the military depotism under which we labour to enforce them called us on the floor of Congress their 'enemies.'" Added the *Mercury*, "They spoke the truth."

At Least Prepare the Freedmen for the Vote

Several newspapers, including some that questioned the right or the ability of the freedman to exercise the franchise, concluded that, if the freedmen were going to be voters, they should be educated and guided in their new duties.

The *Arkansas Gazette*, which (as noted earlier) saw the franchise for the freedmen primarily as "an instrument to perpetuate [the Northerners'] power over the South,"22 argued that it was to the whites' advantage to educate the blacks about politics. "The negro will be a voter in the next election," the *Gazette* said, "and a comprehension of the situation urges that he be put in possession of such information as will influence him to cast his ballot in the interests of the good people of the state."23 It is clear the type of preparation the *Gazette* had in mind:

> It should be impressed upon the minds of the colored population, that they are a part and parcel of the southern people. Born upon the soil, reared up with the white population, their interests are identical with those of their former masters.

A writer for the *Richmond Whig* warned the freedmen: "[B]y the way in which they act will they be judged," then asked: "Is it well for the colored race to offend and make enemies of the white race of Virginia?"24 The writer reminded the freedmen that, not only were the whites "better educated and more intelligent," but they also "own nearly all the property; [and] they must give employment and furnish the means of subsistence to the blacks, or they will starve." The freedmen's "best hope, aye, their only hope for the future," the *Whig* said, "is to conduct themselves as to retain the good will, the confidence and protection of the old native-born Virginians [and avoid] the anger and distrust of those who are now their friends, and without whose continued friendship their destiny is sealed."

Republican Newspapers

The Republican newspapers tended to adopt a more benevolent and optimistic attitude toward the freedman as potential voter.

"The colored man is by nature shrewd, cautious and grateful," the *Nashville Press* said. "He neither forsakes his friends nor confides himself to his enemies."[25]

The *Savannah Republican* stated optimistically that, "in Georgia, candor and justice forces us to admit that the PEOPLE are disposed to give the colored man all of his rights, and to aid him in the cause of education, despite the efforts of a few effete political demagogues to teach them otherwise."[26]

The *Missouri Democrat* (a Republican newspaper), even more optimistically, said it "[beheld] the spectacle of the whole country, almost irrespective of party, practically accepting negro suffrage and wisely seeking to make the best of it." It admonished "the Richmond press" for being "notably emphatic, sententious and solemn in portraying 'the inevitable conflict ['certain to follow upon negro suffrage'] that can only end in the extermination of the colored man.'" Asked the *Democrat*: "Where are there any indications of it?"[27]

Stage 3: Freedmen Suffrage Becomes Certain

When it became clear that the freedmen would get the vote, the conservative editors took two widely divergent stands:

–that (as during the previous period) the freedmen were ignorant, incompetent, and incapable of exercising the vote; that suffrage would result in dire consequences;

–that white conservatives should woo, or threaten, the African-American vote in an attempt to convince the freedmen that their best political interests lay with their former masters.

The Radical editors during this period continued to express confidence in the freedmen's capacity for the franchise, but they added a warning to freedmen against conservative efforts to mislead, threaten, and punish them.

Dire consequences

The *Arkansas Gazette* predicted that "negro social equality will follow close upon negro suffrage." It excoriated "vile white men" who supported "the negro vote" for "sit[ting] side by side with them in [the] state [constitutional] convention, hug[ging] them in the league room" and "refus[ing] to declare themselves unalterably opposed to the amalgamation of the races," which the *Gazette* also referred to a "miscegenation." It added: "When the negro expresses a wish to that effect, they will legislate him into private parlors."28 On another occasion the *Gazette* denounced "the mongrel, hybrid horde" that erected "the African government."29

The *Sentinel* in Raleigh concluded that "the necessary consequence" of "negro suffrage" would be "negro equality in all respects–which, in the case of nearly all the States of the South, means negro *supremacy*." The *Sentinel* warned: "If negroes are to fill Conventions and Legislatures, occupy municipal offices, sit upon the bench and go to Congress, they must have admission to West Point and the Naval Academy, must be allowed front seats at the theatre, a plate at the table *d'Hote*, a state-room in the cars, and even a seat at Presidential and Gubernatorial dinners of State."30 Furthermore, the *Sentinel* said, "the experiment of black suffrage" would lead to a "negro equality [that] will work the material and economical ruin and prostration of the South, and, by consequence, of the whole country, in the end."

The *Charleston Courier* predicted that a "war of races" would result from giving freedmen the vote–and war that the freedmen eventually would lose.31

The *Rome* (Ga.) *Weekly Courier* warned that a vote against the Democrats in the 1868 election would result in "first and foremost universal suffrage and negro equality . . . social and political tyranny . . . miscegenation and all the nameless horrors that follow amalgamation of races . . . wholesale lying, speculation, robbery–with perjury as the highest recommendation for office . . . the subjection of a white majority to a negro minority."32

The *Independent Monitor* in Tuscaloosa, Ala., called the proposed 15th Amendment "the most glaring and stupendous fraud of the age, . . . ruthlessly forc[ing] [negro suffrage] upon the Southern States at the point of the bayonet.33

Woo or Threaten

More optimistically, the *Richmond Whig* expressed the hope that, if the freedmen voted in their "true interests," a substantial number of them would support the conservatives in the fall election of 1867.34 The manner in which they vote "will . . . [ascertain], first whether they have the capacity to appreciate their own interest, and, second, whether they are influenced by hatred [or] good will towards the white race–in other words, whether they have the intelligence and the disposition to exercise the privilege of suffrage to the public advantage." The *Whig* expressed confidence that "[f]ortunately for the experiment the path of interest is so plain that the least intelligent among them ought to be able to see it."

Lest the freedmen miss the direction of this path, the *Whig* warned that following the Radicals "will be exceedingly offensive to nineteen out of every twenty white men in the community."

The *Vicksburg Times* advised the freedmen of Mississippi that "their true policy is to cultivate sentiments of kindness and friendship with the white race–the SUPERIOR RACE!–and the sooner they find out and act upon this established *fact*, the better will it be for all parties." The *Times* warned the freedmen that, "if they are deluded, by wicked and designing men, into a war with the white race, they will be exterminated from the face of the earth!"35

Republican Newspapers

The Radical editors during this period continued to express confidence in the freedmen's capacity for the franchise, but they added a warning to freedmen against conservative efforts to mislead, punish, and threaten them,

When "the colored people of Newbern [became] the first of their race in the State [of North Carolina] to vote," the *Standard*, in Raleigh, expressed confidence that "they will highly appreciate the privilege, and that they will so exercise it as to promote the good and the glory of their country."36 But it warned the freedmen to beware of "[t]he secession leaders [who] are begging you for your votes." It said that these leaders "have lately taken new courage, and they hope to carry the elections, so as to reduce you again to slavery."37 The *Standard* warned further: "They would deny you the right of suffrage. They would make apprentices of you, sell you for debt, sell you for alleged offences, and trample all your manhood out of you."

On another occasion the *Standard* said that "in their desperation [the former rebels had] fondled and embraced colored men for their votes."38 In doing so:

> They invited them into their parlors, in this City, and beslanered [*sic*] them with their fulsome adulation. They went into colored meetings. They addressed colored votes from the stump. They exhausted argument and persuasion to prevail upon them to vote against that party [the Republican] to which they owed all their civil and political rights.

But the *Standard* expressed the confidence that the former rebels' efforts would prove "all . . . in vain."

In an editorial titled "Colored Men Remember!" the *Loyal Georgian* warned its readers that "the Rebel-Copperhead party–sometimes called the Democratic party," which had "fought to keep you in slavery," was now doing "all they could to prevent you from voting."39

The *National Republican* observed that the freedmen were being "asked daily by men whom you have known all your life to vote with them . . . because these men have been known by you for a number of years and that they are your *real* friends."40 The *National Republican* suggested that, in response, the freedmen should "ask them if they will not do as much for you as they ask you to do for them; namely, vote with you and as you vote, and thereby help you to protect your interests." Furthermore, "[t]ell them all you ask is fair play, and if they are really willing to give you that, why are they not willing to help you elevate men who say the right to vote shall not be taken away from you."

The *San Antonio Express* described the Democratic party's "struggle to secure the negro vote" in the South as "surpass[ing] all the past demagogueism of the mother of demagogues."[41] Democratic efforts apparently were having some impact, since the *Express* noted that "the old sinful party" had "formed associations which give preference to the colored Democrat over the white Republican in every relation of life–in bus and in social capacity."

Stage 4: Freedmen Begin Voting for Radical Candidates

Once the freedmen began voting, largely for Radical Republican candidates, the conservative editors usually took one of two stands:
  –that efforts still should continue toward gaining the understanding, sympathy, and support of the freedmen; that, through wooing or threatening, the freedmen eventually would come to see that their true interests lay with the whites
  –that "negro suffrage" was certain to lead to horrible results for the Southern states and for the nation, so horrible, in fact, that scandals might produce a backlash that would lead to the restoration of conservative governments.

African-American and Radical Republican newspapers, generally, were heartened by the freedmen's support for the Radical cause and by the results of the elections. They continued to express confidence in the freedmen as citizens and voters.

Wooing and Threatening

The *Arkansas Gazette* was one of the newspapers that adopted both of these arguments at different times during this period. In September 1868 it attempted to convince African-American voters who had supported the Radical Party that they owed nothing to that political party. "The intelligent negro knows that it was a result of the war, that gave him his freedom. . . not the party that had set the slaves free," the *Gazette* reminded Arkansas freedmen. In fact, the Radical Party owed its electoral successes to the freedmen, not the reverse. The *Gazette* called on "the honest colored man" to consider these points,[42]

The *Missouri Republican* thought it saw signs that the Radicals were losing "control [of] the negro vote" and in fact that, by "forcing upon the

South negro suffrage," the Radicals had "placed in Democratic hands a cudgel with which to smash out Radical brains."[43] The *Republican* saw the conservatives as determined to win the 1868 congressional election: "[T]he means of their triumph, notwithstanding the large number of disenfranchised whites, is to be that negro vote which Radicals intended to be the instrument of the permanent enslavement of the whites."

The *Virginia Free Press* expressed the opinion that "the negroes down South are beginning to wake up . . . to the frauds put upon them by . . . Radical adventurers" and to "begin to see that their true interests are identified with those of the 'white folks at home.'"[44] It found as "striking proof . . . the fact of the organization of negro conservative clubs, and the activity of some of the colored leaders." As an example, the *Free Press* cited "an intelligent negro in Mississippi, Charles W. Fitzhugh, . . . a member of the State Convention," who warned "his colored brethren" of the evils of Northern adventurers who (in the words of the *Free Press*) "foisted themselves into office by the use of the negro votes."

On the eve of municipal elections, the *Charleston Courier* appealed to "the colored voters of Charleston . . . not to aid the cause of misrule, but to unite with ['the white race of Charleston'] in giving a hearty and cordial support to the Citizens' Ticket, . . to cast your votes against a government of ignorance and in favor of one of intelligence and security."[45] Making it clear that it sought the votes of freedmen, but only as long as they were cast for the proper candidates, the *Courier* made this offer: "The white race of your own soil extend to you the hand of fraternity; will you not accept it?"

The results of the election proved a disappointment to the "expectations and . . . hopes" of the *Courier* editors.[46] An editorial said that "[t]he colored voters who endeavored to act as freedmen, and to exercise the ballot according to their own judgments, were intimidated and in many instances driven from the polls." But the editors found "gratification" in knowing that "a large body of colored voters, . . amid obloquy and persecution, adhered to the cause of conservatism and peace." These freedmen had "accepted the hand of fraternity extended to them by the white race of their own soil. And for this they will not be forgotten."

In advance of the same municipal election, the *Charleston Mercury* also urged freedmen to support the Citizens' Ticket, but it followed a harsher line than the *Courier*. The "colored men," it said, should "look at the question of bread," and not partisan politics.[47] It urged them not "to array themselves against the white citizen–in politics [or] out of politics." It warned the freedmen: "If they want peace and quiet–if they want work–if they want money to get bread and meat and coffee and clothes, let them vote at the municipal election with the citizens of Charleston."

Disastrous Results Predicted

Even while urging the conservatives to attempt to woo, or control, the votes of the freedmen, the white Southern editors could see only disaster resulting from votes cast by the freedmen for the Radicals. According to some editors, the results were likely to be so horrible that a backlash soon would restore power to the whites.

As noted earlier, the *Arkansas Gazette*, as the 1868 election approached, spoke up for "those thinking negroes who have made up their minds to vote with . . . the democratic party."[48] But it also referred to "[t]he ignorant deluded negro [as] a fit subject" for control by the radicals, who had "[bred] a hatred on the part of the negros [sic] towards the whites to whom they formerly belonged."[49] The results of "the elections at which they have been allowed to vote and the insolent conduct of the great majority on all occasions show that radicalism has succeeded but too well in its vile work," the *Gazette* concluded.

The *Missouri Republican*, which had suggested "a really systematic effort" to recruit black voters to the conservative party,[50] a month later expressed fear that giving them the vote "would convert the State into a paradise for negroes," that they would flow in from Northern states where they were not allowed to vote.[51] The *Republican* warned that the white laboring man should be concerned about "an influx of negroes" who "would become his rivals and snatch from him the means of supporting life."

The *Richmond Whig* talked about "turn[ing] loose" upon "ten magnificent States . . . three or four millions of black barbarians and a host of unprincipled adventurers." The *Whig* called "the white men of Virginia to trample this wretched instrument [a proposed constitution], the spawn of mingled negroism and carpet-bagism, under foot, and to vote down the alien ticket that accompanies it." Apparently determined to resist at any cost, the *Whig* offered this promise to its readers: "When the rivers shall flow back upon their sources, and the valleys shall tower above the mountains, and not before, will the people of Virginia do or assist in doing this great iniquity."[52]

The *Charleston Courier* had praised the "large body of colored voters" who had supported the conservatives in defeat in the 1868 municipal election.[53] It had nothing but condemnation for the actions of the officials who won the election with the support of the majority of freedman votes. "From the very inception of their entrance into office," the *Courier* said, "the majority have shown an utter contempt of the decent opinions of mankind, a disregard of law, a recklessness of legislation, and a course of conduct not only without self-respect, but with no care either for the sentiments or the interests of the city, which they profess to govern."[54]

African-American and Radical Republican Newspapers

During this time, the African-American and Radical Republican newspapers expressed confidence in the freedmen as voters and generally drew encouragement from the results of the elections.

In June 1868 an editor on the *Missouri Democrat* (a Republican newspaper) wrote "Thank Heaven" that in seven states "loyal governments have been established by negro votes" and expressed the hope that "the murder of loyal men by rebels . . . with Democratic officials to secure impunity to all murders" would end. "[W]ithout the ballots cast by black hands," the *Democrat* said, "there would be no peace, no safety for loyal men, in any of the rebellious States, except under military rule."[55]

An editorial in the *San Antonio Express* hailed the election of Radical Republicans in South Carolina, "the former hot-bed of treason, and the nest from which the apostate of freedom, John C. Calhoun, hatched his dogmas of States Rights and secession."[56] The writer attributed the congressional victories to "colored" voters, who outnumbered whites on the registration rolls, 80,286 to 47,010. "Could Calhoun's ghost revisit his native State and see the utter repudiation of his teachings," the *Express* said, "we fancy that he would hie his ghostship back to the grave to free himself from the obloquy and infamy which hangs over his name."

The *Alabama State Journal* favorably viewed the franchisement of the freedmen but saw the need for education to accompany it. "Now that they have the vote, it is more necessary than ever that knowledge should be disseminated to them," the *Journal* said.[57]

The African-American *Arkansas Freeman* interpreted Radical Republican successes in Little Rock in a different light. It urged the "colored voters . . . to nominate a ticket of their own for the next city election, and appropriate to their own use some of the good, fat offices that have heretofore been monopolized by a few white leaders."[58] The *Freeman* said that "the colored voters . . . have been pack-horses for a few greedy White Radical leaders long enough." It expressed confidence that "[w]e have got plenty of our men among us capable of holding all these fat offices." Furthermore, it said, "It is high time that some of us should begin to live in fine houses, and drive fast horses, and fare sumptuously every day."

As for the Radical politicians, their "loud professions of friendship for the colored man . . . is [sic] all humbug and moonshine," the *Freeman* said.[59] The Radical leaders "love the colored people, or least APPEAR to love them, so far as professions go, simply because through their votes they are put and kept in good paying offices, the *Freeman* said, adding, "Rebels would do the same thing, if the colored voters were to put them back again in office. It is a matter, after all, simply of dollars and cents."

Stage 5: Whites Begin to Win Elections

Near the end of the period under study, white conservatives began to win an election here and there. In response to these elections, the conservative editors tended to make one or both of two points:

– that at least a number of freedmen had seen the light, recognizing that their true friends lay among white conservatives rather than among the Radical carpetbaggers

– that the election results represented long-overdue justice for the conservative cause and a proper putting in their place of the freedmen and the Radicals for daring to think that there might be a place for them in the white man's government.

Freedmen Have Recognized Their True Friends

Both points were made by the *Charleston Courier* when, in 1868, a proposed Alabama state constitution that would have placed Radicals in power failed to receive the required number of votes. The *Courier* concluded that "negro ascendancy has been repudiated in Alabama." The constitution, an editorial said, would have brought the "evils of the ostracism of the intelligence and virtue of the State, and the installation of power of its ignorance and partisanship." But the *Courier* also said it was to the credit of "many of the more respectable of the colored voters" that they recognized these deficiencies and "knew as well as the whites, that security for life, liberty and property means intelligent suffrage."[60] (The defeat of the constitution resulted primarily because the vast majority of white voters stayed away from the polls. Even though the constitution received 70,812 "yes" votes to 1,005 "no" votes, the total number of voters was 13,550 less than the required 50 percent of registered voters.[61])

In Virginia, in 1869, two candidates, both from the North and both claiming to be Republican, ran for governor. Henry H. Wells, who already held the position by appointment, had the support of the more radical Republican wing. Gilbert C. Walker, who was endorsed by the True Republicans, attracted many of the conservative votes, who had not nominated a candidate. The result was a Walker victory. The True Republican-conservative forces made an attempt to encourage African-American votes for Walker and discourage votes for Wells. Conservatives organized biracial barbecues in Richmond to woo the support of freedmen.[62] Reports indicated that Walker-supporting employers threatened to discharge Wells supporters, sent Wells supporters far from the polls on election day, and promised extra pay for those who would not vote.[63]

Rather than excoriating the freedmen who supported Wells, the *Richmond Whig* found pleasure in noting that Walker had received 10 "colored votes" for every white vote that Wells got. "The great bulk of all classes of our population," the *Whig* said, "felt that Wells was a pest, an enemy, an incendiary, seeking to foment discord and contention among us for his own sordid end."[64]

The *Charleston Courier* interpreted the Virginia election as delivering "a death blow" to "the test oaths, disqualifications, penalties and Union Leagues, which have so much distracted the peace of the land, and retarded its interests."[65] The *Courier* also hailed the results as "the second emancipation of the colored race." It said that "[h]undreds of them braved proscription, left their Leagues, and openly voted with the Conservative Republicans and the white race of their own soil." It expressed "gratification to know that many of the colored people stood by the white race of their own State."

A single sentence in an editorial in the *Clarion*, in Jackson, Miss. (referring to the same election in Virginia), reflected both of the sentiments expressed during this period. "[T[he black man may be ignorant" about ballots and government, the *Clarion* said, "but he is not such a fool as not to know that his true interests dictate that he should be on good terms with the great body of the people among whom he expects to spend his days."[66]

Radicals and Freedmen Put in Their Place

In the other half of the sentence, the *Clarion* said that the election showed that "colored people do not intend to permit themselves to be dragooned as a class into an organization of hostility to the whites, by the 'political black-legs and adventurers,' . . . known here as carpetbaggers."[67]

Editorial reactions to two other elections in 1870 put more emphasis on defeating opponents than on winning converts.

The success of the conservatives in Virginia's legislative and congressional elections of 1870 prompted the *Richmond Whig* to state: "The late election demonstrates the fact that on the present line the negroes had as well cease their operations in this State. They have made desperate efforts, under the lead of the carpet-baggers, to get possession of the government, and they have now been beaten in three elections."[68]

The *Virginia Free Press* noted that the conservatives had succeeded even though the Fifteenth Amendment to the Constitution had "enfranchised not less than 700,000 negroes, and it is fair to presume that nine-tenths of these voted the Radical tickets."[69]

In Tennessee, when voters in 1870 approved a new constitution favored by the conservatives, the *Memphis Appeal* said that the three-to-one margin was "really six instead . . . [f]or not less than two-thirds of the votes against the new Constitution were cast by negroes." It described those votes as "having no meaning," as "so many blackballs,... driven that way in a flock by the carpet-baggers."70

Conclusion

These elections, though few number during the period of this study, turned out to foreshadow elections that, especially after 1876, routinely began returning political power to the conservatives. Constitutionally, the former slaves were citizens and voters, but the political mentality that had made possible the decision in *Dred Scott v. Sanford* once again had begun to prevail. By the time of *Plessy v. Ferguson,* two decades after these elections, a dissenting Supreme Court justice (in a case that involved seating on streetcars but could have concerned voting rights) would lament that the states had successfully managed to "interfere with the full enjoyment of the blessings of freedom."

The specter of *Dred Scott* once again was set free in the land.

Notes

1. *Louisville Journal*, Oct. 13, 1865.
2. *Richmond Whig,*,Nov. 24, 1865.
3. *Louisville Journal*, Oct. 13, 1865.
4. *Raleigh Sentinel*, Aug, 11, 1865.
5. *Memphis Appeal*, Feb. 15, 1866.
6. *Memphis Appeal*, Feb. 25, 1866.
7. *Huntsville Advocate*, Aug. 31, 1865.
8. *Livingston Journal*, Aug. 5, 1865.
9. *Brownlow's Knoxville Whig*, March 21, 1866.
10. *Raleigh Standard*, Sept. 26, 1866.
11. *Loyal Georgian*, March 3, 1866.
12. *Colored Tennessean*, Aug. 14, 1865.
13. *Memphis Avalanche*, February 15, 1866.
14. *Memphis Appeal*, March 9, 1867.
15. *Memphis Appeal*, March 21, 1867.
16. *Memphis Appeal*, February 21, 1867.
17. *Richmond Dispatch*, June 28, 1867.
18. *Richmond Dispatch*, October 25, 1867.
19. *Arkansas Gazette*, September 3, 1867.
20. *Memphis Appeal*, March 21, 1867.
21. *Charleston Mercury*, November 4, 1867.
22. *Arkansas Gazette*, September 3, 1867.
23. *Arkansas Gazette*, April 9, 1867.
24. *Richmond Whig*, October 18, 1867.
25. *Nashville Press*, February 11, 1867.
26. *Savannah Republican*, July 27, 1867.
27. *Missouri Democrat*, April 15, 1867.
28. *Arkansas Gazette*, February 4, 1868.
29. *Arkansas Gazette*, February 11, 1868.
30. *Sentinel*, January 6, 1868.
31. *Charleston Courier*, March 25, 1868.
32. *Rome Weekly Courier*, May 27, 1868.
33. *Independent Monitor*, February 15, 1868.
34. *Richmond Whig*, October 18, 1867.

35. *Vicksburg Times*, January 7, 1868.
36. *Standard*, March 20, 1867.
37. *Standard*, November 13, 1867.
38. *Standard*, February 19, 1868.
39. *Loyal Georgian*, February 15, 1868.
40. *National Republican*, September 9, 1868.
41. *San Antonio Express*, September 6, 1868.
42. *Arkansas Gazette*, September 15, 1868.
43. *Missouri Republican*, July 30, 1868.
44. *Virginia Free Press*, September 3, 1868.
45. *Charleston Courier*, November 9, 1868.
46. *Charleston Courier*, November 12, 1868.
47. *Charleston Mercury*, November 7, 1868.
48. *Arkansas Gazette*, September 15, 1868.
49. *Arkansas Gazette*, February 25, 1868.
50. *Missouri Republican*, July 30, 1868.
51. *Missouri Republican*, August 30, 1868.
52. *Richmond Whig*, May 22, 1868.
53. *Charleston Courier*, November 12, 1868.
54. *Charleston Courier*, October 30, 1869.
55. *Missouri Democrat*, June 29, 1868.
56. *San Antonio Express*, May 8, 1868.
57. *Alabama State Journal*, February 2, 1869.
58. *Arkansas Freeman*, October 5, 1869.
59. *Arkansas Freeman*, October 5, 1869.
60. *Charleston Courier*, February 18, 1868.
61. Walter L. Fleming, *Civil War and Reconstruction in Alabama*. Spartanburg, S.C.: The Reprint Co., 1978, pp. 537-44. (Original edition, copyright 1905, by Columbia University Press.)
62. Richard Lowe, *Republicans and Reconstruction in Virginia, 1856-70*. Charlottesville: University of Virginia Press, 1991, p. 174.
63. Lowe, p. 174.
64. *Richmond Whig*, July 9, 1869.
65. *Charleston Courier*, July 10, 1869.
66. *Clarion*, July 13, 1869.
67. *Clarion*, July 13, 1869.
68. *Richmond Whig*, November 15, 1870.
69. *Virginia Free Press*, November 27, 1870.
70. *Memphis Appeal*, April 6, 1870.

31

The Michigan Democratic Press and the Fifteenth Amendment: A Divided Party United

Janice L. Bukovac
Michigan State University

The Fifteenth Amendment
March 30, 1870

SECTION. 1. The right of citizens of the United States to vote shall not be denied or abridged by the United States or by any State on account of race, color, or previous condition of servitude.

SECTION. 2. The Congress shall have power to enforce this article by appropriate legislation.

In 1861 the Democratic party was fighting a number of different battles. Internally, it was struggling with serious divisions that in November 1860 had lost it the presidency. Externally, it was faced with a serious political opponent in the form of the dominant Republican party. Compounding all this was a civil war that demanded cooperation from all Northern political factions just to save the Union. It was a time ripe for disorganization and change. The Radical Republicans reflected this in their innovative philosophies and promotion of revolutionary structural alterations. The Democratic party and its press should have portrayed similar progression. Yet, this research proves such assumptions not only inadequate but incorrect. Throughout the war years and postwar reconstruction the Democrats remained rooted in established philosophies that continued to steer the party. While these hard-line philosophies were argued as a reason for the Democrats' failure to regain political ascendancy for many years, they lent a strength and consistency to a beleaguered political identity.

The Democratic press was an excellent reflection of its party and its principles. Not only were these newspapers the self-proclaimed servants of the party and its ideals, but they also were the primary mode that in the words of one newspaper, "The truths and principles of democracy must be got before the people."[1] The newspapers involved in this research provide an exhaustive and representative sample of Michigan Democratic party papers for the years under consideration. Examination of leading Democratic organs like the *New York World* indicated that the Michigan papers were largely in step with their Northeastern peers and reflected the Northern Democratic party. In the words of the *Detroit Free Press*, "The general truths of Democracy are the same everywhere. They will be found in every Democratic paper."[2] Considering the structural instability of the party the consistency and continuity of the papers' contents and convictions were commendable.

Throughout the war years the Michigan Democratic press maintained two impressive avenues of consistency—its devotion to Democratic principles and ideals, and its uniform method of arguing against black rights legislation. The formation of the arguments and rationale remained consistent and reflected long established principles. Despite internal party divisiveness, the Democratic press remained united in opposition to the Republican policy.[3]

In 1860 the Democratic party experienced a voter realignment—infrequent in American political history—that favored the Republicans.[4] The fracture of the Democratic party in 1860 with two national candidates, serious internal divisions and member disillusionment, resulted in a party suffering serious organization problems. Yet the press did not display this divisiveness. Other than infrequent rallying calls to unite, it portrayed an image of a united party with a consistent philosophy. The fact that the Democrats maintained their forceful political press throughout a difficult time illustrates a powerful loyalty by editors and constituents throughout the state. Nowhere was this more apparent than the debate over the Fifteenth Amendment.

The Fifteenth Amendment to the Constitution was the final legislative action taken during the 1860s concerning the expansion of black rights. Its subject, that of black enfranchisement, was not a new concern in Washington, D.C., or in the nation. The roots of the Fifteenth Amendment lie in the ratification of the Fourteenth Amendment.

Background

Despite Democratic opposition, the Fourteenth Amendment was ratified on 20 July 1868. A total of twenty-eight states was needed to ratify the amendment; twenty-four ratified it within the first year—all Northern states. The Fourteenth Amendment, however, failed to accomplish what Radical Republicans believed to be a necessary privilege of equality—the right to vote. The possible reduction in congressional representation that the Fourteenth Amendment outlined for the Southern states, based on the number of male voters, did not guarantee that blacks would be allowed to vote.[5] Southern states rejected the Fourteenth Amendment, understandably, refusing to voluntarily grant blacks the vote in order to gain representation. The Radical Republicans demanded that congressional intervention was needed to complete the guarantee of civil rights begun with the Thirteenth and Fourteenth amendments.

In partial response to the pressure, Congress passed the Military Reconstruction Act on 2 March 1867. The act divided the Southern states (except Tennessee) into five military districts under military rule, and it outlined the procedure by which states could organize new governments acceptable to Congress.[6] These procedures included manhood suffrage and ratification of the Fourteenth Amendment. With the promise of readmission to Congress and relief from military rule, several Southern states eventually ratified the amendment.[7] The apparent acceptance of enfranchising blacks in the South left the nation with an awkward double standard since blacks in the North were denied the vote. The Fifteenth Amendment sought to resolve this imbalance.

Long before the Military Reconstruction Act pressured the South to accept the Fourteenth Amendment the issue of black suffrage had been a focal point in congressional proceedings. During the debates over the Thirteenth Amendment, the *Detroit Free Press*, Michigan's biggest Democratic paper, spent considerable space discussing the issue. Even before the Emancipation Proclamation, Democrats foresaw that black suffrage was one of the issues that they would have to face.

Opposition to black suffrage was strong in both the Northern and Southern states. Even the Joint Committee on Reconstruction noted that three-fourths of the nation was not yet ready to accept such fundamental change.[8] As a compromise, Congress deleted the words "race and color" from section 2 of the Fourteenth Amendment, and established the terms of representation in Congress based on eligible male voters. The Republicans hoped that this indirect tactic would give blacks the vote. Instead the South showed little inclination to voluntarily enfranchise blacks.

Slowly, Congress continued its efforts to give blacks the right to vote, regardless of public opinion. The elections of 1866 had left the Republicans with an enlarged congressional majority and on the brink of action. The first effort was in Washington. Although the residents of the District of Columbia had voted down black suffrage in a special election in January 1865, Congress enacted a bill granting enfranchising blacks in the district in December 1866.[9] In January 1867, Congress passed legislation requiring manhood suffrage in all federal territories, and as a requirement of statehood for Nebraska.[10]

But the Military Reconstruction Act was Congress's most ambitious legislation on black suffrage. In section 5, black suffrage was a required condition for the readmission of former Confederate states to the Union and representation in Congress.[11] With this piece of legislation only the North and the Border states remained outside federal mandate on black suffrage. Section 2 of the Fourteenth Amendment, which based congressional representation on the number of eligible voters, indirectly promoting black suffrage, was the only legislation that affected those areas. With an insignificant black population the motivation to grant blacks the vote to gain representation was negligible.

Eventually, Southern states accepted the terms, rejoined the Union and sent their representatives to Congress. As Southern representation increased, Radical Republicans feared that they might lose the ability to direct the progress of Reconstruction.[12] Democrats had seen significant gains in the congressional elections of 1867 and hoped for further success in the 1868 elections. Although black suffrage was a key objective of Republican reconstruction, it deliberately was absent from the 1868 Republican platform. The Republicans were well aware of the popular sentiment against black suffrage and believed that it would damage their campaign to openly promote black rights.

The Republicans met in May 1868 in Chicago and nominated Ulysses S. Grant as their presidential candidate. Their platform was a carefully worded document that-—while clear in its criticism of President Johnson and its praise of the late President Lincoln-—was vague on controversial issues. Black suffrage was politically sensitive and, despite the fact that many Radicals favored it nationwide, conservative Republicans recognized Northern opposition to candidates supporting such legislation. Consequently, while the Radical Republicans wished to see Grant run on an outspoken platform that included black suffrage, conservatives were more cautious. The Republican platform justified black suffrage in the Southern states on the basis of the "consideration of public safety, of gratitude, and of justice," leaving the question of black suffrage in the Northern states in the hands of the people. "The question of suffrage in all the loyal States," they reasoned, "properly belongs to the people of those States."[13] Adroitly, the Democratic party was disarmed of one of their more powerful political weapons against the Republicans.

The Democratic convention was held in July 1868; after extensive debate and consideration of numerous candidates, Horatio Seymour of New York received the presidential nomination. Unlike the Republican platform, the Democratic counterpart denounced the efforts of Republican reconstruction as "unconstitutional, revolutionary, and void."[14] It criticized the usurpations of Congress and the Radical Republicans as a "disregard of right, and . . . unparalleled oppression and tyranny which have marked its career."[15] Instead of restoring the Union, the Republican administration had dissolved it, putting the Southern states under military despotism and supremacy. According to the Democrats, it was time for reunion, amnesty, restoration of states' rights and recognition of state control over black suffrage.[16]

Unfortunately for the Democrats, Seymour proved a poor, lackluster choice and his running mate, Francis P. Blair, Jr., of Missouri, proved a liability. Grant easily won the 1868 presidential election, while Democrats made gains in Congress. With the presidential election behind them pro-suffrage Republicans moved to enfranchise blacks.

Michigan

In Michigan sentiment against black suffrage was strong. Unlike the issues concerning earlier congressional efforts to aid blacks, black suffrage was put to a popular vote in the state and suffered a resounding defeat. In 1866, following a mandate that required that the question of constitutional revision be addressed every sixteen years, Michigan voters supported the convening of a convention. The convention's work included the elimination of the word "white" on the matter of voting requirements. Michiganians by a vote of

110,582 to 71,729 roundly defeated the predominately Republican attempt to initiate a new constitution that eliminated race restrictions on voting.[17] Michigan was not the only Northern state to send such a message to Congress, as sentiment ran strong in the Northern states against giving the vote to blacks. Republicans did not need to be told the political consequences of promoting the enfranchisement of the black man.

Legislative History

The third session of the Fortieth Congress met in December 1868. Although the Republican platform had indicated that the issue of black suffrage would be left to the individual states, numerous proposals for a constitutional amendment to give blacks the vote were introduced. Black suffrage proponents recognized the necessity of moving on an amendment, while Republicans still maintained control in most legislatures. If they failed to act quickly, the Democrats could tap Northern sentiment and make black suffrage an issue in the next elections, possibly capturing control of enough state legislatures to block ratification of a constitutional amendment.[18]

On 7 March 1868 Senator John Henderson of Missouri introduced Senate Joint Resolution 8, disallowing states to deny the vote on the basis of color, race or previous condition.[19] In January 1869 it was reported out of the Senate Judiciary Committee. During that time the House was also considering a similar measure. On 17 February 1869 the Senate passed Senate Joint Resolution 8 and, after a slight alteration by the House, a conference was appointed that reported out the final version of the Fifteenth Amendment. The amendment, which guaranteed the right to vote to all male citizens, was sent to the states on 27 February 1869.

The congressional debates did not follow party lines as closely as those concerning the Thirteenth and Fourteenth Amendments. Instead, the question of black suffrage was widely resisted by conservative Republicans, and the morality of taking such action, right after their party's success in the presidential election, bothered many. Democrats and conservative Republicans alike argued that the vocal Radical Republicans were showing bad faith so soon after their election promises.

The Democrats centered their opposition on the issue of states' rights. Congress, they declared, did not have the right through the Constitution to impose black suffrage, nor did the Fourteenth Amendment cover the right to vote.[20] These were familiar arguments questioning the constitutional ability of Congress to force unwarranted legislation on voters, and the related rights of states to control their own institutions.

The Democrats also accused the Republicans of being inconsistent on many levels. In Congress they were accused of inconsistency concerning their stated platform promises and of refusing to consider universal suffrage. Not only were they violating their own promises to leave black suffrage to the discretion of the individual states, but also they intended to deny the vote to Chinese immigrants. It seemed illogical to the Democrats to show concern for blacks, whose level of sophistication they argued was inferior to that of most Chinese immigrants. The Democrats even voted for a proposal of universal suffrage made by Senator Joseph S. Fowler of Tennessee.[21] Although Fowler was a Republican, the proposal was roundly dismissed by his peers, and the sincerity behind the Democratic vote was questioned.[22]

The Democrats continued their efforts to block legislation by playing the devil's advocate. The Fifteenth Amendment appeared a perfect issue over which to divide the Republican party. Many Northern Republican states refused to eliminate voting restrictions and qualifications and congressional Democrats argued on their behalf. Literacy and property restrictions were no different to them than race restrictions. The House Democrats played one fluctuating faction of Republicans against the other with some success.[23]

The Republicans, however, were not so divided as to allow the Democrats to stop the momentum. Recognizing the timeliness of their case, congressional Republicans agreed to a compromise, allowing black suffrage. The Radicals were disappointed with the compromise because it did not provide for universal manhood suffrage, allowing for educational, intelligence, poll taxes and property tests.[24] As the Radicals feared, these tactics were eventually employed by the South to restrict voters. But at the time this was the best compromise that could be reached among Republicans.

Newspaper Editorials

During the debate over the Fifteenth Amendment the Democratic press reflected the party platform more than any other period during the 1860s. This was a direct result of the 1868 platform, which was neither vague nor mild in its support of states' rights and condemnation of the Republican administration and its reconstruction policy. Such forceful language more accurately mirrored the critical and verbal role the papers played in the political arena. The increased criticism and forewarning by the press, indicated a continued healing and strengthening of the Democratic party from its disruption of the late 1850s. Although plagued by divisions, the Democrats were evolving into a strong political adversary. As the *Detroit Free Press* declared: "The minority reserves to itself the inalienable right to find fault . . . to condemn the mistakes of the majority."[25] Buoyed by the party's success in the 1867 and 1868 elections, the Democrats were ready to seriously challenge the Republicans. As indicated by the homogeneity of the newspapers and the continued criticism of the Republican party, the Democrats were doing just that.

The goal of the Fifteenth Amendment—black suffrage—was not a new issue, and consequently the Democratic arguments used familiar terminology. Long before the Fifteenth Amendment was debated, newspapers discussed the possibility of black suffrage. During the debate over the Thirteenth Amendment the *Detroit Free Press* accused the Republican party of such aspirations. With the Fourteenth Amendment all Michigan Democratic papers spoke of the Republican plot to enfranchise blacks. Unlike the Thirteenth and Fourteenth amendments, the Fifteenth Amendment had no redeeming elements for the Democrats, who considered its framing deceitful; its content, revolutionary; and its outcome, destructive. Based on their estimate, as reflected in the vehemence and condemnation of the press, there was no question that the Democratic party perceived the Fifteenth Amendment as the most despotic act the Republican party had ever supported. The amendment according to the Democrats was the most unconstitutional, treacherous and disastrous of all reconstruction legislation.[26]

The Democratic press promoted traditional Democratic philosophies. The structure of their arguments on states' rights and the sanctity of the Constitution was familiar. Their rhetoric, during debate over the Fifteenth Amendment however, grew increasingly violent. With renewed vengeance, Democratic editors denied the constitutional right of Congress to meddle in affairs of the states on this matter. "Democracy," the *Detroit Free Press* declared, "would have no objection to a fair and distinct proposition to amend the Constitution so as to confer political equality, provided the proposition was, as required by the Constitution, submitted to the people of the several States."[27] Not only were the people not accorded a vote, but past elections left no doubt as to their preference.

Since 1865 black suffrage had been defeated at the ballot box in numerous Northern states, including Colorado, Connecticut, Wisconsin, Minnesota, Nebraska, Tennessee, Kansas, Ohio and Michigan.[28] The Republican party, which often justified its policies as the will of the people, was now disregarding public opposition to black suffrage. The Democrats were outraged. The question of black suffrage was for the states to answer, editors claimed. The *Marshall Democratic Expounder* was representative of Michigan Democratic papers when it stated, "It is the right of the State in the exercise of its sovereignty under the Constitution."29 The fact that the Republican Congress was forcing black suffrage on the Northern states, against their wishes, was the worst form of treachery. "What you have solemnly condemned" the *Clinton County Independent* railed, "a radical Congress may impose upon you in spite of your condemnation."30

The Democrats were embittered and frustrated by the Republicans' refusal to consider the will of the people, especially since the Republicans' actions violated their own party platform. The Democratic newspapers expressed their dismay with the Republican treachery, labeling it "Swindle" and "trickery."31 Similar sentiments were voiced across Michigan. This violation of the peoples' trust was even more objectionable to the Democrats because they had lost the 1868 election. The Democrats contended that if the Republicans had run on a black suffrage platform, they would have lost. The *Detroit Free Press* reasoned that recent Democratic political success had left the Democrats confident that the people "voted regardless of that question [black suffrage] and in a different manner from what they would have voted had they supposed it was a question involved in any shape or form." The Democrats could see no rationale for the Republican turnaround but one—self engrandizment. "So much for devotion to principle," mocked the *Detroit Free Press*.32

The Democrats' high hopes for the 1868 presidential elections had been dashed after the Republican party decided not to make black suffrage a campaign issue. It was obvious, at least to the Democrats, that the Republicans, who had lied in their party platform to capture an otherwise uncertain victory, were now promoting black suffrage as a means to maintain power. The Republican party believed in part that they needed the black vote to remain in power. There was clear indication in the congressional debates of the Republicans' political motivation.33 This fueled Democratic criticism, popular during the debate over the Fourteenth Amendment, of the self-interested Republican party. Only too true was the Coldwater Sentinel's warning that "the issue, Negro suffrage, repudiated in this election, like the stone rejected by the builders, will after election become the head of the corner in the Republican edifice."34

The Democrats were unrelenting in their condemnation of the Republican policy and its potential repercussions. Although undeniably in part an effort to improve their own status among

Northern Democrats and Republicans, who opposed black suffrage, there was a continuing adherence to basic Democratic philosophies and the belief that blacks were unqualified for political responsibility. The Democrats considered the white race superior to the black and could not comprehend the Republicans believed otherwise. The Republican Congress, the Democrats reasoned, was violating the laws of nature.35

The Democratic press repeatedly identified blacks as inferior, uneducated, uninterested and incompetent. "A race so inferior to ourselves," the *Detroit Free Press* declared, "that in no other relations of life will they ever be recognized as our equals."36 The Detroit daily spoke for all Democratic papers when it noted: "[We] do not believe . . . Negroes should have any part or parcel in a government for white men. . . . No Democrat . . . proposes such an idea."37

The Democrats exploitation of racial prejudice throughout the 1860s increased as Reconstruction continued. While this activity sought to attract popular support, it also reflected a basic perception. The Democrats' negative opinion of the black man, regardless of political considerations, condemned support for black suffrage. For Democrats there was no rationale for giving in to such a supposedly unworthy group. If the Republicans promoted black suffrage they reasoned, it was only as a stepping stone to maintain power. Here, declared the Democratic press, was a large group whose vote the Republicans could control. According to the *Jackson Eagle*, the Radicals were aware of the blacks' political ignorance and by granting them the right to vote, sought to assure their own ascendancy.38

Democrats continued to criticize the Republicans as false champions of the black man. Republicans were accused of imposing black suffrage on the South for no other reason than "to spite whites."39 Their decision to reject black suffrage in the 1868 campaign platform was only to achieve victory—their wish to extend black suffrage to the rest of the states was, not for the black man, but for themselves. According to the East Saginaw Courier, the Republicans were "schemers and intriguers," offering the black man the vote only to strengthen their own numbers.40 Elsewhere the *Detroit Free Press* charged, "They offer them as a bribe, as pay for services to be rendered."41 And the *Clinton County Independent* contended Republicans were not genuinely concerned with the black man. Instead, they were only willing to accord them rights in principle, so long as they did not claim them in practice.42 Editors mocked that a Republican would no sooner allow a black man into his house as allow him to vote, unless that vote were for him.

To support their accusations, the Democrats pointed to the lack of consideration given to enfranchising women and foreigners. If the Republicans were truly such champions of civil and political rights, queried the Democratic press, why did they do not accord similar rights to women and immigrants? The Democrats were not ready themselves to accord suffrage to women, and such propositions were not to be found in the formal platforms or among congressional proposals. But from a political standpoint it was a logical argument. Women were, claimed the Democratic press, in general more educated, genteel and knowledgeable than blacks. The Coldwater Sentinel argued that "The Negro may vote, but the woman who knows enough to train up a family of boys until old enough to be electors, and finally teach them how to vote, cannot."43 The *Detroit Free Press* queried, why deny to the knowledgeable, intelligent woman what is granted so freely to the unknowledgable black man?44

The argument regarding immigrants, although different from that for women, also had legitimacy. Chinese, German and Irish immigrants were recognized by the Democrats as better educated than blacks and deserving of equal treatment. The *Detroit Free Press* accused the Republicans of believing that "the Negroes are more intelligent than the foreigners."45 The Democratic press did not doubt that the Republican refusal to extend the vote to these groups had nothing to do with the groups themselves, but rather with the Republicans' lack of ability to control them.

The Democratic press hammered the Republicans, portraying them as anti-foreign and anti-woman. Republican actions clearly indicated that women and immigrants were beneath blacks and not worthy of the same rights and privileges. Whether the Democrats believed the Republicans to be anti-foreign and anti-woman was irrelevant. The political motivation for their argument was to present the Republicans as a self-centered party. Women and educated immigrants were not so culpable, and, the Democratic press indicated, would not blindly support that radical political faction.46 It had nothing to do with rights. The *Marshall Democratic Expounder* went even further and proposed promoting suffrage to eighteen-year-old males. Many educated, working eighteen-year-old males had better voting qualifications than most blacks. This was why the Republicans would never consider granting eighteen-year-olds suffrage; their vote could not be controlled.47

These Democratic arguments against the Republicans were an effort to discredit the Republicans rather than promote any strongly held principles. In reality, the Democrats had no intention of promoting suffrage for any of these groups, but the rationale behind their arguments was clear. There was a reason why these groups did not enjoy the same privileges as white American males, and that was because suffrage was a political right not a natural one. And a political right had to be earned. According to the *Detroit Free Press*, "The mind must be emancipated, the intellect must be elevated, the self-reliance must be acquired that grows out of the independent intercourse of man with man."[48] If suffrage was a natural right, there was no reason to deny it to all; if it was a political right, there was no reason to grant it to inexperienced, socially uneducated blacks.

During all the controversy over black suffrage, the Democratic press insisted that suffrage was not a party issue.[49] Regardless of politics, the Constitution and states' rights, black suffrage itself was inherently wrong. It had nothing to do with Democrat versus Republican. Black suffrage, claimed the Democrats, was of personal and state interest. Black suffrage, the Democrats reasoned, would surely bring hardship and violence to all Michigan residents, regardless of political affiliation. This argument benefitted the Democrats because many Northern Republican1s were uneasy with the idea of black suffrage, and their support could not be won by advocating strict party lines. The Democrats realized that a future with black suffrage hit emotional chords and fears that had little to do with party affiliations. Yet Democratic conclusions accurately reflected deep-rooted party principles. So although they argued suffrage was a nonpartisan issue, their stand was a direct result of their beliefs.

The Democratic editorials were frightening in their predictions. If black suffrage was successful, the press foresaw three outcomes. Initially, the Democrats feared that the Michigan legislature would grant black suffrage before any of its Northern neighbors. If this happened, the flood of Freedmen to Michigan would be inevitable. Jobs belonging to white men would be taken by blacks, according to the *Detroit Free Press*, and an economic crisis would befall the state.[50] Even after several Northern states, including Michigan, ratified the Fifteenth Amendment, these fears still existed. The *Marshall Democratic Expounder*, in parodying the poem of the charge of the Light Brigade, declared, "Negroes will be on the right [of] us——Negroes on the left of us——Negroes behind us——Negroes around us."[51]

These concerns were not limited to Michigan. The Democratic press also feared for the South, expressing concern for the viability of the Southern economy. An abstract principle such as black suffrage was not worth, in the opinion of the *Detroit Free Press*, "ruining the prosperity of the most fertile and valuable section of the Union."[52] The Niles Democratic Republican already feared that "the industry and the agriculture of that section have been paralyzed."53

The second, and more frightening, outcome of black suffrage was the possibility of a race war with its accompanying violence and bloodshed. According to the Democrats, this was not just a possibility but a fact. The *Detroit Free Press* claimed that the current congressional policy would "reawaken the prejudices of race" that had died down since the end of the Civil War.54 Republicans were "fools . . . madmen" to encourage such social hostility. "Will they," asked the Detroit editor, "sustain a policy that, as certain as the sun shines, will either lead to a war of races, and the extermination of the blacks in this country, or to the vision of a Negro President, a Negro Congress, and Negro Governors and Legislatures?" The *Jackson Eagle* screamed "Blood, blood! Revolution upon revolution!"55 According to the *Clinton County Independent*, the outcome was certain and the Republicans, who claimed to so adore the black man, were merely leading him to the slaughter. Extermination of the black race was the inevitable result of the radical policy.56

The third fear that the Democratic press expressed was tied to its concern for the democratic system of government. Considering their declarations regarding states' rights, it is understandable that they feared that the Republicans would remain the nation's dominant political party. The Democratic press warned that the Republicans were attempting the "lowest meanest and most contemptible swindling of the people," ushering in a future more bleak than ever before.57 The *Grand Rapids Daily Democrat* referred to the Republican-controlled Congress as a "popular despotism."58 The *Detroit Free Press* accused Congress of "revolutionizing the entire institutions of the country, creating an oligarchy"; it was "an act of tyranny," "despotic" and "crazy fanaticism."59 Democrats could not comprehend how Congress could succeed in this attempt. The *Detroit Free Press* even predicted doom for the white-dominated government if blacks were enfranchised.60

Summary

During the lengthy debate over black suffrage and the Fifteenth Amendment, the Michigan Democratic press portrayed their party as a strong and viable political body. Democratic newspapers depicted a strong, philosophically consistent party that in reality was still mending its tears. Factional differences were not as apparent in the editorials as they were in reality. The predominately hard-line rhetoric, with its promotion of traditional philosophies, belied efforts of compromise. There was continuing praise and promotion of the democracy and its principles. According to the *Coldwater Sentinel*, every Democrat "should now feel that he is anointed of God." The *Detroit Free Press* concurred, confidently proclaiming, "the glorious principles of the Democratic party are still enshrined in the hearts of a majority of the people."[61] The only indication of party differences were the rare calls for unity, as when the *Detroit Free Press* pleaded, "Let us sink all minor issues, bury all past differences, and combine for the one great day of driving from power the faction which is the sole obstacle to the restoration of the republic on a wise, constitutional, and equitable basis."[62] The overall impression, however, was that the Democratic party continued as a strong and united political entity. If it suffered from internal dissention, it was not apparent in the Michigan press.

Beyond supporting the stated party platform and the Congressional arguments, the press increased its attacks and criticism of the Republicans. Different from the assault leveled at the Republicans during the debate over the Thirteenth and Fourteenth amendments, these attacks were better organized and more critical. The rhetoric was vituperative, and a serious effort to discredit the Republicans was pursued. The press demonstrated a concentrated emotion that was only minimally apparent in the platform and congressional records. The fact that the newspapers implied acceptance of ideas that they themselves denied—such as woman suffrage—reflected their goal of discrediting the Republicans at all costs. They clearly recognized the Republicans' weakened condition and knew that there was an opening where none existed only a few years ago. The Democrats were correct in their assessment of the divisiveness of the Republican party on the issue of black suffrage. Their ability to use it to their advantage, however, was not as powerful as the Republicans' rallying cry.

The majority of the Democratic press focused on the Republicans rather than on the mechanics of black suffrage. Although there was no lack of exaggerated predictions of revolution and destruction, they were similar to the predictions made years earlier. Democratic criticism of the Republican's method and motives was more intense. The Republicans, according to the Democratic press, were nothing more than a group of hypocrites at a variety of levels. They said one thing and proceeded with another, whether betraying their party platform or the trust of the black man. Whatever the issue, the Republicans pursued only one thing—self-engrandizment.

The Michigan Democratic press accurately identified the Republicans' political plans for blacks. Considerable research on the framing of the Fifteenth Amendment revealed various theories as to its motivation.63 Central to all was the acknowledgement that the Republicans were moved by the need to attract the black vote. The readmittance of the Southern states and the expected addition of Southern representatives to the Democratic ranks indicated a possible Democratic resurgence. Republicans believed that the black man, particularly in the North, could provide additional Republican votes. Similar to the Democratic fears concerning them, the Republicans harbored strong concerns that a return to a Democratic administration would spell doom for the nation. So, although in part a concern for the equality of blacks, the Republican motivation was something less than altruistic.

The Democrats' lack of success did not adversely affect the press, either in consistency or strength. After the ratification of the Fifteenth Amendment the Democrats simply proceeded, as they had after each controversial piece of legislation, with the issues of the day, and the promotion of the party. As for black suffrage, the *Marshall Democratic Expounder* stated in mid 1870 that it "may be best to let the whole matter drop out of politics."64

Notes

1. *Clinton County Independent*, 19 February 1868.
2. *Detroit Free Press*, 10 November 1867.
3. Lawrence Grossman, The Democratic Party and the Negro (Urbana: University of Illinois Press, 1976), 1.
4. For a discussion on voter realignment in Michigan see Formisano, The Birth of Mass Political Parties, Michigan, 1827-1861.
5. Patrick, The Reconstruction of the Nation, 134.
6. Foner, Reconstruction: America's Unfinished Revolution 1863-1877, 276.
7. Senate Committee on the Judiciary, Amendments to the Constitution: a Brief Legislative History, 35.
8. Ibid., 2766.
9. Patrick, Reconstruction of the Nation, 135.
10. Senate Committee on the Judiciary, Amendments to the Constitution: a Brief Legislative History, 36.
11. Congressional Globe, 40th Cong., 1st Sess., 1868, 13.
12. Senate Committee on the Judiciary, Amendments to the Constitution: a Brief Legislative History, 36.
13. Porter and Johnson, National Party Platforms, 1840-1956, 39.
14. Ibid., 38.
15. Ibid.
16. Ibid., 37-38.
17. Willis Dunbar and William Shade, "Centennial of 'Impartial Suffrage' in Michigan," Michigan History LVI(1) (1972): 46.
18. Avins, The Reconstruction Amendments Debates, xvi.
19. Senate Committee on the Judiciary, Amendments to the Constitution: a Brief Legislative History, 36.
20. Avins, The Reconstruction Amendments Debates, xvi.

21. Equal or impartial suffrage meant either restricted or unqualified suffrage. Universal suffrage meant unrestricted manhood suffrage except for age and residence requirements. Negro or black suffrage could be used to mean either universal or impartial. In Michigan impartial was most commonly used of the loose terms.
22. Avins, The Reconstruction Amendments, Debates, xix.
23. Gillette, The Right to Vote: Politics and the Passage of the Fifteenth Amendment, 78.
24. Dunbar and Shade, "The Black Man Gains the Vote: The Centennial of 'Impartial Suffrage' in Michigan," 50.
25. *Detroit Free Press*, 30 December 1866.
26. Gillette, The Right to Vote: Politics and the Passage of the Fifteenth Amendment, 88-9.
27, *Detroit Free Press*, 18 February 1869.
28. Dunbar and Shade, "The Black Man Gains the Vote: The Centennial of "Impartial Suffrage" in Michigan," 46.
29. *Marshall Democratic Expounder*, 2 November 1865.
30. *Clinton County Independent*, 19 February 1868.
31. *Coldwater Sentinel*, 12 March 1869, and *Detroit Free Press*, 18 February 1869.
32. *Detroit Free Press*, 12 October 1867.
33. LaWanda Cox and John Cox, "Negro Suffrage and Republican Politics: The Problem of Motivation in Reconstruction Historiography," *Journal of Southern History* XXXIX (1954): 304.
34. *Coldwater Sentinel*, 12 October 1866.
35. *Detroit Free Press*, 28 July 1868.
36. Ibid., 28 September 1866.
37. Ibid., 12 July 1867.
38. *Jackson Eagle*, 24 March 1866.
39. *Monroe Monitor*, 1 November 1865.
40. *East Saginaw Courier*, 1 November 1868.
41. *Detroit Free Press*, 26 May 1867.
42. *Clinton County Independent*, 25 December 1867.
43. *Coldwater Sentinel*, 17 January 1868.
44. *Detroit Free Press*, 14 December 1866.
45. Ibid., 12 September 1867.
46. Ibid., 29 November 1868.
47. *Marshall Democratic Expounder*, 16 May 1867 and 23 May 1867.
48. *Detroit Free Press*, 25 July 1868.
49. Ibid., 4 July 1867.
50. Ibid., 25 November 1866.
51. *Marshall Democratic Expounder*, 21 November 1869.
52. *Detroit Free Press*, 28 September 1867.
53. *Niles Democratic Republican*, 28 December 1867.
54. *Detroit Free Press*, 12 September 1867.
55. *Jackson Eagle*, 22 July 1865.
56. *Clinton County Independent*, 19 February 1868.
57. *Coldwater Sentinel*, 12 March 1869.
58. *Grand Rapids Daily Democrat*, 20 March 1869.
59. *Detroit Free Press*, 16 December 1866.
60. Ibid., 29 July 1866.
61. *Coldwater Sentinel*, 20 November 1867, and *Detroit Free Press*, 7 November 1867.
62. *Detroit Free Press*, 22 December 1867.
63. Cox and Cox, "Negro Suffrage and Republican Politics: The Problem of Motivation in Reconstruction Historiography," 330.
64. *Marshall Democratic Expounder*, 14 April 1870.

32

Partisan News in the Early Reconstruction Era: Representations of African-Americans in Detroit's Daily Press

Richard L. Kaplan
University of California at Santa Barbara

For most of the nineteenth century Detroit newspapers deliberately and openly adopted a public posture of loyalty to the Democratic party or its opponent, whether Whig or Republican. Detroit's journals were largely vehicles of partisan communication and persuasion. With newspapers beholden to the two parties, the news agenda remained confined to the debates and issues raised by the Democrats and Republicans in Congress. Each partisan paper in Detroit would repetitively highlight the policy positions of its preferred party. Such partisan publicity worked to consolidate the party's electoral coalition while splintering and weakening the opposed political alliance. America's public-political discussion, at least as represented by newspapers as the central medium of public communication, became absorbed in the politicized and polarized debates between the two parties.[1] Information and issues that did not conform to the parties' interests were often left unreported.

In the early Reconstruction period a central issue separating the two parties and, in turn, Detroit's two Democratic dailies from the two Republican journals, was the question of the proper social status and political rights of the newly freed African-Americans. Democrats, tainted by their less than enthusiastic support for the Union in the Civil War, tried to mobilize a persistent popular racism against the Republican party's Reconstruction policies. Democrats appropriated their racist rhetoric, in part, from a commercial popular culture. But, in addition, the party of Jefferson and Jackson produced their own derogatory stereotypes of black Americans. The press, embroiled in the bitter partisan battles, promulgated these harshly negative depictions in both their news stories and their fiction columns.

This essay explores the nature of news coverage in the Reconstruction period. In this context it analyzes the press' depiction of Black Americans in order to demonstrate how deeply partisan interests penetrated into the reporting of journalists as well as invading the commercial amusements of popular culture. In essence, the paper documents a press that was thoroughly dominated by the battles and polemics of the two parties.

News Selections in the Reconstruction Era

In the early Reconstruction Era, 1865-1872, the overwhelming preponderance of news and editorials filling up the columns of Detroit's dailies was politically biased. The following charts present some measures of the magnitude of this partisanship.[2] Editorials are the genre in which newspapers most directly express their views. During the elections seasons of the nineteenth century, the majority of the sampled editorials were explicitly partisan. The paper would present itself in straightforward fashion as advocate and spokesperson for its party. In non-election seasons the percentage of partisan editorials fluctuated more erratically. The numbers declined over the course of the late nineteenth century from forty to sixty percent in 1860 and 70s, to eighteen to thirty-four percent in the 1880s and 90s.

	Editorials in Presidential Election Seasons						
	1868	1876	1884	1892	1900	1908	1916
Partisanship as a Percentage of Editorials[3]	82%	78%	62%	52%	29%	28%	17%
	Editorials in Non-Election Seasons						
	1867	1875	1883	1891	1899	1907	1915
Partisanship	54%	40%	18%	34%	5%	1%	3%

The Detroit press typically filled about one fourth of their news space with partisan news stories and articles during the presidential election campaigns. In non-election seasons news fluctuated between four and nine percent partisan news.

	News in Presidential Election Years							
	1868	1876	1884	1892	1896	1900	1908	1916
Reporter's Partisan Evaluations as a Percentage of the News Space	9%	12%	17%	9%	30%	12%	7%	0%
Total Partisan News4	15%	21%	39%	16%	40%	14%	7%	5%
	News in Non-Election Years							
	1867	1871	1879	1887	1895	1903	1911	1915
Reporter's Partisan Evaluations	2%	0%	2%	1%	8%	0%	0%	1%
Total Partisan News	18%	4%	4%	3%	9%	3%	0%	3%

What was the nature of newspaper partisanship behind these numbers? In the Reconstruction Era, 1865-1876, Civil War issues were still paramount in the press and the polity, but the two parties defined them differently. As E. E. Schattschneider explains, "...[A]ntagonists can rarely agree on what the issues are...because the definition of the alternatives is the choice of conflicts, and the choice of conflicts allocates pow-er."5 For the Republicans, the issues of course were the national union and treason. They persistently tried to depict the Democrats as the party of the South, of secession and war, for which the citizens of the North had paid dearly with the blood of their boys. In reply, the Democrats redefined the terms of the conflict, repainting the same issue cleavage in different colors, mostly black. Democrats insinuated that the war with its goal of Union and abolition of slavery had a secret motive: the establishment of a despotic government by Republicans in Washington, a centralized military state held up by the support of ignorant black voters. As the Detroit *Free Press* editorialized,

> The Radical [Republican] party, claiming to be the party of pure morality, religion, liberty and progress, has been in power only about seven years, and yet has crowded into that short period instances enough of oppression, violence, fraud, immorality, public robbery and corruption to utterly destroy any government but ours...Its next step may be to proclaim a dictator and openly set aside the constitutional government. In view of the character of the leaders of the party and the alarming outrages already committed by it, we have reason to fear they may resort to any measures no matter how desperate rather than relinquish power and plunder. ...To secure power in the South they have disfranchised great numbers of white men and given the ballot to four millions of ignorant, incompetent negroes, led on by a few

of the meanest white men...[etc., etc.]6

These were the policy views repetitiously advocated by Detroit's Democratic daily press and opposed as best they could by Detroit's two Republican journals.7 Party interests set the partisan news agenda.

The African-American Reconstruction Era Partisan Rhetoric

The status of the African-American, whether as freedman or slave, was a central issue through which partisan politics was articulated in the 1860s and early 1870s.8 The rights and duties of black Americans, their nature and capacities, their social situation and economic disabilities, were all grist for the partisan polemic mill. Moreover, partisan news of the Reconstruction era did not stop with the advocacy of national congressional policies for southern blacks, nor with criticism of the terrorism of the Ku Klux Klan. It encompassed more than views on the proper economic and political relations between the races in the South and on the role of federal troops in unreformed southern state governments. Indeed, the physical bodies of black Americans became a symbolic nexus for the general depiction of the nature, disorders and promises of American society.9

Images of blacks pervaded the Democratic newspapers and were not confined to any single journalistic genre whether editorial, fiction or telegraphic news dispatch. For example, the *Daily Union*, Detroit's junior Democratic daily, carried the following array of articles in a sampled 1868 issue:

-a local crime story headlined "Brutal Murder by Negroes"

-a celebration of a local boy claiming affiliation with the Ku Klux Klan.

-an editorial referring to the Republican goal of "the political supremacy of the negro."

-an editorial attacking Republican presidential nominee Grant for his views on negro suffrage.

-an anecdote caricaturing a wedding of African-Americans replete with dialect speech.

-a letter to the editor attacking Republican newspapers' distortion of the "temper, desires and views of southern whites."

-a reprinted article from the South entitled "Beauties of Jacobinism" which impugns southern blacks and "Yankee carpetbaggers."

-a reprinted letter to the editor which discusses "indolent negroes" and the election.10

The issue of blacks came up repeatedly in the political struggles in the North from the Civil War until the end of Reconstruction, and not only in relation to southern policies. Michigan, like other northern states, had to confront the possibility of enfranchising their local black population which, however minimal in size (1-2%,) seemed to stimulate the active animus of a majority of whites. Between the war's end and the ratification of the Fifteenth Amendment in April 1870, northern states repeatedly rejected extending the franchise to their native black populations. Michigan, an overwhelmingly Republican state, in Spring 1868 defeated a state constitutional charter amendment that promised to remove racial restrictions on the electorate. The vote was 39.3% in favor and 60.7% opposed. Such defeats along with the resurgence of the Democrats in the 1867 elections motivated "the Democracy" to play the race card again in 1868.11 The Michigan Democratic platform for the Fall 1868 election promised "to keep this country as our fathers made it, a white man's government."12 But national and state-wide Democratic losses in 1868 and the *de facto* establishment of black suffrage through the Fifteenth Amendment convinced Michigan Democrats to acquiesce to the black vote. In 1870, a state charter amendment to bring the state constitution in line with national law (as embodied in the Fifteenth Amendment) drew little partisan attention and fewer votes.13

A second local issue through which the status of blacks was contested was the integration of Detroit's public schools. Between 1867 when the state legislature ruled segregation illegal and 1871 when the Detroit School board finally capitulated, school segregation was a simmering issue, repeatedly editorialized upon by the Democratic newspapers and occasionally erupting in confrontation between the Republican state authorities and Democratic city officials.14

Despite these local and the national conflicts, the Democratic odium directed towards blacks did not derive from the actual threat of black suffrage. True, in the South the lack of black political rights was used by congressional Republicans to exclude southern states and their likely Democratic votes from national elections. But in Michigan, the small black population was not large enough to decide any state contests. The importance of the black population cannot explain the obsessive reference to them in Michigan politics.

For Democrats, the Republicans and their Civil War and Reconstruction policies were evidently darkly stained by close proximity to the black man. (The *San Francisco Examiner*, a

Democrat paper, labeled its political adversaries, "the chocolate papers.") Since the origin of the Republican party, the expression "black Republican" had become standard Democratic invective. For example, Wilbur Storey, editor of the Detroit *Free Press*, the main Michigan Democratic organ from 1853 to 1861, and later editor of the important partisan and sensationalist journal the Chicago *Times*, "insisted that the Republican Party was always to be referred to as "Black Republican' Party" in the columns of his paper.15 The expression, because of its polemical edge, implied a measure of political orthodoxy whether pronounced by a Democrat or a Republican. Thus, *Free Press* managing editor William Quinby, upon hiring future Detroit mayor John Lodge in 1883, invoked this cliché of partisan rhetoric to communicate clearly to Lodge the partisan rules of the newspaper game.16

> This is the Democratic state organ. Your father is one of the leading Republicans of the state, and of course you are a Republican also. I want you to see to it that you do not inject any of your Black Republican principles into what you write for the paper.17

References to blacks pervaded the discourse of the Democratic party and its affiliated journals.18 As Jean Baker says:

> ...[N]o matter where they began, Democratic set speeches invariably ended with blacks as the reason for higher taxes and tariff, the impeachment of Andrew Johnson, inflationary greenbacks, and Republican corruption. The Democrats looked at currency and saw the Negro, reviewed the impeachment and ended with the Negro, debated the purchase of Alaska and concluded with the Negro.19

Or as the Republican San Francisco *Chronicle* wrote on June 17, 1869:

> The Democratic Party just now seems to be based entirely upon shins, facial angles, elongated tibias and kinky hair. Without this capital, the party couldn't last a week.

Blacks were thus part of an intricate, convoluted set of representations elaborated by the Democratic party.

Let us untangle some of this imagery. According to Democrats, the project to free the Negro was illegitimate, and to give him the right to vote an absurd endeavor. On the basis of his physical-racial nature the Negro was a foolish, superstitious child. He lacked the reason and the self-control to participate in the white man's republican government. As the *Free Press* intoned, "this inferior race is [not] capable of managing affairs of state..." African-Americans were "a degraded race of ignorant semi-savages..."20

Such partisan sentiments were reinforced by a hammering repetition. On subsequent days the *Free Press* wrote:

"[the Republicans] have given the ballot to 4 million of ignorant, incompetent negroes..." (May 10th, 1868, p.2)

"an ignorant population" (May 12th)

"ignorance and the most inferior of all races" (May 12th, p.4 col.4, a reprinted editorial)

"ignorant negroes" (May 14th p.2.)

"ignorance and vice are placed over intelligence and virtue—the inferior race is made the superior" (May 14th p.2.)

"the white men of the South were deprived of all voice in public affairs while ignorant blacks, fresh from the field.." (May 20th)

"It has placed the ballot in the hands of those negroes, ignorant and unfit as they are" (May 23rd)

"the salvation of the blacks depends upon the infamy of putting the southern whites under the rule of ignorant blacks..." (May 25th)

And on our sampled day—

"the semi-barbarous African" (October 15, 1868 p.2)

"an inferior and uneducated people, who know nothing of their own, let alone the rights and wants of their fellow man." (October 15th, p.4)

To remove the black from the natural hierarchy of races, to remove the slave from white control, was to open up the possibility for license by those incapable of the self-restraint necessary for liberty. The natural outcome of such a lack of internal or external control was, in the jargon of the day, "outrages": black attacks on whites, especially white women. Such outrages were repeatedly described in the Democratic press and were a politically motivated news selection, part of the partisan driven news agenda. Thus, for example, our sampled issue of the *Detroit Union* of October 15, 1868 reports a local crime headed "Brutal Murder by Negroes." And, on January 1, 1868 the *Union* reprinted this story from the Democratic *New York Times*:

Outrage By A Negro In Maryland Upon A White Woman
Late on Sunday afternoon a most violent outrage was committed by a negro man on a most estimable married lady, in Hartford County, Maryland...This is the fourth or fifth affair of this kind which has happened in this county within the past year, in which negroes have been the actors and white women the sufferers. In this instance..."

Meanwhile, throughout May 1868, the *Free Press* publicized "depredations" occurring in the South, news of which was transmitted to them via the wire service and exchanged southern Democratic newspapers.

THE SOUTH.
Official Report of the Florida Elections

...TERRIBLE TRAGEDY IN ARKANSAS

A MAN AND FOUR CHILDREN MURDERED BY A NEGRO...

At a small town called Lincoln...which was settled by freedmen, a negro named Cochrane was detected by another named Wm. Babcock in illicit intercourse with his wife and attacked him. Cochrane killed Babcock in the encounter and immediately took up with Babcock's wife who had four children. Next day all the children were found in the swamp with their throats cut...Ike Martin...informed the civil authorities who have laid the matter before the military. Cochrane is not yet arrested.

NEGRO SHOT AND ARRESTED...[etc.]...

THE STORM...[etc.]

DEPREDATIONS COMMITTED BY NEGROES

Seven negroes attempted to enter [a] cotton shed on Washington street last night. They were fired upon by the watchmen...[etc.][21]

The not-so-veiled logic informing the news selections is spelled out in repetitious detail on the editorial page.[22] In the month of May, the problem of "negro outrages" is invoked in editorials on May 9th and 10th but the fullest statement of the logic appears on May 31st in the following fantasy/editorial.[23]

The True Condition of the Africanized South

The effect of the policy pursued by the Congressional majority in the South can be seen by the condition of that section. In all the late [state constitutional] conventions negro delegations were admitted, and their action has brought disgrace and ridicule upon the nation. Propositions of the most indefensible and monstrous character have been submitted and argued by these men...Two ideas seemed to control the negroes. One was hatred of the white people among whom they reside; the other, to obtain a living without labor...[I]n the constitutions framed by them it is the vital element, in every day life they carry out this platform. Outrages upon white men, women and children are now common occurrences. Scarce a paper comes from that section without containing accounts of offenses committed by negroes at which the heart sickens and blood runs cold. Lesser crimes...are multiplied ten fold since the inauguration of negro equality. Bands of idle and worthless blacks pass through all the country plundering, destroying and burning...Behind these lawless blacks stand the Loyal Leagues [a governmental agency to insure for Blacks the right to vote], and then comes Congress and the Radical party...[etc.]24

Much earlier, in 1863, the *Free Press* had publicized the crimes of a black man accused of outraging a young white woman. Years later all the major witnesses to the crime recanted their testimony, but at the time, the *Free Press* saw fit to headline its article "Horrible Outrage...A negro entraps a little girl into his room and commits fiendish crime upon her person...Full history of the shocking event."25 Once the defendant was pronounced guilty, a share of Detroit's white community went on a rampage described in the pitiful 1863 account: "A Thrilling Narrative from the Lips of the Sufferers of the Late Detroit Riot, March 6, 1863." In the course of the riot several of Detroit's blacks died, many were beaten and hundreds left homeless.26 Commenting on the riot the *Free Press* editorialized,

> We regret the mob. If our voice could have controlled it, it never should have occurred; but what could Democrats do when the Abolition press were raising heaven and earth to claim the rights of white men to the experiment of nigger liberty.27

The Detroit riot was a pale echo of other northern anti-draft riots of 1863, such as the New York City riot which claimed over one hundred lives. Such riots were triggered by popular resentment over the draft, high taxes to support the war, and the (largely mythical) threat of black economic competition in hard economic times. As Jean Baker notes, the anti-draft riots quickly turned into mob attacks on blacks who appeared as the hidden hand behind governmental Civil War policies. Such popular mob action was fueled by the overheated rhetoric of Democrat newspapers and orators, which portrayed blacks as malignant creatures—a threat to the social, political and economic foundations of the social order.28

The political consequences of this selection of the news and its rhetorical treatment were neither hidden nor implicit for the Democratic editors and readers. As the *Union*'s weekly "Letter from New York" makes plain:

The constantly recurring intelligence of NEGRO OUTRAGES in the South does a great deal towards strengthening the Democracy in this section of the country.29

Such stories, as the *Union* suggested, were important for deepening the political cleavages that defined the two parties, and for consolidating the partisan loyalties of Democrats and Republicans.

The purpose of this news was partly to point to Black Americans' lack of capacity for self-rule and partly to counter the massive Republican production of news reports of a reign of Ku Klux Klan terror in the South.30 Democrats argued that, given the biological and cultural deficit that precluded blacks from exercising self-control and autonomous reason, black participation as equals in political rule would not work. Moreover, the Democratic papers suggested that this failure in political democracy was the secret goal of the Radical Republicans in Congress. Blacks, necessarily dependent and incapable of participating independently in republican government, would require the perpetual help of the Republican party and the permanent tutelage of governmental services. Under the control and direction of the Republican party, they would vote for this despotic Radical government.

Blacks were part of a deliberate plan to despoil republican government and the natural rights of free-born whites. Thus, the Detroit *Free Press* drew the invidious, but not coincidental, comparison between Republican policies in the South and North.

> The party that demands that the elective franchise shall be extended to the ignorant negroes of the South, stands equally ready to disfranchise the intelligent voter of a city of the North.31

And Democratic newspapers repeatedly reiterated that the Republican goal was not Negro equality but superiority. As the *Union* explained, the victory by General Grant in the election of 1868 was sure to be taken by Republicans as proof "that the people demand Reconstruction upon the basis of a military dictatorship under congress and the political supremacy of the Negro."32 Generally, says Alexander Saxton, the moralistic claims of abolitionists were regarded with suspicion as stalking horses for the deprivation of white, working-class rights.33

For Democrats, this violation of proper social roles could only have been accomplished by a force from outside civil society, by an excessive political power. Therefore, the *Free Press* equated the Congressional Republicans with French Jacobins and suggested: "Is it not strange that an influence so terribly destructive of sound morality as the rule of Radicalism has not broken up the foundation of civil society."34 And the Detroit *Union* in publishing its annual proclamation of principles or "prospectus" linked governmental despotism to Black civil rights:

> The Union opposes the centralization of governmental power; Opposes the

supremacy of the military over the civic jurisdiction; Opposes the enfranchisement and social equality of the black race by Congressional activity[35]

Thus were linked what one historian of the *Free Press* calls Editor Storey's central political tenets— "racism and states rights."[36]

Imagery of the childlike, permanent dependency of blacks pervaded Democratic accounts, including their criticism of any governmental help to newly independent African-Americans starting out without land, tools or capital. African-Americans were seen as seeking to "obtain a living without labor." In this context, the Democrats launched an attack on the Freedmen's Bureau, a government agency in charge of distributing aid to newly freed southern blacks and some whites.[37] Thus the *Free Press* editorialized on May 10th, 1868:

> They feel certain that with the help of the entire treasury...the army, the Freedman's Bureau and 4 million of negroes they can perpetuate their power indefinitely...

On May 31st it opined:

> Behind these lawless blacks stand the Loyal League and then comes Congress. Clothing and food are supplied them by the Freedmen's Bureau and thus equipped [the blacks] are prepared to act as the ready and willing tools of the conspirators at Washington.

During the same time, the Democratic journal presented a front-page, verbatim account of the Michigan State Democratic Convention and reported various indictments made against the Republicans.

> [The Republicans] declared white men disloyal until the contrary was proved, and declared all black men loyal without proof; it used federal power to control suffrage in the states; it established a Freedmen's Bureau to feed and clothe the blacks as pensioners on the national bounty...[38]

Such rhetoric drew on the classical Jacksonian cultural repertoire that attacked both "corrupt" governmental institutions and indolent people of color using familial imagery. This Democratic imagery of the freed blacks paralleled historical depictions of Indians. In Michael Rogin's psychological account:

The myth of the West establishes male independence through violence against bad children [Indians] of nature too closely, maternally bound. Imposing private property against communally living on the land, Indian policy makers hypostasized the bounded ego of the self-made man. Indian freedom by contrast, would have to succumb to self-restraint, hard work and emulation for these were, from the perspective of the dominant culture, the requisites of maturity.[39]

Democrats wished to separate the Negro in the South from the too easy support of the maternal government and subject him to the harsh discipline of his paternalistic master—the southern white elite.

In Democrat rhetoric, Republicans desired to disrupt the natural laws governing the social order by placing blacks in a position of superiority for which they were racially unfit. Blacks, as Jean Baker expounds, bore through the physical trait of their skin color the visible sign of their inferiority. Black skin as a natural attribute pointed to blacks' natural social position as inferior to whites.[40] Thus the epithet "Black Republican" and the continual recourse to the Negro in Democratic stump speeches emphasized the social disorder being introduced by the political reign of Radical Republicans.

As mentioned previously, *Free Press* owner Storey had ordered his editorial staff always to refer to the opposed party as the Black Republican party. About Storey one historian writes,

> His vitriol was unequaled...when he turned his attention to the Republicans and the abolitionist movement. He called the Republican party "this monster of frightful mien — this party made up of white abolitionists, black abolitionists, and fugitives from slavery—this rabble of discord and destruction."[41]

Storey's use of the expression "monster" in this context is doubtlessly not accidental. For monster refers to "any animal or plant that is out of the usual course of nature" and the word derives from the Latin for divine warning against the violation of God-given natural law.[42] Here we see the imagery of boundary mixing, a disordering of natural categories that consequently results in the creation of a monster, a Frankenstein.

This preoccupation with the violation of natural categories perhaps explains why Democrats and the Detroit *Free Press* obsessively returned again and again to the issue of black-white "amalgamation" and why Democrats equated the granting of political and civil rights to African-Americans with "an indiscriminate, unnatural, loathsome and hated sexual union of the races."[43] The fear of miscegenation in part revealed anxieties over the blurring of sharply defined, supposedly natural, racial differences. The hysteria pointed to the shakiness of the socially erected edifice of a black/white racial dichotomy. This racial system smoothly classified individuals into categories, defined their place in the social hierarchy, and justified white power over blacks, as well as securing the identity of white males in opposition to blacks.44

The normally vitriolic rhetoric of the *Free Press* reached new extremes in this news story in which there is a double violation of the *Free Press'* ideological premises: first, improper black-white sex, and secondly a white woman freely consenting to wed an avaricious black. Reporting on the elopement of a "white girl with a negro," the *Free Press* reporter added this observation:

> [T]he girl is forever lost to decency and respect. Even should her separation from her negro paramou[r] be eternal, the finger of scorn would be pointed to her, to her dying day, as a white woman who disgraced her sex and common decency by consenting to become the wife of a black, ugly looking, disgusting negro.45

Republicans Wave the Bloody Shirt

To this extended racist onslaught from the Democratic newspapers, the Republicans responded as best they could. On the one hand, the Republican journals, the Detroit *Post* and the Detroit *Advertiser and Tribune* stood forthrightly for human equality. The *Post,* the more orthodoxly Republican of the two journals, declared in its Prospectus for 1867 that,

> [The *Post*'s] principles are based upon the immortal truths of the Declaration of Independence and the Divine Laws of the Universal Brotherhood of Man. Hence its motto is Equal Rights, Equal Justice for all Men.46

The *Advertiser and Tribune* too repeatedly editorialized for political rights for the freed slaves.47 Across the country, in San Francisco as in Detroit, Republican journals attempted to rebut the Democrats' racism, to denounce "the ineffable meanness which...[a Democratic journal] is capable in its demagogical appeals to the despicable prejudice of castes and color..."48

Beyond mere assertions of black-white equality, the Republican papers mocked the Democrats' assertions of the absolute superiority of all whites by virtues of their blood. In the weekly letter from Washington the correspondent for the Republican *Advertiser and Tribune* wrote:

> Our Washington Letter
>
> Saulsbury as a White Man of Intelligence...

From Our Own Correspondent
Washington, D.C., Jan. 8, 1867

Coming down from the Capitol last evening,...I had a fine illustration of the character of some of the gentlemen...[defending President Andrew Johnson.] I had just been listening to the solemn warnings of Cowan and Saulsbury against the frightful excesses of the "Radicals," till I almost doubted the propriety of going forward quite so fast. Saulsbury...was positive on one point—the total unfitness of the colored race for elective franchise...When he was speaking I did not notice anything out of the way in his manner, but set him down, as I have one hundred times before, as one honest political bigot. I started home two or three hours afterwards, and to my disgust a drunken man was reeling to and fro on the sidewalk...To my horror as I came up with him I discovered the drunken man was the gentleman in the Senate who warned [Congress] of the unfitness of the negroes for the ballot!49

Other news articles from the South helped to shore up Northern support for the civil rights of African-Americans. The papers reported the violence of Southern whites against the freedmen, particularly in the context of a burgeoning Ku Klux Klan. Here, Republican papers worked hand-in-hand with Republican congressmen in the production of partisan news as they published the results of Congressional investigations into Southern acts of intimidation and terror. For example, the *Post* devoted eight columns (or 24% of its news space) to the verbatim publication of the congressional conclusions of its investigation into a Klan massacre in New Orleans.50 From the Democratic point of view, Republican press accounts of Ku Klux Klan crimes were so much distorted party propaganda. Thus the *Free Press* declared:

. . . [Republican press] organs have undertaken once more to fire the Northern heart, and the consequence is that the columns of those sheets are again filled with police report editorials concerning the alleged lawlessness of the Southern States, especially as regards...the cruel treatment of negroes...Those who desire to test the truth of our remarks need only consult the Detroit *Post* of yesterday morning whose pages fairly reek with that kind of nauseous stuff.51

The wave of both Southern legislation and violence against Blacks and the resultant publicity helped to destroy any Northern support for President Andrew Johnson and his union party of moderate Republicans in 1866-1867.52 The *Advertiser and Tribune* itself turned from lukewarm to ardent supporter of Reconstruction measures.

Despite this strong response to Democratic racism, Republican defense of the besieged Southern black was more often camouflaged in the rhetoric of Southern disloyalty than straight-forward support for equal rights.

Republicans focused on the South's continued recalcitrance and the seditious support they received from "Copperhead" Democrats. Republicans so often invoked the treason of the South that Democrats came to label this standard rhetorical move "waving the bloody shirt." The "bloody shirt" referred to the blood-soaked garments of the Northern soldier who had sacrificed his life to preserve the country. Simple strategic reasons guided the Republicans in their attempt to shift the definition of the Democrat-Republican conflict. The historian David Montgomery explains:

More Americans identified the cause of the Republican party with the cause of the Union than wanted Negroes to vote. It was for this latter reason that the Democrats were the party that talked incessantly of blacks.[53]

Even Southern outrages were said to be aimed at Union soldiers and to demonstrate continued Southern rebellion against the Union. For example, the *Post*, in the sampled edition of 1867, editorializes against the "Rebel Democrats in Tennessee," where Southerners were in a "conspiracy to assassinated Union men and freedmen, particularly soldiers who had serve in the United States Army..."[54] And, in the edition sampled for 1868 the *Post* polemicized against recalcitrant Southerners.

North Carolina papers state that the rebels in that State are arming themselves with improved breach loading...rifles in expectation of a new rebellion in case [Democratic Presidential nominee and VP] Seymour and Blair are successful, for the purpose of trampling the reconstructed state governments into dust...[55]

As already noted, the two Detroit Republican dailies did not always see eye to eye on the proper Reconstruction policies. The *Advertiser and Tribune* was less inclined to support Black rights and punitive reconstruction measures against white Southerners, supporting the polices of President Andrew Johnson until late 1866. They also abandoned Reconstruction before the *Post*. In 1872 the daily flirted with the Liberal Republican party which announced as a plank in its party platform the speedy rehabilitation of the South and an abolition of Reconstruction measures. These policy differences reflected in part the natural competition of two newspapers aimed at the same market segment, but also party factional antagonisms. The *Post* stood with long-time state Republican leader, Senator Zachariah Chandler, while the *Advertiser and Tribune* was allied with Chandler's bitterest enemies.[56] Richard Slotkin, looking at the journals of New York

City in 1874-1877, has shown how each daily paper expressed the views of a party faction and, in turn, the interests of different elite economic groups.57 Thus, the debates in the public sphere between the two political parties were multiplied by the dissonance of competing party factions.

To summarize, the Democratic party through the vehicle of its loyal press organs and stump speeches offered the voters a complex depiction of the problems of American society and, with this portrait, an indictment of the rule of the Republican party and its misguided policies. Republicans responded in defense of their Reconstruction policies and universal civil rights, but also sidestepped the brunt of the Democrats charge by waving the "bloody shirt." They emphasized that the Democrats had defended the secession of the South, which resulted in so much spilt blood, and that Democrats possessed suspect loyalties in the war. Republican and Democratic journals faithfully repeated these party lines, although they doubtlessly innovated in this editorial or improvised in that news story.58 Their editorial pronouncements took up the unfolding events in Congress and in the South and encapsulated them in the political philosophy of the party in daily reiterated arguments. Sociologist Shanto Ingeyar has recently pointed to the overwhelming bias of contemporary news reporting towards the "episodic" over the "thematic."59 The news of today, he claims, neglects to contextualize events in an overarching interpretation, a framework that can help explain the events' occurrence. Journalism of the nineteenth century surely suffered from the opposite malady—the rigorous explanation (as well as selection) of events according to a generalized political picture.

Unlike our contemporary papers, nineteenth-century newspapers stood under the protecting umbrella of a party's political legitimacy. Furthermore, the paper possessed a partisan readership that expected a strong display of partisanship by their journal. The partisan paper was thus free to explore systematically and repeatedly the various social implications of governmental policies in editorials and in feature articles. The news agenda was not dependent upon the occurrence of "news events" to justify the reporter's story selection. What would be forbidden to our contemporary independent and "objective" press as editorializing—as exposing the reporter's subjective point of view—could be thoroughly pursued by the nineteenth-century press.

Partisan newspapers had the merit of forcefully expressing

alternative political views for the public. The *Post* acknowledged this political role in explaining the mission of partisan journals:

The secret of this influence [of papers on the community] is not so much that they furnish people with opinions ready made; but that they keep prominent and engrossing topics constantly before them, and throw all possible life upon these topics from every quarter....[Republican papers] are constantly stimulating this reflection and discussion [by the public.]60

On the other hand, the emphatic public dialogue of parties was contaminated by their strategic political calculations. Their strategic definition of issue cleavages meant that papers directed their attacks not on the positions of the other party but on contrived images thereof. This, at least, was Lord James Bryce's perspective in the late 1800s:

[T]he aim of each party is to force on its antagonist certain issues which the antagonist rarely accepts, so that although there is a vast deal of discussion and declamation on political topics, there are few on which either party directly traverses the doctrines of the other. Each pummels, not his true enemy, but a stuffed figure set up to represent that enemy.61

Popular Culture and the Party Agenda

But if newspaper news choices followed the dictates of party interests, what determined the particular appeal of party policies and propaganda? What determined the cleavages that sliced up the electoral pie between Democrats and Republicans? Party appeals and coalitions were not simply manufactured out of whole cloth. Ignoring for the moment the interests of entrenched political office holders and the influence of wealth, parties appealed to inherited coalitions, which needed to be shored up, and to potential voters dissatisfied with their current political alliances. For example, Alexander Saxton explains that the Democrats' racist ideology fulfilled a number of functions, foremost of which was the need to defend slavery in order to retain the support of the party's southern wing.62 But here I sidestep most of these questions in order to address the popular cultural sources of the Democratic press' political appeals.

Jean Baker and Saxton can both point to the Democratic party's drawing upon, and reiterating, the racialist discourse of a commercial popular culture. Democratic orators and journals could strategically utilize already existing cultural resources in their efforts to split the available vote in ways detrimental to the Republicans. They deployed a repertoire of stereotypical representations of blacks which had been produced by popular commercial culture for the mass entertainment and amusement of whites since the 1840s. As Baker tells us, minstrel shows, were "the preferred entertainment of the northern working-class from 1840 to 1880." Minstrelsy, along with lithographs, songs, et cetera, rendered into concrete and comprehensible form the "abstract notions northerners held about blacks."63 Whites performing in black-face created vivid and supposedly authentic portrayals of the lives, behavior and character of blacks. White audiences may have confused these contrived imitations—crude projective stereotypes—with real black lives.64

Democratic newspapers drew upon popular entertainment conventions and mixed fact with fiction, popular humor and its mimicry of blacks with the news. Typically, journalistic claims of first-hand observation and factual reporting of black behavior conformed to popular cultural conventions and presented African-Americans as amusing, immature, foolish and superstitious.65 The *Free Press* in 1871 reported this incident from the regular news beat of the Detroit court house.

> The case of Elijah Coombs, secretary of the Lincoln Hall Association, a political club composed of blacks...came up for trial before Judge Boynton yesterday. The want of harmony in the camp was occasioned by the alleged incompetence of the secretary, and his refusal to deliver his books in obedience to a vote of the association.
>
> According to a disinterested witness, "Uncle Josh took hole of Coombs and keerfully laid him down on de flor an' Mr. Sorrel, de President, took the books 'way from him." Mr. Coombs 'lowed as he was gwine to cut his livers out and Mr. Prater 'taliated by remarking something 'bout clubbin' Coombs' brains out."66

The use of caricatured dialect is designed to heighten the distance of the narrator (and his reading audience) from the black speaker.67 The quoted black is an unsophisticated primitive who speaks only in order to mangle syntax while his political club deliberates solely for the purpose of exposing its incapacity to engage in reasoned discussion. The narrator juxtaposes in an ironic manner his own formal, correct language to the informal, childish language of the quoted "disinterested witness."68 While the blacks are depicted as a primitive other, they pose no threat but instead are material for comic entertainment. Interestingly enough, this brief news item was probably the original source for the comic column "the Lime Kiln Club," which was a featured attraction at the *Free Press* from 1881 until 1891.69

In another later example, the Detroit *Evening News*, an independent journal with occasional Democratic sympathies, titled one news story

"Doctah Clawk." The headline with its caricatured speech patterns already prepares the reader for this genre of humorous, descriptive feature.70 The sub-head "He Propounds His Views on State, National, and International Law" points to the pomposity of Doctah Clark. Clark, who is on his way to a political convention, is mocked as a self-absorbed and garrulous child, a parody of independent political reasoning. He is irredeemably tied to his "Ethiopian" physical nature.

The reporter explained that he was a NEWS man, en route to the convention. He made a wrong move in so doing, although the game came out all right in the end.

> Oh, well, you know me," said the colored gentleman. "My name is Clawk—Doctor Clawk—you know me for years."
>
> "I should say so," said the reporter, with an aspect of reverential awe. "I have heard your name mentioned as a candidate for the legislature."
>
> The doctor's body dilated visibly, and his face exhibited that genuine gratification which can only be expressed by the facial muscles of the Ethiopian.
>
> "My name, sah, <u>has</u> been mentioned. But I don't care about it. I'm a man that is animated by principle. I go to all the meetings and lectures and political speeches, and I hear everything. I hear a republican speech, and I note it. I hear a democratic speech, and I note it. Then I balance 'em." The doctor swayed his body, and lifted his hands like a grocery scale. "I balance 'em, see."...71

Baker suggests that Democrats mined the dark depths of popular culture to produce electoral gold.

Popular culture, a neglected expression of the historically voiceless, not only defined the nature of the Negro's inferiority but also provided a domain within which Democrats developed specific public policies. By using its language and symbols, party leaders linked popular sentiments to party agenda.72

Beyond "Selectivity": Fiction in the Partisan Press

The partisan news agenda also penetrated into the non-news articles of the Detroit journals. Until now this essay has used the concepts of "news agenda" and "selectivity" to indicate how partisan interests guided the news choices of the press. But when we turn to fiction stories, such concepts no longer illuminate our analysis, instead they obscure the workings of the partisan press. The concepts of "agenda" and "selectivity" assume a number of distinctions from our contemporary era which do not adequately characterize the nineteenth-century press. "Selectivity" takes for granted a separation of the news-collecting organization from the events waiting to be gathered. It assumes the prior existence of news facts separate from journalistic representations and interpretations. The journalist introduces his or her bias merely by a selection of those already existing facts and events. However, Detroit newspapers' publication of literary stories and comic features call into question these distinctions. In their fiction columns, Democratic papers did not just select, "borrow from," or "draw upon" the facts and representations from an already existing reality (or an already existing popular culture, as Baker suggests).[73] Rather, they <u>actively created</u> the representation of that reality. They actively produced stereotypical images of blacks.

Throughout its news and fiction stories (in examples such as the above), Detroit's Democratic press constructed blacks as objects of disdain and derision. More generally, as Saxton suggests, popular cultural conventions were influenced by the Democratic party. The founders of minstrelsy were disproportionately Democratic.[74] In the case of newspapers, the merging of popular cultural conventions and party agenda was most smoothly melded in humorous, fictional columns.

Alongside racist "news" and "sketches," which mixed in unequal proportions the creative talents of the writer with the strategic agenda of the party and the popular prejudices of the citizenry, were regular humor columns that featured black characters. The Democratic *Free Press* became specifically renowned for the weekly comic column of Charles B. Lewis under the pseudonym M. Quad. M. Quad's most famous column "Brother Gardner's Lime Kiln Club" provided a broad comic burlesque of the antics of a black social club debating such topics as the aesthetics of barber poles, the number of dogs owned by Detroit's colored population, and "de goneness of de past."[75] One contemporary of M. Quad remarks:

> "The Lime Kiln Club" purported to be the discussion of a group of colored gentlemen with odd names like "Give-a-damn-Jones," etc. of various local types. Its dialect was not of the genuine southern negro but near enough to that of the northern to make it interesting and amusing.[76]

M. Quad's column along with that of fellow writer Barr's "Luke Sharp" achieved for the *Free Press* a national reputation as suggested by *Harper's* in an 1888 survey of "Western Journalism."

> The *Free Press* may be said to have a dual character—to be sort of a Dr. Jekyll and Mr.

> Hyde in journalism. It is a strong Democratic newspaper... this for its local constituency; it is also a weekly literary and family paper, with a funny department that has given it a reputation and circulation in every part of the United States...The writer of the most popular humorous articles and sketches for the *Free Press* is Charles B. Lewis [whose nom-de-plume is M. Quad]...the expectation of finding something funny in the "Bijah" or "Lime Kiln Club" papers may cause one to buy it to read upon the cars or in a leisure hour.[77]

Charles B. Lewis' column rode the crest of a wave of humorists which emerged in the 1850s and swept over the pages of American journalism in the second half of the century.[78] Such humorists included Marcus M. ("Brick") Pomeroy and Artemus Ward. While M. Quad was syndicated in Democratic newspapers across the country, equally partisan comics lambasted the Democratic party in the Republican press.[79] One such column was David Locke's "The Struggles of Petroleum V. Nasby" consisting of letters from an almost illiterate "copperhead" who resided at "Confederit X Roads," Kentucky. Nasby was "[illiterate,] hypocritical, cowardly, loafing, lying, dissolute."[80] Locke would wickedly lampoon Nasby's writing and speech as the crude dialect of a poor, southern white Democrat, a sort of mirror of the speech being attributed by Democrat humorists to blacks. Locke's Nasby paraded typical Democratic views such as negrophobia and a hatred for the Union, opinions which in Nasby's case, as archetypical Democrat, were taken to be a product of ignorance, foolishness and partisan venality. As popular tradition has it, Nasby kept up the spirits of the President during the war. Lincoln would insist on reading various comic tidbits from the latest Nasby to his cabinet.[81]

While The Lime Kiln Club did not begin officially until 1878, M. Quad did humor parodies of blacks starting from 1869 and his column was largely derivative of other humorists who did Democratic pieces such as Artemus Ward and Marcus M. ("Brick") Pomeroy.[82] Part and parcel of this vogue of newspaper comedy was a tradition of comic burlesque of blacks. According to Kenneth O'Reilley:

> During the postwar years the freedman often found himself and his speech patterns caricatured by southern writers. Northern writers spurred by a growth of "Negrophobia," soon followed suit and Lewis emerged as one of the first and most widely read writers to caricature northern negro speech.[83]

Conclusion

Throughout the period of Reconstruction, Democrats and

Republicans fought over the right to lead the country. They battled for the hearts and minds of American voters by presenting opposed policies for the post bellum South and contrasting images of Black Americans. Journalism's close ties with the political system meant that the polarized rhetoric of the two parties was imported into its pages. One of the central propaganda ploys of the Democratic party was the continual, vicious portrayal of newly enfranchised African-American citizens. Detroit's Democratic journals followed suit by editorializing against civil rights for blacks, by selecting news that depicted the negative consequences of Republican southern policies, and by elaborating stereotyped images of the emancipated blacks. To advance its strategic interests, the party extracted the unrefined racism of popular culture and processed and polished it in order to heighten racial antagonism and thereby gain votes.

Since early Reconstruction the Republican party had defended equal rights. However, by 1876 a combination of reasons, including enduring popular prejudices, convinced the Republican party to abandon their Reconstruction policies.[84] In effect the Republicans acceded to the racist depiction promulgated by the Democratic media. After 1876, Black Americans were no longer a political issue dividing Democratic newspaper from Republican. Black citizens retained their public-journalistic presence only as the object of comic parody as the humor tradition developed by M. Quad and minstrelsy spread across the pages of the press without apparent regard for any journal's partisan preferences.[85]

Notes

1. The classic discussion of the ideal political role of public discussion in modern mass democracies can be found in Juergen Habermas, *The Structural Transformation of the Public Sphere.* trans. by T. Burger (Cambridge: MIT Press, 1989.)
2. Here I discuss some methodological issues. My most general systematic measure was designed to capture changes in partisanship of the Detroit dailies over a twenty-five year period. I constructed a stratified sample of Detroit's daily newspapers for my content analysis. A copy of the October 15th issue of all journals was analyzed for the presidential election years, 1868-1900. And a copy of all dailies in the electoral off-season was analyzed 1867-1899 (February 15th of the year preceding the presidential election year.) The presidential election season generally lasted four months, from the beginning of July to the start of November.
  All the stories of all the dailies for the selected dates were coded for partisanship. I coded for two different aspects of "political bias," that is—journalistic political preference in the news and other articles. We can call these two dimensions of partisanship "latent" and "manifest" partisanship, or "covert" and "overt." This distinction is important in capturing the full extent of nineteenth-century press politics. The manifest aspects of partisanship refer to statements of evaluation and preference by a writer-narrator.

However, even when a reporter makes no evident political evaluation, a story can support the interests and policies of a party. This type of partisan support would be the latent bias of a newspaper. In the late 1800s, the most evident form of this covert preference was the grossly unequal amounts of news space that the partisan paper gave to the words and deeds of one party over the other. More subtle forms of preference were shown in the reporting of news events that supported the policy positions of one party at the expense of its foe. As my paper discusses, this was a typical tactic of the nineteenth-century partisan press. Adequate coding of these stories depends upon historical background knowledge of the articulated policy divisions between the two parties. (Klaus Krippendorf calls this background knowledge in coding "context units." See his *Content Analysis* (Beverly Hills: Sage Publications, 1980) pp. 59-60.) Fortunately for the historical researcher, these policy cleavages are explicitly and repeatedly elaborated on the editorial page of the partisan paper. In considering the distinction of covert and overt bias, one should note that often the sheer quantity of the stories of covert bias grows so overwhelming that the preference becomes evident and overt, a proudly displayed badge of party loyalty by the newspaper. (In general, compare the coding procedures in John Merrill, "How Time Stereotyped Three U.S. Presidents," *Journalism Quarterly*, V. 42 (1965) and Donald L. Shaw, "News Bias and the Telegraph: A Study of Historical Change," *Journalism Quarterly* V. 44, no. 1 (Spring 1967). However, Shaw focuses exclusively on manifest bias. He writes: "A biased news story was any which had as a referent a presidential or vice-presidential candidate and which contained value statements in such a way the overall impression created upon today's reader was a positive or negative feeling toward that referent. An unbiased news story did not create this positive or negative feeling, regardless of whether or not such value statements including adjectives, adverbs, nouns or verbs phrases or statements were used." p. 5.) In addition to measuring the extent of partisanship, this essay analyzes the news agenda. It documents the correspondence of news and editorial topics to the expressed policy positions of the two parties. In this quantitative measure of themes, I examine the Democratic papers in the month of May 1867 in addition to the February 15, 1867 issue of my more general sample. Furthermore, I analyze these journalistic themes—specifically the stereotypical representation of African American—in a great deal of detail. To a quantitative measurement of the news agenda I add the qualitative explication of the internal logic of political representations. In demonstrating the coherence and organization of a political ideology, the mere quantitative citing of motifs is inadequate. Instead, such a content analysis demonstrates the adequacy of the interpretation by using representative quotes. These examples illustrate the logic and connections of a thinking that has grown foreign to us.

3. In the sampled issues all editorials were coded for their political bias and their length was measured. The percentage is a percentage of the paper's space devoted to editorials.

4. Includes both the percentage of news space with explicit partisan evaluations by the journalist writer, and news coverage that highlights the views and policy stands of the affiliated party (without explicit evaluative stands by the reporter.) For example, a report of a speech made by an official of the favored party without a matching story from the opposed party would count as a partisan selection.

5. E. E. Schattschneider, *The Semisovereign People: A Realist's View of Democracy in America* (Hinsdale, Ill.: Dryden Press, 1975) p. 66.

6. *Detroit Free Press*, May 10, 1868, p. 2. And see James C. Mohr, "Introduction" in James C. Mohr (ed.) *Radical Republicans in the North* (Baltimore: Johns Hopkins University Press, 1976) pp. xiii-xiv.

7. Also see the elaboration of Democratic party ideology in Jean Baker, *Affairs of Party: The Political Culture of Northern Democrats in the Mid-Nineteenth Century* (Ithaca: Cornell University Press, 1983.)

8. Kenneth Burgess-Jackson argues instead that "constitutional issues" were the "most fundamental issue" of partisan dispute of this period. See his "Democracy Versus Republicanism: Detroit Press Reaction to the Reconstruction Act of 1867," *Southern Studies* V. 1, no. 4 (Winter 1990) pp. 306, 311.
9. Baker, *Affairs of Party*, p. 257.
10. *Detroit Daily Union*, Oct. 15, 1868, during presidential election season.
11. Morton Keller, *Affairs of State: Public Life in Late Nineteenth-Century America* (Cambridge, Mass.: Harvard University Press, 1977) pp. 71, 81 on the 1867 results.
12. Harriette Dilla, *The Politics of Michigan, 1865-1878* (New York: Columbia University, 1912) pp. 92-3.
13. Willis Dunbar and William Shade, "The Black Man Gains the Vote: The Centennial of 'Impartial Suffrage' in Michigan," *Michigan History* V. 56, no. 1 (1972) pp. 53-5.
14. David Katzman, *Before the Ghetto: Black Detroit in the Nineteenth Century*, (Chicago: University of Illinois Press, 1973) pp. 84-90 and 22-25.
15. Frank Angelo, *On Guard: A History of the Detroit Free Press* (Detroit: Detroit Free Press, 1981) p. 65 and James E. Scripps, "Wilbur F. Storey, Detroit's's First Great Journalist" *Detroit News-Tribune* (Sept. 16, 1900) p. 14.
16. For example, William Allen White, the famous Emporia, Kansas editor, in his 1946 autobiography writes "...and my mother, loyal to her dead husband and still a black abolitionist Republican who feared the rebels..." to indicate the strength of his mother's political convictions. And to describe his boss' partisan loyalties: "He was a stalwart, wool dyed black radical Republican who was still fighting the battles of the Civil War." William Allen White, *The Autobiography of William Allen White*, (New York: MacMillan Co., 1946) pp. 163, 207.
17. John C. Lodge with the collaboration of M. M. Quaife, *I Remember Detroit* (Detroit: Wayne State University, 1949) p. 56.
18. In a manner reminiscent of the continual, albeit veiled, racism in our current political speech. See Stuart Alan Clarke, "Fear of a Black Planet," *Socialist Review* V. 91 no. 3-4 (July 1991); Thomas B. Edsall and Mary D. Edsall, "When the official subject is presidential politics, taxes, welfare, crime, rights or values...the real subject is Race," *Atlantic Monthly* (May 1991.)
19. Baker, *Affairs of Party*, p. 256; Keller, *Affairs of State*, pp. 51-2, 81-3.
20. *Free Press*, May 9 and 10, 1868. Also see Oct. 15, 1868 p. 2.
21. *Free Press*, May 30, 1868.
22. Cf. Richard Slotkin, *The Fatal Environment* (New York: Atheneum, 1985) p. 440.
23. I extensively scrutinized the pages of the *Free Press* in May 1868 to determined the repetition and continuity of news-editoiral motifs. "The most respectable residents leave and their places are supplied by adventurers who encourage negroes to commit the greatest outrages." May 9, 1868, p. 2 c. 2. They fear for their wives and children, for their material prosperity..." May 10, 1868.
24. *Free Press*, May 31, 1868, p. 2 col. 2.
25. Angelo, *On Guard*, pp. 86-7 cites the *Free Press* of Feb. 27, 1863. The court verdict coincided with Congress' authorization of a draft to replenish the ranks of the Union army, March 3, 1863.
26. This account is presented in Melvin Holli (ed.) *Detroit* (New York: New Viewpoints, 1976) pp. 86-92 and cf. other accounts of the Detroit Riot in James McPherson (ed.) *Anti-Negro Riots of the North, 1863* (New York: Arno Press, 1969) pp. 1-24; and Milton A. McRae, *Forty Years in Newspaperdom* (New York: Bretano's Inc., 1924) pp. 4-5.
27. Quoted in the preface of McPherson, *Anti-Negro Riots*, p. iv.
28. See the account of the New York riot in David Montgomery, *Beyond Equality: Labor and the Radical Republicans, 1862-1872* (Chicago: University of Illinois Press, 1981) pp. 102-7. "Military suppression of strikes, greenback inflation, the specter (for it was

never more than that) of liberated Negroes flocking North, and the ubiquitous draft—what could have been better grist for the Coppery [i.e. Democratic] mill?...[At a Fourth of July rally against conscription] Copperhead orators pounded home the themes that the government's war effort was undermining the Constitution, that conscription claimed the lives of the poor in a rich man's war, and that emancipated Negroes were flooding the North." p. 102.
29. *Daily Union*, October 13, 1868.
30. See for example the *Union*'s commentary on the *Post*'s coverage of elections in the South, Nov. 6 1868, p. 2; Also, the *Free Press*, Aug. 28, 1880; And the *News*, Oct. 15, 1874 p. 2; Montgomery tells of the impact of such news reports on Northern Republicans in 1866. *Beyond Equality*, pp. 69-70. Also see the *News*, Jan. 5, 1875, p. 2.
31. Feb. 15, 1867 and Oct. 15, 1868 p. 2. cols. 2 and 3; Oct. 9. 1868.
32. Oct. 15, 1868.
33. Alexander Saxton, *The Indispensable Enemy; Labor and the Anti-Chinese Movement in California* (Berkeley: University of California Press, 1971) pp. 27, 132-6. Keller discusses fears of "money-power." *Affairs of State*, pp. 51-2.
34. Quote from the *Free Press* of Feb. 15, 1867. References to the Republicans as "Jacobins" in the *Free Press* of Oct. 15, 1868 and May 7, 1868, p. 2, c. 2.
35. *Union*, Dec. 15, 1868.
36. Angelo, *On Guard*, p. 72
37. Quoted from the *Free Press*, May 31, 1868. Other attacks on the Freedmen's Bureau in the *Free Press* in May 1868 besides those quoted below are May 4, p. 2, c. 2 and May 28, 1868. Also see Dec. 18, 1868. Other payoffs to blacks are mentioned May 20, 1868, p. 2, c. 3.
38. *Free Press* May 31, 1868, p. 1.
39. Michael Rogin, *Fathers and Children: Andrew Jackson and the Subjugation of the American Indian,* (Second edition) p. 14. Of course, northern Republicans too were motivated by republican imagery to try and impose a model of disciplined liberal society on the bad social relations of the South. See Eric Foner, *Free Soil, Free Labor, Free Men* (New York: Oxford University Press, 1970) ch. 2; Burgess-Jackson "Democracy Versus Republicanism," pp. 37-8.
40. Baker, *Affairs of Party*, p. 256.
41. Angelo, *On Guard*, p. 72.
42. Clarence Thorndike (ed.) *Thorndike-Barnhart Comprehensive Desk Dictionary* (Garden City: Doubleday and Co., 1958.)
43. See, for example, the *Free Press* of Jan. 23 p. 4 and Jan. 29, 1867 p. 4 and Feb. 9, 1867, p. 4 as cited in Burgess-Jackson, "Democracy Versus Republicanism."
References to amalgamation were repetitiously invoked in the press, and indeed any black participation in politics was labelled miscegenation. For example, the state governments of the South that permitted Black participation were called in the *Free Press* variously "miscegenation governments" May 14, p. 2 and May 4, 1868 p. 4; "mongrel constitution" May 9 p. 2, col. 2, May 10th p. 2; "miscegenation constitution" May 12th p. 2; "mongrel senators" May 20th p. 2. Also on May 9th the *Free Press* editorialized against "...Hayti, Jamaica, Mexico or any other country which illustrates the evils of amalgamation."
44. Michael Rogin, *Ronald Reagan: The Movie* (Berkeley: University of California Press, 1987) pp. 51-5 and 279; Susan Gillman, *Dark Twins* (Chicago: University of Chicago Press, 1989) pp. 81-6; Eric J. Sundquist, "Mark Twain and Homer Plessy," *Representations* no. 24 (Fall 1988). Furthermore, in Rogin's analysis, the sexualization and demonization of black men as uncontrollable rapists and white women as helpless, virtuous victims fulfilled the purpose of policing the boundaries and depriving both women and blacks of power. pp. 51-2.
45. Angelo, *On Guard*, p. 86.

46. The prospectus was repeatedly published in January through May 1867. See the *Post*, Jan. 5, 1867, p.3 and May 7, 1867.
47. *Advertiser and Tribune*, Jan. 10, 1867 p. 2; Feb. 19, 1867, p. 2; Feb. 16, 1867 p. 2.
48. So wrote the San Francisco *Chronicle* (Republican) regarding the San Francisco *Call* (Democrat.) Feb. 16, 1869 and see June 17, 1869.
49. *Post*, Jan. 10, 1867.
50. *Post*, Feb. 15, 1867, p. 2.
51. *Free Press*, Oct. 15, 1868, p. 4, c. 1. And see Aug. 24, 1880 p.4 and Sept. 24, 1880 p. 4. American historians from 1890 through 1950 tended to adopt the Democrats' point of view. The news accounts of KKK terror, right or wrong, only had the purpose of strengthening Republican power and prolonging the mistaken experiment of Reconstruction. See, for example, Paul Buck, *The Road to Reunion* (Boston: Little, Brown and Co., 1937.) The revised point of view is strongly represented by Eric Foner, *Reconstruction: America's Unfinished Revolution, 1863-1873* (New York: Harper & Row, 1988)
52. Montgomery, *Beyond Equality*, pp. 66-72.
53. Montgomery, *Beyond Equality*, p. 84.
54. *Post*, Feb. 15, 1867.
55. *Post*, Oct. 15, 1868.
56. I further discuss the history of these papers and their factional differences next chapter.
57. Richard Slotkin, *The Fatal Environment*, pp. 332-4. Montgomery describes the elite economic interests manifest in different party factions and policies. Montgomery, *Beyond Equality*, ch. 2. These linkages of class and faction in Michigan can probably be traced out through the figure of James Joy. Joy, as a leading Michigan Republican and a major owner of railroads, was a central player in the more conservative faction of the Republican party.
58. While the speeches reported verbatim by the *Free Press* often tried to cast the Republicans as the party of the corrupt rich who were trying to exploit political power for private gain, the *Free Press* rarely invoked such motifs in its editorials.
59. Shanto Iyengar, *Is Anyone Responsible? How Television Frames Political Issues* (Chicago: University of Chicago, 1991.)
60. *Post*, Jan. 24, 1867, p. 4.
61. James Bryce, *The American Commonwealth* (New York: The Macmillan Company, 1909) V. 2, p. 214. For a more genral discussion of the constraints on free expression posed by political and economic institutions see Jeffrey Goldfarb, *On Cultural Freedom: An Exploration of Public Life in Poland and America* (Chicago: University of Chicago Press, 1982.)
62. Alexander Saxton, "Blackface Minstrelsy and Jacksonian Ideology," *American Quarterly* V. 27, no. 1 (1975) p. 17. And, more generally, see Alexander Saxton, *The Rise and Fall of the White Republic: Class, Politics and Mass Culture in Nineteenth-Century America* (New York: Verso, 1990) pp. 148-54, 105, 136-42.
63. Baker, *Affairs of Party*, p. 214, and Saxton, "Blackface Minstrelsy," p. 4.
64. *Ibid.* pp. 218, 220. "White southerners, who lived in closer contact with blacks had no need to visualize..., but Northerners...What they saw...was their own imposition. With few exceptions blacks were not allowed on white stages..." p. 218.
65. Chapter 6 in Baker's *Affairs of Party* is an extensive catalogue of the conventions and logic of these stereotypes.
66. *Free Press* Feb. 15, 1871.
67. An important discussion of the nineteenth-century use of dialect to portray African-Americans is Eric Sundquist, *To Wake the Nations: Race in the Making of American Literature* (Cambridge, MA: Harvard University Press, 1993) ch. 4.
68. Cf. June Howard, *Form and History in American Literary Naturalism* (Chapel Hill: University of North Carolina Press, 1985) pp. 104-106.

69. (To be discussed more later.) Charles Lewis, the author of the comic column "The Lime Kiln Club," was a reporter at the Detroit Central Station Court early in his career according to Kenneth O'Reilly, "M. Quad and Brother Gardner: Negro Dialect and Caricature in Nineteenth Century Detroit," *Detroit In Perspective* V. 3, no. 2 (Winter 1979) p. 119.
70. As Frederic Jameson notes, "[A]mong the most important indices of generic expectations" are "the shifting in our distances from the characters, the transformation of the very categories through which we perceive characters..." Quoted in Howard, *Form and History*, p. 105.
71. *Evening News* October 12, 1874, p. 4. The *News* at this time was attacking Republican reconstruction policies.
72. Baker, *Affairs of Party*, p. 213
73. Quoted expressions from Baker, *Affairs of Party*, pp. 252, 253 and 257.
74. Saxton, "Blackface Minstrelsy"; Saxton, *The Rise and Fall of the White Republic*, pp. 95, 102-5, 127.
75. One collection among others of Lime-Kiln comedy columns is M. Quad (Charles B. Lewis,) *Brother Gardner's Lime-Kiln Club* (Chicago: Belford, Clarke & Co., 1882.) Other columns of Charles Lewis are reprinted in *Quad's Odds* (Detroit, R.D.S. Tyler & Co., 1875.)
76. Edward Holden, Little Journeys in Journalism: Recollections of Some Prominent Members of the Free Press Staff," *Michigan History Magazine*, V. 11, no. 3 (1927) p. 424.
77. Z. L. White "Western Journalism," *Harper's Magazine* V. 77 (October 1888) p. 690. And on the *Free Press'* reputation see O'Reilly, "M. Quad and Brother Gardner" p. 130; Holden, "Recollections," pp. 424, 428.
78. George Catlin, "Adventures In Journalism: Detroit Newspapers Since 1850," *Michigan History Magazine* V. 29, no. 3 (July-Sept. 1945) pp. 355 and 350; O'Reilly, "M. Quad and Brother Gardner" p. 114.
79. O'Reilly, "M. Quad and Brother Gardner" pp. 126-7. O'Reilly tells us that Charles B. Lewis' column the Lime Kiln Club lasted from 1877 to 1891 whereupon he departed from the *Free Press* for Pulitzer's Democratic *New York World*. In New York Lewis initiated a new feature parodying blacks which was titled "Cotton Blossoms." The *World* induced Lewis to leave Detroit with a salary reputed to be at least $8,000.
80. Keller, *Affairs of State*, p. 47. On the Democrat "Brick" Pomeroy see pp. 49-50.
81. *Ibid.*, pp. 47-9; Buck, *The Road to Reunion*, pp. 20-1.
82. Keller, *Affairs of State*. Cf. M. Quad's *Free Press* column for Dec. 7, 1878.
83. O'Reilly, "M. Quad and Brother Gardner" p. 117; Saxton, "Blackface Minstrelsy," p. 26.
84. The main reasons for the Republican party's abandonment of Reconstruction were: the *de facto* seizure of control of most Southern state governments by whites; the displacement of "Radicals" from positions of power in Northern Republican parties; a lack of popular support for continued federal military intervention in the South; and lastly a new political philosophy articulated by the northern, genteel intelligentsia that melded a racist Social Darwinism with economic liberalism. See Foner, *Reconstruction*, pp. 483-4, 488-99; Keller, *Affairs of State*, ch. 7. On the case of California see Saxton, *The Indispensable Enemy*, chs. 4-6. On this new political philosophy also see: Thomas Bender, *New York Intellect* (New York: Alfred Knopf, 1987) ch. 5; Montgomery, *Beyond Equality*, ch. 9; George Fredrickson, *The Inner Civil War: Northern Intellectuals and the Crisis of the Union* (New York: Harper & Row, 1965) pp. 192-4.
85. *Ibid.*, p. 118.

33

Wanted Dead or Alive: How Nineteenth Century Missouri Journalists Framed Jesse James

Cathy M. Jackson
University of Missouri

From the Old West have sprung anti-heroes of mythical proportions. Out of the once vast and untamed land that was the nineteenth century frontier came lawless men and women, who over time have shed their tattered and stained reputations, and through a "...melange of fact, fiction, fantasy and sheer nonsense...," have become larger than life heroes and heroines, according to Michael Malone.[1]

Onto that ahistorical landscape steps Jesse Woodson James, who lived from 1847-1882. A year after the Civil War ended in 1865, James began his outlaw career with a bank robbery in Liberty, Missouri. During the next six years, James reportedly committed 23 criminal acts ranging from killing to train and bank robberies to stagecoach holdups in Kentucky, Minnesota, Iowa, Arkansas, Texas, Kansas, and Alabama. Historians Paul Wellman, James D. Horan, and a nineteenth-century James biographer Frank Triplett, wrote that 10 people were killed during the James' gang robberies.[2] Wellman wrote that during the robbery of the Gallatin, Missouri bank on December 7, 1869, James "With a swift movement, fired at the cashier. The bullet entered the victim's right eye and passed out the back of his head. (Former Union Captain John W.) Sheets was instantly dead...."3

Yet somewhere in the 16 years of infamy, James became an American legend and folk hero.4 Scholars credit Theodore Roosevelt with writing that James was America's Robin Hood.5 Kent L. Steckmesser wrote that James became a folk hero, or a person so admired and revered that his exploits have become folklore, because he operated outside the law during the post-Civil War days, a time when Reconstruction laws and conquering Unionists were considered unjust by many Southerners, including western Missourians.6

Horan writes that the legend of James as a Robin Hood-like figure aiding beleaguered Missourians, is mythmaking at its best, because "...Jesse was a thief and a callous killer."7 For more than a century that false image has persisted. Numerous James accounts, including those by Horan, Steele, Dyer, and Steckmesser have claimed that James firmly believed charity began and ended at home.8

Despite the scholarly assessments of James' outlaw exploits by Horan, William Settle, and Steel, Jesse James can still fixate an audience. In July 1995, a media frenzy surrounded an exhumation of James' corpse to determine authenticity of the remains. That year over 1,000 articles referred to James, an indication of the public's continuing fascination with him, 103 years after his death.9 Reporters from around the nation and other countries attended the October reburial of James.10

Perhaps by understanding how nineteenth-century print journalists depicted James while he was alive, we also may be able to understand why society and to some extent, the media are still fascinated with James. More importantly, a strictly qualitative perusal of a sampling of nineteenth- century Missouri newspapers may shed light on one aspect of how an outlaw can become a folk hero, and the print media's historical role in that transformation. The object is to peruse nineteenth-century newspaper articles published in Missouri, the state where James committed most of his crimes and which he called home.11

According to David Nord, journalism historians have paid little attention to the information function of nineteenth-century newspapers. He calls for studies that explore whether editors and reporters informed or actually persuaded readers to adopt their journalistic perceptions of what the rightful ideological order of thinking should have been for that time.12 Lance Strate wrote, "...as a general rule, members of a society are separated from their culture heroes by time, space, and social class and therefore know their heroes only through stories, images, and other forms of information. In this sense, there are no such things as heroes, only communication about heroes. Without communication, there would be no hero."13 This statement by Strate perhaps indirectly placed print journalists, as the only mass media practitioners existing at that time, at the center of mythmaking. As the official purveyors or disseminators of communication, nineteenth century journalists, may have had a pivotal role in perpetuating the James' hero legend. This study suggests that historically, newspapers have played a role in turning Jesse James into a legendary hero and thus a figure worthy of cultural and folkloric iconoclasm..

The term hero is used in this study, because as David Bryan McLennan wrote: "The hero myth has stood through time as the expression of the relationship of individuals with their communities. Heroes, however fleeting in modern times, symbolize the need and desires of people, especially in turbulent times."14 Heroes are created to fill some societal void and help people make sense of their world. While heroes can be defined as the best a society has to offer, there are times when the worst, or criminal elements have worn that mantle. Strate suggested that to understand how heroes are made, one must probe the channels or the means by which hero information is transmitted.15 Thus, this study researches one of the possible purveyors of the Jesse James hero image; the Missouri newspapers in the latter 1800s.

Literature Review

According to Frank Richard Prassel, it is impossible to separate fact from fiction when it comes to outlaws of the Old West.16 This study utilizes an interdisciplinary approach that weaves media theory, and cultural and folkloric theories to better understand the nineteenth-century Missouri newspapers' role in creating the James legend. This study also attempts to foster a fuller understanding of how James has become established as what Blaine Harden of the *Washington Post,* wrote: "...a quasi-fictional, quasi-admirable icon who's been sentenced to wander forever through our collective consciousness. His abiding undeadness owes less to achievement or villainy or verifiable fact than to accident.... Jesse James unintentionally sated a populist hunger for anti-heroes."17 To understand that anomaly, or how James somehow shed his past to rise as any type of hero, is to probe the depths of how myths and legends come to be.

Any analysis of nineteenth century history, both real and legendary of the Old West, must address violence as an element deeply ingrained in the imagery. In film, fiction, and on television the dominant symbol has been the six-gun, and the prototypical westerner has been the gunfighter. Cultural and intellectual historians, who have examined the fact and fiction of violence in the Old West, have concluded that the violence is vastly distorted. In that light, it is not hard to image how James, who supposedly thrived on violence, could become weaved into the legendary fabric of the Old West, or how his misdeeds still could be a source of much discussion among contemporaries who are bombarded by images of the wild and wooly West of the nineteenth century.

Other studies conducted by scholars have been to probe, "...the violent western experience — as mediated through folklore, fiction, and film —in relation to the broader context of American values. Researchers of Old West outlaws and gunfighters, such as James, cannot avoid tracing the relationship between myth and reality.[18] They have pondered America's fascination with outlaws, gangsters, and how reports of criminals' exploits have been handed down through generations of storytellers who inevitably weave in more fiction than fact, especially when there are incidents of violence to be reported. But lacking in such research is evidence providing a definitive link between history, media, and the perpetuation of heroic folklore. Historians such as Richard Maxwell Brown, have argued that the "contradictory folklore of Western heroism," can be traced from newspapers to other print mediums then to Hollywood.[19] But he does not account for the oral narrative tradition that often focused on the violent exploits of nineteenth-century outlaws.

Hollon chronicled the violence of the Old West, postulating that although America has always had a violent past, the frontier has been violence's most powerful magnet. He wrote:

> Without exception, the history of every Western state is replete with lawlessness, from the arrival of the early Mountain Men to the appearance of the twentieth-century Minutemen. In between, we find a wide range of individual types — claim jumpers, miners, cowboys, cattle rustlers, Indian haters, Border ruffians, Mexican banditti, mule skinners, highwaymen, racial bigots of various colors, professional outlaws, homicidal maniacs, and hired gunslingers. Each group had more than a speaking acquaintance with violence, for the rough life on the frontier prior to 1900 produced scant recognition of the law as law.[20]

Hollon wrote that the 19th century general public expected the West to be violent because of its distance from civilized societies and the problems inherent in attempting to conquer a wilderness where established law was often left to the discretion of Sam Colt's invention. And citizens of that wilderness did not disappoint the general public, often weaving tale after tale of the fictitious, violent characteristics of its outlaws. Billy the Kid was a murderer, but Brown contended he killed less than half the 21 victims attributed to him.21

William A Settle, Jr. is credited by scholars with doing the most to debunk the James myth by analyzing newspaper and eyewitness accounts of James's crimes; and perusing documents contained in various state historical societies, including Kansas and Missouri. His book, *Jesse James Was His Name*, was based on his 1945 Ph.D dissertation at the University of Missouri.22 Dyer and Joseph Snell of the Kansas Historical Society, who was the editor of a 1992 reprint of Triplett's 1882 biography of James, wrote Settle did much to shed a truthfull light on James's life, and cast doubt on his Robin Hood image.23

Dyer and Snell wrote that early biographers of James, especially Joseph A. Dacus, author of the *Life and Adventures of Frank and Jesse James and the Younger Brothers Noted Western Outlaws* (1880); and J.W. Duel, *The Border Outlaws* (1881); and posthumous books like Triplett's *The Life times and Treacherous Death of Jesse James* (1882); and Jacob Spencer's *The Life and Career of Frank and Jesse James* (1882) quoted verbatim from newspapers, and in the process repeated many erroneous facts that now comprise the James' legendary legacy. Snell writes that Spencer was the editor of the *St. Joseph News* and wrote his version less than a week after James's death.24 For example, newspaper accounts claim James was fast with a gun and a dead shot. Horan wrote that Dick Liddil, a member of James's gang, stated in his memoirs that James could not be trusted to hit the side of a barn with any accuracy. Yet, the deadly shot myth appears in Weilman's and Triplett's biographies.25

The ties to Robin Hood, a legendary English character, who Steckmesser wrote never existed, are pervasive and lasting, despite efforts to debunk the myth.26 According to Steckmesser, the Robin-Hood/hero/outlaw must possess benevolence towards the poor and downtrodden, have a pleasing countenance, a fun-loving nature, unusual intelligence and leadership skills, boundless courage, and a non-aggressive, peace-loving disposition. The Robin Hood-outlaw only shoots in self defense and has the uncanny ability to always be betrayed by a close friend or acquaintance.[27] Early and later biographers, and nineteenth-century journalists have attributed these characteristics or qualities to James, whom they wrote was assassinated by a trusted gang member, Robert Ford, who shot an unarmed James while his back was turned.[28]

Another criterion for hero-making is societal upheaval. Scholar Helena Huntington Smith's "Myth Machine" is "fueled by credulity and emotions; by old men's expansive memories, and by hatreds — the hatred of the poor for the rich, and the rich for the poor, or such hatreds as the terrible postwar bitterness in Missouri, which helped to make a hero of Jesse James."[29]

Tangherlini described why legends are spawned during times of social upheaval. He wrote:

> Since legends are intended to be believable and believed, they act as an unconscious fictionalizing. Legend addresses real psychological problems associated with the geographic and social environments, acting as a reflection of commonly felt pressures. However, it is not only fears which are addressed but also desires. Much of folk narrative is the human fantasy engaging in wishful thinking.[30]

To deal with the social upheaval, Tangherlini postulated that society takes real events and weaves fantasies from them as a sort of escape valve from the problems indigenous to such periods — economic, political, loss of social status, etc. Nineteenth-century journalists also experienced the post-Civil War societal stress. It is a small leap to assume that they, too, needed heroes. But unlike the average citizen, they had the power to insure that their heroes would be remembered, according to Strate.

Robert N. Mullen and Charles E. Welch, Jr., who explored the myth of Billy the Kid, another nineteenth-century outlaw, stated it was publicity and not his deeds that made Henry McCarty, alias William Bonney, alias Billy the Kid, a well-known scourge of the Old West. In reality, Mullen and Welch wrote he was not the leader of his band, he mostly ambushed to kill, and was better known for stealing cattle and horses. Although, his sensational escape from a New Mexico jail hardly merited any printer's ink, Mullen and Welch wrote that his death at the hands of a reputed friend, Pat Garrett, and some of his adventures received press recognition that elevated him far above the more noteworthy outlaws of his time.[31]

Other folkloric scholars link specific historical events and rumors to creations of legends, which Max Luthi defines as an apparition of reality that has some believable aspects. At the heart of the legend is some piece of reality based on a real event, and it is this actualization that "...accounts for the episodic nature of legend." Luthi espouses that legends tell the story of what happened to man.32 Ernst Bernheim noted how rumor merges into legend,33 and Gordon Allsport researched how legends owe their immortality to their abilities to mirror what society embraces unquestionably, no matter whether it is true. In the James myth, his many criminal exploits, which were reportedly documented by newspaper accounts became the basis for many embroidered rumors and stories that grew into legend.34

Richard M. Ohmann wrote that myths and legends take on lives of their own because they are part of the very fabric of any culture. "Myths comment on the world and in a deeper way they comment on man. To understand myths and the needs they serve is to understand something about ourselves."35 Campbell wrote that "...myths are the nature of dreams, and that, as dreams arise from an inward world unknown to waking consciousness, so do myths: so indeed, does life."36

Ancona wrote that myths exist or have their origins in the "secondary mind," or the unconscious, where longings and images form.37 Ausband wrote that when "myths die, gods die."38 He said:

> If we can do without tales of the gods, we cannot do without tales of heroes and villains, of monsters and the human courage it takes to face them. Those tales are the myths we live by, because they show us that life means something after all. The names of the monsters change, and so do those of the heroes and of the struggle itself as our ways of perceiving the world change, but every society must have its heroes and its monsters, perhaps some gods, too, if it can afford them — because it must find meaning in the world.39

The scholarly works of Campbell, Ancona, Ausband, and Ohmann help us to understand why nineteenth-century Missourians and other Americans embraced James, despite his nefarious deeds. Why they clasped him to their bosoms and held on tight to a man, who murdered and robbed, but who nevertheless gave an image, a god they could cling to in the war-torn, ravished, economically depleted land that was theirs after the Civil War.

The language and words used by journalists and repeated in early James' biographies are important to understanding the progression of the myth. The study of semantics, which is the study of how persons respond to words and other symbols, is also the study of the meanings of words and their symbolic arousals in readers.40 Several scholars, including John C. Condon, Jr., and Geoffrey Wagner postulate that "The structure of our language often does our thinking for us."[41] Condon, Jr. wrote, "The ability to use language means the ability to transfer experience into symbols and through the symbolic medium to share experiences.... It is totally false to assume that language does not affect behavior." Wagner wrote, "Words are to reality what a map is to its territory. Language contains the past for us — its time-binding function. Language stores literature, historical events, truth, error, scientific theory,... on our behalf. It is thus a map of the past."[42]

Such scholarly work makes it easy to assume that the laudatory, highly descriptive adjectives and adverbs used to describe James' criminal deeds had an impact on nineteenth-century readers and early biographers. The oft-repeated descriptions which have been published in 20th-century works, like Wellman's, serve to perpetuate a myth that puts James in a favorable, heroic light. And according to the work of Condon, Jr. and Wagner, journalists of that era must have looked admirably at James' exploits to have written about him in such terms. Their newspaper articles have contributed to how James is viewed historically.

Media scholars, especially journalism historians, and journalism practitioners have long agreed that newspapers are pieces of history and reporters are history makers. Media managers shape the western world's view of reality. Such manipulations, Herbert Schiller implies have directed the course of American history. [43] Allan Nevins in a 1955 *Saturday Review* article, writes that newspaper reporters are in good positions to create heroes by partisan coverage, or giving more ink to one source or subject. Therefore they must be vigilant in how they treat "heroes," he argued.[44] Sidney Hook wrote, "Whoever controls the microphones and printing presses can make or unmake history overnight." Hook contended that the hero is noted more often in news stories and written about to emphasize unique abilities."[45] Many aspects of the James myth, such as his intelligence, his good looks, good taste in horseflesh, fast gun hand, and wily ability to outsmart lumbering lawmen was mentioned repeatedly in nineteenth-century news articles and early biographers.

The mythmaking capabilities of the mass media have been documented by Marshall McLuhan, who wrote, "The newspaper will serve as an example of the Babel of myths or language."[46] In *The Unreality Industry*, Mitroff and Bennis wrote that the mass media ". . .have degraded our general level of education and debased our national discourse. Instead of grappling honestly with our problems, i.e., of dealing directly with reality itself the inevitable drift to unreality reaches new lows."47 Boorstin in *The Image* wrote that pseudo-events and images, which are created by the media, are flooding our consciousness. The flooding is as old as history, going back to the early nineteenth century when ". . .the great modern increase in the supply and the demand for news began. . ."48

The unreality aspect of the mass media industry has played havoc with history. Many history scholars have traditionally used newspaper archives for research. Inaccurate stories not only create biases and myths, but they can distort reality for generations of readers. "Historians must learn that words are as dangerous as bullets, and that each must be carefully weighed to detect the nuances of meaning that might prejudice the viewpoints of their readers," wrote Ray Billingsley.49 The research emphasized in the preceding pages strengthens this study by showing a causal link between the media, their word usage and mythmaking, especially when the news articles contained false information about outlaws like James.

But to achieve fuller understanding of the nineteenth-century newspapers' roles in creating the James legend; some attempt must be made to comprehend the working conditions of the reporters. Journalists of that era employed sensationalism as a means to pad their pay checks, because many were paid by the column inch.50 Libel as defined by twentieth-century standards did not mean the same thing in the latter part of the 1800s. If newspapers were inaccurate, few people sued during a time when such lawsuits were subjected to common law rulings rather than contemporary constitutional mandates. In the nineteenth century, newspaper publishers only had to prove good motives and justifiable ends to beat a libel suit.51 Such a climate could have fostered a news environment that did not fear lawsuits and thus had little regard for the truth when writing about James.

Barbara Cloud wrote about the frontier editor's ties to politics. While, she wrote it was usually the second paper established in frontier towns that catered to partisan politics,52 in nineteenth-century Missouri, many newspapers tended to take political sides no matter whether the competition was located next door or across the state. The James outlawry was a particular sore spot for nineteenth-century Missouri politicians. The crimes of Jesse and his brother Frank, and their gang had been a campaign issue splitting the state's Democratic Party, which was composed of both pro-Confederate and pro-Union men. Horan explained:

> Indirectly, the James and the Youngers [members of the outlaw gang] also influenced national elections. In the 1870s the Republicans —ironically then called the Radicals— had a fragile hold on important political posts; it was important that as many states as possible be won. In an attempt to drive a wedge between the northern and southern Democrats, the Republicans gleefully used every state convention to blast the Democratic administration for its incompetence in ridding the state of banditry.53

According to Dyer and Horan, stories in papers across the nation, especially the eastern states, pointed to Missouri as "The Outlaw State," "Poor Old Missouri," "The Outlaw's Paradise," and "Haven for Outlaws,"54 In 1882, Missouri Governor Thomas T. Crittenden, who was tired of the criticism and slurs aimed at his administration, offered a $25,000 reward for Jesse James dead or alive and a $15,000 bounty for his brother Frank.55 No one attempted to collect the money, according to Wellman, until Crittenden made a deal offering clemency to Robert Ford if he could eliminate Jesse James by any means necessary.56 It was a pact that was to cost him his reelection bid and hopes of becoming president when Ford's assassination of James caused a statewide outcry that was echoed by members of Crittenden's own party. Crittenden even netted the criticism of President Grover Cleveland, who refused to appoint him to a diplomatic post, saying, "he had bargained with the Fords for the killing of Jesse James," according to Horan.57

Thus, it was in that volatile, political climate that journalists and editors, some of whom clearly stated their political leanings in their mastheads, covered the crimes and death of Jesse James. John P. Ferre writes that moralists decried the late nineteenth-century newspapers for their pandering to sensationalism, glorification of criminals and crimes, and fixations with murder.58 In 1896, Aline Gorren wrote that instead of educating society, news reporting was a reflection of the half-tamed, socially deprived masses.59 It was a society that was ripe for legend making. A time when Jesse James, outlaw and murderer, could warm hearts and give hope.

Methodology

The social reconstructivist theory of Gamson and Modigliani (1989) will be utilized for this research to understand the media's role in the legend-making of James. This theory views the media as having their most significant effects by constructing meanings and offering these constructs in a systematic way to audiences, where they may be incorporated into personal meaning structures, often shaped by prior collective identifications.60 This process often engages strong social institutions and is influenced by the social environment of the receiver. "Such a theory is in line with new research that has two main thrusts: First, that media construct social formations and history itself by framing images of reality (in fiction as well as news) in a predictable and patterned way; and secondly that people in audiences construct for themselves their own view of social reality and their place in it in interaction with the symbolic construction offered by the media," according to Denis McQuail in *Mass Communication Theory: An Introduction*.61 In addition Gaye Tuchman's 1978 definition of framing, which is depicted as the media's ability to set the stage for how citizens will discuss public events, will be utilized for this study.62

The social reconstructivist theory is utilized in this study to show how nineteenth-century newspapers constructed James as a hero by favorably describing him using descriptive adjectives and adverbs. Once James was portrayed as a hero by the journalists, post-Civil War Missouri society, which was in need of such an anti-hero, eagerly embraced James as he was presented to them by the print media. Missouri in the latter 1800s was reeling from the bloody border wars and guerilla tactics of Quantrill and Bloody Bill Anderson. Accepting the violence of James, especially if it was depicted favorably by the newspapers, would have been an easy conquest for a social reconstructivist-inclined print media.

Tuchman's framing arguments will be employed for studying the adjectives and adverbs used to describe James and his exploits. Adjectives and adverbs when used favorably can give insight into the feelings of the writer or journalist, and do much to persuade readers that the subject is worthy of praise or disdain. For example, it would be easy to assume that the journalist who used favorable adjectives and adverbs to depict James must have wanted to frame the outlaw in a heroic light. Such a favorable frame could have led nineteenth-century readers to embrace James as a champion, a Robin Hood figure, who robbed the despised Union banks and railroads and gave to poor Missourians.

The method to prove the aforementioned theories will be a perusal of the contents of a sampling of nineteenth-century Missouri newspapers, compiled from a collection maintained by the State Historical Society of Missouri. The sampling was taken from newspapers published during the time of James' reign of outlawry: February 13, 1866 until the days following his death on April 3, 1882. This strictly qualitative study will be done to determine how journalists and editors wrote about James and his exploits when he was alive, and how they covered his death. Coding the newspapers for adjectives, adverbs, and other supercilious words, this study hopefully will shed light on which articles — the ones written while he was alive or the ones written after his death contributed most to the James legend.

Specifically this study seeks to determine whether the journalists' coverage was favorable and heroic, despite the criminality of James' activities. In other words, did newspaper journalists write good things about James? Did they write about his crimes in ways befitting such acts? Or did they depict him in such a way as to rouse sympathy among readers, a sympathy that made James seem like a hero? Hero is defined as a person who has done something brave and noble. Was James depicted as being a good, old, Southerner and former guerrilla raider, who in the aftermath of the Civil War, took up outlawry not only to revenge the South for its defeat at Union hands, but to strike back at the Reconstruction carpetbaggers, who came to Missouri? Answers to these questions should provide evidence to determine whether nineteenth-century Missouri journalists played a pivotal role in the creation of the James legend and significantly contributed to the transformation of the outlaw into a cultural icon and folk hero.

According to Horan, *Kansas City Times* editor Edwards, a native Virginian, and adjutant to Confederate General Joe Shelby, was a Southern sympathizer, who endowed James with heroic characteristics, and created fictitious news articles that made James a champion of the poor. If Edwards and other Missouri journalists of that era were responsible for what would be called framing approximately 100 years later, a perusal of their writings and especially of the adjectives and adverbs used, should reveal how they presented James and his criminal activities to their readers.

Ten nineteenth-century Missouri newspapers were selected either in a random sample according to the time period (1866-1882) or because of their locations in towns where James committed robberies. Four newspapers, *The North Missourian*, Gallatin; *The Liberty Tribune*, Liberty; the *Missouri Valley Register,* Lexington; and *The Conservator*, Richmond, were chosen because banks in those towns were robbed by James.[63] In addition, *The Liberty Tribune* and *The Liberty Advance* were located in Clay County, where Kearney, James' boyhood home was located. Other microfilm editions of the aforementioned newspapers and *The Democrat*, Savannah; *The Missouri Valley Register,* Lexington; and *The Weekly Record*, New Madrid; were scanned for stories about robberies that occurred in other parts of the state to determine if distance from the mayhem made a difference in the way articles were written. In contrast, an attempt will be made to scan for death stories on James all the newspapers previously mentioned, and *The Kansas City Times*, Kansas City; *The Missouri Republican*, St. Louis; *The Bates County Record*, Butler; and *The Democrat*, Savannah; and *The Kansas City Journal*, Kansas City.

Several cultural, folkloric scholars including Beverly Stoeltje have theorized how the media can help birth legends or stories which are connected to some real events.[64] Legends are historically based, fictionally enhanced stories that focus on real people. Therefore such studies will be utilized in this research. In addition, scholarly work about framing or organizing a story line around a central idea by selecting, emphasizing, and excluding information;[65] and research that explores the working conditions and reporting mores of nineteenth-century journalists will be used. Early and later biographies on James and other historical research on James also are vital to this study.

Findings

Of the ten newspapers examined, only one of the robbery accounts mention the James brothers by name. One story does mention other gang members, who were suspected as taking part in the crimes. *The Missouri Valley Register*, March 19, 1868, chronicled the lynching of Andy McGuire and Jim Deavers for the 1867 robbery of the Hughes and Wasson bank in Richmond.[66] Although the crime later was credited to the James gang by Horan, and Triplett, James was not mentioned in the article.[67] Savannah's *The Democrat* referred to the James gang in an account of an 1881 train robbery in Blue Cut, Mo., but noted that two members of that gang said they were Jesse James while committing the crime.[68]

The first major usage of James' name appears in his death stories, which were written after April 3, 1882. In comparison to the robbery stories, the death stories were full length with decked headlines proclaiming that James had been killed. On April 4, *The Missouri Republican* in St. Louis ran one full page and a half page on James' death.[69] A collection, *Goodbye Jesse James: A Reprinting of Six of* the *Best News Stories Concerning the Career and Death of America's Most Famous Outlaw,* only featured articles from *The Kansas City Daily Journal.* From April 4-9, 1882, the *Daily Journal* ran multi-decked, full-page stories on the death of James, who was killed on April 3 in St. Joseph, Missouri. The *Daily Journal* sent a reporter to the scene, who in an April 4 account lavishly used laudatory prose. The reporter wrote James was the "best shot among Quantrill's raiders, . . who distinguished themselves with reckless courage." He had "...a quality of mercy.. .fought with the relentless air of a hungry tiger, and it was his death-dealing weapon that sent its leaden message to Capt. Wagner's (a Union officer) heart and thus gave victory to the guerrilla band."[70]

Of the seven newspapers examined for death stories, including *The Kansas City Journal*, Kansas City; *Bates County Democrat*, Butler; *The Democrat,* Savannah; *The Missouri Republican*, St. Louis; the *North Missourian*, Gallatin; *The Weekly Record*, New Madrid; *The Liberty Advance*, Liberty: all, except the *Liberty Advance*, noted the treachery used by Robert Ford to kill James. The six papers also noted the excitement, surprise, and anguish expressed by Missourians when they heard of the death. Dyer, Horan, and Wellman wrote that many newspaper stories published nationwide did much to turn James' life and death into a legend

The *Bates County Democrat* noted the crowds that rushed to St. Joseph to view the body. This account said James was "a fine looking man... and his physiognomy was that of an intelligent as well as a resolute and daring man.... In fact nothing in the appearance of the remains indicated the desperate career of the man or the many bloody scenes of which he has been the hero." The article noted James was in the "...habit of wearing two belts with a brace of very fine revolvers.... In the barn were fine horses, the property of James."[71] Horan wrote the horses had been stolen from a neighbor.[72]

Although a death story from a correspondent, which appears to be an editorial in the *Liberty Advance* (April 14, 1882), vilified James' crimes, it used complimentary adjectives. "Jesse W. James... outshone, in the crimson flame of his murderous achievements, any fiend that the imaginative mind of [Sir Walter] Scott could ever have imagined." The article also condemned the foreign and national press, especially Chicago's *TheTribune* and *The Inter-Ocean*, which hailed the justice of James' killing.[73]

But the surveyed newspapers through their use of laudatory adjectives contained many more tributes to James' prowess and bravery. Each one noted Ford and how his bullet entered the back of James' head. According to Triplett, the honor code of the Old West stated there was no greater dreg on society than a bushwhacker or a man who shoots an unarmed or unaware man from the back.[74] Jesse James' wound became subheads for three newspapers: "THE BLOODY HOLE OVER THE LEFT EYE;" *The Kansas City Journal* (April 4, 1882); "BULLET THROUGH HIS BRAIN," *Bates County Democrat* (April 6, 1882); and a subhead in the *Missouri Republican* (April 4) read "CRASHED THROUGH THE OUTLAW'S SKULL." Two separate decks in that same April 4 issue of the *Missouri Republican* read, "MYSTERIOUS BOB'S BULLET," "SENT CRASHING THROUGH THE BRAIN OF JESSE JAMES." All the death stories note that James was unarmed, "I'LL TAKE OFF MY PISTOLS," was one subhead in the *Bates County Democrat* (April 6, 1882); and referred to the shooter as a mere boy or lad, who was staying at the home of the James. Such headlines and stories fit the basic characteristics of Robin Hood-heromaking outlined by folklorist Steckmesser.

Each of the death stories mention crimes committed by the James gang, in contrast to no mention of the brothers in the same newspapers' accounts of the robberies that were surveyed for this study. Edwards' *The Kansas City Times*, not only mentioned the robberies, but published letters from Jesse James in which James denied he committed the crimes. Edwards backed up the denials in editorials that proclaimed James an upstanding citizen. Edwards placed James at the sacking of Lawrence, Kansas with Quantrill's raiders, but Horan wrote that historians have proved James was never there. Edwards has James not only participating in the raid, but sparing the life of a Union soldier at the pleas of a young girl. Other inaccurate facts Horan attributed to Edwards include the churchgoing nature of James, his Robin Hood image of giving money to a widow to pay her mortgage, but then waylaying the loan collector and recouping his funds. It is Edwards who Horan and Dyer blamed for the enduring image of James as a man driven to a life of crime by the unforgiving Northern carpetbaggers who swarmed into Missouri after the Civil War.

Horan, who cites a telegram housed in the State Historical Society of Missouri, wrote that Edwards was so protective of the James brothers and the Youngers that he wired his paper to stop printing stories on their involvement in the robbery of a train at Gads Hill. Edwards called the report, "...remarkable for two things — utter stupidity and total untruth." Edwards established a trust fund seeking public donations to help James' widow and children. Horan wrote he was aghast at the audacity of someone who started a similar fund for the widow of William Westfall, an unarmed train conductor gunned down by Jesse James.[75]

Horan and Dyer wrote it was Edwards' articles exonerating James from crimes, and his grief-stricken death stories that contained much of the antedotal information on James that has since become part of the legend.[76] Some of those same inaccurate images were found in Triplett's 1882 biography and over 79 years later in Wellman's 1961 *A Dynasty of Western Outlaws*. Perhaps some of the newspapers surveyed for this study aided in that mythmaking. *The Democrat* recorded how he used hair dye to perfect his disguise, which was more evidence of his wily, intellectual abilities to outwit the law. [77] *The Liberty Advance* noted his hearty and playful nature as the "...domesticated guerrilla train-robber . . ." participated in a snowball fight with his young female neighbors, who knew him as Mr. Howard in St. Joseph. [78] The newspapers appeared to print all information they could find on James after his death, even the sale of his dog for $15.[79]

This sampling of nineteenth-century Missouri newspapers reveals that the death stories could have provided more fodder for the James legend than the stories published about his crimes. Although a more thorough analysis of all the Missouri newspapers in operation during James' years of infamy, 1866-1882, would be called for before any broad-reaching conclusions could be reached, the consistent usage of descriptive adjectives and adverbs shows that nineteenth-century journalists favorably framed James. Even his criminal exploits were depicted in heroic tones.

The social reconstructivist theory of Gamson and Modigliani is evidenced by such framing which served to systematically construct James as a heroic, admirable figure deserving of legendary status. The acceptance of the nineteenth-century journalists' work can be evidenced from the proliferation of early biographies, dime novels, historical treatises, and other written material that appeared shortly after James' death.

One main source for the James' mythmaking was John Newman Edwards, a nineteenth-century newspaperman, who was the editor of the *Kansas City Times*. James' historians, including Dyer, Steele, and Horan identify Edwards as the major force behind creation of James' Robin Hood image. Edwards, a close friend of the James family, became the namesake for the James' only surviving son Jesse Edwards.[80] Edwards, who consistently published in the *Kansas City Times* letters from James denying his part in any criminal activities, wrote editorials and articles glorifying James, and created such a vivid image that early James biographers and other journalists copied Edwards' partisan opinions almost verbatim.

Horan wrote that the legends surrounding James have been long lasting: "He will always be the boy eternal, the merry-eyed outlaw who rides across the western plains on a magnificent bay, the bag of gold stolen from the hated railroads slung across his saddle horn while behind him, helplessly outclassed, come the lumbering posse,"[81] This kind of laudatory prose echoed Edwards, who in 1873, wrote: "Jesse James, .. .has a face as smooth and innocent as the face of a school girl. The blue eyes, very clear and penetrating, are never at rest. There is always a smile on his lips, and a gracefull word or a compliment for all with whom he comes in contact."[82]

The same laudatory description echoed in nineteenth-century biographies of James, including Triplett's *The Life Times & Treacherous Death of Jesse James* and in Dacus' *Illustrated Lives and Adventures of Frank and Jesse James.* In the twentieth century, Wellman's *A Dynasty of Western Outlaws* continued the laudatory tradition in its depiction of James.

Wellman wrote that when the James gang was scouting towns for future bank robberies, "...they proceeded on their leisurely way, stopping at the best hotels, dining luxuriously, smoking the finest cigars, and spending money freely, though not ostentatiously.... It was more like an outing, a sort of picnic, than a grim foray.... Eight bold, athletic young men, superb horsemen, skylarking at times in sheer exuberance."[83]

Triplett wrote that in 1873, the bank robbery at St. Genevieve, Missouri, must have been the work of the James' gang, because, "The staying qualities of the band; their coolness in danger; their perfect nerve in the most trying situations; their rallying around a disabled comrade,...show it to be the work of..." the James gang.[84]

According to Kansas historian Snell, Triplett merely repeated newspaper accounts of James' death in his biography of James, which was published seven weeks after the outlaw's death in 1882. Snell wrote, "With caretul comparison one can find page after page of text, which agrees completely, except for minor word and punctuation changes, with news stories from (Edwards' Kansas City) *Times* of April 1882." For example, Triplett used Edwards' entire article titled

"The Murder of Jesse James," which begins:

"Not one among the hired cowards, hard on the hunt for blood money, dared face this wonderful outlaw until he had disarmed himself and turned his back to his assassins — that first and only time in his career, which has passed from the realms of an almost fabulous romance into that of history."[85]

Discussion and Conclusion

Initially this study attempted to analyze for framing all news stories published in the same Missouri towns where James committed twelve of his crimes; and compare those articles with stories written about his death in those same newspapers. However, records at the Missouri historical society were not complete in some cases, including most of the pre- and post-death stories written by Edwards. The faded nature and otherwise poor quality of some microfilms also prevented scrutiny of some editions of newspapers. Only a sample of articles and newspapers spanning the life and death of James could be studied given the task of viewing primary documents that are not categorized by subject. However, even such a small sample can shed a glimmer of light on how nineteenth-century Missouri journalists covered James, and determine whether those reports helped foster myths.

It is puzzling how three papers, the *Missouri Valley Register*, Lexington; *The Tribune*, Liberty; and *The Conservator*, Richmond; chronicled the bank robberies at Richmond, Liberty, Savannah, Independence, and Lexington, but failed to mention James. Only *The Democrat* in Savannah included James in the 1881 robbery of a Chicago & Alton train at Blue Cut. But it offered somewhat of a mystery by noting that two men in the same gang said they were James. However, when surveyed for his death stories, the same papers contained many details about his crimes. Did they reprint what was written in the larger St. Louis and Kansas City papers, or was there some other newsgathering characteristic preventing attribution of the crimes to James? Much research can be done to explore this aspect in terms of news values like timeliness; and how newspapers covered breaking stories in other communities during a time when the telegram was the only technological mode of transmission. Did the societal/cultural mores created by the post-Civil War time spawn a news value and ideology that influenced editors' and reporters' decisions about attributing the crimes to James?

It has been noted that modern historians should employ literary writing techniques to imbue their work with creativity. Perhaps the early James historians imbued their biographies with so much creativity, it was copied and passed down through the generations in songs and legends, eventually becoming fact for many contemporary historians, who do not examine the information for credibility. Did the historians' way of writing help create the myth of James or did it merely reflect the media's? Research tracing the exact phrasing of words from news story to biography to song to contemporary accounts could trace this literary progression.

Another avenue for research could explore contemporary accounts which claim that nineteenth-century Missouri residents knew that the James brothers had committed crimes. Yet, only one paper surveyed for this study mentioned James in connection to a crime. How did Missouri residents know James was a robber, and if they did not know, who told the reporters, who wrote such lengthy death stories outlining all James' outlaw ventures? The external communication system of a region that was bereft of telephone, television, or radio has been mentioned repeatedly in western novels, films, and scholarly articles without adequate explanation as to how information was passed from town to town and state to state. Did the habit of oral storytelling spread the work of James' exploits?

The unstructured, communication system of the frontier is an area ripe for exploration into how facts and rumors are weaved into legends, and how the frontier media, products of their societal environments, sometimes became disseminators of more legend than fact. Strate writes that oral transmission, which was an integral part of the frontier means of communication, spawned a hero who in order to be memorable had to be "larger than life, superhuman or supernatural beings. Oral heroes are the heroes of myth and legend."[86] Considering the paucity of details on James' crimes that appeared in the pre-death stories, it appears the nineteenth century press may have relied on oral narratives as a source for the after-death stories. Due to the lack of attribution in any of the stories, it remains for further research to determine whether oral folklore about James was incorporated into the newspapers and thus legitimatized for historical posterity.

Prassel postulated that within the context of Anglo-Saxon myth, many labels are used to describe the outlaw: Bandit, pirate, highwaymen, desperado, rebel, hoodlum, gunman, gangster, renegade, moll, etc.[87] Death stories in the *Missouri Republican* referred to James as an outlaw, bandit, and train robber. Other newspaper accounts labeled him a desperado, freebooter, and just plain robber.[88] Many of these labels have stuck with James and become synonymous with the man in contemporary culture, but seemingly not in an infamous way befitting a murderer of his status.

"The figures around whom knowledge is made to cluster, those about whom stories are told or sung, must be made into conspicuous personages, foci of common attention,....." wrote Ong.[89] Wellman wrote that the way Jesse Woodson James died, "...the cowardly treachery of it, completed the James legend and gave him an imperishable place in American folklore."[90]

And it was a folkloric place that was built by the creative, descriptive writing of the nineteenth-century Missouri press, which did much to help spread the James legend via other print-related industries. When the media depicted James as a hero, those "facts" were taken at face value and became the basis for early and later biographies and historical research about the outlaw.

To understand the press' historical role in the transformation of James from outlaw to folk hero is to understand how journalists, when they operate outside the realm of objectivity, can promulgate falsehoods and half-truths, and in the process legitimize a legend that can distort history for generations of readers. It is not a role of which newspapers, which have traditionally prided themselves on accuracy and truthfulness, can be proud. Yet it is a historical legacy the press must bear and one it should remember as it glorifies other criminals and turns them into heroes.

Notes

1. Michael Malone, *Historians and the American West* ed. by Malone with a forward by Rodman Paul, (Lincoln, Nebraska, University of Nebraska Press, 1983), 1-3. Also see Paul, *Historians and the American West* vii-ix; Richard Slotkin, *Gunfighter Nation: The Myth of the Frontier in Twentieth-Century America* (New York: HarperPerennial, 1992), 4-5, 82-3.
2. James D Horan, *The Outlaws* (New York, Grammercy Books, 1977), 36-54,64-84. Paul I. Wellman, *A Dynasty of Western Outlaws* (Garden City. New York: Doubleday & Company, Inc.), 1961, 120-1 Dems Mcloughlin, *Wild and Woolly: An Encyclopedia of the Old West* (New York Barnes and Noble Books, 1975), 225-53 For a listing of crimes, see Frank Triplett, *The Life Times & Treacherous Death of Jesse James* introduction by Joseph Snell, reprint ed., (Stanford, Conn Longmeadow Press. 1992), 294-5.
3. Wellman, *A Dynasty*, 81.
4. Slotkin, *Gunfighter Nation,* 127-128. William E. Parrish, Charles T. Jones, Jr., Lawrence O. Christensen, *Missouri The Heart of the Nation* (Arlington Heights, Illinois: Harlan Davidson Inc, 1992), 222, Bruce A, Rosenberg, *The Code of the West* (Bloomington, Indiana: Indiana University Press, 1982) 172.

5. Horan, *The Outlaws,* 29, and Kent L Steckmesser. "Robin Hood and the American Outlaw," *Journal of American Folklore,* vol 79, 1966, 348-355.
6. Steckmesser. "Robin Hood and the American Outlaw," 348-9. James was also called Robin Hood by Rosenberg, *The Code of the West* 169. Other cultural scholars, who support Steckmesser on the theory that stressful societal times breed outlaw/heroes are Orrin Kapp, "The Folk Hero," *Journal of American Folklore,* vol 62 (1949), 236; Klapp, *Heroes Villains and Fools The Changing American Character* Englewood Cliffs, New Jersey: Prentice-Hall, Inc., 1962), 53; and Stephen Ausband, *Myth and Meaning Myth and Order* (Macon, Georgia: Mercer University Press, 1983). 2-3.
7. Horan,*The Outlaws,* p. 29.
8. *Ibid.*, 30, Phillip Steele, *Jesse and Frank James: The Family History* (Gretna, Louisiania: Pelican Publishing Company, 1992), 15; Robert L. Dyer, *Jesse James and the Civil War in Missouri* (Columbia, Missouri: University of Missouri Press, 1994), 2-5; and Steckmesser, "Robin Hood and the American Outlaws," 350.
9. Lexis/Nexis news service, which lists approximately 200 newspapers, contained over 1,000 entries citing Jesse James' name in 1995.
10. *The Kansas City Star.* 21 October 1995, 1(A).
11. Robert L. Dyer, *Jesse James and the Civil War in Missouri,* (Columbia, Missouri University of Missouri Press, 1994). 1-5.
12. David Paul Nord, "The Politics of Agenda-Seting in Late 19th-Century Cities," *Journalism Quarterly,* 1992,567-7.
13. Lance Strate, "Heroes: A Communication Perspective," chapter in *American Heroes in a Media Age*, eds Susan J. Drucker and Robert S. Cathcart (Cresskill, New Jersey: Noyes Publications, 1994), 16.
14. David Bryan McLennan, "Autobiography, Cultural Mythology and the Modern Hero," chapter in Drucker and Cathcart, *American Heroes in a Media Age,* 113.
15. Strate, *American Heroes in a Media Age,* 17.
16. Frank Prassel, *The Great American Outlaw: A Legacy of Fact and Fiction* (Norman: University of Oklahoma Press, 1993), xi-xii.
17. Blaine Harden, "Jesse James: Dead or Alive. Why America Won't Let Its Outlaw Celebrities Rest in Peace," *The Washington Post Magazine,* 19 Nov.1995, 18(W).
18. Richard M. Brown, "Historiography of Violence in the American West," chapter in Malone, *Historians and the American West,* 235.
19. Richard M. Brown, "Desperadoes and Lawmen: The Folk Hero," chapter in *The Culture of Crime* , eds. Craig L. LaMay and Everette E. Dennis (New Brunswick, New Jersey: Transaction Publishers, 1995), 138.
20. W. Eugene Hollon, *Frontier Violence: Another Look* (New York: Oxford University Press, 1974), vii.
21. Brown, *The Culture of Crime.*, 142.
22. Dyer, *Jesse James and the Civil War in Missouri* 69; Snell, in Triplett, *The Life Times*, xix.
23. *Ibid*, Snell introduction, xix.
24. *Ibid*, Snell introduction, x-xiu, Dyer, *Jesse James and the Civil War in Missouri,* 69.
25. Triplett, *The Life Times & Treacherous Death of Jesse James,* 112: Wellman, *A Dynasty of Western Outlaws,* 104.
26. Steckmesser, "Robin Hood and the American Outlaw," 349.
27. *Ibid.* 350-54; Kent L. Steckmesser, *The Western Hero in History and Legend* (Norman, Oklahoma: University of Oklahoma Press, 1965), 250.
28. Ibid, Steckmesser, *The Western Hero in History and Legend.* See also Dyer, *Jesse James and the Civil War in Missouri*, 63-5, Triplett, *The Life Times & Treacherous Death of Jesse James,* 224.
29. Helena Huntington Smith, "Sam Bass and the Myth Machine," *The American West,* 7 (January 1970), 32. See also Beverly Crane, "The Structure of Value in 'The Roommate's

Death': A Methodology for Interpretative Analysis of Folk Legends," *Journal of Folklore Institute*, 14, 133-51,cited by Timothy R. Tangherlini, "It Happened Not Too Far From Here...": A Survey of Legend Theory and Characterization," *Western Folklore,* 49 (October 1990), 381; Wellman *A Dynasty of Western Outlaws* 65, and Steckmesser. "Robin Hood and the American Outlaw," 349.

30. Tangherlini, "It Happened Not Too Far From Here," 381.
31. Robert N. Mullin and Charles E. Welch, Jr., "Billy the Kid: The Making of a Hero," *Western Folklore,* 46 (March 1984), 105.
32. Max Luthi, "Aspekte des Marchens und der Sage," *Germanische Ronische Montasschrift,* 16, quoted by Tangherlini, "It Happened Not Too Far From Here".372
33. Ernst Berriheim, *Einleitung in Der Geschichtswissenschaft* (Berlin: Walter de Gruyter, 1920), quoted by Tarigherlini, "It Happened Not Too Far From Here...," 372.
34. Gordon Misport, *The Psychology of Rumor* (New York: Holt Publishing Company, 1947), 130.
35. Richard M. Olimarn, ed *The Making of Myth* vol 1.3rd edition, (New York: G.P. Putnam's Sons, 1962), 2-3.
36. Joseph Campbell, *The Hero With a Thousand Faces,* Bollingen Series XVII, (Princeton, New Jersey: Princeton University Press, 1949), 3-10.
37. Francesco Aristide, *Ancona, Myth: Matter of Mind?,* (Lanham. Maryland University Press of America, Inc., 1994), 50.
38. Stephen C. Ausband, *Myth and Meaning, Myth and Order,* (Macon, Georgia, Mercer University Press, 1983), 36.
39. *Ibid,* 115.
40. Arthur C. Hastings, forward to *Semantics and Communications,* ed John C. Condon, Jr., (New York:The MacMillan Co. 1966). 1-2.
41. Geofrey Wagner and Sanford R Radner, *Language & Reality: A Semantics Approach to Writing* (New York: Thomas Y. Crowell Company. 1974). ix.
42. *Ibid,* 115, 130.
43. Herbert I. Schiller, *The Mind Managers.* (Boston. Massachussetts: Beacon Press, 1973), 8, 31.
44. Allan Nevins, "Is History Made by Heroes," *Saturday Review,* November 5, 1955, p.43.
45 Sidney Hook, *The Hero in History* (New York: The John Day Company. 1943). quoted by William H. Talt, *Newspapers as Tools for Historians,* (Columbia, Mo.: Lucas Brothers Publishers, 1970), 32.
46. Marshall McLuhan, "Myth and the Mass Media," chapter in *Myth and Mythmaking,* ed. Henry Murray, (New York: George Braziller. 1960), 298.
47. Ian I. Mitroff and Warren Bennis, *The Unreality Industry,* (New York Birch Lane Press Book, 1989). xii.
48 Daniel J. Boorstin, *The Image: A Guide to Pseudo-Events in America,* (New York: Atheneum, 1961), 11-13.
49. Ray Allen Billingsley, "History is a Dangerous Subject," *Saturday Review,* Jan.15, 1966, 59-61, 80-81.
50. Ted Symthe, "The Reporter, 1880-1900: Working Conditions and Their Influence on the News," *Journalism History*, 7:1 (Spring 1980), 1-8.
51, Timothy Gleason, "19th-Century Legal Practice and Freedom of the Press: An Introduction to an Unfamiliar Terrain," *Journalism History* 14:1 (Spring 1987), 26-31.
52. Barbara Cloud, "A Party Press? Not Just Yet! Political Publishing on the Frontier," *Journalism History* 7:2 (Summer 1980), 54.
53. Horan, *The Outlaws*,34.
54. Dyer, *Jesse James and the Civil War in Missouri,* 3,8: Horan, *The Outlaws,* 34.
55. 1882 Reward Poster authorized by Governor Thomas Crittenden and sold as a souvenir at the Jesse James Museum in St. Joseph, Mo.

56. Wellman, *A Dynasty of Western Oulaws*, 122.
57. Horan, *The Outlaws*, 35.
58. John P. Ferre, "The Dubions Heritage of Media Ethics: Cause-and-Effect Criticism in the 1890s," *American Journalism* (1988), 5.
59. Aline Gorren, The Ethics of Modem Journalism," *Scribner's Magazine*. April 1896, 20.
60. William Gamson, and A. Modigliani, "Media Discourse and Public Opinion on Nuclear Power: Constructivist Approach," *American Journal of Sociology,* 95 (1989), 1-37.
61. Denis McQuail, *Mass Communication Theory: An Introduction*. 3rd edition. (London: Sage Publications, 1994), 333.
62. Gaye Tuchman, "Making News By Doing Work: Routinizing the Unexpected," *American Journal of Sociology*, 79, 110-131.
63. Triplett, *The Life Times & Treacherous Death of Jesse James*, 294.
64. Beverly J. Stoeltje, "Making the Frontier Myth: Folklore Process in a Modem Nation," *Western Folklore*, 46 (October 1987), 235-253.
65. Zhongdang Pan and Gerald M. Kosicki, "Framing Analysis: An Approach to News Discourse," *Political Communication,* 1 0(1993),56.
66. The Missouri Valley Register, Gallatin, Mo., 19 March 1868.
67. Horan, *The Outlaws*, 38; Triplen, *The Life Times & Treacherous Death of Jesse James*, 294.
68. *The Democrat,* Savannah, Mo., 16 Sept. 1881.
69. *The Missouri Republican*, St. Louis, Mo., 4 April 1882.
70. The *Kansas City Daily Journal*, Kansas City, Mo., 4-9 April 1882.
71. *Bates County Democrat*, Butler, Mo., 6 April 1882.
72. Horan, *The Outlaws*, ,34.
73. *The Liberty Advance,* Liberty, Mo., 28 April 1882.
74. Triplett, *The Life Times & Treacherous Death of Jesse James*, 212.
75. Horan, *The Outlaws*, 35-6. Also see Steckmesser, "Robin Hood and the American Outlaw," 351.
76. Horan, *The Outlaws*, 36, Dyer, *Jesse James and the Civil War in Missouri,* 66.
77. *The Democrat,*. Savannah,Mo., 11April1882.
78. *The Liberty Advance,* Liberty, Mo., 14 April 1882.
79. *Weekly Record,* New Madrid, Mo., 15 April 1882.
80. Steele, *Jesse and Frank James The Family History*, 55.
81. Horan *The Outlaws,* .29.
82. John Edwards, *Memoirs Reminiscences and Recollections bv John Edwards,* privately printed (Kansas City, Mo., 1889), 23.
83. Wellman, *A Dynasty of Western Outlaws*, 100.
84. Triplett, *The Life Times and Treacherous Death of Jesse James*, 66.
85. *Ibid*, Snell introduction, xiv.
86. Strate, *American Heroes in a Media Age*, 17.
87. Prassel, *The Great American Outlaw*, vii.
88. *The Democrat*. Savannah, Mo., 11 April 1882, *The Missouri Republican* and the *Bates County Democrat*, 6 April 1882.
89. William J. Ong, *The Presence of the Word* (Minneapolis, Minn.: University of Minnesota Press, 1981). as quoted by Strate, *American Heroes in a Media Age,* 17.
90. Wellman, *A Dynasty of Western Outlaws*, 123.

Index

A

Abbott, Reverend John S. C. 128
Abolition 37, 51, 52, 54, 56, 57, 59, 66, 75-92, 95, 107-109, 111,113, 114, 119, 120, 209, 217, 218, 223, 226, 295, 296, 302, 305, 379, 460
Abolitionists 64, 65, 95, 101, 103, 141, 142, 144, 149, 277, 445
Adams, Governor James H. 95
Advertising 4, 6, 7, 8, 11, 12, 13, 15, 16, 39, 102, 247, 248, 349-358, 361, 350, 352-361, 367-371, 471, 472, 47-477
Advertiser and Tribune 531, 532, 533, 544
Advertising agencies 5
Advertising agents 352
African-American newspapers 53, 485, 486, 494, 497
African-American press 485, 488
African-Americans 51, 52, 54, 60, 68, 217, 218, 235, 349, 473, 479, 519, 520, 522, 524, 529, 530, 532, 536, 544
Agate type 352
Agenda-setting theory 148
Alabama State Journal 498
Albany Patriot 245, 247-250, 252-256
Alcorn, James Lusk 137
Alexander, P. W. 442
Alexander, Peter 384
Alien and Sedition Acts of 1798   300
Allen, William 298
American Anti-Slavery Society 78, 80, 83-85, 88
American Jews 227, 229, 230, 232, 239, 241-244, 346, 449
American Jewish Advocate 449
American Jewish history 327
American Medical Times 317, 323
American Revolution 67, 258
Anderson, Gen. Robert 409
Anderson, General Robert 409
Andersonville Prison 250, 256
Andrew, John 57
Andrews, L. F. M. 279

Andrews, Sidney 473
Annexation of Texas 111, 120
Antebellum journalism 65
Anti-abolitionists 66
Anti-Jewish attitude 327
Anti-secessionists 138
Anti-Semitism 233, 234, 238, 325, 326, 334, 337, 346, 461, 462
Anti-slavery periodicals 81
Antietam 321
Antislavery movement 76, 78, 79, 84, 85, 89, 95, 117
Appomattox 183, 254, 321, 325, 390
Aristotle 180
Arkansas Freeman 498
Arkansas Gazette 489-491, 494, 496, 501
Army chaplains 462
Army of Pensacola 45
Army of Tennessee 279, 414
Army of the Potomac 321, 409
Army of the Tennessee 439
Asmonean, The 334, 450, 456, 466, 467
Associated Press 54, 57, 61, 162, 182, 183, 201, 203
Athens Post 150
Atlanta 245, 250, 251, 253, 255, 256, 437, 439, 440
Atlanta Daily Confederacy 377
Atlanta Daily Intelligencer 375
Atlanta Register 445
Atlantic Monthly 104, 353
Augusta Chronicle 276, 277, 281, 283, 284, 285, 288, 289, 441, 443
Augusta Constitutionalist 439, 445, 446, 448
Augusta Register 445
Austin Daily State Journal 481
Austin, Texas Daily State Journal 476

B

Baltimore American 59, 60
Baptist Convention 123, 127
Baptist press of North Carolina 125
Baptists   123, 124, 125, 126, 127, 128, 129, 130, 132, 133, 134

Barksdale, Ethelbert 38, 39, 137-144
Barksdale, Gen. William 138
Barnum, P. T. 311, 312, 313, 320, 404
Barton, Clara 211
Bates County Democrat 559, 560, 568
Bates County Record 558
Bates, David 193
Battlefield Relief Society 250
Beach, A.E. 311
Beach, H.D. 311
Beauregard Defenders 45
Beauregard, Gen. P. G. T. 284, 440
Beauregard, Pierre 382
Becker, Joseph 312, 322
Beecher, Catharine 128
Beecher, Henry Ward 265
Bell, John 141-143, 145, 147, 156
Benajmin, Judah P. 234, 461, 465
Benneyt, James Gordon 179, 311
Berea College 108, 121
Bias 183
Bible 233, 235, 242, 244
Biblical Recorder 124-136
Bill of Rights 241, 407
Billy the Kid 550, 552, 567
Birney, James G. 85, 108, 111, 112
Black Republicans 147
Bloch, Edward 453
Bloch, Therese 449
Bloomer, Amelia 210, 219
Bonaparte, Napoleon 408, 415
Bonney, William 552
Booth 389, 393, 394, 395
Booth John Wilkes 185, 389
Boston Female Anti-Slavery Society 79
Boston Traveler 103, 123
Botts, Lawson 50
Brady, Mathew 321
Bragg, Gen. Braxton 284, 382, 383, 384
Breckinridge, John C. 139, 141-145, 147
Bridgeport, Conncecticut Republican Farmer 277
Brooke, Walter 43
Brown, Gov. Joseph 50-61, 63, 66, 67, 69, 70, 72, 73, 277, 285, 295, 318, 438, 440, 444, 448
Brown, Old Osawatomie 50
Brown, Owen and Ruth Mills 53
Brown, Sam 110
Brownlow, Parson 149, 150, 155, 158

Brownlow's Knoxville Whig 156, 501
Brunell, Lizzie 222, 223
Buchanan, James 53, 188, 295
Buchanan, President James 233
Buell 410
Bull Run 321
Bunker Hill 8
Bunnel, Lizzie 210, 220
Bunnell, Lizzie 210, 213-216, 218, 219, 221, 222
Burke, Edmund 179
Burkitt, Lemuel 126
Burnside, Gen. Ambrose E. 300, 301, 304
Burr, Colonel A. P. 247
Bush, Isidor 232

C

Calhoun, John C. 22, 23, 25, 26, 28, 86
Camden (S.C.) Daily Journal 442
Cameron, Simon 188, 409
Carlisle, William 94
Carolina Art Association 103
Carter, Henry 309, 310, 315
Carvalho, Solomon Nunes 231
Cary, Mary Ann Shadd 260
Cassius Marcellus Clay 107, 121
Castalia Female Institute 130
Censorship 63, 66, 73, 181, 192, 198, 284, 292, 296, 297, 385, 471
Census 350
Chancellorsville, Battle of 195
Changing reportage 181
Chapman, Maria 88, 89
Chapman, Maria Weston 80
Charleston Courier 94, 266, 361, 367, 368, 439, 445 492, 495, 497,499, 501
Charleston Mercury 33, 94, 137, 360, 367, 368, 374, 383, 442, 443, 489, 496, 501
Chattanooga Advertiser, The 150
Chattanooga Daily Rebel 375
Chattanooga Gazette 148, 150
Chattanooga Reflector, The 150
Chicago Globe 180
Chicago Inter-Ocean 560
Chicago Journal 215
Chicago Times 293,301, 304, 412
Chicago Tribune 187, 335, 393, 397, 399, 404, 560

Index 573

Chichester, Thomas 276, 277
Chickamauga, Battle of 384, 385
Child, David Lee 77, 80, 88, 90
Child, Lydia Marie 75-82, 84-90
Chillicothe Advertiser 298
Chilton, Samuel 57, 58
Chowan Female Institute 129
Christianity 325, 328, 329, 331, 337, 338, 341
Christian history 125
Christmas 16
Christy, John 443, 444
Churches 113
Cincinnati Commercial 357, 359, 360, 367-369, 411
Cincinnati Enquirer 293, 303
Cincinnati Gazette 335, 411
Civil equality for Jews 241
Civil liberties 63
Civil liberty 236
Civil War 108, 127, 161, 163, 165, 167, 169, 173, 181, 227, 231, 233, 238, 239, 240, 346, 350, 438, 484, 486
Civil War correspondents 319
Clay, Cassius Marcellus 108, 109, 112-120
Clay, Green and Sally 109
Clay, Henry 28, 32, 76, 111, 120, 285
Cleveland Banner 150
Cleveland, President Grover 556
Clinton County Independent 511, 513, 515, 518
Clinton, Hillary 419
Clisby, Joseph 278
Coldwater Sentinel 512, 513, 516, 518
Collins, John A. 88, 89
Colonization Society 9, 10
Colored Tennessean 488
Colt, Sam 550
Columbus Enquirer 441
Columbus, Ohio, Crisis 291
Commercial Culture 12
Commercialization of gender 354
Committee, Joint on Conduct of War 425
Confederacy 278, 279, 281, 287, 288, 325, 350, 378, 395, 425, 471, 473, 476, 477, 479
Confederate army 245, 246, 250-254, 281, 282, 285, 287, 301, 378, 439, 440, 443

Confederate Baptist 259
Confederate cavalry 276, 279-281
Confederate Congress 138, 144, 266, 437, 438, 440, 442, 447, 448
Confederate Constitution 442, 443
Confederate government 287
Confederate House of Representatives 444
Confederate leaders 285
Confederate military sites 282
Confederate morale 282, 287, 438
Confederate Peace Movemeny 277
Confederate press 285, 286, 437, 443
Confederate Press Association 275, 384
Confederate States of America 148, 234, 237, 245, 250, 253, 280, 285, 293
Confederate troops 246, 253
Congressional Medal of Honor 325
Conscription 437, 440, 445-448
Conservator, The 558
Constitutional Convention 37-41, 45, 138, 141
Constitutional convention 138, 143
Constitutional liberties 298
Constitutional Union Party 141, 142, 147, 154, 156
Consumer society 352, 353
Conway, Rev. Moncure D. 461
Cook, John 57
Coope, F. T. 144
Cooperation Party 39, 40, 42-44
Copeland, John 50, 68, 69
Copperheads 233, 291, 293, 298,
Coppic, Edwin 50, 58, 68
Cotton 9, 10
Cotton speculators 328
Countryman, The 279
Crayon, Porte 66
Cremieux, Adolphe 230
Crisis 291, 293, 295-307
Crockett, David Myers 45
Cult of true womanhood 257, 267
Cumberland Democratic Alleganian 9
Curtis, George William 70, 71
Curtis, Cyrus H. K. 353

D

Daily Enquirer 462
Dana, Charles A. 184, 185, 190, 193, 196, 199, 421
David Crockett Myers 45

Davidson, James W. 279
Davis, Jefferson 192, 250, 278, 284-287, 389-405, 430, 436-448
Davis, Reuben 139
Davis, Varina 399, 400, 401
Dayton Daily Empire 293, 298
De Bow's Review 94, 104
Declaration of Independence 8, 483, 531
Delegates of American Israelites 233, 239, 244
Democratic National Convention, 1860 138, 140, 295, 302
Democratic Party 29, 76, 85, 111, 114, 138, 140, 141, 145, 146, 150, 152, 196, 294, 302, 472, 473, 503-519, 524, 534, 535, 538-540, 542, 555
Democratic press 153, 154, 157, 158, 246, 294, 471-473, 477, 479, 480, 504, 510, 512-517, 522, 523, 526, 528, 531, 534-536, 538-540,
Denominational newspapers 127
Department of Tennesse 345
Department of Tennessee 326
Department of the Ohio 300
Der Deutsche Republicaner 451
Detroit Free Press 293, 504, 505, 510-516, 518, 521, 524, 528, 530, 541, 542
Detroit newspapers 519, 538, 545
Detroit Post 531, 532
Detroit Union 525, 528
Dickinson, Anna 265
Disunionists 88, 95, 139-142
Dix, Dorothea 259, 350
Domestic Intelligence 65-67, 72-74
Douglas Democrats 65
Douglas, Stephen A. 140-144, 147, 457
Douglass, Frederick 60
Draft riots 262
Dred Scott v. Sanford 483, 501
Dreiser, Theodore 180
Dropsie, Moses 237

E

Eastern Clarion 38, 41, 47
Eaton 476, 480, 481
Edinburgh Review 102
Editing pictures 321
Edwards, Jesse 562
Election of 1856 94

Election of 1860 138, 148, 150, 457
Emancipation 79, 108-115, 117-121, 304
Emancipation Proclamation 297, 299
Emancipator, The 83
Emerson, Ralph Waldo 60
Enfranchisement 507, 513, 217
Engravers and engraving 310, 313, 318, 320, 321
Equal opportunity 214
Equal rights 214, 216, 332, 484, 531 532, 540
Everett, Edward 198
Ewing, Ellen 408
Ewing, Phil 415
Ewing, Thomas 408, 411
Examiner, The (Frederick) 15

F

Fairbank, Calvin 114
Faulkner, C. J. 50
Fears, J. W. 245, 247, 248, 250-253, 256
Federal cavalry 282
Feminist movement 90
Fifteenth Amendment 502-505, 508-511, 515-518
Fillmore, Abigail 422
First Amendment 112, 416, 303, 412, 443
First Ladies 419-435
Flash, Henry Lynden 276-288, 442-444
Fold-out engravings 314
Foote, Rep. Henry S. 438, 444, 448
Forbes, Edwin 319
Ford, Robert 551, 556, 560
Ford's Theatre 183-186, 194, 389
Forestville Female Institute 130
Forsyth, John 383, 385
Fort Fisher 200
Fort McHenry 191
Fort Sumter 73, 246, 265, 295, 325, 379, 409, 461
Forth Estate 408
Fourteenth Amendment 505, 506, 508-510, 512
Fourteenth amendment 505, 510, 516
Fowler, Senator Joseph S. 509
Framing 547, 556, 557, 558, 562, 563, 568
Francis P. Blair 507
Franciscans 229

Frank Leslie's Gazette of Fashion 315
Frank Leslie's Illustrated 411
Frank Leslie's Illustrated Newspaper 60, 73, 313, 314, 318, 321, 322
Frank Leslie's Illustrirte Zeitung 315
Frank Leslie's Lady's Magazine 311
Frank Leslie's Monthly 311
Frank Leslie's New Family Magazine 311, 315
Frank Leslie's New York Journal of Romance 312
Frank Leslie's Portfolio of Fancy Needlework 311
Frederick Examiner 14, 16
Free blacks 67
Free speech 475, 476
Free thought 476
Freedmen 483-500
Freedom of expression 479
Freedom of the press 63, 95, 112, 118, 144, 198, 261, 292, 305 407, 442, 471, 472, 477
Freedom of religion 241
Freedom of speech 63, 95, 144, 261, 407, 442, 475, 476, 479
Freedom of thought 94, 479
Freesoilism 95
Function of the press 5

G

Gag, Francis D. 219
Gales, Joseph 22
Garrett, Pat 552
Garrison 86
Garrison, William Lloyd 56, 60, 77-80, 83, 88-90, 108, 109
Gazette of Fashion 311
Gendered commercial discourse 354
Georgetown College 279
Georgia Analytical Repository 126
Georgia Legio 384
Georgia Legislature 444
Gettysburg 277, 278
Gettysburg Address 198
Gettysburg, Battle of 416
Gleason, Frederick 310
Gleason's Pictorial Drawing-Room Companion 310
Gobright, Lawrence 182, 183, 184, 186
Godey's Lady Book 211
Graham's 105
Gran 412

Grand Rapids Daily Democrat 516
Grant, Gen. Ulysses S. 183, 186, 192, 193, 199, 200, 203, 204, 238 325-390, 411, 412, 414, 462
Grant's Order #11 238, 239, 325, 327, 344, 345, 462
Grayson, William 97, 98
Great Awakening 125, 126, 134
Great Revival 125, 126, 134
Greeley, Horace 56, 111, 297, 409, 464
Green, Duff 22, 24-29, 33
Green, Shields 50, 68
Green, Thomas C. 55
Greeneville Democrat 150
Griffin Independent South 247
Griswold, Henry 58

H

Habeas corpus 196, 292, 407
Hackenburg, W.B., 331
Hale, Sarah Josepha 76
Halftones 310, 316
Halleck, Gen. Henry 329, 333, 335, 339, 344, 345, 410, 411
Hamilton, Gov. James A. 33
Hamlin, Hannibal 144
Hammond, Col. J. H. 416
Handbill No. IV 115
Hardee, Gen. William J. 200, 276, 279
Harding, Charles B. 50
Harlan, John M. 483, 484
Harper's Ferry 50, 52-57, 65, 67, 71, 318
Harper's Monthly 66
Harper's New Monthly Magazine 105
Harper's Weekly 64-67, 69, 70, 72, 73, 314, 315, 318, 321, 322, 353
Harris, Joel Chandler 279
Harrison, Anna 422
Hartford Courant 161-174, 390-398, 400, 404
Hayne 98
Hayne, Paul Hamilton 94, 97-105
Hebrew Education Society of Philadelphia 237
Henry, Mayor Alexander 237
Henry, R. H. 139
Herald of Freedom 11, 12, 13, 14, 16
Hienan, F. 245, 248, 249, 254, 256
Higginson, Thomas Wentworth 52
Hill, Sen. B. H. 441
Holcombe, Henry 126

Holy Congregation of the Sons of Israel 451
Home Journal 279
Hood, Gen. John B. 253, 439, 440
Hood, James 148
Hopper, Isaac 78, 82, 89
House, Edward H. 64
House Military Affairs Committee 444
Howe, Julia Ward 109
Hoyt, George H. 57
Hume, David 285
Hunter, Andrew 50, 52, 66
Hunter, Henry 57
Huntsville Advocate 487
Huntsville Advocate 501

I

Iliad 179
Illowy, Rev. Dr. Bernard 462
Illustrated American News 310
Illustrated London News 309, 310
illustrated publications 316
Illustrations 310-323
Illustrators 63
Independent Monitor 492, 501
Independent press 162
Indianapolis Sentinel 293
Individual rights 294, 304, 457
Individualism 4, 5, 6, 7, 12
Industrial Revolution 161
Industrialization 4
Ingram, Herbert 310
Intellectual freedom 95
Inverted pyramid 163, 167, 169, 170, 175, 180-183, 186, 187, 198, 200, 203
Isham, Warren P. 412
Israelite, The 328, 334, 335, 338, 449, 451-458, 461-467
Israels Herold 451

J

J.V., Colonel DuBois 335
Jackson, Andrew 22, 25, 26, 29, 32, 294, 442
Jackson Clarion 500
Jackson Clarion-Ledger 139, 145
Jackson Eagle 512, 515
Jackson Mississippian 37, 138, 140, 141, 144
Jackson, President Andrew 311
Jackson, Thomas 408
Jacksonian Globe 22
Jacksonians 22, 31
Jacksonville New South 476, 481
Jacob, Harriet 260
Jay, John 238
James, Frank 566
James, Jesse 547, 548, 549, 551, 552, 556, 559, 560-563, 566-568
Jefferson Davis 437, 439, 445, 448
Jefferson, Thomas 9, 294
Jewish chaplaincy 238, 241
Jewish civil rights 228
Jewish culture 241
Jewish immigrants 229
Jewish Institute of Muenster 228
Jewish Messenger 326, 333, 340, 348
Jewish newspapers 231, 325, 326, 334, 345
Jewish periodicals 227
Jewish religious life 229
Jewish religious pedagogy 228
Jewish women 335
Job printing 249
John Brown's Raid 65, 67, 72
Johnson, President Andrew 185, 189, 486
Johnston, Albert Sydney 409
Johnston, Gen. Joseph E. 251, 253, 254, 415
Jonesborough Union 150
Journal of Commerce 191
Journalism Hall of Fame 291
Judaism 228, 230-232, 241, 242
Judge Parker 55
July fourth 462
Juvenile Miscellany 78

K

Kansas 70, 98, 100
Kansas and Nebraska Act 100
Kansas City Journal 558, 559, 560
Kansas City Times 558, 561, 562
Keckley, Elizabeth 261
Kendall, Postmaster General Amos 108
Kennesaw Mountain, Battle of 251, 253, 256, 300
Kentucky Constitution 112
Kentucky Gazette 114
Kentucky General Assembly 109, 110, 120
Kentucky Senate 117
Key, Philip Barton 188

Index 577

Key, Thomas M. 410
K'hillah K'dosha Bene Yeshurun 451
Kilpatrick, Hugh Judson 282
Kimball, A. N. 144
Knickerbocker 105
Knox, Thomas W. 413
Knoxville Register, The 150
Knoxville Southern Citizen 102
Knoxville Whig 149, 156, 487
Knoxville Whig and Independent Journal 156
Ku Klux Klan 522, 528, 532
Kursheedt, Gershom 231

L

Lacrosse Democrat 293
Ladies Home Journal 211, 353, 354
Ladies' Magazine 76
LaFayette, La Marquis 8
Lead paragraphs 180, 182, 184
Leavitt, Joshua 85
Ledger, The 330, 332, 345
Lee, Gen. Robert E. 54, 68, 183, 186, 187, 195, 200, 201, 254, 321, 389, 390, 397, 402, 404, 405
Leeser, Isaac 227-244, 326-347
Leslie, Frank 309-323
Lexington Observer and Recorder 112, 116, 122
Liberalism 71
Liberator 60, 61, 83, 84, 86, 88, 108
Liberia 9, 10
Liberty Advance 558, 559, 561
Liberty Party 83, 85, 111, 120
Liberty Tribune 558, 564
Library of Congress 321
Lilienthal, Rabbi Dr. Max 449, 454
Lily, The 210, 218, 221
Lincoln, Abraham 37, 40, 108, 111, 137, 141-144, 181-198, 201 202, 238-240, 265, 276, 286, 292, 293 296-307, 327, 329, 330,332, 337-339, 346, 376, 379, 389, 395, 398, 399, 403, 404, 405, 414, 419-436, 444, 445
Lincoln, Abraham, assassination of 181, 182, 185-187, 206, 240, 390-396, 404, 405
Lincoln's death and funeral 393
Lincoln, Mary Todd 185, 261, 420-435
Lind, Jenny 310
Literary journalism 97

Literary magazines 102, 103
Living Writers of the South 279
Livingston Journal 487, 501
llustrated London News. 313
llustrated News 311
Lodge, John 524
London Quarterly Review 228
London Times 423
Loring, Ellis Gray 80
Louisiana State Seminary 409
Louisville Examiner 118
Louisville Journal 337, 486, 501
Lovejoy, Elijah 51, 108, 112, 121
Loyal Georgian 487, 488, 493, 501
Lynching 54

M

Macon Daily Confederate 278, 279
Macon Intelligencer 443
Macon Telegraph 276, 278, 285, 289, 441-443
Madison, Dolly 422
Magnolia, The 96
Maine Argus 403
March on Atlanta 201
March to the Sea 275, 277, 440
Marketing 73
Marshall Democratic Expounder 511, 514, 515, 518
Martineau, Harriett 89
Mass media 5
Massachusetts Anti-Slavery Society 77
Mather, Cotton 128
Mayer, Isaac Wise 326, 334, 347
Mayflower, The 209-226
McCarthy, A. J. 246, 247
McCarty, Henry 552
McClellan, Gen. George 189, 190, 200, 302, 410
McClernand, Major Gen. John 414
McDowel, Gen. Irvin 409
McLean, Washington 303
McMinnville, Tennessee Enterprise 476
McPherson, Edward M. 477
Meade, Gen. George 477
Medary, Samuel A. 291-307
Medary, Charles 297
Memphis Appeal 282, 375, 378, 412, 487, 489, 500, 501
Memphis Avalanche 487, 488, 501

578   The Civil War and the Press

Memphis Morning Post 478
Memphis Post 474, 476, 481
Mercury 94
Meredith, Thomas 123, 124, 127-132
Merrimac 193
Messenger 326, 333, 340-345, 348
Metcalfe, Gov. Thomas 114
Metropolitan Female Seminary 130
Mexican War 85, 108, 118, 119, 304, 381, 408
Michelbacher, Rev. J. M. 234
Mikveh Israel 228, 229, 242
Military Reconstruction Act 505, 506
Militia 64, 66, 68, 72
Milton, John 129
Mississippi 138, 139, 140-145, 239
Mississippi Legislature 37, 38
Mississippi Ordinance of Secession 46
Mississippian 37, 38, 40, 41, 42, 47
Missouri Democrat 491, 497, 501
Missouri Republican 495, 558-560, 565, 568
Missouri Valley Register 558, 559
Mobs 72, 79, 108, 112, 118, 277, 409
Mobile Advertiser 375, 383
Mobile Daily Advertiser and Register 375, 382
Mobile Daily Tribune 375, 383
Mobile Register 143, 279, 378, 383
Mobile Tribune 375, 385
Monteflore, Sir Moses 229
Montgomery Advertiser 375
Montgomery Appeal 442
Montgomery, Col. James 261
Montgomery Mail 443
Moore, Henry 277
Mordecai, Jacob 228
Morris, U.S. Senator Thomas 294
Morse, Nathan 276-288, 441, 442
Motherhood 212, 214
Mother's Monthly Journal 128
Mott, Lucretia 80
Mrs. Cornwald Barry Wilson 128
Myers, Porter Jacob 37-47

N

N.W. Ayer & Son Advertising Agency 354
Nashville Press 490
Nat Turner Rebellion 63
Natchez Courier 39, 40, 47, 142
Natchez Free Trader 37, 41, 42
National Anti-Slavery Society 77
National Anti-Slavery Standard

76, 80, 81, 84, 85, 88, 89, 90
National Freedmen's Relief Bureau 265
National Intelligencer 22, 24, 26, 28, 30, 31, 32, 33, 391, 394, 395
National Republican 494
Native Americans, images of 349
Nebraska 100
Nevada Gazette 291
New England Anti-Slavery Society 79
New Madrid (Missouri) Weekly Record 559
New Nation 474, 475, 480
New Orleans Daily Picayune 52, 60
New Orleans Delta 279
New Orleans Picayune 375, 376, 382, 391, 397, 399
New Orleans Times-Democrat 71
New York Academy of Medicine 317
New York Daily News 200
New York Herald 54, 60, 64, 65, 180, 182, 185, 189, 190, 197, 198, 201, 204, 311, 413, 414, 423, 426, 430
New York Illustrated News 318, 321
New York Journal of Romance 311
New York Letters 81
New York Post 182
New York Sun 182, 185, 426
New York Sunday Times 101
New York Times 52, 60, 103, 163-165, 174, 175, 182, 201, 262, 358, 360, 361, 367, 369, 391, 392, 397-399, 401, 404, 408, 413, 419, 426-436
New York Tribune 56, 59, 60, 61, 64, 111, 182, 185, 190, 195, 199, 201, 202, 329, 358, 359, 361, 367-369, 409, 410, 421, 426
New York World 191, 504
Newby, Dangerfield 53
News 275, 276, 277, 278, 279, 282, 284, 285, 286, 288
News agenda 519, 522, 525, 534, 537, 541
News boys 319
News exchanges 250, 275
Newspapers 63, 64, 73, 76
Newswriting 180, 188
Nightingale, Florence 259
Niles Democratic Republican 515
Non-slaveholders 117
Non-partisan press 197
North Carolina Baptist Convention

124, 129
North Carolina Magazine, or Universal Intelligence 126
North Missourian 558, 559
Northern newspapers 292
Northern press 63, 282
Nullification 21, -33, 86, 94
Nullification crisis 21, 22, 30, 33
Nullification Proclamation 22

O

Objective journalism 306
Objectivity 181, 182, 187, 197, 199, 534
Occident and American Jewish Advocate 227, 230, 231, 232, 236, 238, 239, 241, 242, 243, 244, 327, 328, 329, 330, 332, 334, 449, 450, 456, 466, 467
Ohio House of Representatives 294
Ohio Legislature 296
Ohio State Journal 293
Ohio Statesman 294
Ohio Sun 294, 305, 306
Olcott, Henry S. 64
Olds, Dr. Edson 298
Opinion leaders 148
Ordinance of Secession 43-46
Osawatomie, Kansa 53
Oxford Female College 130

P

Partisan newspapers 50, 54, 105, 197, 306, 471, 477, 478, 519-527, 532, 534, 535, 537, 539, 540-542, 554, 555, 562
Partisan politics 496
Partisan press 105, 162, 276, 292, 471, 537, 541
Partisanship 97, 519, 520, 521, 522, 534, 537
Party politics 100
Patriotism 7-9, 12, 60, 65, 128, 212, 237, 245-256
Patronage 22, 23, 25, 28, 30, 472, 478, 479
Peace Democrats 293, 297-301, 303, 304, 307
Peace Democratic newspapers 293, 295, 305
Peake, Mary S. 261
Pendleton, George 298

Pendleton, W. N. 438
Penny Press 39, 161-163, 168, 172, 174, 179
Personal journalism 138, 276
Peterson's Magazine 279
Philadelphia Inquire 200
Philadelphia Inquirer 239, 332
Philadelphia Press 353
Philadelphia Public Ledger 330, 345
Philanthropist, The 108
Phillips, Wendell 57
Photographic realism 320
Photography 310, 316, 320-322
Pierce, Franklin 294
Plantations 104
Plessy v. Ferguson 483, 501
Political and civil liberties 231
Politics 472, 475, 480, 481, 482
Polk, James K. 111, 117, 118
Polk, Sarah 422
Pope, John 477
Popular sovereignty 140, 141
Portage, Ohio Sentinel 59
Porter, Admiral David Dixon 414
Postal censorship 221
Postal distribution 63, 64
Powell 329, 330, 333, 338, 339
Powell, Lazarus 329, 330
Presbyterian Church, General Assembly 113
Presbyterian Church, Synod 239
Presbyterian, The 126, 127
Press agencies 203
Press influence 148
Press pass restrictions 191, 192, 198
Press releases 181
Press responsibility 447
Prince, Thomas 125
Printer's Ink 352
Printing contracts and subsidies 22, 478
Providence Journal 329
Public Ledger 239
Public life
Public opinion 5, 79, 99, 148, 230
Public role of women 90
Pugh, Senator George 298

Q

Quinby, William 524
Quincy, John Adams 23, 32

R

Racism 9, 65, 67, 69
Radical Republican newspapers 485, 486, 494
Radical Republican party 521, 484-497, 503-509, 555
Rags 249
Raleigh Progress 443, 444, 445
Raleigh Sentinel 487, 501
Raleigh Standard 487, 501
Raphall, Rabbi Dr. Morris J. 233, 328
Raymond, Henry J. 427
Reconstruction 471, 472, 475, 447, 478, 480-489, 504-507, 510, 512, 518-534, 540, 542, 544, 545, 548, 558
Redpath, James 60
Rehine, Zalma 228
Reid, Samuel 386, 374, 375, 377-384
Reid, Samuel Chester, Jr. 373, 383-387
Religious equality 241
Religious freedom 237, 239, 241, 333
Religious journalism 123, 125
Religious newspapers 125, 126, 127
Religious periodicals 126, 127
Religious press 126, 127
Reporters 63, 67
Repository of Israel 228
Republic, The 313
Republican Banner 8, 12, 16
Republican National Committee 427, 476, 481
Republican newspapers 94, 150, 293, 409, 471, 472-482, 487, 490, 493, 497
Republican Party 32, 46, 64, 70, 188, 189, 237, 265, 293, 295, 296, 301, 425, 457, 458, 471, 472, 473, 476, 480, 481, 482, 503-535, 540-545
Revolutionary War 168, 304
Rhett, Robert Barnwell 137
Richmond (Missouri) Conservator 564
Richmond Dispatch 360, 361, 367, 374, 489
Richmond Enquirer 52, 71, 360, 361, 367, 368, 443, 444
Richmond Sentinel 445
Richmond Whig 228, 396, 443, 486, 490, 492, 497, 499, 500, 501
Rome Weekly Courier 492
Roosevelt, Theodore 548
Rowell, George 352
Russell 93, 94, 96-106, 422, 423
Russell's 96, 97, 98
Russia 108

S

Sabbath 241
San Antonio Express 474, 480, 494
Saturday Evening Post 354
Saturday Review 554
Savannah, fall of 287
Savannah Democrat 558, 559
Savannah Daily Herald 476, 481
Savannah Republican 439, 445, 490
Sawyer, Samuel 412
Schmidt, Charles F. 451
Scot, Thomas 410
Scott, Anne Firor 209
Scott, Dred 483, 484, 501
Scott, Walter Dill 353
Scott, Winfield 85, 86
Scribner's (Century) Monthly 353
Seaton, William W. 22
Secession 25-29, 37-47, 95, 137-148, 150, 152, 156, 158, 246, 292, 457, 461
Secession crisis 147, 149
Secessionist press 103
Secessionists 100
Second Bank of the United States 23, 28, 32
Second Great Awakening 125, 126, 134
Second South Carolina volunteers 261
Sectarianism 236
Sectional journalism 102
Sectionalism 65, 66, 71, 73, 95-99, 104, 105, 304, 305
Seneca Falls 209
Seventh Battalion of the Mississippi Infantry 45
Seward, Frederick 186
Seward, William 184
Seymour, Horatio 507
Sheftal, Mordecai 232
Shelby, Gen. Joe 558
Sherman, Ellen Ewing 411
Sherman, Gen. William T. 192, 200, 245, 251-256, 275, 276, 278, 280-289, 407-417, 439-441, 444, 447
Sherman, Sen. John 413
Sherman, Judge Charles 408
Shiloh, Battle of 248, 378, 382
Sickles, Daniel 188

Simms, William Gilmore 96
Slavery 50-60, 82, 107-121, 233-235, 244, 249, 260, 261, 330, 351, 370, 473, 476, 483,-487, 493, 495, 501
Slaveholders 51, 52, 76, 86, 87, 107, 115
Slavery 23, 38, 40, 43, 46, 50, 51, 53-58, 60, 63, 65-67, 69-73, 79, 81, 83-87, 93, 94-106, 124, 134, 137, 140, 148, 149, 217, 218, 233-235, 297, 298, 304, 330, 332, 391, 456, 458-460, 465
Smith, Gen. Kerby 384
Smith, J. Henly 377
Social control 181
Soldiers, African-American 351
Soldiers, Jewish 325, 335, 340, 341, 343
South Carolina 21-27, 30-33, 94, 100, 137, 138, 142
South Carolina Legislature 95
Southern and Western Monthly Magazine and Review 96
Southern Cooperationists 40
Southern editors 96
Southern Jews 234, 237
Southern Literary Messenger 96, 104
Southern magazines 95
Southern mind 93, 94, 98, 246
Southern morale 260, 447
Southern nationalism 103
Southern periodicals 96
Southern press 96, 284, 378, 441, 484
Southern Quarterly Review 94, 96, 104
Southern rights 140
Southern Watchman 441, 443, 444, 448
Southern writers 98
"Sparta" 375
Spiritualism 10
Springfield Republican 60, 163
St. Louis Observer 108
Stanton, Edwin 181-203, 335, 339
Stanton, Elizabeth Cady 209
States' rights 142, 218, 294, 304, 378, 457
Stearns, Martha Shubal 124
Stephen, Alexander 285, 438
Stephens, Aaron 49
Stevenson, Wellington 277

Stoddard, Richard 100
Storey, Wilbur 301, 412, 524
Stowe, Harriet Beecher 52
Strong, T.W. 310
Strother, David Hunter 65, 66, 67, 68, 69, 71, 72, 73
Stuart, J. E. B. 68
Submission party 42, 44
Suffrage 210, 211, 217, 218, 222-226, 483-495, 499, 505-518, 523
Sumner, Sen. Charles 189

T

Tabloid journalism 314
Tabloid-size newspaper 313
Taliaferro, General William B. 64, 107
Talmud 235
Tariff of 1828 28
Tariff of Abominations 23, 29
Taylor, Margaret 422
Taylor, Zachary 236
Technology 14
Telegraph 127, 162-164, 167, 169, 173, 174, 182, 183, 189, 190, 191, 198 203, 250, 276, 278, 281, 284,-287, 289, 292, 408
Telegraph bureaus 191
Telegraphic news 247, 254
Texas annexation 118
Texas Rangers 381
Third Party Political Scheme 84
Thomas, Dr. Mary 210
Thompson, John R. 96
Tift, Nelson 246
Times of London 422
Timrod, Henry 105
Tod, Governor David 293
Transylvania University 109
Treason Act of 1862 300
Treasury Departmen 326
Trotter, Judge George R. 116
True American 107, 108, 112-122
Truth, Sojourner 261
Tubman, Harriet 261
Tucker, Attorney General John Randolph 64
Turner, Joseph Addison 104
Turner, Nat 51
Two-step flow theory 148
Typewriters 162

U

U. S. Senate 120
U.S. Congress 69, 85, 115, 238, 239, 265, 296, 300, 329, 330, 339, 344, 407, 421, 462, 477, 484, 486, 488, 489, 329, 407, 421, 503, 505-509, 511-513, 515-518
U.S. Constitution 112, 140, 141, 217, 239, 240, 292, 297, 298, 304, 329, 461, 463, 505, 507 511, 514, 516, 518
U.S. House of Representatives 138, 139, 265, 330
U.S. Senate 139, 239, 329
U.S. Supreme Court 69, 85, 483
U.S. Treasury Department 238
Uncle Tom 52
Uncle Tom's Cabin 95
Underground Railway 84
Union Appeal 412
Union army 238, 245, 250, 251, 253, 254, 259, 281, 292, 297, 300, 325, 328, 333, 350, 375, 477
Union military 301
Unionists 40, 46, 100, 149, 301
Unitarian Universalist Church 71
United States Army 68
United States Census 127
United States Government Printing Office 197
United States Marines 53, 68
United States military 489
United States Military Academy 408

V

Vallandigham, Rep. Clement 298, 300, 301, 304
Valley, Missouri Register 564
Van Buren, Pres. Martin 27, 28, 29, 230
Vaughan, John C. 118
Vesey, Denmark 51
Vicksburg, Mississippi 277, 278
Vicksburg Daily Times 474, 481
Vicksburg Sun 37
Vicksburg Times 493
Vicksburg Whig 39, 40, 41, 47, 142
Vietnam War 286
Villard, Henry 190
Virginia Free Press 495, 500

Virginia militia 64

W

Wake Forest College 130
Walke, William. F. 248, 249
War, as a gendering activity 211, 258, 351
War Between the States 231, 278
War Department 169, 185, 187, 190, 191, 192, 195, 199, 204, 206
War of 1812 304
Warren, Robert Penn 404
Washington Chronicle 330, 331, 338
Washington D.C. Intelligencer 398
Washington Daily Globe 345
Washington, George 8, 9
Washington Monument 8
Washington Post 549, 567
Washington Star 331
Watchman, Southern 444
Watson, Peter 190
Waud, A.R. 320
Waud, Alf 321
Waud, Alfred 321
Waud, Alfred Rudolph 320
Webster, Delia 114
Webster, Daniel 10
Welles, Gideon 184, 192, 193, 196
West Point 68, 282, 409
Wheeler 276, 279
Wheeler, Gen. Joseph 383, 440
Whig newspapers 156, 157, 158
Whig party 85, 111, 114, 120, 150, 151, 155, 156, 451
Whitaker's Magazine 104
White Hall 107, 110, 121
Whitefield, George 125
Whittier, John Greenleaf 109
Wickliffe, Robert 110
Wickliffe, Robert, Jr 110
Wickliffe, Robert, Sr 110, 114
Wilberforce, William 279
Wilkie, Franc B. 413
Willarson, Samuel 410
Williamsport, Maryland 4, 6, 8, 16
Willis A. Hodges 53
Wilson, Senator Henry 461
Wing, Henry 195
Winthrop, Robert 109
Wire services 182, 203
Wise, Isaac Mayer 326, 328, 334-348, 449-467
Wise, Governor Henry 63, 64, 66

Womanhood
　Conceptualization of 222
　Cult of true 350
　Notions of 211
Women, activities during the Civil War 350
Women and gender roles 350
Women, and morality 128
Women and patriotism 212, 258, 260, 262, 263, 264, 266, 268, 271, 351, 356
Women and religion 124
Women and straight news reporting 264
Women and the press 211
Women, as consumers 355
Women, as the weaker sex 263
Women, as wage-earners 216
Women, cardinal virtues of 257
Women, civic and political identity 210, 212
Women, Civil War as a turning point 259
Women, coverage of their public activities 350
Women, divisions between Northern and Southern 218, 223
Women, domestic sphere 212
Women editors 76
Women, education of 125, 128, 129, 131, 132, 210
Women, images of 210, 212, 213, 215, 257, 262, 265, 349, 350, 351, 355, 356
　self-image 211, 222
　women, evangelic image 270, 356,
　women, image as altruistic 216, 263, 266, 271
　women, image as committed to the home 213
　women, image as equal to man 212, 214, 223, 263, 264, 267, 356
　women, image as morally superior 212, 257, 263, 264, 268, 356
　women, image as mother 215, 263, 268, 356
　women, image as ornamental 212, 265, 267, 355
　women, image as radical 262, 270, 355, 356
　women, romanticized image 212, 262, 270, 356
Women, images of, linked to wartime experiences 213
Women, images of proper behavior 431
Women, images of, Proper vs. Public Sphere 368
Women, importance of 125
Women, increased opportunities for 222
Women, media images of 350
Women, newsworthiness of 264
Women, private sphere 271, 356, 368, 370
Women, post-war images of 212
Women, promotion of 132
Women, proper sphere 130, 133, 258, 262, 351, 357, 435
Women, public sphere 264, 269, 356
Women, role of 124, 125, 130-132, 212, 260, 265, 351, 422
　Motherhood as the ideal role 215
　preserver of religion 129
Women, Southern 260
Women, sphere of 128
Women, sphere of influence 125
Women, spiritual role of 260
Women, virtues of 131
Women's history, influence of the Civil War on 258
Women's influence 214
Women's Loyal League 218
Women's Missionary Union 125, 132
Women's movement 75
Women's network 90
women's periodicals 221
Women's publications 211, 212, 219
Women's rights 125, 132, 209-212, 214, 217, 219, 220-222, 257
Women's rights conventions 267
Women's rights movement 75, 76, 209, 210, 218, 219, 222, 223
Women's rights periodicals 210
Women's suffrage movement 217
Women's wartime experiences 210
Wood block printing 310, 313, 318
Woods, George 249
Woods, Lt. Col. W. B. 414
World War I 258
World War II 258
Worthington, Col. Thomas 416

Y

Yale 109, 110
Yazoo City Democrat 138
Yerger, J. Shall 43

York, New Herald 191
York, New Times 267
York, New Tribune 195
Young Men's Christian Association 71
Youth's Companion 353

Z

Zion College 455, 457
Zion Collegiate Association 456